CAPITAL BUDGETING
Planning and Control
of Capital Expenditures

THIRD
EDITION

JOHN J. CLARK
Royal H. Gibson, Sr., Professor of Business Administration
Drexel University

THOMAS J. HINDELANG
Professor of Finance and Head, Department of Finance
Drexel University

ROBERT E. PRITCHARD
Professor of Finance
Glassboro State College

PRENTICE HALL, Englewood Cliffs, New Jersey 07632

Library of Congress Cataloging-in-Publication Data

Clark, John J.
    Capital budgeting : planning and control of capital expenditures /
John J. Clark, Thomas J. Hindelang, Robert E. Pritchard. -- 3rd ed.
        p.   cm.
    Includes bibliographies and indexes.
    ISBN 0-13-114877-X : $31.50
    1. Capital budget. 2. Cash flow. 3. Capital assets pricing
model.   I. Hindelang, Thomas J. II. Pritchard, Robert E., 1941-
. III. Title.
HG4028.C4C6 1989
658.1'54--dc19   88-38361
                                                               CIP

Editorial/production supervision and interior design: **Maureen Wilson**
Cover design: **Photo Plus Art**
Manufacturing buyer: **Ed O'Dougherty**

 © 1989, 1984, 1979 by Prentice-Hall, Inc.
A Division of Simon & Schuster
Englewood Cliffs, New Jersey 07632

Printed in the United States of America

10 9 8 7 6 5 4 3 2 1

ISBN 0-13-114877-X

Prentice-Hall International (UK) Limited, *London*
Prentice-Hall of Australia Pty. Limited, *Sydney*
Prentice-Hall Canada Inc., *Toronto*
Prentice-Hall Hispanoamericana, S.A., *Mexico*
Prentice-Hall of India Private Limited, *New Delhi*
Prentice-Hall of Japan, Inc., *Tokyo*
Simon & Schuster Asia Pte. Ltd., *Singapore*
Editora Prentice-Hall do Brasil, Ltda., *Rio de Janeiro*

For Margaret, Chris, Jody

Contents

PART II   Evaluation of Projects Under Conditions of Unchanging Risk

PART V   Capital Asset Pricing Applied to Capital Budgeting

15   INTRODUCTION TO CAPITAL ASSET PRICING   269

16   CAPITAL ASSET PRICING, PROJECT SELECTION, AND THE COST OF CAPITAL   293

17   A CRITIQUE OF THE CAPITAL ASSET PRICING MODEL   310

PART VI   Mathematical Programming and Multiperiod Analysis

PART VII   Strategic Management

PART VIII   Special Applications

26   CAPITAL BUDGETING FOR THE MULTINATIONAL FIRM   536

27   LEASE ANALYSIS: LEASE-BUY / LEASE-SELL   560

APPENDIXES

Preface

In the second edition of *Capital Budgeting*, we sought to implement three objectives: to improve the text as a teaching tool, to expand certain topics and introduce new materials to keep the subject matter abreast of the times, and to correct deficiencies culled from the generally favorable reviews earned by the first edition.

To maintain and enhance the strengths of the text for student use, we also pledged to avoid that bane of second (and subsequent) editions, namely, the proliferation of chapter appendixes that undermine the continuity of subject matter. Returning readers found in *Capital Budgeting*, second edition, that new and revised materials were completely integrated with the subject matter under discussion. Moreover, the manuscript had been partitioned into modules. This aspect enabled the instructor to pick up the discussion at a level commensurate with the backgrounds of his or her student group. In addition, when the instructor believes that he or she has examined a topic in sufficient depth, the remaining chapters in the module can be skipped without loss of continuity.

In this, the third edition of *Capital Budgeting*, we have reinforced the objectives of the second edition to extend the scope of the subject matter covered and to provide greater depth and variety in the teaching materials at the end of each chapter. Specifically, the third edition has the following added features:

1 The evolving discussion of capital budgeting in relation to strategic management is examined in the introductory chapter and in a module devoted exclusively to the topic.

2 We have developed computer support materials for the text in the form of six LOTUS 1-2-3 templates. These templates can be utilized in the chapters on project evaluation, risk analysis, leasing, business combinations, and sustainable growth. Adopters of the text may obtain this package from Prentice Hall.

3 Where appropriate to the subject matter, case studies complement the conventional discussion question and computational problem format for end-of-chapter assignments. This permits the instructor to plan assignments which match course learning objectives and the progress of his or her class. A propos of the case studies, we have based the cases on actual business experience, situations, and reports. In some instances, this is referenced to enable students to dig further if

they choose. For example, the case study at the end of the chapter on business combinations can be expanded by having the student refer to the company's 10K report to the Securities and Exchange Commission. Most of the case studies also call upon the LOTUS templates mentioned earlier.

4   All examples and illustrations have been revised to reflect the Tax Reform Act of 1986. However, the reader will appreciate that all authors of finance textbooks have had to grapple with the problems of updating materials given the sequence of changes in the tax law over the past five years. Some authors have chosen simply to assume certain rates in their problems and let Congress go "merrily" on its way. We have chosen another path, namely, to review and update to the present code all text and problem materials. For example, in the crucial area of asset cost recovery, we have stepped back in time to compare the tax accounting methodologies (straight line, double declining balance, sum of the years' digits) with the later ACRS allowances and the present code. At least, the student will be in a better position to experience and evaluate the impact of these formidable changes in the tax law.

5   In response to editorial comments from our colleagues, we have shortened the extensive bibliography at the end of the second edition to concentrate on selected seminal articles and publications of recent vintage. This selection should be more pertinent to the needs of junior–senior undergraduate and graduate students. We have also moved the references to the end of each chapter. We agree with the observation that the widespread use of the computerized data bases to locate relevant references made the detailed bibliography of the first two editions somewhat obsolete.

We offer the following observations to provide an overview of the coverage throughout the text. Part I, the first module, introduces the subject and reviews basic tools and concepts relevant to capital budgeting. If the student has had prior exposure to these tools and concepts, the instructor may wish to assign these chapters for the student to read as a refresher and spend only limited classroom time for review.

Part II explores the evaluation of capital projects under conditions of "unchanging risk." The module commences with the problem of properly identifying the after-tax cash flows traceable to the proposed capital project. In putting the cash flows on an after-tax basis, the provisions of the Tax Reform Act of 1986 are applied. Next, the basic capital project evaluation techniques are examined in two chapters devoted to this purpose.

The discussion initiated in Part II is continued in Part III by an in-depth analysis of the assumptions underlying the use of net present value, internal rate of return, and the profitability index. An extended discussion is presented on the question of possible conflicts in rankings between the different methodologies, and the superiority of net present value is carefully delineated subject only to stated assumptions. All financial models are built upon assumptions. The majority are static models which make no attempt to trace movements in the variables through time. Unless aware of such underlying qualifications, the future practitioner of the art may be entrapped into conclusions that do not square with the reality of a dynamic business environment. More so than in competing texts, emphasis is placed on the role of forecasting in developing the cash flows. Forecasting represents an integral part of capital budgeting. In addition, we treat explicitly the issue of adjusting cash flows for the price trends, that is, long-term upward or downward swings in the general price level. "Inflation" or "deflation," to use the terms loosely, impact cash flows, costs of capital, sustainable growth rates, and so forth.

The student is now ready to approach the issue of risk in project evaluation (Part IV). The essence of the discussion lies in the determination of expected return and standard deviation for portfolios of securities and capital projects. An ample number of illustrations and problems depict the use of decision trees in risk analysis, the utilization of probabilities, and the calculation of expected risk-adjusted NPV, variances, and covariances. The subject matter of Part V leads ineluctably to a study of the capital asset pricing model (CAPM). The three chapters of Part V are devoted to the theoretical constructs of CAPM, to its application to the capital asset evaluation, and to a critique of CAPM theory. The last incorporates the contributions of earlier research and the dissents of Roll and others. In this module we offer a balanced presentation of pros and cons, supported by a bibliography to assist the assignment of research papers.

Part VI turns to mathematical programming as an effective tool to evaluate feasible portfolios of capital projects and the determination of the capital budget. Linear, integer, and goal programming, are described and illustrated with emphasis on the assumptions of each formulation and the interpretation of optimal solutions. Our objective in this module is to prepare the student for the ever-growing use of such computer-aided models by making him or her capable of stating a capital budgeting problem in terms of an objective function and constraints, interpreting the results of the program, and performing the ever-important sensitivity analysis on the "optimal" solution.

Part VII introduces the student to the basic analysis employed in strategic management. This is a comprehensive type of analysis comprising quantitative and qualitative information as compared to the primarily quantitative analysis characteristic of capital budgeting. Business combinations, divestitures, capital abandonment, and sustainable growth are viewed in the context of strategic management.

The last module, Part VIII, treats several significant topics in capital budgeting of particular concern in today's economy. These include leasing, expanded to include both lessor and lessee perspectives, and capital budgeting in the multinational firm. Each chapter is a self-contained unit, and the instructor may use these chapters according to the inclinations of the student body.

Collectively, we express our appreciation to reviewers of the earlier editions who identified areas of improvement as well as to our colleagues who devoted time and effort to assessing the present manuscript prior to publication. We are especially indebted to

Randolph Pohlman
Kansas State University

George Tsetsekos
Drexel University

John F. Muth
Graduate School of Business,
Indiana University

Arthur C. Gudikunst
Amherst Management Group,
Amherst, MA

Richard H. Bernard
North Carolina State University

Michael J. Gombola
Drexel University

Dennis E. Logue
The Amos Tuck School
Dartmouth College

George W. Hettenhouse
Graduate School of Business
Indiana University

Francis S. Yeager
University of Houston

In addition, our students at Drexel University provided valuable feedback to the authors on this edition as in previous ones which was extensively class texted at both the graduate and undergraduate levels. To all our students goes a collective thanks. Several of our graduate students deserve special acknowledgment for their contributions: Maureen Breen, Joan Bretz, Jane Rabbitt, Tom Sheridan, Louise Weber, Pamela Wohlschlegel, and An-Hwa Wu.

Besides the reviewers and our students, we appreciate the contributions of: Dr. George Tsetsekos, Drexel University, who authored Chapter 22, "Strategic Planning for Capital Investment Decisions"; Zaher Zantout, Drexel University, who provided valuable assistance on the case studies; Arthur H. Rosenfeld of Warren, Gorham, and Lamont, Inc., for the use of that firm's comprehensive annuity and discount tables; Dean Paul E. Dascher, College of Business and Administration, Drexel University, for his continuing encouragement and support, and for providing clerical help during the preparation of all three editions; and finally Scott Barr, editor in finance, at Prentice Hall, as well as his staff, for providing capable and efficient assistance in producing the final product. Numerous other individuals have helped to improve the quality of the text; to them we offer a collective thank you.

Comments from readers of the third edition are welcomed and encouraged.

John J. Clark
Thomas J. Hindelang
Robert E. Pritchard

Introduction to the Management of Capital Assets

1

Capital budgeting is the decision area of financial management that establishes criteria for investing resources in long-term projects. Such projects commonly include land, buildings, facilities, equipment, and vehicles. The decisions made regarding the acquisition, maintenance, or abandonment of capital assets are vital to most companies for the following reasons:

1　These assets normally represent relatively large expenditures of funds.
2　The funds are generally committed for lengthy periods of time. Furthermore, capital investment decisions are difficult or very costly to reverse.
3　Capital investment decisions usually have a significant impact on whether or not the firm achieves its most important financial objectives.
4　The decision to replace existing capital assets or to abandon previously accepted investment projects determines the company's future course of development.
5　Working capital requirements closely relate to the size and utilization of fixed assets.

However, capital budgeting should not be considered as primarily or exclusively concerned with investments in property, plant, and equipment. The decision to accept or reject originates in a *project* analysis, and the techniques employed apply equally to a variety of long-term commitments: leasing contracts, mergers and acquisitions, budgeting of research and development expenditures, management of the firm's financial structure (e.g., the decision to refund debt), and valuation of multi-period advertising contracts. The methodology of capital budgeting applies equally to issues of project termination, divestiture of a poorly performing division, or the total liquidation of the business.

Although historically the literature on capital budgeting has been business oriented, the subject matter offers a method of project analysis as well as decision criteria pertinent to governmental and not-for-profit institutions (hospitals, universities, etc.). In the former case, the technique is most often referred to as *cost-effec-*

tiveness studies or, when set in a larger framework, *systems analysis*. In the latter case, the application of capital budgeting techniques may require modification to accommodate traditional practices which affect the pattern of cash inflows and outflows.

Although a very large number of expenditure problems lend themselves to capital budgeting analysis, the process absorbs time and money, especially the more sophisticated techniques of ranking and risk evaluation. The cost of these approaches must be justified by the perceived benefits. Theory adapts to circumstances. Conceptually appealing but costly techniques of analysis do not merit across-the-board application. Hence, in establishing a capital budgeting program within the firm, management must first set a cutoff by size of expenditure. That is, projects requiring investment of funds over a specified amount will be subject to the scrutiny of capital budgeting analysis; below the cutoff, the outflow on the asset will be expensed.

In summary, capital budgeting is simply a set of tools to assess the returns and risks associated with the commitment of funds to long-term projects. It is a specialization within the field of financial management. The reader will note that the latter expression has two components: finance and management. Finance theory cannot be a pursuit of abstract, deductive knowledge divorced from real-world experience. It exists to formulate criteria which assist managers in making decisions relating to the financing of operations. Equally important are the other contributors to firm performance: procurement, production, distribution, and personnel. These, too, management must integrate into the decision process. Thus, the financial manager needs to appreciate the implications of his/her analysis for the other facets of the business and for management's goals. He/she must quantify the financial effects of these diverse activities to assure that maximum benefits are derived from corporate endeavors.

The interdisciplinary nature of financial management/capital budgeting, too frequently neglected in the literature, is traceable to the assumptions underlying the field.

BASIC ASSUMPTIONS OF FINANCIAL MANAGEMENT / CAPITAL BUDGETING

Assumption 1. The primary function of management is to increase the value of the firm as reflected by the price of the common stock. Some would contend that management must satisfy the needs of many competing interest groups to whom the firm has responsibility, while sustaining a "satisfactory" level of profits. The problems associated with "maximizing" and "satisficing" are handled through the use of mathematical programming and, specifically, goal programming. (See Chapters 18 through 21.)

Whether the financial manager should base his or her calculations on "maximizing" or "satisficing" depends on whether the firm's management is characterized by a separation of ownership from control (typical of large corporations with scattered stock ownership) or on a unity of stockholder and management interests. In the former circumstance, stock ownership may constitute a relatively small proportion of managerial compensation; in the latter, management compensation may be closely related to performance of the common stock and "maximizing" would represent the dominant decision criterion.

Assumption 2.   Owners have a preference for current, as opposed to future, cash flows. Investors must be compensated for postponing the recovery of their investments and their returns on investment. Since the benefits of a capital acquisition are received over a future period, the time element lies at the core of capital budgeting. The firm must time the start of a project to take advantage of short-term business conditions and finance the project to benefit from trends in the capital markets. In addition, the longevity of capital assets and the substantial outlays required for their acquisition suggest that the estimated inflows and outflows anticipated from the project be discounted from the time they are received or paid out. The discounting of cash inflows and outflows to their present value constitutes the foundation for evaluating and ranking projects. The methodologies involved are introduced in Chapters 2 and 3 and used throughout the remainder of the text.

Assumption 3.   Shareholders are risk averters. Economists explain risk aversion by the theory of diminishing marginal utility. As an individual acquires more units of any asset (including money), the value of each additional unit to the person declines. Therefore, present dollars have greater value than do future dollars. In the case of capital investments, if an investment fails, the value of the funds lost would be greater than the value of the funds gained should the investment have succeeded. Accordingly, investors and business firms demand higher returns as the perceived risks of a project increase. Utility theory and the risk-return equation form the subject matter of Chapters 11 and 14.

Assumption 4.   In the evaluation of capital budgeting projects, the analysis is based upon the incremental cash flows directly attributable to the project. These cash inflows and outflows would not exist if the project were rejected. Historical or sunk costs are not relevant to the analysis. As discussed in Chapter 4, the incremental cash flows are forecasted estimates. Again we note that depreciation is not a cash flow item, but the tax savings from the depreciation deduction do create a cash inflow.

Assumption 5.   Cash flow analysis may differ from accounting income reporting. Projects may also be analyzed by the principles of financial accounting, and by the end of the project's life, the cash flow and the accounting-based analysis will come together. However, in any given fiscal period, the net return calculated on a cash or accounting basis may significantly differ. A project that appears worthy of investment in the long run may show negative accounting effects in the early periods. This might create political problems for management if shareholders and investors believe accounting values determine stock prices. As we shall see, the evidence on this point is not conclusive. In any event, the financial manager must be alert to the effects of capital project analysis on the company's accounting statements. We deal with the problems of reconciling project cash flows and accounting income in Chapter 20, where goal programming (a multiple-criteria model) is examined.

Assumption 6.   Since capital investment decisions rest upon multi-period estimates of cash flows, a formalized forecasting procedure is essential to the process. Experience tells us, on the other hand, that forecasts err, and the degree of error may correlate with the duration of the project. Short-term forecasts generally display less risk than do long-term forecasts. The future dimly seen entails risk, and any appraisal of a capital project must necessarily comprehend some assessment of the risk accompanying the project.

Assumption 7. The trend in asset acquisition by the firm indicates management's risk posture. The annual capital budget reflects the benefits, costs, and risks of the projects contained therein and, over time, molds the composition of the firm's total assets as well as the business risk complexion of the enterprise. The capital budget also shapes the operating budgets of future periods.

It follows that although the project is the focus of planning, the firm—its continued existence and development—is the primary interest. Hence, while analysis may yield "reliable" estimates of the expected risk and return from projects, the question arises as to what impact these have on the firm's return on assets and risk posture. If a project enhances the firm's return on assets but multiplies operating risks or adds to the perils of insolvency, should it be accepted? The answer may be affirmative, but the question cannot be avoided. Investors do not simply add new shares to their portfolios without regard to their current holdings. In like manner, financial managers should view the firm as a portfolio of previously accepted projects and view new investment proposals in light of their impact on the overall performance of the company. A high rate of return on a project is not enough to justify its acceptance. The key question is: Will the acceptance of the project add to the market value of the common shares?

Assumption 8. Every capital project has to be financed, and there are no free sources of capital. Most firms strive to maintain a capital structure (some combination of debt capital and equity capital) that will minimize their financing costs. Accordingly, we need to know not only whether the adoption of a particular project increases the market value of the common shares, but also how the acceptance of the project affects the debt-carrying capacity of the firm.

In Chapter 10, we examine the traditional methodology of determining the firm's cost of capital and the optimal financial structure. The problem of establishing the firm's cost of capital is then reexamined in Chapter 16 as part of our study of capital asset pricing.

Another aspect to managing the cost of capital is the growth rate in sales. Management and stockholders are pleased to see the firm's product line accepted by the market. They are even more pleased with the tangible rewards from capital gains and/or higher dividend payouts. However, paradoxical as it may seem, rising growth rates in sales (as well as negative growth rates) can have undesirable consequences for the firm. What management needs to know is: What growth rate is sustainable over a specified time frame without necessitating a change in the firm's financial structure or dividend policy? Modifications of the company's financial structure mandated by higher than sustainable growth rates in sales can alter the cost of capital and, in turn, the ranking of capital projects. Sustainable growth is covered in Chapter 24.

Assumption 9. Capital budgeting always involves allocating scarce resources among competing investment opportunities. The constraints are twofold: financial and managerial. Capital is a scarce and costly resource, as noted in Assumption 8. Yet projects have to be managed and management talent is manifestly a scarce resource. In fact, the major constraint on the implementation of new capital projects may be not financial but managerial.

Finally, there are other aspects of the capital acquisition process that warrant serious consideration. These emanate from the macroeconomic environment and include the fluctuations of the business cycle, the interest rate structure, and extended periods of inflation or deflation. Apropos of the business cycle, projects that appear to be sound investments in prosperity may look quite different in recession. Interest rate fluctuations affect the timing of capital proposals. Similarly, periods of inflation or deflation complicate the process of forecasting cash flows, undermine the utility of financial statements, and distort financial ratios derived from these statements.

CAPITAL BUDGETING AND STRATEGIC MANAGEMENT

Capital budgeting functions within an overall plan which outlines the expected development of the firm. It is at this point that the dividing line between capital budgeting and strategic management blurs.

It is convenient to think of strategic management as having three elements: (1) defined goal(s), (2) strategy, and (3) a set of tactics.

Goal(s)

In the broadest sense, firms strive for security, that is, a set of conditions harmonious with the survival of the organization. We may think of these conditions as "barriers to competition" or unique characteristics which create a superior market position. Thus, IBM's hold on the mainframe computer market confers on that firm a special competitive advantage. "Barriers to competition" may also arise from size, impediments to entering the industry, diversity of product line, research and development capability, vertical or horizontal integration, or conglomerate diversification. The list is as extensive as the possible solutions to the challenges that confront the business firm. From a financial perspective, it is these "barriers to competition" that generate positive net present values or above-market returns on investment.

Top management has the responsibility to define firm goals. It is this definition of goals that constitutes the dividing line between capital budgeting and strategic management. If management's vision of firm development is merely to support the existing product line, simply to keep the company on course, then conventional capital budgeting techniques constitute the appropriate decision tools. However, if management has defined a set of goals which change the direction of firm development, then it has crossed over the line into the realm of strategic management and must employ alternative decision models, discussed in Chapters 22 to 25.

Yet before setting a course to steer the enterprise, one must first know its present position. This requires close examination of the company's market share, an audit of the physical plant to assess the capability of achieving market objectives and securing the necessary inputs to production, and an appraisal of the organization's human resources.

Strategy

Strategy translates firm goals into specific policies in the pursuit of concrete objectives. It coordinates the management of scarce resources in the direction of the stated goals. Strategy tells second-level management the potential areas of business development to investigate, sets priorities, and guides the planning process. To illustrate, if top management wishes to diversify operations by entering markets that promise a lower covariance of cash flows, then which industries merit investigation to achieve the goal? Among the industries worthy of analysis, in which do we find firms that best link up with the managerial skills and technology of the acquiring firm? Is it preferable to accomplish firm goals by direct investment in new assets or by indirect investment through merger? Is the plan to be financed by internal resources (retained earnings) or by external financing? These are questions of strategy.

Tactics

Tactics relate to the nitty-gritty of implementing the company's goals and strategy, namely, the analysis of specific projects for investment. At this level, the circle closes and capital budgeting techniques may be applied to evaluate projects delineated by the strategic plan.

If we relate the assumptions of financial management to the requirements of strategic planning, we can identify the major decision points in the capital budgeting process:

1. Has management examined the current position of the firm? Strategic planning presupposes a clear understanding of the firm's current position, its sources of strength and actual or potential weaknesses. In developing long-range plans, a cost-effective audit of current operations is in order. The survey should cover at least the following major areas:

- ☐ The size of the market for each product line and the firm's share of each market segment.
- ☐ The capacities, locations, adaptability, and condition of existing plant and equipment, viewed in terms of accessibility to distribution points and to input sources (labor, raw materials, fuel, utilities, transportation, and so on) and the types and kinds of managerial and technological skills likely to be attracted to these locations.
- ☐ Potential new markets for the existing product line by product extension or market extension forms of business combinations. Alternatively, are there advantages in horizontal or vertical combinations that promise economies of scale from specialization? Are there opportunities for diversification from the pure conglomerate form?
- ☐ What are the basic economic trends, favorable or unfavorable, affecting the future of the industry and the company? Ponder, if you will, the last two decades of experience in the worldwide steel industry.
- ☐ Is the political environment, existing and forthcoming legislation, and tax law helpful or harmful to the prospects of the industry and the company? For example, given prevailing attitudes, the future of the tobacco industry does not inspire confidence.
- ☐ Based upon the foregoing estimates, what changes appear likely in the firm's business and financial risk posture.

Strategic planning does not establish, at the outset, a detailed set of expenditures. Rather, it is an interactive process of setting goals, surveying current operations, soliciting feedback opinion and relevant data, and then finalizing company objectives. For example, after Philip Morris acquired the Miller Brewing Company, the former decided to modernize and relocate Miller facilities. This required detailed analysis of all combinations of location and plant design. Precise cost estimates for each combination had to be devised. The combinations had to be evaluated also in terms of the existing and anticipated pattern of demand as well as distribution facilities. Only after this comprehensive analysis could specific "go/no-go" decisions be made.

The capital budget incorporates two classes of investment projects: mandatory investments, which are essential if the firm is to remain in business (for example, projects required by government regulatory agencies or necessary to the continuance of the business), and discretionary investments, which represent the aspirations or goals of management. This distinction leads to our second decision point.

2. Are the objectives of the capital budget defined? Each annual capital expenditure program is a step in the direction of the firm's strategic plan. This suggests (a) that management prioritize specific projects so that they come on line in a rational sequence and (b) that a time frame be established for the accomplishment of the strategic plan.

3. How is the capital budget to be financed? Will the budget be financed predominantly by retained earnings or by some combination of debt and equity? There are arguments pro and con for each approach.

As noted, business firms refer to the "cost of capital." The term defines the weighted average cost of all the different types of capital included in the firm's financial structure (short- and long-term debt, preferred stock, common stock, and retained earnings). Since the cost of each type of capital in the firm's financial structure interrelates with the amount and cost of every other type, there exists for each company an optimum financial structure, that is, a combination of debt and equity which yields the lowest weighted average cost of funds.

The cost of capital, on the other hand, is not a static figure. It is a dynamic calculation responsive to conditions in the money and capital markets and the fortunes of the enterprise. The cost of capital forms the base line or benchmark for evaluating proposed projects. It would be incorrect to evaluate a project on the basis of the financing costs attached to that project, given the interaction among the different types of capital in the company's financial structure. Using the cost of capital to discount the cash flows of all projects, therefore, assures an equitable and uniform evaluation for purposes of ranking the projects.

4. Have all alternatives been identified? Control of capital assets can be acquired in different ways: by purchase of new assets, purchase of existing assets, leasing, merger, participation in joint ventures, and so on. These alternative modes of acquisition affect the costs of ownership and need to be explored with an eye to minimizing investment outlays.

Similarly, in the case of an asset already owned by the company, it may be replaced by a new asset with the same function, modernized by additional investment, rebuilt to its original condition, disposed of without replacement, or simply left on line in an as-is condition. The notion to stress is that all alternatives be examined, for any project can look good when compared with a sufficiently poor alternative.

Evaluation, accordingly, requires the calculation of a return from each of the available alternatives. However, firms have different evaluation procedures, and these may result in different rankings of the capital projects under review. Common evaluation procedures include net present value, internal rate of return, payback, discounted payback, and average rate of return. Since these procedures do not necessarily produce similar project rankings, a good rule to follow is to use more than one method of evaluation and investigate the differences, if any. Chapters 5 and 6 discuss evaluation techniques, and Chapter 7 examines the superiority of the net present value technique.

The greatest proportion of capital expenditures is allocated for the replacement of worn-out or obsolete plant and equipment. The analyses required for replacement investments are simplified if accurate records on past performance are available. Management, having had experience with the existing equipment, is aware of wage rates, material costs, product demand characteristics, and so on. This expertise improves the quality of the analyses and tends to reduce the inherent risk of investment.

When making replacement decisions, five factors warrant particular attention:

☐ The operating costs of existing plant and equipment and of alternative investments.

☐ The cost-effectiveness of rebuilding or overhauling versus replacement (including tax ramifications).

☐ The potential alternative uses and the marketability of replacement plant and equipment should demand for the output decline. The product life cycle must be projected.

☐ The probability that technological innovation may quickly make obsolete newly acquired plant and equipment. This contingency would suggest leasing rather than the purchase of new equipment.

☐ If new facilities are acquired on the assumption of growth in demand, the level of growth the company can sustain without a fundamental restructuring of operating and financial policies.

Peoples Express illustrates the dangers of excessive growth. In this case, rapid and enthusiastic growth upset the company's strategic plan, generated a financial crisis, and forced a contraction in operations. As mentioned in Assumption 8, the issue relates to the concept of sustainable growth.

Moreover, the replacement problem does not involve simply inserting new facilities into an existing production line. There is a need to balance the productivity of individual components to minimize idle time. Industrial engineers, for example, view production in terms of processes and look at plant and equipment as systems rather than as unit-by-unit items. Relatively simple questions, such as the replacement of an aging boiler, grow more complex when the boiler is viewed as part of an aging plant, each component of which will ultimately have to be overhauled or replaced in the near term.

Replacement projects are frequently classified as mandatory investments. Discretionary investments are more likely to involve expansion into closely related product lines (product extension conglomerates), expansion into new geographic areas (market extension conglomerates), or diversification into unrelated product lines (pure conglomerates). Mandatory and discretionary investments have to be evaluated for each fiscal year. The former, though essential, may not promise an expected return, and the selection criterion is to minimize cost. The latter can be ranked by return and risk. The budget will include both types of projects, and the challenge to management is to select from an array of mandatory and discretionary projects that combination that will constitute the year's budget. Capital budgeting thus progresses from the evaluation of projects to the evaluation of alternative budget combinations.

5. Have the cash flows of each project proposed been identified? As a corollary to the foregoing, the analyst must estimate the incremental cash inflows and outflows of each capital project. This is not an easy assignment. Are the projects dependent or independent? If the cash flow of one project depends upon the acceptance of another, the two projects should be treated as a single proposal for evaluation purposes. Since

the capital budget addresses future cash inflows and outflows, how were the estimates formulated and what level of confidence can be placed in the projections? One cannot divorce capital budgeting from the underlying forecasting methodology. Also, in properly identifying the cash flows, the analyst must isolate the after-tax effects of noncash items, such as depreciation, losses on the disposal of fixed assets, and losses on the disposal of spare parts inventories.

6. Has management assessed the risks inherent in the strategic plan? Risk can be viewed in several ways. As the strategic plan unfolds with each year's capital budget, the business risk of the company will change complexion. The *business risk*, or the degree of operating leverage (DOL), depends upon the mix of fixed and variable costs in the production process. The higher the DOL, the more sensitive is net operating income to any percentage change in sales. Similarly, the way management finances the strategic plan affects the *financial risk* of the enterprise. The latter refers to the ratio of debt to equity or the degree of financial leverage (DFL). As the DFL increases, the percentage change in net income after taxes will be greater for any given percentage change in net operating income.

Another view of risk envisions the firm as a portfolio not of stocks and bonds but of capital projects incorporated into operations at different times. How the cash flows from these projects *covary* with business conditions will mitigate or intensify risk. For example, the merger of two steel companies will probably intensify the risk of the combination since, as capital goods companies, they are similarly affected by the business cycle. The question for analysis is: How will the cash flows from new projects conceived by the strategic plan affect the *covariance* of cash flows for the business as an entity?

In turn, these concepts of risk are reflected in the market price of the firm's common stock through P/E ratios and beta value (see Chapter 15). This process compels management to ask itself how much additional risk can be accepted in pursuit of higher returns. The stockholder profile of the firm is not without relevance to this judgment.

7. How do nonquantitative factors impact the budget? The capital budget results from a quantitative analysis of monetary costs and benefits. However, dollar values do not capture all the real benefits and real costs of business operations. Depletion of natural resources, pollution of air and water supplies, and the costs of labor displacement are mostly nonquantifiable. On the other hand, management must be alert to these "intangibles" or face the prospect of having a refined quantitative analysis being strongly opposed by community and pressure groups. The recent history of the nuclear power industry is an object lesson in the complications which can arise from not fully considering the "intangible" consequences of new projects.

8. Is the capital budget consistent with the short-term plan and the cash budget? The dreams of tomorrow are enticing and essential to the development of the firm. All the same, the firm must survive in the present, or there will be no tomorrow. The capital budget has to be managed so as to maintain the viability of current operations and the financial health of the company. An important consideration here is whether the firm has a reserve of liquidity to handle unforeseen contingencies and/or to take advantage of unanticipated opportunities.

So also, the cash budget should reflect expected cash flows based upon short- and long-term business plans and should include plans for acquisition of funds from external sources, payment of obligations, and so on. Development of a cash budget is necessary because the timing of the actual capital expenditures must be correlated to correspond with the funds available within the business.

9. Has the company developed a capital budgeting manual? A budget is simply a plan for spending and not an authorization to spend. The authorization procedure is described in the capital budgeting manual. A complete manual will also cover project evaluation criteria, the required data, and the format for presentation of capital proposals; key dates in the budgeting cycle; establishment of priorities; and the line of authority for approval of projects and the formulation of the capital budget. The rationale for the capital budgeting manual is to impart an appreciation to all management personnel of the nature and significance of the capital budget. People do not take seriously that which they do not understand.

10. Has provision been made to monitor the implementation of the budget? This topic should also be covered in the capital budgeting manual. In general, once expenditures have been authorized, strict cost controls should be put in place. Monitoring costs and establishing crucial "go" and "no-go" decision points are vital in limiting cost overruns. PERT/critical-path-monitoring systems are effective tools for controlling larger projects. The lessons learned from close cost control help to improve future estimating procedures as well as point to problems with projects under completion.

11. Are capital projects periodically reassessed? Finally, after a project has been completed and put on line, the actual revenues and costs must be compared with the forecasted figures. This facet of capital budgeting has met with minimal enthusiasm in most companies. Yet, if we are to rely on future estimates, we must determine the deviations between actual and projected cash flows and seek out the causes of these deviations. For individuals and companies, the process of recognizing and understanding the sources of past errors is a most valuable learning experience. But learning from past successes and failures is only one benefit of the monitoring function; the more important benefit is the contribution made to the ongoing evaluative process. Should the project be continued or liquidated in favor of a potentially more valuable investment. Nothing is static. Project abandonment is as much a part of capital budgeting as asset acquisition.

This brief discussion alludes to the numerous facets and intricacies of capital asset management. Our goal is to provide the analytical tools necessary to the process and offer some illustrations as to how the process is actually carried out by business. Initially, we shall rely on a pervasive tool of financial management—discounted cash flow. This takes the form of interest calculations and the reverse function of discounting cash flows back to their present values. The subject matter is discussed in Chapters 2 and 3.

INSTITUTIONAL BACKGROUND

The business firm buys, sells, and invests within a framework of law and the conceptual foundations of the private enterprise system. The latter include custom and traditions, ethical codes, and generally accepted philosophic principles. This system of values influences the set of available investment opportunities and the network of firm interactions. Mandatory capital investments must be made if the firm is to remain in business. In this regard, for instance, the Environmental Protection Agency (EPA) mandated certain investments by the steel industry to prevent air pollution. Or public utility commissions require utilities to service all customers within a defined area as a franchise obligation without regard to the economics of servicing some regions. These investments may produce no revenues and entail only the expenditure of funds. In these cases, the analyst should recommend the project which minimizes discounted cash outlays.

Federal and state tax laws have a pervasive influence on the decision to invest in new capital assets and/or accept the risks of business enterprise. Supplemented by IRS and Tax Court interpretations, the federal tax code has at various times granted investment tax credits and at other times revoked the provision. The same ambivalence is present in the treatment of the depreciation tax deduction. Until the passage of the Economic Recovery Act of 1981 (ERTA) and the Tax Equity and Fiscal Responsibility Act of 1982 (TEFRA), two forms of depreciation were allowed for tax purposes: straight-line depreciation (SLD) or accelerated depreciation using either the sum-of-the-years-digits method (SYD) or the double-declining-balance method (DDB). The purpose of accelerated depreciation, like the investment tax credit, was to encourage capital formation. The passage of ERTA revised the method of computing accelerated depreciation by substituting the accelerated cost recovery system (ACRS). Under ACRS (as modified by the Tax Reform Act of 1986) the depreciation allowance depends upon which of eight classes the asset falls under.

ERTA, TEFRA, and the Tax Reform Act of 1986 also affected leasing arrangements. Other pertinent areas covered by these changes included taxation of ordinary income (net operating income), capital gains and losses, capital loss carrybacks and carryforwards, and the expensing of depreciable assets.

However desirable tax reform may seem, frequent changes in the tax code constitute unsettling events which add to the risk of business. The instability is compounded when we realize that changes in federal tax law are oft-times followed by modifications in state laws. The most recent changes in the federal code are summarized in Chapter 4.

Traditions are harder to change than laws. In this respect, we can rest assured that the evaluation of capital projects will continue to depend upon the discounting of cash flows. The distinctions between simple and compound interest, between present value and terminal value, and between annuities and perpetuities will persist. They are part of the warp and woof of our financial system and are discussed in Chapter 3.

SUMMARY

We have attempted in this introduction to discuss, albeit with a broad brush, the conceptual basis of capital budgeting, the interaction of managerial and financial considerations, and the supporting institutional structure of society. We have discussed in some detail the assumptions of capital budgeting, for no theory can be better than the assumptions upon which the theory rests. The assumptions also alert the user to the limitations of the financial analysis.

1. What are the basic steps required to evaluate a capital project adequately?
2. Cite several reasons why capital budgeting decisions are vital to firms.
3. Give a simple definition or description of capital budgeting.
4. How can you, as financial manager, explain the role of financial management in the strategic planning process?
5. The novice to capital budgeting may interpret the term *project* to mean only a new investment in plant and equipment. Evaluate this assumption as it relates to the overall theory of the firm.
6. What are the basic assumptions underlying capital budgeting theory?
7. If a project that enhances the rate of return on a firm's assets is rejected because it increases the possibility of insolvency, other goals of the firm have been brought into the decision process. What are some of the goals of a firm that should be considered in evaluating a capital investment project?
8. Explain the significance of a business plan and indicate how it relates to capital budgeting.
9. Given the constantly changing tax laws, why are taxes not just ignored in capital budgeting analysis?
10. Chapter 1 discusses the necessity of integrating the capital budgeting process into the firm's overall strategic plan. Outline and discuss the most important steps which should be implemented in the capital budgeting process to help achieve this integration.

REFERENCES

Ang, J. S. "A Graphical Presentation of an Integrated Capital Budgeting Model." *Engineering Economist* (Winter 1978).

Anthony, R. N. "The Trouble with Profit Maximization." *Harvard Business Review*, 38 (November–December 1960), 126–134.

Balachandran, Bala V., Nandu J. Nagarajan, and Alfred Rappaport. "Threshold Margins for Creating Economic Value." *Financial Management* (Spring 1986).

Branch, Ben. "Corporate Objectives and Market Performance." *Financial Management*, 2 (Summer 1973), 24–29.

Ciscel, David H., and Thomas M. Carroll. "The Determinants of Executive Salaries: An Econometric Survey." *Review of Economics and Statistics*, 62 (February 1980), 7–13.

Davis, Keith. "Social Responsibility Is Inevitable." *California Management Review*, 19 (Fall 1970), 14–20.

De Alessi, Louis. "Private Property and Dispersion of Ownership in Large Corporations." *Journal of Finance*, 28 (September 1973), 839–851.

Dean, J. *Capital Budgeting*. New York: Columbia University Press, 1951.

De Angelo, Harry, and Linda De Angelo. "Managerial Ownership of Voting Rights: A Study of Public Corporation with Dual Classes of Common Stock." *Journal of Financial Economics* (Winter 1985).

De Angelo, Harry, and Edward M. Rice. "Anti-Takeover Charter Amendments and Stockholder Wealth," Working paper, Graduate School of Business Administration, University of Washington, 1980.

Dewing, A. S. *Financial Policy of Corporations*, 5th ed. New York: The Ronald Press Company, 1953.

Donaldson, Gordon. "Financial Management in an Affluent Society." *Financial Executive*, 35 (April 1967), 52–60.

Downs, Thomas W. "The User Cost and Capital Budgeting." *Financial Review* (Spring 1986).

Fama, E. F. "Agency Problems and the Theory of the Firm." *Journal of Political Economy* (April 1980), 288–307.

_____. "The Effects of a Firm's Investment and Financing Decisions on the Welfare of Its Security Holders." *American Economic Review*, 68 (September 1978), 272–284.

_____. *Foundations of Finance*. New York: Basic Books, 1976.

Fama, Eugene, and Michael Jensen. "Organizational Forms and Investment Decisions." *Journal of Financial Economics* (Winter 1985).

Findlay, M. Chapman, III, and G. A. Whitmore. "Beyond Shareholder Wealth Maximization." *Financial Management*, 3 (Winter 1974), 25–35.

_____, and Edward E. Williams. "Capital Allocation and the Nature of Ownership Equities." *Financial Management*, 1 (Spring 1972), 72–96.

Galbraith, J. K. *The New Industrial State*. Boston: Houghton Mifflin Company, 1967.

Gitman, Lawrence, and Charles E. Maxwell. "Financial Activities of Major U.S. Firms: Survey and Analysis of *Fortune*'s 1,000." *Financial Management* (Winter 1985).

Grabowski, Henry G., and Dennis C. Mueller. "Managerial and Stockholder Welfare Models of Firm Expenditures." *Review of Economics and Statistics*, 54 (February 1972), 9–24.

Hakansson, Nils H. "The Fantastic World of Finance: Progress and the Free Lunch." *Journal of Financial and Quantitative Analysis*, 14 (November 1979), 717–734.

Hibdon, J. E. *Price and Welfare Theory*. New York: McGraw-Hill Book Company, 1969.

Hill, Lawrence W. "The Growth of the Corporate Finance Function." *Financial Executive*, 44 (July 1976), 36–43.

Hodder, James E. "Evaluation of Manufacturing Investments: A Comparison of U.S. and Japanese Practices." *Financial Management* (Spring 1986).

Jennergren, I. Peter. "On the Design of Incentives in Business Firms—A Survey of Some Research." *Management Science* (February 1980).

Jensen, Michael C., and William H. Meckling. "Theory of the Firm: Managerial Behavior, Agency Costs and Ownership Structure." *Journal of Financial Economics*, 3 (October 1976), 305–360.

Kester, W. Carl. "Capital and Ownership Structure: A Comparison of United States and Japanese Manufacturing Corporations." *Financial Management* (Spring 1986).

Lee, Sang M., and A. J. Lerro. "Capital Budgeting for Multiple Objectives." *Financial Management* (Spring 1974).

Levy, Haim, and Marshall Sarnat. "A Pedagogic Note on Alternative Formulations of the Goal of the Firm." *Journal of Business*, 50 (October 1977), 526–528.

Lewellen, W. G. "Management and Ownership in the Large Firm." *Journal of Finance*, 26 (May 1969), 299–322.

Lloyd, William P., John S. Jahera, Jr., and Steven J. Goldstein. "The Relation Between Returns, Ownership Structure and Market Value." *Journal of Financial Research* (Spring 1986).

McConnell, John J., and Chris J. Muscarella. "Corporate Capital Expenditure Decisions and the Market Value of the Firm." *Journal of Financial Economics* (Fall 1985).

Moag, J. S., W. T. Carleton, and E. M. Lerner. "Defining the Finance Function: A Model-Systems Approach." *Journal of Finance*, 22 (December 1967), 543–556.

Moore, J. R. "The Financial Executive in the 1970s." *Financial Executive*, 35 (January 1967), 28–36.

Osteryoung, J. S. "A Survey into the Goals Used by *Fortune*'s 500 Companies in Capital Budgeting Decisions." *Akron Business and Economic Review* (Fall 1973).

Petty, J. W., D. F. Scott, Jr., and M. M. Bird. "The Capital Expenditure Decision-Making Process of Large Corporations." *The Engineering Economist* (Spring 1975).

Pinches, George E. "Myopia, Capital Budgeting and Decision Making." *Financial Management*, 11 (Autumn 1982), 6–19.

Pogue, G. A., and K. Lall. "Corporate Finance: An Overview." *Sloan Management Review* (Spring 1974), 19–38.

Rappaport, A. "A Fatal Fascination with the Short Run." *Business Week*, May 4, 1981.

Sanger, Gary C., and John J. McConnell. "Stock Exchange Listings, Firm Value, and Security Market Efficiency: the Impact of NASDAQ." *Journal of Financial and Quantitative Analyses* (March 1986).

Simkowitz, Michael A., and Charles P. Jones. "A Note on the Simultaneous Nature of Finance Methodology." *Journal of Finance*, 27 (March 1972), 103–108.

Solomon, Ezra. "What Should We Teach in a Course in Business Finance?" *Journal of Finance*, 21 (May 1966), 411–415.

Summers, Laurence. "On Economics and Finance." *The Journal of Finance* (July 1985).

Weston, J. Fred. "New Themes in Finance." *Journal of Finance*, 24 (March 1974), 237–243.

_____. "Developments in Finance Theory." *Financial Management*, 10th Anniversary Edition (1981), 5–22.

Interest and Annuities

2

In Chapter 1 we indicated that central to the process of evaluation of capital investments is the discounting of cash flows to be recovered in the future to their present values. In this chapter dealing with the mathematics of *discounted cash flow*, we detail the computations involving simple and compound interest and the future value of an annuity. Here, we start with a present sum and determine its value in the future. In the following chapter, we reverse the process and ascertain the present value of sums to be received in the future.

SIMPLE AND COMPOUND INTEREST

Since the computations for simple and compound interest form the basis for discounted cash flow analysis, we examine these first. *Simple interest* is computed using Equation (1),

$$I = (P)(i)(t) \tag{1}$$

where I = dollar amount of simple interest earned
    P = principal
    i = rate of return (interest rate)
    t = time period over which funds are invested

The accumulated fund at the end of the time period in question would simply be the amount of interest earned (I) plus the original principal (P).

When we speak of simple interest, it is assumed that the interest will be withdrawn and paid as soon as it is earned. *Compound interest*, on the other hand, is earned on the fund consisting of both the principal and previously earned interest; thus we are earning "interest on interest" to produce the compounding effect. The time of calculation could be the end of a month, quarter, year, and so on. The compound sum after one period is calculated using Equation (2),

$$S = P(1 + i) \qquad (2)$$

where S = compound sum.

Funds may be compounded annually or more frequently. The easier case of annual compounding is considered first. If funds are invested with annual compounding, the compound sum after n years is found using Equation (3),

$$S_n = P(1 + i)^n \qquad (3)$$

where S_n = compound sum after n years
     n = number of years

It should be mentioned that the calculations required throughout the text can be carried out using present/future value tables (such as those we have provided in Appendix B at the back of the text), financial calculators, or spreadsheet packages on micro-computers. The tables we have included in Appendix B were selected because of their extensive nature and because they have a written description and a mathematical formula at the top of each column. These latter two characteristics assist the user in understanding what the factors in any given column mean and in determining appropriate factors for interest rates or number of periods not shown in the tables. We encourage the reader to gain first a clear understanding of the correct analytical process to be used to solve the problem at hand. Once this is accomplished, carrying out the calculations is by-and-large mechanical. We suggest that the reader achieve experience and facility in using the most recent and efficient problem-solving technology. To this end, we have developed a set of LOTUS 1-2-3 templates to accompany this text and have endeavored to make them very usable even for spreadsheet novices.

EXAMPLE 1
Compound Interest

A depositor puts $3,000 in a bank at 5%, compounded annually, for 3 years. Determine the amount that will have accrued at the end of 3 years.

SOLUTION: Use Equation (3), as follows:

$$S_3 = \$3,000(1 + 0.05)^3$$
$$= \$3,000(1.157625)$$
$$= \$3,472.88$$

At the end of 3 years, the depositor will have $3,472.88.

Use of the first column in Appendix B, "Compound Interest and Annuity Table," provides the factors that are referred to as *single payment/compound interest factors*. In Example 1, for instance, reference to the 5% page, 3-year row gives the interest factor 1.157625.

EXAMPLE 2
Simple versus Compound Interest

> An investor places $20,000 in an 8% account. How much will he have at the end of 6 years?
>
> SOLUTION:
>
> $$S_6 = \$20,000(1.586874)$$
>
> $$= \$31,737.48$$
>
> The investor will have $31,737.48 in 6 years. Thus he has earned $11,737.48 in interest, since he left the interest along with the original principal to earn additional interest. The amount of simple interest earned each year would be $1,600, which means that $9,600 of simple interest would have been earned over the 6-year period. The extra $2,137.48 of interest is the result of the compounding.

INTEREST COMPOUNDED MORE THAN ONCE A YEAR

In many instances, interest is compounded more frequently than annually. If this is the case, then the compound sum is found using Equation (4),

$$S_n = P\left(1 + \frac{i}{m}\right)^{m \times n} \tag{4}$$

where m = number of times interest is compounded per year.

Appendix B may be helpful in solving for the compound sum, but its usefulness is limited. See Example 3.

EXAMPLE 3
Interest Compounded More Than Once A Year

> An investor places $1,000 at 8% interest. Determine the amount that will have accrued after 3 years if the interest is compounded annually, semiannually, quarterly, and monthly.
>
> SOLUTION: *Consider annual compounding first*: Use Column 1 from Appendix B as in Example 1.
>
> $$S_3 = \$1,000(1.259712) = \$1,259.71$$

Consider semiannual compounding next: First, solve using Equation (4).

$$S_3 = \$1,000\left(1 + \frac{0.08}{2}\right)^{2\times 3}$$

$$= \$1,000(1.04)^6$$

$$= \$1,000(1.2653189)$$

$$= \$1,265.32$$

Appendix B can be used to solve this problem, which involves the equivalent of 4% for 6 years. Thus the factor for 4% and 6 years is obtained from Appendix B.

$$S_3 = \$1,000(1.265319) = \$1,265.32$$

Consider quarterly compounding next: First, solve using Equation (4).

$$S_3 = \$1,000\left(1 + \frac{0.08}{4}\right)^{4\times 3}$$

$$= \$1,000(1.02)^{12}$$

$$= \$1,000(1.2682418)$$

$$= \$1,268.24$$

Appendix B can also be used to solve this problem, which involves the equivalent of 2% for 12 years. Thus the factor for 2% and 12 years is obtained from Appendix B.

$$S_3 = \$1,000(1.268242) = \$1,268.24$$

Finally, solve for monthly compounding: First, solve using Equation (4).

$$S_3 = \$1,000\left(1 + \frac{0.08}{12}\right)^{12\times 3}$$

$$= \$1,000(1.006666)^{36}$$

$$= \$1,000(1.2702321)$$

$$= \$1,270.23$$

Appendix B cannot be used to solve this problem, since it involves the equivalent of two-thirds of 1% interest for 36 years and the compound interest factor for this is not included in Appendix B.

It is interesting to note in Example 3 how more frequent compounding leads to higher effective interest yields. The initial change in the frequency of compounding (yearly to semiannual) results in a greater increase in effective yield than do subsequent changes (semiannual to quarterly). At the limit, interest may be compounded continuously.

Table 2–1   Values of e^x

x	e^x	x	e^x	x	e^x
0.01	1.0101	0.08	1.0833	0.35	1.4191
0.02	1.0202	0.09	1.0942	0.40	1.4918
0.03	1.0305	0.10	1.1052	0.45	1.5683
0.04	1.0408	0.15	1.1618	0.50	1.6487
0.05	1.0513	0.20	1.2214	0.55	1.7333
0.06	1.0618	0.25	1.2840	0.60	1.8221
0.07	1.0725	0.30	1.3499	0.65	1.9155

CONTINUOUS COMPOUNDING

Some financial institutions utilize continuous compounding. Equation (4) then becomes Equation (5):

$$S_n = P\left[\lim_{m \to \infty}\left(1 + \frac{i}{m}\right)^{mn}\right] \tag{5}$$

Equation (5) can be rearranged as follows:

$$S_n = P\left\{\lim_{m \to \infty}\left[\left(1 + \frac{i}{m}\right)^{m/i}\right]^{in}\right\}$$

The limit as m approaches infinity of $(1 + i/m)^{m/i}$ is e, the base of the natural or Naperian logarithmic system. An irrational number, e has an approximate value of 2.7182.

Equation (5) can be rewritten as Equation (6):

$$S_n = Pe^{in} \tag{6}$$

Values of e^x are contained in Table 2–1.

EXAMPLE 4
Continuous Compounding

A depositor placed $2,000 at 10% interest compounded continuously for 5 years. Determine the compound sum at the end of the 5-year period.

SOLUTION: Use Equation (6) and Table 2–1.

$$S_5 = \$2,000\,e^{(0.10)5}$$
$$= \$2,000\,e^{0.50}$$
$$= \$2,000(1.6487)$$
$$= \$3,297.40$$

If interest had been just compounded annually, the compound sum would have been $2,000(1.610510) = $3,221.02. The continuous compounding resulted in an additional $76.38 of interest.

EXPONENTIAL EFFECTS OF COMPOUNDING

Equation (3) is an *exponential function*, which is significant for two reasons. First, the compound sum (S_n) increases at an increasing rate. For example, if $100.00 were invested at 10%, the compound sum would be $110.00, $121.00, and $133.10 after 1, 2, and 3 years, respectively. Second, the compound sum increases at an increasingly faster rate at higher rates of interest. For example, consider the compound sum of $100.00 after 20 years invested at the following rates: 6%, 8%, 10%, and 12%. The compound sums are $320.71, $466.09, $672.75, and $964.63, respectively. Notice that the difference between the compound sum at 6% and 8% is $145.38, while the difference between the compound sum at 10% and 12% is $291.88—more than twice the former. The exponential effects of compounding are graphically demonstrated in Figure 2–1.

COMPOUND INTEREST AND THE REINVESTMENT RATE

Throughout the sections on compound interest, we have implicitly assumed a *constant reinvestment rate*. This means that all interest obtained from an investment is

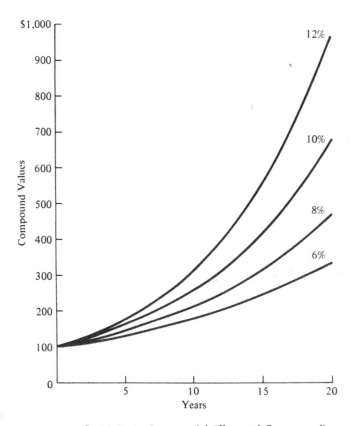

FIGURE 2–1   Exponential Effects of Compounding.

reinvested at the stated rate of return for that investment during the life of the investment. This is a very important assumption, as all interest, annuity, and present value tables are constructed based on a constant reinvestment rate.

Most investments do *not* have a constant reinvestment rate. An example of one that does is a bank certificate—interest is normally either paid at specified periods *or* may be reinvested at the rate paid on the certificate. In the latter case, the interest is returned to the investor when the certificate matures. An example of an investment that does not have a constant reinvestment rate is a bond. There is a periodic payment of interest (generally semiannually). The reinvestment rate for the interest depends upon the market return available on a security of comparable risk at the time the interest is paid.

FUTURE VALUE OF AN ANNUITY

Sometimes deposits are made regularly on an annual basis into a savings or pension fund (such as an IRA). To determine the amount which will accumulate after a number of years, we use Equation (7),

$$F = A \left[\frac{(1 + i)^n - 1}{i} \right] \qquad (7)$$

where F = future value of an annuity payment
  A = annual *year-end* annuity payment
  i = rate of return (interest rate)
  n = number of years

Values of $[(1 + i)^n - 1]/i$, commonly referred to as *future value of an annuity factors* and symbolized by S_n, are provided in Appendix B, second column. Equation (7) is derived in the appendix to this chapter.

EXAMPLE 5
Future Value of an Annuity

An investor places $1,400 per year at the *end* of each year into an IRA for 25 years. Interest is compounded annually at 8%. Determine the amount in the account at the end of the period.

SOLUTION: Use Equation (7) and Appendix B, 8% page, 25-year row:

$$F = \$1,400(73.015940)$$

$$= \$102,348.31$$

The investor will have $102,348.31 in 25 years.

EXAMPLE 6

Future Value of an Annuity

> Repeat Example 5 using 6% and 10% interest rates.
>
> SOLUTION:
>   At 6%, $F = \$1,400(54.864512) = \$76,810.32$.
>   At 10%, $F = \$1,400(98.347059) = \$137,685.88$.

The results of Examples 5 and 6 are tabulated for comparison:

INTEREST RATE	FUTURE VALUE OF ANNUITY	INCREMENTAL DIFFERENCE
6%	$76,810.32	
8	102,348.31	$25,537.99
10	137,685.88	35,337.57

The differences between the future values resulting from the three interest rates selected are very substantial. The differences become greater as the interest rate is increased. If, for example, we selected a 12% rate, the increase over 10% would be $48,981.53. The reason for the size of the differences is that the compound interest factors increase exponentially as noted earlier in this chapter.

EXPONENTIAL EFFECTS OF COMPOUNDING OF ANNUITIES

The exponential effects of compounding of annuities are very important, especially in the area of pension planning. The rate of return has a very significant effect on the amount accumulated in a fund. The values shown in Table 2–2 represent the accumulations in an annuity based on payments of $2,000 per year at the end of each year.

START-OF-YEAR ANNUITIES

Sometimes annuities are paid at the beginning of the year rather than at the end. If this is the case, the future value will be substantially greater. Finding the future value

Table 2–2   Annuity Values — $2,000 Year-End Payments

INTEREST RATE	ACCUMULATION		
	10 YEARS	20 YEARS	30 YEARS
8%	$28,973	$91,524	$226,566
10	31,875	114,550	328,988
12	35,097	144,105	482,665
14	38,675	182,050	713,574

of an annuity paid at the start of the year involves the use of both the compound interest (column 1) and future value of an annuity (column 2) of Appendix B. The procedure is demonstrated in Example 7.

EXAMPLE 7
Future Value of an Annuity Paid at the Start of the Year

An investor pays $1,400 per year into an IRA for 25 years. Interest is compounded annually at 8%. Determine the amount in the account in 25 years assuming payments are made at the start of each year.

SOLUTION: Since future value tables are computed for *end-of-year payments*, it is necessary to use the compound interest table for the initial payment and then the future value tables for 25 years, subtracting 1, corresponding to the final year-end payment which is not made (since payments are made at the start of each year).

$$F = \$1,400(6.848475 + 73.105940 - 1)$$

$$= \$1,400(78.954415) = \$110,536.18$$

The difference between the year-end payment annuity found in Example 5 and the start-of-the-year payment annuity just determined is $8,187.87 ($110,536.18 − $102,348.31).

SINKING-FUND PAYMENTS

A *sinking fund* is a fund created to provide for payment of a debt or other obligation by setting aside a certain amount at stated intervals, usually at the end of each year. Sinking-fund payments may be determined using *sinking-fund factors*, which are the reciprocals of the future value of annuity factors. Sinking-fund factors are found in Appendix B, column 3,

sinking-fund payment = fund obligation × sinking-fund factor

$$A = F\left[\frac{i}{(1 + i)^n - 1}\right] \tag{8}$$

where the sinking-fund factor is the expression in brackets.

EXAMPLE 8
Sinking Fund Payments

A corporation needs $15,000,000 in 15 years to pay off a bond issue. The bond indenture requires the establishment of a sinking fund with annual year-end payments. If the corporation can earn 6% annually on its sinking fund, how much must it put into the fund for 15 years to accumulate the full $15,000,000?

SOLUTION: Use Equation (8) and the sinking-fund factor from Appendix B, column 3, for 6% and 15 years:

$$\text{sinking-fund payment} = \$15,000,000 \times 0.04296276$$
$$= \$644,441.40$$

The corporation must put $644,441.40 into the fund each year for 15 years to accumulate $15,000,000.

QUESTIONS

PROBLEMS

1. A sum of $3,000 is invested at 8% for one year. Determine the interest received.

2. The XYZ Company needs $5,000 at the end of 5 years. If the interest rate is 8%, determine the end-of-year payment for each of the 5 years.

3. Peter Jones will receive a 12% return on a $6,000 investment for 4 years. How much will he have at the end of the 4-year period if we assume the following:

    (a) The interest is compounded yearly.

    (b) The interest is compounded semiannually.

    (c) The interest is compounded quarterly.

    (d) The interest is compounded monthly.

4. If $1,000 is invested for 5 years at 6%, compounded continuously, determine the compound sum.

5. Sharon O'Conner has a 6% passbook account at a local savings and loan association. If the interest is compounded semiannually, how much will she have at the end of 1 year if she has $100 on deposit at the start of the year?

6. Sandy Weber has an 8% growth certificate purchased from a bank. Interest is compounded quarterly. If she lets the interest accumulate, it will also be compounded at the same rate. The certificate costs $5,000 and has a life of 4 years. How much will she receive from the bank when the certificate matures?

7. If $1,000 is invested at 6%, 8%, and 10%, determine the compound sum after a period of 20 years and draw graphs for each of the relationships.

8. Mr. Jones wants to know what the compound sum of his $5,000 bank balance will be in 10 years. The interest rate is 5%. He has compound interest tables for 4% and 6%. If he averages the compound interest factors from his tables and uses the average to compute the compound sum, how much error will result?

9. How much must be deposited at the end of each year to have $10,000 in 10 years? Assume the funds earn 8% annual interest.

10. An investor placed $1,000 in an 8% investment trust for 20 years, compounded continuously. How much did the investor have at the end of the period?

11. Suppose compounding was semiannual in Problem 10. Calculate the difference between the compound sum and continuous compounding after 20 years.

12. The Joneses are planning for their retirement. If they have $10,000 now and will add $1,500 at the end of each year for 10 years, how much will they have in 10 years if the funds are invested at 8%? Suppose they invest the funds at the start of the year. How much will they accumulate in 10 years?

13. Ted and Joan want to build up an estate for their children. If they save $1,000 per year for 30 years, and the money is compounded annually at 6%, how much will they have?

    (a) Assume they save the $1,000 at the end of each year.

    (b) Assume they save the $1,000 at the start of each year.

14. John and Melissa Smith have a savings account of $8,500. John is to retire in 10 years. If they save $2,000 per year for the next 10 years and their original savings plus the yearly savings are compounded annually at 6%, how much will they have when John retires? Assume end-of-year savings of $2,000.

15. Crothers, Inc., must have $300,000 in 15 years to pay off a bond issue. How much must it put into a sinking fund at the end of each year to accumulate the $300,000 if funds are compounded at an annual rate of 8%?

16. Kline Industries needs to put a certain amount in a sinking fund each year for 15 years to pay off a $4.5 million bond issue. Determine the yearly payments for each of the following sinking funds based on a 6% rate of return.

    (a) The payments are made at the end of the year.

    (b) The payments are made at the beginning of the year.

17. A sinking fund is needed to pay off $10,000,000 in 20 years. If payments are made at the end of each year, determine the amount of each payment for the last 5 years, assuming $250,000 is placed in the fund for the first 15 years and all funds earn 7% interest compounded annually.

18. The state has determined actuarially that it will require $100,000 to fund Ms. Smith's pension. If Ms. Smith has 20 years until retirement, how much must the state place in the retirement system at the end of each year to fund Ms. Smith's retirement, assuming the return is 10% compounded annually?

19. An individual has $2,000 that can be invested in one of two ways. One investment will pay 10% for the next 15 years. As an alternative, the individual can put the investment in an initial 8% savings certificate for 5 years. The expectation is that savings certificate rates will increase 2% every 5 years. Which alternative would you choose? Ignore income taxes.

20. National Bank and Trust advertises passbook accounts paying 5% with a higher effective interest rate. Compute the effective annual yield based on quarterly, monthly, and continuous compounding.

21. Samuel Drucker put $1,000 in the bank 3 years ago. During the first year he received 5% interest compounded semiannually. During the last 2 years the rate was 6% compounded quarterly. How much did Drucker have at the end of 3 years?

22. You are debating the importance of placing funds into your individual retirement account at the beginning versus the end of the year. Suppose you put $2,000 in your IRA and obtain a 9% return. Determine the accumulation after 25 years assuming start-of-year and end-of-year payments and compare the accumulations.

23. An investor is considering the purchase of a bond which is currently selling for $800 and will mature in 10 years, being redeemed at that time for $1,000. In the interim it will pay $100 in interest per year. The interest will be paid at the end of each year. The investor plans to reinvest the interest payments. Suppose the investor reinvests the interest received each year at 12%. What will be the accumulation, including the redemption value of the bond? Perform the same calculations based on a return of 8% on the interest payments received. [Note: This problem is designed to demonstrate the importance of the reinvestment rate in determining the actual return on investment over the life of the asset. In succeeding chapters we will examine further the significance of the reinvestment rate.]

REFERENCES

See Chapter 3 for references on interest and annuities

APPENDIX: DERIVATION OF FORMULA
FOR FUTURE VALUE OF AN ANNUITY

Frequently, it is necessary to save a certain sum each year to accumulate a required amount within a given time period. In general, savings are made *at the end of the year* and the annuity tables are constructed in that manner.

When a payment is made each year for a period of n years, at interest rate i, the future value is expressed as follows,

$$F = A_1(1 + i)^{n-1} + A_2(1 + i)^{n-2} + \cdots + A_n(1 + i)^0 \qquad (\text{I-1})$$

where
$$F = \text{future value of the annuity}$$
$$A_1, A_2, \ldots, A_n = \text{amounts paid into the annuity at the end of the year}$$
$$i = \text{rate of return}$$
$$n = \text{number of years}$$

If the payments are equal each period, then Equation (I-1) may be rewritten as Equation (I-2):

$$F = A(1 + i)^{n-1} + A(1 + i)^{n-2} + \cdots + A \qquad (\text{I-2})$$
$$= A\left[(1 + i)^{n-1} + (1 + i)^{n-2} + \cdots + (1 + i) + 1\right]$$

Multiplying both sides of the equation by $(1 + i)$,

$$F(1 + i) = A\left[(1 + i)^n + (1 + i)^{n-1} + (1 + i)^{n-2} + \cdots + (1 + i)\right] \qquad (\text{I-3})$$

Subtracting Equation (I-2) from Equation (I-3),

$$Fi = A\left[(1 + i)^n - 1\right]$$

Dividing by i results in Equation (7), provided earlier in this chapter.

$$F = A\left[\frac{(1 + i)^n - 1}{i}\right] \qquad (7)$$

Present Value, Present Value of Annuities, and Perpetuities

3

Chapter 2 illustrated how to determine the future value of single payments and the future value of an annuity. In this second chapter on discounted cash flow, we examine the reverse processes of finding the *present value* of an amount to be received in the future as well as the *present value of an annuity* of future payments.

The goal of present value calculations is to determine the amount of money which a firm or investor would accept at present in place of a given amount at some future date. We also deal with *perpetuities* (future payments received over an indefinite future) and *capital recovery* in this chapter. The concepts and computations of present value are extremely important to the capital acquisition process as most projects are expected to yield cash flows over some number of periods in the future.

PRESENT VALUE

When using the discounted cash flow procedures for capital investment evaluation, it is necessary to know the present value of a sum to be received at a future time. The present value of a sum to be received in the future may be obtained using Equation (3) of Chapter 2, reproduced here as Equation (1):

$$S_n = P(1 + i)^n \qquad (1)$$

Solving Equation (1) for P results in Equation (2), which is the present value (PV) of the sum S_n to be received in n years:

$$\text{PV} = \frac{S_n}{(1 + i)^n} \quad \text{or} \quad \text{PV} = S_n\left(\frac{1}{1 + i}\right)^n \quad \text{or} \quad \text{PV} = S_n V^n \qquad (2)$$

Values for the factor $[1/(1 + i)]^n$, symbolized by V^n and called *single payment/ present value factors*, are found in Appendix B, column 4.

In our discussion of compound interest in Chapter 2, we indicate that we are assuming a constant reinvestment rate throughout the life of a given investment and that compound interest, annuity, and present value tables are developed on this assumption. Thus, we define the present value as an amount that, when compounded at a constant rate over the life of the investment, will equal the future value (compound sum).

EXAMPLE 1

Present Value of a Single Future Payment

A corporation expects to receive $10,000 in 3 years as payment for a note from a customer. The corporation needs cash now and has decided to sell the note to a bank. If the bank discounts the note at 10%, how much will the corporation receive?

SOLUTION: Utilize Equation (2) and Appendix B, column 4, at 10% as follows:

$$PV = \$10,000(0.751315)$$

$$= \$7,513.15$$

The corporation will receive $7,513.15 from the bank. Stated another way, the present value of $10,000 to be received in 3 years, discounted at 10%, is $7,513.15.

EXAMPLE 2

Present Value of Multiple Unequal Payments

A corporation expects a certain investment to yield cash flows as follows: year 1, $2,000; year 2, $3,000; year 3, $4,000; and year 4, $6,000. If the present value of these cash flows represents the *productive value* of the investment to the corporation, determine the productive value, assuming the company requires a 14% return.

SOLUTION: Use Equation (2) for each of the four cash flows and Appendix B, column 4, at 14% and then add together the present values as shown in the tabular format below:

Solution Table for Productive Value at 14%

TIME	CASH FLOW	DISCOUNT FACTOR	PRESENT VALUE
Year 1	$2,000	0.877193	$1,754
2	3,000	0.769468	2,308
3	4,000	0.674972	2,700
4	6,000	0.592080	3,552
		Productive value =	$10,314

If the corporation requires a 14% return, the productive value of the asset is $10,314. Said differently, the present value of the investment's future cash flows is $10,314 if the firm requires a 14% return.

EXAMPLE 3
Present Value at Different Discount Rates

A corporation has estimated the salvage value of a certain plant to be $1,000,000 in 20 years. Determine the present value of the salvage value at 5-year intervals using 10%, 12%, 14%, and 16% discount rates, and graph the relationships.

SOLUTION: Using Appendix B, the present values are tabulated in Table 3–1. Figure 3–1 shows that as the discount rate increases, the present value of cash flows to be received many periods in the future becomes increasingly smaller. Thus, at 16%, the importance of the salvage value to the question of acquiring an asset is much less than if the required return were 10%. Since this is the case, we would want to *allocate more resources* to estimating the salvage value of an asset if the required return were 10% than if it were higher. Also, at higher rates of return, the *relative significance* of an error in estimating the salvage value would be much less important than at lower rates. For example, suppose we made a 20% error in estimating the salvage value to occur at the end of year 20; the actual amount turns out to be $1,200,000, not the estimated $1,000,000. At a 10% discount rate, the error in present value would be $178,397 − $148,664 = $29,733. If, however, the discount rate were 16%, the error in present value would be $61,642 − $51,386 = $10,256. The error in the latter case is about one-third of the error at 10%. Thus, we can conclude that at 16% the error in present value is only about one-third as sensitive to an error in the estimation of the salvage value as at 10%. This is an example of the application of *sensitivity analysis*, an analytical technique that we will be using throughout the remainder of the text.

Table 3–1 and Figure 3–1 also demonstrate the anomaly stated in Chapter 1: the need for long-term accuracy in forecasting decreases as the discount rate employed is increased.

Table 3–1 Present Value of $1,000,000

DISCOUNT	PRESENT VALUE (YEARS TO SALVAGE)			
RATE	5	10	15	20
10%	$620,921	$385,543	$239,392	$148,644
12	567,427	321,973	182,696	103,667
14	519,369	269,744	140,096	72,762
16	476,113	226,684	107,927	51,386

PRESENT VALUE OF AN ORDINARY ANNUITY

Frequently, funds are received uniformly from year to year as a result of investment in equipment or pension funds and the like. When the first cash flow occurs at the end of the first period, the annuity is referred to as an ordinary annuity or an annuity in arrears. The present value of an ordinary annuity is found using Equation (3):

$$PV = A\left[\frac{(1+i)^n - 1}{i(1+i)^n}\right] \tag{3}$$

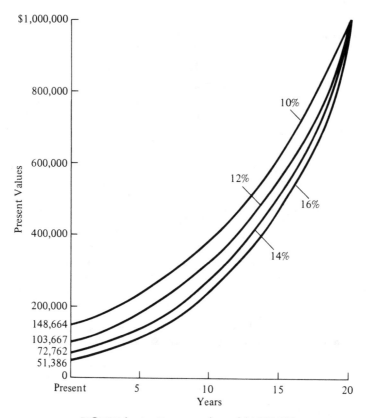

FIGURE 3–1   Present value of $1,000,000

Values corresponding to the bracketed portion of Equation (3) may be found in Appendix B, column 5. Equation (3) is derived in the appendix to this chapter.

The bracketed portion of Equation (3) can be simplified, resulting in an expression which is easier to evaluate using a calculator. The simplified expression is shown in Equation (4):

$$\frac{1 - (1 + i)^{-n}}{i} \tag{4}$$

Recall that the exponent "$-n$" means the reciprocal of the expression. That is, $(1 + i)^{-n}$ equals $1/(1 + i)^{n}$.

EXAMPLE 4

Present Value of an Annuity

A corporation expects to receive cash inflows of $3,000 each year for 10 years as the result of implementing a new project. Determine the present value of the sum discounted at 8%.

SOLUTION: Utilize Equation (3) and Appendix B, column 5, 8% for 10 years, as follows:

$$PV = \$3,000(6.710081)$$
$$= \$20,130.24$$

The present value of $3,000 to be received each year for 10 years, discounted at 8%, is $20,130.24.

EXAMPLE 5
Present Value of an Annuity

A corporation expects to receive $5,000 per year for 5 years and $8,000 per year for the following 5 years. Determine the present value of these funds at 18%.

SOLUTION: Utilize Equation (3) and Appendix B; write the solution in tabular format, as shown:

Solution Table for Present Value at 18%

TIME	AMOUNT	DISCOUNT FACTOR	PRESENT VALUE
Years 1–5	$5,000	3.127171	$15,636
6–10	8,000	1.366915	10,935
		Present value =	$26,571

The discount factor for years 6–10 may be obtained in two ways. One way is to subtract the annuity factor for years 1–5 from the factor for years 1–10: $4.494086 - 3.127171 = 1.366915$. The second requires discounting the discount factor for years 1–5 back 5 years: $3.127171(0.437109) = 1.366915$.

EXAMPLE 6
Present Value of an Annuity

Assuming the cash flows tabulated here are discounted at 10%, determine their present value.

YEARS	AMOUNT
1–5	$1,000
6–10	1,200
11–20	900

SOLUTION: The answer may be determined using the factors in Appendix B, column 5, adjusted as follows.

1 The factor for years 1–5 is obtained directly from the tables: 3.790987.
2 The factor for years 6–10 is obtained by subtracting the factor for years 1–5 from the factor for years 1–10: $6.144567 - 3.790787 = 2.353780$.

3 The factor for years 11–20 is obtained by subtracting the factor for years 1–10 from the factor for years 1–20: 8.513564 − 6.144567 = 2.368997.

Present Value

AMOUNT	FACTOR	PRESENT VALUE
$1,000	3.790787	$3,790.79
1,200	2.353780	2,824.54
900	2.368997	2,132.10
		$8,747.43

The present value of the stream of cash inflows shown in this example is $8,747.43.

PRESENT VALUE OF AN ANNUITY DUE

Sometimes annuity payments are received at the start of the year rather than at the end. If this is the case, the annuity is called an annuity due or an annuity in advance and the present value of the annuity will be greater than if payments are received at the end of the year (i.e., an ordinary annuity). The procedure for determining the present value of an annuity due is demonstrated in Example 7.

EXAMPLE 7
Present Value of an Annuity Due

A firm will receive $2,000 each year at the *start of each year* for 8 years. Using an 8% discount rate, determine the present value of the cash inflows.

SOLUTION: The cash flows consist of an initial $2,000 payment plus *seven* annual year-end payments. The present value is determined as follows:

$$PV = \$2,000 + \$2,000(5.206370)$$

$$= \$2,000 + \$10,412.74$$

$$= \$12,412.74$$

The cash inflows have a present value of $12,412.74 when discounted at 8%. Notice that the factor (5.206370) is taken from the 7-year row for 8% in column 5, Appendix B, since the cash flows in question will have an initial payment and then one at *the end of each of the next 7 years*.

PERPETUITIES

A *perpetuity* is an annuity or series of periodic payments that runs indefinitely, differing, therefore, from the annuities previously discussed in terms of duration only. The most common example of a perpetuity is the establishment of an endowment, although bonds lacking any maturity also qualify.

The value of a perpetuity is determined simply by dividing the yearly payment by the rate of return being received on the principal as shown in Equation (5),

$$PV = \frac{P}{i} \qquad (5)$$

where PV = present value of the perpetuity
       P = annual payment
       i = rate of return

EXAMPLE 8
Present Value of Perpetuity

If a perpetuity yields $1,000 per year, determine the present value based on a 14% required return.

SOLUTION: Use Equation (5) as shown:

$$PV = \frac{\$1,000}{0.14}$$

$$= \$7,143$$

An investor requiring a 14% return would be willing to pay $7,143 for a perpetuity yielding $1,000 per year. From another vantage point, if someone wanted to establish a perpetual endowment of $1,000 per year, $7,143 would be required if the funds could be invested at 14%.

CAPITAL RECOVERY

In financial problems it is frequently necessary to find the yearly payment needed to repay a debt such as a mortgage. Recall that Equation (3) found the present value of an annuity. If Equation (3) is solved for the yearly payment (A), we arrive at Equation (6):

$$A = PV\left[\frac{i(1+i)^n}{(1+i)^n - 1}\right] \qquad (6)$$

The *capital recovery factor*, which is the reciprocal of the uniform series/present worth factor, is the factor in brackets in Equation (6). These factors are found in Appendix B, column 6:

$$\text{capital recovery factor} = \frac{i(1+i)^n}{(1+i)^n - 1} \qquad (7)$$

EXAMPLE 9
Capital Recovery

> A borrower needs $20,000. A bank will provide a mortgage at 8% for 25 years with equal annual year-end payments. Determine the amount of the year-end payment.
>
> SOLUTION: Use Equation (6) and Appendix B, column 6, 8% for 25 years.
>
> $$\text{mortgage payment} = \$20,000(0.09367878)$$
> $$= \$1,873.58$$
>
> A borrower would pay $1,873.58 each year for 25 years to repay the $20,000 mortgage.

OTHER APPLICATIONS OF DISCOUNTED CASH FLOW PROCEDURES

The concepts of present and future value can be combined to perform useful functions such as determining the payments which must be made to a pension fund to be able to draw a given amount upon retirement (a defined benefit plan). This is demonstrated in Example 10.

EXAMPLE 10
Present and Future Value

> Smith wants to retire in 25 years with an annual pension of $30,000 for a period of 20 years. Assuming Smith can obtain a 9% return, determine the amount he must place in his pension each year at year-end.
>
> SOLUTION: First, determine how much Smith must have in 25 years to be able to draw $30,000 per year for 20 years at 9% return; that is, determine the present value of the $30,000 for 20 years.
>
> $$PV = \$30,000 \times 9.128546 = \$273,856.38$$
>
> The payments over 25 years required to yield the needed $273,856.38 are determined using the future value tables, column 2.
>
> $$FV = \$273,856.38$$
> $$\text{payment} \times FV \text{ factor} = \$273,856.38$$
> $$\text{payment} \times 84.700896 = \$273,856.38$$
> $$\text{payment} = \frac{\$273,856.38}{84.700896}$$
> $$= \$3,233.22$$
>
> Smith must contribute $3,233.22 for 25 years to be able to draw $30,000 for 20 years from his defined benefit pension plan.

The pension of $30,000 in Example 10 may seem rather high. However, if inflation were 7% a year for the 25-year period, the purchasing power of the $30,000 in terms of today's dollars would be only $0.184249 \times \$30,000 = \$5,527.47$. The discount factor corresponds to the present value at 7% for 25 years. If inflation were to average 10% for the 25-year period, the $30,000 payment would be worth only $0.092296 \times \$30,000 = \$2,768.88$. Further, note that the present values for the pension fund payments are for the *first year* of payment only. If inflation continued, subsequent years' payments would have even less purchasing power.

EXAMPLE 11
Defined Contribution Pension Plan

An executive aged 40 plans for retirement at age 65. His current earnings are $40,000 per year. He estimates that his earnings will average as tabulated here:

AGE	AVERAGE EARNINGS
41–45	$47,000
46–50	55,000
51–55	63,000
56–60	70,000
61–65	78,000

Assuming that he places 10% of his salary into a defined contribution plan at the end of each year, determine how much will have accrued at a 9% return. Then determine how much he will be able to draw each year for the next 20 years.

SOLUTION: Use Appendix B, column 2. Since the average salary is given for 5-year periods, the annuity factors may be added for each 5-year increment. The first (for years 41–45) corresponds to years 21–25 in column 2. Table 3–2 shows the resulting figures.

At age 65 the executive would have $477,933.85 in his pension fund. The amount that he will be able to draw for the next 20 years is computed as

$$\text{payment} = \frac{\$477,933.85}{\text{PV factor}}$$
$$= \frac{\$477,933.85}{9.128546}$$
$$= \$52,355.97$$

The annual pension would be $52,355.97.

Table 3–2   Funding of Defined Contribution Pension Plan

AGE	YEARS TO RETIREMENT	AVERAGE CONTRIBUTION	COMPOUND INTEREST FACTOR	VALUE AT AGE 65
41–45	25–21	$4,700	33.540776*	$157,641.64
46–50	20–16	5,500	21.799204	119,895.62
51–55	15–11	6,300	14.167986	89,258.31
56–60	10–6	7,000	9.208219	64,457.53
61–65	5–1	7,800	5.984711	46,680.75
				$477,933.85

*$33.540776 = 84.700896 - 51.160120$ (year 25 less year 20 from Appendix B, column 2).

Note: Exercises 1–11 adapted from Certified Public Accountant examinations.

1. On May 1, 1984, a company purchased a new machine for which it does not have to pay until May 1, 1986. The total payment on May 1, 1986 will include both principal and interest. Assuming interest at a 10% rate, the cost of the machine would be the total payment multiplied by what time value of money concept?
   (a) Future value of annuity of $1.
   (b) Compound sum of $1.
   (c) Present value of annuity of $1.
   (d) Present value of $1.

2. The figure 0.9423 is taken from the column marked 2% and the row marked three periods in a certain interest table. From what interest table is this figure taken?
   (a) Compound sum of $1.
   (b) Future value of annuity of $1.
   (c) Present value of $1.
   (d) Present value of annuity of $1.

3. A businesswoman wants to withdraw $3,000 (including principal) from an investment fund at the end of each year for 5 years. How should she compute her required initial investment at the beginning of the first year if the fund earns 6% compounded annually?
   (a) $3,000 times the future value of an annuity factor for $1 at 6% at the end of each year for 5 years.
   (b) $3,000 divided by the future value of an annuity factor for $1 at 6% at the end of each year for 5 years.
   (c) $3,000 times the present value of an annuity factor for $1 at 6% at the end of each year for 5 years.
   (d) $3,000 divided by the present value factor for an annuity of $1 at 6% at the end of each year for 5 years.

4. An accountant wishes to find the present value of an annuity of $1 payable at the beginning of each period at 10% for 8 periods. He has only one present value table which shows the present value of an annuity of $1 payable at the end of each period. To compute the present value factor he needs, the accountant would use the present value factor in the 10% column for
   (a) Seven periods.
   (b) Seven periods and add $1.
   (c) Eight periods.
   (d) Nine periods and subtract $1.

5. What amount should an individual have in her bank account today before withdrawal if she needs $2,000 each year for 4 years, with the first withdrawal to be made today and each subsequent withdrawal at one-year intervals? (She is to have exactly a zero balance in her bank account after the fourth withdrawal.)
   (a) $2,000 + ($2,000 × 0.926) + ($2,000 × 0.857) + ($2,000 × 0.794).
   (b) $2,000/(0.735 × 4).

    (c) ($2,000 × 0.926) + ($2,000 × 0.857) + ($2,000 × 0.794) + ($2,000 × 0.735).

    (d) $2,000/(0.926 × 4).

6. If an individual put $3,000 in a savings account today, what amount of cash would be available 2 years from today?

    (a) $3,000 × 0.857.

    (b) $3,000 × 0.857 × 2.

    (c) $3,000/0.857.

    (d) $3,000/(0.926 × 2).

7. What is the present value today of $4,000 to be received 6 years from today if discounted at 10%?

    (a) $4,000 × 0.926 × 6.

    (b) $4,000 × 0.794 × 2.

    (c) $4,000 × 0.681 × 0.926.

    (d) $4,000 × 0.5645.

8. Calculation of the amount of the equal periodic payments which would be equivalent to a present outlay of $1,000 is most readily effected by reference to a table which shows the

    (a) Compound sum of $1.

    (b) Present value of $1.

    (c) Future value of an annuity of $1.

    (d) Present value of an annuity of $1.

9. On January 1, 1984, Robert Harrison signed an agreement to operate as a franchise of Perfect Pizza, Inc., for an initial franchise fee of $40,000. Of this amount, $15,000 was paid when the agreement was signed, and the balance is payable in 5 annual payments of $5,000 each beginning January 1, 1985. The agreement provides that the down payment is not refundable, and no future services are required of the franchisor. Harrison's credit rating indicates that he can borrow money at 12% for a loan of this type. Information on present and future value factors is as follows:

Present value of $1 at 12% for 5 periods	0.567
Compound sum of $1 at 12% for 5 periods	1.762
Present value of a year-end annuity of $1 at 12% for 5 periods	3.605

Harrison should record the acquisition cost of the franchise on January 1, 1984 at

    (a) $29,175

    (b) $33,025

    (c) $40,000

    (d) $44,050

10. What amount should be deposited in a bank today to grow to $1,000 3 years from today?

    (a) $1,000/0.794.

    (b) $1,000 × 0.926 × 3.

    (c) ($1,000 × 0.926) + ($1,000 × 0.857) + ($1,000 × 0.794).

    (d) $1,000 × 0.794.

11. A businessman wants to invest a certain sum of money at the end of each year for 5 years. The investment will earn 6% compounded annually. At the end of 5 years, he will need a total of $30,000 accumulated. How should he compute his required annual investment?

    (a) $30,000 times the future value of an annuity factor for $1 at 6% at the end of each year for 5 years.

    (b) $30,000 divided by the future value of an annuity factor for $1 at 6% at the end of each year for 5 years.

    (c) $30,000 times the present value of an annuity factor for $1 at 6% at the end of each year for 5 years.

    (d) $30,000 divided by the present value of an annuity factor for $1 at 6% at the end of each year for 5 years.

12. A corporation expects an investment to yield cash inflows as follows: year 1, $3,000; year 2, $5,000; years 3–9, $4,000; year 10, $6,000. If the present value of these cash flows represents the productive value of the asset, determine the maximum amount the corporation can pay for the asset assuming a required 15% return.

13. A company is considering acquisition of several assets that are expected to last 10 years. When its cost of funds was 8%, management devoted about 20 labor-hours per asset to the estimation of salvage values. Assuming a linear relationship between labor-hours applied to forecasting salvage values and the accuracy of those salvage values, how many labor-hours would you allocate to such activities if the cost of funds increased to 16%?

14. What amount must be deposited today so that $10,000 may be withdrawn at years 12, 13, 14, and 15 if the funds are invested at 8%?

15. A bond pays interest semiannually in the amount of $40.00. If the bond will mature in 10 years paying $1,000 (in principal) at that time, determine the present value of the bond using a 15% discount rate.

16. Mr. Jones wants to purchase a perpetuity that will pay $15,000 per year commencing in 8 years. If perpetuities such as these have 14% yields, determine how much he must pay to purchase the perpetuity now.

17. A bank will provide a $50,000 mortgage at 13% interest for 30 years with equal annual year-end payments. Determine the amount of the year-end payment. Suppose the borrower decides to pay back the remaining loan over a 20-year period after only $2,000 in principal has been repaid. Determine the new year-end payment.

18. An investor bids on a 3-year annuity paying $300 each year at the end of the year. The investor requires a 10% return, but wants an increase in return of 1% per year to compensate for inflation. Determine the amount the investor will pay for the annuity.

19. You have just won the "millionaire" first prize of $50,000 per year for 20 years in the state lottery. You receive your first prize installment immediately and will receive the remaining 19 installments annually. Determine the amount you would accept now in lieu of the $50,000 for 20 years if funds can be invested at 14%. (Ignore tax effects.)

$377,518.50

20. You have just won the top prize of $1,000 per week for life in a state lottery. Assuming an investment rate of 13%, how much of the current lottery proceeds must be invested to fund your prize? (Assume a perpetuity.)

21. Ms. Sharpe is 40 years old, anticipates retirement at age 65, and may invest up to $3,500 per year in a Keogh plan. She expects to live to age 80. If she can invest the funds at year's end at an annual rate of 14% and receive a return of 8% after retirement, determine the lump-sum value of her Keogh fund at 65 and the annual pretax payment after retirement.

Lump sum
A) 636,547.90
B) 74,367.59

22. Referring to Problem 21, if Ms. Sharpe wants to receive $100,000 per year, how large an initial payment must she make into a retirement fund in addition to the $3,500 yearly payments?

23. Mr. Jones plans to place $2,500 per year into a retirement fund at the end of each year for 20 years. He has $10,000 in the fund at present. If he obtains a 10% return prior to retirement and an 8% return after retirement, determine his pension based on a 20-year payment. *216,462.50*

Equation #6
21,436.07

24. Ms. Smith started working for ABC Corporation at age 35. ABC has a defined benefit plan, in which employees receive 2% of their final year's earnings for each year worked. ABC expects salaries to increase an average of 8% a year, and Ms. Smith currently earns $30,000. Most employees retire at age 65. The life expectancies for a person at several ages are given.

AGE	LIFE EXPECTANCY	YEARS BEYOND 65
35	37 years	7 years
50	24	9
60	16	11
65	13	13

Assume ABC will receive an average annual return on its pension fund of 8% and that contributions are made at year-end.

(a) Based on Ms. Smith being 35 years old, determine ABC's annual contribution to the pension fund.

(b) When Ms. Smith reaches 50, ABC revises their contribution. Determine the amount needed in the fund when Ms. Smith is 65 based on the assumption that Ms. Smith's salary will continue to increase 8% annually.

(c) If ABC does not change its contribution after Ms. Smith is 50, by how much will the pension fund be overfunded or underfunded?

(d) Determine the revised contribution assuming Ms. Smith's actual salary is then $100,000.

25. ABC Corporation has established a defined benefit pension plan, which provides that at retirement each employee will receive a pension equal to his or her final year's salary multiplied by the number of years employed at the company divided by 60. Thus, if a person were employed for 20 years, the pension would be 20 ÷ 60, or one-third of the last year's salary. The company has been obtaining a 9% return on its pension contributions and it (conservatively) expects the funds to get a 6% return after each employee retires.

Mr. Green, a new employee, is hired. He is age 45 and his life expectancy is 28 years. He is expected to retire at age 65 (giving an expected pension period of 8 years). His current salary is $30,000 per year, and it is expected to increase at an average annual rate of 8% per year. Determine the following.

(a) The expected pension at age 65.
(b) The amount needed at age 65 to fund the pension.
(c) The annual contribution to the pension fund.

26. The dividend-valuation model used to determine the cost of common stock equity is:

$$K_e = \frac{D_1}{P_0} + g \tag{8}$$

where K_e = the cost of common stock equity in the present period
D_1 = the dividend in the following period
P_0 = the market price of the common stock in this period
g = the annual expected growth rate of the dividend

Start with Equation (3) in the chapter, assume that A increases at the rate of g each year, and derive Equation (8).

Information for Problems 27–29:

During the life of a firm it is not unusual for the rate of growth of the dividend to change. If the growth rate changes, the value of the firm may be expressed as Equation (9),

$$P_0 = D_0 \sum_{t=1}^{k} \frac{(1+g_1)^t}{(1+r)^t} + D_1 \sum_{t=k+1}^{\infty} \frac{(1+g_2)^{t-k}}{(1+r)^t} \tag{9}$$

where g_1 = dividend growth rate for periods 1 through k
g_2 = growth rate for periods $k+1$ through infinity
$D_1 = D_0(1+g_1)^k$

For computational purposes, Equation (9) may be rewritten as Equation (10):

$$P_0 = D_0 \sum_{t=1}^{k} \frac{(1+g_1)^t}{(1+r)^t} + D_0 \left(\frac{1+g_1}{1+r}\right)^k \sum_{t=1}^{\infty} \frac{(1+g_2)^t}{(1+r)^t} \tag{10}$$

In addition to a changing rate of growth for the dividends, the rate of discount may change from period to period. The more general case is described in Equation (11),

$$P_0 = D_0 \sum_{t=1}^{k_1} \frac{(1+g_1)^t}{(1+r_1)^t} + D_1 \sum_{t=1}^{k_2} \frac{(1+g_2)^t}{(1+r_2)^t} + \cdots + D_n \sum_{t=1}^{k_n} \frac{(1+g_n)^t}{(1+r_n)^t} \tag{11}$$

where n = number of intervals, an interval consists of one or more periods

$g_1, g_2, \ldots, g_n$ = dividend growth rate in intervals $1, 2, \ldots, n$

$r_1, r_2, \ldots, r_n$ = discount rate in intervals $1, 2, \ldots, n$

k_n = number of periods in interval n

D_0 = initial dividend

$D_1, D_2, \ldots, D_n$ = dividend at the beginning of each interval calculated using Equation (12):

$$D_n = D_{n-1} \frac{(1 + g_{n-1})^{k_{n-1}}}{(1 + r_{n-1})^{k_{n-1}}} \tag{12}$$

27. A newly formed corporation is offering stock with projected dividends of $2 for the first 3 years and a yearly increase in dividend of 5% per year thereafter. At what current price can the stock be valued, assuming a 10% discount rate and dividend payments at the end of each year?

28. An investor plans to value a stock over a 10-year period. The current dividend is $2. The investor expects dividend growth rates as follows: years 1–3, 8%; years 4–7, 9%; years 8–10, 7%. Determine the dividend valuation for the stock for the 10-year period if the investor's discount rate is 8%.

29. A corporation's dividend is presently $3; it is expected to grow at an annual rate of 5% for 10 years and at an annual rate of 10% thereafter. A shareholder, in valuing the corporation's stock, plans to use an 8% discount rate for the first 5 years and 12% for the next 20 years. Determine the amount at which the shareholder would value the stock.

REFERENCES

Bauman, W. Scott. "Investment Returns and Present Values." *Financial Analysts Journal*, 25 (November–December 1969), 107–118.

Brigham, Eugene, and T. Craig Tapley. "Financial Leverage and Use of the Net Present Value Investment Criterion." *Financial Management* (Summer 1985).

Buser, Stephen A. "Laplace Transforms as Present Value Rules: A Note." *Journal of Finance* (July 1986).

de la Mare, R. F. "An Investigation into the Discounting Formulae Used in Capital Budgeting Models." *Journal of Business Finance & Accounting* (Summer 1975).

Friend, Irwin. "Recent Developments in Finance." *Journal of Banking and Finance*, 1 (October 1977), 103–117.

Golbe, Derra L., and Barry Schachter. "The Net Present Value Rule and an Algorithm for Maintaining a Constant Debt-Equity Ratio." *Financial Management* (Summer 1985).

Greene, T. L. *Corporation Finance*. New York: G. P. Putnam's Sons, 1897.

Haley, Charles W., and Lawrence D. Schall. *The Theory of Financial Decisions*. New York: McGraw-Hill Book Company, 1973, Chap. 5.

Jean, William H. "Terminal Value or Present Value in Capital Budgeting Programs." *Journal of Financial and Quantitative Analysis*, 6 (January 1971), 649–652.

_____. "On Multiple Rates of Return." *Journal of Finance*, 23 (March 1968), 187–192.

Lerner, Eugene, M., and Willard T. Carleton. *A Theory of Financial Analysis*. New York: Harcourt Brace Jovanovich, 1966.

_____, and A. Rappaport. "Limit DCF in Capital Budgeting." *Harvard Business Review*, 46 (September–October 1968), 133–138.

Lewellen, Wilbur G., Howard P. Lanser, and John J. McConnell. "Payback Substitutes for Discounted Cash Flow." *Financial Management*, 2 (Summer 1973), 17–23.

Lindsay, R. J., and A. W. Sametz. *Financial Management: An Analytical Approach*. Homewood, Ill.: Richard D. Irwin, Inc., 1967.

Logue, Dennis E., and T. Craig Tapley. "Performance Monitoring and the Timing of Cash Flows." *Financial Management* (Autumn 1985).

Mao, J. C. T. *Quantitative Analysis of Financial Decisions*. New York: Macmillan Publishing Co., 1969.

Masson, Robert Tempest. "Executive Motivations, Earnings, and Consequent Equity Performance." *Journal of Political Economy*, 79 (November–December 1971), 1278–1292.

Petty, J. William, and Oswald D. Bowlin. "The Financial Manager and Quantitative Decision Models." *Financial Management*, 4 (Winter 1976), 32–41.

Ruback, Richard S. "Calculating the Market Value of Riskless Cash Flows." *Journal of Financial Economics* (Fall 1986).

Simkowitz, Michael A., and Charles P. Jones. "A Note on the Simultaneous Nature of Finance Methodology." *Journal of Finance*, 27 (March 1972), 103–108.

Weingartner, H. M. "The Excess Present Value Index—A Theoretical Basis and Critique." *Journal of Accounting Research*, 1 (Autumn 1963), 213–224.

Welter, P. "Put Policy First in DCF Analysis." *Harvard Business Review*, 48 (January–February 1970), 141–148.

Weston, J. Fred. "New Themes in Finance." *Journal of Finance*, 24 (March 1974), 237–243.

_____. *The Scope and Methodology of Finance*. Englewood Cliffs, N.J.: Prentice Hall, Inc., 1966.

_____. "Developments in Finance Theory." *Financial Management*, 10 (Summer 1981), 5–22.

Yarrow, G. K. "On the Predictions of Managerial Theories of the Firm." *Journal of Industrial Economics* (June 1976).

APPENDIX: DERIVATION OF FORMULA
FOR PRESENT VALUE OF AN ANNUITY

In many capital budgeting problems, funds are expected to be received at the end of each year for a period of years. The present value of a series of payments is the sum of the individual payments to be received each year. The sum is expressed in Equation (I-1),

$$PV = \frac{S_1}{1 + i} + \frac{S_2}{(1 + i)^2} + \cdots + \frac{S_n}{(1 + i)^n} \tag{I-1}$$

where PV is the present value of the funds to be received.

If the payments are equal and the discount rate (i) is held constant, Equation (I-1) can be reduced to Equation (I-2),

$$PV = \sum_{t=1}^{n} \frac{S}{(1 + i)^t} \tag{I-2}$$

where PV is the present value of a stream of funds to be received in equal amounts at year end, discounted at rate i.

To obtain the *uniform series/present worth factors* located in Appendix B, column 5, start with Equation (7) from Chapter 2,

$$F = A \left[\frac{(1 + i)^n - 1}{i} \right] \tag{I-3}$$

where F = future amount of an annuity
      A = equal yearly payment

Recall in Chapter 3 that

$$PV = S \left[\frac{1}{(1 + i)^n} \right] \tag{I-4}$$

Since we are concerned with the present value of an annuity, substitute Equation (I-3) for S in Equation (I-4):

$$PV = A \left[\frac{(1 + i)^n - 1}{i} \right] \left[\frac{1}{(1 + i)^n} \right]$$

$$= A \left[\frac{(1 + i)^n - 1}{i(1 + i)^n} \right] \tag{I-5}$$

Equation (I-5) is Equation (3) provided earlier in this chapter. In addition, Equation (I-6) is the expression for the present worth of $1 per period:

$$\frac{(1 + i)^n - 1}{i(1 + i)^n} = \frac{1 - V^n}{i} \tag{I-6}$$

These factors are found in Appendix B, column 5, and are commonly referred to as uniform series/present worth factors or present value annuity factors.

Analysis of Capital Project Cash Flows

4

The analysis of capital projects rests upon *incremental* cash flows, that is, *all the cash inflows and outflows traceable to a given project and cash inflows and outflows that would disappear if the project disappeared*. Historical costs (accounting costs) previously incurred are not part of the analysis. Put it this way: investing funds to modernize a previously acquired asset is not justified by the "sunk" cost represented by the asset unless the new funds (the incremental funds) promise a return greater than their cost. One would not modernize the S.S. *United States* simply because the steamship company had in the past made a substantial investment in constructing the vessel. Even though the write-off of large assets would have significant effects on the financial statements of the company, such write-offs would not have any nontax effects on cash flows.

It is also important to note that in capital budgeting, we are concerned with *future* cash flows extending over 5, 10, 15 years or more. Hence, cash flow analysis cannot be separated from the subject of *business forecasting* (treated in Chapter 9). Furthermore, the one certainty of a long-term forecast is that it will in some degree fall wide of the mark. This uncertainty creates the risk that the project's outcome may be more or less favorable than anticipated. *Risk analysis*, therefore, is one of the most important component subjects studied in capital budgeting.

The methods for analyzing risk discussed in Chapters 11–14 provide a framework for comparing projects that have inherently different levels of risk. In essence, the methods described permit the use of common denominators so that projects of varying risk can all be reduced to the same baseline for comparison. Use of the procedures depends, of course, on having both the best available estimates for cash flows and the best estimates of the degree of risk or error associated with those cash flows. Even the most sophisticated of mathematical evaluation techniques applied to poor estimates will yield poor-quality results. Accurate estimates of cash flows are essential to a quality capital investment program.

CLASSIFICATION OF PROJECT CASH FLOWS

The operating cash flows of a project fall into three categories:

Cash Inflows

These may be associated with incremental sales receipts or *savings* in operating costs through investment in new equipment or the modernization of existing equipment. To reduce cost is to create a cash inflow. It is fair to recognize that projects involving savings in operating costs are the most common type of capital project. ✱ However, the cash flows from savings in operating costs are usually difficult to forecast. On the other hand, cash inflows from increased sales from the current product line or from the introduction of a new product are more dramatic and can be forecasted based upon past performance and/or market surveys. In sum, the firm may obtain incremental cash inflows from either new sales or savings in operating costs.

Cash Outflows

These generally originate from incremental expenditures on labor, material, selling expenses, and so forth. It follows that:

1   Depreciation and other amortization charges on fixed assets are noncash charges and not part of the cash outflows. However, the particular method of depreciation adopted will have an *indirect* influence on the tax expense of the company. For example, the various forms of accelerated depreciation have the effect of reducing the tax expenses (or creating tax savings) in the early years of the project. Compared with straight-line depreciation, and allowing for the time value of money, this will increase the present value of the project.

2   Remaining depreciation on old equipment or the *after-tax loss* on the disposal of prior assets are not chargeable against the new venture; that is, it does not add to or subtract from the cash flow of the new investment. *All sunk costs are irrelevant to the choice among economic alternatives.*

3   Incremental interest charges attributable to financing the project are not deducted from the cash flow. The general principle in capital budgeting, although in certain cases exceptions may be made, is that the return on the project should be determined independently of the means of financing. Moreover, by putting the project on a net present value basis, we will be allowing for the time value of money and the return of investment.

4   Additional federal, state, and local taxes may result from the implementation of the project. The proper tax factor chargeable to the project is the difference between the company's present tax bill and the tax bill that would result if the project were undertaken. A change may be positive or negative. It is important to remember, however, that taxable income does not equate to the net cash flows and may not correspond with income computed under conventional accounting principles. Depreciation, for example, is not deducted from the cash flow but is vital in the computation of taxable income. Interest also is not deducted from the project cash flows, for reasons explained in consideration 3 but is figured in the calculation of the firm's tax liability. The tax effects of interest are recognized by putting the cost of capital on an after-tax basis.

The cash inflows and outflows discussed earlier are repetitive; that is, they recur in each period over the life of the project, although not necessarily in the same

Table 4–1   Comparison of Accounting and Cash Flow Results, Project X

		ACCOUNTING INCOME	CASH FLOW
Additional sales receipts		$20,000	$20,000
Savings in labor and materials		10,000	10,000
Cash benefits		$30,000	$30,000
Less: Depreciation on new equipment	$6,000		
Less: Depreciation on old equipment	3,000		
Additional depreciation expense		3,000	—
Additional administrative expenses		4,000	4,000
Additional selling expenses		4,000	4,000
Additional interest on debt		1,000	—
Additional taxes		2,000	2,000
Net accounting income		$16,000	
Cash outflow			$10,000
Net recurring cash inflow			$20,000

amounts. *The difference between the cash inflows and outflows* of each period is termed the *net operating cash flow per period*.

Table 4–1 compares the accounting and cash flow results of project X for a given period. Note that the *net cash flow is on an after-tax before-depreciation-and-interest basis*. In addition, the firm could see the incremental cash flow effects of a project by preparing a cash-basis statement of changes in financial condition before and after the project's implementation.

Cash Flows Related to Investment in the Capital Project

In addition to these repetitive cash inflows and outflows, consideration must be given to the cash outflow represented by the investment in the project (see Table 4–2). This investment may take place in one period or be spread over several periods over the life of the project. Accordingly, both the repetitive items in cash flow and the investment expenditures will eventually be put on a present value basis. The investment expenditure is also an incremental outlay which may be adjusted for the following factors:

1   The salvage value of old equipment disposed of as a consequence of the new project will reduce the investment outlay.
2   Tax gains or losses on disposal of old equipment, if they result in tax increases or savings, also will impact the investment required.
3   The liquidation value of inventories (such as spare parts) no longer needed should also be credited to the new project.
4   However, the investment in the new project will include any additional commitment of working capital that is necessary. It should be noted that this additional working capital investment might take place over several years, tied to the life cycle of the product.

Table 4 – 2 Incremental Investment, Project X

Cost of new equipment		$50,000
Additional working capital		10,000
Total		60,000
Less: Salvage value of old equipment	$5,000	
Liquidation value of parts inventory	2,000	
Tax savings on disposal of old equipment	3,000	$10,000
Investment cash outflow		$50,000

Timing of cash outflows. In the analysis of a large project, the development of a time-flow chart such as the one shown is useful:

TIME	ACTIVITY	CASH FLOW
0	Purchase land	– $2,200,000
3 months	Start construction	– 900,000
6 months	Property taxes	– 20,000
1 year	Construction project	– 2,000,000
	Property taxes	– 25,000
	Loan interest	– 80,000
18 months	Complete construction	– 700,000
	Property taxes	– 30,000
	Purchase machinery	– 1,600,000
21 months	Install machinery	– 400,000
24 months	Sell old plant	+ 2,271,800
	Property taxes	– 35,000
	Interest	– 100,000
	Working capital	– 250,000
	Net cash outflow	– $6,068,200

The timing of both the cash outflows and the cash inflows is critical to capital budgeting analysis.

In many instances cash flows must be adjusted to reflect the actual time of receipt of payment. Consider a firm opening a new plant with projected yearly sales, operating expenses, and related costs. During the first year, the lags in accounts receivable and payable, inventory buildups, and accruals warrant special attention. The first-year and subsequent yearly cash flows are developed in Example 1:

EXAMPLE 1

Operating Cash Flows

A corporation anticipates additional sales of $1,000,000 per year resulting from its new plant. Cost and revenue projections are as follows:

☐ *Revenues*: All sales on credit with a 60-day average collection period.
☐ *Costs*: Materials are 30% of sales with 2 months' safety stock, payment made 30 days after monthly deliveries. Labor costs are 25% of sales with payment 2 weeks after the end of salary period, which is monthly.

☐ Utilities and fuels are 15% of sales with bills received at end of month and paid 30 days after receipt.

☐ Administrative costs are 10% of sales and paid in month of occurrence.

Determine the pretax cash flows for the first and subsequent years, ignoring depreciation and taxes.

SOLUTION: Consider the initial year first. Sales are projected at $1,000,000, but with a 60-day collection period, cash received can only be expected to be $833,333. Materials cost $25,000 per month and a 2-month safety stock is required. With payment in 30 days, the first-year cost would be $50,000 plus $25,000 × 11 months, or $325,000. Monthly labor costs amount to $20,833. With a 2-week lag in payment, the first-year cost is $229,163, with the next salary payment due 2 weeks after the start of the second year of operation. Utilities and fuels cost $12,500 per month. A 30-day payment lag results in a first-year cost of $137,500. Administrative costs are paid in the month they occur, so the yearly cost is $100,000. The first year is summarized as follows:

Cash receipts	$833,333
Materials	− 325,000
Labor	− 229,163
Utilities and fuel	− 137,500
Administrative costs	− 100,000
Earnings before depreciation and taxes	$41,670

In subsequent years the cash flows would be as follows:

Cash receipts	$1,000,000
Materials	− 300,000
Labor	− 250,000
Utilities and fuel	− 150,000
Administrative costs	− 100,000
Earnings before depreciation and taxes	$200,000

Whenever a plant is expanded or a new operation undertaken, lower earnings and cash flow may result during the initial period of operation. In addition to the lags in collections and payments, start-up costs may reduce profitability.

THE DEPRECIATION DEDUCTION

Methods of Depreciation

Historically, there have been three primary methods of depreciation: straight line, declining balance, and sum of the years' digits. The last two are termed *accelerated methods*. Another, less frequently used, method is based on units of production. There are specific methods of depreciation that must be used as part of the *accelerated cost recovery system* (*ACRS*), as shown in Table 4–3. It should be noted that the total profitability and cash flows over the entire life of an asset are not affected by the choice of a method of depreciation. Only the timing of the profits and cash flows is affected.

The simplest method of depreciation, *straight line*, involves dividing the depreciable value by the number of years in the asset's depreciable life. The result is an amount that is constant over the asset's depreciable life. While this method is easy to use, it does not result in any tax advantages. However, it tends to smooth earnings, provided that expenses and revenues remain relatively constant during the period the asset is being depreciated.

Prior to the passage of the Economic Recovery Tax Act in 1981, *declining-balance depreciation* was the most commonly used accelerated method. With the passage of the Tax Reform Act of 1986, declining balance will again be used extensively. Declining balance involves multiplying a constant decimal by a reducing base. The original base is the total cost of the asset (not the depreciable value). The original base is reduced each year by the cumulative depreciation taken to date. The decimals are obtained by multiplying the straight-line rate by 2, $1\frac{1}{2}$, or $1\frac{1}{4}$, depending on whether double-, one-and-one-half-, or one-and-one-quarter declining balance is being used. The process stops when the salvage value is reached. This may result in depreciating an asset fully in fewer years than the asset's depreciable life. If an asset does not have a salvage value, it is necessary to switch from the declining-balance method being used to straight-line. The switch to straight-line depreciation takes place in the first year that it results in a higher write-off than the declining balance method.

The third basic method, the *sum-of-the-years'-digits depreciation* (SYD), does not give as rapid an acceleration as does double declining balance. In addition, SYD depreciates *against the depreciable value*, whereas the declining-balance methods depreciate against the total cost of the asset.

Sum-of-the-years'-digits depreciation applies a changing rate to the depreciable value. Each year a fraction is multiplied by the depreciable value to obtain that year's depreciation. The numerator, which changes from year to year, represents the number of years remaining in the asset's useful life. The denominator is the sum of the digits representing the useful life. The denominator may be found using Equation (1),

$$S = N\frac{(N + 1)}{2} \tag{1}$$

where S = sum of the years' digits
N = number of years in useful life

Thus, if an asset had a depreciable life of 5 years, the denominator of the fraction would be $5(5 + 1)/2 = 15$. The depreciation for each year would be as tabulated:

YEAR	SYD DEPRECIATION
1	5/15
2	4/15
3	3/15
4	2/15
5	1/15

Units-of-production depreciation is useful when the wearing of an asset is primarily a function of output as opposed to age. The total output of the asset in some measurable unit is first estimated. Then depreciation is taken each year on the basis of the fraction of the total output produced in that year. The method has the advantage of accurately reflecting costs against output, which should correspond to revenue.

Table 4–3 compares the three basic methods of depreciation. Assume that project X has a required investment outflow of $100,000; the required equipment has a 10-year useful life. The firm's cost of capital is 10%, and the combined federal and state marginal tax rate is 40%. No salvage value is taken.

The financial manager will prefer the method of depreciation that gives the highest present value of the tax shield. In this instance, SYD is the preferred option. As the reader will observe, the analysis is sensitive to three variables: the firm's marginal tax rate, the period of time over which the asset is depreciated, and the option of which accelerated depreciation methods can be used. Of course, the tax law can restrict or change the depreciation methods which can be used. The following section explores this topic.

The Impact of Tax Legislation on the Depreciation Tax Shield

Computing depreciation for an asset requires three pieces of information: the asset's depreciable value, the asset's depreciable life, and the method of depreciation to be used. Each of these is discussed in the paragraphs that follow.

The asset's depreciable value.   The depreciable value represents the difference between the total cost to acquire the asset and its expected salvage value. The cost of the asset includes the purchase price and any other expenditures, such as shipping and installation, that are incurred to prepare the asset for its intended use. The salvage value is the amount expected to be realized upon disposal of the asset. Net salvage value rather than salvage value may be used. Net salvage value takes into consideration any costs of removal. Salvage value is based on an estimate, given the expected life, working conditions, maintenance policy, etc.

The asset's depreciable life.   An asset's depreciable life is the period of years during which the asset will be depreciated to its expected salvage value. There may be two different depreciable lives. The first is the depreciable life used for tax purposes. Generally, this is the shortest period permitted by law for the depreciation of the asset in question. The second is the depreciable life used to compute depreciation for the purpose of reporting earnings to shareholders. For the latter, the asset's *useful* (productive) *life* is generally used. This is the period of time that the asset can reasonably be expected to operate in the manner and at the level of efficiency intended.

An asset's useful or productive life is the period during which the present value of the cash inflows expected to be derived from the asset's use (that is, its productive value) exceeds the asset's abandonment value. Obviously, when an asset is acquired, its productive value exceeds its abandonment value, or it would not be acquired. However, during the life of the asset, its productive value may change appreciably due to changes in costs and/or revenues attributable to its use. Thus, an asset may be abandoned or may be kept for a period longer than originally planned.

Table 4–3   Comparison of Depreciation Methods

A. Straight-Line Depreciation (SLD)

(1) PERIOD	(2) DEPRECIATION	(3) DEPRECIATION RATE	(4) TAX RATE	(5 = 2 × 4) TAX SHIELD	(6) DISCOUNT FACTOR (0.10)	(7 = 5 × 6) PV OF TAX SHIELD
1	$ 10,000	0.10	0.40	$4,000	0.909	$ 3,636
2	10,000	0.10	0.40	4,000	0.826	3,304
3	10,000	0.10	0.40	4,000	0.751	3,004
4	10,000	0.10	0.40	4,000	0.683	2,732
5	10,000	0.10	0.40	4,000	0.621	2,484
6	10,000	0.10	0.40	4,000	0.564	2,256
7	10,000	0.10	0.40	4,000	0.513	2,052
8	10,000	0.10	0.40	4,000	0.467	1,868
9	10,000	0.10	0.40	4,000	0.424	1,696
10	10,000	0.10	0.40	4,000	0.386	1,544
Total	$100,000					$24,576

B. Double Declining Balance (DDB)

Double the SLD rate, 0.10 to 0.20, and apply the 200% rate to the adjusted book value (cost less accumulated depreciation) for each period in the life of the project.

(1) PERIOD	(2) ADJUSTED BOOK VALUE	(3) DDB RATE	(4) DEPRECIATION	TAX RATE	(5 = 2 × 4) TAX SHIELD	(6 = 4 × 5) DISCOUNT FACTOR (0.10)	(7) PV OF TAX SHIELD (8 = 6 × 7)
1	$100,000	0.20	$20,000	0.40	$8,000	0.909	$7,272
2	80,000	0.20	16,000	0.40	6,400	0.826	5,286
3	64,000	0.20	12,800	0.40	5,120	0.751	3,845
4	51,200	0.20	10,240	0.40	4,096	0.683	2,798
5	40,960	0.20	8,192	0.40	3,277	0.621	2,035
6	32,768*	0.20	6,554	0.40	2,622	0.564	1,479
7	32,768	0.20	6,554	0.40	2,622	0.513	1,345
8	32,768	0.20	6,554	0.40	2,622	0.467	1,224
9	32,768	0.20	6,554	0.40	2,622	0.424	1,112
10	32,768	0.20	6,554	0.40	2,622	0.386	1,012
Total			$100,000				$27,408

*Switch to straight-line at this point.

C. Sum of the Years' Digits (SYD)

The sum of the years' digits (S) equals $N(N + 1)/2$ or, in our illustration, $10(10 + 1)/2 = 55$. A fraction of 55 (i.e., $10/55, 9/55, 8/55$) is applied successively to the depreciable value.

(1) PERIOD	(2) DEPRECIABLE VALUE	(3) SYD FRACTION	(4) DEPRECIATION	TAX RATE	(5 = 2 × 4) TAX SHIELD	(6 = 4 × 5) DISCOUNT FACTOR (0.10)	(7) PV OF TAX SHIELD (8 = 6 × 7)
1	$100,000	10/55	$ 18,182	0.40	$7,273	0.909	$ 6,611
2	100,000	9/55	16,364	0.40	6,546	0.826	5,407
3	100,000	8/55	14,545	0.40	5,818	0.751	4,369
4	100,000	7/55	12,727	0.40	5,091	0.683	3,477
5	100,000	6/55	10,910	0.40	4,364	0.621	2,710
6	100,000*	5/55	9,091	0.40	3,636	0.564	2,051
7	100,000	4/55	7,273	0.40	2,909	0.513	1,492
8	100,000	3/55	5,454	0.40	2,182	0.467	1,019
9	100,768	2/55	3,636	0.40	1,454	0.424	616
10	100,768	1/55	1,818	0.40	727	0.386	281
Total			$100,000				$28,034

*Switch to straight-line at this point.

Historically, an asset's depreciable life was the period during which the asset was expected to remain in use. Since depreciation is a tax-deductible expense, there is an incentive to depreciate assets over as short a period as allowed by law. Regardless of the method of depreciation used, a shorter life will result in a higher present value of the after-tax depreciation cash throw-offs.

By permitting a shorter depreciable life for tax purposes than an asset's productive life, Congress may provide a tax incentive to encourage investment in capital equipment. Whether such tax incentives actually result in added capital investment is debatable. Investments should be based on a thorough economic analysis as described in later chapters. Use of a shorter depreciable life for tax purposes does affect the decision, but firms normally will not purchase assets unless there is clear economic justification based on expected sales, reduction of costs, etc. Tax incentives may affect a decision but should not be the basis for a decision.

By contrast, if tax incentives such as shortened depreciable lives do exist, and management is accustomed to employing them within the overall capital budgeting decision process, removal of such incentives may result in postponement or rejection of proposed purchases. This is especially important in periods of slow economic growth when management is not sure future sales will meet targeted expectations. Removal of economic incentives during periods of slow economic growth may have a negative impact on the economy overall if their removal results in a decrease in capital expenditures.

Over the years, the depreciable life was based on the owner's experience or on the class-life asset depreciation range (ADR) system provided by the IRS. This system permitted the taxpayer to select a useful life within a designated range of years. It was designed to reduce conflict between taxpayers and the IRS over the concept of the useful life of an asset. The IRS published guidelines for thousands of assets, providing an asset depreciation range (ADR) for each asset. The ADR specified a range of years from which the depreciable life for tax purposes could be chosen. For example, printing presses had a range from 9 to 13 years, with an ADR midpoint of 11 years.

In 1981, the useful life was defined in the Economic Recovery Tax Act (ERTA) by dividing all assets into six depreciable life categories. This "categorization" represented a significant departure from past practices. Prior to the ERTA, each type of asset was depreciated for tax purposes over a period that reasonably approximated the actual period during which the asset would be used. The ERTA depreciation categories really had little to do with an asset's useful life. Rather, they were established as a means of permitting businesses to depreciate assets over shorter periods of time. This allows the recovery of the asset's cost more rapidly and thereby makes the acquisition more attractive to a company.

The Tax Reform Act (TRA) of 1986 modified the ACRS system for property placed in service after 1986. Eight ACRS classes are provided, based generally on the asset depreciation range (ADR) system used prior to 1981. The eight ACRS classes as defined by the Tax Reform Act of 1986 are shown in Table 4-4.

Thus far in our discussion, we have described the selection of an asset's depreciable life only as it relates to federal income tax computations. In general, *for tax purposes*, it is most beneficial to maximize depreciation in the early years of the asset's life. This may be accomplished by using an accelerated depreciation method, as described shortly, and a depreciable life that is as short as allowable by the IRS. The rationale for using a short depreciable life and accelerated depreciation is to postpone

Table 4–4   Eight ACRS Classes Defined by the Tax Reform Act of 1986

RECOVERY PERIOD	RECOVERY METHOD	ASSETS
3-year	Double declining balance	ADR midpoint life of 4 years and less excluding cars and light trucks
5-year	Double declining balance	ADR midpoint life of more than 4 years and less than 10 years plus cars and light trucks, qualified technological equipment, certain renewable resource property, R & D property
7-year	Double declining balance	ADR midpoint life of 10 years and less than 16 years plus property without an ADR life
10-year	Double declining balance	ADR midpoint life of 16 years and less than 20 years
15-year	150% declining balance	ADR midpoint life of 20 years and less than 25 years plus sewage plants
20-year	150% declining balance	ADR midpoint life of 25 years or more, other than real property with an ADR life of 27.5 or longer
27.5-year	Straight-line	Residential rental real estate, elevators, and escalators
31.5-year	Straight-line	Other real property

payment of tax. This has the effect of increasing cash inflows in the earlier years of the asset's life and thus permits recovery of the cost of the asset as soon as possible. Early recovery of costs reduces risk and permits reinvestment of funds in other profitable projects.

For purposes of financial reporting, electing an accelerated method of depreciation and/or short asset life may not be desirable. For *financial reporting purposes*, it is important to reflect the costs inherent in the use and ownership of an asset as accurately as possible. Suppose, for example, that an asset may be depreciated over a 3 year recovery period for tax purposes but, given the maintenance program established by the firm, will probably last for 7 years. For reporting to shareholders, creditors, and other interested parties, the 7-year life should be used. In addition to providing a more realistic picture, using the longer life and straight line rather than accelerated depreciation will tend to result in smoother earnings patterns. A consistent earnings pattern is favored by shareholders and creditors.

The method of depreciation to be used.   The third dimension of determining the impact of tax legislation on the depreciation tax shield is the consideration of what

Table 4–5   ACRS Rates Under TRA 1986*

RECOVERY YEAR	3-YEAR (200% DDB)	5-YEAR (200% DDB)	7-YEAR (200% DDB)	10-YEAR (200% DDB)	15-YEAR (150% DDB)	20-YEAR (150% DDB)
1	33.0%	20.0%	14.3%	10.0%	5.0%	3.8%
2	45.0	32.0	24.5	18.0	9.5	7.2
3	15.0	19.2	17.5	14.4	8.6	6.7
4	7.0	11.5†	12.5	11.5	7.7	6.2
5		11.5	8.9†	9.2	6.9	5.7
6		5.8	8.9	7.4	6.2	5.3
7			8.9	6.6†	5.9†	4.9
8			4.5	6.6	5.9	4.5†
9				6.5	5.9	4.5
10				6.5	5.9	4.5
11				3.3	5.9	4.5
12					5.9	4.5
13					5.9	4.5
14					5.9	4.5
15					5.9	4.5
16					3.0	4.5
17						4.5
18						4.5
19						4.5
20						4.5
21						1.7
Total	100%	100%	100%	100%	100%	100%

*Half-year convention is incorporated into all categories.
†Switchover to straight-line depreciation over remaining useful life.

depreciation or cost recovery (the preferred terminology under the Tax Reform Act of 1986) methods can be used by corporate taxpayers. Table 4–4 specifies the eight ACRS classes as well as the only accelerated method of cost recovery which can be used on assets in each class. Thus, for assets acquired after 1986, taxpayers can use either straight-line cost recovery or the recovery method which is specified in Table 4–4. In addition, the 1986 Tax Reform Act imposes a mandatory half-year convention and allows a switchover from declining balance to straight-line depreciation where it becomes advantageous to do so.

The half-year convention assumes that assets are acquired and disposed of in the middle of the taxable year. Thus, current depreciation rules call for recovering the total value of 3-year assets over 4 years, 5-years assets over 6 years, and so on. For a 3-year asset, only half of the usual depreciation is allowable in the first year; the full amount is allowable in year 2; only half of the usual depreciation is allowable in year 3 —the year the asset is disposed of; the remainder of the depreciation is allowable in year 4.

Table 4–5 shows depreciation percentages for all personal property classes from 3 years to 20 years. To facilitate calculations, Table 4–5 has already incorporated the half-year convention and the switch from accelerated cost recovery to straight-line at the optimal time (i.e., the first year in which the straight-line depreciation would exceed the accelerated depreciation). The percentages shown in Table 4–5 are multiplied by the depreciable cost of the asset. If the asset has no salvage value, then the total depreciable cost is written off as depreciation expense over the life of the asset. If the asset has a salvage value, only the difference between the asset's depreciable cost and its salvage value is written off as depreciation expense. Example 2 illustrates the use of Table 4–5.

EXAMPLE 2
Accelerated Cost Recovery under Tax Reform Act of 1986

The Pohlman Corporation is evaluating the acquisition of two assets:

a) an asset which costs $200,000 has a zero salvage value, and would be classified as a 5-year asset for cost recovery purposes; and

b) an asset which has a depreciation basis of $140,000 has a $20,000 estimated salvage value, and would be classified as a 7-year asset for cost recovery purposes.

For each of these assets, determine the amount of straight-line depreciation which would be written off for tax purposes (remember the half-year convention) and the amount of accelerated cost recovery using Table 4–5.

SOLUTION:

a) For the first asset described, we would find:

	STRAIGHT-LINE COST RECOVERY			ACCELERATED COST RECOVERY		
PERIOD	BASIS	PERCENTAGE	COST RECOVERY	BASIS	PERCENTAGE[†]	COST RECOVERY
1	$200,000	10%*	$ 20,000	$200,000	20%	$ 40,000
2	200,000	20	40,000	200,000	32	64,000
3	200,000	20	40,000	200,000	19.2	38,400
4	200,000	20	40,000	200,000	11.5	23,000
5	200,000	20	40,000	200,000	11.5	23,000
6	200,000	10*	20,000	200,000	5.8	11,600
Total	—	100%	$200,000	—	100%	$200,000

*Half-year convention
[†]From Table 4–5

Of course, it can easily be seen that there is a much more rapid write-off under the accelerated method than under straight-line. Under ACRS, $104,000 of the cost of the asset is recovered by the second year versus only $60,000 under straight-line. The tax shield provided by the cost recovery write-off would be the appropriate tax rate times the amount of the cost recovery. The present value of the tax shield would be much higher for the accelerated method than for straight-line.

b) Turning to the second asset described, we have:

	STRAIGHT-LINE COST RECOVERY			ACCELERATED COST RECOVERY		
PERIOD	BASIS	PERCENTAGE	COST RECOVERY	BASIS	PERCENTAGE[†]	COST RECOVERY
1	$140,000	7.142%*	$ 10,000	$140,000	14.3%	$ 20,000
2	140,000	14.286	20,000	140,000	24.5	34,300
3	140,000	14.286	20,000	140,000	17.5	24,500
4	140,000	14.286	20,000	140,000	12.5	17,500
5	140,000	14.286	20,000	140,000	8.9	12,460
6	140,000	14.286	20,000	140,000	8.9	11,240
7	140,000	14.286	10,000	140,000	8.9	0
8	140,000	7.142*	0	140,000	4.5	0
Total	—	100 %	$120,000	—	100 %	$120,000

*Half-year convention
[†]From Table 4–5

   As shown in the table, the total cost recovery under each method is limited to the original cost less the estimated salvage value. As always, the accelerated method is very attractive compared with straight-line on the basis of the present value of the tax shield provided by the cost recovery.

TAXATION ON ORDINARY INCOME

One of the major changes relative to capital investments implemented by the TRA of 1986 was the repeal of the investment tax credit (ITC), which provided up to a 10% credit on capital expenditures. The ITC has been repealed and reintroduced several times over its 25-year history. The purpose of the ITC (like that of accelerated cost recovery) was to stimulate investment in capital assets. It is debatable whether the ITC achieved its stated purpose.

   To partially offset the repeal of the ITC, the TRA of 1986 significantly reduced the corporate tax rates on ordinary income. Corporate taxable income (earnings before taxes) is that portion of the total income remaining after all operating and administrative expenses and interest are paid and depreciation is deducted. The calculation of tax payable is a simple matter once taxable income has been determined. All corporations bear federal income tax on ordinary income at the rates shown in Table 4–6 plus a surtax of 5% on taxable income between $100,000 and $335,000.

   The benefits of the graduated rate structure are phased out as taxable income increases from $100,000 to $335,000, with an effective marginal tax rate of 39% in this income range. Corporations with income in excess of $335,000 will, in effect, pay a flat tax at a 34% rate.

   There is little uniformity in the taxation of corporate income by states, but it should be noted that state income tax is included as an income statement expense for computing federal income taxes. As such, its impact on earnings after taxes depends

Table 4–6   Corporate Federal Income Tax Rates

TAXABLE INCOME	1987 AND LATER YEARS
First $50,000	15%
Next $25,000	25
Over $75,000	34

to a great extent on the rate of federal tax being paid. For example, in a state that imposes a 10% tax, the effective state tax rate would be only 6.6% if a firm has a 34% marginal federal tax rate. The reader should be cognizant of state taxes, but because of the large variation among states and the detailed computations involved, we do not include them in our cash flow calculations. Rather, we assume a combined federal and state tax rate in our illustrations and problems.

SUMMARY

Accurate estimates of cash flows, including all provisions for depreciation and taxation, are essential as inputs to the evaluation of proposed capital expenditures. In this chapter we have described how the cash flows are computed based on cost estimates. We further examined the implications of accelerated depreciation on the capital acquisition decision and noted that the use of accelerated depreciation may provide some tax incentive for capital investment.

Throughout the chapter we have emphasized that capital budgeting decisions are based upon the evaluation of relevant incremental benefits and costs affected by the project under consideration. In each instance, we estimate the costs and anticipated revenues relating to the project within the context of the firm as a whole.

QUESTIONS
_____
PROBLEMS

1. List the kinds of items which are relevant under each of the three categories of cash flows relative to capital investments.

2. Why is depreciation considered in cash flow analysis? Why do financial managers prefer accelerated depreciation methods over straight-line depreciation?

3. Suppose Congress is considering a revenue-neutral tax act that would reduce corporate tax rates and concurrently eliminate accelerated depreciation and the use of shortened depreciable lives. How would a change in the tax laws affect capital spending?

4. A company having a 40% marginal tax rate and using a 10% discount rate is considering the acquisition of an asset costing $50,000. Calculate the present value of the after-tax depreciation cash throw-offs assuming
   (a) Straight-line depreciation over 10 years.
   (b) Straight-line depreciation over 5 years.
   (c) Sum-of-the-years'-digits depreciation over 5 years.
   (d) ACRS depreciation over 5 years.
   (e) One-and-one-half declining-balance depreciation over 5 years.

5. A firm with a 40% tax rate is contemplating the purchase of a machine which costs $100,000. As a consequence of its use, revenues are expected to increase $25,000 per year while operating costs increase $10,000 during its useful life of 10 years. Determine the after-tax cash flows based on the following:
   (a) Straight-line depreciation over 10 years.
   (b) Sum-of-the-years'-digits depreciation over 5 years.
   (c) ACRS depreciation over 5 years.

6. ABC Corporation is using a labor-intensive production process. Current equipment has been completely depreciated to its projected salvage value of $10,000. New equipment costs $250,000 and has a useful life of 10 years. While revenues are not expected to change, labor costs are anticipated to decrease by $50,000 per year if the new equipment is used. Assuming ABC has a 40% marginal tax rate, determine the cash outflow necessary to acquire the equipment and the annual cash inflows based on the following:
   (a) Straight-line depreciation over 10 years.
   (b) ACRS depreciation over 5 years.

7. A2Z Corporation is expanding its Hoboken, New Jersey, chemical cleaning products plant to increase sales and market share. Construction will be completed in September, and the plant will be in full operation October 1. A tabulation of projected incremental costs and revenue follows. Determine the incremental cash flows for the first 2 years (ignoring depreciation and taxes).

ITEM	$/YEAR	NOTES
Sales	$2,520,000	Collection experience on sales: month 1, 20%; month 2, 70%; month 3, 10%.
Raw material A	408,000	3 months' initial stock (includes permanent 2 months' safety stock), required; payment net 30 (end of month)
Raw material B	144,000	2 months' initial stock required (includes permanent 1 month safety stock); payment net 30 (end of month)
Miscellaneous raw materials	180,000	Average 1 month stock required; net 25
Electricity	9,600	Net 25 (first billing Nov. 1)
Fuel oil	12,000	Net 30 (first billing Nov. 1)
Water	6,000	Net 30 (first billing Nov. 1)
Labor, hourly	144,000	Paid weekly, 1-week lag
Salaried supervision	60,000	Paid monthly on last working day
Packages, containers, and so on	210,000	2 months' initial supply required (includes permanent 1 month safety stock); net 30 (end of month)

8. A corporation is considering replacing an older truck with a newer model, which, owing to more efficient operation, will reduce costs from $20,000 to $16,000 per year. Sales are $30,000 per year. The old truck cost $30,000 when purchased nearly 5 years ago, had an estimated useful life of 15 years, zero salvage value, and is being depreciated straight-line. At present its market value is estimated to be $20,000 if sold outright. The new truck costs $40,000 and would be depreciated straight-line to a zero salvage value over a 10-year life. The corporation has a 40% marginal tax rate. Determine the following:

   (a) The cash outflow required to acquire the new truck assuming the old truck is sold at the present time.

   (b) The yearly cash flows from operations resulting from the old truck and the new truck.

   (c) Summarize the cash flows and calculate the differential cash flows over the 10-year period.

9. A corporation has decided to purchase a new machine for its business. The following are the facts relating to the disposal of the old machine and purchase of the new:

   (a) The original cost of the old machinery was $2,000,000.

   (b) The book value of the old machinery is $400,000 and it can be traded in for $900,000. It is fully depreciated.

   (c) The cost to remove the old machinery is $30,000.

   (d) The cost for the new machine is $3,500,000.

   (e) Wiring by a contractor will cost $15,000.

   (f) The cost of installation by an outside contractor is $145,000.

   (g) The legal fees are $115,000.

   (h) The costs of wiring, installation, and legal fees will be capitalized.

   (i) The added working-capital requirements are $50,000.

   (j) The depreciation method used for financial and tax accounting is straight-line.

   (k) The marginal tax rate is 40%.

   (l) The expected useful life of the new machine is 20 years.

   Determine the out-of-pocket cost to purchase the new machine.

REFERENCES

Bierman, Harold, Jr. "A Reconciliation of Present Value Capital Budgeting and Accounting." *Financial Management*, 6 (Summer 1977), 52–54.

Campbell, David R., James M. Johnson, and Leonard Savoie. "Cashflow, Liquidity and Financial Flexibility." *Financial Executive* (August 1984).

Gentry, James A., and Jesus M. De La Garza. "A Generalized Model for Monitoring Accounts Receivable." *Financial Management* (Winter 1985).

Gilmer, R. H., Jr. "The Optimal Level of Liquid Assets: An Empirical Test." *Financial Management* (Winter 1985).

Golub, Steven J., and Harry D. Huffman. "Cashflow: Why it should be stressed in financial reporting." *Financial Executive* (February 1984).

Gombola, Michael, and J. Edwards Ketz. "A Note on Cash Flow and Classification Patterns of Financial Ratios." *Accounting Review* (January 1983).

Hespos, Richard F., and Paul A. Strassmann. "Stochastic Decision Trees for the Analysis of Investment Decisions." *Management Science* (August 1965).

Jacob, David P., Graham Lord, and James A. Tilley. "A Generalized Framework for Pricing Contingent Cash Flows." *Financial Management* (Autumn 1987).

Kamath, Ravindra R., Shahriar Khaksari, Heidi Hylton Meier, and John Wonklepeck. "Management of Excess Cash: Practices and Development." *Financial Management* (Autumn 1985).

Kodde, David, and Hein Schreuder. "Forecasting Corporate Revenue and Profit: Time-Series Models Versus Management and Analysts." *Journal of Business, Finance and Accounting* (Summer 1984).

Kroll, Yoram. "On the Differences Between Accrual Accounting Figures and Cash Flows: The Case of Working Capital." *Financial Management* (Spring 1985).

Lanser, Howard P., and John A. Halloran. "Evaluating Cash Flow Systems Under Growth." *Financial Review* (Summer 1986).

Logue, Dennis E., and T. Craig Tapley. "Performance Monitoring and the Timing of Cash Flows." *Financial Management* (Autumn 1985).

Magee, J. F. "How to Use Decision Trees in Capital Investment." *Harvard Business Review* (September–October 1964).

Mao, James C. T. "The Internal Rate of Return as a Ranking Criterion." *Engineering Economist*, 11 (Winter 1966), 1–13.

Meyer, Richard L. "A Note on Capital Budgeting Techniques and the Reinvestment Rate." *Journal of Finance*, 34 (December 1979), 1251–1254.

Miller, Tom W., and Bernell K. Stone. "Daily Cash Forecasting and Seasonal Resolution: Alternative Models and Techniques for Using the Distribution Approach." *Journal of Financial and Quantitative Analysis* (Fall 1985).

Moore, William T., and Son-Nan Chen. "Implementing the IRR Criterion When Cash Flow Parameters are Unknown." *Financial Review* (Winter 1984).

Oblak, David J., and Roy J. Helm, Jr. "Survey and Analysis of Capital Budgeting Methods Used by Multinationals." *Financial Management*, 9 (Winter 1980), 37–41.

Otley, David T. "The Accuracy of Budgetary Estimates: Some Statistical Evidence." *Journal of Business, Finance and Accounting* (Summer 1985).

Petry, Glenn H. "Effective Use of Capital Budgeting Tools." *Business Horizons*, 19 (October 1975), 57–65.

Pogue, Gerald A., and Kishore Lall. "Corporate Finance: An Overview." *Sloan Management Review*, 15 (Spring 1974), 19–38.

Renshaw, E. "A Note on the Arithmetic of Capital Budgeting Decisions." *Journal of Business*, 30 (July 1957).

Wilkens, E. N. "Forecasting Cash Flow: Some Problems and Applications." *Management Accounting* (October 1967), 26–30.

Evaluation of Alternative Investment Opportunities

5

Once the firm's management has established its goals and priorities for capital expenditures, it must address the question of evaluating proposed expenditures in some systematic manner. Since in all organizations the amount of funds available for capital expenditures is limited, *management is faced with the dual problems of establishing some basic criteria for the acceptance, rejection, or postponement of proposed investments, and then ranking the projects that meet the criteria for acceptance in order of their value to the firm.* Our studies indicate that at least 35 methods have been devised to guide management in the acceptance or rejection of proposed investments. Some of the methods are general in nature and readily applicable to many firms. Others are designed for particular industries such as utilities. Some are special applications of more general procedures and have been developed to deal, for example, with the question of variability of risk among proposals.

To provide a point of departure, we cite three factors that Norman E. Pflomm[1] has noted as basic to the capital project evaluation process:

1 The computed measures of project attractiveness should be *consistently* applied to all projects.

2 The quantitative measure(s) should be used as a guide rather than as the sole basis for approval or rejection of capital projects.

3 Management should completely understand the assumptions made in the analysis, how the computations were carried out, and what the final results really mean.

Each of these points is sound advice to management. Consistency in evaluation is very important—the same measure(s) should be applied to each proposed project. The results of the analysis should be used as guides for management, but in the final rounds of decision making, it is the all-important management judgment that must carry the day. The results of the quantitative analysis are important inputs, but they

[1]Norman E. Pflomm, *Managing Capital Expenditures* (New York: The Conference Board, 1963).

Table 5 – 1   Reasons for Using the Various Capital Budgeting Techniques

REASONS CITED	NUMBER OF CORPORATIONS CITING REASONS	PERCENTAGE OF TOTAL
Recognizes time value of money	37	17%
Required for regulated business	27	12
Easy to use	26	12
Familiar to management	22	10
Accepted in our industry	20	9
Capital-intensive industry	18	8
Ease of comparison	15	7
Long-lived investments	15	7
Appropriate	9	4
Other	9	4
High rate of equipment or merchandise obsolescence	8	4
High risks	5	2
Labor-intensive industry	4	2
High cash flow in early years	3	1
Volatile product prices or demand	3	1
Total	221	100%

are only *inputs*. Expert judgment based on experience will have the final say. Finally, it is very important for management to understand fully just how the quantitative results were obtained. Without this understanding, misinterpretation and misapplication of the results may occur.

Many different methods for evaluating proposed projects have been developed. Each has particular strengths that make it especially useful depending upon the particular circumstances. Most companies therefore use more than one method; some companies use several. Naturally, for larger-sized projects the desirability of using more than one evaluation criterion increases.

Glen H. Petry [2] has studied the reasons for managements' choices of techniques and for employing multiple methods. The reasons cited for selecting a particular evaluation method are summarized in Table 5–1, while the reasons for using multiple techniques are summarized in Table 5–2.

The tables indicate that managers differ with respect to how proposed capital investments should be evaluated. There *should* be differences because companies are different. Thus it becomes very important to understand how and why each method is used. With this knowledge, the most appropriate evaluation technique can be selected. We will introduce six commonly used techniques, indicating the importance and shortcomings of each.

---

[2] Glen H. Petry, "Effective Use of Capital Budgeting Tools," *Business Horizons* (October 1975), and Patrick J. Davey, *Capital Investments: Appraisals and Hints* (New York: The Conference Board, 1974).

Table 5–2   Reasons for Using Multiple Techniques

REASON	NUMBER OF RESPONSES	PERCENTAGE OF TOTAL
Multiple criteria	46	21%
Different types of projects	43	20
Different types of products	32	15
Different project lives	25	12
Different divisions	19	9
Different sizes of projects	12	6
Different cash flow patterns	8	4
Different approval levels	8	4
Different project locations	7	3
Different personal preferences	6	3
Other	7	3
Total	213	100%

AN OVERVIEW OF PROJECT EVALUATION TECHNIQUES

In the course of our study of the methods used to evaluate capital investments, we explore six alternatives: payback, return on investment, net present value, profitability index, internal rate of return and equivalent annual charge (also called equivalent annual cash flow). The latter four are called *discounted cash flow procedures* because they consider the time value of money by discounting expected cash flows to their present value. Each method has its own story to tell; consequently, most companies use two or more to provide management with the information necessary to make acquisition and abandonment decisions.

1   *Payback.* This method involves determining the number of years necessary to recover the cost of a project and comparing the recovery period with the *maximum payback period* acceptable to management.

2   *Return on investment.* This name has been given to a variety of methods that divide yearly cash inflows or net income (either before or after taxes) by the project's cost or book value.

3   *Net present value.* This method requires discounting all expected after-tax cash flows to present value and taking the difference between the sum of the discounted cash inflows and outflows. This difference is called the *project's net present value.*

4   *Profitability index.* This method involves dividing the present value of the cash inflows by the present value of the cash outflows. The quotient provides an index for measuring *return per dollar of investment.*

5   *Internal rate of return.* This method involves determining the discount rate that will exactly equate the present value of the cash inflows with the present value of the cash outflows so that the net present value will be zero. That discount rate is called the project's internal rate of return.

6   *Equivalent annual charge.* This method involves discounting all the expected after-tax cash inflows to present value and then determining their equivalent annual charge over the project's life.

In this chapter, we commence with payback and return on investment. The discounted cash flow methods are examined in Chapter 6.

CLASSIFICATION OF PROJECTS

The construction of a capital budget must take note of interrelationships among proposed projects. If the acceptance or rejection of one project does not affect the cash flows of another project, the two are said to be *independent*. On the other hand, dependency effects occur whenever the cash flows of one project influence or are influenced by the cash flows of another. Three situations involving dependency warrant examination:

1   *Mutually exclusive projects.* If the acceptance of one project precludes the acceptance of another project, the two are mutually exclusive. An airline pondering the future of its fleet may have to choose between the slower 747, which has a larger seating capacity, and the SST, which has a lower passenger capacity but supersonic speed.

2   *Complementary projects.* If the acceptance of one project enhances the cash flows of another project, the two are complementary. Thus, the cash flows from an automobile service station on a superhighway might ᵀ increased by the construction of restaurant facilities at the same location.

3   *Prerequisite or contingent projects.* If the acceptance of one project depends upon the prior acceptance of another project, the acceptance of the former is prerequisite to the acceptance of the latter. The construction of an oil refinery at a given location may depend upon the prior commitment to construct port facilities.

Obviously, dependent projects must be presented together if the manager is to consider the full range of alternatives. In this respect, one of the major problems in capital budgeting lies in the identification of all viable alternatives. *The ranking process is relative and any capital project may appear attractive when compared against a sufficiently poor alternative.*

Some projects are mandatory; they must be accepted if the firm wishes to remain in business. Others are discretionary, acceptable if financially attractive. Utilities, for example, are required by law to make investments needed to provide service on demand, even though more rewarding projects may be available. For the telephone company, switching equipment would fall into the mandatory category, while the installation of new, lower-cost generating equipment would constitute a discretionary investment. On the other hand, *the evaluation of mandatory investments does not exclude the possibility of abandonment, based on a discounted cash flow analysis. One has the option of going out of business.*

BASIC ASSUMPTIONS

In our initial discussion of capital budgeting, we make several assumptions which will be relaxed in later chapters. The assumptions are listed here:

1   *Projects being evaluated have the same risk posture as the firm overall. We shall assume that the investment decisions made will not alter the firm's existing risk complexion.* This does not mean that we are operating in a risk-free atmosphere. *Rather, it means that projects accepted have the same average risk, which characterizes the firm.*

All firms operate under some degree of business and financial risk. The unique combination of risk elements determines the firm's risk complexion. The risk complexion is integrated by the securities markets and results in the rate at which the market discounts the price of the firm's securities. Types of investments that generally will not affect the risk complexion or market discount rate include replacements for equipment currently in use, where the market and economic structure surrounding the use of the equipment are expected to maintain stable. In Chapters 11 through 14, we examine decision-making techniques that permit us to evaluate the impact of risk on the capital investment decision.

2   *Management must set benchmarks for the evaluation of capital expenditures.* The benchmark for payback is the maximum number of years required by the firm for the complete recovery of the investment in a project. For rate of return, the benchmark is the minimum rate of return required by management, which may vary appreciably depending on the method used to compute the rate of return. Several methods are in common use, as noted later.

For the discounted cash flow methods, the major criterion for evaluation will initially be assumed to be the firm's marginal cost of capital, commonly referred to as the *cost of capital*. This represents the cost of funds used to acquire the firm's total assets and is found by averaging the rates of return expected to be received by all parties contributing to the firm's financial structure. Actual computation of the firm's cost of capital is discussed in Chapter 10. Application of the evaluative criteria to the discounted cash flow procedures is discussed in the following chapter.

3   *The firm's cost of capital is constant over time and is not affected by the amount of funds that is invested in capital projects.* This assumption avoids the problems imposed by *capital rationing* and varying money and capital market rates.

There are two types of capital rationing: internal and external. *Internal capital rationing* involves the constraints resulting from the limitations of existing managerial ability in assuming any new project or expansion responsibilities. Some firms attempt to circumvent this constraint by expanding through the acquisition of ongoing companies and thereby purchasing the needed managerial expertise along with the physical assets. *External capital rationing* originally referred to a lack of capital available to finance desirable projects. While this aspect of external capital rationing remains a primary consideration in the capital acquisition process, other external constraints also require close attention. Such constraints include lack or potential unavailability of critical materials, skilled labor, water and sewer supplies, and government permits to carry out construction and operate facilities.

4   *Investment opportunities are independent of each other. There are no interrelationships among projects under consideration* (mutually exclusive, contingent, and complementary projects do not exist); furthermore, *there is no correlation between the cash flows of any pair of projects under consideration by the firm or between the cash flows of any project and the ongoing operations of the firm.* This assumption is necessary to avoid the potential conflicts that may arise in ranking projects falling into the several categories of dependent projects. We discuss these conflicts in Chapter 8.

5   *Borrowing and lending rates are equal.* This means that the rate that must be paid by the firm to obtain funds from the capital markets (borrowing) is equal to the rate the firm can earn if it purchases securities in the capital markets (lending). This assumption is necessary to assure that a firm will be able to reinvest the incremental cash flows resulting from the use of an asset at the *same rate* that is used to discount those incremental cash flows to their present value. As noted earlier, the use of the compound interest, annuity, and present value tables is predicated on reinvesting intermediate cash flows at a constant rate over the life of the investment. The reason that it may not be possible to reinvest intermediate cash inflows at the same rate used to discount the project is that the market level of interest rate varies (sometimes appreciably) over the life of the project. A methodology for evaluating projects during periods when interest rates and reinvestment rates are expected to vary is included in Chapter 8.

6   *Perfect capital markets exist.* This means that (a) no lender or borrower in the markets possesses sufficient power to influence prices; (b) any participant in the markets can lend or borrow as much as desired without affecting security prices (i.e., there is not an upward-sloping supply curve for capital); (c) bankruptcy and transaction costs do not exist; (d) all participants in the markets have access to the same cost-free information, this information is interpreted in exactly the same way by all participants, and such information is immediately incorporated into all security prices; and (e) capital rationing does not exist.

CERTAINTY, RISK, AND UNCERTAINTY — AN INTRODUCTION

We have assumed that the projects being evaluated would not change the risk complexion of the firm overall. That is, the projects being evaluated have the same degree of risk as the firm. To understand this assumption better, we will define the three states of certainty, risk, and uncertainty and the different types of risk with which the decision maker must deal.

Certainty postulates that the decision maker knows in advance the exact future values of all the parameters that may affect the decision.

Risk postulates that the decision maker is (1) aware of all possible future states of the environment, including the economy and business, that may occur and thereby affect relevant decision parameters and (2) able to place a probability on the value of each parameter given the occurrence of each of these states.

Uncertainty postulates that the decision maker may or may not (1) be aware of all the possible states that affect the decision and (2) be able to place a probability distribution on the occurrence of each.

In Part IV we examine the problems inherent in project selection under conditions of changing risk and describe procedures that are useful in selecting portfolios of projects in order to minimize risk. At this juncture it is useful to review three kinds of risk faced by financial managers.

1   *Business risk* is the variability in earnings that is a function of the firm's normal operations (as impacted by the changing economic environment) and management's decisions with respect to capital intensification. The use of more capital equipment generally results in higher fixed costs and thereby increases the variability of earnings before interest and taxes (EBIT) with output. It should be noted that business risk considers only the variability in EBIT and does not consider the effect of debt or other financing on the firm's risk posture.

2   *Cataclysmic risk* is the variability in earnings that is a function of events beyond managerial control and anticipation. Such events would include expropriation, erratic changes in consumer preferences, severe energy shortages, and the like.

3   *Financial risk* is the variability in earnings resulting from the firm's financial structure and the necessity of meeting obligations on fixed-income securities. The use of more debt or preferred stock results in greater obligatory payments and thereby increases the variability of earnings after taxes and earnings per share.

We now undertake our examination of each of the non-DCF methods.

PAYBACK

Payback, especially, is a widely used criterion for evaluating projects. Its popularity stems in large part from the fact that it is simple to use and the results are easy to understand. Little explanation is required. Payback just measures the period of time required to recover the investment in the project. It is the period during which the cumulative net cash inflows generated by the project just equal the net cash outflows necessary for the project.

Since payback measures only the time period necessary to recover the investment, it is really a measure not of profitability but rather of the *particular project's expected liquidity*. The degree of project liquidity is viewed as important by many managers, but since payback does *not* measure profitability, it is almost always used in conjunction with another evaluation criterion. Using the payback method to determine the payback period is illustrated in Examples 1 and 2.

EXAMPLE 1
Payback with Equal Annual Cash Inflows

> A corporation is evaluating a project that requires a $60,000 cash outlay, and is expected to generate annual net cash inflows of $8,000 over its 15-year useful life. Determine the payback period for the project.
>
> SOLUTION: The payback period is equal to the net cash outlay divided by the annual net cash inflow:
>
> $$\text{payback period} = \frac{\text{net cash outlay}}{\text{annual net cash inflow}} = \frac{\$60,000}{\$8,000} = 7.5 \text{ years}$$
>
> The result indicates that after $7\frac{1}{2}$ years the firm's $60,000 cash outlay will be recovered.

When net cash inflows are not equal from year to year, the payback period is found by cumulating the cash inflows until they equal the net cash outlay, as shown in Example 2.

EXAMPLE 2
Payback with Unequal Annual Cash Inflows

> ABC Company is evaluating a capital project that requires a $38,000 net cash outlay and will generate net cash inflows of $10,000 for each of the first 2 years, $8,000 each for years 3 and 4, and $6,000 for each of years 5 through 10. Determine the payback period.
>
> SOLUTION: Table 5–3 is helpful in determining the payback period. As can be seen, the cumulative net cash inflows become equal to $38,000 sometime during year 5. If the cash inflows occur equally throughout the year, this point would be one-third of the way into the year ($2,000 ÷ $6,000). Thus the payback period for this project is $4\frac{1}{3}$ years.

Table 5 – 3   Annual and Cumulative Expected Cash Inflows

YEAR	NET CASH INFLOW	CUMULATIVE CASH INFLOWS
1	$10,000	$10,000
2	10,000	20,000
3	8,000	28,000
4	8,000	36,000
5	6,000	42,000
6	6,000	48,000
7	6,000	54,000
8	6,000	60,000
9	6,000	66,000
10	6,000	72,000

Once the payback period is determined, projects are accepted or rejected depending on the length of the period required to recover their investments. For example, management may feel that it wants to recover investments in discretionary projects within 3 years. If this benchmark were established, then projects having a payback period in excess of three years would be rejected. It is also possible to rank projects using the payback period wherein the ordering is from shorter to longer payback period. In practice, however, we find that *the payback criterion is more frequently used as a method for identifying potentially undesirable projects than for ranking projects.*

As with other evaluation methods, the use of payback requires a benchmark for acceptability. The benchmark is the maximum number of years permitted for recovery of the project's cost. Establishing this constraint is frequently somewhat arbitrary but should not be. *If payback is used, it should be used as a device to identify the projects which management feels will require a long period for cost recovery.* These projects may be of above-average importance to the company, since they will tie up capital for an extended period of time. Thus the payback method is useful to alert management to a long-term commitment of capital.

If payback is to be used as a constraint to eliminate some proposed projects, the acceptable payback period should be established consistent with the life cycle of the product being produced, potential for obsolescence due to changes in technology or consumer preference, and the like. Thus the same cutoff should *not* be applied to all projects. Rather, the cutoff should be consistent with the project's expected and intended use and useful life.

When payback is used as demonstrated in Examples 1 and 2, cash flows are considered only up to the time that the initial investment is recovered. As a result, the only question answered concerns the length of time needed to recover the initial investment. Weingartner notes: "Generally, the break-even point is a point of indifference—with qualifications—beyond which an accounting profit is expected to be generated by the operation under analysis, and below which loss is expected."[3] If the net revenues are constant, the aggregate profit will be proportional to the project's life after the payback period has elapsed. "Thus, a longer anticipated life yields a higher initial profit, other things remaining equal, because depreciation expense will be lower. Indeed, the life of the project may be overestimated by the proposer not only to enhance its total profitability, but also to reduce the payback period on the accounting profit basis. A bias countering this one may arise in the selection of the shortest project or asset life which the tax authorities permit to improve the actual after-tax cash flow profitability. Cash flow payback, the usual concept, is less affected since depreciation enters only as a tax shield."[4]

The use of payback, then, depends on the importance to management of knowing the capital recovery period. Merritt and Sykes note that: "It [payback] causes assessors to concentrate on unimportant and often irrelevant characteristics of an investment project to the detriment of its significant characteristics. It has harshly, but not unfairly, been described as the 'fish bait' test, since effectively it concentrates

---

[3] H. Martin Weingartner, "Some New Views on the Payback Period and Capital Budgeting Decisions," *Management Science*, 15, no. 12 (August 1969), p. B-599.

[4] Ibid., p. B-601.

on the recovery of the bait (the capital outlay) paying no attention to the size of the fish (the ultimate profitability), if any."[5]

The payback method has been further discredited for at least five reasons:

1   It fails to consider the expected revenues beyond the payback period established by the firm. Frequently, such payback periods are set from 2 to 5 years. The time period established generally is not based on an economic measure that would attach a cost to the use of funds and to the application of managerial effort, but rather may depend to a great extent on the firm's risk preferences for liquidity. Thus, for example, if a firm established a 3-year payback period requirement, revenues generated after the third year would not be considered when applying this method.

2   It fails to consider the time value of money.

3   It does not differentiate between projects requiring different cash investments.

4   While it does measure a project's rate of capital recovery or liquidity, it does not consider the firm's liquidity position as a whole, which is a much more important question. As Weingartner points out: "The usually designated speculative and/or precautionary motive of firms to hold liquid or near liquid funds in order to seize upon unexpected opportunities is a different motive from that which requires each new investment separately to recover its original cost within a short time."[6]

5   It ignores the cost of funds used to support the investment, even during the payback period. By ignoring the cost of funds, a very important cost is overlooked. Reconciliation of this problem is considered below.

A somewhat different approach to the application of payback, which takes into consideration the cost of funds necessary to support an investment, is demonstrated in the following section.

Payback Including the Cost of Funds

The payback method described earlier may be modified to incorporate the cost of funds used to support the project.[7] This procedure overcomes the fifth shortcoming just given and also proves useful in dealing with certain classes of cataclysmic risk. The methodology of incorporating the cost of funds into the payback method is demonstrated in Example 3.

---

[5]A. J. Merritt and A. Sykes, *The Finance and Analysis of Capital Projects* (London: Longmans Green and Co. Ltd., 1963).

[6]Weingartner, "Some New Views on the Payback Period," p. B-599.

[7]W. G. Lewellen, H. P. Lanser, and J. McConnell, "Payback Substitutes for Discounted Cash Flow," *Financial Management*, II, no. 2 (Summer 1973), present a procedure for establishing a one-to-one conversion of zero net present value conditions into counterpart payback maxima. This approach renders the two approaches of discounted cash flow and payback operationally equivalent.

EXAMPLE 3
Payback

A corporation requires a rate of return of 15%. Using the project with cash flows as shown, determine the period necessary to recover both the capital expenditures and the cost of funds required to support those expenditures.

TIME	EXPECTED CASH FLOWS
Present	− $10,000
1	− 4,000
2–6	+ 3,000
7–15	+ 6,000
15*	+ 2,000

*Recovery of working capital.

SOLUTION: Construct a table showing cash flows and costs of capital to support those funds.

TIME	EXPECTED CASH FLOW	DOLLAR COST OF FUNDS AT 15%	CUMULATIVE NET CASH FLOW
Present	− $10,000	0	− $10,000
1	− 4,000	− $1,500	− 15,500
2	+ 3,000	− 2,325	− 14,825
3	+ 3,000	− 2,224	− 14,049
4	+ 3,000	− 2,107	− 13,156
5	+ 3,000	− 1,973	− 12,129
6	+ 3,000	− 1,819	− 10,948
7	+ 6,000	− 1,642	− 6,590
8	+ 6,000	− 939	− 1,579
9	+ 6,000	− 237	+ 4,184

The total investment will be recovered in 9 years, assuming that all cash flows are year-end.

When the payback is used as shown in Example 3, it provides the period of time for the project to provide a return just equal to the cost of capital. The reader may verify this by discounting the expected cash flows to their present value at 15% for the 9-year payback period. We can conclude that the project must remain in use 9 years for the firm to cover its cost of capital and recover the funds invested in the project.

Since the payback, when employed as demonstrated in Example 3, indicates the period for recovery of both capital and the associated cost of funds, it can be used to advantage for analysis of cataclysmic risks. Examples of such risks include the probability of major technological changes that render ongoing processes valueless and sudden plant takeovers by foreign governments. These are risks associated with the possibility of the business going on for a period and then collapsing entirely.

Thus, payback is an all-or-nothing risk indicator and may be used to advantage in assessing risks relative to the time period during which an investment is expected to remain in use. For example, suppose that a firm were considering a project in a foreign country having the cash flows in Example 3. Payback shows that if the project remains in use and delivers the expected cash flows for 9 years, the firm will not suffer because it will have met its cost of capital. If the project operates more than 9 years, it will yield a return in excess of the firm's cost of capital. If management could estimate the possibility of the project's expropriation in terms of time from implementation, then payback, as used in Example 3, would provide an excellent cutoff time for risk analysis.

Why Payback Is Used

Although payback suffers from some severe limitations, it is frequently used by many companies. Furthermore, in periods of tight money and high interest rates, when capital is very expensive, the use of payback tends to increase since cash flows expected beyond a short time horizon are of limited importance. Various other reasons attributed to its frequent use include the following:

1   It is very simple.

2   Many managers have severe reservations about the estimates of expected cash flows to be received beyond the next 2 to 5 years and feel from past experience that if they can recover their investment in, for instance, 3 years, they will make a profit.

3   Many firms have liquidity problems and are very concerned about how rapidly invested funds will be recovered.

4   Some firms have high costs of external financing and must look to internally generated funds to support their future ventures. Hence, they are especially interested in the rate at which their investment will be recovered.

5   It is a simple matter to compensate for the differences in risk associated with alternative proposed projects: projects having higher degrees of risk are evaluated using shorter payback periods.

6   Some firms are involved in areas where the risk of obsolescence as a result of technological changes and severe competition is great. Therefore, they are anxious to recover funds rapidly.

7   Some firms manufacture products that are subject to model period changes and therefore must recover their investment within the model life.

While payback does have severe limitations and is not a measure of profitability, it has been widely accepted for the reasons just described. We recommend that payback be used as a supplemental evaluation tool, in conjunction with a discounted cash flow procedure. When payback is employed as in Example 3, we recommended its use in the following situations:

1   As a measure of a project's liquidity if such liquidity is of particular importance to the firm. Project liquidity should not be confused with profitability or with the firm's overall liquidity preference, as discussed.

2   For projects involving very uncertain returns, especially when those returns become increasingly more uncertain in future time periods.

3   During periods of very high external financing costs, which make capital recovery very important.

4 For projects involving a high degree of cataclysmic risk.

5 For projects subject to model-year changes or obsolescence resulting from technological changes, changing consumer preferences, and the like.

RETURN ON INVESTMENT

The return-on-investment (ROI) method compares the yearly after-tax (or pretax) income with the investment in the asset. The underlying idea is to compare the return expected to be received from a project with some preestablished requirement. Pflomm notes four methods in common use (see Table 5–4).[8] The simplest is to divide the average annual income by the total investment, as shown. The three other methods noted by Pflomm are also shown in the table.

Table 5 – 4 Return on Investment Computed by Four Different Methods

PROPOSAL—BENCH LATHE	
Investment	$1,000.00
Estimated useful life	5 years
Income: Year 1	300.00
Year 2	300.00
Year 3	300.00
Year 4	300.00
Year 5	300.00
Total	$1,500.00

RETURN-ON-INVESTMENT COMPUTATIONS

Method 1: Annual return on investment:

$$\frac{\text{annual income}}{\text{original investment}} \times 100 = \frac{300}{1,000} \times 100 = 30\%$$

Method 2: Annual return on average investment:

$$\frac{\text{annual income}}{\text{original investment}/2} \times 100 = \frac{300}{500} \times 100 = 60\%$$

Method 3: Average return on average investment:

$$\frac{\text{total income} - \text{original investment}}{(\text{original investment}/2) \times \text{years}} \times 100 = \frac{500}{(1,000/2) \times 5 \text{ years}} \times 100 = 20\%$$

Method 4: Average book return on investment:

$$\frac{\text{total income} - \text{original investment}}{\text{weighted average investment*}} \times 100$$

$$= \frac{500}{(1,000 + 800 + 600 + 400 + 200)/5 \times 5 \text{ years}} \times 100 = 16\tfrac{2}{3}\%$$

*Sum of book values of asset each year, straight-line depreciation over life of the project.
SOURCE: Norman E. Pflomm, *Managing Capital Expenditures* (New York: The Conference Board, 1963).

[8] Pflomm, *Managing Capital Expenditures*.

In each calculation, the income figure refers to additional after-tax profits and may include depreciation cash throw-offs or may be net of those throw-offs. Example 4 illustrates four possible ROI calculations.

EXAMPLE 4

Return on Investment Calculations

A firm is evaluating a project which has an original investment of $24,000 and a projected salvage value of $4,000 at the end of its 6-year life. The net income before taxes generated by the project each year is

YEAR	NET INCOME BEFORE TAX
1	$2,000
2	3,500
3	4,000
4	2,400
5	2,000
6	1,000

The firm's marginal tax rate is 40%. Determine
(a) ROI before tax on original investment.
(b) ROI before tax on average investment.
(c) ROI after tax on original investment.
(d) ROI after tax on average investment.

SOLUTION: For parts (a) and (b), we start by determining the average annual net income (NI) before taxes:

$$\text{average NI before tax} = \frac{\$2,000 + 3,500 + 4,000 + 2,400 + 2,000 + 1,000}{6}$$

$$= \$2,483.33$$

(a) $\text{ROI before tax on original investment} = \dfrac{\$2,483.33}{\$24,000} = 10.35\%$

(b) $\text{ROI before tax on average investment} = \dfrac{\$2,483.33}{(\$24,000 + \$4,000)/2} = \dfrac{\$2,483.33}{\$14,000}$

$$= 17.74\%$$

For parts (c) and (d), we must determine average annual net income after taxes. If the firm's marginal tax rate is assumed to remain constant at 40% over the 6-year life of the project, then the average annual net income after tax will merely equal the average annual before-tax figure multiplied by 1 minus the 40% tax rate:

$$\text{average NI after tax} = (\text{average NI before tax})(1 - \text{tax rate})$$

$$= (\$2,483.33)(1 - 0.4)$$

$$= \$1,490.$$

(c) $\text{ROI after tax on original investment} = \dfrac{\$1,490}{\$24,000} = 6.21\%$

(d) $\text{ROI after tax on average investment} = \dfrac{\$1,490}{(\$24,000 + \$4,000)/2} = \dfrac{\$1,490}{\$14,000}$

$$= 10.64\%$$

There is nothing too challenging about computing the return on investment. However, as pointed out at the beginning of this chapter, management should understand how the ROI benchmark figures have been calculated so that a relevant comparison can be made for the project under evaluation.

There are three major weaknesses of the ROI criterion. *The primary shortcoming of all the rate-of-return procedures is that they do not consider the timing of the expected profits.* Thus, a project with low initial profitability and high future profitability would have the same average return as a project with higher initial profitability and lower future profitability. The former project would have much less value to the firm than the latter. The difference between the average rate of return and the project's internal rate of return becomes increasingly significant for projects with relatively large inflows in the later years of their lives.

A second fault is much more insidious and warrants special attention, as it demonstrates a very important aspect of capital expenditure management. The real value of any asset to a firm is a function of management's ability to employ the asset in a productive manner. The firm's balance sheet (which indicates the book value of assets) is only a listing of the investments that the firm has made and the sources of capital used to obtain and maintain those investments. The amounts listed on the balance sheet reflect accounting values, which may differ substantially from both market values and productive values.

Since the balance sheet book values neither reflect the value of assets in terms of their earning ability nor their market value, the return-on-investment method may be extremely misleading. Consider, for example, an apartment house having an original cost of $1 million 10 years ago, currently producing cash inflows (after-tax profits plus depreciation cash throw-offs) of $250,000 per year, and having a book value of $500,000. Based on the book value, the rate of return would be 50%. However, experience indicates that apartment house values, in general, have doubled over the last 10 years, so that the fair market value is probably close to $2 million. A $250,000 return on a $2 million investment is only 12.5%. This simple example clearly demonstrates two important facts: the rate-of-return method may give very misleading results and, *in any capital investment problem, it is the fair market value or the productive value of the asset to the firm, not the book value, that must be considered. The book value is not relevant because it merely represents sunk costs and comes into play only when computing the tax impact of investments.*

Third, *there is no benchmark for project acceptance* (as there is for payback and the discounted cash flow criteria). The cost of capital is based on the after-tax cost of funds used for financing. Comparing pretax ROI with the cost of capital is therefore erroneous. Further, even if ROI is computed on an after-tax basis, the fact that the time value of money is ignored renders the cost of capital invalid as a benchmark.

The Conference Board's survey indicates that about one-fourth of the firms surveyed use the method, but generally only as a supplemental tool. While rate of return is still used by some firms, we do not recommend it. The results frequently are erroneous, as it seldom, if ever, indicates the real value or earning power of a project.

QUESTIONS

PROBLEMS

1. A corporation plans to invest funds in a new machine. The initial after-tax cash outflow amounts to $10,000 and yearly cash inflows over its 6-year life are $2,200. Determine the payback period for the machine.

2. A certain project has yearly after-tax cash outflows and inflows as follows:

YEAR	OUTFLOW	INFLOW
Present	− $10,000	0
1	− 5,000	$3,000
2	0	4,000
3–6	0	5,000

Determine the payback period.

3. A corporation has a policy of rejecting any investment that does not result in recovery of cost within 4 years. Management is considering three projects:

TIME	PROJECT A	PROJECT B	PROJECT C
Present	− $10,000	− $12,000	− $3,000
1	4,000	0	500
2	4,000	5,000	500
3	2,000	4,000	500
4	2,000	3,000	2,000
5	2,000	3,000	2,000
6	2,000	3,000	2,000
7	2,000	3,000	2,000

Determine the acceptable projects and rank them by payback period.

4. If a corporation requires a 10% after-tax return on its investments, determine the payback period for each investment listed in Problem 3.

5. The Johnson Company is considering the acquisition of a small company that will fit nicely into its present distribution system and complement present operations. Senior management requires a maximum 9-year payback period. The acquisition cost of the company is $8 million and the company yielded after-tax cash flows of $750,000 in the past year. A 5% after-tax growth rate has been projected. Additionally, the Johnson Company can save $50,000 per year by combining the two distribution systems. Should the acquisition be made assuming that the Johnson Company has a cost of capital of 9%?

6. Obel International Corporation is considering manufacturing a new product line in one of its three plants. The plants are located in the United States, Canada, and Mexico and the cost of capital at each location is 8%, 9%, and 14%, respectively. Expected cash flows at each location are as follows:

TIME	UNITED STATES	CANADA	MEXICO
Present	− $25,000	− $28,000	− $32,000
1	− 9,000	− 12,000	− 16,000
2	− 6,000	+ 2,000	+ 1,000
3	+ 1,000	+ 8,000	+ 13,000
4	+ 8,000	+ 16,000	+ 18,000
5–10	+ 18,000	+ 18,000	+ 18,000

Provide a payback period chart based on net cash flow from each country and indicate your choice of location for the management.

7. The Green Thumb Sod Company has a required rate of return of 12%. Pete Moss, the company's financial wizard, must decide between two different heavy-duty, sod-cutting machines. Sod-cutter A will cost $8,000 to purchase this year, plus an additional $2,000 next year for testing and tuning. After this period, Pete estimates cash inflow generated by the machine will be $3,000 for the next 4 years, $2,000 the next 3 years, and $1,000 per year to the end of its 12-year useful life. Sod-cutter B will cost $15,000, with no additional costs, and is expected to generate an income of $4,000 for the first 3 years, $3,000 the next 6 years, and $900 per year to the end of its 10-year useful life. Which machine should Pete recommend purchasing, assuming that he wants to recover both the capital expenditures and the cost of funds required to support these funds as soon as possible? All cash flows are year-end.

8. A project will provide cash inflows of $1,000 for 10 years. What is the maximum amount that could be invested in the project if capital recovery can take no more than 5 years? The cost of capital is 12%.

9. A project that has a 10-year life costs $5,000. It is expected to generate income of $800 per year each year of its life. Determine the project's return on investment using the four methods of Table 5–4.

10. Why is the payback method used? What information does it provide? Briefly discuss the major shortcomings of the payback method.

REFERENCES

Ang, J. S., and J. H. Chua. "Composite Measures for the Evaluation of Investment Performance." *Journal of Financial and Quantitative Analysis* (June 1979).

Beedles, William L. "A Note on Evaluating Non-Simple Investments." *Journal of Financial and Quantitative Analysis*, 13 (March 1978), 173–176.

Bernhard, Richard H. "'Modified' Rates of Return for Investment Project Evaluation—A Comparison and Critique." *Engineering Economist*, 24 (Spring 1979), 161–167.

_____. "Some New Capital Budgeting Theorems: Comment." *Journal of Financial and Quantitative Analysis*, 13 (December 1978), 825–829.

Breck, Ivan E., and Daniel G. Weaver. "A Comparison of Capital Budgeting Techniques in Identifying Profitable Investments." *Financial Management* (Fall 1984).

Dearden, John. "The Case Against ROI Control." *Harvard Business Review*, 47 (May–June 1969), 124–135.

Fogler, H. Russell. "Ranking Techniques and Capital Rationing." *Accounting Review*, 47 (January 1972), 134–143.

Gitman, Lawrence J., and John R. Forrester, Jr. "A Survey of Capital Budgeting Techniques Used by Major U.S. Firms." *Financial Management*, 6 (Fall 1977), 66–71.

Grinyer, J. R. "Relevant Criterion Rates in Capital Budgeting." *Journal of Business Finance and Accounting*, 1 (Autumn 1974), 357–374.

Grossman, Elliott S. *A Guide to the Determinants of Capital Investment.* Conference Board Report No. 721 (New York: Conference Board, 1977).

Hastie, Larry K. "One Businessman's View of Capital Budgeting." *Financial Management*, 3 (Winter 1974), 36–44.

Haynes, W. Warren, and Martin B. Solomon, Jr. "A Misplaced Emphasis in Capital Budgeting." *Quarterly Review of Economics and Business* (February 1962).

Hoskins, Colin G., and Glen A. Mumey. "Payback: A Maligned Method of Asset Ranking." *Engineering Economist*, 25 (Fall 1979), 53–65.

Howe, Keith M., and James A. Patterson. "Capital Investment Decisions Under Economies of Scale in Flotation Costs." *Financial Management* (Summer 1985).

Kim, Suk H., and Edward J. Farragher. "Current Capital Budgeting Practices." *Management Accounting*, 28 (June 1981), 26–30.

King, Paul. "Is the Emphasis of Capital Budgeting Theory Misplaced?" *Journal of Business Finance and Accounting* (Winter 1975).

Kruschwitz, Lutz. "The Role of the Payback Period in the Theory and Application of Duration to Capital Budgeting: A Comment." *Journal of Business Finance and Accounting* (Winter 1985).

Kwan, Clarence C. Y. "Optimal Sequential Selection in Capital Budgeting: A Shortcut." *Financial Management* (Spring 1988).

Lindsay, R. J., and A. W. Sametz. *Financial Management: An Analytical Approach.* Homewood, Ill.: Richard D. Irwin, Inc., 1967.

Lorie, J. H., and L. J. Savage. "Three Problems in Rationing Capital." *Journal of Business*, 28 (October 1955).

Luckett, Peter F. "ARR and IRR: A Review and an Analysis." *Journal of Business, Finance, and Accounting* (Spring 1984).

Pratt, John W., and John S. Hammond, III. "Evaluating and Comparing Projects: Simple Detection of False Alarms." *Journal of Finance*, 34 (December 1979), 1231–1242.

Robichek, A.A., Donald G. Ogilvie, and John D. C. Roach. "Capital Budgeting: A Pragmatic Approach." *Financial Executive*, 37 (April 1969), 26–38.

_____, and James C. Van Horne. "Abandonment Value and Capital Budgeting." *Journal of Finance*, 22 (December 1967), 577–590.

Rosenblatt, Meir J. "A Survey and Analysis of Capital Budgeting Decision Process in Multi-Division Firms." *Engineering Economist*, 25 (Summer 1980), 259–273.

Statman, Meir, and Tyzoon T. Tyebjee. "Optimistic Capital Budgeting Forecasts: An Experiment." *Financial Management* (Summer 1985).

Searby, Frederick W. "Return to Return on Investment." *Harvard Business Review*, 53 (March–April 1975), 113–119.

Taggart, Robert A., Jr. "Capital Budgeting and the Financing Decision: An Exposition." *Financial Management*, 6 (Summer 1977), 59–64.

Trippi, Robert R. "Conventional and Unconventional Methods for Evaluating Investments." *Financial Management*, 3 (Autumn 1974), 31–35.

Weingartner, H. Martin. "Some New Views on the Payback Period and Capital Budgeting Decisions." *Management Science* (August 1969).

Discounted Cash Flow Evaluation Techniques

6

The analytical discounted cash flow methods are based on the concept of discounting cash inflows and outflows to their present values, thus fully considering the time value of money. In this chapter we describe four methods: net present value, profitability index, internal rate of return, and equivalent annual charge.

NET PRESENT VALUE

The present value criterion for evaluating proposed capital investments involves summing the present values of cash outflows required to support an investment with the present value of the cash inflows resulting from operations of the project. The inflows and outflows are discounted to present value using the firm's required rate of return for the project. The *net present value* (NPV) is the difference in the present value of the inflows and outflows,

$$\text{NPV} = \sum_{t=0}^{n} \frac{CI_t}{(1+k)^t} - CO_0 \tag{1}$$

where CO_0 = present value of the after-tax cost of the project
CI_t = the after-tax cash inflow to be received in period t
k = appropriate discount rate or hurdle rate
t = time period
n = useful life of asset

If the project cost is incurred over a period of time, then CO_0 represents the present value of those cash outflows and may be expressed as shown in Equation (2),

$$CO_0 = \sum_{t=0}^{n} \frac{CO_t}{(1+k)^t}. \qquad (2)$$

where CO_t = the after-tax cash outflow in period t.

If the NPV is positive, it means the project is expected to yield a return in excess of the required rate; if the NPV is zero, the yield is expected to exactly equal the required rate; if the NPV is negative, the yield is expected to be less than the required rate. Hence, except in unusual circumstances, only those projects that have a positive or zero NPV meet the criterion for acceptance.

It should be noted that the cash inflows (CI_t), which are discounted in the NPV method according to Equation (1), result from two sources: (1) using the asset over its productive life and (2) disposing of the asset at the end of its life. The net salvage value obtained from the disposal of the asset is the final cash inflow generated by the asset and must be included in the determination of the asset's NPV.

A difficulty encountered with NPV is in deciding the appropriate hurdle rate to use in discounting the cash flows. The accuracy of the forecasts of cash flows influences the selection of a hurdle rate, so the use of NPV also depends on the accuracy of those forecasts. While the firm's cost of capital may be used as the discount rate, questions exist concerning how the cost of capital should be calculated. These are examined in Chapters 10 and 16. Also, there may be difficulty in obtaining the data needed to perform the calculations, even after the procedural questions are resolved.

EXAMPLE 1

Determination of Net Present Value

ABC Company is evaluating project Z, which requires a present cash outflow of $10,000 and generates cash inflows of $4,000 each year over its 6-year useful life. The asset is projected to have no salvage value at the end of its life. The company has set its required rate of return at 16%. Determine the NPV for project Z.

SOLUTION: We can determine the NPV for project Z either by using Equation (1) directly or by constructing the equivalent table.

In equation form the solution is

$$NPV = \sum_{t=0}^{n} \frac{CI_t}{(1+k)^t} - CO_0$$

$$= \sum_{t=1}^{6} \frac{\$4,000}{(1+0.16)^t} - \$10,000$$

Since project Z has equal annual cash inflows, we can evaluate the first term on the right-hand side of this equation by using the annuity factors from Appendix B, column 5.

Thus,

$$NPV = (\$4,000)(3.684736) - \$10,000$$
$$= \$4,739$$

Using the tabular format, we find

TIME	CASH FLOW	DISCOUNT FACTORS FOR 16%	PRESENT VALUE
0	− $10,000	1.0000	− $10,000
1–6	+ 4,000	3.684736	+ 14,739
			NPV = $ 4,739

Of course, we arrive at the same result using either approach. Therefore, the reader can utilize whichever method is more easily understood. If the project under evaluation has cash inflows that differ year by year over its life, the process of determining the project's NPV is slightly more complicated. Under such conditions, we need a separate term in the equation method for each cash inflow or a separate line for each cash inflow in the table. In addition, single-payment discount factors from Appendix B, would be used rather than the annuity factor used here. We illustrate the treatment of this additional complexity in Example 3.

Two other factors about NPV deserve mention.

1   The NPV model implicitly assumes that the *incremental cash inflows* will be *reinvested* to earn the firm's required rate of return throughout the life of the project. For example, project Z in Example 1 had an NPV of $4,739 when the project's cash flows are discounted at the firm's required rate of return of 16%. This NPV value implicitly assumes that ABC Company can reinvest project Z's cash inflows to earn 16% compounded annually between the time that they occur and the end of the project's life. In practice, the reinvestment rate frequently differs from the discount rate. This results from the fact that the general level of interest rates normally changes (sometimes substantially) over the life of a project. We deal with this problem as a part of our discussion of terminal value in Chapter 8.

2   The NPV of a project reveals the amount by which the productive value (present value of the cash inflows) exceeds or is less than the cost. Naturally, if we have a choice (if discretionary projects are involved), we choose only those projects whose productive values exceed or at least equal their costs. If the NPV of a project is positive, the amount of the NPV is the amount by which the project will *increase the value of the firm making the investment*. Thus, selecting that group of projects with the highest total NPV, other things being equal, should *maximize* the market value of the firm.

NPV Profiles

Recall that one difficulty with the NPV model is the determination of the appropriate required rate of return, or hurdle rate, to use in discounting the project's cash flows. One helpful approach to addressing this difficulty is the construction of an *NPV profile* for any given project. An NPV profile is a graphic representation of a project's NPV as the hurdle, or discount, rate is allowed to take on various values. The NPV profile shows how much the firm's required rate of return could increase and still yield a project attractive to the firm.

We illustrate the construction of an NPV profile in Example 2.

EXAMPLE 2

NPV Profile for Project Z

For project Z (Example 1), compute the NPV at discount rates from 0% to 40% at 5% intervals. Then graph the results by showing the NPVs on the vertical axis and the discount rates on the horizontal axis (join the plotted points with a smooth curve).

SOLUTION: The table summarizes the results of the NPV calculations.

DISCOUNT RATE	PROJECT Z'S ANNUAL CASH INFLOWS	PRESENT VALUE ANNUITY FACTOR FOR 6 YEARS AT THE GIVEN DISCOUNT RATE	DISCOUNTED CASH INFLOWS	PROJECT Z'S COST	NPV AT THE GIVEN DISCOUNT RATE
0%	+$4,000	6.000000	$24,000	$10,000	+ $14,000
5	+ 4,000	5.075692	20,303	10,000	+ 10,303
10	+ 4,000	4.355261	17,421	10,000	+ 7,421
15	+ 4,000	3.784483	15,138	10,000	+ 5,138
20	+ 4,000	3.325510	13,302	10,000	+ 3,302
25	+ 4,000	2.951424	11,806	10,000	+ 1,806
30	+ 4,000	2.642746	10,571	10,000	+ 571
35	+ 4,000	2.385157	9,541	10,000	− 459
40	+ 4,000	2.167974	8,672	10,000	− 1,328

The following figure shows the NPV profile for project Z.

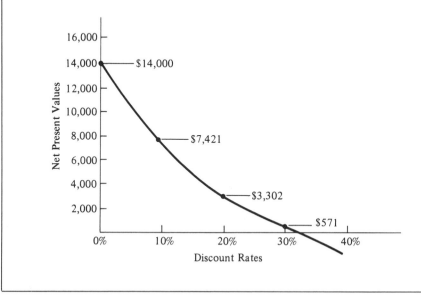

Several points about the NPV profile deserve mention. First, the profile for project Z shown in Example 2 is downward sloping. This will be the usual NPV profile for investment projects that have one or more cash outflows initially followed by an uninterrupted series of cash inflows over the project's life. Second, the NPV profile intersects the vertical axis at a value representing the sum of the undiscounted cash flows for the project. For project Z, this value is $14,000: (6 × $4,000) − $10,000. Third, the smooth NPV profile consists of the project's NPVs at all discount rates. Thus, for project Z, the NPV found in Example 1 at the firm's 16% required rate of return—$4,739—is found on the profile at the 16% discount rate. Finally, we see that the profile crosses the horizontal axis at about 32.5%; NPV equals zero at this discount rate. Later in the chapter, we see that this rate is called the *internal rate of return*. The significance of this point is that as long as the ABC Company's required rate of return does not exceed 32.5%, project Z is a candidate for acceptance.

NPV for More Complex Projects

We next turn to the determination of NPV for a project with a more involved pattern of cash flows over its useful life.

EXAMPLE 3

Net Present Value

A certain investment is expected to take several years to develop and implement. If the costs and cash flows are as tabulated, determine the NPV at 14%.

TIME		AMOUNT	
Present	− $	10,000	
1	−	60,000	
2	−	3,000,000	
3	−	350,000	
4	+	550,000	
5–20	+	800,000	
20	+	300,000	Net salvage value

SOLUTION: As mentioned in Example 1, we can determine a project's NPV utilizing either an equation or a table. Both methods are illustrated here.

Using Equations (1) and (2) for this project, we find

$$NPV = \sum_{t=0}^{n} \frac{CI_t}{(1+k)^t} - \sum_{t=0}^{n} \frac{CO_t}{(1+k)^t}$$

$$= \frac{\$550,000}{(1.14)^4} + \sum_{t=5}^{20} \frac{\$800,000}{(1.14)^t} + \frac{\$300,000}{(1.14)^{20}}$$

$$- \$10,000 - \frac{\$60,000}{(1.14)^1} - \frac{\$3,000,000}{(1.14)^2} - \frac{\$350,000}{(1.14)^3}$$

$$= \$387,731$$

Using a tabular form, we find

Solution Table for NPV Using 14% Discount Rate

TIME	CASH FLOW	DISCOUNT FACTOR	PRESENT VALUE
Present	− $ 10,000	1.0	− $ 10,000
1	− 60,000	0.877193	− 52,632
2	− 3,000,000	0.769468	− 2,308,404
3	− 350,000	0.674972	− 236,240
4	+ 550,000	0.592080	+ 325,644
5–20	+ 800,000	3.309419	+ 2,647,534
20	+ 300,000	0.072762	+ 21,829
			NPV = $ 387,731

Since the NPV is positive, this project is a viable candidate for acceptance. Its acceptance is expected to increase the value of the firm by $387,731 in present value terms.

PROFITABILITY INDEX

The *profitability index* (PI) is the ratio of the present value of the after-tax cash inflows to the outflows. A ratio of 1 or greater indicates that the project in question has an expected yield equal to or greater than the discount rate. The profitability index is a measure of a project's profitability per dollar of investment. As a result, it may be used to rank projects of varying costs and expected economic lives in order of their profitability. But a word of caution is in order. If projects are ranked just by the profitability index, the investment in a typewriter might appear better than one in a steel mill. The size of projects is ignored. And, as previously noted, the group of projects having the greatest combined net present value should be selected within the constraints of budget limitations, project interdependency, mutual exclusivity, and the like.

$$PI = \frac{\text{present value of cash inflows}}{\text{present value of cash outflows}} \qquad (3)$$

$$PI = \frac{\sum_{t=0}^{n} \dfrac{CI_t}{(1 + k)^t}}{CO_0} \qquad (4)$$

The relationship among net present value, profitability index, and the required rate of return is as follows:

NET PRESENT VALUE	PROFITABILITY INDEX	EXPECTED RETURNS
Negative	Less than 1	Less than required return
Zero	Equal to 1	Exactly equal to required return
Positive	Greater than 1	Greater than required return

EXAMPLE 4

Ranking Projects Using the Profitability Index

Three projects have been suggested to a corporation. The after-tax cash flows for each are tabulated here. If the corporation's cost of capital is 12%, rank them in order of profitability.

After-Tax Cash Flows

TIME	PROJECT A	PROJECT B	PROJECT C
Present	− $10,000	− $30,000	− $18,000
1	2,800	6,000	6,500
2	3,000	10,000	6,500
3	4,000	12,000	6,500
4	4,000	16,000	6,500

SOLUTION: Each project must be evaluated to obtain the present value of the cash inflows and outflows. The present values of the inflows and outflows are as follows:

	PROJECT A	PROJECT B	PROJECT C
PV of outflows	− $10,000	− $30,000	− $18,000
PV of inflows	10,281	32,040	19,743

The profitability indices are:

$$PI_A = \frac{\$10,281}{\$10,000} = 1.0281$$

$$PI_B = \frac{\$32,040}{\$30,000} = 1.068$$

$$PI_C = \frac{\$19,743}{\$18,000} = 1.0968$$

The projects would be ranked as follows: C, B, and A.

Note that the ranking using profitability indices measures return per dollar of investment. Thus, although project B in Example 4 has the highest NPV, it is not the most profitable per dollar of investment. Rather, project C is the most profitable per dollar of investment. Note further that all the projects have positive net present values, and hence all meet the 12% required rate of return.

INTERNAL RATE OF RETURN

By definition, the *internal rate of return* (IRR) is that rate which exactly equates the present value of the expected after-tax cash inflows with the present value of the after-tax cash outflows. This is expressed in Equation (5):

$$\sum_{t=0}^{n} \frac{CI_t}{(1+r)^t} = \sum_{t=0}^{n} \frac{CO_t}{(1+r)^t} \tag{5}$$

where r is the internal rate of return. Thus, at the internal rate of return, the NPV is zero.

The internal rate of return recognizes the time value of money and considers the anticipated revenues over the entire economic (useful) life of an investment. Referring back to the NPV profile for Project Z shown in Example 2, the IRR for Project Z would be the discount rate at which the NPV profile crosses the horizontal axis. Historically, analysts have solved for the IRR of a project on a trial-and-error basis. Today, programmed calculators which solve any IRR problem are readily available. In addition, spreadsheet packages such as LOTUS 1-2-3 have an IRR function which can easily handle even the most elaborate set of project cash flows. We will not dwell on IRR calculations but rather encourage the reader to develop skills using the LOTUS 1-2-3 templates which we have provided with the text. The development of skill in using the micro-computer and the most popular spreadsheet packages available will definitely serve the reader's long-run goals more effectively than tedious calculations by hand.

The next example illustrates the search process which spreadsheet packages and calculators use to arrive at the IRR result.

EXAMPLE 5
Internal Rate of Return

A new project has an after-tax cost of $10,000 and will result in after-tax cash inflows of $3,000 in year 1, $5,000 in year 2, and $6,000 in year 3. Determine the internal rate of return.

SOLUTION: First, set up a solution table.

TIME	CASH FLOW		DISCOUNT FACTOR	PRESENT VALUE
Present	− $10,000	×	1	− $10,000
1	3,000	×	Unknown	Unknown
2	5,000	×	Unknown	Unknown
3	6,000	×	Unknown	Unknown
			NPV =	$ 0.00

Since only the sum of the present values of the three cash inflows is known to be $10,000, there is no direct way of obtaining the answer. Therefore, it must be estimated and then checked. In order to make a first estimate of the answer, *it is possible to reconstruct the problem using an average cash inflow each year rather than the exact amounts given.* The average of $3,000, $5,000, and $6,000 is $4,666 per year. Based on the amount of $4,666, we can reconstruct a solution table.

TIME	CASH FLOW		DISCOUNT FACTOR	PRESENT VALUE
Present	− $10,000	×	1	− $10,000
1–3	4,666	×	Unknown	10,000
			NPV =	$ 0.00

Now there is only one unknown, and this may be found as follows:

$$\$4,666 \times \text{d.f.} = \$10,000$$

$$\text{d.f.} = \frac{\$10,000}{\$4,666} = 2.1431$$

The discount factor (d.f.) is 2.1431. To determine the corresponding internal rate of return, refer to Appendix B, column 5. The closest factor is 2.139917, which corresponds to 19%. Thus, 19% is the estimate to be used in solving the problem. Refer back to the original solution table, and replace the unknown discount factors with the discount factors corresponding to 19%. Then multiply these by the cash inflows to determine the present values. The table is as follows:

Solution Table for NPV Using 19% Discount Rate

TIME	CASH FLOW		DISCOUNT FACTOR	PRESENT VALUE
Present	− $10,000	×	1	− $10,000
1	3,000	×	0.840336	2,521
2	5,000	×	0.706165	3,531
3	6,000	×	0.593416	3,560
			NPV =	− $ 388

The NPV is negative. This means that the discount factors applied to the inflows are too small. Larger discount factors are obtained by using *lower* rates of return. The solution table for 17% is as follows:

Solution Table for NPV Using 17% Discount Rate

TIME	CASH FLOW		DISCOUNT FACTOR	PRESENT VALUE
Present	− $10,000	×	1	− $10,000
1	3,000	×	0.854701	2,564
2	5,000	×	0.730514	3,652
3	6,000	×	0.624371	3,746
			NPV =	− $ 38

The NPV is much closer to zero, but still negative. Therefore, the rate of return must be lower than 17%. The solution table for 16% is as follows:

Solution Table for NPV Using 16% Discount Rate

TIME	CASH FLOW		DISCOUNT FACTOR	PRESENT VALUE
Present	− $10,000	×	1	− $10,000
1	3,000	×	0.862069	2,586
2	5,000	×	0.743163	3,716
3	6,000	×	0.640658	3,844
			NPV =	$ 146

The NPV for 16% is positive. Therefore, we can conclude that the actual internal rate of

> return is between 16% and 17%. This range is close enough for most purposes. Again, this example is aimed at illustrating the process of finding the IRR rather than of finding the precise result.

Once the IRR of a project has been determined, it is a simple matter to compare it with the required rate of return to decide whether or not the project is acceptable. If the IRR equals or exceeds the required rate, the project is acceptable. Ranking the projects is also a simple matter. Projects are ranked according to their IRRs: the project with the highest IRR is ranked first, and so on.

In Example 5, the cash flows were conventional—one or more outflows followed by a series of uninterrupted cash inflows. If there are changes in the signs of the cash flows over the asset's life, then there may be more than one internal rate of return. This is an unusual problem that demonstrates an anomaly of IRR. Since we recommend NPV as a more useful evaluative method than IRR, we do not discuss the methods for determining multiple IRRs.

AGREEMENT AMONG NPV, PI, IRR

When a firm is evaluating a *single, independent, conventional* project, the three discounted cash flow methods—NPV, PI, and IRR—*always* agree with respect to the attractiveness of the project. Notice the conditions we are placing on this statement. We must be evaluating only *one* project, whose cash flows or acceptance are not related to other projects under evaluation. Further, that project must have a conventional cash flow pattern; that is, the project must have one or more cash outflows in the first years of its life and then have an uninterrupted series of cash inflows until the end of its useful life.

We can see that the three methods *must* agree by referring to the NPV profile. Consider again the NPV profile for project Z shown in Example 2. It is modified in Figure 6–1.

In Figure 6–1, we can see that project Z has a positive NPV and is therefore attractive at the 16% required rate of return. If a project's NPV is greater than 0 at the required rate of return, the project's IRR must exceed the required rate of return which signals that the project is attractive. This is true since the only way that the project's NPV can be reduced to zero, thereby obtaining the IRR, is to use a higher discount rate. Thus, IRR must exceed the firm's required rate of return. Figure 6–1 shows that the IRR of project Z is 32.5%, which exceeds the firm's 16% required rate of return.

To verify that the PI must also agree, recall the definitions of NPV and PI:

$$NPV = \text{discounted cash inflows} - \text{discounted cash outflows}$$

$$PI = \frac{\text{discounted cash inflows}}{\text{discounted cash outflows}}$$

If a project has a positive NPV, then its discounted cash inflows (DCI) necessarily exceed its discounted cash outflows (DCO). Furthermore, if NPV is greater than 0, then PI must be greater than 1 thereby signalling project attractiveness. For project Z,

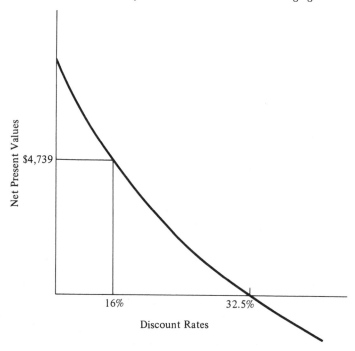

FIGURE 6–1   NPV Profile for Project Z

$NPV_{16\%}$ = $4,739 since DCI = $14,739 and DCO = $10,000; thus, PI = 1.4739 or $14,739 ÷ $10,000.

Therefore, if one of the three DCF models (NPV, PI, or IRR) determines that a single, independent, conventional capital project is a candidate for acceptance, *all three of these models will agree*. Conversely, if any of these three DCF models find that the project should be rejected, then *all three of these models will agree*.

However, if the firm is *ranking mutually exclusive projects, conflicts in project ranking can arise, depending on whether NPV, PI or IRR is used*. Conditions under which such conflicts can arise and the resolution of these conflicts are treated in depth in Chapters 7 and 8.

At this juncture, we turn to the final DCF model, which has special applications for regulated industries.

EQUIVALENT ANNUAL CHARGE

The annual capital charge method involves discounting all the cash inflows and outflows to present value and determining the equivalent annual charge over the life of the project. The method is of particular importance in the areas of public price regulation such as for utilities. A utility may, for example, construct a power-generating station at great cost. Project life and annual operating costs may also be forecasted. The annual capital charge method is used to find the equivalent annual charge that should be made to customers to cover the construction and operating costs, while also providing a required rate of return. The required rate of return may be the firm's cost of capital or another appropriate rate. The process is demonstrated in Example 6.

EXAMPLE 6
Equivalent Annual Charge

A utility has spent $10,000,000 on a new facility. Operating costs are expected to be $800,000 per year over its 30-year life. If the utility requires a 9% return, determine the equivalent annual charge.

SOLUTION: The equivalent annual charge consists of two parts: the $800,000 per year and the periodic payment needed to amortize $10,000,000 over 30 years at 9%. For the latter, refer to Appendix B, column 6.

$$\text{annual charge} = 0.09733635 \times \$10,000,000$$
$$= \$973,363.50$$

The total equivalent annual charge is $973,363.50 + $800,000 = $1,773,363.50.

In many problems a salvage value or recovery of working capital will be involved. This may be handled easily by multiplying salvage value by the appropriate sinking-fund factor (Appendix B, column 3). The product is then subtracted from the annual equivalent charge for the entire cost. The process is demonstrated in Example 7.

EXAMPLE 7
Equivalent Annual Charge with Salvage Value

Suppose in Example 7 that the facility had a $1,000,000 salvage value. Recompute the equivalent annual charge.

SOLUTION: First, find the present value of the salvage value:

$$PV = 0.075371 \times \$1,000,000 = \$75,371$$

Second, subtract the present value of the salvage value from the original cost:

$$\$10,000,000 - \$75,371 = \$9,924,629$$

Third, determine the equivalent annual charge:

$$\text{annual charge} = 0.09733635 \times \$9,924,629 = \$966,027.16$$

Last, add the equivalent annual charge to the $800,000 yearly operating cost to obtain the total annual charge:

$$\$800,000 + \$966,027.16 = \$1,766,027.16$$

The equivalent annual charge method is also useful for comparing alternatives that have unequal lives, as demonstrated in Example 8.

EXAMPLE 8

Equivalent Annual Charge

Two mutually exclusive projects have projected cash flows as shown:

TIME	PROJECT A	PROJECT B
Present	− $10,000	− $8,000
1	− 2,000	− 2,500
2	− 2,000	− 2,500
3	− 2,000	− 2,500
4	− 2,500	− 3,800
5	− 2,500	− 3,800
6	− 2,500	− 3,800
7	− 3,000	
8	− 3,000	
9	− 3,000	
10	− 3,000	

In addition, project A will recover salvage value of $1,500 in year 10, while project B will recover $1,000 in year 6. Determine the equivalent annual charge for each project at 10% required rate of return.

SOLUTION: Consider project A. The equivalent annual charge of the initial cost and salvage value are determined as in Examples 6 and 7.

$$\text{annual charge} = 0.16274539 \times \$10,000$$
$$= \$1,627.45$$
$$\text{equivalent payment} = 0.06274539 \times \$1,500$$
$$= \$94.12$$

The equivalent annual charge of the initial cost less salvage value is $1,533.33.
   Next, find the present value of the outflows over the 10-year operating life:

$$\text{present value} = 2.48685 \times \$2,000 + 1.868409 \times \$2,500 + 1.789306 \times \$3,000$$
$$= \$4,973.70 + \$4,671.02 + \$5,367.92$$
$$= \$15,012.64$$

The present value of the outflows is $15,012.64. The equivalent annual charge is found in the same manner as that used for the initial investment:

$$\text{annual charge} = 0.16274539 \times \$15,012.64$$
$$= \$2,443.24$$

The total equivalent annual charge is, therefore, $1,533.33 + $2,443.24 = $3,976.57.
   Consider project B. The equivalent annual charge of the initial cost and salvage values are determined in the same manner as for project A.

$$\text{annual charge} = 0.22960738 \times \$8,000$$
$$= \$1,836.86$$
$$\text{equivalent payment} = 0.12960738 \times \$1,000$$
$$= \$129.61$$

The equivalent annual charge of the initial cost less the salvage value is $1,707.25. The present value of the outflows is determined as follows:

$$\text{present value} = 2.486852 \times \$2,500 + 1.868409 \times \$3,800$$

$$= \$6,217.13 + \$7,099.95$$

$$= \$13,317.08$$

The present value of the outflows is $13,317.08. The equivalent annual charge is

$$\text{annual charge} = 0.22960738 \times \$13,317.08$$

$$= \$3,057.70$$

The total equivalent annual charge is therefore $1,707.25 + $3,057.70 = $4,764.95. Project A is clearly superior to project B, as its equivalent annual cost is lower.

The annual capital charge method just described is a valuable managerial tool in that it does consider the time value of money and the flows over the entire asset life. Further, it is especially useful in serving as a baseline for setting rate structures as previously indicated, for evaluating nondiscretionary expenditure alternatives that are not profit producing, and for comparing projects having unequal lives. For example, to meet clean water requirements, a firm may have to install pollution-control equipment, but there may be choice as to the particular equipment to be installed and its associated operating costs. The annual capital charge method is ideal for comparing the costs of alternatives of this type.

CHANGING RESIDUAL VALUES OVER TIME — THE ABANDONMENT DECISION

When a decision is made to accept a given project, it is implicitly assumed that the asset will generally decrease in value over its useful life. A discretionary project is accepted if it has a productive value to the firm that exceeds its cost. For most projects, the productive value continues to exceed the residual value of the asset throughout its useful life and abandonment never becomes an issue. There are two instances, however, when abandonment may be appropriate.

The first arises when costs and/or benefits change over the life of the project. An example of this is the rapid decrease in the productive values of automobile tooling as oil prices escalate. We deal with the question of capital abandonment under conditions of changing risk in Chapter 25. The second is when the market value of an asset is *expected* to rise during its life at a more rapid rate than the cash inflows resulting from the firm's use of the asset. Examples of the latter are easily found in both commercial and residential real estate. Depending upon the rate and method of depreciation permitted for a structure, the optimum abandonment time normally ranges from 7 to 12 years after acquisition. The timing of abandonment is of critical concern to the managers of limited real estate partnerships.

When investment opportunities are initially considered, key variables are identi-fied and assumptions are made to arrive at some choice. As time passes, changes can occur that could affect these key variables. Assumptions made initially may prove incorrect, or perhaps some additional unforeseen new investment opportunities may arise. *Failure to abandon projects that are no longer desirable could be very costly. By the same reasoning, failure to abandon projects that could make funds available for substantially better investment opportunities might also be costly from an opportunity standpoint.* Therefore, the prudent financial manager must incorporate abandonment values (at various points throughout the life of the project) into the analysis for capital project evaluation and selection.

As a first approach to the abandonment problem, assume that the firm has the option to abandon the project at various points throughout its useful life. The methodology basically finds the maximum NPV of the project cash flows and the abandonment value considering all possible periods when the project can be aban-doned.

In equation form, we want to determine the time period m that maximizes NPV^m,

$$NPV^m = \sum_{t=0}^{m} \frac{A_t}{(1+k)^t} + \frac{AV_m}{(1+k)^m} \qquad (6)$$

where A_t = operating cash flow of the project in period t, which can be either a cash inflow (positive value) or a cash outflow (negative value)
k = firm's cost of capital
AV_m = abandonment value in period m
m = period when abandonment is being considered
NPV^m = net present value of the cash flows from operating the project for m periods, as well as the abandonment value of the project at the end of the mth period

The use of Equation (6) is illustrated in Example 9.

EXAMPLE 9

Abandonment Decision

Consider that project Z has the following cash flows and abandonment values over its useful life:

	PERIOD					
	0	1	2	3	4	5
Cash flows	− $7,500	$2,000	$2,000	$2,000	$2,000	$2,000
Abandonment values	—	$6,200	$5,200	$4,000	$2,200	0

The firm's cost of capital is 10%. Determine the optimal time for project Z to be abandoned if it is accepted.

SOLUTION: The analysis proceeds by preparing the following table:

PERIOD	10% DISCOUNT FACTOR	CASH FLOWS	ABANDONMENT AFTER PERIOD				
			1	2	3	4	5
1	0.909	$2,000	$1,818	$1,818	$1,818	$1,818	$1,818
2	0.826	$2,000		1,652	1,652	1,652	1,652
3	0.751	$2,000			1,502	1,502	1,502
4	0.683	$2,000				1,366	1,366
5	0.621	$2,000					1,242
PV of operating cash flows			$1,818	$3,470	$4,972	$6,338	$7,580
PV of abandonment value			5,636	4,295	3,004	1,503	0
PV of total flows			$7,454	$7,765	$7,976	$7,841	$7,580
Investment outflow			7,500	7,500	7,500	7,500	7,500
NPV^m			($46)	$ 265	$ 476	$ 341	$ 80

As can be seen, the NPV is maximized by abandoning project Z at the end of period 3. It should also be noted that the abandonment option makes project Z considerably more attractive than if the firm had to maintain the project until the end of its five-period useful life; that is, the NPV of the optimal holding period ($476 for three periods) is almost six times the NPV of the project if it is held to the end of its useful life ($80).

Example 9 demonstrates the importance of selecting the optimum time for the disposal of an asset. Naturally, the analysis must be ongoing because costs, revenues, and the market price of an asset will change from year to year. Consequently, it is necessary to recalculate the net present value and reconsider abandonment periodically throughout the life of an asset. The review of existing projects should take place at regular intervals and especially when events in the economy (for instance, changes in interest rates, changes in project replacement costs, or changes in projected revenues) dictate. Again, the primary objective is to maximize the present value of the firm's entire portfolio of assets.

QUESTIONS
PROBLEMS

1. What is the decision rule for accepting projects using each of the following methods of project evaluation?
   (a) payback period
   (b) net present value
   (c) profitability index
   (d) internal rate of returns
   (e) equivalent annual charge

2. The Fisher Beer Company is evaluating two brewing projects. The after-tax cash flows for the alternative proposals are summarized in the table.

TIME	PROJECT A	PROJECT B
Present	− $20,000	− $28,000
1	5,000	8,000
2	5,000	8,000
3	6,000	8,000
4	6,000	8,000
5	6,000	8,000

Using a 10% rate, determine the NPV and PI for each project.

3. Leisure Incorporated is evaluating two investment opportunities and will pick one. Project Fun requires an investment of $10,000, while Project Lazy requires an investment of $19,000. The after-tax cash flows are as follows:

	CASH FLOWS	
YEAR	FUN	LAZY
1	$2,000	$4,000
2	3,000	5,000
3	4,000	6,000
4	3,000	4,000
5	3,000	3,000

Determine the NPV and the profitability index associated with each opportunity given a hurdle rate of 10%.

4. A project costs $75 and will yield after-tax cash flows of $5 in years 1 and 2, $20 in years 3 and 4, and $25 in years 5 to 10. Find the IRR of the project.

5. Referring to Problem 4, determine the equivalent annual inflows which, when discounted at the IRR, will give a NPV of zero.

6. An investor paid $65,000 for a duplex that she intends to keep 5 years and then sell. In the first years she knows that she will have to spend a considerable amount for repairs. If she desires a 9% after-tax return and the cash flows are as tabulated, will she achieve this return? Determine the net present value and profitability index.

YEAR	CASH FLOWS
1	− $ 100
2	4,900
3	5,300
4	4,800
5	74,500

7. A utility company is considering building a new generating facility for $50,000,000 with inflation-adjusted operating expenses of $1,000,000 annually for 30 years, the life of the installation after completion of construction. The salvage value is estimated at $1,500,000, and construction will take 2 years before the new facility can be brought on line. Consider the cost of construction to represent outflows of $25,000,000 each at the end of the first

2 years. Alternatively, the company can rebuild the present facility for $10,000,000 and reduce annual operating expenses from $2,000,000 to $1,500,000. If this alternative is chosen, power will have to be bought from a network grid for a year at a cost of $30,000,000 until the work is finished. Consider the costs of construction and purchase of power to be paid in equal installments at the start and end of the current year. This rebuilding project has an expected life of 15 years after rebuilding with no salvage value. Ignore investment tax credits and depreciation and determine the equivalent annual cost of each project based on a 7% return.

8. Inner City Memorial Hospital has been plagued with continuous operating deficits. Based on a study made by an outside consulting firm, it is decided that the deficits are due to the outdated structure of the current facility. The hospital's consultants have made the following recommendation. They indicated that they can update the current facility for $10,000,000. With these renovations the hospital's annual budget will be $8,000,000. They also state that they can build an entirely new facility for $15,000,000. This new facility would have an annual operating budget of $7,000,000. A state health care planner has been called in to decide which project would be less costly to the consumer. The planner has accumulated the following facts:

☐ Both projects would have a useful life of 25 years with no salvage value.
☐ Expenses are expected to increase equally over the years for both projects due to inflation.
☐ A 10% discount rate is assumed.

Prepare an analysis that would indicate the least costly alternative on a present value basis.

9. Project Gamma has the following cash flows and abandonment values over its useful life:

PERIOD	0	1	2	3	4	5
Cash Flows	− $6,000	$1,750	$1,750	$1,750	$1,750	$1,750
Abandonment Values	—	$5,500	$4,500	$3,500	$2,000	0

The firm's cost of capital is 12%. Determine NPV^m and the optimal time for project Gamma to be abandoned.

10. Construct a net present value profile for the following project. At approximately what discount rates would management accept the project? Reject the project?

DISCOUNT RATE	NET PRESENT VALUE
0%	$5,000
5	3,079
10	1,669
15	609
20	− 204

11. For the two projects shown in Problem 2 and with the help of the LOTUS templates, determine the IRR for each project and construct an NPV profile for each project.

12. For the two projects shown in Problem 2 and with the help of the LOTUS templates, perform a sensitivity analysis on the two projects. Determine the NPV, PI, and IRR for each project if the cash inflows decrease by: a) 10% each year and b) 20% each year. Discuss your results.

REFERENCES

Aggarwal, Raj. "Corporate Use of Sophisticated Capital Budgeting Techniques: A Strategic Perspective and a Critique of Survey Results." *Interfaces*, 10 (April 1980), 31–34.

Bauman, W. Scott. "Investment Returns and Present Values." *Financial Analysts Journal* (November–December 1969).

Beenhakker, Henri L. "Sensitivity Analysis of the Present Value of a Project." *Engineering Economist*, 20 (Winter 1975), 123–149.

Bernardo, J. J., and H. P. Lanser. "A Capital Budgeting Decision Model with Subjective Criteria." *Journal of Financial and Quantitative Analysis* (June 1977).

Bernhard, R. H. "Discount Methods for Expenditure Evaluation—A Clarification of Their Assumptions." *Journal of Industrial Engineering* (January–February 1962).

Brick, Ivan E., and Daniel G. Weaver. "A Comparison of Capital Budgeting Techniques in Identifying Profitable Investments." *Financial Mangement* (Winter 1984).

Brick, John R., and Howard E. Thompson. "The Economic Life of an Investment and the Appropriate Discount Rate." *Journal of Financial and Quantitative Analysis*, 13 (December 1978), 831–846.

Brief, R. P. "Limitations of Using the Cash Recovery Rate to Estimate the IRR." *Journal of Business Finance and Accounting* (Fall 1985).

Brigham, Eugene F., and T. Craig Tapley. "Financial Leverage and Use of the Net Present Value Investment Criterion: A Reexamination." *Financial Management* (Summer 1985).

de Faro, Clovis. "On the Internal Rate of Return Criterion." *Engineering Economist*, 19 (April–May 1974), 165–194.

_____. "A Sufficient Condition for a Unique Nonnegative Internal Rate of Return: A Comment." *Journal of Financial and Quantitative Analysis*, 8 (September 1973), 683–684.

de la Mare, R. F. "An Investigation into the Discounting Formulae Used in Capital Budgeting Models." *Journal of Business Finance and Accounting* (Summer 1975).

Doenges, R. Conrad. "The 'Reinvestment Problem' in a Practical Perspective." *Financial Management*, 1 (Spring 1972), 85–91.

Donaldson, Gordon. "Strategic Hurdle Rates for Capital Investments." *Harvard Business Review*, 50 (March–April 1972), 50–58.

Dorfman, Robert. "The Meaning of the Internal Rate of Return." *Journal of Finance*, 36 (December 1981), 1010–1023.

Dudley, Carlton L., Jr. "A Note on Reinvestment Assumptions in Choosing Between Net Present Value and Internal Rate of Return." *Journal of Finance*, 27 (September 1972), 907–915.

Dyckman, Thomas R., and James C. Kinard. "The Discounted Cash Flow Investment Decision Model with Accounting Income Constraints." *Decision Sciences*, 4 (July 1973), 301–313.

Emery, Gary W. "Some Guidelines for Evaluating Capital Investment Alternatives with Unequal Lives." *Financial Management*, 11 (Spring 1982), 14–18.

Ezzell, John R., and William A. Kelly, Jr. "An APV Analysis of Capital Budgeting Under Inflation." *Financial Management* (Autumn 1984).

Fama, Eugene F. "Risk-Adjusted Discount Rates and Capital Budgeting under Uncertainty." *Journal of Financial Economics*, 5 (1977).

Golbe, Devra L., and Barry Schachter. "The Net Present Value Rule and an Algorithm for Maintaining a Constant Debt-Equity Ratio." *Financial Management* (Summer 1985).

Greenfield, R. L., M. R. Randall, and J. D. Woods. "Financial Leverage and Use of the Net Present Value Investment Criterion." *Financial Management* (Autumn 1983).

Green, Willis R., Jr. "Capital Budgeting Analysis with the Timing of Events Uncertain." *Accounting Review* (January 1970).

Herbst, Anthony. "The Unique, Real Internal Rate of Return: Caveat Emptor!" *Journal of Financial and Quantitative Analysis*, 13 (June 1978), 363–370.

Hoskins, Colin G., and Glen A. Mumey. "Payback: A Maligned Method of Asset Ranking," *Engineering Economist*, 25 (Fall 1979), 53–65.

_____. "Benefit Cost Ratios vs. Net Present Value: Revisited." *Journal of Business, Finance and Accounting* (Summer 1974).

_____. "On Multiple Rates of Return." *Journal of Finance*, 23 (March 1968), 187–192.

Jeynes, Paul H. "The Significance of Reinvestment Rate." *Engineering Economist*, 9 (Fall 1965), 1–9.

Keane, Simon M. "The Internal Rate of Return and the Reinvestment Fallacy." *Journal of Accounting and Business Studies*, 15 (June 1979), 48–55.

Klammer, Thomas. "Empirical Evidence on the Adoption of Sophisticated Capital Budgeting Techniques." *Journal of Business* (July 1972).

Lere, John C. "Deterministic Net Present Value as an Approximation of Expected Net Present Value." *Journal of Business Finance and Accounting* (Summer 1980).

Lewellen, Wilbur G., Howard P. Lanser, and John J. McConnell. "Payback Substitutes for Discounted Cash Flow," *Financial Management*, 2 (Summer 1973), 17–23.

Longbottom, David, and Linda Wiper. "Capital Appraisal and the Case for Average Rate of Return." *Journal of Business Finance and Accounting*, 4, no. 4 (Winter 1977).

Mehta, Dileep R., Michael D. Curley, and Hung-Gay Fung. "Inflation, Cost of Capital, and Capital Budgeting Procedures." *Financial Management* (Winter 1984).

Merville, L. J., and L. A. Tavis. "A Total Real Asset Planning System." *Journal of Financial and Quantitative Analysis* (January 1974).

Moore, William T., and Son-Nan Chen. "Implementing the IRR Criterion When Cash Flow Parameters Are Unknown." *Financial Review*, 19, no. 4 (1984).

Myers, Stewart C. "Procedures for Capital Budgeting Under Uncertainty." *Industrial Management Review* (Spring 1968).

Peasnell, K. V. "Capital Budgeting and Discounted Cash Equivalents: Some Clarifying Comments." *Abacus* (December 1979).

Petty, J. William, and Oswald D. Bowlin. "The Financial Manager and Quantitative Decision Models." *Financial Management*, 4 (Winter 1976), 32–41.

Rapp, Birger. "The Internal Rate of Return Method—A Critical Study." *Engineering Costs and Production Economics*, 5 (1980).

Roll, Richard, and Marcus C. Bogue. "Capital Budgeting of Risky Projects with Imperfect Markets for Physical Capital." *Journal of Finance* (May 1974).

Russell, Allen M., and John A. Rickard. "An Algorithm for Determining Unique Nonnegative Internal Rates of Return." *Journal of Business Finance and Accounting* (Fall 1984).

Schwab, Bernhard, and Peter Lusztig. "A Comparative Analysis of the Net Present Value and the Benefit-Cost Ratios as Measures of the Economic Desirability of Investments." *Journal of Finance*, 24 (June 1969), 507–516.

Siegel, Jeremy J. "The Application of the DCF Methodology for Determining the Cost of Equity Capital." *Financial Management* (Spring 1985).

Stephen, Frank. "On Deriving the Internal Rate of Return from the Accountant's Rate of Return." *Journal of Business Finance and Accounting*, 3 (Summer 1976), 147–150.

Van Horne, James C. "Capital-Budgeting Decisions Involving Combinations of Risky Investments." *Management Science* (October 1966).

Weingartner, H. M. "The Excess Present Value Index—A Theoretical Basis and Critique." *Journal of Accounting Research*, 1 (Autumn 1963), 213–224.

Welter, P. "Put Policy First in DCF Analysis." *Harvard Business Review*, 48 (January–February 1970), 141–148.

Whisler, William D. "Sensitivity Analysis of Rates of Return." *Journal of Finance*, 31 (March 1976), 63–70.

CASE STUDY 6–1

Hilton Industries, Inc.:
The Information Technology Division
(Abandonment decision and behavioral finance)

Hilton Industries, Inc., is a large technologically oriented firm. It has subsidiaries and divisions in Western Europe, North America, and the Far East. During 1986, this company had a budget of U.S. $3,176 million for R & D. Approximately 95% of Hilton Industries' products stems from its own R & D. Products developed during the past 15 years account for 55% of sales. Ongoing development work on the company's products, which are already of a high standard, forms a major part of the research activities. This enables the company to safeguard the existing product lines.

Hilton Industries also endeavors to take advantage of opportunities for tackling unsolved problems. Examples of such areas include new therapeutic principles in human medicine, new crop protection systems, new inorganic and organic high-performance materials, and new information systems based on the combination of photography and electronics.

In 1986, total sales of Hilton Industries were U.S. $56.7 billion, which represented a 4.3% decline from 1985 sales. However, the company was able to boost unit sales slightly beyond the high level of 1985, thus making good use of its worldwide production capacity. The 4.3% decline in sales is due to shifts in international currency parities coupled with a leveling-off of the worldwide economic recovery.

Given only a slight decline in operating profit and a further improvement in the nonoperating income, Hilton Industries income before taxes stood at a record high of U.S. $5.016 billion, representing a 4.9% increase from the excellent figure for 1985.

In its fourth successive year of healthy business development, Hilton Industries took the opportunity to strengthen its financial base. Significant improvements in the balance sheet structure were achieved. In 1986, U.S. $757 million was allocated to retained earnings and U.S. $250 million to the free reserve. Moreover, the financial leverage of the company was reduced by satisfying many debt contracts and a debt/equity ratio of 42.3% was achieved at the end of 1986. This figure compares favorably with the historical figures of the company and to industry averages.

In its year-end meeting, the board of directors expressed satisfaction with the results of 1986 operations and discussed whether any fine-tuning was required for the company's strategy. It was decided that Hilton Industries should continue its efforts to be an innovative worldwide company. Long-term considerations would have priority over short-term profitability and results. As such, the R & D budget would continue to grow, and research into new technologies would be encouraged and rewarded. Technology gives this company its admirable status. The lead in R & D and the frequent introduction of new technologies maintain the competitive advantage over existing firms. To compete, Hilton Industries must remain innovative. With respect to short-term profitability, the Board expressed confidence that maintaining the high current plant utilization and continuously approving and abandoning emerging technologies that did not show good prospects would ensure high earnings and dividends to stockholders. The objective of this strategy was twofold: (1) growth—internal and through acquisitions and (2) long-term profitability.

The acquisition policy of Hilton Industries aimed at two goals:

1   to round out traditional fields of business and regional activities, and
2   to enter new future-oriented fields related to those with which the company is already familiar.

Finally, the board of directors formed a group of three vice presidents from the planning and budgeting department and assigned to the group the responsibility of continuously reappraising the emerging technologies of the company. The group was asked to start its duties shortly after the decision was reached.

The three VPs had different backgrounds. The first, Ms. Jones, was a V.P. of Finance with an MBA from a leading university. Mr. Frank was a V.P. of Marketing with previous work experience and education in sales management. Finally, Mr. Clifford, was a V.P. of Technological Forecasting with an engineering education and previous work experience in a research laboratory. This committee had to submit a report at the next meeting of the Board on the newly formed Information Technology Division.

The first few experiments in the field of electronically assisted photographic techniques were done through boot-legging in the Amagasaki lab of Compugraphic Corporation, a Japanese subsidiary of Hilton Industries. When these experiments showed good prospects, Dr. Saarime, the Amagasaki lab director, championed the technology for an entire year until a separate division with its own lab and budget was established in January 1985 to develop this technology.

The features of this technology are the following:

☐   Photographic films and papers give a much higher information density and involve significantly lower costs than nonchemical image recording techniques.

☐ The photographically produced image is first converted into electronic signals and then exposed on color negative paper. This method creates a wide range of possibilities for image manipulation and enhancement.

The division's basic research focused on the structure of the light-sensitive crystals which determine speed, graininess, sharpness, and color rendition. The division's goals also include faster and simpler processing. Photographic materials were being developed for new light sources such as laser diodes. Finally, the latest electronic systems are used to increase the reliability and user-friendliness of the equipment.

Despite the enthusiasm the employees of the Information Technology Division have shown about the prospects of the technology, Ms. Jones and Mr. Frank think it would be better to abandon further development of this technology. The budget of this division was U.S. $4 million in 1985 and 1986. This year the division requested an additional budget of U.S. $3 million. The initial schedule using the PERT network was that the development of this technology needed only 2 years and U.S. $7.5 million. During 1986, this division presented the initial prototype of the CRT printer at the "Compugraphic 86" exhibition. Based on a consumer survey at the exhibition, Mr. Frank was not sure that total demand would be as great as expected. In addition, Mr. Clifford was not sure that the diffusion of this technology was likely to succeed because the core design concepts of the products that will rely on this technology were not yet clear. Some time may elapse before this technology starts to be a financial success.

In brief, the committee presented an economic justification for selling off this technology to a small, emerging information company that proposed to buy it for a lump sum of U.S. $4.5 million. All committee members believed that it would be foolish to throw good money after bad money.

QUESTIONS

1. What is wrong with the belief of the committee?
2. What is wrong with the asset recovery issue?
3. Do you need more data to make a decision about the further development of this technology? If yes, what kind of data?
4. Determine under what conditions you would support the request of the Head of the Information Technology Division for an additional budget of U.S. $3 million.

The Superiority
of the Net Present Value
Technique

7

In the two previous chapters, we introduced the most widely used discounted cash flow (DCF) and non-DCF models used in capital budgeting. We argued that the DCF methods are superior to the non-DCF models because the former take the time value of money into account. In this chapter, we support our preference for the NPV model as the unique evaluation technique that consistently helps firms to maximize common shareholders' wealth positions. Whenever mutually exclusive projects are being evaluated, only the NPV model will consistently show the firm the project or set of projects that will maximize the value of the firm. The use of any other evaluation technique can lead the firm to select projects that leave the shareholders in inferior wealth positions.

We begin with a review of surveys that provide insight into the actual use of evaluation techniques in industry.

TRENDS IN THE USE OF
PROJECT EVALUATION TECHNIQUES

Over the last 25 years, various surveys have provided information concerning the use of capital project evaluation techniques in practice. Table 7–1 presents results obtained by eight major studies. All the surveys cited sampled large U.S. industrial firms, usually the *Fortune* 500 or *Fortune* 1000 companies for the years listed. In general, the surveys were mailed to the vice president of finance, the treasurer, or the controller of each company. The response rates varied from a low of 22% to a high of 71%. These survey results provide an indication of historical trends as well as a rough idea of current practice by large U.S. firms.

As can be seen in Table 7–1, in 1959 the two non-DCF techniques, payback and average rate of return (AROR), were the most popular primary techniques used, each accounting for 34% of the respondents. Only 13% of the respondents reported using a

Table 7–1 Historical Trends in the Use of Project Evaluation Techniques (Percent of Respondents Using Each Technique)

	KLAMMER			FREMGEN	PETTY, SCOTT, AND BIRD	KIM AND FARRAGHER	GITMAN AND FORRESTER	KIM AND FARRAGHER	HENDRICKS	KIM, CRICK, AND KIM
TECHNIQUE	1959	1964	1970	1971	1972	1975	1977	1979	1981	1986
Primary Method:										
NPV	5%	15%	27%	5%	15%	26%	13%	19%	10%	21%
IRR	8	17	30	38	41	37	53	49	66	49
PI				1	2					
PAYBACK	34	24	12	11	11	15	9	12	11	19
AROR	34	30	26	31	31	10	25	8	9	8
Secondary Method:										
NPV	2%	3%	7%	21%	14%	7%	28%	8%	30%	24%
IRR	1	2	6	33	19	7	14	8	16	15
PAYBACK	18	21	32	53	37	33	44	39	38	35
AROR	4	9	11	27	24	3	14	3	15	19

SOURCES: T. Klammer, "Empirical Evidence on the Adoption of Sophisticated Capital Budgeting Techniques," *Journal of Business*, July 1972, 387–97; J. Fremgen, "Capital Budgeting Practices: A Survey," *Management Accounting*, May 1973, 19–25; J. W. Petty, D. F. Scott, and M. M. Bird, "The Capital Budgeting Decision Making Process of Large Corporations," *The Engineering Economist*, Spring 1975, 159–72; S. H. Kim and E. J. Farragher, "Capital Budgeting Practices in Large Industrial Firms," *Baylor Business Studies*, November 1976, 19–25; L. J. Gitman and J. R. Forrester, "A Survey of Current Capital Budgeting Techniques Used by Major U.S. Firms," *Financial Management*, Fall 1977, 66–71; S. H. Kim and E. J. Farragher, "Current Capital Budgeting Practices," *Management Accounting*, June 1981, 26–30; J. A. Hendricks, "Capital Budgeting Practices Including Inflation Adjustments," *Managerial Planning*, February 1983, 22–28; S. H. Kim, T. Crick, and S. H. Kim, "Do Executives Practice What Academics Preach?" *Management Accounting*, November 1986, 49–52.

AUTHOR AND YEAR SURVEY WAS TAKEN

DCF technique (NPV or IRR) as their primary evaluation method. Through the 1960s, 70s, and 80s, there has been a significant decrease in the use of non-DCF techniques as the primary evaluation method with a corresponding increase in the use of the two DCF methods—NPV and IRR. However, it is instructive to note that even the most recent three studies show that at least 20% of the *Fortune* 500 or *Fortune* 1000 firms still use either payback or average rate of return as their primary evaluation method. We certainly hope that these firms do not use the other non-DCF technique as their secondary evaluation method.

Another unfortunate fact shown in the results presented in Table 7–1 should also be discussed. Namely, among the DCF techniques used as the primary evaluation method, at least twice as many companies use IRR as use NPV (e.g., 49% vs. 21% in the Kim et al. 1986 survey). This persistent and dominant use of IRR in preference to NPV is very unfortunate because IRR has several significant shortcomings, the most important of which is that it fails to assist firms in achieving their primary objective—the maximization of shareholders' wealth. Nevertheless, financial managers say that they prefer to measure project attractiveness with IRR percentages because such values are familiar to them and are easy to compare across projects.

Our major goal in this chapter is to shed greater light on the shortcomings of IRR and its inability to contribute to the maximization of shareholders' wealth. We demonstrate that IRR does *not* convey what most practitioners who use it *think* it does. Further, we show that, in general, the ranking of two or more projects by their IRRs makes little sense because these figures are not comparable unless the time patterns of the projects' cash flows are identical (in which case we would not need to rank the projects). It is to be hoped that this chapter may play a part in a widespread rejection of the IRR approach in practice and its replacement by the far superior NPV technique.

DIFFERENCES AMONG THE DCF TECHNIQUES

Among the three DCF techniques—NPV, PI, and IRR—there are two *major* differences in the techniques that warrant discussion:

1   The *absolute* versus the *relative* measurement of project attractiveness
2   The *reinvestment assumption*

Each of these points is discussed in turn.

As we can tell by observing the three DCF models, the NPV model results in an *absolute* measure of the project's worth, while both PI and IRR are *relative* measures of project viability. Specifically, NPV shows the dollar amount by which the project's discounted cash inflows (DCI) exceed its discounted cash outflows (DCO). On the other hand, PI computes the ratio of DCI to DCO and IRR determines a percentage return figure. As you might expect, a model that ranks projects using an absolute figure of merit may very well arrive at a different ranking than the one obtained by a model that compares projects on a relative basis.

The major question that will be addressed in later sections of this chapter is: Can firms maximize shareholders' wealth (the primary objective of financial management) equally well with a relative or an absolute measure of project attractiveness? To remove some of the surprise element, the answer to this question is no! We show that NPV is *clearly superior* to either of the relative measures (PI and IRR) of project attractiveness in helping firms to maximize shareholders' wealth. Further, we recommend that the two relative models should be abandoned in favor of the NPV model.

Turning to the second major difference, we can state a general rule that is often overlooked by users of DCF models: all DCF models make the implicit assumption that the project's cash inflows can be reinvested to earn a return that is *equal to the rate used to discount the cash flows*. This reinvestment assumption is made for *each* cash inflow between the time it occurs and the end of the project's life. Thus, the NPV and PI models make the implicit assumption that the project's cash inflows can be reinvested at the firm's required rate of return. Analogously, the IRR model makes the implicit assumption that the cash inflows can be reinvested at the computed IRR rate.

In order to illustrate the implicit reinvestment assumptions, we introduce the concept of *terminal value*. The terminal value (TV) of a project is the value that would accumulate by the end of the project's life if the project's cash inflows were invested to earn a specified compounded return between the time the cash inflows occurred and the end of the project's life. The TV of a project is calculated using Equation (1),

$$\text{TV} = \sum_{t=0}^{n} CI_t (1 + i)^{n-t} \tag{1}$$

where CI_t = the cash inflow that occurs at the end of period t
     i = the reinvestment rate
     n = the useful life of the project

Example 1 demonstrates the respective reinvestment assumptions for NPV and IRR.

EXAMPLE 1

An Illustration of Reinvestment Assumptions

A firm with an after-tax required rate of return of 14% is evaluating the following two projects:

	PROJECT CASH FLOWS	
YEAR	A	B
0	− $10,000.00	− $10,000
1	+ 3,862.89	0
2	+ 3,862.89	0
3	+ 3,862.89	0
4	+ 3,862.89	+ 20,736

The firm has computed the NPV and IRR for each project:

	PROJECT	
	A	B
$NPV_{14\%}$	$1,255	$2,277
IRR	20%	20%

(a) Show that project A will achieve a terminal value of $20,736 (which is exactly the final cash inflow for project B) when the reinvestment rate is 20% (which is exactly the IRR for both projects).

(b) Compute the TV for each project using a reinvestment rate of 14%.

(c) Show that each project's NPV is exactly the present value of the TV less its cash outflow.

SOLUTION: (a) We determine the TV for project A using Equation (1):

$$TV_A = \sum_{t=0}^{n} CI_t (1 + i)^{n-t}$$

$$= \$3,862.89(1.20)^{4-1} + 3,862.89(1.20)^{4-2}$$

$$+ 3,862.89(1.20)^{4-3} + 3,862.89(1.20)^{4-4}$$

$$= \$6,675.07 + 5,562.56 + 4,635.47 + 3,862.89$$

$$= \$20,736$$

This terminal value for project A exposes IRR's implicit reinvestment assumption that the entire cash inflow is reinvested to earn the IRR rate. Projects A and B are equivalent only if the terminal values are equivalent, and this occurs only if *project A's cash inflows are reinvested at the 20% IRR.*

(b) Turning to the NPV model, the TV for project A assuming a 14% reinvestment rate is:

$$TV_A = \$3,862.89(1.14)^{4-1} + 3,862.89(1.14)^{4-2}$$

$$+ 3,862.89(1.14)^{4-3} + 3,862.89(1.14)^{4-4}$$

$$= \$19,010$$

The TV for project B is $20,736 because there are no intermediate cash inflows (i.e., those between the investment in the project and the end of its life) to reinvest.

(c) We compute the NPV of each project by discounting the TV using the firm's required rate of return and then subtracting the cost of the project, as shown in Equation (2),

$$NPV = \frac{TV}{(1+k)^n} - CO_0 \tag{2}$$

where CO_0 = the cash outflow

k = the firm's required rate of return

For project A,

$$NPV_A = \frac{\$19,010}{(1.14)^4} - \$10,000$$

$$= \$11,255 - \$10,000 = \$1,255$$

This value equals the NPV for project A using the conventional NPV model introduced in Chapter 6. (To see that the NPV found using Equation (2) is equivalent to the NPV using Equation (1) from Chapter 6, see Problem 11 at the end of this chapter.)

For project B,

$$NPV_B = \frac{\$20,736}{(1.14)^4} - \$10,000$$

$$= \$12,277 - \$10,000 = \$2,277$$

Therefore, these two last computations show that the NPV model makes the implicit assumption that a project's cash inflows are reinvested at the firm's required rate of return.

We now turn to a discussion of what the computed IRR value really conveys.

THE TRUE MEANING OF IRR

It is our contention that a majority of the users of the IRR model do not fully understand its implications. When we have asked users to describe the meaning of a computed IRR value, the almost unanimous response is that IRR shows the compounded annual rate of return that is earned on the original investment in the asset over its entire life. This is *wrong*!

At this juncture, there are three definitions that can be offered for IRR:

1   It is the discount rate that equates a project's discounted cash inflows with its discounted cash outflows.
2   It is the return on investment that allows the project's cash inflows to reduce the value of the investment to zero at the end of the project's life.
3   It is the return earned on the funds that remain internally invested in the project.

The first definition is used and illustrated in Chapter 6 and probably requires no further elaboration. However, the second and third descriptions call for additional discussion.

The second and third definitions view a project or investment as analogous to a mortgage. That is, when an individual has a mortgage, the payments (cash inflows from the investment) go first toward interest (return from the investment); only after that do they reduce the outstanding principal (i.e., reduce the value of the investment). By the end of the life of the mortgage (investment) the outstanding principal (value of the investment) is reduced to zero. Over the life of the mortgage (investment) the lending party (the firm) has earned interest (a return) only on the outstanding principal (the amount of funds that remain invested in the investment).

An illustration should help clarify this discussion.

EXAMPLE 2
A Project Viewed as a Mortgage

For project A shown in Example 1, which has an IRR equal to 20%, complete the following table, which views the project as a mortgage. Show that the project cash flows reduce the value of the investment to zero by the end of year 4.

YEAR	(1) BEGINNING VALUE OF THE INVESTMENT	(2) CASH INFLOW	(3) 20% RETURN ON VALUE OF THE INVESTMENT 20% × (1)	(4) REDUCTION IN THE VALUE OF THE INVESTMENT (2)–(3)	(5) ENDING VALUE OF THE INVESTMENT (1)–(4)
1	$10,000	$3,862.89			
2		3,862.89			
3		3,862.89			
4		3,862.89			

The ending value of the investment in any year is the beginning value of the investment in the following year. Thus, the value from column 5 is carried back to column 1 for the next year. Once the table is complete, explain project A's IRR using the third definition.

SOLUTION: Carrying out the calculations, the completed table appears as follows:

YEAR	(1) BEGINNING VALUE OF THE INVESTMENT	(2) CASH INFLOW	(3) 20% RETURN ON VALUE OF THE INVESTMENT 20% × (1)	(4) REDUCTION IN THE VALUE OF THE INVESTMENT (2)–(3)	(5) ENDING VALUE OF THE INVESTMENT (1)–(4)
1	$10,000.00	$3,862.89	$2,000.00	$1,862.89	$8,137.11
2	8,137.11	3,862.89	1,627.42	2,235.47	5,901.64
3	5,901.64	3,862.89	1,180.33	2,682.56	3,219.08
4	3,219.08	3,862.89	643.81	3,219.08	0

Looking at the table we see that 20% is earned on $10,000 during year 1, 20% is earned on $8,137.11 during year 2, 20% is earned on $5,901.64 during year 3, and 20% is earned on $3,219.08 during year 4. Project A does not earn a 20% rate of return on $10,000 for the entire 4-year useful life; the return of 20% is earned only on funds that remain *internally invested in the project* (i.e., the value of the investment in each of the 4 years). Thus the IRR criterion makes the assumption that cash inflows are reinvested at the same rate, so that it can *claim a true compounded rate of return on the entire original investment for the entire useful life of the project*. However, it can be said that project A will generate a true compounded rate of return of 20% on $10,000 for 4 years if and only if the cash inflows of $3,862.89 each year can be reinvested at a 20% return for the rest of the project's useful life. This was demonstrated in the computation of the terminal value for project A in Example 1.

As mentioned in Example 2, all that the computed IRR value shows is the rate of return on the funds that remain internally invested in the project. However, IRR users are under the misapprehension that IRR conveys the true compounded annual rate of return on the project. In reality, the true compounded rate of return on the project is related to IRR, as shown in Equation (3):

$$\text{true rate of return on a project} = \text{weighted average of} \begin{bmatrix} \text{IRR and} & \text{reinvestment rate earned on the project's cash inflows} \end{bmatrix} \qquad (3)$$

The weights used in Equation (3) are the cash inflows generated by the project. The *lower* the cash inflows early in the project's life, the longer the funds remain internally invested in the project; this dictates that IRR be the more heavily weighted factor in Equation (3). On the other hand, the *higher* the cash inflows early in the project's life, the earlier the funds have to be reinvested in other projects; this makes the reinvestment rate increasingly significant in the determination of the project's true rate of return.

Obviously, the true rate of return earned on a project is much more relevant than the project's IRR. However, even the project's true rate of return suffers from the limitation that rates of return are *relative* measures of project attractiveness that may or may not have anything to do with the maximization of shareholders' wealth. This is the topic explored in the final section of this chapter.

THE INABILITY OF IRR TO MAXIMIZE SHAREHOLDERS' WEALTH

When firms are evaluating mutually exclusive projects, two questions arise. First, can a conflict exist in ranking the projects using NPV, PI, and IRR? Second, if a conflict can and does arise, which technique should the firm utilize to maximize shareholders' wealth?

Fisher's Intersection

The answer to the first question is: Yes, it is possible for a conflict to arise in ranking mutually exclusive projects if the assets require different discounted cash outflows (a size disparity exists), if the projects have differing cash inflow patterns (a time disparity exists), or if the projects have unequal useful lives.

Notice that we said that a conflict is *possible*. That is, even if we have two or more mutually exclusive projects and even if one of the three disparities (size, time, or useful life) exists, there may or may not be a conflict between the rankings given the projects by NPV, PI, and IRR. Consider Figure 7–1.

Part (a) shows that project B dominates project C. This means that project B's NPV profile is everywhere above the NPV profile of project C. Thus, project B will have a greater NPV and PI than project C, regardless of the cost of capital; project B also has a higher IRR than project C. In part (b), the NPV profiles of projects D and E are tangent at only one point, but project D's profile is everywhere else above project E and project D has a higher IRR. Thus, there will again be no conflict between the rankings given D and E by the three techniques. In part (c), we see that (1) the profiles for projects F and G have a single point of intersection, (2) the NPV for project F at a zero discount rate is greater than the NPV at a zero discount rate for project G, and (3) the IRR for project G is greater than the IRR for project F. Under these conditions, *there will be a conflict between NPV and IRR if the firm's cost of capital is less than the discount rate at which the intersection in NPV profiles occurs. Also, there may be a conflict between NPV and PI only if there is a size disparity between projects F and G, and there will be a conflict between PI and IRR only if NPV and PI agree in their rankings of the projects.*

The intersection shown in Figure 7–1(c) is of some importance. It is called *Fisher's intersection* after the great economist Irving Fisher, who was among the first

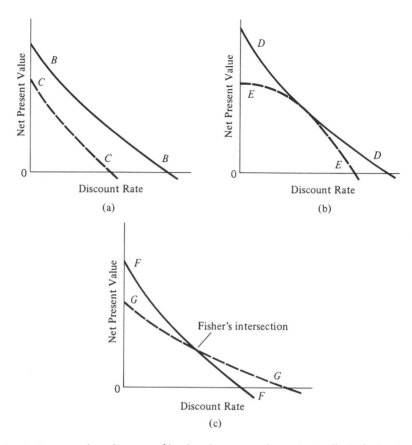

FIGURE 7–1   Examples of NPV Profiles for Three Sets of Two Mutually Exclusive Projects

to point out conflicts among NPV, PI, and IRR.[1] Fisher's intersection occurs at the interest rate where the NPVs of the two projects are equal; it is of significance because it is the *hurdle rate at which the preferred project using NPV shifts from one project to the other*. In addition, as we mentioned before, at required rates of return less than Fisher's intersection, NPV and IRR conflict in their ranking of the two projects. On the other hand, if the required rate of return is greater than Fisher's intersection, no conflict between NPV and IRR exists.

We can determine the discount rate at which Fisher's intersection occurs between the NPV profiles for two projects (call them I and II) using Equation (4):

$$NPV_I = NPV_{II}$$

$$\sum_{t=0}^{n} \frac{(CI_t)_I}{(1+f)^t} - (CO_t)_I = \sum_{t=0}^{n} \frac{(CI_t)_{II}}{(1+f)^t} - (CO_0)_{II} \qquad (4)$$

[1]See especially Irving Fisher, *The Rate of Interest* (New York: Macmillan Publishing Co., 1907) and *The Theory of Interest* (New York: Macmillan Publishing Co., 1930).

where $(CI_t)_I$, $(CI_t)_{II}$ = the cash inflow in period t for project I and project II, respectively
$(CO_0)_I$, $(CO_0)_{II}$ = the discounted cash outflow for project I and project II, respectively
f = the discount rate at which Fisher's intersection occurs

Notice that Equation (4) can be simplified by bringing all terms over to the left-hand side. Thus, the calculation of Fisher's rate (f) is similar to an IRR calculation. In addition, as with IRR, there can be zero, one, or multiple values for f. However, we limit our attention to cases in which there is zero or one intersection because these are the more usual cases. The reader interested in the problem of the existence and uniqueness of the Fisher's intersection is referred to that literature.[2]

The illustration of the calculation of Fisher's rate is the task of Example 3, which is adapted from an example originally presented by Hirshleifer.[3]

EXAMPLE 3
Fisher's Intersection

A firm is evaluating the following two mutually exclusive, but quite profitable, projects:

	PROJECT	
t	I	II
0	− $10,000	− $10,000
1	0	+ 20,000
2	+ 40,000	+ 10,000

As an aside, we can tell just by looking at the cash flow patterns of the two projects which would be preferred by the NPV criterion at low to moderate discount rates and which project would have the higher IRR (see Problem 14 at the end of this chapter).

(a) As a review of Chapter 6, compute each project's IRR.

(b) Based on the cash flow patterns for the two projects and the answer to part (a), can we determine whether these two projects will have a Fisher's intersection? Explain.

(c) Using Equation (4), determine f (the discount rate at Fisher's intersection) and the NPV at f for both projects. Comment on the significance of f.

(d) Using these results, sketch the two NPV profiles.

SOLUTION: (a) Computing the two IRR's, we find:

$$\text{IRR}_I \Rightarrow \frac{-\$10,000}{(1+r_I)^0} + \frac{0}{(1+r_I)^1} + \frac{\$40,000}{(1+r_I)^2} = 0$$

---

[2] See J. C. T. Mao, "The Internal Rate of Return as a Ranking Criterion," *The Engineering Economist* (Summer 1966), pp. 1–13; J. C. T. Mao, *Quantitative Analysis of Financial Decisions* (New York: Macmillan Publishing Co., 1969), Chap. 7; W. H. Jean, *The Analytical Theory of Finance* (New York: Holt, Rinehart and Winston, 1970), Chap. 2; and E. F. Fama and M. H. Miller, *The Theory of Finance* (New York: Holt, Rinehart and Winston, 1972), Chap. 3.

[3] J. Hirshleifer, "On the Theory of Optimal Investment Decisions," *Journal of Political Economy*, 66 (August 1958), 329–352.

Therefore,

$$r_I = 100\%$$

$$\mathrm{IRR_{II}} \Rightarrow \frac{-\$10{,}000}{(1+r_{II})^0} + \frac{\$20{,}000}{(1+r_{II})^1} + \frac{\$10{,}000}{(1+r_{II})^2} = 0$$

Therefore,

$$r_{II} = 141.4\%$$

(b) By looking at the cash flow patterns for the two projects, we can tell that project I has a higher NPV than project II at a zero discount rate. This can be seen by taking the undiscounted sum of the cash flows for the two projects: the NPV at 0% for project I is $-\$10{,}000 + 0 + \$40{,}000 = \$30{,}000$; the NPV at 0% for project II is $-\$10{,}000 + \$20{,}000 + \$10{,}000 = \$20{,}000$. In addition, the results of part (a) show that project II has a higher IRR than project I. Therefore, we can conclude that the NPV profiles for these two projects must intersect at a discount rate somewhere to the left of the smaller IRR (i.e., somewhere less than 100%). We compute this rate, f, in part (c).

(c) Using Equation (4), we find

$$\mathrm{NPV_I} = \mathrm{NPV_{II}}$$

$$\frac{-\$10{,}000}{(1+f)^0} + \frac{0}{(1+f)^1} + \frac{\$40{,}000}{(1+f)^2} = \frac{-\$10{,}000}{(1+f)^0} + \frac{\$20{,}000}{(1+f)^1} + \frac{\$10{,}000}{(1+f)^2}$$

$$\frac{-\$20{,}000}{(1+f)^1} + \frac{\$30{,}000}{(1+f)^2} = 0$$

Therefore,

$$f = 50\%$$

The NPV level achieved by both projects at $f = 50\%$ is determined by substituting 50% into the NPV equation for k using either project's cash flows:

$$\mathrm{NPV_I} = -\$10{,}000 + \frac{0}{(1.50)^1} + \frac{\$40{,}000}{(1.50)^2}$$

$$= \$7{,}778$$

We would find the same NPV value at $k = 50\%$ for project II.

The significance of the f value is that for any required return less than 50%, the NPV model will prefer project I, while the IRR model will prefer project II. For required returns above 50%, both NPV and IRR will rank project II higher than project I. Thus, depending on the level of the required rate of return relative to 50%, there either will or will not be a conflict between NPV and IRR in ranking these two projects. In addition, the more the firm's required rate of return is below 50%, the greater the NPV dominance of project I over project II.

(d) We now have sufficient data to plot the two NPV profiles.

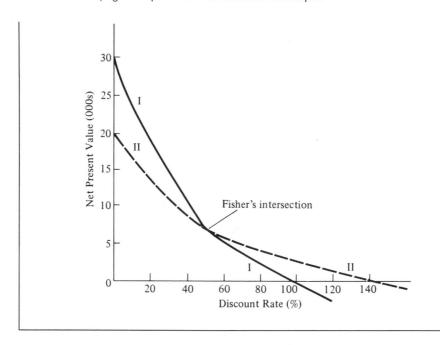

How IRR Selects the Wrong Project

Let's take a closer look at our results in Example 3. For required rates of return less than 50% (where a conflict in project ranking between NPV and IRR occurs), one of the two models will clearly lead the firm to select the *wrong* project, which will result in the common shareholders being worse off than they would have been if the better project had been accepted.

It is important for us to determine whether it is the NPV model or the IRR model that has the inherent flaw that occasionally produces a conflict, and therefore an error, in project ranking. The answer to this question is the focus of Example 4.

EXAMPLE 4

The Inability of IRR to Maximize Shareholders' Wealth

For the two projects shown in Example 3, we want to show that one project clearly dominates the other. This will indicate which model leads the firm astray by showing a preference for an inferior project.

Consider the following tabulation of the project cash flows:

	PROJECT		
t	I	I MODIFIED	II
0	− $10,000		− $10,000
1	0		+ 20,000
2	+ 40,000		+ 10,000

Notice that the two projects have the same cash outflow in year 0. In addition, in year 2, the cash inflow of project I exceeds that of project II. One way of showing the dominant project is to modify the cash flows of one of the projects. We will demonstrate by modifying project I. First, equate the cash flows for project I in year 2 with those of project II. Then discount the remainder of the second year cash flow of project I ($40,000 − $10,000 = $30,000) back one year using the firm's required rate of return. Thus, project I modified and project II will have equal cash flows in year 0 and year 2 and we can determine the *dominant* project by comparing the year 1 cash inflows.

(a) Using a 16% required rate of return, complete the table.

(b) On the basis of part (a), which project dominates and will NPV or IRR lead the firm to accept the wrong project? Can you generalize the results found in part (a): For what required rates of return will project I dominate II? Discuss.

(c) Some IRR proponents might argue that project II is preferred because it generates a $20,000 cash inflow in period 1, which can be used for reinvestment in attractive opportunities. However, if such attractive opportunities exist, the firm would still be able to accept project I and borrow $20,000 in period 1 at the cost of capital.

The loan can be repaid in period 2 with part of the $40,000 cash inflow. For this firm, with a 16% cost of capital, prepare a table similar to the one given, which has a column for the original project I cash flows, the loan cash flows just discussed, the total of these two sets of cash flows (which is actually a revised set of cash flows for project I), and the cash flows of project II. Which project dominates? Generalize your results.

SOLUTION: (a) The completed table is as follows:

	PROJECT		
t	I	I MODIFIED	II
0	− $10,000	− $10,000	− $10,000
1	0	+ 25,860	+ 20,000
2	+ 40,000	+ 10,000	+ 10,000

We arrive at the value of $25,860 for the year 1 cash inflow of modified project I by multiplying the $30,000 of the cash inflow of year 2 ($30,000 remains after $10,000 of the original $40,000 is left in year 2) by the 1-year discount factor for 16% (0.862). This results in a modified, *but equivalent*, cash flow series for project I.

(b) We can thus see that project I dominates project II and that any rational decision-maker would prefer project I to II. The project preferred by the NPV criterion (project I) would leave the firm with greater wealth than the project preferred by the IRR criterion (project II). In fact, by examining the modified cash flow series, we can see that the firm would be throwing away $5,860 of wealth in year 1 dollars if it followed the IRR criterion rather than the NPV criterion.

Recall from Example 3 that Fisher's intersection occurs at $f = 50\%$. The NPV model would continue to prefer project I at all required rates of return up to 50%. Thus, the modified project I cash flows would continue to dominate project II for all required rates of return up to 50% (see Problem 12 at the end of this chapter for a demonstration of this). For required rates of return in excess of 50%, the cash flows of project II will dominate the cash flows of modified project I because at such required rates of return, the NPV criterion prefers project II (see Problem 13 for a further development of this). At discount rates greater than 50%, the IRR criterion is correct in ranking project II higher than project I; however, the IRR criterion is correct only because it agrees with the NPV criterion, not because it is a valid evaluation criterion. We saw that IRR was clearly wrong in ranking projects where it conflicted with NPV (i.e., at discount rates lower than 50%.)

(c) For a firm with a 16% cost of capital, we prepare a table comparing the two projects given that the firm can accept project I and take out a loan for $20,000 at the end of year 1:

			PROJECT	
			I AND	
t	I	LOAN	LOAN COMBINED	II
0	− $10,000		− $10,000	− $10,000
1	0	+ $20,000	+ 20,000	+ 20,000
2	+ 40,000	− 23,200*	+ 16,800	+ 10,000

*This value includes $3,200 in interest plus the principal of $20,000.

Again, we see that project I plus the loan clearly dominates project II. Under both alternatives, the firm has $20,000 to invest in those attractive opportunities at the end of year 1. The additional returns earned on the $20,000 are added to the returns on each project and project I will, of course, continue to dominate. Project I will continue this domination over project II even if the firm has an opportunity to invest more than $20,000 at the end of year 1 and given that loans are available if the firm accepts either project (see Problem 16 at the end of this chapter).

Consistent with our generalized results in part (b), project I with the loan continues to dominate project II as long as the firm can borrow funds at a rate less than 50%, Fisher's rate for these two projects found in Example 3.

As noted in Example 4, IRR can have a detrimental impact on shareholders' wealth. This fact can also be demonstrated by showing how much the shareholders' wealth would increase at the end of the life of the project as a result of accepting that project. This is done for two mutually exclusive projects in Example 5.

EXAMPLE 5
Inability of IRR to Maximize Shareholders' Wealth, Revisited

A firm with a 10% cost of capital is evaluating projects A and B which have the following after-tax cash flows:

t	A	B
0	− $200,000	− $200,000
1	+ 50,000	+ 102,500
2	+ 50,000	+ 102,500
3	+ 235,000	+ 102,500
$NPV_{10\%}$	$ 63,335.84	$ 54,902.33
$PI_{10\%}$	1.31668	1.2745
IRR	23.0%	25.03%

NPV and PI rank project A higher, while IRR prefers project B. Somewhat artificially, assume that the firm will obtain the $200,000 required to purchase either project at its cost of capital and that any amount can be repaid each year. Show the impact on shareholders' wealth at the end of the life of each project, where cash inflows over the life are used to pay interest and principal on the $200,000 required.

SOLUTION: The analysis proceeds by preparing the following tables for each project:

PROJECT A

YEAR	BEGINNING BALANCE	INTEREST AT 10%	CASH INFLOW	RETIRMENT OF PRINCIPAL	ENDING BALANCE	INCREASE IN SHAREHOLDERS' WEALTH*
1	$200,000	$20,000	$50,000	$30,000	$170,000	
2	170,000	17,000	50,000	33,000	137,000	
3	137,000	13,700	235,000	137,000	0	$84,300

*Cash inflow in year 3 less the interest in year 3 less the beginning balance for year 3.

PROJECT B

YEAR	BEGINNING BALANCE	INTEREST AT 10%	CASH INFLOW	RETIRMENT OF PRINCIPAL	ENDING BALANCE	INCREASE IN SHAREHOLDERS' WEALTH*
1	$200,000	$20,000	$102,500	$82,500	$117,500	
2	117,500	11,750	102,500	90,750	26,750	
3	26,750	2,675	102,500	26,750	0	$73,075

*Cash inflow in year 3 less the interest in year 3 less the beginning balance for year 3.

Project A increases shareholders' wealth by $84,300, compared with $73,075 for project B. So again, if the firm followed the IRR criterion and accepted project B, it would lead to a sacrifice of $11,225 in the shareholders' wealth position at the end of the 3-year life of both projects. IRR is clearly an inferior criterion in maximizing shareholders' wealth compared with NPV.

It is important to note the relationship between each project's increase in shareholders' wealth at the end of year 3 and its NPV; *namely, if we discount each project's increase in shareholders' wealth back to time zero at the firm's required rate of return, we get precisely the NPV for that project.* To illustrate,

$$
\begin{aligned}
\text{NPV for project A} &= \left(\begin{array}{c}\text{increase in share-}\\ \text{holders' wealth for}\\ \text{project A}\end{array}\right) \times \left(\begin{array}{c}\text{present value}\\ \text{factor for 3}\\ \text{years and 10\%}\end{array}\right)\\
&= (\$84,300) \times (0.751315)\\
&= \$63,335.84
\end{aligned}
$$

Parallel results can be found for project B.

If it is argued that there are attractive reinvestment opportunities in years 1 and 2 for the $102,500 cash inflows of project B, it can again easily be shown that project A is still superior when an additional loan is obtained (at the cost of capital) to have this amount of funds available in each year. The comparison is as follows:

PROJECT A

TIME	ORIGINAL	LOAN	REVISED	PROJECT B
0	− $200,000		− $200,000	− $200,000
1	+ 50,000	+ $ 52,500	+ 102,500	+ 102,500
2	+ 50,000	+ 52,500	+ 102,500	+ 102,500
3	+ 235,000	− 121,275*	+ 113,725	+ 102,500

*The loan repayment of $121,275 consists of $105,000 in principal, $5,250 in interest for the loan outstanding in period 2, and $11,025 in interest for the loan outstanding in period 3 of $110,250; this last amount equals the amount of outstanding principal for the two loans (2 × $52,500) plus the unpaid interest at the end of period 2 ($5,250).

> Project A clearly dominates project B, and any rational decision maker would select A rather than B.

At this juncture we might question why such difficulties arise in the use of IRR. It could be said that IRR does a good job of measuring the *compounded rate of return over time on the funds that remain invested in an asset, but the problem is that this figure has nothing at all to do with maximizing shareholders' wealth.* A firm that attempted to *maximize IRR* could very well find that the highest IRR project had an original cost of $100 and a return next year of $150, leading to a 50% IRR; shareholders would be pleased over the $50 net return, but would raise more questions about how the remaining portion of the capital budget was invested. If management replied that they did not want to invest any more than $100 because to do so would cause the IRR to fall below the very attractive 50% level achieved, they would be looking for new jobs. *The NPV criterion shows clearly and unambiguously the impact of projects on shareholders' wealth or the present value of the firm. However, the same is obviously not true for IRR.*

If three projects have NPVs of $10,000, $14,000, and $16,000, these figures show the magnitudes of the increase in shareholders' wealth if the respective investments are accepted. On the other hand, if these same projects have IRRs of 40%, 30%, and 25% and PIs of 1.68, 1.22, and 1.53, respectively, we have no idea which of the three will lead to the greatest increase in shareholders' wealth by looking at their IRRs and PIs. In fact, as has been illustrated in many examples in this chapter, the increase in shareholders' wealth can be the opposite of the rankings indicated by either the IRR or PI criterion. In an informative and hard-hitting article, Keane points out:

> The internal rate of return, therefore, is invalid not because of any implicit reinvestment assumption or because of the possibility of producing multiple yields, but simply because a rate of return expressed in percentage terms is inappropriate for discriminating between projects of different sizes. All but *identical* projects have different sizes whatever their initial outlays or expected lives may suggest, and although the rate of return method might appear at times to give correct investment advice, it is *never* in fact correct in principle.[4]

Weingartner also has a number of uncomplimentary things to say about the profitability index.[5] He demonstrates that given a size disparity between two mutually exclusive projects, there will be a conflict between NPV and PI whenever

$$\frac{b_1}{b_2} < \frac{c_1}{c_2}$$

where b_j = net present value of project j
       c_j = cost of project j

Assume that $b_1 > b_2$, which means that the NPV criterion prefers project 1. Under the condition specified, PI will rank project 2 higher than 1, which is in conflict with

---

[4]S. M. Keane, "Let's Scrap IRR Once and for All!," *Accountancy* (February 1974), 78–82.

[5]H. Martin Weingartner, "The Excess Present Value Index—A Theoretical Basis and Critique," *Journal of Accounting Research* (Autumn 1963), 213–224.

NPV. This can be seen by noting that since all the b's and c's are positive, the following inequality exists.

$$\frac{b_1}{c_1} < \frac{b_2}{c_2}$$

The relationship between the PIs is as follows:

$$PI_1 = \frac{b_1 + c_1}{c_1} < \frac{b_2 + c_2}{c_2} = PI_2$$

To obtain this expression, we simply added unity to both sides of the inequality. In such circumstances, as Weingartner points out, the PI criterion "would lead to selection of the project with the *lower net present value which would make a lower contribution to the wealth of the owners of the firm*" [emphasis added].[6] Finally, Weingartner concludes his article by stating

> Our examples of mutually exclusive alternatives reinforce the conclusion that PI does not provide aid in the choice among such alternatives. In two examples, ranking by means of PI and by IRR led to the same *incorrect choice*. In the third example, these rankings were different, and the PI criterion resulted in the wrong choice. In all these instances, *the NPV criterion and Fisher's rate of return yield similar answers which are correct* in the absence of capital rationing or more complex interrelationships between investments. [emphasis added][7]

To conclude this section, the next example demonstrates in another way that utilizing the NPV criterion will lead to wealth maximization even when NPV conflicts with IRR and PI in the ranking of mutually exclusive projects. Irving Fisher was probably the first to use rigorously the type of analysis called upon in the demonstration; hence, it is referred to as two-period Fisherian analysis.

EXAMPLE 6
Inability of IRR and PI to Maximize Shareholders' Wealth (Second Revisit)

> A firm with a cost of capital of 10% has a current wealth position of $250,000. The accompanying graph shows combinations of consumption this year and consumption next year that can be obtained given the firm's current wealth position, the cost of capital (or market rate of interest), and the assumptions of equal borrowing and lending rates. Notice that one possible consumption pattern would be $250,000 this year and $0 next year; another would be $0 this year and $275,000 next year [$275,000 would be available for consumption next year since the $250,000 could be invested at the market rate of interest, 10%—$275,000 = $250,000(1.10)]. Consider that the firm has determined its desired consumption pattern and that is to consume $150,000 this year and $110,000 next year. Notice, of course, that this consumption pattern, as is true for all others on the line, has a present value of $250,000 (using the market discount rate of 10%) and a future value next

[6] Ibid., p. 220.
[7] Ibid., p. 224.

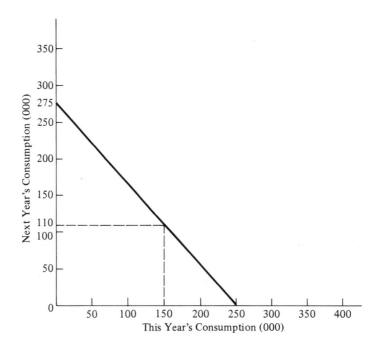

year of $275,000. The firm is evaluating two mutually exclusive projects:

YEAR	I	II
0	− $40,000	− $ 80,000
1	+ 80,000	+ 150,000
$NPV_{10\%}$	$32,727	$ 56,364
$PI_{10\%}$	1.82	1.70
IRR	100%	87.5%

Both PI and IRR rank project I above project II, whereas NPV reverses this order.

Using a graph similar to the one shown, demonstrate that project II, if accepted by the firm, will place the firm in a superior wealth position than if project I were accepted (i.e., demonstrate that following the NPV criterion maximizes shareholders' wealth, whereas PI and IRR fail to do so).

SOLUTION: The graph indicating the original wealth position, that achieved by accepting project I (labeled I), and that achieved by accepting project II (labeled II) is as shown. Note in the figure that the lines for projects I and II are determined geometrically by two points: (1) the point found by first moving horizontally to the left along the line $110,000 of consumption next year in the amount of the investment for each project and then moving vertically upward in the amount of the cash inflow in period 1, and (2) the point on the horizontal axis at $250,000 (the firm's original wealth position) plus the NPV of the project.

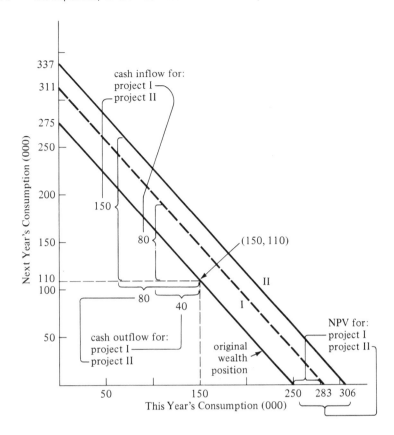

The wealth position of the firm (in terms of current dollars) after accepting either project I or project II is equal to the firm's current level of wealth ($250,000) plus the NPV of either project. Thus, as we can clearly see, the wealth position of the firm after *accepting project II dominates* the wealth position of the firm if project I were accepted. The graph shows that the wealth line of project II is above and to the right of that of project I; therefore, the firm with project II can achieve any level of current and future consumption that could be achieved by accepting project I *and still have wealth left over.* A quantification of the level of the *dominance in current wealth position is the difference in the NPVs of the two projects*—$23,630 (NPV for project II is $56,360 minus the NPV for project I of $32,730). This difference shows the amount by which the firm is *wealthier* by following the NPV criterion rather than either PI or IRR. That is, if the firm used either PI or IRR, shareholders' wealth would be decreased by $23,630 compared with the selection of projects using the superior NPV criterion.

Hence, the *direct link between the NPV criterion and shareholder wealth maximization has been established* using yet another type of analysis (two-period Fisherian analysis). The selection of the project or projects that *maximize NPV will lead to shareholder wealth maximization.* This is obviously not the case for either PI or IRR.

In addition to the points discussed, Example 6 demonstrates the inferiority of the basic rationale behind PI and IRR. We have discussed that these models rank projects using a *relative criterion*. These two relative evaluation techniques use the rate of change in the firm's wealth position (IRR) or the number of dollars of DCI per dollar of DCO (PI) to rank projects. Unfortunately, though, both of these relative ranking techniques totally ignore the *number of dollars invested in competing projects* and, *more importantly, the resulting absolute change in the firm's wealth position after accepting either of the alternatives*. It is nice to have a rapid rate of change in wealth or a high number of dollars of DCI per dollar of DCO, but neither of these characteristics buys shareholders anything—only wealth can do that! Therefore, since the firm is trying to maximize the shareholders' wealth position, we strongly recommend that the NPV criterion be used because it is the only model capable of helping the firm achieve this goal; both IRR and PI should be abandoned because they totally ignore shareholders' wealth.

SUMMARY

The several examples included in our analysis should convince even the skeptical reader that the NPV criterion is clearly superior to either the IRR or PI criterion in maximizing shareholders' wealth.

In the following chapter, we demonstrate how the NPV model is rich enough to handle the evaluation of mutually exclusive projects under a wide variety of conditions. We call solely upon the NPV model to select the preferred project from a mutually exclusive set because only this model leads to shareholder wealth maximization.

QUESTIONS
PROBLEMS

1. Briefly discuss the difference between relative and absolute capital budgeting evaluation techniques. Classify NPV, PI, and IRR.

2. Discuss the general assumption that discounted cash flow models make concerning the reinvestment of cash inflows. What reinvestment assumptions do NPV, PI, and IRR make?

3. Name two major reasons why the DCF models may conflict when ranking mutually exclusive projects. Could both these reasons be an explanation for a conflict between NPV and PI in ranking mutually exclusive projects? Discuss.

4. Give four verbal definitions for the internal rate of return.

5. Where does the word *internal* in IRR come from? Is there any difference between a project's IRR and its true compounded annual rate of return? Discuss.

6. What is meant by *Fisher's intersection*? Why is it important in evaluating mutually exclusive investments?

7. True or false: There will always be a conflict between NPV and IRR for two mutually exclusive projects with NPV profiles having a Fisher's intersection. Justify your answer.

8. True or false: By observing the NPV profiles for two mutually exclusive projects, we can determine whether there will be a conflict between NPV and PI. Justify your answer.

9. Answer the following true-false questions based on the two-period Fisherian analysis shown in Example 6.

   (a) The original wealth position of the firm is 250 units of this year's consumption and 0 units of next year's consumption or 0 units of this year's consumption and 275 units of next year's consumption; this means that the market rate of interest is 10% and any other market rate of interest would lead to a different amount available for next year's consumption.

   (b) The desired consumption pattern of 150 this year and 110 next year has a present value of 250 units, which is also true of all other points on the line.

   (c) As can be seen from the graph, project I has an NPV of 283, while project II has an NPV of 306.

   (d) The wealth position of the firm after accepting project II dominates that after accepting project I because the firm could throw away 23 units of current consumption if it had accepted project II and still be as well off as if it had accepted project I.

   (e) Given these two projects, NPV and PI conflict in their rankings because NPV prefers project II, while PI prefers project I.

   (f) In this type of analysis, the only time when PI could lead to an inferior wealth position in comparing mutually exclusive projects would be when a size disparity exists between the projects.

   (g) Similarly, in this type of analysis, the only time that IRR could lead to an inferior wealth position would be when a size disparity exists between the projects.

   (h) In this type of analysis, neither IRR nor PI can distinguish between different size investments because each is a relative measure of project attractiveness.

   (i) Neither IRR nor PI has anything in particular to do with maximizing wealth position because each is a relative measure that ignores the absolute magnitude of the wealth generated by an investment.

   (j) A project with a negative NPV would be rejected by this type of analysis because the wealth line after accepting the investment would be lower and to the left of the current wealth line, which means that the former would be dominated.

   (k) In this type of analysis, the terminal value criterion would give rankings that are *always* consistent with the NPV criterion.

10. Two of the most widely used methods of evaluating capital investment projects are the net present value technique and the internal rate of return method. When two or more mutually exclusive investments are being evaluated, conflicts can arise between the rankings given the projects by

NPV and IRR. The following questions point to potential difficulties that can arise.

Consider the following two mutually exclusive investment proposals,[8] which are graphed here:

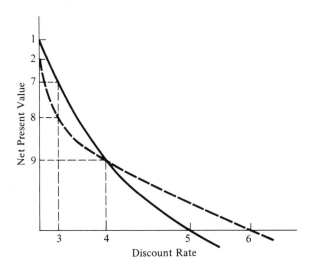

Project A

| | NET CASH | DISCOUNTED AT | | |
| | FLOWS | 6% | 15.5% | 28.5% |
YEAR				
0	− $100			
1	+ 30	$28.29	$25.95	$23.34
2	+ 30	26.70	22.50	18.18
3	+ 70	58.80	45.36	32.97
4	+ 70	55.44	39.34	25.69
		$169.23	$133.15	$100.18

Project B

| | NET CASH | DISCOUNTED AT | | |
| | FLOWS | 6% | 15.5% | 34% |
YEAR				
0	− $100			
1	+ 60	$56.58	$51.90	$44.82
2	+ 60	53.40	45.00	33.42
3	+ 30	25.20	19.44	12.48
4	+ 30	23.76	16.86	9.30
		$158.94	$133.20	$100.02

[8]The two projects used in this problem originally appeared in an example in R. Conrad Doenges, "The 'Reinvestment Problem' in a Practical Perspective," *Financial Management* (Spring 1972), 85–91.

(a) The project whose discounted cash flow pattern is shown by the curve intersecting the axes at points 1 and 5 is
   (i)   project A.
   (ii) project B.

(b) The dollar value that point 1 on the graph equals is
   (i) $169.23.
   (ii) $158.94.
   (iii) $200.00.
   (iv) $100.00.
   (v) $69.23.

(c) The dollar value that point 2 on the graph equals is
   (i) $158.94.
   (ii) $169.23.
   (iii) $58.94.
   (iv) $180.00.
   (v) $80.00.

(d) The discount rate that point 5 on the graph equals is
   (i)   0%.
   (ii) 6%.
   (iii) 15.5%.
   (iv) 28.5%.
   (v) 34%.

(e) The dollar amounts that points 7 and 8 equal, respectively, are
   (i) $200 and $180.
   (ii) $169.23 and $158.94.
   (iii) $100 and $80.
   (iv) $69.23 and $58.94.
   (v) none of the above.

(f) Using the NPV criterion, project B would be preferred to project A for all discount rates
   (i)   greater than 0%.
   (ii) less than 6%.
   (iii) less than 15.5%.
   (iv) greater than 15.5%.
   (v) less than 28.5%.

(g) Using the NPV criterion, *only one* project would be *acceptable* at the following rate:
   (i)   6%.
   (ii) 15.5%.
   (iii) 28.5%.
   (iv) 32%.
   (v) 40%.

(h) Using the IRR criterion, project A would be preferable to project B when the discount rate is
   (i)   greater than 0%.
   (ii) greater than 15.5%.
   (iii) less than 15.5%.
   (iv) greater than 28.5%.
   (v) none of the above.

(i) There would be a conflict between the rankings of the two projects using NPV versus IRR when the discount rate is
  (i) greater than 0%.
  (ii) greater than 6%.
  (iii) less than 15.5%.
  (iv) greater than 15.5%.
  (v) none of the above.

(j) Using the IRR criterion, project B would be preferable to project A when the discount rate is
  (i) greater than 0%.
  (ii) greater than 6%.
  (iii) less than 15.5%.
  (iv) greater than 15.5%.
  (v) greater than 28.5%.

(k) At a discount rate of 32%, there would be a conflict between the preferred investment using NPV versus IRR:
  (i) True
  (ii) False

(l) At a discount rate of 40%, there would be a conflict between the preferred investment using NPV versus IRR:
  (i) True
  (ii) False

(m) The value for point 9 on the graph would equal

  (i) $$\frac{-100}{(1+r)^0} + \frac{30}{(1+r)^1} + \frac{30}{(1+r)^2} + \frac{70}{(1+r)^3} + \frac{70}{(1+r)^4},$$

  where $r =$ point #4.

  (ii) $$\frac{-100}{(1+r)^0} + \frac{60}{(1+r)^1} + \frac{60}{(1+r)^2} + \frac{30}{(1+r)^3} + \frac{30}{(1+r)^4},$$

  where $r =$ point #4.

  (iii) expression (i), where r will equate it to zero.
  (iv) expression (ii), where r will equate it to zero.
  (v) both (i) and (ii).
  (vi) none of the above.

(n) Referring to question (m), the value for point 4 on the graph will be
  (i) the value of r that will equate expression (i) with that of (ii).
  (ii) the value of r that will equate expression (i) to zero.
  (iii) the value of r that will equate expression (ii) to zero.
  (iv) both (ii) and (iii).
  (v) none of the above.

11. Show that if NPVs reinvestment assumption is met (i.e., the reinvestment rate i equals the firm's required rate of return k), then Equation (2) in this chapter is equivalent to Equation (1) in Chapter 6.

12. For the two projects shown in Examples 3 and 4, show that the cash flow series for project I modified as discussed and illustrated in Example 4 will continue to dominate project II for required rates of return of 20%, 30%, 40%, 45%, and 49%.

13. Consider two firms that have required rates of return of 60% and 70%. Compute the NPV for both project I and project II shown in Examples 3 and 4 using a 60% and a 70% required rate of return. For both of these rates, demonstrate that project II will dominate project I modified using the approach illustrated in Example 4.

14. For the two projects shown in Example 3, the NPV criterion will prefer project I at low and moderate discount rates, whereas project II has a higher IRR than project I. Discuss what project characteristics would lead the NPV model to prefer project I and why this is the case based on the way this model evaluates projects. Similarly, discuss the project characteristics that would lead the IRR model to prefer project II and why this is the case based on the way this model evaluates projects.

15. Part (a) of the solution to Example 4 shows that project I modified dominated project II in the amount of $5,860 (rounded) in cash flow terms at the end of year 1. What is the relationship of this amount to the NPVs of the two projects? [*Hint*: Determine the present value of $5,860 using a 16% discount rate; next determine the NPV of each project using a 16% discount rate.]

16. For the two projects shown in Example 3 and 4, show that project I still dominates project II if the firm has the opportunity to invest $30,000 at the end of year 1 and a loan bearing interest at 16% can be obtained in conjunction with either project.

17. For the two projects shown in Examples 3 and 4, show that project I no longer dominates project II if a firm must pay 60% to obtain the $20,000 desired at the end of year 1 (if project I is accepted).

18. For the conditions described in Problem 17, show why project II dominates project I plus the loan in the amount of the answer to Problem 17.

19. For the two projects shown in Example 1, discuss the conditions under which each of the following occurs.
    (a) The true rate of return [as computed by Equation (3)] on project A will be *exactly equal* to the true rate of return on project B.
    (b) The true rate of return on project A will be *greater than* the true rate of return on project B.
    (c) The true rate of return on project A will be *less than* the true rate of return on project B.

20. Based on your discussion in Problem 19, demonstrate by using terminal value [Equation (1)] that shareholders would (a) be indifferent between projects A and B under the condition you specify in part (a) of your answer to Problem 19; (b) prefer project A to project B under the condition you specify in part (b) of your answer to Problem 19; and (c) prefer project B to project A under the condition you specify in part (c) of your answer to Problem 19.

21. Based on projects A and B in Example 1, is the 20% return on project B the true guaranteed rate of return, but is the 20% return on project A not guaranteed and is the true rate of return dependent upon the reinvestment rate which can be earned on the cash flows that take place at the end of years 1, 2, and 3? Discuss.

REFERENCES

Bauman, W. Scott. "Investment Returns and Present Values." *Financial Analysts Journal*, 25 (November–December 1969), 107–118.

Beaves, R. G. "Net Present Value and Rate of Return: Implicit and Explicit Reinvestment Assumptions." *The Engineering Economist* (Summer 1988), 275–302.

Beenhakker, Henri L. "Sensitivity Analysis of the Present Value of a Project." *Engineering Economist*, 20 (Winter 1975), 123–149.

Beidlemen, C. R. "Discounted Cash Flow Reinvestment Rate Assumptions." *Engineering Economist* (Winter 1984).

Bernhard, R. H., and Carl J. Norstrom. "A Further Note on Unrecovered Investment, Uniqueness of the Internal Rate, and the Question of Project Acceptability." *Journal of Financial and Quantitative Analysis* (June 1980).

Brick, Ivan, and Daniel G. Weaver. "A Comparison of Capital Budgeting Techniques in Identifying Profitable Investments." *Financial Management* (Winter 1984).

Capettini, R., R. A. Grimlund, and H. R. Toole. "Comment: The Unique, Real Internal Rate of Returns." *Journal of Financial and Quantitative Analysis* (December 1979).

Carlson, C. Robert, Michael Laurence, and Donald H. Wort. "Clarification of the Reinvestment Assumption in Capital Analysis." *Journal of Business Research* (April 1974).

de la Mare, R. F. "An Investigation into the Discounting Formulae Used in Capital Budgeting Models." *Journal of Business Finance and Accounting* (Summer 1975).

de Faro, Clovis. "On the Internal Rate of Return Criterion." *Engineering Economist*, 19 (April–May 1974), 165–194.

_____. "A Sufficient Condition for a Unique Nonnegative Internal Rate of Return: A Comment." *Journal of Financial and Quantitative Analysis*, 8 (September 1973), 683–684.

Dorfman, Robert. "The Meaning of the Internal Rate of Return." *Journal of Finance*, 36 (December 1981), 1010–1023.

Dudley, Carlton L., Jr. "A Note on Reinvestment Assumptions in Choosing Between Net Present Value and Internal Rate of Return." *Journal of Finance*, 27 (September 1972), 907–915.

Fogler, H. Russell. "Ranking Techniques and Capital Rationing." *Accounting Review*, 47 (January 1972), 134–143.

Franklin, Peter J. "The Normal Cost Theory of Price and the Internal Rate of Return Method of Investment Appraisal: An Integration." *Journal of Business Finance and Accounting* (Spring 1977).

Hajdasinski, M. M. "A Complete Method for Separation of Internal Rates of Return." *Engineering Economist* (Spring 1983).

Herbst, Anthony. "The Unique, Real Internal Rate of Return: Caveat Emptor!" *Journal of Financial and Quantitative Analysis*, 13 (June 1978), 363–370.

Jean, William H. "Terminal Value or Present Value in Capital Budgeting Programs." *Journal of Financial and Quantitative Analysis*, 6 (January 1971), 649–652.

_____. "On Multiple Rates of Return." *Journal of Finance*, 23 (March 1968), 187–192.

Jeynes, Paul H. "The Significance of Reinvestment Rate." *Engineering Economist*, 9 (Fall 1965), 1–9.

Keane, Simon M. "The Internal Rate of Return and the Reinvestment Fallacy." *Journal of Accounting and Business Studies*, 15 (June 1979), 48–55.

Lohmann, J. R. "The IRR, NPV and the Fallacy of the Reinvestment Rate Assumptions." *The Engineering Economist* (Summer 1988), 303–330.

Mao, James C. T. "The Internal Rate of Return as a Ranking Criterion." *Engineering Economist*, 11 (Winter 1966), 1–13.

_____. "A New Graphic Analysis of Fisher's Rate of Return." *Cost and Management*, 44 (November–December 1970), 24–27.

McDaniel, W. R., D. E. McCarty, and K. A. Jessell. "Discounted Cash Flow With Explicit Reinvestment Rates: Tutorial and Extension." *The Financial Review* (August 1988), 369–385.

Meyer, Richard L. "A Note on Capital Budgeting Techniques and the Reinvestment Rate." *Journal of Finance*, 34 (December 1979), 1251–1254.

Norstrum, C. "A Note on 'Mathematical Analysis' of Rates of Return Under Certainty." *Management Science* (January 1976).

_____. "A Sufficient Condition for a Unique Nonnegative Internal Rate of Return." *Journal of Financial and Quantitative Analysis*, 7 (June 1972), 1835–1839.

Oakford, R. V., S. A. Bhimjie, and J. V. Jucker. "The Internal Rate of Return, the Pseudo Internal Rate of Return, and the NPV and Their Use in Financial Decision Making." *Engineering Economist* (Spring 1977).

Peasnell, K. V. "Capital Budgeting and Discounted Cash Equivalents: Some Clarifying Comments." *Abacus* (December 1979).

Petty, J. William, and Oswald D. Bowlin. "The Financial Manager and Quantitative Decision Models." *Financial Management*, 4 (Winter 1976), 32–41.

Rapp, Berger. "The Internal Rate of Return Method—A Critical Study." *Engineering Costs and Production Economics*, 5 (1980).

Schwab, Bernhard, and Peter Lusztig. "A Comparative Analysis of the Net Present Value and the Benefit-Cost Ratios as Measures of the Economic Desirability of Investments." *Journal of Finance*, 24 (June 1969), 507–516.

Wiar, Robert C. "Economic Implications of Multiple Rates of Return in the Leveraged Lease Context." *Journal of Finance*, 28 (December 1973), 1275–1286.

CASE STUDY 7-1

National Motors, Inc.

(Evaluation of capital budgeting projects using different profitability measures)

National Motors, Inc., is a leading manufacturer of large transportation vehicles and was incorporated in Delaware on August 15, 1932. It is a publicly owned company with some 30,000 shareholders. The common shares of National Motors, Inc., are listed on the New York, Midwest, and Pacific stock exchanges. During the fourth quarter of 1986, the price of a common share was between a high of $32 1/8 and a low of $27 5/8. This company outperformed all its competitors during 1986 and had dividends per share of $0.20 and an EPS of $1.83, although its dividends per share and common share price compared to 1983 and 1984 were lower.

To restore the profitability of National Motors, Inc., management designed a manufacturing strategy that aims at cutting costs. A committee comprised of the vice president and representatives of the Financial Planning department was asked to review the firm's operations. The committee was to advise management as to what assets the company should retire and determine the needed increase in capital expenditures for remodelling and renovating the company's manufacturing process.

Among its beginning tasks, this committee had to submit a report to the chief executive officer on the recommended capital expenditures needed in the painting station in the plant. Four mutually exclusive projects were initially proposed and this committee had to determine which one to choose. (See Exhibit 1.) The committee has determined that 12% is an appropriate hurdle rate for all four of these projects.

Exhibit 1
Yearly Net Cash Flows

TIME	PROJECT A	PROJECT B	PROJECT C	PROJECT D
0	− $200,000	− $70,000	− $200,000	− $40,000
1	+ 45,000	+ 50,000	+ 102,500	+ 75,000
2	+ 55,500	+ 40,000	+ 102,500	—
3	+ 60,000	+ $20,000	+ $102,500	—
4	+ $ 92,500	+ $10,000	—	—
5	+ $110,000	+ $10,000	—	—

QUESTIONS

1. Using spreadsheet software, compute the NPV, PI, IRR, and discounted payback period for each of these four projects.
2. Conduct a sensitivity analysis and design a best case scenario (future cash flows are increased by 10%) and a worst case scenario (future cash flows are decreased by 10%). Present all the results in a tabular form together with the results you found in Question 1.
3. Help National Motors decide which project should be implemented. Explain all your underlying assumptions.

Capital Budgeting
for Mutually Exclusive Projects

8

In Chapter 7, we demonstrated the superiority of the NPV criterion over the other DCF approaches, IRR and PI. In the current chapter, we illustrate how the NPV model effectively handles the evaluation of mutually exclusive projects. In addition, we demonstrate the enrichment of the NPV model to handle changing required rates of return in the future as well as changing reinvestment rates.

ELABORATIONS OF THE BASIC NPV MODEL

Chapter 6 introduced the basic NPV model, which assumes that the firm's required rate of return remains constant over the project's life. We reintroduce this model as Equation (1),

$$\text{NPV} = \sum_{t=0}^{n} \frac{CI_t}{(1+k)^t} - \sum_{t=0}^{n} \frac{CO_t}{(1+k)^t} \qquad (1)$$

where CI_t = the after-tax cash inflow in period t
CO_t = the after-tax cash outflow in period t
n = the useful life of the project
k = the firm's required rate of return

Of course, the NPV model does not encounter any major difficulty if the firm estimates that its required rate of return will change in future years. In fact, the straightforward elaboration of Equation (1) merely calls upon the geometric sum to determine the appropriate discount factor. Equation (2) determines the NPV for a project under the assumption that the firm will have a changing required rate of return,

$$\text{NPV} = \sum_{t=0}^{n} \frac{CI_t}{\prod_{j=1}^{t}\left(1 + k_j\right)} - \sum_{t=0}^{n} \frac{CO_t}{\prod_{j=1}^{t}\left(1 + k_j\right)} \tag{2}$$

where k_j = the firm's required rate of return in period j
Π = the product operator which requires the multiplication of the terms which follow

The perceptive reader has already suspected that Equation (1) is a special case of Equation (2). And this is the case. If all the values of k_j are equal, Equation (2) reduces to the simpler Equation (1).

As discussed in Chapter 7, both Equations (1) and (2) make the implicit assumption that the reinvestment rate (i) will be equal to or a close approximation for the firm's required rate of return (k). If the firm's reinvestment rate is *not* approximately equal to its required rate of return, then the NPV model's calculations are based upon an erroneous assumption. The greater the deviation of the reinvestment rate from the firm's required rate of return, the greater the error that the basic NPV model makes in evaluating the attractiveness of a given project.

To overcome the error that the basic NPV model makes when i does not equal k, we must call upon the terminal value (TV) calculation introduced in Chapter 7. Recall that the TV calculation shows the total value of a project's cash inflows under the assumption that they are reinvested to earn a specific annual rate of return i. We repeat the TV model here for convenience as Equation (3):

$$\text{TV} = \sum_{t=0}^{n} CI_t(1 + i)^{n-t} \tag{3}$$

Equation (3) determines the TV under the assumption that the reinvestment rate (i) remains constant over the life of the project.

Once the TV is computed using Equation (3), a modified NPV value (which we call NPV*) can be computed using Equation (4):

$$\text{NPV*} = \frac{TV}{\left(1 + k\right)^n} - \sum_{t=0}^{n} \frac{CO_t}{\left(1 + k\right)^t} \tag{4}$$

Two characteristics should be noted about Equation (4). First, we call equation (4) a modified NPV model (NPV*) because we are no longer assuming that the reinvestment rate equals the firm's required rate of return, as in Equations (1) and (2). In Equation (4), we are assuming the project's cash inflows can be reinvested at the annual rate of return i and the firm's required rate of return is k. Second, Equation (4) assumes the firm's required rate of return remains constant over the life of the project.

As we saw, it is a straightforward extension of the NPV model to allow the required rate of return to change over the life of the project. Applying the same methodology to Equation (4) that we did to Equation (1) in arriving at Equation (2), we derive Equation (5):

$$\text{NPV*} = \frac{\text{TV}}{\prod\limits_{j=1}^{n}\left(1 + k_j\right)} - \sum_{t=0}^{n} \frac{CO_t}{\prod\limits_{j=1}^{t}\left(1 + k_j\right)} \tag{5}$$

Equation (5) determines the modified NPV value (NPV*) under the assumption that the firm's required rate of return changes over the life of the project. Further—along the same lines as our earlier discussion about the relationship between Equations (1) and (2)—Equation (4) is just a special case of Equation (5) under the assumption that the firm's required rate of return is constant over the project's life.

Finally, the calculation of TV in Equation (3) makes the assumption that the reinvestment rate (i) remains constant over the project's life. Of course, this reinvestment rate could very well change over time. Under such conditions, a project's TV is computed using Equation (6),

$$\text{TV} = \sum_{t=0}^{n} CI_t \left[\prod_{j=t+1}^{n} \left(1 + i_j\right) \right] \tag{6}$$

where i_j is the reinvestment rate that can be earned in period j.

The compounding process shown by the geometric sum begins in period $t + 1$ because we are making the usual assumption that the cash flows CI_t occur at the *end* of period t. Hence, each cash inflow can be reinvested starting in period $t + 1$. It should also be mentioned that Equation (6) reduces to Equation (3) if the reinvestment rate remains constant over the project's life.

Once TV has been computed using Equation (6), the modified NPV value can be computed using (1) Equation (4), if the firm's required rate of return remains constant over the project's life, or (2) Equation (5), if the required rate of return changes over time.

With these elaborations of the basic NPV model, we can handle all possible conditions relative to the firm's expected future required rate of return, as well as its expected reinvestment rate. Although these values of k and i present forecasting difficulties, we must address the prospect that such values are not very likely to remain constant at their current levels over project lives of 5, 10, or 20 years.

The NPV and NPV* models presented can be applied to the evaluation of independent projects, as well as to sets of mutually exclusive projects. The evaluation of independent projects requires only the application of the decision rule that the project is a candidate for acceptance if NPV (or NPV*) is greater than or equal to zero because projects satisfying this condition will increase shareholders' wealth. The ranking of mutually exclusive projects using NPV and NPV* is the task of the next section. Equations (1)–(6) are illustrated throughout the remainder of this chapter.

EVALUATING MUTUALLY EXCLUSIVE PROJECTS

So that we can correctly evaluate mutually exclusive projects to select the one that will maximize shareholders' wealth, there are three major questions to be addressed. Over the lives of the mutually exclusive projects:

1   Is the firm's reinvestment rate (i) expected to *differ significantly* from the firm's required rate of return (k)?

2   Is the reinvestment rate (i) expected to *change* over the projects' lives or is it expected to *remain constant*?

3   Is the firm's required rate of return (k) expected to *change* over the projects' lives or is it expected to *remain constant*?

Depending on the answers to these three questions, the firm can select the appropriate version of the NPV model to choose the preferred project from a mutually exclusive set of projects.

In addition to these three questions, we have the preliminary consideration of whether or not the firm is subject to capital rationing. If the firm is subject to capital rationing, then all feasible *portfolios* of capital projects must be evaluated in order to select the one maximizing NPV or NPV* without violating any of the firm's resource limitations. Mathematical programming techniques provide an efficient mechanism by which feasible portfolios can be evaluated. We explore mathematical programming approaches to capital budgeting in Chapters 19 and 20.

If capital rationing does not exist, then each set of mutually exclusive projects can be evaluated on its own merit. Where firms have conditions of *no capital rationing*, the only decisions necessary are which project in each mutually exclusive set is best and whether it has a positive NPV or NPV*. All the best projects with positive NPV or NPV* values should be undertaken to maximize shareholders' wealth.

Figure 8–1 presents a flow chart that guides the firm in the selection of the appropriate model to evaluate mutually exclusive projects.

As can be seen, the first question that must be answered in the flow chart is whether capital rationing exists. Once this question is handled, we next address the three major questions about the equality of i and k and whether each remains constant or changes over time. The appropriate version of the correct model to use (NPV or NPV*), as well as the choice of how TV is computed, depends upon the answers to these three major questions. Thus, the flow chart merely presents a map for the selection of Equations (1)–(6), depending on prevailing conditions.

Figure 8–1 is a *general* tool, which can be used to rank mutually exclusive projects that exhibit *any* of the three types of disparities: *size, time, or useful life.* Each of these disparities imposes different difficulties on the project-ranking process; however, the flow chart properly handles the difficulties by selecting the appropriate model. In the next three sections, we apply the flow chart to mutually exclusive sets of projects that possess each of these disparities.

Projects with a Size Disparity

A size disparity is exhibited in a set of mutually exclusive projects if a difference exists in the original cash outflow required by the projects. Such projects are

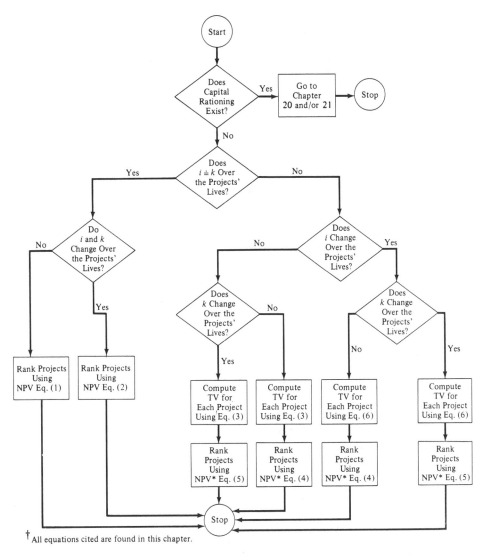

† All equations cited are found in this chapter.

FIGURE 8–1   Flow Chart for Ranking Mutually Exclusive Projects†

comparable and can be handled with the techniques presented in this chapter, as long as capital rationing does not exist (i.e., the first question posed in Figure 8–1). Where capital rationing does not exist, the firm can obtain *any amount* of capital funds at the same cost of capital. Thus, differences in cash outlays between (or among) mutually exclusive projects are irrelevant because the firm can obtain sufficient funds to accept all attractive investments; and the one that generates the greatest increase in shareholders' wealth should be selected.

Consider the two projects shown in Example 1.

EXAMPLE 1
Ranking Two Mutually Exclusive Investments Which Exhibit a Size
Disparity

Alpha Company is evaluating two projects:

	PROJECT	
CHARACTERISTIC	X	Y
Original investment	$240,000	$180,000
Annual cash inflows	$80,000	$62,000
Useful life	6 years	6 years

Given a 16% required rate of return, these values are computed by Alpha to rank the
two projects:

	PROJECT	
CRITERION	X	Y
$NPV_{16\%}$	$54,779	$48,454
$PI_{16\%}$	1.23	1.27
IRR	24%	26%

Alpha Company sees that there is a conflict in the ranking of these two projects
using NPV versus PI and IRR. The firm determines the discount rate at which Fisher's
intersection occurs and finds $f = 20\%$. A sketch of the NPV profile for each project is
shown in Figure 8–2.

Alpha Company estimates that its cost of capital will be closely approximated by the
reinvestment rate it is able to earn over each of the next 10 years. In addition, the firm
feels that the actual value for i and k would remain constant over the lives of projects X
and Y and could range from a low of 12% to a high of 18%. Using Figures 8–1 and 8–2,
help Alpha Company select the correct project.

SOLUTION: Referring to Figure 8–1, we see that Alpha Company should use the basic
NPV model shown in Equation (1) to rank projects X and Y because $i = k$ and both will
remain constant over the lives of these two projects. Using Equation (1), the NPV of each
project at each of the rates in the range 12% to 18% is

	12%	13%	14%	15%	16%	17%	18%
NPV_X	$88,913	$79,804	$71,093	$62,759	$54,779	$47,135	$39,808
NPV_Y	74,907	67,848	61,097	54,638	48,454	42,529	36,851

We see that project X dominates project Y over the entire range of 12% to 18%. The
excess of NPV for project X over that for project Y is greater at the lower rates in the
range. Notice also that the NPVs computed in the table correspond to the NPV profile for

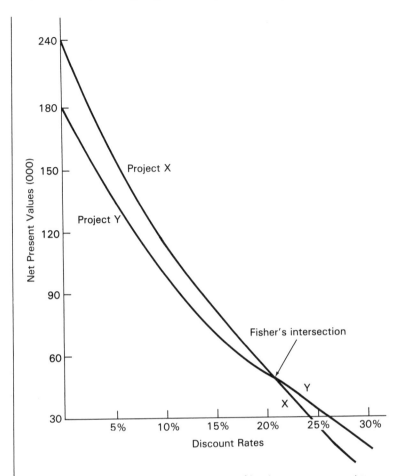

FIGURE 8–2   NPV Profiles for Projects X and Y

each project shown in Figure 8–2. The NPV profiles are relevant or exact for *only one branch shown in Figure 8–1—the branch where i = k and where they do not change over the lives of the projects.* These are the conditions that Alpha Company estimates will prevail for the two projects in question. Therefore, we can use Figure 8–2 or the table to rank projects X and Y.

Thus, given the estimated future conditions, Alpha Company should select project X rather than project Y because the NPV of project X exceeds that of project Y for all rates between 12% and 18%. The shareholders of Alpha Company will be *wealthier* in the amount of the difference between the two NPVs if the firm selects project X rather than project Y. This is true *even though project Y has a higher IRR.* In addition, as Figure 8–2 shows, project X continues to dominate project Y for all values of $i = k$ less than 20%. At rates in excess of Fisher's intersection, the preferred project shifts to project Y because at such rates for i and k, project Y has a greater NPV. This again shows the importance of Fisher's intersection and its utility in performing sensitivity analysis to rank mutually exclusive projects.

The ranking of the two projects in Example 1 was straightforward because the future conditions estimated by the firm enabled us to rank the projects using the basic NPV model. The firm could very well have envisioned a series of events that necessitated the computation of TV and NPV* properly to rank the projects under evaluation. For a slightly more complex problem setting, consider Example 2.

EXAMPLE 2

A Size Disparity with Changing Cost of Capital and
Reinvestment Rates

Alpha Company wants to rank the two projects under evaluation in Example 1 for the following conditions. First, the company estimates that i will equal k over the lives of the two projects. Second, rather than remaining constant at 16%, these two values (i and k) are estimated to be 16% for the first 2 years, 18% for the next 2 years, and 21% for the last 2 years of the projects' lives. Help Alpha Company select the correct evaluation technique and then rank projects X and Y.

SOLUTION: Using Figure 8–1, we see that NPV computed with Equation (2) is appropriate where $i = k$ and the values are changing over time. Thus, for project X:

$$\text{NPV}_X = \sum_{t=0}^{n} \frac{CI_t}{\prod_{j=1}^{t}(1 + k_j)} - \sum_{t=0}^{n} \frac{CO_t}{\prod_{j=1}^{t}(1 + k_j)}$$

$$= \frac{\$80,000}{1.16} + \frac{\$80,000}{(1.16)^2} + \frac{\$80,000}{(1.16)^2(1.18)} + \frac{\$80,000}{(1.16)^2(1.18)^2} + \frac{\$80,000}{(1.16)^2(1.18)^2(1.21)}$$

$$+ \frac{\$80,000}{(1.16)^2(1.18)^2(1.21)^2} - \$240,000$$

$$= \$68,966 + \$59,453 + \$50,384 + \$42,698 + \$35,288 + \$29,163 - \$240,000$$

$$= \$45,952$$

This calculation is slightly more involved than the one in Example 1. Here, even with a constant cash inflow over the project's life, the discount factors for each year must be computed rather than simply taken from tables of annuity discount factors. As we would expect, the NPV for project X here ($45,952) is less than that of Example 1 with a constant 16% rate ($54,779). This result occurs because the project contributes less to the value of the firm as the firm's cost of funds increases to 18% and 21% over the project's life.

For project Y,

$$\text{NPV}_Y = \frac{\$62,000}{1.16} + \frac{\$62,000}{(1.16)^2} + \frac{\$62,000}{(1.16)^2(1.18)} + \frac{\$62,000}{(1.16)^2(1.18)^2}$$

$$+ \frac{\$62,000}{(1.16)^2(1.18)^2(1.21)} + \frac{\$62,000}{(1.16)^2(1.18)^2(1.21)^2} - \$180,000$$

$$= \$53,448 + \$46,076 + \$39,048 + \$33,091 + \$27,348 + \$22,602 - \$180,000$$

$$= \$41,613$$

Given these calculations, we see that Alpha Company should rank project X first and project Y second. The difference of $4,339 in the NPV values again shows the amount by which the shareholders benefit by accepting project X rather than the project with the higher IRR (project Y). Recall that we are operating under the condition that capital rationing does not exist. Thus, the aditional expenditure required for project X is justified by the returns generated.

Projects with a Time Disparity

In addition to projects with differences in the original cash outflows, firms often encounter projects with the same cash outflow but differing patterns of cash inflows. In this latter case, the projects are called *mutually exclusive projects that exhibit a time disparity*. To rank such projects, we again use Figure 8–1 to arrive at the appropriate model.

EXAMPLE 3

Ranking Projects with a Time Disparity and Unequal (But Constant over Time) Values of i and k

Delta Company is evaluating projects A and B:

	PROJECT A	PROJECT B
Cash outflow	$70,000	$70,000
Cash inflows		
Year 1	10,000	50,000
2	20,000	40,000
3	30,000	20,000
4	45,000	10,000
5	60,000	10,000

Delta Company has a cost of capital of 14% and has computed the NPV, PI, and IRR for the two projects:

CRITERION	PROJECT A	PROJECT B
$NPV_{14\%}$	$32,219	$29,252
$PI_{14\%}$	1.46	1.42
IRR	27.2%	37.6%

Over the coming 5 years, Delta Company estimates that its cost of capital will remain constant at 14% but that its reinvestment rate will be 20%. Recall that all three models cited earlier would be in error relative to the reinvestment rate that Delta expects to experience. In particular, the NPV and PI assume that the cash inflows of each project will be reinvested at 14%, while the IRR model assumes that the cash inflows of project A can be reinvested at 27.2% while those of B can be reinvested at 37.6%. Provide assistance to Delta Company in selecting the right model and in ranking projects A and B.

SOLUTION: Referring to Figure 8–1, we see that if $i \neq k$ and both i and k are constant over the lives of the projects, we should use Equation (3) to compute the TV for each project and Equation (4) to compute the NPV*. The terminal value calculations would be as follows:

$$TV_A = \sum_{t=0}^{n} CI_t(1 + i)^{n-t}$$

$$= \$10,000(1.20)^{5-1} + \$20,000(1.20)^{5-2}$$

$$+ \$30,000(1.20)^{5-3} + \$45,000(1.20)^{5-4}$$

$$+ \$60,000(1.20)^{5-5}$$

This terminal value can either be computed directly or through the use of compound interest factors from column 1 on the 20% page in Appendix B,

$$TV_A = \$10,000(2.0736) + \$20,000(1.7280) + \$30,000(1.44)$$

$$+ \$45,000(1.20) + \$60,000$$

$$= \$212,496$$

For project B,

$$TV_B = \$50,000(2.0736) + \$40,000(1.7280) + \$20,000(1.44)$$

$$+ \$10,000(1.20) + \$10,000$$

$$= \$223,600$$

Ranking the projects, we find

$$NPV_A^* = \frac{TV_A}{(1 + k)^n} - CO_0$$

$$= \frac{\$212,496}{(1.14)^5} - \$70,000$$

$$= \$40,364$$

$$NPV_B^* = \frac{\$223,600}{(1.14)^5} - \$70,000$$

$$= \$46,131$$

Thus, we see that Delta Company should prefer project B to project A since $NPV_B^* = \$46,131$ is greater than $NPV_A^* = \$40,364$. Given that the firm can reinvest cash inflows at 20% over the next 5 years, project B will result in a net increase in the value of the firm of $46,131, while project A will yield a net increase of only $40,364 (both these figures are based on the firm's cost of capital being 14% over the next 5 years).

In Example 3, we assumed that, although $i \neq k$, both values remained constant over the lives of the two projects. The more usual case is when both values vary in the future depending on economic conditions, the level of interest rates, the competitive environment faced by the firm, and the like. Figure 8–1 and Equations (1)–(6), on which Example 3 is based, provide substantial flexibility in the treatment of changing values for i and k, as well as in the performance of sensitivity analysis. The next example illustrates this flexibility.

EXAMPLE 4

Time Disparity with Changing Cost of Capital and
Reinvestment Rates

Gamma Company is evaluating two mutually exclusive projects:

t	C	D
0	− $1,000,000	− $1,000,000
1	+ 300,000	+ 600,000
2	+ 700,000	+ 700,000
3	+ 1,500,000	+ 1,000,000

Gamma estimates that these values for i and k will prevail during each of the next 3 years:

t	k_t	i_t
1	12%	15%
2	13	18
3	14	20

Using Figure 8–1, rank projects C and D for Gamma Company.

SOLUTION: From Figure 8–1, we see that if $i \neq k$, and both i and k vary over the project lives, we should utilize Equation (6) to compute the TV of each project and then rank the projects using Equation (5) for NPV*. Equation 6 is

$$\text{TV} = \sum_{t=0}^{n} CI_t \left[\prod_{j=t+1}^{n} (1 + i_j) \right]$$

Note again that the compounding process starts in the year following each cash inflow (CI_t) because such flows take place at the end of each year t. Thus, in the given table of i- and k-values, the value for $i_1 = 15\%$ is extraneous information because the earliest that cash flows can be reinvested is during year 2, when $i_2 = 18\%$. We find

$$\text{TV}_C = \$300,000(1.18)(1.20) + \$700,000(1.20) + \$1,500,000$$

$$= \$2,764,800$$

$$\text{TV}_D = \$600,000(1.18)(1.20) + \$700,000(1.20) + \$1,000,000$$

$$= \$2,689,600$$

We next determine the NPV*:

$$NPV_C^* = \frac{TV_C}{\prod\limits_{j=1}^{n}(1+k_j)} - CO_0$$

$$= \frac{\$2,764,800}{(1.12)(1.13)(1.14)} - \$1,000,000$$

$$= \$916,295$$

$$NPV_D^* = \frac{\$2,689,600}{(1.12)(1.13)(1.14)} - \$1,000,000$$

$$= \$864,174$$

Thus, we see that Gamma Company should rank project C higher than project D because $NPV_C^* = \$916,295$ is greater than $NPV_D^* = \$864,174$. In present value terms, project C will increase shareholders' wealth by $52,121 more than will project D.

We have dealt with the treatment of mutually exclusive projects that have had either a size disparity or a time disparity. The ranking of such projects has been illustrated under a variety of conditions relative to the firm's required rate of return (or cost of capital) and the estimated reinvestment rate. The final type of disparity is that of unequal useful lives. This type of disparity combines the first two, in that projects with unequal lives usually require different cash outflows and have varying cash inflow patterns.

Projects with Unequal Useful Lives

It is sometimes argued that projects with unequal useful lives are inherently noncomparable because they have different durations of cash flows. Our position is that projects with unequal lives *are comparable* as long as the firm evaluating such projects can adequately address the critical question: *What will take place at the end of the shorter-lived project?* It can generally be assumed that at the end of the shorter-lived project, one of two types of reinvestment will occur: (1) the asset will be replaced with another possessing similar characteristics, or (2) the funds will be reinvested elsewhere by the firm at a specified reinvestment rate.

If the type of reinvestment can be pinpointed, we can rank mutually exclusive projects with unequal lives by calling upon the familiar approach outlined in Figure 8-1. To utilize the flow chart effectively, we must discuss several points.

First, we must compare the projects with a *common termination date*. This date can be *no earlier* than the *end of the longer-lived project* (if project abandonment is ruled out). If we assume that each project is replaced by another with similar characteristics, then the period over which the two *replacement chains*—the series of replacements of each asset by another with similar characteristics—must be compared is the *least common multiple of the lives of the two assets*. If we assume that at the end of the life of the shorter-lived asset the funds are reinvested elsewhere at a specified reinvestment rate, then the two assets should be compared over the period of the *longer-lived project*.

Second, the magnitude of the funds available for reinvestment elsewhere in the firm each year must be incorporated into the analysis through the TV calculation. This analysis will be demonstrated in Example 5.

Third, as we see in Figure 8–1, we must address three questions to appropriately discount the cash flows: (1) What is the firm's reinvestment rate? (2) What is the firm's cost of capital? (3) Will each of these values change over time?

We illustrate the application of this methodology in Example 5, which calls upon two projects originally cited by Solomon.[1]

EXAMPLE 5
The Evaluation of Replacement Chains for Two Assets

Mew Company is evaluating two projects:

t	PROJECT G	H
0	− $10,000	− $10,000
1	+ 12,000	0
2	0	0
3	0	0
4	0	+ 17,490

Mew computes these evaluation criteria based on its cost of capital of 12%:

CRITERION	PROJECT G	H
$NPV_{12\%}$	$714	$1,115
$PI_{12\%}$	1.07	1.11
IRR	20%	15%

Based on the foregoing analysis, it appears as though project H is more attractive on an NPV and a PI basis, and project G is more attractive using the IRR criterion.

However, this analysis ignores what takes place at the end of the life of project G. It is rather inequitable to compare project G, which has a 1-year life, with project H, which has a 4-year life; no consideration is given to the fact that the funds generated at the end of year 1 by project G can be reinvested until the end of year 4 (i.e., the end of project H's life).

When confronted with the above challenge, Mew states that if project G is implemented it will be replaced each year for four years with a similar machine by the same manufacturer. In addition, Mew states that excess cash flows generated by project G can be reinvested to earn 14% during year 2, 15% during year 3, and 16% during year 4.

Rank these two projects using the appropriate models.

[1]See Ezra Solomon, "The Arithmetic of Capital Budgeting Decisions," *The Journal of Business*, 29, no. 2 (April 1956), 124–129.

SOLUTION: Project H is unaffected by any of the factors given earlier since it is the longer-lived project and has no intermediate cash inflows. Thus, the terminal value of project H is $17,490 and its NPV* = $1,115.

On the other hand, to analyze project G we must perform three steps: (1) determine the net cash flows when considering the annual replacements, (2) determine the TV given the reinvestment of the net cash flows at the relevant rates stated above, and (3) compute NPV* based on the firm's cost of capital.

To determine the net cash flows for project G, this table is helpful:

TIME	REPLICATION OF PROJECT G				OVERALL NET CASH FLOW
	1	2	3	4	
0	− $10,000				− $10,000
1	+ 12,000	− $10,000			+ 2,000
2		+ 12,000	− $10,000		+ 2,000
3			+ 12,000	− $10,000	+ 2,000
4				+ 12,000	+ 12,000

To determine the terminal value of project G, we utilize the overall net cash flows generated by project G and the estimated reinvestment rates. We do this as follows:

$$\mathrm{TV}_G = \sum_{t=0}^{n} CI_t \left[\prod_{j=t+1}^{n} \left(1 + i_j \right) \right]$$

$$= \$2,000(1.14)(1.15)(1.16)$$

$$+ \$2,000(1.15)(1.16) + \$2,000(1.16) + \$12,000$$

$$= \$20,030$$

Finally, we compute NPV* for project G:

$$\mathrm{NPV}_G = \frac{\mathrm{TV}_G}{(1 + k)^n} - CO_0$$

$$= \frac{\$20,030}{(1.12)^4} - \$10,000$$

$$= \$2,729$$

Therefore, we see that $\mathrm{NPV}_G^* = \$2,729$ and $\mathrm{NPV}_H^* = \$1,115$. Clearly, the successive replacements of project G over four years dominate the performance of project H. Mew Company should select project G.

Example 5 illustrates the treatment of unequal project lives, wherein it is assumed that the shorter-lived project is replaced at the end of its life with an asset with the same cost and benefits as the original asset.

The recommended methodology encounters no difficulties in handling any other pattern of costs and benefits associated with the replications of the shorter-lived project. In times of high rates of inflation, it is unlikely that future project-related costs and benefits will remain unchanged. Although we treat the problem of inflation in depth in Chapter 9, at this point it is sufficient to state the simple rule that one way to handle inflation is to discount the inflated costs and benefits at a rate that also incorporates the impact of inflation on the firm's cost of capital. Example 6 demonstrates how unequal, useful-lived projects are handled to incorporate the effects of inflation.

EXAMPLE 6

The Evaluation of Replacement Chains with Inflation Factored In

The Sigma Company is evaluating two projects:

t	J	K
0	− $40,000	− $54,000
1	+ 30,000	+ 25,000
2	+ 33,000	+ 27,750
3		+ 30,802

Sigma needs the use of this type of asset for at least the next 6 years (which happens to be the least common multiple of the lives of these two assets); thus, each asset will be replaced at the end of its life with a similar one from the same manufacturer.

Sigma has observed purchase prices of these two assets over the last decade. Project J has had price increases that average 12% compounded annually, while project K has had compounded annual price increases of 14%. Sigma expects these trends to continue over the next 6 years.

In addition to the differing effects of inflation on the purchase prices of these two assets, inflation impacts the operating costs—and thus the cash inflows—of the two assets differently. Sigma estimates (as shown in the table) that the cash inflows for project J will grow at 10% compounded annually, while project K's cash inflows will grow at 11% compounded annually. Again, this pattern is expected to continue over the next 6 years.

Finally, Sigma estimates that its cost of capital after the impact of inflation and its reinvestment rates over the next 6 years will be as follows:

t	i_t	k_t
1	18%	12%
2	14	13
3	15	14
4	17	16
5	20	17
6	22	19

Use Figure 8–1 to help Sigma rank projects J and K.

SOLUTION: We begin the analysis by preparing for each project a table that determines the overall net cash flow given the necessary number of replications to cover 6 years. A similar table was prepared in Example 5.

For project J,

t	REPLICATION OF PROJECT J			OVERALL NET CASH FLOW
	1	2	3	
0	− $40,000			− $40,000
1	+ 30,000			+ 30,000
2	+ 33,000	− $50,176		− 17,176
3		+ 36,300		+ 36,300
4		+ 39,930	− $62,941	− 23,011
5			+ 43,923	+ 43,923
6			+ 48,315	+ 48,315

For project K,

t	REPLICATION OF PROJECT K		OVERALL NET CASH FLOW
	1	2	
0	− $54,000		− $54,000
1	+ 25,000		+ 25,000
2	+ 27,750		+ 27,750
3	+ 30,802	− $80,003	− 49,201
4		+ 34,191	+ 34,191
5		+ 37,952	+ 37,952
6		+ 42,126	+ 42,126

Using the final column in each of these tables, we can now compute the terminal value at the end of year 6. Referring to Figure 8–1, we see that Equation (6) should be used to compute these TV values due to the changing reinvestment rates over the next 6 years. In addition, recall that only the *cash inflows* will be compounded in the TV calculation. Once computed, the TV will be used in Equation (5) for NPV*.

For project J,

$$TV_J = \sum_{t=0}^{6} CI_t \left[\prod_{j=t+1}^{6} (1 + i_j) \right]$$

$$= \$30,000(1.14)(1.15)(1.17)(1.2)(1.22)$$
$$+ \$36,300(1.17)(1.2)(1.22) + \$43,923(1.22)$$
$$+ \$48,315$$
$$= \$67,368 + \$62,178 + \$53,586 + \$48,315$$
$$= \$231,447$$

For project K,

$$TV_K = \sum_{t=0}^{6} CI_t \left[\prod_{j=t+1}^{6} (1 + i_j) \right]$$

$$= \$25,000(1.14)(1.15)(1.17)(1.20)(1.22)$$
$$+ \$27,750(1.15)(1.17)(1.20)(1.22)$$
$$+ \$34,191(1.20)(1.22) + \$37,952(1.22) + \$42,126$$
$$= \$56,140 + \$54,662 + \$50,056 + \$46,301 + \$42,126$$
$$= \$249,285$$

Finally, we are ready to compute NPV* for each project. Figure 8–1 indicates that Equation (5) is appropriate based on the changing k-values over the next 6 years.

$$NPV^* = \frac{TV}{\prod\limits_{j=1}^{n}\left(1+k_j\right)} - \sum_{t=0}^{n}\frac{CO_t}{\prod\limits_{j=1}^{t}\left(1+k_j\right)}$$

Notice that both projects will require discounting the cash outflows using the second term on the right-hand side of the preceding equation. That is, any cash outflows shown in the table prepared for each project in the *overall net cash flow* column beyond year 0 must be discounted back to time 0.

$$NPV_J^* = \frac{\$231{,}447}{(1.12)(1.13)(1.14)(1.16)(1.17)(1.19)} - \$40{,}000$$

$$- \frac{\$17{,}176}{(1.12)(1.13)} - \frac{\$23{,}011}{(1.12)(1.13)(1.14)(1.16)}$$

$$= \$99{,}325 - \$67{,}321$$

$$= \$32{,}004$$

$$NPV_K^* = \frac{\$249{,}285}{(1.12)(1.13)(1.14)(1.16)(1.17)(1.19)} - \$54{,}000$$

$$- \frac{\$49{,}201}{(1.12)(1.13)(1.14)}$$

$$= \$106{,}980 - 88{,}101$$

$$= \$18{,}879$$

Thus, we see that project J is significantly more attractive to Sigma than is project K, based on the NPV* values. The analysis that led to this conclusion has incorporated the effects of inflation, the sequence of replacements necessary to have 6 years of service from each asset, the varying reinvestment rates over time, and Sigma Company's changing cost of capital with inflation reflected.

The approach illustrated in Example 6 provides an appropriate methodology for ranking projects with unequal lives as long as the assumption is valid that each project will be replaced by one of similar profitability until a common horizon date. If this is not the case, we need to know the best estimate for the rate at which cash flows from each project can be reinvested up to a common horizon date (usually the end of the useful life of the longer-lived project). Given this estimate (which could vary from year to year), we can call upon the techniques of the previous section and find the terminal value (TV) and NPV*. As shown in Figure 8–1, the latter approach should be implemented any time that projects with unequal lives are analyzed and the reinvestment rate differs from the cost of capital.

EXAMPLE 7

Unequal Useful Lives with Differing Reinvestment Rates

The Tau Company, with a present cost of capital of 14%, is evaluating two mutually exclusive projects that have different useful lives:

t	P	Q
0	− $10,000	− $12,000
1	+ 5,506	+ 4,991
2	+ 5,506	+ 4,991
3	+ 5,506	+ 4,991
4		+ 4,991
IRR	30%	24%
$NPV_{14\%}$	$2,783	$2,542
$PI_{14\%}$	1.278	1.212

As can be seen by the three measures of project attractiveness computed above, project P dominates project Q. However, management believes that during the next 4 years there will be changes in business conditions that will result in the reinvestment rates and costs of capital shown in the following table:

t	i_t	k_t
1	16%	14%
2	18	10
3	19	10
4	20	10

Rank the two projects for Tau Company under the assumption that the cash inflows for each project will be reinvested at the rates shown and that neither project will be replaced at the end of its life. Recall that a common terminal horizon (i.e., the life of the longer project) must be used to evaluate the projects.

SOLUTION: Based on Figure 8–1, we use Equation (6) to compute the terminal value for each project:

$$TV = \sum_{t=0}^{n} S_t \left[\prod_{j=t+1}^{n} (1 + i_j) \right]$$

$$TV_P = \$5,506[(1.18)(1.19)(1.20)]$$
$$+ \$5,506[(1.19)(1.20)] + \$5,506(1.20)$$
$$= \$9,278 + \$7,863 + \$6,607$$
$$= \$23,748$$

$$TV_Q = \$4,991[(1.18)(1.19)(1.20)]$$
$$+ \$4,991[(1.19)(1.20)] + \$4,991(1.20)$$
$$+ \$4,991$$
$$= \$8,410 + \$7,127 + \$5,989 + \$4,991$$
$$= \$26,517$$

Finally, we rank the two projects with NPV* using Equation (5):

$$NPV^* = \frac{TV}{\prod_{j=1}^{n}(1+k_j)} - \sum_{t=0}^{n}\frac{CO_t}{\prod_{j=1}^{n}(1+k_j)}$$

$$NPV_P^* = \frac{\$23{,}748}{(1.14)(1.10)(1.10)(1.10)} - \$10{,}000$$

$$= \$5{,}651$$

$$NPV_Q^* = \frac{\$26{,}517}{(1.14)(1.10)(1.10)(1.10)} - \$12{,}000$$

$$= \$5{,}476$$

Thus, we see that, based on the new estimates for i_t and k_t, project P is slightly more attractive than project Q.

This concludes our examination of mutually exclusive projects. We have shown how Figure 8–1 provides the financial analyst with the proper model to rank any set of mutually exclusive projects under any conditions relative to costs of capital and reinvestment rates.

SUMMARY

Preceding sections focus on the complications frequently encountered in practice when the financial manager grapples with formulation of the firm's capital budget. The issues presented really represent a set of signals suggesting further investigation. The financial manager should exercise caution whenever the following situations arise:

1   The projects analyzed are different in size.
2   The projects have different life spans.
3   The cash flow patterns (increasing, decreasing, or uniform) vary from one project to the next.
4   The company's future reinvestment opportunities are expected to change significantly from the present set of investment options.
5   The firm's marginal cost of capital is expected to rise significantly over time.
6   There exist capital and/or labor constraints on the budget.

Under any of the foregoing circumstances, the mechanical application of ranking techniques without regard to the underlying assumptions can trap the financial manager into manifestly wrong decisions. Therefore, we present Figure 8–1 to provide a framework for the correct analysis and ranking of mutually exclusive projects. The approach of Figure 8–1 is couched in NPV and NPV* terms because of the *uniquely consistent superiority of this approach in maximizing shareholders' wealth.*

The financial manager will construct the capital budget to maximize the present value of the firm; this suggests the acceptance of new capital projects as long as the project shows a positive NPV or NPV*. The preferred capital budget is that combination of projects which maximizes total NPV or NPV*. The strategy holds even if the firm must resort to new financing to absorb all viable projects. In reality, new financing may not be feasible for several reasons, such as delays entailed in marketing new securities, problems of corporate control created by new stockholders, and restrictive provisions in bond indentures.

More important perhaps than the limits imposed by financing arrangements is the ability of the firm to digest new projects due to labor bottlenecks and scarce management talent. A capital budget is not simply an exercise in applied finance, but comprises a host of technological and managerial problems. Consequently, for a variety of reasons, the firm may be pragmatically stopped from accepting more than a restricted number of projects in a given time period.

What principle should guide the preparation of a capital budget in the presence of such constraints? Within the limits imposed by the constraints, the firm should select that combination of projects which maximizes the NPV of the budget. To accomplish that objective, management might have to look beyond the present fiscal period to a longer planning horizon. These problems—the need to allocate resources to projects over several fiscal periods, limited financial and managerial resources, and technological uncertainties—become critically important in constructing a capital budget and modify the strict adherence to the NPV criterion implied by Figure 8–1. The problem of maximizing NPV subject to such stated constraints is best described and resolved by mathematical programming techniques discussed in Chapters 20 and 21.

QUESTIONS
PROBLEMS

1. Discuss four aspects of the capital budgeting problem setting that must be addressed to select the appropriate model to rank mutually exclusive projects.

2. Discuss those characteristics of capital projects and the firm that warrant special attention when making capital investment decisions.

3. When projects have unequal useful lives, what are the two major alternatives that the firm has at the end of the life of the shorter project? How is each of these alternatives treated in ranking mutually exclusive projects with unequal lives?

4. If a firm estimates that $i = k$ over the life of the two mutually exclusive projects under evaluation, can the NPV profiles be used to rank the projects? Why or why not? If so, how would this be done?

5. Can NPV profiles be drawn when the firm feels that either i or k or both will change over the projects' lives? Why or why not?

6. State one approach for the treatment of capital investment evaluation under inflationary conditions.

7. The following two mutually exclusive projects are under evaluation:

YEAR	PROJECT A	PROJECT B
Present	– $25,000	– $25,000
1	10,000	0
2	10,000	5,000
3	10,000	10,000
4	10,000	30,000

(a) Determine the NPV of projects A and B. The firm's cost of capital is 10%.
(b) Determine the IRR of projects A and B.
(c) What is the reinvestment rate assumed under IRR?
(d) State *completely* the reasons for the conflict in ranking these two projects by NPV and IRR.
(e) Assume that the firm estimates that its cost of capital will remain at 10% but that the reinvestment rates over the next 4 years will be

t	i_t
1	10%
2	12
3	14
4	16

Rank the two projects.

8. XYZ Company is evaluating the following two mutually exclusive projects:

YEAR	PROJECT A	PROJECT B
Present	− $20,000	− $20,000
1	5,000	17,000
2	9,000	5,000
3	16,000	5,000

Over the coming 3 years, the firm estimates that the following reinvestment rates and costs of capital will be encountered:

t	i_t	k_t
1	12%	12%
2	14	13
3	18	16

Rank these two projects using the appropriate methodology.

9. The Rinky Dink Rickshaw Transport Company has a capital budget of $15,000. There are two alternative projects in which the entire sum may be invested: Graffiti Remover and a Roach Zapper. Each project has an initial cost of $15,000 and an estimated life of 4 years. The Roach Zapper will produce greater returns later in the project life, owing to the tenacious quality of Rickshaw roaches and the difficulty in extermination. The Graffiti Remover will produce greater returns at the beginning of the project, because the machine will become less efficient as it gets older.

ROACH ZAPPER		GRAFFITI REMOVER	
YEAR	CASH FLOWS	YEAR	CASH FLOWS
0	− $15,000	0	− $15,000
1	3,500	1	8,000
2	5,000	2	6,500
3	6,000	3	4,000
4	8,000	4	2,000

Rinky Dink's cost of capital is 14% and the reinvestment rate is 17%. Rank these two projects using the appropriate methodology.

10. Ms. Surekill, the administrator of Savelife Hospital, a small general-care hospital in the Appalachian Mountains, is in a quandary. She has alleviated all her capital budgeting problems for the coming fiscal year except for the electrocardiology and stress-testing departments.

EKG is an established department, which prefers to buy a new electrocardiograph machine every 4 years. It has two machines at present. The newest machine has been the primary machine for the past 4 years, with the older machine used as backup. Most of the income from a new machine, if purchased, would be in the first 4 years.

Stress Testing, on the other hand, is a new department that wants a treadmill device used to measure stress on the cardiovascular system. Since it is a new department, not yet in operation, its estimated income would be low initially but would increase as the availability of the new test became known to the house staff and was accepted by them.

The following table illustrates the expected after-tax cash flows by year for the two machines, each of which would cost $10,000:

YEAR	EKG	STRESS TEST
Present	− $10,000	− $10,000
1	4,000	1,000
2	4,000	1,000
3	4,000	1,000
4	4,000	3,000
5	1,000	3,000
6	1,000	3,000
7	1,000	7,000
8	1,000	7,000

Savelife faces an increasing reinvestment rate over the coming 8 years, starting at 12% and increasing by 2% per year. The hospital's cost of capital is 18% and will remain constant over the next 10 years. Rank these two projects for Ms. Surekill.

11. Mr. I. M. Kool, a manager at the NoSweat Air Conditioning Company, is faced with the prospect of having to replace one of the large machines used in the plant. Two machines currently on the market will perform the job satisfactorily—the Hi-Grade and Superior machines. The expected after-tax cash flows for each machine are

YEAR	HI-GRADE	YEAR	SUPERIOR
0	− $60,000	0	− $80,000
1	15,000	1	24,000
2	16,500	2	24,000
3	20,000	3	20,000
4	20,000	4	20,000
5	20,000	5	18,000
6	20,000	6	18,000

The firm's cost of capital is 16%, and its reinvestment rate is 20%. Rank the two projects.

12. The Waltzer Company is evaluating the following two mutually exclusive projects:

TIME	PROJECT A	PROJECT B
0	− $20,000	− $20,000
1	+ 5,000	+ 16,000
2	+ 8,000	+ 10,000
3	+ 10,000	+ 5,000
4	+ 20,000	+ 5,000

(a) Based only on observation, which project would you expect IRR to prefer? Which project would you expect NPV to prefer? Assuming $i = k = 15\%$. Explain why.

(b) Compute the IRR and NPV of projects A and B.

(c) $k = 15\%$ over the life of the project and $i = 18\%$ over the life of the project. Which project is preferred?

13. For the two projects under evaluation by the Waltzer Company in Problem 12, assume the following changes in i and k over the life of the projects:

t	i_t	k_t
1	20%	15%
2	15	12
3	12	10
4	10	10

Which project is preferred? Show your work.

14. For the two projects under evaluation by the Waltzer Company in Problem 12, assume $i = 18\%$ over the life of the projects, but k varies as follows:

t	k_t
1	15%
2	12
3	10
4	10

Which project is preferable?

15. For the two projects under evaluation by the Waltzer Company in Problem 12, assume $k = 10\%$ over the life of the project, but i varies as follows:

t	i_t
1	20%
2	15
3	12
4	10

Which project is preferred?

16. For the two projects under evaluation by the Waltzer Company in Problem 12, assume the following changes in i and k over the life of the project:

t	i_t	k_t
1	20%	10%
2	15	12
3	15	12
4	10	10

Which project is preferred?

17. The Philly Bus Service wants to add to its fleet in order to improve its service. It has a choice of two models:
   (a) Model O: 3-year life, cost of $26,000, and cash inflow of $12,000 per year.
   (b) Model P: 4-year life, cost of $38,000, and cash inflows of $19,000 per year.

   Assume that each bus will be replaced at the end of its life by a model with the same cost and future benefits. Assume further that Philly's cost of capital is 14% and its reinvestment rate is 18%. Rank the two projects.

18. For the two projects shown in Problem 17, assume that the cost of model O will increase by 12% per year, while model P will increase by 10% per year. In addition, assume that the benefits of model O are $12,000 in the first year and will increase at 8% each year thereafter. Benefits of model P are $19,000 in the first year and will increase at 11% each year thereafter. The firm's reinvestment rate remains at 18%, but its cost of capital starts at 14% and increases by 1% each year thereafter. Rank the two projects under these new conditions reflecting inflationary effects.

19. Edna Finn, restaurateur de premier classe, has $10,000 to invest in round-lot purchases of French red wine. She may buy $10,000 shipments of freshly bottled Bordeaux or Beaujolais. Beaujolais matures quickly and must be consumed within the first several years of bottling. Bordeaux takes a longer time to mature and its value is greater in later years. The cash flows resulting from the two mutually exclusive purchases and subsequent sale are as follows:

YEAR	BEAUJOLAIS	BORDEAUX
0	– $10,000	– $10,000
1	8,000	0
2	5,000	0
3	3,000	0
4	2,000	0
5	1,000	0
6	1,000	0
7		7,000
8		7,000
9		11,000
10		11,000
11		18,000
12		18,000

The restaurateur expects a reinvestment rate of 12% in the first 3 years, 14% in years 4–6, and 16% for the duration of the Bordeaux. Cost of capital is expected to be 12% for 6 years and 15% for the last 6 years. Rank the two projects.

20. For the two projects shown in Example 1 and for the values $i = k = 12\%$, 15%, and 18%, show that (a) the TV [using Equation (3)] for project X is greater than the TV for project Y, and (b) the NPV* [using Equation (4)] for project X is greater than the NPV* for project Y. [The NPV* values will equal NPV for each project demonstrating that when $i = k$ and these values remain constant, Equation (1) is just a simplification of Equations (3) and (4).]

21. Show the following:
(a) Equation (1) will result when all k_j are equal in Equation (2).
(b) Equation (2) results when $i_j = k_j$ in Equation (5).
(c) Equation (1) results when $i = k$ in Equation (4).

REFERENCES

Bacon, Peter W. "The Evaluation of Mutually Exclusive Investments." *Financial Management*, 6 (Summer 1977), 55–58.

Balachandran, Bala V., Nandu J. Nagarajan, and Alfred Rappaport. "Threshold Margins for Creating Economic Value." *Financial Management* (Spring 1986).

Beranek, William. "Some New Capital Budgeting Theorems." *Journal of Financial and Quantitative Analysis*, 13 (December 1978), 809–829.

Carter, E. Eugene. "Designing the Capital Budgeting Process." *TIMS Studies in the Management Sciences*, 5 (1977), 25–42.

Downs, Thomas W. "The User Cost and Capital Budgeting." *Financial Review* (May 1986).

Emery, Gary W. "Some Guidelines for Evaluating Capital Investment Alternatives with Unequal Lives." *Financial Management*, 11 (Spring 1982), 14–18.

Ezzell, John R. and William A. Kelly, Jr. "An APV Analysis of Capital Budgeting Under Inflation." *Financial Management* (Autumn 1984).

Fama, Eugene F. "Components of Investment Performance." *Journal of Finance*, 27 (June 1972), 551–557.

Gordon, Myron. *The Investment, Financing, and Valuation of the Corporation.* Homewood, Ill.: Richard D. Irwin, Inc., 1962.

Hirshleifer, J. *Investment, Interest and Capital.* Englewood Cliffs, N.J.: Prentice Hall, 1970.

_____. "On the Theory of Optimal Investment Decision." *Journal of Political Economy*, 66 (August 1958).

_____. "Hurdle Rate for Screening Capital Expenditure Proposals." *Financial Management*, 4 (Autumn 1975), 17–26.

Porterfield, J. T. *Investment Decisions and Capital Costs.* Englewood Cliffs, N.J.: Prentice Hall, 1965.

Pratt, John W., and John S. Hammond, III. "Evaluating and Comparing Projects: Simple Detection of False Alarms." *Journal of Finance*, 34 (December 1979), 1231–1242.

Statman, Meir, and T. Craig Tapley. "Optimistic Capital Budgeting Forecasts: An Experiment." *Financial Management* (Autumn 1985).

Solomon, Ezra. "The Arithmetic of Capital-Budgeting Decisions." *Journal of Business*, 29 (April 1956), 124–129.

Teichroew, Daniel, Alexander A. Robichek, and Michael Montalbano. "An Analysis of Criteria for Investment and Financing Decisions under Certainty." *Management Science*, 12 (November 1965), 151–179.

Trueman, Brett. "The Relationship between the Level of Capital Expenditures and Firm Value." *Journal of Financial and Quantitative Analysis* (June 1986).

Weaver, James B. "Organizing and Maintaining a Capital Expenditure Program." *Engineering Economist*, 20 (Fall 1974), 1–36.

The Management of Forecasting, Sensitivity Analysis, and Adjustment for Price Trends

9

This chapter deals with estimating the cash flows that form the basis of capital budgeting. During the first eight chapters we assumed that the cash flows were given and evaluated the attractiveness of proposed projects. But, forecasting cash flows is probably the most critical part of the entire capital budgeting process. If these estimates are not accurate, then any analysis, regardless of its detail and sophistication, will probably lead to less than optimal decisions.

In theory, estimating cash flows is a reasonably simple and straightforward process consisting of two steps:

1   Forecast the costs, sales, and expenses as they relate to a particular project.
2   Include in these estimates depreciation and other tax factors, and compute the after-tax cost (cash outflows) and revenues (cash inflows) expected to result from the implementation of the project over its useful life.

As a practical matter, the first step is more difficult and more critical. We discuss it in this chapter. The second step (dealing with depreciation and the tax laws) is complicated, but can be accomplished by a good tax accountant or attorney. We examined these topics in depth in Chapter 4.

THE ROLE OF FORECASTING IN THE CAPITAL BUDGETING PROCESS

The entire capital budgeting process hinges on the precision of the forecasts of the cash outflows and inflows surrounding a project. Thus, it is important for the analyst to obtain accurate forecasts and have some measure of the *reliability of those forecasts* regardless of the fact that he or she is seldom responsible for actually generating the forecasts. Rather, the analyst must do two things:

1   Identify all the variables that factor into the cash flows and determine which of those variables are critical to the success of the project. The latter part of this process is called *sensitivity analysis.* As an example, we noted earlier that the sensitivity of a project's NPV to inaccurate estimates of salvage value decreases rapidly as increasingly higher discount rates are used. Consequently, in periods of high interest rates, we should not allocate much time or other resources to refining the forecasts of salvage value. Rather, *at the onset it is essential to identify those elements of a project which will have a pronounced effect on its success.* These are the elements that warrant the allocation of resources necessary to obtain accurate forecasts and these are the elements that warrant close monitoring both during the acquisition process and after the project's implementation.

2   Indicate to those generating the estimates the degree of forecasting accuracy required and plan to analyze the design of the forecasting systems used to produce the estimates.

In carrying out these two steps, the analyst must keep in mind that the "riskiness" surrounding any project may result from the *inherent riskiness of the project itself,* as in basic research and development (R & D), and/or from *the use of forecasting methods that yield erroneous estimates.* The replacement of an existing machine may turn out to be more risky than implementing an R & D project if the sales forecasts used to base the demand for the machine's output are poorly designed and lead to exaggerated estimates of cash inflows.

Thus, the goal of this chapter is to describe methods that may be used to identify those factors critical to a project's success or failure and to indicate how to evaluate forecasts in terms of their probable reliability with respect to the project being evaluated.

DETERMINING THE KEY VARIABLES — SENSITIVITY ANALYSIS

To start the process of determining key variables, consider Example 1 which represents a typical industrial capital budgeting replacement decision, including forecasts for inflation.

EXAMPLE 1
Replacement Investment Decision

A corporation is considering the acquisition of a machine with an estimated cost of $30,000. The machine is to replace an existing machine, which has been fully depreciated and is estimated to have negligible salvage value but can be used for the foreseeable future. The new machine is expected to have a 10-year useful life. The rationale for the purchase of the new machine has been presented by the plant engineer, who anticipates two advantages:

1   Reduction in down-time and maintenance. Down-time for the existing machine is about 3 hours per week. This results in one worker sitting idle while repairs are made. It is expected that regular off-shift maintenance could keep the new machine operating a full 40 hours per week.

2 Increased output and reduced unit labor cost. Output could be increased to 12,800 units per year from the current 10,000, while dropping unit labor costs in current dollars to $1.40 from the current $2.30.

The internal cost accountants have provided the following cost analysis for the output currently produced:

	PER UNIT	PER YEAR (10,000 UNITS)
Sales	$10.00	$100,000
Cost of goods sold		
Labor	$2.30	$23,000
Materials	1.00	10,000
Utilities/fuel	0.80	8,000
Other	1.70	17,000
	− $ 5.80	− $ 58,000
Sales expenses	− 2.80	− 28,000
Depreciation*	− 0.10	− 1,000
Earnings before taxes	$ 1.30	$ 13,000
Taxes (46%)	− 0.60	− 6,000
Earnings after taxes	$ 0.70	$ 7,000

*Depreciation for other facilities is allocated at $0.10 per unit.

The sales department indicates that there have been some back orders for the product and that it could sell 10,500 units per year now with a 4% annual increase in unit sales volume until the capacity volume of 12,800 units per year is reached. It expects that the per unit sales expense will be the same for any additional volume sold, before considering the impact of inflation.

The treasurer's office requires a 15% after-tax hurdle rate at present for projects of this type, but the treasurer expects both the hurdle rate and reinvestment rates to change over the 10-year project life as follows:

YEAR	HURDLE RATE	REINVESTMENT RATE
Present	15%	—
1	16	16%
2	15	16
3	14	15
4–10	13	14

The corporate economist has estimated the following average inflation rates for the next 10-year period:

ITEM	AVERAGE ANNUAL INCREASE
Sale price	8%
Labor	7
Materials	10
Utilities/fuel	15
Other	7
Sales expense	8
Depreciation	N/A
Taxes	N/A

Based on the information provided, develop pro forma income and cash flow statements with and without the new machine for the 10-year expected life. Compute the project's terminal value, net present value, and internal rate of return.

SOLUTION: The solution is straightforward, but requires numerous tedious calculations; it is thus most appropriately solved using a LOTUS 1-2-3 template such as that provided with this text. Pro forma profit and loss statements and cash flow reports for years 1 and 10 are given, along with an income and cash flow summary. On the income and cash flow summary, the net present value was determined by subtracting $30,000 (purchase cost) from the present value of the difference in cash inflows between the new and old machines. The net present value is $27,779.30, indicating that the new machine is a viable candidate and should be considered for acceptance.

INCOME AND CASH FLOW SUMMARY

	WITHOUT PROJECT		WITH PROJECT	
PERIOD	NET INCOME	CASH FLOW	NET INCOME	CASH FLOW
1	$7,020.00	$ 8,020.00	$10,044.00	$15,594.00
2	7,430.40	8,430.40	10,228.60	17,920.60
3	7,832.59	8,832.59	11,812.50	19,248.20
4	8,219.09	9,219.09	13,337.60	20,818.70
5	8,580.77	9,580.77	14,963.40	22,491.70
6	8,906.55	9,906.55	20,085.80	21,363.30
7	9,183.05	10,183.10	21,090.10	22,370.10
8	9,394.26	10,394.30	22,013.90	23,293.90
9	9,521.00	10,521.00	22,875.40	24,155.40
10	9,540.13	10,540.13	23,648.06	24,928.06

Terminal value	$210,379.00
Present value	$ 57,779.30
Net present value	$ 27,779.30
Internal rate of return	23%

PROFIT AND LOSS STATEMENT
PERIOD 1

	WITHOUT PROJECT			WITH PROJECT		
		UNIT	10,000 UNITS		UNIT	10,500 UNITS
Sales		$10.00	$100,000.00		$10.00	$105,000.00
Cost of goods sold						
Labor	$2.30	$23,000.00		$1.40	$14,700.00	
Material	1.00	10,000.00		1.00	10,500.00	
Utilities/fuel	0.80	8,000.00		0.80	8,400.00	
Other	1.70	17,000.00		1.70	17,850.00	
	− $ 5.80		−$ 58,000.00	− $ 4.90		− $ 51,450.00
Sales exp.	− 2.80		− 28,000.00	− 2.80		− 29,400.00
Depreciation	− 0.10		− 1,000.00	− 0.53		− 5,550.00
Earnings before taxes	$ 1.30		$ 13,000.00	$ 1.77		$ 18,600.00
Taxes (46%)	− 0.60		− 5,980.00	− 0.81		− 8,556.00
Earnings after taxes	$ 0.70		$ 7,020.00	$ 0.96		$ 10,044.00

CASH FLOW REPORT FOR PERIOD 1

	WITHOUT PROJECT	WITH PROJECT	DIFFERENCE
Net income	$7,020.00	$10,044.00	$3,024.00
Depreciation	1,000.00	5,550.00	4,550.00
Cash flow	$8,020.00	$15,594.00	$7,574.00

PROFIT AND LOSS STATEMENT
PERIOD 10

	WITHOUT PROJECT		WITH PROJECT	
	UNIT	10,000 UNITS	UNIT	12,800 UNITS
Sales	$19.99	$199,900.00	$19.99	$255,872.00
Cost of goods sold				
Labor	$4.23	$42,284.60	$2.57	$32,945.20
Material	2.36	23,579.50	2.36	30,181.70
Utilities/fuel	2.81	28,143.00	2.81	36,023.10
Other	3.13	31,253.00	3.13	40,004.90
	− $12.53	− $125,260.90	− $10.87	− $139,154.90
Sales exp.	− 5.60	− 55,972.20	− 5.60	− 71,644.40
Depreciation	− 0.10	− 1,000.00	− 0.10	− 1,280.00
Earnings before taxes	$ 1.76	$ 17,666.90	$ 3.42	$ 43,792.70
Taxes (46%)	− 0.81	− 8,126.77	− 1.57	− 20,144.64
Net income	$ 0.95	$ 9,540.13	$ 1.85	$ 23,648.06

CASH FLOW REPORT FOR PERIOD 10

	WITHOUT PROJECT	WITH PROJECT	DIFFERENCE
Net income	$ 9,540.13	$23,648.06	$14,107.93
Depreciation	1,000.00	1,280.00	280.00
Cash flow	$10,540.13	$24,928.06	$14,387.93

The next step is to determine which of the variables are critical to the success of the project. This requires a sensitivity analysis—asking how much the final outcome (net present value) would change as a result of errors in the estimates or changes in the decision environment. One of the significant capabilities of spreadsheet packages such as LOTUS 1-2-3 is the ease of performing a detailed sensitivity analysis which considers numerous modifications and determines the final results within seconds of computer time. In Example 2, we examine each variable to determine its sensitivity.

EXAMPLE 2

Key Variable Determination — Sensitivity Analysis

Recompute the net present value based on each of the following changes to original estimates. Tabulate the results showing the dollar and percentage change in net present value. Analyze the results and indicate the key variables.

1 Volume increases to 10,500 units and remains level (does not increase yearly to 12,800 units).

2 Unit labor cost decreases to $1.68 rather than to $1.40.

3 The hurdle rates and reinvestment rates are 2% higher than estimated in each of the 10 years.

4 The hurdle rates and reinvestment rates are as anticipated for years 1–3, but are 2% higher than estimated in each of the succeeding years.

5 The sales price increases only 6.4% annually rather than the estimated 8%.

6 Labor costs increase 8.4% annually rather than the estimated 7%.

7 Materials costs increase 12% annually rather than the estimated 10%.

8 Utilities and fuel costs increase 18% annually rather than the estimated 15%.

SOLUTION: The results are tabulated as follows:

CHANGE	REVISED NPV	DECREASE IN NPV DOLLAR	DECREASE IN NPV PERCENTAGE
1. Volume of 10,500	$17,507	$10,272	37%
2. Unit labor of $1.68	16,319	11,460	41
3. Hurdle and reinvestment rates plus 2%	13,190	4,589	17
4. Hurdle and reinvestment rates plus 2%, years 4–10	26,224	1,555	6
5. Sale price increases 6.4% annually	19,500	8,279	30
6. Labor increases 8.4% annually	16,320	11,459	41
7. Materials increase 12% annually	26,489	1,290	5
8. Utilities and fuel increase 10% annually	26,511	1,268	5

The results of the sensitivity analysis indicate that the key variables are volume, labor cost, and annual changes in sale price and labor costs. If sales volume does not increase as anticipated, the project's NPV will decrease by 33%. A further sensitivity analysis might be advisable to determine the outcome if, for example, sales volume fell from the current 10,000 units to a "worst case." At this point, the analyst should suggest some possible volumes, such as 7,000 or 8,000, and ask the sales department to estimate the probability of such volumes. Corresponding NPVs will indicate to management the potential for downside risk resulting from reductions in volume.

The estimate in unit labor costs is another crucial factor. If unit labor decreases to $1.68 rather than $1.40, the NPV will decrease 37%. The remaining two most sensitive variables are the annual increase in sales price and the annual increase in labor costs. Twenty percent errors in these estimates will result in 27% and 37% reductions in NPV. Interestingly, increasing the hurdle rates and reinvestment rates by 2% for each year impacts NPV by only 15%. The analyst may want to consider increasing these by 4% for each year to further gauge the impact of potentially high costs of money.

Example 2 clearly pinpoints the critical, or most sensitive, variables. Consequently, it is the estimates for these inputs that the analyst must check most carefully. In our discussion of risk we suggest obtaining a set of estimates for each sensitive variable and attaching corresponding probabilities to each. Then, using a computer, it is possible to consider alternative sets of potentially undesirable (and desirable) scenarios. In most instances management is concerned primarily with downside risk, so that appropriate contingency plans may be developed to deal with those possibilities. Certainly, the possibility of outcomes better than anticipated must be considered. But, the problems associated with higher than expected cash flows are generally easier to solve than those resulting from lower cash flows—thus, our interest lies primarily in potential downside risk. In Example 3 we consider two downside risk scenarios and their impact on the capital budgeting problem in Examples 1 and 2. The first is a recession model, the second an inflation model.

EXAMPLE 3

Sensitivity Analyses of Several Variables

Consider two possible economic scenarios: recession and inflation. In the recession case, hold volume constant at 10,500, increase sales price 6.4% yearly, and start with unit labor costs of $1.68. Determine the cash flow, terminal value, and net present value.

In the inflation case, allow volume to expand to 12,800, increase the hurdle rates and reinvestment rates by 4% for each year, use unit labor of $1.68, increase sales price 8% annually, and increase labor, materials, utilities and fuel, other, and sales expenses by 8.4%, 12%, 18%, 8.4%, and 9.6%, respectively. Determine the cash flows, terminal value, and net present value.

SOLUTION: The results are tabulated as follows:

RECESSION CASE
INCOME AND CASH FLOW SUMMARY

	WITHOUT PROJECT		WITH PROJECT	
PERIOD	NET INCOME	CASH FLOW	NET INCOME	CASH FLOW
1	$7,020.00	$8,020.00	$8,456.40	$14,006.40
2	6,566.40	7,566.40	7,092.20	14,742.20
3	5,980.17	6,980.17	6,901.96	14,252.00
4	5,240.35	6,240.35	6,406.88	13,756.90
5	4,322.99	5,322.99	5,745.11	13,095.10
6	3,200.80	4,200.80	8,291.37	9,341.37
7	1,842.63	2,842.63	7,210.43	8,260.43
8	212.98	1,212.98	5,868.60	6,918.60
9	− 1,728.62	− 728.62	4,225.06	5,275.06
10	− 4,028.35	− 3,028.35	2,233.15	3,283.15

Terminal value		$119,103.00
Present value		$ 32,711.10
Net present value		$ 2,711.10
Internal rate of return		16%

INFLATION CASE
INCOME AND CASH FLOW SUMMARY

	WITHOUT PROJECT		WITH PROJECT	
PERIOD	NET INCOME	CASH FLOW	NET INCOME	CASH FLOW
1	$7,020.00	$8,020.00	$ 8,456.40	$14,006.40
2	6,648.48	7,648.48	7,659.26	15,351.30
3	6,113.08	7,113.08	8,008.37	15,444.10
4	5,380.74	6,380.74	7,990.13	15,471.20
5	4,412.61	5,412.61	7,696.62	15,225.00
6	3,163.02	4,163.02	10,442.30	11,719.80
7	1,578.39	2,578.39	8,973.31	10,253.30
8	− 404.18	595.82	7,019.68	8,299.68
9	− 2,858.46	− 1,858.46	4,511.32	5,791.32
10	− 5,870.97	− 4,870.97	1,341.59	2,621.59

Terminal value		$173,282.00
Present value		$ 33,688.50
Net present value		$ 3,688.50
Internal rate of return		20.4%

> Note that the NPVs are still positive but that profit and cash flows without the new machine become negative in the later periods of the analysis. Thus, the new machine looks good—but in comparison with a poor alternative.

Throughout our discussion of sensitivity analysis, we have assumed that inflation will impact each input by a different amount. Such is the situation in any company; to talk of *an* inflation rate is meaningless. Composite inflation rates, such as the CPI and PPI, are useful only if the inputs employed by the firm are the same and used in the same proportion as the inputs used to compute the composite index. Since this never happens, it is necessary to forecast inflation rates for each input. If there were several alternative projects available to accomplish the same goal, logic would argue toward selection of the project which, on the average, would tend to use less of those inputs with high expected inflation rates.

THE METHODOLOGY OF FORECASTING

The reader will recall that in Example 1 the corporate economist presented to the analyst average inflation rates for a number of significant variables which were applied to the cost accountant's analysis of how the current net cash flows would be altered by the acceptance of the project. The results in period 1 were then projected over the life of the project without allowance for the variances and covariances at play in all financial statements. Each period's net cash flow represented a point estimate, with the risks of the project considered in the designation of a hurdle rate.

The reader will also recognize, upon reflection, that certain assumptions underlie all business forecasts. Financial forecasts involve certain explicit and implicit assumptions. These include:

☐ *Methodological assumptions* accompany forecasting techniques, whether quantitative or qualitative. As an example, different statistical techniques, applied to the same data base, may yield different forecasts. Conversely, the same technique may yield divergent results for different time spans or if other explanatory variables are included. Thus, forecasts vary according to the particular assumptions about the behavior and interrelationships of the variables used to project sales and costs. National and industry statistics (originating with governmental, trade, or monetary agencies) are frequently used as inputs to company forecast models. These contain additional methodological assumptions. Variances in macrolevel data work down to compound the variances intrinsic to company forecasting procedures.

☐ *Planning assumptions* relate to marketing and production strategies as well as to erratic events (e.g., outcome of litigation) and perhaps the intuitive adjustments of top officers. Production strategies merit special comment. The bridge that leads from sales to net income is distinct from the external link of sales to the market. Sales projections only initiate the design of a comprehensive operating plan, for management has considerable latitude in responding to the market environment. It may, for example, alter the product mix, adjust production schedules, modify inventory policies, regulate discretionary expenditures, and so on. Consequently, *any single projected sales level can translate into a broad range of net income estimates.*

☐ There exists a group of *continuity assumptions*, akin to the "going concern" principle in financial accounting, which are vital to appraisal of the forecast, yet merit explicit mention only by exception. Unless alerted to the contrary, the reader of a financial forecast properly assumes the projections are prepared in a manner consistent with the applicable accounting principles adopted by the firm in the annual report. Likewise, the composition of top corporate management, the continuing availability of normal sources of supply, reasonable stability of the tax environment, and so on, are implied unless the reader is informed to the contrary.

Clearly, a full array of assumptions would constitute a sizable document. Moreover, since the underlying events may each assume a variety of different outcomes and these may occur in diverse combinations, a large number of projections can result from very few assumptions. The complexity obscures the impact on estimated net income of changes in a single assumption and underscores the difficulty in deciding which assumptions merit specific comment. However, at a minimum the user of the forecasted cash flows in a project analysis should

☐ Understand the implications of assumptions and so help in forming a judgment as to the reasonableness of the forecast and to the main uncertainties attached to it.
☐ Be acquainted with the assumptions that are, wherever possible, specific rather than general, definite rather than vague.
☐ Not be encumbered by all-embracing assumptions relating to the general accuracy of the estimates.
☐ Be alert to the assumptions that relate to matters that have a material bearing on the forecast.

As illustrated, sensitivity analysis is a common device in the internal review of business plans to isolate those factors which *all things equal* may induce variations greater than a specified range. Some authorities advocate a range of 10% to 15% of net income as the line of demarcation. Accepting 15% as a working hypothesis, management would alert the analyst to those assumptions which may cause net income to depart by 15% or more from the published estimate. But a 10% or 15% standard is not sacrosanct. The standard could also be set probabilistically to identify a range of variation with, for example, a 95% chance of containing the actual net income. Circumstances (the nature of the market, technological and financial characteristics of the industry) alter cases, and it is for management to judge what is "material" in the company's projections.

It is reasonable to inquire how the sales department made its estimates. Merely surveying the opinion of the sales force tends to result in underestimates. And how did the corporate economist arrive at his or her set of interest rates—difficult variables to predict under any circumstances?

There are two principal approaches to forecasting these variables: subjective and objective (see Figure 9–1). The objective approach divides into noncausal (naive) and causal techniques. Since the subjective approach is almost self-explanatory, we shall concentrate on the objective methods:

Noncausal techniques.   These techniques extrapolate the historical record (time series) to obtain the forecast for the next period or periods. On the assumption that past patterns will continue, no attempt is made to isolate the causes which have shaped past sales behavior. Basically, the data are averaged to eliminate irregular variations and describe a recurrent pattern.

Various types of averaging, depending on the characteristics of the data, are available. But, as illustrated by Table 9–1A, different methods of averaging applied to the same data base yield different projections. For example, the *arithmetic moving average* allows equal weight to sales in all periods averaged. An *exponentially weighted moving average* gives predominant weight to the most recent sales and

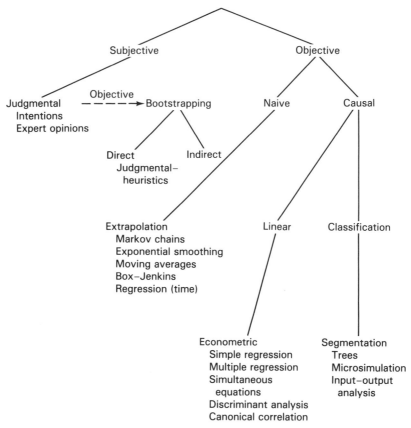

Source: Adapted from J. Scott Armstrong, *Long-Range Forecasting: From Crystal Ball to Computer, 2nd ed., p. 77.* New York: John Wiley and Sons, Inc.

FIGURE 9–1   Forecasting Methods (and Techniques)

progressively smaller importance to earlier experience. Computer programs can select the "smoothing constant" which minimizes the forecasting error. Both approaches presume that averaging over several periods will cancel irregular influences and so reveal the "normal" trend of sales or costs. The irregularities, however, do provide an indication of how far the actual results may depart from the projection. Hence, it is useful to measure these variances by obtaining either the *mean absolute deviation* (*MAD*) or the *standard deviation* (*SD*). The result is a predicted figure accompanied by a range within which future values may fall if past experience prevails. Chapter 11 examines these and other measures of risk in detail

A third form of averaging (Table 9–1B) involves the fitting of a regression line to the historical time series depicting the average movement of sales or costs per unit of time. The particular equation applied—arithmetic straight-line trend, geometric straight line, or polynomial—is a matter of obtaining the curve best fitting the data. The results may show a *constant absolute amount* of change per time period, a *constant rate of change*, or *variation in the amount or rate of change.*

Table 9 – 1

PERIOD*	SALES	A: MOVING AVERAGE FORECASTS		B: CURVE FITTING		
		3-YEAR MOVING AVERAGE (1)	EXPONENTIAL SMOOTHING (2)	LEAST SQUARES (3)	POLYNOMIAL (4)	GEOMETRIC (5)
1	$50.2			$59.78	$55.40	$59.20
2	62.8			61.75	60.64	61.10
3	76.4	$63.1	$56.5	63.72	64.94	63.05
4	63.8	67.7	58.49	65.69	68.31	65.07
5	67.1	69.1	59.02	67.66	70.75	67.15
6	72.9	67.9	59.83	69.33	72.25	69.30
7	66.8	68.9	61.14	71.60	72.82	71.52
8	77.7	72.5	61.70	73.57	72.46	73.80
9	71.1	71.9	63.30	75.54	71.16	76.17
Mean absolute deviation		$ 2.73	$10.83	$ 3.63	$ 5.3	$ 4.87
Standard deviation		3.99	26.53	4.42	6.2	4.38

*Time interval may represent monthly, quarterly, annual data as appropriate to the analysis.

MOVING AVERAGE FORECASTS	CURVE FITTING
Advantages	Advantages
1. Data are easy to obtain within the company.	1. Data are minimal and easy to acquire within the company.
2. Calculations are easily computerized.	2. Calculations are readily computerized.
3. Little analytical skill is required.	3. Little analytical skill is required.
4. Forecast is economical.	4. Curve fitting is economical.
5. Forecast is easily understood.	5. Curve fitting averages out cyclical and irregular influences.
6. Forecast is reasonably accurate in the short term, 12 months ahead	6. Curve fitting is readily understood in general terms.
7. Estimates of error are easily obtained from calculations.	7. Curve fitting is reasonably accurate in short term if market conditions are relatively stable.
	8. Estimates of error are obtained from calculations.
Disadvantages	Disadvantages
1. Forecast will not catch turning points.	1. Curve fitting will not catch turning points.
2. Forecast cannot be used for new products.	2. Coefficients a and b are computed from historical data and do not respond quickly to new influences changing trend and cyclical factors.

Table 9–1 (cont.)

MOVING AVERAGE FORECASTS	CURVE FITTING
3. Forecast assumes future to be very much like the past.	3. Curve fitting cannot be used in new product forecasting.
4. There is no analysis of variables influencing company sales.	4. Curve fitting strongly assumes that the future is very much like the past.
	5. Curve fitting provides no information about the response of sales to new market strategies by company, or by competitors.
	6. Selecting the most appropriate curve requires exercise of analysts' judgment. Generally, the best curve is one minimizing the standard deviation.

(1) Each three-period average in effect is used to forecast sales two periods ahead. For example, $63.1 is the average for the first three-period interval and is used as the sales forecast in period 4. With a mean absolute error of $2.73, the forecast for period 10 may then be stated at $71.9 − $2.73, thereby setting control limits.

(2) The forecast for each period from 4 onward is computed by

$$F = \text{old average} + L\,(\text{current sales} - \text{old average})$$

where L = a smoothing constant between 0 and 1 that determines the influence of the most recent data in computing the forecast.

Assume that $L = 0.10$, then period 4 projection =

$$\$58.49 = \$56.50 + 0.10(\$76.40 - \$56.50)$$

Forecast for period 10 becomes

$$\$64.08 = \$63.30 + 0.10(\$71.10 - \$63.30)$$

Analyst must experiment to determine the value of alpha (L) that provides the minimum mean absolute deviation or standard deviation.

(3) Least squares (Y_c) values are computed from

$$Y_c = a + bx$$

where Y_c = forecasted sales values from the model
  a = value of line at point of origin in period 0
  b = average change in sales per period of time
  x = a particular time period as 0, 1, 2, 3, and so on.

Values of a and b are derived from historical data by the following simultaneous equations:

$$EY = Na + bEx$$
$$EXY = aEX + bEx,$$

where Y = historical sales
  EY = the sum of all sales values
  N = total number of values in series

Table 9–1 (cont.)

For the series illustrated

$$Y_c = \$59.76 + \$1.97x$$

and the forecast for period 10 would be

$$Y_c = \$59.76 + \$1.97(9)$$
$$= \$77.49$$

The curve assumes that the best description of the historical sales data is a projection which allows a $1.97 *absolute change accumulated for each time period.*
(4) Values (Y_c) are computed from $Y_c = a + bx + cx^2$. The curve will swing upward if c is positive or downward if c is negative. Yields a curve with one change of direction. For the data, the equation reads

$$Y_c = \$68.39 + \$1.97x - \$0.467x^2,$$

and the forecast for period 10 becomes

$$Y_c = \$78.51$$

(5) The geometric trend allows for a *constant rate* of change from period to period with the parameters a and b computed according to the least squares curve from the logarithms of the historical sales data, after the computation of a and b, the relationship can be eressed in natural numbers.

$$Y_c = ab^x$$

where for the assumed data $a = \$58.59$ and $b = \$1.032$.
    The forecast for period 10, thus becomes

$$Y_c = (\$58.59)(1.032)^9$$

$$= \$77.79$$

A time series of historical values reflects four influences: trend, cyclical, seasonal, and irregular. Computer programs, utilizing the averaging methods discussed are available to isolate and measure each of these influences. In this approach, trend and seasonal components are forecasted separately to show the underlying direction of the data with the pattern of seasonal fluctuations superimposed.

All the averaging methods described provide management with a single-point estimate of sales plus or minus an average deviation. The latter is used to set control limits for comparison with actual monthly or quarterly sales reports. Repeated violation of the control limits signals the need for a recomputation of the forecast by modifying the weighting system or the averaging technique selected.

The fundamental assumption of these techniques (existing patterns will continue into the future) is more likely to be correct over the short term and provide reasonably accurate forecasts for the immediate future. The techniques usually do quite poorly further into the future and ordinarily cannot predict when the rate of growth in a trend will change significantly. Of course, any time series will ultimately catch new patterns of growth, but the lag may be such as to dilute the quality of the short-term forecast. Thus, forecasters frequently supplement noncausative methods with *leading statistical indicators* for the economy or industry performance. Leading indicators portend departures from the norm before they surface in the historical record of company sales.

Causal techniques. These techniques suggest more than a mere extrapolation of historical data. They involve the identification of forces which have caused the time series to behave in a certain way in past years. If these explanatory variables can be measured, they can assist in predicting future outcomes. The problem shifts initially to forecasting the causal factors which in turn aid the analyst to predict sales or costs. However, causal models still assume an historical continuity in the relationship between sales or cost and the explanatory variables.

The regression analysis is modified in the causal approach by substituting for time a single explanatory variable (Table 9–2A) or a number of variables (Table 9–2B) to derive a workable equation relating the behavior of sales to the underlying system of causation. To illustrate, in Table 9–2 sales are forecast by predicting the values in the regression equation and calculating the projected levels of sales. The model also generates a *standard error of the estimate* (*SEE*), that is, the variation in sales over and above that explained by the causal variables. Packaged computer programs carry through the computations in a minimum of time. Chapter 15 examines the details of regression analysis and its related statistics.

Table 9–2

	A: SIMPLE CORRELATION			B: MULTIPLE CORRELATION*†			
PERIOD	SALES (Y)	DISPOSABLE CUSTOMER INCOME (X)	FORECASTED SALES (Y_C)	SALES (Y)	DISPOSABLE PERSONAL INCOME (X_1)	HOUSING STARTS (X_2) (000,000)	FORECASTED SALES (X_C)
1	$50.2	$200	$54.63	$50.2	$200	1.0	$54.50
2	62.8	215	62.43	62.8	215	1.5	61.05
3	76.4	220	65.03	76.4	220	2.5	69.16
4	63.8	210	59.83	63.8	210	1.1	57.20
5	67.1	230	70.23	67.1	230	1.7	65.47
6	72.9	235	72.83	72.9	235	2.2	70.02
7	66.8	225	67.63	66.8	225	1.6	63.76
8	77.7	240	75.43	77.7	240	2.8	75.29
9	71.1	235	72.83	71.1	235	2.0	68.60
Mean absolute deviation			3.13				3.59
Standard error of the estimate			4.51				4.07

Table 9–2 (cont.)

(1) Projected from the regression equation, $Y_c = a + bx$, except that x now symbolizes the independent variable (disposable customer income) presumed to explain changes in company sales. The parameters are

$$Y_c = -\$49.37 + \$0.52(x)$$

If the forecast of disposable income in period 10 were $260, company sales would be projected as

$$Y_c = -\$49.37 + \$0.52(260)$$
$$= \$85.83$$

The standard error of the estimate measures the dispersion of the forecasted sales from actual sales in prior years. The standard error serves the same function as the standard deviation providing one indicator of the accuracy achieved by the model. The forecast, plus and minus, the standard error also establishes a control band to monitor the forecast as sales data develops in the period projected.

(2) Projected from the regression equation:

$$Y_c = a + bx_1 + cx_2$$

The parameters are:

$$Y_c = \$7.38 + \$0.20x_1 + \$7.11x_2$$

If the forecast of disposable income in period 10 were $260 and 3 for housing starts, the company sales forecast would be projected as

$$Y_c = \$7.38 + (\$0.20)(260) + (\$7.11)(3)$$
$$= \$80.71$$

*Advantages

1. Allows for quantitative evaluation of market forces and company marketing actions. Permits inclusion of company marketing plans (perhaps, advertising expenditures) as predictors of sales levels;
2. If turning points in the explanatory variable can be foreseen, then turning points in company sales can be predicted.
3. Will lead to more accurate forecasting, if independent variables can be projected with reasonable accuracy;
4. May be only quantitative technique for new products or for long term forcasts;
5. Subject to cumulative improvement over time;
6. Allows for isolation and analysis of errors.

†Disadvantages

1. More in-depth knowledge of market forces required than in extrapolation techniques;
2. More costly in computation time, extent of data required, and competence of personnel;
3. May not be possible to forecast independent variables with the accuracy required to improve on extrapolation techniques;
4. Historical data may not be available on many important variables;
5. Coefficients still based upon historical relationships and may not quickly respond to new influences entering the market;
6. Not easily understood by personnel unfamiliar with statistical techniques.

Computer technology has extended the power of causal analysis through simulation models that calculate expected sales levels under assumed market conditions. A series of equations describe the seller's relationship to the market by identifying the factors behind the decisions of customers; the resulting flow of orders, production, and shipments; and associated adjustments in inventories and unfilled orders. Interactions between company marketing decisions (price, promotions, selling effort, and so forth) and the responses of customers are also incorporated. Primary inputs to the model include historical data, technological factors, and macroeconomic assumptions. The computer reruns the model under various conditions as to external forces (the national economy) and/or marketing and production actions of the company to forecast sales. Of course, any such models should be tested for validity.

Causal models are generally more sophisticated, hence, more costly in terms of personnel outlays and computer time. Adding to the number of *significant* explanatory variables improves the accuracy of the model. Introduction of leads/lags may further improve the model and sensitize it to changes in rates of growth (turning points). The more elaborate causal models—econometric models—incorporate certain general "leading" econometric indicators that change direction before industry and company sales.

SUMMARY

This brief excursion into business forecasting should at least convince the reader that business forecasting is a field of study in itself but one that is inextricably linked to capital budgeting.

QUESTIONS
PROBLEMS

1. Differentiate between the risk inherent in a project and forecasting risk.
2. In Example 1 different values were used for the hurdle rate and the reinvestment rate. In general, would these values be the same or would they differ? Explain.
3. If the same values for the hurdle rate and the reinvestment rate were used, would the project's NPV be more or less sensitive to changes in those rates as compared with the situation in Example 2 wherein they are assumed to be different?
4. The examples in this chapter provide for the computation of the project's internal rate of return based on assumed reinvestment rates. Explain the meaning of the calculated internal rate of return using these assumptions.
5. "Any project can be made to look attractive when compared with a sufficiently undesirable alternative." Such a statement could be applied to the "Inflation Case" in Example 3. When comparing the two mutually exclusive alternatives, "Without Project" and "With Project," is it fair to compare the two as shown or would you abandon the "Without Project" alternative prior to the tenth period? Assume that if abandonment did take place, any cash flows would be reinvested in other projects at the assumed reinvestment rates rather than replacing the project.

REFERENCES

Agrawall, S. P. "Accounting for the Impact of Inflation on a Business Enterprise." *Accounting Review* (October 1977).

Bohren, Oyvond. "The Validity of Conventional Valuation Models Under Multiperiod Uncertainty." *Journal of Business Finance and Accounting* (Summer 1984).

Brennan, M. J. "An Approach to the Valuation of Uncertain Income Streams." *Journal of Finance* (June 1973).

Brenner, Menachem, and Itzhak Venezia. "The Effects of Inflation and Taxes on Growth Investments and Replacement Policies." *Journal of Finance* (December 1983).

Carlson, John A. "Expected Inflation and Interest Rates." *Economic Inquiry*, 17 (October 1979), 597–608.

Carter, E. Eugene. "Designing the Capital Budgeting Process." *TIMS Studies in the Management Sciences*, 5 (1977).

Chang, Eric C., and J. Michael Pinegar. "Risk and Inflation." *Journal of Financial and Quantitative Analysis* (March 1987).

Chant, P. D. "On the Predictability of Corporate Earnings per Share Behavior." *Journal of Finance* (March 1980).

Chen, Son-Nan. "Capital Budgeting and Uncertain Inflation." *Journal of Economics and Business* (August 1984).

_____, and William T. Moore. "Multi-Period Asset Pricing: The Effects of Uncertain Inflation." *Financial Review* (May 1984).

_____, and_____. "Uncertain Inflation and Optional Portfolio Approach." *Financial Review* (November 1985).

Comiskey, Eugene E., Charles W. Mulford, and Thomas L. Porter. "Forecast Error, Earnings Variability and Systematic Risk: Additional Evidence." *Journal of Business Finance and Accounting* (Summer 1985).

Cross, Stephen, M. "A Note on Inflation, Taxation and Investment Returns." *Journal of Finance* (March 1980).

Fama, Eugene F. "Short-Term Interest Rates as Predictors of Inflation." *American Economic Review*, 65 (June 1975), 269–282.

_____, and G. William Schwert. "Asset Returns and Inflation." *Journal of Financial Economics*, 5 (November 1977), 115–146.

Feldstein, Martin, Jerry Green, and Eytan Sheshinski. "Inflation and Taxes in a Growing Economy with Debt and Equity Finance." *Journal of Political Economy*, 86 (April 1978), S53–S70.

_____, and Lawrence Summers. "Inflation, Tax Rules and the Long-Term Interest Rate," *Brookings Papers on Economic Activity*, 1 (1978), 61–109.

Gitman, Laurence J., and John R. Forrester, Jr. "Forecasting and Evaluation Practices and Performance: A Survey of Capital Budgeting." *Financial Management* (Fall 1977).

Hendershott, Patric H. "Inflation, Resource Utilization, and Debt and Equity Returns." Working paper, National Bureau of Economic Research (June 1981).

_____, and James C. Van Horne. "Expected Inflation Implied by Capital Market Rates." *Journal of Finance*, 28 (May 1973), 301–314.

Higgins, Robert C. "Sustainable Growth Under Inflation." *Financial Management*, 10 (Autumn 1981), 36–40.

Hochman, Shalom, and Ramon Rabinovitch. "Financial Leasing Under Inflation." *Financial Management* (Spring 1984).

Hong, Hai. "Inflation and the Market Value of the Firm: Theory and Tests." *Journal of Finance*, 32 (September 1977), 1031–1048.

Howe, Keith M. "Does Inflation Change Affect Capital Asset Life?" *Financial Management* (Summer 1987).

_____, and Harvey Lapan. "Inflation and Asset Life: The Darby versus the Fisher Effect." *Journal of Financial and Quantitative Analysis* (June 1987).

Ibbotson, Roger G., and Rex A. Sinquefield. *Stocks, Bonds, Bills, and Inflation*. Charlottesville, Va.: Financial Analysts Research Foundation, 1979.

Jacob, David P., Graham Lord, and James A. Tilley. "A Generalized Framework for Pricing Contingent Cash Flows." *Financial Management* (August 1987).

Kelly, William A., Jr. and James A. Miles. "Darby and Fisher: Resolution of a Paradox." *Financial Review* (February 1984).

Kim, M. K. "Inflationary Effects in the Capital Investment Process: An Empirical Examination." *Journal of Finance* (September 1979).

Kistler, L. H., and C. P. Carter. "Replacement Cost Measures: Their Impact on Income, Dividends, and Investment Return." *Quarterly Review of Economics and Business* (Spring 1979).

Kodde, David A., and Hein Schreuder. "Forecasting Corporate Revenue and Profit: Time-Series Models Versus Management and Analysts." *Journal of Business Finance and Accounting* (Autumn 1984).

Mehta, Dileep R., Michael D. Curley, and Hung-Gay Fung. "Inflation, Cost of Capital, and Capital Budgeting Procedures." *Financial Management* (Winter 1984).

Modigliani, Franco, and Richard A. Cohn. "Inflation, Rational Valuation and the Market." *Financial Analysis Journal*, 35 (March–April 1979), 24–44.

Nelson, C. R. "Inflation and Capital Budgeting." *Journal of Finance* (June 1976).

Poengsen, Otto H., and Hubert Straub. "Inflation and the Corporate Investment Decision." *Management International Review*, 16, no. 4 (1976).

Rappaport, Alfred, and Robert A. Taggart, Jr. "Evaluation of Capital Expenditure Proposals Under Inflation." *Financial Management*, 11 (Spring 1982), 5–13.

Statman, Meir, and Tyzoon T. Tyebjee. "Optimistic Capital Budgeting Forecasts: An Experiment." *Financial Management* (Autumn 1985).

Stulz, René M. "Asset Pricing and Expected Inflation." *Journal of Finance* (July 1986).

Tanzi, Vito. "Inflation Expectations, Economic Activity, Taxes, and Interest Rates." *American Economic Review*, 70 (March 1980), 12–21.

Tatom, John A., and James E. Turley. "Inflation and Taxes: Disincentives for Capital Formation." *Review of the Federal Reserve Bank of St. Louis*, 60 (January 1978), 2–8.

Turnbull, S. M. "Discounting the Components of an Income Stream: Comment." *Journal of Finance* (March 1977).

Van Horne, James C. *Financial Market Rates and Flows*. Englewood Cliffs, N.J.: Prentice Hall, 1978, Chap. 5.

_____, and William F. Glassmire, Jr. "The Impact of Unanticipated Changes in Inflation on the Value of Common Stocks." *Journal of Finance*, 27 (December 1972), 1081–1092.

_____. "A Note on Biases in Capital Budgeting Introduced by Inflation."' *Journal of Financial and Quantitative Analysis* (January 1971).

Wilkens, E. N. "Forecasting Cash Flow: Some Problems and Applications." *Management Accounting* (October 1967), 26–30.

CASE STUDY 9 – 1

Bellcamp Soups, Inc.

The Bellcamp Soup Company's annual reports for 1978 to 1987 showed:

YEAR	NET SALES	MARKETING AND SALES EXPENSE	OFFICERS' SALARY EXPENSE
1978	$2,944,779	$305,700	$441,717
1979	2,797,663	256,213	332,959
1980	2,560,569	213,703	369,585
1981	2,248,692	181,229	344,585
1982	1,983,659	163,054	370,635
1983	2,135,341	206,662	381,779
1984	2,068,135	227,329	374,144
1985	2,143,135	238,695	387,549
1986	2,357,449	264,952	369,657
1987	2,448,845	253,947	417,707

Perform two simple regressions with the two variables and state whether, in your opinion, marketing and sales expenses might be a good forecast variable for net sales. State whether, in your opinion, officers' salary expenses might be a good forecast variable for net sales. Use the mean absolute deviation and the standard error of the estimate to evaluate the degree of confidence you can place in the two expenses as a predictor of net sales. Perform a multiple regression analysis. Interpret your results.

Cost of Capital

10

The four discounted cash flow procedures used to evaluate alternative investments (internal rate of return, net present value, profitability index, and annual capital charge) all measure cash flows in terms of a required rate of return (hurdle rate) to determine their acceptability. This hurdle rate was referred to earlier as the firm's cost of capital, and as noted in our discussion of risk analysis, the actual hurdle rate applied may be the cost of capital adjusted to compensate for project risk differing from that of the normal risk complexion of the firm. But what exactly is the cost of capital and how do we go about determining it? These are the questions that will be addressed in this chapter. This will necessitate an examination of the general problem of managing the financial structure and the valuation of the firm.

We shall confront the problems initially utilizing traditional methodology. Later (in Chapter 16), we examine the capital asset pricing model and discuss an alternative procedure for calculating the firm's cost of capital utilizing this model.

CONVENTIONAL WISDOM

The *cost of capital* refers to the rates of return expected by those parties contributing to the financial structure: preferred and common shareholders as well as creditors. It represents the cost of funds used to acquire the total assets of the firm. Thus, it is generally calculated as a weighted average of the cost associated with each type of capital included in the financial structure of the enterprise. Several factors merit additional comment and examination.

1   *The cost of capital, considered as a rate of return, disaggregates into a risk-free rate plus a premium for risk*. The risk premium covers the business and financial risk of the firm relative to available, alternative investments. Since the risk-free rate is common to all firms, differences in the cost of capital among firms originate in their riskiness. *The cost of capital embodies the*

average risk posture of the firm, that is, the composite risk of the firm as a portfolio of operational projects which makes up its risk complexion.

2   Since the firm's capital cost is the security holders' income, *the cost of capital represents a rate of return that will maintain the market value of the outstanding securities within the context of overall market movements.* Investors have available to them a wide range of investment options, from risk-free government securities to common stocks of varying quality. Hence, in arranging their portfolios, they expect to receive a risk premium appropriate to the quality of a given investment. If the security concerned does not appear to promise such a yield at its current price, the price will drop until the yield equates with investor expectations.

3   *The cost of capital is that rate which will enable the firm to sell new securities at current price levels.* The firm must have the potential of using the new funds in ways that generate yields sufficient to cover the risk-free rate and the required premium for risk.

The reader will note that we have expressed the concept of the cost of capital in three different ways. But there is an underlying commonality: the firm must manage its assets and select capital projects with the goal of obtaining a yield at least sufficient to cover its cost of capital. If it fails in this objective, the market price of its outstanding securities will decline. If it achieves yields greater than the cost of capital, it is likely that the price of securities, especially the common stock, will be bid upward. Consequently, *the cost of capital is seen as an opportunity cost.* As an opportunity cost, it has dual aspects. From the investment standpoint, the firm competes against a variety of alternative uses of funds to attract investor capital, while internally the firm must select business projects with estimated yields that maintain the market value of its securities by promising returns commensurate with investor expectations (i.e., cover the required risk premium).

As a final note, a firm does not calculate the cost of capital and post it on the company bulletin board. Nor does the firm calculate it by picking up the annual report. Rather, it is a *dynamic concept, a synthesis of the costs of new equity and debt.* It conforms to the *marginal cost* of each, a weighted average cost for the next dollar of capital apportioned between debt and equity securities. Capital budgeting deals with future cash flows and calculates net present values (NPV) using the marginal cost of capital, based on the next dollar of invested capital. The cost of capital stresses the cost of that dollar based upon market expectations. The theory of marginal cost pricing dictates, therefore, the acceptance of projects to the point at which NPV equals zero for the last project accepted using the hurdle rate based upon the cost of capital.

The discussion of the cost of capital thus far has assumed some optimum balance of the financial mix, but the question is yet to be addressed. The following sections examine those factors which affect the financial structure and indicate how we may go about selecting a financial structure. But again it is important to note that the firm's optimum financial structure is not fixed, but dynamic.

We conclude this section by providing an overview of several surveys which indicate how large U.S. firms determine the hurdle rates they use to evaluate capital projects. Table 10–1 provides the results of four surveys over the last 15 years. As can be seen, a higher percentage of large U.S. firms call upon the weighted average cost of capital to determine their hurdle rates. This is the preferred approach, according to finance theory. A significant percentage of firms also use the cost associated with one element of their capital structure as a hurdle rate. This chapter presents the finance theory related to the correct determination of capital project hurdle rates and the

Table 10–1 Determination of Capital Investment Hurdle Rates, Percentage of Respondents Using Each Method

METHOD USED	AUTHOR AND YEAR SURVEY PUBLISHED			
	BRIGHAM 1975	PETTY, SCOTT, AND BIRD 1975	SCHALL, SUNDEM, AND GEIJSBEEK 1978	GITMAN AND MERCURIO 1982
Weighted Average Cost of Capital	61%	30%	46%	83%
Cost of a Specific Source of Funds (i.e., Cost of Debt or Cost of Equity)	13	17	26	17
Historical Rates of Return	10	13	20	
Subjectively Determined by Management	12	40	6	

SOURCES: E. F. Brigham, "Hurdle Rates for Screening Capital Expenditure Proposals," *Financial Management*, Fall 1975, 17–26; J. W. Petty, D. F. Scott, and M. M. Bird, "The Capital Budgeting Decision Making Process of Large Corporations," *The Engineering Economist*, Spring 1975, 159–72; L. D. Schall, G. L. Sundem, and W. R. Geijsbeek, Jr., "Survey and Analysis of Capital Budgeting Methods," *Journal of Finance*, March 1978, 281–87; L. J. Gitman and V. A. Mercurio, "Cost of Capital Techniques Used by Major U. S. Firms: Survey and Analysis of *Fortune's* 1000," *Financial Management*, Winter 1982, 21–29.

appropriate methodologies to carry out the needed calculations. However, we believe that it is also important for our readers to be aware of current practice.

MARKET VALUE VERSUS BOOK VALUE

For the ongoing business, the primary sources of funding are the earnings retained from profits and the funds generated through depreciation. Various types of debt are also used. For most firms, issues of new common stock are infrequent, and the use of preferred stock is practically nonexistent except for regulated utilities.

To discuss the sources of financing, we need to first examine the balance sheet as it reflects, in an historical setting, the current financial mix of the firm. We will then contrast balance sheet values with market values.

The right-hand side of the balance sheet is a presentation of the firm's debt and equity portfolios in an historical sense. The book value of equity seldom is related directly to the market value, and the same holds true for *some* types of debt. This being the situation, one might ask why we examine the balance sheet at all. The answer is that the balance sheet does reflect accurately *some* debt obligations, and using other information from it, we may determine the market values of the remaining components of debt and of equity.

Consider the section of the balance sheet shown in Table 10–2. The current liabilities section accurately indicates the amounts owed. Further, while current liabilities do turn over, they often form a *permanent* part of the firm's financing package. When one is paid, another is generated. Also, as the firm expands, it is usual for the current liabilities to expand proportionately.

The amounts shown for long-term debt indicate the dollar amount of the obligation at the time of maturity. The notes payable listed probably have a market

Table 10 – 2   Sample Balance Sheet

	(IN THOUSANDS)	(IN PERCENT)
Accounts payable	$ 4,000	9.88%
Accrued taxes	1,000	2.47
Accrued wages	500	1.23
Current liabilities	$ 5,500	13.58%
Note payable (2 years)	3,000	7.41
Bonds (7% due 2000)	8,000	19.75
Long-term debt	$11,000	27.16%
Total liabilities	$16,500	40.74%
Common stock ($1 par 2,000,000 shares outstanding)	$ 2,000	
Paid-in capital	8,000	
Retained earnings	14,000	
Owners' equity	$24,000	59.26%
Total liabilities and owners' equity	$40,500	100.00%

value close to the $3 million shown *because* their maturity is near at hand. However, the bonds mature in some 20 years. If current interest rates are significantly different from the 7% listed, the market price of the bonds will differ from the book value. For example, if the current interest rate for newly issued, comparable-quality bonds is 10%, the outstanding bonds might be selling for $800. This means that the actual outstanding bond debt is only 80% of that shown on the books, or $6,400,000.[1]

The values shown in the common stock and paid-in capital accounts indicate how much the firm realized when the stock was originally sold. Retained earnings tells us how much the firm has retained out of all its after-tax profits since its inception.[2] *The true value of the equity is the market price, which represents the collective judgment of all the participants in the marketplace.* The book value of the common stock has little bearing on the market value, which reflects primarily current and expected earnings and dividends. The book value in this example is $12 per share ($24 million ÷ 2 million shares outstanding). Suppose the market value of the common stock is $20. Then the *market-valued* liability and owners' equity would be as shown in Table 10–3. The market value of the common stock captures *all* the owners' equity accounts.

Note how the total amount of financing has changed. The book value is $40,500,000, whereas the market value is $54,900,000. The market value indicates the true value of the business. Note also how the debt-to-equity ratios have changed. Based on book values, the ratio is $16,500,000 : $24,000,000, or 0.69 : 1. That is, for every dollar of equity, the *balance sheet* shows 69 cents of debt. The situation is dramatically altered when market values are used: $14,900,000 : $40,000,000, or 0.37 : 1. The *market* indicates only 37 cents of debt for each dollar of equity.

---

[1]This explains why when interest rates are very high, some companies actually repurchase their own debt on the open market. This method, while using cash, reduces debt at a discount.

[2]Unless there have been stock dividends, in which case the common stock and paid-in capital accounts would have been increased at the expense of retained earnings.

Table 10–3   Balance Sheet Adjusted to Reflect Market Values

	(IN THOUSANDS)	(IN PERCENT)
Accounts payable	$ 4,000	7.29%
Accrued taxes	1,000	1.82
Accrued wages	500	0.91
Current liabilities	$ 5,500	10.02%
Notes payable (2 years)	3,000	5.46
Bonds (7% due 2000)	6,400	11.66
Long-term debt	$ 9,400	17.12%
Total liabilities	$14,900	27.14%
Common stock (2,000,000 shares at		
$20/share)	$40,000	72.86%
Total liabilities and owners' equity	$54,900	100.00%

Thus far in this chapter we have established that the true financing picture of the firm is shown by the *market values*, and that the debt-to-equity ratios are provided by *market* and not by *book* values. One further observation needs to be made. The market has valued this firm's assets as being worth $54,900,000, not the $40,500,000 which is shown on the balance sheet. The market says that the productive value of the assets is some $14,400,000 greater than the book value. This implies that the book values shown for *some* of the assets on the balance sheet are not consistent with their market valuations.

INTERNALLY AND EXTERNALLY GENERATED FUNDS

The financing of a company from *external* sources such as the issuance of new debt and equity tends to be lumpy in nature. Due to the prohibitively high costs of issuing securities, it is necessary to either issue stock or borrow—but almost never both at the same time. When stock is sold, enough is issued to support another increment of debt at a later date. As a consequence, the firm's debt-to-equity ratio will vary over time. Funds generated *internally* tend to flow in relatively constantly throughout the year, with exceptions, of course, for seasonal fluctuations in business and periodic issuance of cash dividends. Internally generated funds which are retained in the firm must be invested judiciously. If this takes place and is manifested by increases in earnings and perhaps dividends at a rate greater than that anticipated by the market, then the market price of the stock is likely to rise. The higher market price means that the equity base has increased and may permit further borrowing without adversely changing the financial risk posture of the firm. As a consequence, for many firms the financing program includes little use of new equity but rather reinvestment of internally generated funds to increase the equity base and then increase borrowing consistent with the preplanned debt-to-equity ratio.

The selection of debt instruments depends to a great extent on the availability of money and the relative terms of the different types. In periods of high interest, short-term or intermediate-term notes may be preferable to lower-interest-rate long-term bonds. Or a higher-interest-rate callable bond may be useful because it has dual advantages of providing for a long-term commitment if interest rates should increase and being callable at a stated price if interest rates should decrease. With the rapid changes in the structure of the money and capital markets, pat answers to the question of the best type of debt instrument to use do not exist. Each case must be evaluated individually, using the counsel of commercial and investment bankers.

FINANCIAL STRUCTURE

The firm manages assets and selects capital projects to secure the maximum return appropriate to the level of acceptable risk. Conversely, it manages the financial structure to minimize the cost of capital (i.e., to obtain the lowest weighted average cost of capital). Assuming that both business risk and financial risk influence the weighted average cost of capital, the introduction of debt into the financial structure lowers the weighted average cost up to some point. Debt capital has cost advantages:

1   Owing to higher priority in the order of payment, the interest of debt *normally* is lower than the other types of capital.
2   Unlike payments to equity, interest qualifies as a tax deduction so that some portion of these charges is borne by Uncle Sam. Tax deductibility reduces the effective cost of debt capital.
3   Given a long-term upward trend in the price level, inflation makes debt cheaper in real terms if the rate of increase in the price level exceeds the anticipated inflation rate at the time of flotation.

The use of debt incurs financial risk. As a consequence, the cost of debt may be divided into two parts: the *explicit* cost, which is the interest, and the *implicit* cost, which represents the additional return that equity investors (common shareholders) will require when debt is used and the risk posture of the firm is changed toward a more risky position. The implicit cost is expressed in the marketplace by a bidding downward of the price of the common stock. This comes about by an excess of supply over demand for the stock in the marketplace. When the market price of the stock declines, two significant events take place; *the total equity base decreases* (and with it, the ratio of debt to equity increases), and the *cost of equity* (that is, the return required by shareholders) *increases*. As will be noted later in this chapter, these two simultaneous events tend to *increase* the overall cost of the equity component of the financial package. Within limits, however, the use of debt may have the net result of reducing the firm's overall cost of funds.

Therefore, in managing the financial structure, the firm strives to achieve that combination of debt and equity that results in the lowest weighted average cost of capital. This is the optimum financial structure. For any given level of earnings after taxes, it will also maximize the value of the firm. Thus, cost of capital is inextricably linked to the valuation of the firm and its capital projects.

To determine the optimum capital structure (i.e., debt-to-equity ratio) it is necessary to know investor preferences for risk, that is, their utility functions for risk versus return. This subject will be discussed at some length in Part IV. Assume that we know the investor risk preferences in terms of both the interest rates charged and the return on equity required for different financial mixes. Given this information, we may find the optimum financial mix by determining the weighted average cost of capital for each possible mix and selecting that mix with the lowest cost.

Table 10 – 4 Developing an Optimum Financial Structure

TOTAL FINANCING	EQUITY PORTION	EQUITY RATE	DOLLAR COST	DEBT PORTION	RATE*	DOLLAR COST	TOTAL COST
$100	$100	14%	$14.00	0	—	0	$14.00
100	90	14	12.60	$10	6%	$0.60	13.20
100	80	14.5	11.60	20	6.25	1.25	12.85
100	70	15	10.50	30	6.5	1.95	12.45
100	60	16	9.60	40	7	2.80	12.40
100	50	18	9.00	50	7.5	3.75	12.75
100	40	20	8.00	60	8	4.80	12.80

*This refers to the after-tax cost of debt. This will be discussed in greater detail later in this chapter.

Table 10–4 demonstrates the concept of optimum financial structure. Note that $100 of financing is needed and that various proportions of equity and debt may be used. As more debt is used, both the implicit and explicit costs start to increase. The goal is to adopt that particular combination which will result in the lowest total cost.

The optimum financial structure is the one which results in the lowest total cost of funds. In the example demonstrated in Table 10–4, the best mix is 60% equity and 40% debt, with a total cost of $12.40. In general, the *implicit cost of debt*, which is reflected by increases in the cost of equity, goes up only slightly at first. However, since most investors are risk averse, the cost tends to rise at an increasing rate as greater amounts of debt are used.

The selection of the financial structure that results in the lowest cost of financing should also produce the highest earnings per share and thereby maximize the market value of the common stock. The next logical question is how to determine the optimum financial structure (that is, ratio of debt to equity) for a given firm. In theory one could experiment using different amounts of debt and note the results, but this is obviously not feasible, at least over a broad range of values. The more useful approach is to study the ratios within the industry as well as those of major firms within the industry and then seek the advice of competent investment bankers.

A Modifying Position

To this point, the discussion has assumed that both operating and financial risk influence the cost of capital. Thus, the way the company is financed—the debt-to-equity ratio—can raise or lower the cost of capital and, in turn, the market value of the common shares. Not everyone shares these views.

Some authorities look to business risk as the basic risk of the business which determines the cost of capital. All things equal, the cost of capital responds only to a change in business risk (i.e., the variability of net operating income). The segment of the income statement after net operating income deals simply with "financial packaging"; it cannot alter the amount of funds available or their variability. The position does not deny the reality of financial risk, but instead holds that it is discounted solely against the common stock and does not affect the valuation of the firm.

Both the modifying proposition and the conventional wisdom recognize that financial leverage affects the required yield on the common shares. The issue is whether a firm can lower its cost of capital by manipulating the financial structure, or whether it can raise the market value (within limits) of the common shares by additions of debt to the financial structure. Probably the weight of practitioner opinion would answer yes, but the available research does not give a definitive response. The issue is of major importance in the evaluation of projects that involve revision of the financial structure (refunding projects or conglomerate mergers).

CALCULATING THE MARGINAL COST OF CAPITAL

The marginal cost of capital is determined by taking a weighted average of the marginal costs of each of the components in the firm's financial structure. Initially, we examine how the marginal costs of each of the components may be determined. Then we discuss the averaging process.

Throughout our discussion of the cost of capital, we use current market values, as opposed to historical book values, to represent the amount of each component in the financial structure. Our choice is based on the fact that the book values represent only historical amounts. For example, the dollar amount of common stock reflected on the firm's balance sheet is not indicative of its current market value. Similarly, the market values of preferred stock and many forms of debt may change appreciably from their book values as market interest rates and money supplies fluctuate.

Common Stock Equity

Chapter 3 develops Equation (1), which relates the firm's cost of equity to the price of the common stock and its dividend, where it is assumed that the dividend will grow at the given rate g for the foreseeable future,

$$K_e = \frac{D_1}{P_0} + g \tag{1}$$

where K_e = cost of common stock equity
D_1 = expected dividend in the next period
P_0 = current market price
g = annual growth rate of the dividend

Because the marginal cost of capital represents the amount that the firm must earn on the net proceeds derived from new issues, it is necessary to consider flotation costs. Therefore, for new issues Equation (1) is rewritten as Equation (2),

$$_nK_e = \frac{D_1}{P_0(1 - F)} + g \tag{2}$$

where $_nK_e$ = cost of new equity capital
F = flotation cost expressed as a percentage of the market price

The value $_nK_e$ discounts the anticipated return on new common stock to equal the net proceeds of the issue. However, once new common is issued, there is no distinction on the security markets between the cost of new and old common. The earnings on the funds raised by the sale of additional shares must be sufficient to cover flotation costs and reward risk or the price of the common shares will decline.

As an alternative to Equation (2), the cost of common stock equity capital may be thought to consist of the return on a risk-free investment such as that available from Treasury notes plus premiums to compensate for the business and financial risks associated with the particular investment.

Retained Earnings

The market value of the common stock reflects the residual value of the firm as perceived by the investors. As such, it encompasses the total common equity portion and therefore includes the firm's retained earnings. Thus, we argue that retained earnings are not relevant to the calculation of the cost of capital since when using market weights, the value of the common stock includes the retained earnings. We are not interested in book values and rather argue that the market discounts retained earnings as a part of the value of common stock. Others take a differing view.

After-tax profits either may be retained in the firm or distributed as cash dividends. Retention of profits presumes the availability of sufficient investment opportunities (either internal or external) to make it more attractive to shareholders for the firm to retain rather than distribute the earnings. As a practical matter, there is generally an upper limit to the amount of earnings a firm may retain. This limit is predicated on the need for the firm to maintain a stable cash dividend policy.

The cost of retained earnings is also a meaningful factor in determining the firm's optimal capital structure. Its computation is significant principally for internal planning: choosing the proportion of new debt, new common, and retained earnings that will minimize the marginal cost of capital. Internally, the cost of *new* common will be greater than the cost of financing by retained earnings, since the funds raised from the new common must earn an amount sufficient to cover the flotation costs plus the yield required to maintain the market value of the common shares.

Cost of Preferred Stock

Most preferred stocks are perpetual, and therefore their explicit costs may be viewed in the same terms as a perpetuity. However, in the same manner as debt, preferred affects financial risk. Accordingly, the true cost of preferred from the perspective of the common shareholders is the rate that must be earned on the assets acquired through preferred financing to cover the yield on the preferred plus the increased yield on the common. The cost of the firm's outstanding preferred is simply its dividend divided by its current market price,

$$K_p = \frac{D_p}{P_p} \qquad (3)$$

where K_p = cost of preferred stock
D_p = preferred dividend
P_p = price of the preferred stock

As was the case for common stock, we must consider flotation costs for new issues of preferred. Thus, Equation (3) is modified as Equation (4),

$$_nK_p = \frac{_nD_p}{_nP_p(1 - F)} \qquad (4)$$

where $_nK_p$ = cost of new preferred equity capital
$\quad _nD_p$ = dividend on the new issue
$\quad F$ = flotation cost expressed as a percentage of the market price
$\quad _nP_p$ = sale price of the new preferred issue

Cost of Debt

Firms have both short- and long-term debts, and it is therefore necessary to consider all forms of debt financing to determine the cost of capital. Some authorities argue that certain short-term obligations are "free" (noninterest bearing) and also that capital budgeting relates only to long-term commitments of invested capital. We reject that position. First, accounts payable and some accruals are only superficially free if the debts are discharged within a defined payment period. At times, firms make regular use of trade credit and choose not to accept the discount for prompt payment. Second, some firms consistently resort to commercial credit to finance current assets, and these finance charges must be covered by earnings just as interest on long-term debt. Third, many capital projects drain working capital and require additional short-term financing. Fourth, the financial structure has interchangeable components. The amount and cost of one type of capital depend upon the proportions raised from other sources. The combination, in turn, shapes the firm's financial risk and the cost of capital. Fifth, accounts payable and accruals, while classified as short term liabilities, tend to roll over and thereby are a part of the firm's permanent financing.

The cost of debt represents an estimate of the yield required to raise designated amounts of short- and/or long-term financing. The firm's commercial banker or investment banker would provide the estimates based on market conditions. The projected yield is placed on an after-tax basis. *However, the total cost of debt involves two elements: the nominal yield based on the face amount of the securities issued when sold at par and the implicit cost or the yield increment on the common needed to maintain its market value in view of the added financial risk.* Note in Table 10–4 the increased return required of the common as debt is added to the capital structure. *Thus, from the viewpoint of the equity holders, the cost of debt is the rate that must be earned on debt-financed assets to cover the net cost of borrowed funds and the incremental yield on the common stock.*

Since we have already dealt with the question of optimum structure with respect to amounts of debt and equity, it is necessary to examine the overall debt structure to ascertain the marginal cost of debt at a given point in time. We assume that the firm has attempted to achieve an optimum debt structure consisting of varying amounts and types of long- and short-term obligations. The optimum structure will, of course, vary over time.

Since interest is tax deductible, the after-tax cost of debt is found using Equation (5),

$$K_i = K(1 - t) \qquad (5)$$

where K_i = after-tax cost of debt
      K = pretax cost of debt (coupon rate on the debt)
      t = firm's marginal tax rate on operating income

For new issues of debt, when flotation costs are involved, Equation (5) is modified to Equation (6),

$$K_i = \frac{I(1 - t)}{P(1 - F)} \qquad (6)$$

where I = dollar amount of interest
     P = sale price of debt
     F = flotation cost as a percentage of the sale price

Equations (5) and (6) are demonstrated in Example 1.

EXAMPLE 1
Cost of Debt

A firm with a 40% marginal tax rate needs $1 million, of which $500,000 is to be funded using debt with the following characteristics:

DEBT	AMOUNT	PRETAX COST	FLOTATION COST
Current liabilities	$200,000	5%	0
Long-term debt	300,000	12	1/2%

Determine the after-tax cost of debt.

SOLUTION: Equation (5) applies to current liabilities, since a flotation cost is not involved:

$$K_i = 0.05(1 - 0.40)$$
$$= 0.030$$
$$= 3\%$$

Equation (6) applies to the long-term portion.

$$K_i = \frac{\$36,000(1 - 0.40)}{\$300,000(1 - 0.005)}$$
$$= \frac{\$21,600}{\$298,500}$$
$$= 0.072$$
$$= 7.2\%$$

Last, the two costs are averaged in proportion to these amounts as shown:

DEBT	AMOUNT	PROPORTION	COST	WEIGHTED COST
Current liabilities	$200,000	0.4	0.030	0.012
Long-term debt	300,000	0.6	0.072	0.043
	$500,000	1.0		0.055

The after-tax cost of debt is 5.5%.

Cost of Depreciation

Depreciation provides a source of funds if the firm generates sufficient sales to cover the costs of production and interest. This is usually the case, and in most instances depreciation is an important source of funds. Depreciation may be used as a source of funds to replace plant and equipment, improve liquidity, or be returned to stockholders by means of the mechanism of stock purchase or, if law permits, through dividends. Since there are a variety of uses for the funds generated through depreciation, they are certainly not free, but rather have an opportunity cost.

Central to the argument of the cost of funds generated through depreciation is the question of how the funds will be used. If the funds are not going to be used to replace assets, but rather to repay debts or distributed to shareholders, the whole process of determining the firm's cost of capital comes into question. The reason for determining the cost of capital is to use it as a benchmark in the evaluation of proposed capital investments. If the firm is not making capital investments, which includes external expansion, the important question is not how to obtain the cost of capital but rather how to otherwise use the funds to best increase shareholder wealth. This might be accomplished by means of reduction of debt (with concurrent reduction of interest expense and financial risk), improving liquidity balances (which also reduces financial risk), distributing funds as dividends (which automatically increases shareholder wealth), or repurchasing stock (which should result in an increase in the market price). All the choices enumerated should increase shareholder wealth.

With respect to utilization of funds generated by means of depreciation, the question to be addressed is: Which use or combination of uses will result in the greatest increase in shareholder wealth? The question may be further expanded to deal with that portion of funds generated through profits but which is not normally distributed as dividends. In general, management who cannot find appropriate uses for funds as investment in capital equipment and the like must then develop plans for using the funds in some other manner to increase shareholder wealth. Since this text deals with capital investment, the subject of alternative uses for funds will not be discussed except as a part of the topic of capital abandonment.

Assuming that funds generated through depreciation are to be utilized as a part of the capital expenditure process, what is their cost? *Since the funds generated through depreciation are a return of investment and since the investment was composed of funds obtained from equity and debt, it is therefore reasonable to use the cost of capital as the cost of depreciation. If this line of reasoning is followed, it is not necessary to include depreciation in the calculation of the cost of capital.* With respect to obtaining the cost of capital, funds generated through depreciation may be ignored, but in making capital expenditures, we should require the same return on investments using funds generated by means of depreciation as we do for all other funds.

The Marginal Cost of Capital

The marginal cost of capital is calculated by taking a weighted average of the marginal cost of each component in proportion to the respective amounts of each that the firm will raise. The process is demonstrated in Example 2.

EXAMPLE 2
Marginal Cost of Capital

A corporation plans to raise $400,000 of new capital as follows:

Current liabilities $20,000 at 11% (assume no flotation or service charge)
Long-term debt $50,000 at 9% (flotation costs, $\frac{1}{2}$ of 1%)
Preferred stock B $30,000, flotation cost ($F$) estimated at 2%; sold at $42 per share with a stated dividend of $2.50
Common stock $300,000, flotation cost (F) estimated at 10%, dividend $1 per share; market price $50 per share, anticipated growth rate of dividend, 10%

The firm's marginal tax rate is 40%. Determine the cost of each component and the marginal cost of capital.

SOLUTION: Cost of long-term debt:

$$K_i = \frac{I(1-t)}{P(1-F)} = \frac{\$4,500(1-0.4)}{\$50,000(1-0.005)} = \frac{\$2,700}{\$49,750} = 0.0543$$

Cost of preferred:

$$_nK_p = \frac{_nD_p}{_nP_p(1-F)} = \frac{\$2.50}{\$42(1-0.02)} = \frac{\$2.50}{\$41.16} = 0.0607$$

Cost of new common:

$$_nK_e = \frac{D_1}{P_0(1-F)} + g = \frac{\$1.00}{\$50(1-0.10)} + 0.10 = \frac{\$1.00}{\$45} + 0.10 = 0.1222$$

MARGINAL COST OF CAPITAL (K_{MC})

	MARKET VALUES	MARKET WEIGHTS	AFTER-TAX COST	WEIGHTED AFTER-TAX COST
Current liabilities	$ 20,000	0.050	0.0660	0.00300
Long-term debt	50,000	0.125	0.0543	0.00679
Preferred stock B	30,000	0.075	0.0607	0.00455
New common	300,000	0.750	0.1222	0.09165
	$400,000		Marginal cost of capital =	0.106

The marginal cost of capital is 10.6%.

1. Why is it necessary to use market rather than book values when computing the cost of capital?

2. The cost of capital is dynamic—changing from period to period. Explain the underlying reasons for this statement.

3. What is meant by the "implicit" cost of debt?

4. When computing the cost of capital, why is it unnecessary to compute the costs of depreciation and retained earnings?

5. Since debt generally has a nominal cost that is less than the cost of common stock and since interest is tax deductible, it would seem reasonable that the use of debt should reduce the cost of capital. Discuss.

6. While we advocate computing the cost of capital based upon the firm's anticipated mix of debt and equity, financial analysts utilize book values to compute debt-to-equity and similar ratios. Given the frequent significant difference between market- and book-based values for ratios which measure financial leverage, do analysts "force" a firm to use a non-optimum financial structure?

7. Abcom, Inc., expects to pay dividends on its common stock of $3.50 per share next year. The dividend has been growing at an annual rate of 4%. If the market price of the stock is $65.00, determine the cost of its common stock equity. If Abcom decides to issue additional stock and the flotation cost is 11%, determine the cost of its common stock equity.

8. Alexander Utilities, Inc., plans to issue preferred stock. The price will be $100.00 per share, the dividend $9.00 and the flotation cost 12%. Determine the cost of the new preferred stock.

9. Manufacturing Company plans to issue long-term bonds. It will pay 9.5% interest and will have a 4% flotation cost. If Manufacturing Company's marginal tax rate is 40%, determine the cost of the new debt.

10. The Kay Manufacturing Corporation plans to raise $2,000,000 of new capital for a plant expansion. The debt structure it plans is as follows:

Current liabilities	$100,000 at 12%
Long-term debt	$550,000 at 9.25%, flotation costs 0.75%
Preferred stock	$350,000, flotation cost 2.5%; sold at $35 per share with a $1.75 dividend
Common stock	$1,000,000, flotation cost estimated at 10%, dividend $1.25 per share; market price $47, anticipated growth in dividend, 8%

The firm's marginal tax rate is 40%. Determine the cost of each component and the after-tax marginal cost of capital.

11. The Lemanski Corporation intends to raise $6,000,000 of new capital by the following methods:

Current liabilities	Increase by $600,000 at 13.46% financing
Long-term debt	$1,800,000 at 7.78% financing with a flotation cost of 9%
Preferred stock	$600,000 with a flotation cost of 15%; stock will be sold at $50 per share with a stated dividend of $4
Common stock	$3,000,000 with a flotation cost of 12%; stock will be sold at $50 per share; the expected dividend per share is $2.50, with a dividend growth rate of 12%

The corporation tax rate is 40%.

(a) Determine the cost of each component and calculate the marginal cost of capital.

(b) What is the marginal cost of capital if all flotation costs are reduced by one-third?

REFERENCES

Agmon, T., A. P. Ofer, and A. Tamir. "Variable Rate Debt Instruments and Corporate Debt Policy." *Journal of Finance* (December 1980).

Aivazian, V. A., and J. L. Callen. "Investment, Market Structure, and the Cost of Capital." *Journal of Finance* (March 1979).

Arditti, Fred D. "The Weighted Average Cost of Capital: Some Questions on Its Definition, Interpretation and Use." *Journal of Finance* (September 1973).

_____, and Haim Levy. "The Weighted Average Cost of Capital as a Cutoff Rate: A Critical Analysis of the Classical Textbook Weighted Average." *Financial Management* (Fall 1977).

_____, H. Levy, and M. Sarnat. "Taxes, Capital Structure, and the Cost of Capital: Some Extensions." *Quarterly Review of Economics and Business* (Summer 1977).

_____, and J. M. Pinkerton. "The Valuation and Cost of Capital of the Levered Firm with Growth Opportunities." *Journal of Finance* (March 1978).

_____, "Risk and the Required Return on Equity." *Journal of Finance*, 22 (March 1967), 19–36.

_____, and Stephen A. Tysseland. "Three Ways to Present the Marginal Cost of Capital." *Financial Management* (Summer 1973), 63–67.

Barges, Alexander. *The Effect of Capital Structure on the Cost of Capital.* Englewood Cliffs, N.J.: Prentice Hall, 1963.

Barnea, A., R. Haugen, and L. Senbet. "An Equilibrium Analysis of Debt Financing under Costly Tax Arbitrage and Agency Problems." *Journal of Finance* (June 1981).

Baron, David P., and Holmström Bengt. "The Investment Banking Contract for New Issues Under Asymmetric Information: Delegation and the Incentive Problem." *Journal of Finance* (December 1980).

_____. "Default Risk and the Modigliani-Miller Theorem: A Synthesis." *American Economic Review*, 66 (March 1976), 204–212.

_____. "Default Risk, Homemade Leverage, and the Modigliani-Miller Theorem." *American Economic Review*, 64 (March 1974), 176–182.

Baumol, William, and Burton G. Malkiel. "The Firm's Optimal Debt-Equity Combination and the Cost of Capital." *Quarterly Journal of Economics*, 81 (November 1967), 547–578.

Ben-Horim, Moshe. "Comment on 'The Weighted Average Cost of Capital as a Cutoff Rate'." *Financial Management* (Summer 1979).

Ben-Shahar, Haim, and Abraham Ascher. "Capital Budgeting and Stock Valuation: Comment." *American Economic Review*, 57 (March 1967), 209–214.

Beranek, William. "The Cost of Capital, Capital Budgeting, and the Maximization of Shareholder Wealth." *Journal of Financial and Quantitative Analysis* (March 1975).

_____. "The Weighted Average Cost of Capital and Shareholder Wealth Maximization." *Journal of Financial and Quantitative Analysis* (March 1977).

Black, Fischer, and John C. Cox. "Valuing Corporate Securities: Some Effects on Bond Indenture Provisions." *Journal of Finance*, 31 (May 1976), 351–368.

_____, and Myron Scholes. "The Pricing of Options and Corporate Liabilities." *Journal of Political Economy*, 81 (May–June 1973), 637–654.

Bodenhorn, Diran. "On the Problem of Capital Budgeting." *Journal of Finance*, 14 (December 1959), 473–492.

Boudreaux, Kenneth J., and Hugh W. Long. "The Weighted Average Cost of Capital as a Cutoff Rate: A Further Analysis." *Financial Management* (Summer 1979).

Brigham, Eugene F., and Myron J. Gordon. "Leverage, Dividend Policy, and the Cost of Capital." *Journal of Finance*, 23 (March 1968), 85–104.

_____, and Keith V. Smith. "The Cost of Capital to the Small Firm." *The Engineering Economist* (Fall 1967).

Chambers, Donald R., Robert S. Harris, and John J. Pringle. "Treatment of Financing Mix in Analyzing Investment Opportunities." *Financial Management* (Summer 1982).

Chen, Andrew H., and John W. Kensinger. "Innovations in Corporate Financing: Tax-Deductible Equity." *Financial Management* (Winter 1985).

De Angelo, Harry, and Ronald W. Masulis. "Optimal Capital Structure under Corporate and Personal Taxation." *Journal of Financial Economics*, 8 (March 1980), 3–29.

Elliott, Walter J. "The Cost of Capital and U.S. Capital Investment: A Test of Alternative Concepts." *The Journal of Finance* (September 1980).

Ezzamel, Mahmoud A. "Estimating the Cost of Capital for a Division of a Firm, and the Allocation Problem in Accounting: A Comment." *Journal of Business Finance and Accounting* (Spring 1980).

Ezzell, J. R., and R. B. Porter. "Flotation Costs and the Weighted Average Cost of Capital." *Journal of Financial and Quantitative Analysis* (September 1976).

_____, and _____. "Correct Specification of the Cost of Capital and Net Present Value." *Financial Management* (Summer 1979).

Fabozzi, F. J., and R. A. Hershkoff. "The Effect of the Decision to List on a Stock's Systematic Risk." *Review of Business and Economic Research* (Spring 1979).

Fama, Eugene F. "Risk-Adjusted Discount Rates and Capital Budgeting Under Uncertainty." *Journal of Financial Economics*, 5 (1977).

_____. "The Effects of a Firm's Investment and Financing Decisions on the Welfare of Its Security Holders," *American Economic Review*, 68 (June 1978), 272–284.

_____, and Merton H. Miller. *The Theory of Finance*. New York: Holt, 1972, Chap. 4.

Findlay, M. Chapman, III. "The Weighted Average Cost of Capital and Finite Flows." *Journal of Business Finance and Accounting* (1977).

Frank, J. R., and J. J. Pringle. "Debt Financing Corporate Financial Intermediation and Firm Valuation." *Journal of Finance* (June 1982).

Gitman, Lawrence, and Vincent A. Mercurio. "Cost of Capital Techniques Used by Major U.S. Firms: Survey and Analysis of *Fortune*'s 1000." *Financial Management*, 11 (Winter 1982), 21–29.

Gordon, Myron J., and Clarence C. Y. Kwan. "Debt Maturity, Default Risk, and Capital Structure." *Journal of Banking and Finance*, 3 (December 1979) 313–329.

_____, and Paul J. Halper. "Cost of Capital for a Division of a Firm." *Journal of Finance* (September 1974).

_____, and L. I. Gould. "The Cost of Equity Capital: A Reconsideration." *Journal of Finance* (June 1978).

_____, and Eli Shapiro. "Capital Equipment Analysis: The Required Rate of Profit." *Management Science* (October 1956).

Greenfield, Robert L., Maury R. Randall, and John C. Woods. "Financial Leverage and Use of the Net Present Value Criterion." *Financial Management* (Autumn 1983).

Gup, Benton E., and Samuel W. Norwood, III. "Divisional Cost of Capital: A Practical Approach." *Financial Management*, 11 (Spring 1982), 20–24.

Haley, Charles W. "Taxes, The Cost of Capital, and the Firm's Investment Decisions." *Journal of Finance* (September 1971).

_____, and L. D. Schall. "Problems with the Concept of the Cost of Capital." *Journal of Financial and Quantitative Analysis* (December 1978).

Hamada, Robert S., and Myron Scholes. "Taxes and Corporate Financial Management" in Edward I. Altman and Marti Subrahmanrjam, eds. *Recent Advances in Corporate Finance.* Homewood, Ill.: Richard D. Irwin, 1985, Chapter 8.

Harris, Robert S., and John J. Pringle. "Implications of Miller's Argument for Capital Budgeting." *Journal of Financial Research* (Spring 1983).

Heins, A. James, and Case M. Sprenkle. "A Comment on the Modigliani-Miller Cost of Capital Thesis." *American Economic Review*, 59 (September 1969), 590–592.

Henderson, Glenn V., Jr. "Shareholder Taxation and the Required Rate of Return on Internally Generated Funds." *Financial Management* (Summer 1976).

_____. "In Defense of the Weighted Average Cost of Capital." *Financial Management* (Autumn 1979), 57–61.

Howe, Keith M. "A Note on Flotation Costs and Capital Budgeting." *Financial Management* (Winter 1982).

_____, and James H. Patterson. "Capital Investment Decisions under Economies of Scale in Flotation Costs." *Financial Management* (Autumn 1985).

Keane, Simon M. "The Cost of Capital as a Financial Decision Tool." *Journal of Business Finance and Accounting* (Autumn 1978).

Kim, Moon H. "Weighted Average vs. True Cost of Capital." *Financial Management* (Spring 1974).

Lerner, Eugene M., and Willard T. Carleton. "Financing Decisions of the Firm." *Journal of Finance*, 21 (May 1966), 202–214.

_____, and_____. "The Integration of Capital Budgeting and Stock Valuation." *American Economic Review*, 54 (September 1964), 327–346.

_____, and_____. *A Theory of Financial Analysis*. New York: Harcourt Brace Jovanovich, 1966.

Levy, Haim, and Robert Brooks. "Financial Break-Even Analysis and the Value of the Firm." *Financial Management* (Autumn 1986).

Lewellen, Wilbur G. *The Cost of Capital*. Belmont, Calif.: Wadsworth Publishing Co., Inc., 1969, Chaps. 3, 4.

Lintner, John. "Dividends, Earnings, Leverage, Stock Prices and the Supply of Capital to Corporations." *Review of Economics and Statistics*, 44 (August 1962), 243–269.

Litzenberger, Robert H., and James C. Van Horne. "Elimination of the Double Taxation of Dividends and Corporate Financial Policy." *Journal of Finance*, 33 (June 1978), 737–749.

_____, and Rao, C. U. "Portfolio Theory and Industry Cost-of-Capital Estimates." *Journal of Financial and Quantitative Analysis* (March 1972).

Livingston, M. "Taxation and Bond Market Equilibrium in a World of Uncertain Future Interest Rates." *Journal of Financial and Quantitative Analysis* (March 1979).

_____. "The Pricing of Premium Bonds." *Journal of Financial and Quantitative Analysis* (September 1979).

Malkiel, Burton G. *The Debt-Equity Combination of the Firm and the Cost of Capital: An Introductory Analysis*. Morristown, N.J.: General Learning Press, 1971.

_____, and John G. Cragg. "Expectations and the Structure of Share Prices." *American Economic Review*, 60 (September 1970), 601–617.

Miles, James A., and John R. Ezzell. "The Weighted Average Cost of Capital, Perfect Capital Markets, and Project Life: A Clarification." *Journal of Financial and Quantitative Analysis* (September 1980).

Modigliani, Franco, and M. H. Miller. "The Cost of Capital, Corporation Finance and the Theory of Investment." *American Economic Review*, 48 (June 1958), 261–297.

_____, and _____. "The Cost of Capital, Corporation Finance and the Theory of Investment: Reply." *American Economic Review*, 49 (September 1958), 655–669; "Taxes and the Cost of Capital: A Correction." ibid., 53 (June 1963), 433–443; "Reply." ibid., 55 (June 1965), 524–527; "Reply to Heins and Sprenkle." ibid., 59 (September 1969), 592–595.

Nantell, Timothy J., and Robert C. Carlson. "The Cost of Capital as a Weighted Average." *Journal of Finance* (December 1975).

Porterfield, James T. S. *Investment Decisions and Capital Costs*. Englewood Cliffs, N.J.: Prentice Hall, 1965.

Resek, Robert W. "Multidimensional Risk and the Modigliani-Miller Hypothesis," *Journal of Finance*, 25 (March 1970), 47–52.

Robichek, Alexander A., and Steward C. Myers. *Optimal Financing Decisions*. Englewood Cliffs, N.J.: Prentice Hall, 1965.

Schneller, Meir I. "Taxes and the Optimal Capital Structure of the Firm." *Journal of Finance*, 35 (March 1980), 119–127.

Schwartz, Eli. "Theory of the Capital Structure of the Firm." *Journal of Finance*, 14 (March 1959).

_____, and J. Richard Aronson. "Some Surrogate Evidence in Support of the Concept of Optimal Capital Structure." *Journal of Finance*, 22 (March 1967), 10–18.

Seitz, Neil. "Shareholder Goals, Firm Goals, and Firm Financing Decisions." *Financial Management*, 11 (Autumn 1982), 20–26.

Shapiro, Alan C. "In Defense of the Traditional Weighted Average Cost of Capital as a Cutoff Rate." *Financial Management* (Summer 1979).

Siegel, Jeremy F. "The Application of the DCF Methodology for Determining the Cost of Equity Capital." *Financial Management* (Spring 1985).

Smith, Richard L. "The Choice of Issuance Procedure and the Cost of Competitive and Negotiated Underwriting: An Examination of the Impact of Rule 50." *Journal of Finance* (July 1987).

Stiglitz, Joseph E. "A Re-examination of the Modigliani-Miller Theorem." *American Economic Review*, 59 (December 1969), 784–793.

_____. "On the Irrelevance of Corporate Financial Policy." *American Economic Review*, 64 (December 1974), 851–866.

Titman, Sheridan, and Roberto Wessels. "The Determinants of Capital Structure Choice." *Journal of Finance* (March 1988).

Whitington, G. "The Profitability of Retained Earnings." *Review of Economics and Statistics* (May 1972).

Wippern, Ronald F. "Financial Structure and the Value of the Firm." *Journal of Finance*, 21 (December 1966), 615–634.

Zhu, Yu, and Irwin Friend. "The Effects of Different Taxes on Risky and Risk-Free Investment and on the Cost of Capital." *Journal of Finance* (July 1986).

CASE STUDY 10-1

Best Foods, Inc. (A)

(Cost of capital)

Best Foods, Inc., was incorporated under the laws of Texas on March 19, 1956, and became a Delaware Corporation on August 30, 1983. Best Foods processes and markets frozen vegetables and also transports general commodities in all states except Alaska and Hawaii.

Exhibit 1 presents a five-year comparison of the important financial indicators on the performance of the company. The 26.9% decrease in 1987 revenues was primarily the result of the sale of the Freezer Queen Division which had revenues in fiscal year 1986 of approximately $44 million. Net income in fiscal year 1986 amounted to $20 million, including a gain on the sale of division assets amounting to $29.6 million. However, in fiscal year 1987, net income was a high $4.3 million with no sale or gain of any division assets. Earnings per share in fiscal year 1987 were higher than any of the previous five years. Common stock prices at the end of fiscal year 1987 were much higher than the preceding year. Finally, the price–earnings ratio of the common stock at fiscal year-end 1987 was much higher than at fiscal year-end 1986, though much lower than the fiscal years ending 1984 and 1985.

Sales of frozen vegetables are somewhat seasonal. Historically, sales have been lower during the summer months, when fresh products are available to the consumer. Also vegetable crops are seasonal and their availability is always subject to unpredictable changes in growing conditions and adverse weather conditions.

The company is faced with substantial competition in all aspects of its business. The frozen food industry is highly competitive, and competition has increased as the industry has matured over the years. The company believes the total production capacity of the industry is now in excess of 120% of current requirements. At the company itself the overall utilization of production capacity is approximately 70%.

On February 28, 1987, the company had approximately 1,400 full-time employees, of whom approximately 1,250 were engaged in processing and service activities and 150 in sales and administration. The company has labor agreements covering employees in Fairmont, Minnesota; Salinas, California; and Rossville, Tennessee. In order to remain competitive, the company must reduce its labor costs. However, the company's competitors have experienced strikes in the course of their efforts to reduce labor costs.

Faced with these market conditions, management is considering making a number of capital investments that would reduce operating costs as well as acquiring existing businesses in order to boost the profitability of the company and smooth out the seasonality of sales. A number of potential target companies were identified and possible capital investments were determined. The question that arose was how to evaluate each of these target companies and determine which one(s) would be most desirable to acquire. In order to evaluate these companies, management is using the net present value method which requires the analyst to discount the projected stream of future dividends of the target companies at the acquirer's cost of capital to obtain a theoretical market price on the shares of the proposed acquisitions. This theoretical price would then be compared with the actual market price in order to make a decision of whether the potential candidate is worth further investigation. Therefore, the first task of management is to calculate the cost of capital of Best Foods, Inc.

The chief financial officer (CFO) at Best Foods has suggested the use of the weighted average cost of capital. This is calculated by taking into account the implicit and explicit costs of the different sources of funds and by using market value weights and nominal yields. However, the chief executive officer (CEO) argues that since the debt-to-equity ratio of the company is very low, the proposed acquisitions should be debt financed and the discount rate would be the cost of the new debt to be acquired. He also contends that Best Foods' stockholders will benefit by the increase in the company's debt-to-equity ratio, since the firm can borrow capital for less than it earns on its equity capital and the increased earnings will ultimately revert to the common shareholders. Finally, the CEO has pointed out to the CFO that the proposed acquisitions have different risk postures than the company and therefore the weighted average cost of capital of the company is inappropriate as a cutoff rate in the evaluation of the target companies.

The CFO's reply is to agree on the difference of risk postures between the company and the proposed acquisitions but he cannot find a relationship between the profitability of the firm and its market value on one hand and its capital structure on the other hand. A firm cannot change the total value of its securities just by splitting its cash flows into different streams. The company's value is determined by its real assets, not by the securities it issues. Moreover, if the stockholders want to maintain a certain leverage level, they can do it on their own by borrowing and buying unlevered shares. However, the CEO has presented an opposing argument. Debt financing is advantageous since it is a tax-deductable expense. Dividends and retained earnings are not.

The CFO quickly indicates the invalidity of the CEO's argument. If tax shields are valuable assets, why is it that firms are not 90% debt-financed or higher? The CFO believes that it is more appropriate to finance the acquisitions by new equity issuance and/or the use of the excess cash available currently and therefore he cannot justify the use of any discount rate except the weighted average cost of capital of the company. However, again the CEO cannot agree with the CFO. If these acquisitions are to be financed by the issuance of new shares, then the discount rate to be used in evaluating the proposed acquisitions should be the cost of this new capital alone and not the weighted average cost of capital (old and new) of the company.

The CFO and CEO have different points of view but agree on the importance of determining accurately the appropriate discount rate to be used in the evaluation of the proposed acquisitions. For instance, one of the target companies had $3.00 of dividends during the last fiscal year with an expected growth rate of 10% during the following years and had a price per share of $123.50 at fiscal year-end. If the cost of capital to the company is 13% then the theoretical price per share of this proposed acquisition would be:

$$\frac{\$3 \times 1.1}{(0.13 - 0.10)} = \$110.00$$

and therefore this firm would not appear to be worth more investigation. If the cost of capital to the company is 12% (only 1% less) then the theoretical price per share of this proposed acquisition would be

$$\frac{\$3 \times 1.1}{(0.12 - 0.10)} = \$165.00$$

and therefore this firm would be a good acquisition. As such, management might end up considering unworthy acquisitions if its discount rate is lower than the actual cost of capital or foregoing good investments because the discount rate used is higher than the actual cost of capital.

QUESTIONS

1   Calculate the weighted average cost of capital of Best Foods.
2   Discuss the appropriateness of using the WACC as a cutoff rate in the evaluation of capital projects. Would the marginal cost of capital be more appropriate? Explain.
3   Use the CAPM to calculate the required return on the shares of the company. Would you use this figure as a proxy for the cost of capital of the company? Explain.
4   If management wants to acquire companies whose returns exceed Best Foods' cost of capital, would it not be increasing its risk posture on the argument that higher return is associated with higher risk? Explain.
5   Based on the financial position of the firm, would you recommend that management finance the acquisitions by new debt as opposed to new equity? Would you rather recommend internal financing? Which financial strategy would increase the market value of the firm? Explain.
6   What factors should Best Foods consider when deciding what its target capital structure should be and in deciding whether or not to add more debt to its capital structure? Discuss.

Exhibit 1   Five-Year Financial Highlights Year Ended February 28 or 29
(in thousands U.S. $ unless per share or percentage)

	1987	1986	1985	1984	1983
Sales	119,182	163,056	177,238	183,630	166,540
Net income	4,309	20,061	1,325	2,276	6,465
Earnings per share	0.32	1.44	0.10	1.16	0.46
Dividends per share					
Class A common share	0.10	0.31	0.10	0.05	—
Class B common share	—	0.20	—	0.05	0.10
Net income/Net worth %	8.27	56.3	3.8	6.8	22.0
Current ratio	3.32	2.45	4.50	3.68	4.31
Property and equipment (net)	30,503	31,782	32,782	35,473	36,889
Long-term debt	16,326	15,494	50,640	50,702	64,501
Stockholders' equity	52,459	52,121	35,634	34,886	33,481
Common stock price					
Class A common share	$2\frac{1}{8}$	$1\frac{7}{8}$	$1\frac{7}{8}$	3	—
Class B common share	$2\frac{7}{8}$	2	$1\frac{3}{4}$	3	$2\frac{3}{8}$
Price/Earnings ratio					
Class A common share	6.6	1.3	18.8	18.8	—
Class B common share	9.0	1.4	17.5	18.8	5.2
Riskless rate of return	5.56%	5.97%	7.49%	9.57%	8.62%
Market rate of return	12.7%	13.7%	14.3%	14.8%	14.6%
β of Best Foods	0.8	0.9	1.2	1.2	1.4

Exhibit 2   Statement of Income (in thousands of U.S. $)

	YEAR ENDED FEBRUARY 28		
	1987	1986	1985
Sales	$119,182	$163,056	$177,238
Cost of sales	91,987	117,669	129,057
Gross profits	$ 27,195	$ 45,387	$ 48,181
Selling, administrative and general expenses	25,110	41,600	38,820
Operating income	$ 2,085	$ 3,787	$ 9,361
Other income (expense)	6,444	29,720	(1,346)
Earnings before interest and taxes	$ 8,529	$ 33,507	$ 8,015
Interest expense	2,329	5,094	5,851
Earnings before taxes	$ 6,200	$ 28,413	$ 2,164
Taxes on Income	1,891	8,352	839
Net Income	$ 4,309	$ 20,061	$ 1,325

Exhibit 3   Balance Sheets (in thousands of U.S. $)

ASSETS	FEBRUARY 28	
	1987	1986
Current		
Cash	$ 618	$ 1,755
Accounts and notes receivable	13,869	14,657
Inventories	32,516	36,677
Prepaid expenses and miscellaneous	1,658	2,125
	$48,661	$55,214
Property and Equipment		
Land	$ 3,196	$ 8,798
Buildings	16,780	18,768
Equipment	36,708	38,355
Less: accumulated depreciation and amortization	(21,240)	(28,285)
	$35,444	$37,636
Total assets	$84,105	$92,850

LIABILITIES	FEBRUARY 28	
	1987	1986
Current		
Accounts payable	$ 6,886	$ 5,219
Accruals	2,894	4,767
Dividends payable	166	2,949
Income taxes payable	2,969	7,025
Current maturities of long-term debt	$ 1,731	$ 2,551
Total current liabilities	$14,646	$22,511
Long-term debt	16,326	15,494
Deferred income taxes	674	2,724
Total liabilities	$31,646	$40,729

STOCKHOLDERS' EQUITY

Common stock, Class A	$ 7,590	$ 7,576
Common stock, Class B	7,156	7,169
Additional paid-in capital	3,171	6,432
Retained earnings	34,542	30,944
Total stockholders' equity	$52,459	$52,121
Total liabilities and stockholders' equity	$84,105	$92,850

Exhibit 4   Long-Term Debt (in thousands of U.S. $)

	FEBRUARY 28	
	1987	1986
Notes and Contracts:		
Revolving credit note to bank collateralized by trade receivables and inventories; borrowing limit $55 millions; due November 1989, with interest at the bank's base rate (7.5% at February 28, 1987) plus 1%.	$ 3,940	$ —
First mortgage notes due May 2002 ($8\frac{1}{2}$% per annum)	5,061	5,617
$7\frac{3}{4}$% mortgage notes due to 1999	8,243	9,376
Total Notes and Contracts	$17,244	$14,993
Capital Lease Obligations:		
$4\frac{5}{8}$ to $6\frac{1}{4}$% mortgage revenue bonds due to 1989	$ 670	$ 2,780
$4\frac{1}{4}$ to $7\frac{3}{4}$% capital lease obligations due to 1993	143	272
Total capital lease obligations	$ 813	$ 3,052
Totals	$18,057	$18,045
Less current maturities	$ 1,731	$ 2,551
Long-term debt	$16,326	$15,494

Introduction to Risk Analysis

11

During the first part of our study of capital investments (in Part II of the text), we assumed that any decisions involving investments would not alter the risk complexion of the firm. This is not to say that we were operating under conditions of certainty, but rather that we held risk constant. However, it is a truism that it is frequently difficult to make either short- or long-term estimates of the cash flows for capital investments with a high degree of accuracy. As a consequence, in this and the following chapters, we examine capital investment decisions under conditions of risk and uncertainty. Initially, we direct our attention to individual projects and then to portfolios of projects.

CERTAINTY, RISK, AND UNCERTAINTY

Up to this point we have assumed that projects being considered have a risk posture consistent with that of the firm overall. This means that the acceptance of projects would not change the firm's risk complexion (i.e., risk has been held constant). A decision maker may be faced with conditions of certainty, risk, or uncertainty; these are differentiated as follows:

☐ *Certainty* postulates that the decision maker knows in advance the precise values of all the parameters possibly affecting the decision.

☐ *Risk* postulates that the decision maker is (1) aware of all possible future states of the economy, business, and so on, which may occur and thereby affect relevant decision parameters and (2) able to place a probability on the value of the occurrence of each of these states.

☐ *Uncertainty* postulates that the decision maker (1) may not be aware of all the possible states that affect the decision and/or (2) may not be able to place a probability on the occurrence of each.

We deal with conditions of certainty and risk, assuming for the present that it is possible to reduce problems under conditions of uncertainty to those of risk by collecting additional data (at some cost). We recognize that techniques such as adaptive and optimal control processes, heuristic programming, and artificial intelligence methods are currently being developed to deal with capital investment evaluation under conditions of uncertainty. Although we shall not deal with any of these, we expect, as they become more fully developed, that they will become an integral part of the risk analysis methodology.

At this juncture it is useful to review the general kinds of risk faced by financial managers. Although the types of risk tend to be interrelated, it is helpful in financial planning, decision making, and control to identify various categories. We shall refer to these in this and the following chapters as we examine the capital investment decision under conditions of risk.

1   *Business risk* is the variability in earnings that is a function of the firm's normal operations (as impacted by the changing economic environment) and management's decisions with respect to capital intensification. The use of more capital equipment (increasing operating leverage) generally results in higher fixed costs and thereby increases the variability of earnings before interest and taxes (EBIT) with output (as measured by the degree of operating leverage). It should be noted that business risk considers only the variability in EBIT, and does not consider the effect of debt or other financing on the firm's risk posture. Although business risk encompasses the variability in earnings due to economic changes and management investment policies, it is instructive to view these as investment and portfolio risk.

2   *Investment risk* is the variability in earnings due to variations in the cash inflows and outflows of capital investment projects undertaken. This risk is associated with forecasting errors made in market acceptance of products, future technological changes, the degree of intertemporal relationship of cash flows, changes in costs related to projects, and other environmental risks discussed shortly.

3   *Portfolio risk* is the variability in the earnings due to the degree of efficient diversification that the firm has achieved in its operations and its overall portfolio of assets. The risk is reduced by the firm seeking out capital projects and merger candidates that have a low or negative correlation with its present operations. The full impact of portfolio effects is discussed in Chapter 14.

4   *Cataclysmic risk* is the variability in earnings that is a function of events beyond managerial control and anticipation. Such events would include expropriation, erratic changes in consumer preferences, severe energy shortages, and the like. Insurance may provide some protection against such risks.

5   *Financial risk* is the variability in earnings that is a function of the financial structure and the necessity of meeting obligations on fixed-income securities. The use of more debt or preferred stock (increasing financial leverage) results in greater obligatory payments and thereby increases the variability of earnings after taxes (EAT) and earnings per share (EPS) (as measured by the degree of financial leverage).

Business and financial risk and the effects of operating and financial leverage were discussed in Chapter 10. Our next objective is to discuss methods of measuring expected return and the possible dispersion of return resulting from the various risks facing the firm.

RISK AND RETURN

Since risk is an inherent part of almost all capital investment decisions, it is necessary to consider it as well as the expected return associated with various decision alternatives. The probability distribution, which describes all possible outcomes, must be defined along with the mean or expected value of cash flows in order to evaluate alternative courses of action. The expected value of a probability distribution is defined in Equation (1),

$$\overline{R} = \sum_{i=1}^{N} (R_i P_i) \qquad (1)$$

where $\overline{R}$ = expected value
   R_i = return associated with the ith outcome
   P_i = probability of occurrence of the ith outcome
   N = number of possible outcomes

Calculation of the expected return for an investment is demonstrated in Example 1.

EXAMPLE 1

Expected Return

A financial manager faces conditions of risk in terms of economic strength in the coming year. Three different states may occur: strong economy with probability 0.3; moderately strong economy, 0.5; and weak economy, 0.2. Three alternative 1-year investments are under consideration offering returns as follows:

STATE OF ECONOMY	PROBABILITY	EXPECTED INVESTMENT OUTCOMES		
		A	B	C
Strong	0.3	$1,800	$1,600	$2,000
Moderately strong	0.5	1,500	1,200	1,600
Weak	0.2	800	1,000	900

Determine the expected return for project A.

SOLUTION: For investment A, using Equation (1) we find:

$$\overline{R} = (0.3)(\$1,800) + (0.5)(\$1,500) + (0.2)(\$800)$$

$$= \$540 + \$750 + \$160$$

$$= \$1,450$$

The mean return for investment A is $1,450. This return is determined by weighting the return for each state of the economy by its respective probability of occurrence. The expected return for investment B is $1,280 and for investment C is $1,580.

The amount of variability or dispersion that is present in the probability distribution of returns associated with a decision alternative is referred to as the risk of that decision alternative. There are several measures of risk that have been advocated for use by financial managers. Statisticians speak of both *absolute* and *relative measures of risk* (variability or dispersion). *Absolute measures of dispersion* include the range, mean absolute deviation, variance, standard deviation, and semivariance. The *relative measure of dispersion is the coefficient of variation*. Each of these measures is defined in equation form and then illustrated and discussed in Example 2.

The range (R_g) is found by

$$R_g = R_h - R_l \tag{2}$$

where R_g = range of the distribution
R_h = highest value in the distribution
R_l = lowest value in the distribution

The mean absolute deviation (MAD) equals

$$\text{MAD} = \sum_{i=1}^{N} P_i \left(|R_i - \overline{R}| \right) \tag{3}$$

The variance (σ^2) is found using Equation (4):

$$\sigma^2 = \sum_{i=1}^{N} P_i \left(R_i - \overline{R} \right)^2 \tag{4}$$

The standard deviation (σ) is the square root of the variance:

$$\sigma = \sqrt{\sum_{i=1}^{N} P_i \left(R_i - \overline{R} \right)^2} \tag{5}$$

The semivariance (SV) is computed using Equation (6),

$$\text{SV} = \sum_{j=1}^{K} P_j \left(R_j - \overline{R} \right)^2 \tag{6}$$

where j = index set, which includes all values of the random variable that are less than the expected value
K = number of outcomes less than the expected value

Finally, the coefficient of variation (v) equals

$$v = \frac{\sigma}{\overline{R}} \tag{7}$$

The calculation of the various measures of risk or dispersion is demonstrated in Example 2.

EXAMPLE 2
Measurement of Risk

Using the information in Example 1, determine the value for each measure of risk as just defined for investment A.

SOLUTION:

$$R_g = \text{range} = \$1,800 - \$800 = \$1,000$$

This value simply means that there is a $1,000 difference between the lowest return that could be earned with investment A and the highest possible return. The range for investment B is $600 and for investment C is $1,100.

$$\text{MAD} = (0.3)(|\$1,800 - \$1,450|) + (0.5)(|\$1,500 - \$1,450|) + (0.2)(|\$800 - \$1,450|)$$

$$= (0.3)(\$350) + (0.5)(\$50) + (0.2)(\$650)$$

$$= \$260$$

The MADs for investments B and C are $192 and $272, respectively. MAD shows the average variability of the values of the distribution from the mean without regard to the sign of the deviation.

$$\sigma^2 = (0.2)(\$800 - \$1,450)^2 + (0.5)(\$1,500 - \$1,450)^2 + (0.3)(\$1,800 - \$1,450)^2$$

$$= (0.2)(-\$650)^2 + (0.5)(\$50)^2 + (0.3)(\$350)^2$$

$$= 122,500$$

$$\sigma = \sqrt{\sigma^2} = \$350$$

The standard deviation is a measure of how representative the expected return is of the entire distribution. The larger the standard deviation, the less representative the mean is because of the greater scatter around the mean. The variance and standard deviation for investment *B* are 49,600 and $222.71, respectively, and for investment C are 145,600 and $381.58.

    The final absolute measure of dispersion is the semivariance, which is similar to the variance but considers only deviations below the mean, since these are the unfavorable deviations that quantify the downside risk.

$$\text{SV} = (0.2)(\$800 - \$1,450)^2 = (0.2)(422,500)$$

$$= 84,500$$

    Note that the downside risk as measured by the semivariance is about 70% of the total variability as measured by the variance for investment A (84,500 as compared with 122,500). The semivariances for investments B and C are 18,880 and 92,480, respectively. Finally,

$$\nu = \frac{\$350}{\$1,450} = 0.2414$$

    The coefficient of variation is 0.2414 for investment A and 0.1742 and 0.2418 for investments B and C, respectively. The coefficient of variation shows the amount of risk (as measured by the standard deviation) per dollar of expected return. That is, the lower the coefficient of variation, the smaller is the amount of relative risk. When evaluating alternatives that have different expected returns, a relative measure of variability such as the coefficient of variation is required to compare accurately the riskiness of the alternatives.

The expected value of return and measures of risk for all three investments in Example 2 are as follows:

COMPARISON OF EXPECTED RETURN AND RISK FOR THREE INVESTMENT ALTERNATIVES

	INVESTMENT A	INVESTMENT B	INVESTMENT C
Expected return	$1,450	$1,280	$1,580
Range	$1,000	$600	$1,100
Mean absolute deviation	$260	$192	$272
Variance	122,500	49,600	145,600
Standard deviation	$350	$223	$382
Semivariance	84,500	18,880	92,480
Coefficient of variation	0.2414	0.1742	0.2418

Given the expected value and various measures of risk surrounding each investment, we now interpret the measures within the context of Example 2. The range simply measures the total variability in possible returns for each investment. It establishes the upper and lower limits of possible outcomes. It is rarely used in practice because it (1) considers only the extreme values (and, by default, ignores all the others) and (2) ignores the probabilities attached to any of the values within the distribution.

The variance, its counterpart the standard deviation, and MAD all measure dispersion in terms of the probabilities associated with each possible outcome. The variance and standard deviation are preferred in decision making under conditions of risk, since the value provided by MAD is distorted by disregard for the signs of the deviations of each value from the mean. As a practical matter, *the standard deviation is used most commonly as it has the same units as the original variable and is the measure of dispersion used with the expected value to characterize several distributions, including the normal distribution.* The semivariance is a special case of the variance, used to measure downside risk. Advocates of the semivariance say that deviations above the mean add to an investment's attractiveness, but since investors frequently tend to avoid downside risk, only deviations below the mean need be quantified. Risk aversion will be further addressed in the following sections.

Thus far, our discussion has been limited to measures of absolute dispersion. While these are statistically valid, their use in financial decision making requires evaluation of risk within the framework of the expected return. Therefore, it is necessary to consider simultaneously both risk and return by means of the measure of relative dispersion, the coefficient of variation. Refer to the preceding table and note that investments A and C have equal coefficients of variation, indicating equal risk per dollar of expected return, whereas investment B has a significantly lower coefficient of variation, indicating a lower risk per dollar of expected return.

Given all this, which of the three alternatives should the financial manager select? In this problem setting, as in most under conditions of risk, the statistics provide additional information about the alternatives, but they do not specify which should be selected by all decision makers. *None of the alternatives is dominant; that is, it simultaneously has a higher expected value and a lower level of risk.* The final decision would have to be made in terms of the decision maker's utility function, that is, his or her specification of preferences considering all relevant aspects of the problem setting. We present a formal discussion of utility theory, after a brief introduction to tree diagrams and decision trees.

DECISION TREES

A technique that has been recommended to handle complex, sequential decisions over time involves the use of decision trees. A *decision tree* is a formal representation of available decision alternatives at various points through time which are followed by chance events that may occur with some probability. A ranking of the available decision alternatives is usually achieved by finding the expected returns of the alternatives. This requires multiplying the returns earned by each alternative for various chance events by the probability that the event will occur and summing over all possible events. To illustrate the use of decision trees in a very simple problem setting, consider Example 3.

EXAMPLE 3

Decision Tree Example

A firm is considering three alternative single-period investments, A, B, and C, whose returns are dependent upon the state of the economy in the coming period. The state of economy is known only by a probability distribution:

STATE OF THE ECONOMY	PROBABILITY
Fair	0.25
Good	0.40
Very good	0.30
Super	0.05
	1.00

The returns for each alternative under each possible state of the economy are as follows:

	STATE OF THE ECONOMY			
ALTERNATIVE	FAIR	GOOD	VERY GOOD	SUPER
A	$10	$40	$ 70	$ 90
B	− 20	50	100	140
C	− 75	60	120	200

Use a decision tree to evaluate the three alternatives.

SOLUTION: The decision tree for this problem is shown in the table. Notice that we have followed the somewhat standard convention of using a square node to represent decision alternatives and round nodes to show chance events. On the far right side of the tree, the returns for each state of the economy have been weighted by the probability that the state will occur. The sum of these values for all possible states of the economy is the expected return associated with each of the three decision alternatives. Thus, once the decision tree has been "folded back," the selection of the alternative that maximizes expected return is immediate.

DECISION ALTERNATIVE	EXPECTED RETURN
A	$44.00
B	52.00
C	51.25

Alternative B maximizes the expected return, alternative C is a close second, and alternative A is a rather distant third.

DECISION ALTERNATIVE	STATE OF THE ECONOMY	PROBABILITY OF STATE OF ECONOMY	RETURN EARNED	WEIGHTED RETURN
A	fair	0.25	$10	$ 2.50
	good	0.40	40	16.00
	very good	0.30	70	21.00
	super	0.05	90	4.50
			$E(R_A)$ =	$44.00
B	fair	0.25	−$20	−$ 5.00
	good	0.40	50	20.00
	very good	0.30	100	30.00
	super	0.05	140	7.00
			$E(R_B)$ =	$52.00
C	fair	0.25	−$75	−$18.75
	good	0.40	60	24.00
	very good	0.30	120	36.00
	super	0.05	200	10.00
			$E(R_C)$ =	$51.25

The decision tree analysis illustrated in Example 3 is an initial step in the evaluation of investments. Of course, several additional dimensions of the problems require further analysis:

1   The degree of *risk* associated with each of the alternatives, as computed by one or more of the six measures illustrated in the previous section.

2   The requisite performance of *sensitivity analysis* by determining both of the following factors:
(a) The degree to which the estimated *probabilities* of the various states of the economy would have to change for the current "optimal" solution to be no longer optimal.
(b) The extent to which the estimated *returns* associated with the alternatives and the states of the economy would have to change for the current optimal solution to no longer be optimal.

3   The need to consider the multiperiod returns on capital projects with their resulting effects on the risk of the project over its life.

4   The need to consider the *utility* that the firm attaches to each of the alternatives based on the firm's goals, risk posture, risk-return preferences, and so on. (Again, the area of utility theory will be discussed momentarily.)

Later chapters will treat each of these four aspects in detail. However, as a preview of the later analysis and to illustrate the usefulness of decision trees, we present the following elaborations.

There is a technical difference between the problems handled with tree diagrams and those handled with decision trees. *Tree diagrams* are used to evaluate a *single project* over one or more periods, where returns on the project are based on chance events that can be conditioned on prior outcomes. *Decision trees* are used to select the *best project from among two or more projects* based on chance events.

Using either tree diagrams or decision trees enables the analyst to compute the mean and standard deviation of a project's discounted cash flows with models that have been recommended in the literature.[1] Namely, the expected discounted cash flow ($\overline{A}$) for a project is determined using Equation (8):

$$\overline{A} = \sum_{s=1}^{M} A_s P_s \tag{8}$$

The standard deviation of the discounted cash inflows is determined using Equation (9),

$$\sigma_A = \sqrt{\sum_{s=1}^{M} \left(A_s - \overline{A} \right)^2 P_s} \tag{9}$$

where A_s = discounted cash inflow associated with series s in the distribution $\sum_{t=1}^{N} A_t^s$

A_t^s = discounted cash inflow which occurs in series s during period t

P_s = joint probability of a single-line series s, which equals

$$P\{ A_1^s \} \left[\prod_{t=2}^{N} P\{ A_t^s | A_{t-1}^s \} \right]$$

s = given series in the distribution

t = given period in the life of the project

M = number of line series in the distribution

N = number of periods in the life of the project

It should be noticed that P_s is a joint probability found by multiplying several conditional probabilities for successive chance events. Computation of these parameters is illustrated in Example 4.

EXAMPLE 4
Tree Diagram for Three-Period Project

Consider project P, which has a three-period useful life. The financial analyst feels that a tree diagram and Equations (8) and (9) are the most efficient and accurate ways to evaluate the project.

[1] See J. F. Magee, "How to Use Decision Trees in Capital Investments," *Harvard Business Review* (September–October 1964), 79–96; and R. D. Hespos and P. A. Strassmann, "Stochastic Decision Trees for the Analysis of Investment Decisions," *Management Science* (August 1965), 244–259.

The possible cash inflows for each period (which are already discounted back to the present) and their associated probabilities are as follows:

PERIOD 1 $A_1^s P\{A_1^s\}$	PERIOD 2 $A_2^s P\{A_2^s|A_1^s\}$	PERIOD 3 $A_3^s P\{A_3^s|A_2^s\}$

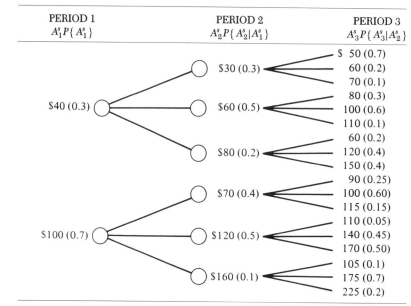

Using these data, determine the expected discounted cash inflow and its standard deviation.

SOLUTION:

SERIES	PERIOD 1 A_1^s	$P\{A_1^s\}$	PERIOD 2 A_2^s	$P\{A_2^s|A_1^s\}$	PERIOD 3 A_3^s	$P\{A_3^s|A_2^s\}$	$A_s = \sum_{t=1}^{3} A_t^s$	P_s	$(A_s \times P_s)$
1	$ 40	0.3	$ 30	0.3	$ 50	0.7	$120	0.063	$ 7.56
2	40	0.3	30	0.3	60	0.2	130	0.018	2.34
3	40	0.3	30	0.3	70	0.1	140	0.009	1.26
4	40	0.3	60	0.5	80	0.3	180	0.045	8.10
5	40	0.3	60	0.5	100	0.6	200	0.090	18.00
6	40	0.3	60	0.5	110	0.1	210	0.015	3.15
7	40	0.3	80	0.2	60	0.2	180	0.012	2.16
8	40	0.3	80	0.2	120	0.4	240	0.024	5.76
9	40	0.3	80	0.2	150	0.4	270	0.024	6.48
10	100	0.7	70	0.4	90	0.25	260	0.070	18.20
11	100	0.7	70	0.4	100	0.60	270	0.168	45.36
12	100	0.7	70	0.4	115	0.15	285	0.042	11.97
13	100	0.7	120	0.5	110	0.05	330	0.0175	5.775
14	100	0.7	120	0.5	140	0.45	360	0.1575	56.70
15	100	0.7	120	0.5	170	0.50	390	0.175	68.25
16	100	0.7	160	0.1	105	0.1	365	0.007	2.555
17	100	0.7	160	0.1	175	0.7	435	0.049	21.315
18	100	0.7	160	0.1	225	0.2	485	0.014	6.79
								1.000	$291.725

$$\bar{A} = \sum_{s=1}^{18} A_s P_s = \$291.725$$

It should be pointed out that in the first table, the A_s column is the sum of the three columns A_1^s, A_2^s, and A_3^s; furthermore, the P_s column is the product of the three probabilities $(P\{A_1^s\})(P\{A_2^s|A_1^s\})(P\{A_3^s|A_2^s\})$ and that the latter two probabilities are conditional on prior period outcomes.

The following table is helpful in computing σ_A:

SERIES	A_s	$A_s - \bar{A}$	$(A_s - \bar{A})^2$	P_s	$(A_s - \bar{A})^2 P_s$
1	$120	− $171.725	29,489.476	0.063	$1,857.837
2	130	− 161.725	26,154.976	0.018	470.790
3	140	− 151.725	23,030.476	0.009	207.184
4	180	− 111.725	12,482.476	0.045	561.711
5	200	− 91.725	8,413.476	0.090	757.213
6	210	− 81.725	6,678.976	0.015	100.185
7	180	− 111.725	12,482.476	0.012	149.790
8	240	− 51.725	2,675.476	0.024	64.211
9	270	− 21.725	471.976	0.024	11.327
10	260	− 31.725	1,006.476	0.070	70.453
11	270	− 21.725	471.976	0.168	79.292
12	285	− 6.725	45.226	0.042	1.899
13	330	38.275	1,464.976	0.0175	25.637
14	360	68.275	4,661.476	0.1575	734.182
15	390	98.275	9,657.976	0.175	1,690.146
16	365	73.275	5,369.226	0.007	37.585
17	435	143.275	20,527.726	0.049	1,005.859
18	485	193.275	37,355.226	0.014	522.973
				1.000	$8,348.274

Now,

$$\sigma_A = \sqrt{8,348.274}$$
$$= \$91.37$$

Thus, the expected discounted cash inflow for project P is $291.73 and the standard deviation of cash inflows is $91.37. These values for $\bar{A}$ and σ_A are used to determine if this project is sufficiently attractive to be undertaken by the firm evaluating it.

Next, we turn to an introduction to utility theory, which is the premier criterion for decision making under risk.

UTILITY THEORY

As discussed, the relaxation of the certainty assumption necessitates consideration of both the expected return and risk criteria for evaluating decision alternatives. However, decision makers will view varying degrees of risk and return differently, hence will select divergent decision alternatives. Utility theory is an attempt to formalize rational decision making, where preferences among alternatives are specified by a given decision maker. The utility value attached to various alternatives represents an integration of all aspects relevant to the decision.

In this section we provide an introduction to the theory of utility analysis. Our particular interest lies in its application to the trade-off between risk and return, which is developed further in Chapter 12 in our coverage of certainty equivalents. The treatment of utility theory contained herein is very brief. The reader should refer to the list of additional readings at the end of this chapter to obtain further details.

When faced with a decision, the decision maker must consider the following within the framework of personal preferences.

1   The opportunity set of all relevant goals and objectives.
2   The hierarchy of goals and acceptable trade-offs among the goals within the hierarchy.
3   The perceptions of risk per se and risk-return preference (i.e., the incremental expected return required to justify acceptance of an additional unit of risk).
4   The preferences for current versus future consumption as affected by present wealth position, liquidity requirements, and so on.

To be able to specify and differentiate among various classes of risk preference (or aversion), it is useful to define the decision maker's utility function with respect to required return and risk. This necessitates acceptance of the *axioms of coherence*.[2]

1   Given any two payoffs (which may involve nonmonetary, as well as monetary values), a decision maker can specify preference for one over the other or indifference between the two.
2   If a given decision maker prefers payoff P_1 to P_2 and P_2 to P_3, then necessarily P_1 is preferred to P_3 (*transitivity or consistency of preferences*).
3   If a decision maker prefers P_1 to P_2 and P_2 to P_3, there is some probabilistic mixture of P_1 and P_3 that is preferred to P_2, some other probabilistic mixture of P_1 and P_3 that is inferior to P_2, and a third probabilistic mixture of P_1 and P_3 that will leave the decision maker indifferent relative to P_2.
4   If a decision maker prefers P_1 to P_2 and P_3 is some other payoff, a probabilistic mixture of P_1 and P_3 will be preferred to the same probabilistic mixture of P_2 and P_3.
5   If a decision maker is indifferent between payoffs P_4 and P_5, they may be substituted for each other in any decision setting.
6   If a decision maker prefers P_1 to P_2, two probabilistic mixtures of P_1 and P_2 will find the former preferred if and only if the former has a larger proportion of P_1.

If the decision maker accepts the axioms of coherence, it is reasonable to assume that he or she will act to *maximize utility*. This means selection of those available decision alternatives that will lead to the greatest level of satisfaction. Since preferences are necessarily subjective, the exact specification of a decision maker's utility function is fraught with operational difficulties. Further, individual utility preferences are likely to change over time. However, we can specify three general categories of decision makers based on their risk preferences: risk averse, risk indifferent, and risk taking. The utility functions for each category of decision maker are shown in Figure 11–1.

With respect to risk, decision makers may be classified as follows:

1   *Risk-averse* decision makers have decreasing marginal utilities for increases in wealth. For the risk-averse decision maker, the chances to enjoy additional wealth are less attractive than the possibility of the pain associated with a decrease in wealth or income.

---

[2]Robert L. Winkler, *Introduction to Bayesian Inference and Decision* (New York: Holt, Rinehart and Winston, 1972), pp. 260–264.

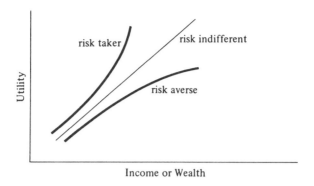

FIGURE 11 – 1   Relationship Between Income or Wealth and Utility

2   *Risk-indifferent* decision makers have constant marginal utilities; hence, their utility curves are linear.

3   *Risk-taking* decision makers have increasing marginal utilities for larger potential increases in wealth.

Within each of the three categories, decision makers demonstrate varying degrees of preference or aversion to risk. Thus, we can anticipate a different utility function for each individual decision maker. Further, each decision maker has a whole family of nonintersecting utility curves, showing successively higher levels of satisfaction. To maximize expected utility, the decision maker will strive to achieve the highest feasible curve within the available alternatives and constraints.

Within the arena of capital investment decision making, experience indicates that the great majority of managers are risk-averters, but again the specific degree of aversion varies over a wide spectrum. Figure 11–2 shows risk-return utility functions (indifference curves) for two managers. Manager A is less risk averse than is manager B. Both managers are willing to accept a 6% risk-free rate of return, but manager B requires increasingly greater returns as risk increases than does manager A. Thus, Figure 11–2 shows the risk-return preferences for two managers at one point in time.

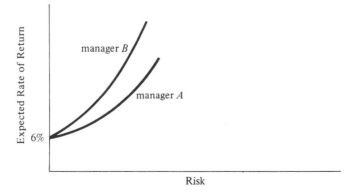

FIGURE 11 – 2   Risk-Return Indifference Curves

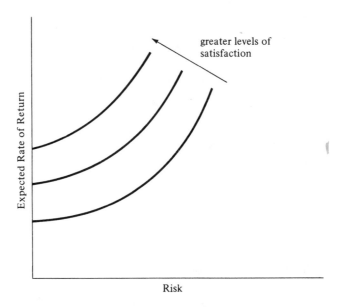

FIGURE 11 – 3   A Family of Indifference Curves for One Manager

As described, each manager has a whole set of indifference curves, indicating successively higher levels of satisfaction. Such a family of indifference curves is shown in Figure 11–3. As we move up and to the left, each curve indicates a higher level of satisfaction.

Given the risk-return preferences, we are now in the position to discuss methods used to compensate for risk in the capital investment process. *There are three formal approaches commonly used to incorporate risk into the analysis: the risk-adjusted discount rate technique, the certainty equivalent method, and the capital asset pricing model.* The first two approaches are discussed in the next chapter and the third is treated in Chapter 16.

SUMMARY

This chapter provides an introduction to risk analysis. We first define conditions of certainty, risk, and uncertainty, as well as five major types of risk faced by financial managers. Next, we present several alternative measures that are helpful in quantifying risk. Following this, we illustrate the use of decision trees and tree diagrams in handling conditions of risk. Finally, we introduce the important area of utility theory. Although there are practical problems related to the use of utility theory, it provides a strong conceptual foundation for financial decision making under conditions of risk.

QUESTIONS
_____
PROBLEMS

1. Contrast conditions of *certainty*, *risk*, and *uncertainty*.

2. Discuss the characteristics of the six major measures of risk introduced in this chapter.

3. Discuss the difference between the types of problems handled by decision trees and those handled by tree diagrams.

4. Discuss the strengths and weaknesses of utility theory in decision making under conditions of risk.

5. A petrochemical company has two investment proposals under the following states of the economy: normal, deep recession, mild recession, minor boom, and major boom. The probabilities of various states of the economy are as follows:

	PROPOSAL A		PROPOSAL B	
STATE	PROBABILITY	CASH FLOW	PROBABILITY	CASH FLOW
Deep recession	0.10	$3,000	0.10	$2,000
Mild recession	0.20	3,500	0.20	3,000
Normal	0.40	4,000	0.40	4,000
Minor boom	0.20	4,500	0.20	5,000
Major boom	0.10	5,000	0.10	6,000

Determine and interpret the following measures:
(a) Expected return.
(b) Mean absolute deviation.
(c) Variance.
(d) Standard deviation.
(e) Semivariance.
(f) Coefficient of variation.

6. A hospital administrator is faced with the problem of having a limited amount of funds available for capital projects. She has narrowed her choice to two pieces of X-ray equipment, since the radiology department is the greatest producer of revenue. The first piece of equipment (project A) is a fairly standard piece of equipment that has gained wide acceptance and should provide a steady flow of income. The other piece of equipment (project B), although more risky, may provide a higher return. After deliberation with the radiologist and director of finance, the administrator has developed the following table:

EXPECTED CASH INFLOW PER YEAR			
PROBABILITY	PROJECT A	PROBABILITY	PROJECT B
0.6	$2,000	0.2	$4,000
0.3	1,800	0.5	1,200
0.1	1,000	0.3	900

Discovering that the budget director of the hospital is taking graduate courses in business, the hospital administrator has asked him to analyze the two projects and make his recommendations. Prepare an analysis that will aid the budget director in making his recommendations.

7. The Hatchet Company is evaluating four alternative single-period investment opportunities whose returns are based on the state of the economy. The possible states of the economy and the associated probability distribution are

as follows:

	STATE		
	FAIR	GOOD	GREAT
Probability	0.2	0.5	0.3

The returns for each investment opportunity and each state of the economy are as follows:

	STATE OF ECONOMY		
ALTERNATIVE	FAIR	GOOD	GREAT
W	$1,000	$3,000	$6,000
X	500	4,500	6,800
Y	0	5,000	8,000
Z	− 4,000	6,000	8,500

(a) Using the decision tree approach, determine the expected return for each alternative.

(b) As a method of performing sensitivity analysis on the decision tree drawn in part (a), it could be determined how much the probabilities of the various states of the economy would have to change in order for the best alternative current to be replaced by one of the others. For this problem, consider the two alternatives with the highest expected returns (i.e., those ranked 1 and 2 by expected returns). Assume that the probability of a "great" economy will remain constant at 0.3. What would the probability of a "fair" and a "good" economy have to be in order for alternative 2 to become the better choice?

8. For the three-period project shown here, compute the expected value and the standard deviation for the discounted cash inflow over the project's useful life.

PERIOD 1	PERIOD 2	PERIOD 3
$A_1^s P\{A_1^s\}$	$A_2^s P\{A_2^s|A_1^s\}$	$A_3^s P\{A_3^s|A_2^s\}$

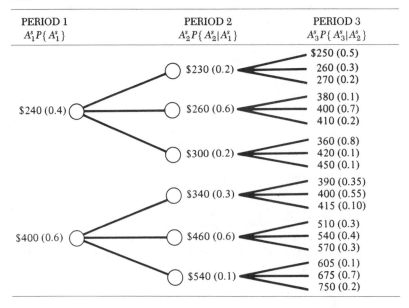

9. The Wee Producem Company is deciding whether to introduce a new product on the market. At the present time it has two decisions to make: (1) the overall decision of whether to introduce the product with additional production costs of $15,000,000 or to drop the project and simply suffer the loss of the $2,500,000 already invested, or (2) to do further market research at a cost of $1,500,000 and then make the introduction decision (with the same costs as given). Wee Producem estimates that the market research group will assign a probability of 0.7 that the product will be introduced. Because of the unusual nature of the product, only two final outcomes are possible: outcome A derives $40,000,000 profit while outcome B derives a $5,000,000 loss. The present estimated likelihood of outcome A is 0.6 and 0.4 for outcome B.

Determine the optimal strategy by using a decision tree to compare the expected returns of the possible alternatives.

REFERENCES

Adler, F. Michael. "On Risk-Adjusted Capitalization Rates and Valuation by Individuals." *Journal of Finance* (September 1970).

Alexander, Gordon J., and Bruce G. Resnick. "More on Estimation Risk and Simple Rules for Optimal Portfolio Selection." *Journal of Finance* (March 1985).

Arditti, Fred D. "Risk and the Required Return on Equity." *Journal of Finance* (March 1967).

Arzac, Enrique R. "Structural Planning Under Controllable Business Risk." *Journal of Finance* (December 1975).

Baker, H. K., M. B. Hargrove, and J. A. Haslem. "An Empirical Analysis of the Risk-Return Preferences of Individual Investors." *Journal of Financial and Quantitative Analysis* (September 1977).

Baron, David P. "On the Utility Theoretic Foundation of Mean-Variance Analysis." *Journal of Finance*, 32 (December 1977), 1683–1698.

_____. "Investment Policy, Optimality, and the Mean-Variance Model: Review Article." *Journal of Finance* (March 1979).

Beaver, William, Paul Kettler, and Myron Scholes. "The Association between Market Determined and Accounting Determined Risk Measures." *Accounting Review*, 45 (October 1970), 654–682.

_____, and James Manegold. "The Association between Market Determined and Accounting Determined Measures of Systematic Risk: Some Further Evidence." *Journal of Financial and Quantitative Analysis*, 10 (June 1975).

_____, and _____. "The Association between Market Determined and Accounting Determined Measures of Systematic Risk: Some Further Evidence." *Journal of Financial and Quantitative Analysis*, 12 (December 1977), 859–878.

Bernoulli, D. "Exposition of a New Theory on the Measurement of Risk." *Econometrica* (January 1954).

Berry, R. H., and R. G. Dyson, "On the Negative Risk Premium for Risk-Adjusted Discount Rates: A Reply and Extension." *Journal of Business Finance and Accounting* (Summer 1984).

Borch, K. *The Economics of Uncertainty*. Princeton, N.J.: Princeton University Press, 1968.

Chang, Eric C., and J. Michael Pinegar. "Risk and Inflation." *Journal of Financial and Quantitative Analysis* (March 1987).

Crum, Roy L., Dan J. Laughhunn, and John W. Payne. "Risk-Seeking Behavior and Its Implications for Financial Models." *Financial Management*, 10 (Winter 1981), 20–27.

Ferson, Wayne E., Shmuel Kandel, and Robert T. Stambaugh. "Tests of Asset Pricing with Time-Varying Expected Risk Premiums and Market Betas." *Journal of Finance* (June 1987).

Friedman, M., and L. J. Savage. "Utility Analysis of Choices Involving Risk." *Journal of Political Economy* (August 1948), 279–304.

_____, and_____. "The Expected Utility Hypothesis and the Measurability of Utility." *Journal of Political Economy* (December 1952).

Gehr, A. K., Jr. "Risk and Return." *Journal of Finance* (September 1979).

Green, Richard C., and Sanjay Srivastava. "Risk Aversion and Arbitrage." *Journal of Finance* (March 1985).

Grinyer, John R. "On the Negative Risk Premium for Risk Adjusted Discount Rates: A Further Comment." *Journal of Business Finance and Accounting* (Summer 1984).

Hakey, Charles W. "Valuation and Risk Adjusted Discount Rates." *Journal of Business Finance and Accounting* (Autumn 1984).

Hillier, Frederick S. "The Derivation of Probabilistic Information for the Evaluation of Risky Investments." *Management Science* (April 1963).

Meyer, Richard L., and Murad J. Antia. "A Note on the Calculation of Probabilistic Betas." *Financial Review* (February 1986).

Simonds, Richard R., Lynn Roy La Motte, and Archer McWhorter. "Testing for Nonstationarity of Market Risk: An Exact Test and Power Considerations." *Journal of Financial and Quantitative Analysis* (June 1986).

Spence, James G. "CML to SML: A Graphical Approach." *Financial Review* (November 1984).

Van Zijl, Tony. "Risk Decomposition: Variance or Standard Deviation—A Reexamination and Extension." *Journal of Financial and Quantitative Analysis* (June 1987).

Project Selection
Under Conditions of Risk

12

In the previous chapter we provided the basics of measuring risk and decision making under conditions of risk. We are now prepared to examine the evaluation of capital projects under conditions of risk. We illustrate the use of two models: the certainty equivalent method and the risk-adjusted discount approach. As we shall see, each method requires the computation of the expected value and the standard deviation of the distribution that quantifies the returns of the project over its useful life. This chapter concentrates on the determination of the expected value, while Chapter 13 examines the computation of the standard deviation of the distribution.

CERTAINTY EQUIVALENT METHOD FOR RISK ADJUSTMENT

The certainty equivalent method permits adjustment for risk by incorporating the manager's utility preference for risk versus return directly into the capital investment process. The method is especially useful when management perceives different levels of risk associated with the estimated annual cash flows over the life of a project. Given the limitations of economic forecasting, it is reasonable to assume that the estimates of cash flows during the early periods in a project's life are likely to be more accurate than those corresponding to the latter years. It is just this reasoning that motivates many firms to rely on payback as a surrogate measure of risk to supplement the discounted cash flow methods. However, the formal methods discussed in this and the following sections overcome all the drawbacks associated with payback while permitting management to impute its risk preference directly into the capital budgeting decision.

When the certainty equivalent method is used, the estimated annual cash flows (which represent the expected value of a probability distribution of returns) are multiplied by a certainty equivalent coefficient (CEC), designated in equation form as α.

The CEC reflects management's perception of the degree of risk associated with the estimated cash flow distribution as well as management's degree of aversion to perceived risk, as evidenced by their utility function. The product of the expected cash flow and the CEC represents the amount that management would be willing to accept for certain in each year of the project's life as opposed to accepting the cash flow distribution and its associated risk. Hence, the name *certainty equivalent method*.

The CECs range in value from zero to 1. The higher values indicate a lower penalty assigned by management to that cash flow distribution. A value of 1 indicates that management does not associate any risk with the estimated cash flow and therefore is willing to accept the expected value of the cash flow estimate as certain. *Since the certainty equivalent method compensates for risk in its entirety, it is therefore appropriate to discount all certainty equivalent-adjusted cash flows at the risk-free rate of return as opposed to the firm's cost of capital.* The risk-free rate of return is that return normally associated with the return available from Treasury bills, since these are short term and have guaranteed return and principal repayment at maturity. The risk-free rate of return is an accurate representation of the time value of money given that the cash flows are not subject to variability.

In our discussion of the NPV technique, we employed a cost of capital as the discount rate. *The cost of capital reflected the normal risk posture of the firm and included the risk-free rate of return plus additional return requirements to compensate for the business and financial risk as defined.* Conversely, the certainty equivalent method compensates for business and financial risk with the CEC and then discounts at the risk-free rate.

The certainty equivalent model is defined in Equation (1),

$$\overline{CE} = \sum_{t=0}^{n} \frac{\alpha_t \overline{R}_t}{(1 + i)^t} \tag{1}$$

where $\overline{CE}$ = expected certainty equivalent value over the life of the project
$\overline{R}_t$ = expected cash flow in period t
α_t = certainty equivalent factor which converts the expected risky cash flow $\overline{R}_t$ into its perceived certainty equivalent value
i = risk-free rate which is assumed to remain constant over the life of the project
n = number of years in the project's life

The value of the certainty equivalent coefficient equals one only for risk-free investments, such as Treasury bills. The values for the certainty equivalent coefficients corresponding to projects falling within the firm's normal risk posture are less than 1.

Note again that the NPV approach lumps together the discounting for time and the adjustment for risk, whereas the certainty equivalent method disaggregates the two by adjusting for risk with the α factor and discounting for the time value of money at the risk-free rate.

In utilizing the certainty equivalent method, it is important to have a valid approach for approximating the certainty equivalent coefficients. One procedure for ascertaining CEC values for different time periods is to undertake an historical review

Table 12–1 Certainty Equivalent Factors for Different Investment Groups Developed by XYZ Company

INVESTMENT GROUPING	COEFFICIENT OF VARIATION, v	CERTAINTY EQUIVALENT COEFFICIENT			
		YEAR 1	YEAR 2	YEAR 3	YEAR 4
Replacement investments—category I	$v \le 0.10$	0.95	0.92	0.89	0.85
Replacement investments—category II	$0.10 < v \le 0.25$	0.90	0.86	0.82	0.77
Replacement investments—category III	$v > 0.25$	0.84	0.79	0.74	0.68
New investment—category I	$v \le 0.10$	0.92	0.88	0.85	0.80
New investment—category II	$0.10 < v \le 0.25$	0.86	0.82	0.78	0.73
New investment—category III	$v > 0.25$	0.80	0.75	0.70	0.64
Research and development—category I	$v \le 0.20$	0.82	0.76	0.70	0.60
Research and development—category II	$v > 0.20$	0.70	0.60	0.50	0

of project performance. Projects are first divided into general categories, such as normal replacement, expansion, and R & D. Then, within each category, on a year-by-year basis, the measures of risk and return are determined. The result is a probability distribution of cash flows by year of project life, from which the coefficient of variation may be obtained. The CEC for each year and each category of project is then assigned according to the magnitude of the coefficient of variation weighted by managers' preference for risk aversion.

An example of the result of dividing projects into categories, determining coefficients of variation based on historical preference, and assigning CECs is shown in Table 12–1 for a 4-year period based on *the utility preferences for one firm at a point in time*. It should be noted that the logical choice for categories of investments is predicated on the historical values of the coefficient of variation. Thus, in Table 12–1, "Replacement investments—category I" groups all projects of that type that *normally* have a coefficient of variation in year 1 of less than 0.10. However, from year to year over a project's life, it is possible for the project to change categories. That is, its projected CEC is determined based on the expected coefficient of variation for each year of the project's life. Further, the factors are for a point in time given a risk-free rate of return and cost of capital. A change in the risk-free rate, cost of capital, or management's utility preferences will result in a revision of the CEC values. *The results of evaluating a project having the same risk complexion as the firm should be consistent when using either the firm's cost of capital or the risk-free rate with certainty equivalent adjustment.*

The change in a project's expected coefficient of variation from year to year depends on the intertemporal correlation (i.e., the degree of correlation that exists between the annual cash flow distributions over time) of expected cash flows. This leads to multi-period and portfolio analyses, which are discussed in subsequent chapters. As a final note, the CEC value assigned to year 4 for "Research and development—category II" in our sample firm is zero. This implies that management is completely disregarding the cash flows for year 4, and the analysis thereby approaches the payback method, wherein *all* cash flows are ignored after a stated period.

The procedure for using certainty equivalent coefficients is demonstrated in Example 1.

EXAMPLE 1

Certainty Equivalent Method

XYZ Company, which developed the CEC values shown in Table 12–1, is evaluating a *new investment* project with expected returns and standard deviations during its 4-year life as follows:

YEAR	EXPECTED RETURN	STANDARD DEVIATION	COEFFICIENT OF VARIATION
1	$1,000	$200	0.20
2	1,200	216	0.18
3	1,200	168	0.14
4	1,800	144	0.08

The cash outflow is $3,000 and the risk-free rate of return is 6%. Find the certainty equivalent factors corresponding to the coefficient of variation listed (see Table 12–1). Then, determine the expected certainty equivalent value, $\overline{CE}$.

SOLUTION: The following table is helpful in computing $\overline{CE}$:

TIME	$\overline{R}_t$	α_t	$\alpha_t \overline{R}_t$	DISCOUNT FACTOR AT 6%	DISCOUNTED $\alpha_t \overline{R}_t$
Present	− $3,000	1.00	− $3,000	1.000	− $3,000
1	+ 1,000	0.86	860	0.943	811
2	+ 1,200	0.82	984	0.890	876
3	+ 1,200	0.78	936	0.840	786
4	+ 1,800	0.80	1,440	0.792	1,140
					$\overline{CE} = \$613$

The meaning of $\overline{CE}$ is discussed shortly.

The certainty equivalent value is analogous to the net present value in that the decision rule for both methods is to reject projects that have negative $\overline{CE}$s or NPVs. In Example 1, since the project in question had a positive $\overline{CE}$ (i.e., $613), it represents a candidate for acceptance. However, further analysis is required.

In our earlier discussions, we pointed out that to maximize shareholders' wealth, the set of projects that maximized NPV should be accepted. If we limit our examination of certainty equivalents to $\overline{CE}$, we should select that set of projects having the highest total $\overline{CE}$. However, another powerful evaluation tool is available to us: *we may ascertain the probability distribution for the certainty equivalent of each project and then develop acceptance criteria in keeping with both risk aversion and maximization of shareholders' wealth.* For example, we might select a decision rule requiring rejection of any project that has a probability less than 90% of achieving a positive CE value. Then, from the remaining group, select the set of projects having the largest total $\overline{CE}$. We treat the probability distribution of certainty equivalents in Chapter 13.

Thus far in our discussion, we have assumed that the risk-free rate remains constant over time. If this assumption is relaxed, Equation (1) may be rewritten in its more general form as Equation (2),

$$\overline{CE} = \sum_{t=0}^{n} \frac{\alpha_t \overline{R}_t}{\prod_{k=1}^{t}(1 + i_k)} \tag{2}$$

where i_k = risk-free rate in year k
$\prod$ = the product operator

The application of Equation (2) is demonstrated in Example 2.

EXAMPLE 2
Certainty Equivalent Value for a Change in Risk-Free Rates

Suppose that the estimated cash flows for a project, the risk-free rates of return, and the certainty equivalent coefficients are as follows:

TIME	α_t	$\overline{R}_t$	RISK-FREE RETURN
Present	1.00	$- \$3,000$	—
1	0.95	1,000	0.05
2	0.92	1,500	0.06
3	0.89	1,700	0.07

Determine $\overline{CE}$.

SOLUTION:

$$\overline{CE} = -\$3,000 + \frac{0.95(\$1,000)}{1 + 0.05} + \frac{0.92(\$1,500)}{(1 + 0.05)(1 + 0.06)}$$

$$+ \frac{0.89(\$1,700)}{(1 + 0.05)(1 + 0.06)(1 + 0.07)}$$

$$= -\$3,000 + \$905 + \$1,240 + \$1,270$$

$$= \$415$$

RISK-ADJUSTED DISCOUNT RATE

The rationale underlying the use of the risk-adjusted discount rate (RADR) technique is that projects which have greater variability in the probability distributions of their returns should have these returns discounted at a higher rate than projects having less variability or risk. A project that had no risk associated with it would be discounted at the risk-free rate, since this is the appropriate rate just to account for the time value of money. Any project that has risk associated with it has to be discounted at a rate in excess of the risk-free rate to discount both for futurity (the time value of money) and for the risk associated with the project (a risk premium). Projects that are of average riskiness vis-à-vis the firm's normal operations should be discounted at the firm's normal hurdle rate or cost of capital, since this figure reflects the normal risk faced by the firm. Those projects having greater than normal risk should be discounted at a rate in excess of the cost of capital; conversely, projects that exhibit less risk than that associated with a firm's normal operations should be discounted at a rate between the risk-free rate and the cost of capital. The risk-adjusted rate is found by Equation (3),

$$r' = i + u + a \qquad (3)$$

where r' = risk-adjusted discount rate
 i = risk-free rate
 u = adjustment for the firm's normal risk
 a = adjustment for above (or below) the firm's normal risk

It should be noted that the sum of i and u in Equation (3) is the firm's cost of capital, since that discount rate is appropriate for projects having average, or "normal," risk. Notice that the term for the abnormal risk adjustment could either be positive or negative, based on whether the project has more or less risk associated with it than the average project for the firm in question.

Equation (4) may be used to determine the expected present value when employing a risk-adjusted discount rate,

$$\overline{\text{RAR}} = \sum_{t=0}^{n} \frac{\overline{R}_t}{(1 + r')^t} \qquad (4)$$

where $\overline{\text{RAR}}$ = expected value of the distribution of discounted cash flows over the life of the project (risk-adjusted net present value)
 $\overline{R}_t$ = expected value of the distribution of cash flows in year t
 r' = risk-adjusted discount rate based on the perceived riskiness of the project under consideration
 n = number of years in the project's life

The amount of risk adjustment is based on management's utility preference for risk aversion, so that this adjustment reflects the management's perception of the risk associated with the project per se, its risk-return preferences, the firm's wealth position, and the impact of the project on the firm's other goals. Table 12–2 provides risk adjustments for the categories of investments defined in Table 12–1, reflecting the utility preferences for a particular firm (XYZ Company) at a particular time. Although all the project types shown in Table 12–2 are generally required to achieve the firm's cost of capital as a minimum return, there may be some categories of projects that have a risk sufficiently low to warrant their implementation, even though their projected return is below the firm's cost of capital.

Table 12 – 2   Return Requirements for Various Investment Groups Developed by XYZ Company

INVESTMENT GROUPING	REQUIRED RETURN
Replacement investments—category I	Risk-free rate plus 2%
Replacement investments—category II	Risk-free rate plus 4%
Replacement investments—category III	Risk-free rate plus 6%
New investment—category I	Risk-free rate plus 8%
New investment—category II	Risk-free rate plus 10%
New investment—category III	Risk-free rate plus 15%
Research and development—category I	Risk-free rate plus 10%
Research and development—category II	Risk-free rate plus 20%

Reference to Table 12–2 indicates that estimating a risk-free rate of 10% would apply a 16% hurdle rate to a project falling into "Replacement investment—category III." *It should also be noted that unlike the certainty equivalent method, the RADR technique as it is generally used in practice applies the same discount rate to the project throughout its useful life.*

The application of Equation (4) is demonstrated in Example 3.

EXAMPLE 3

Calculation of $\overline{\text{RAR}}$

XYZ Company, which developed the risk-adjusted returns shown in Table 12–2, is considering the adoption of a "Replacement investments—category II" project which has the cash flows as shown by the following distributions:

		CASH INFLOWS			
ORIGINAL COST		YEARS 1–5		YEARS 6–10	
PROBABILITY	AMOUNT	PROBABILITY	AMOUNT	PROBABILITY	AMOUNT
0.3	$13,000	0.2	$2,000	0.2	$2,600
0.4	14,000	0.4	2,400	0.6	3,200
0.3	15,000	0.3	2,800	0.1	3,400
		0.1	3,400	0.1	3,600

The risk-free rate is 10%. Determine the risk-adjusted net present value.

SOLUTION: First, determine the mean value for each of the cash flow distributions and incorporate into Equation (4) as follows:

$$\overline{\text{RAR}} = -\ \$14,000 + \sum_{t=1}^{5} \frac{\$2,540}{(1.14)^t} + \sum_{t=6}^{10} \frac{\$3,140}{(1.14)^t}$$

$$= -\ \$14,000 + \$8,720 + \$5,599$$

$$= \$319$$

Since the $\overline{\text{RAR}}$ is positive, this project represents a candidate for acceptance.

In addition to the expected value of the return, we may also examine the probability distribution in a manner similar to that discussed for the certainty equivalent method. This task will be addressed in Chapter 13.

The following section compares the certainty equivalent and risk-adjusted methods and describes some conflicts that may arise when using the two methods.

COMPARING CERTAINTY EQUIVALENT AND ADJUSTMENT OF THE DISCOUNT RATE

Risk adjustment using the risk-adjusted discount rate method has been criticized primarily for two reasons:

1   The method does not examine the riskiness associated with each project or the changes in riskiness over its life, but rather groups projects into general risk categories. It applies the same discount rate risk premium over the entire life of the project. Certainty equivalent requires individual examination of projects in each time period since riskiness associated with a given project may change over its life. In fact, investment uncertainty may be concentrated in only a few years of the project's life, and once this uncertainty is resolved, all future years have a much more moderate risk posture.

2   Risk adjustment combines the two parts of the discounting process: the risk-free return for time and the risk premium. The use of a high constant discount rate over a project's entire useful life implies that its riskiness is increasing over time. The implication results from the fact that discounting equates to an exponential decay of the value of cash as a function of time. The difference between the present value of cash flows discounted at the risk-free rate and the present value of those same cash flows when discounted at a risk-adjusted hurdle rate increases exponentially with the passage of time. The process is illustrated in Example 4.

EXAMPLE 4
Risk-Adjusted Discount Rate and Certainty Equivalent

A project costing $10,000 has a 12-year life and expected cash inflows of $1,800 each year. The risk-free rate of return is 7%, the firm's cost of capital is 10%, and the hurdle rate to be applied for this project is 15%. (The project is a "New investment—category I," as previously defined in Tables 12–1 and 12–2.) Management anticipates that the dispersion of earnings after the fifth year will be relatively constant given that all start-up problems will be resolved by that time. Therefore, they will apply the CECs from Table 12–1 for the first four periods and 0.75 thereafter. Determine the project's NPV using the risk-adjusted discount rate and the certainty equivalent, and compare the two.

SOLUTION: First consider the risk-adjusted discount method.

TIME	$\bar{R}_t$	DISCOUNT FACTOR AT 15%	PRESENT VALUES
Present	− $10,000	1	− $10,000
1–12	1,800	5.420619	9,757
		RAR = −	$ 243

Next consider the certainty equivalent method.

TIME	$\bar{R}$	α_t	$\alpha_t \bar{R}_t$	DISCOUNT FACTOR AT 7%	DISCOUNTED $\alpha_t \bar{R}_t$
Present	$-\$10,000$	1.00	$-\$10,000$	1	$-\$10,000$
1	1,800	0.92	1,656	0.934579	1,548
2	1,800	0.88	1,584	0.873439	1,384
3	1,800	0.85	1,530	0.816298	1,249
4	1,800	0.80	1,440	0.762895	1,099
5–12	1,800	0.75	1,350	4.555475	6,150
					$\overline{CE} = \$\ 1,430$

The two solutions demonstrate the contrasting results of using the two methods. The project would be rejected using the risk-adjusted method, but accepted using certainty equivalent. The difference can be highlighted by looking at the next table, which compares the discounted cash flows using the certainty equivalent method, the risk-adjusted discount rate (15%), and the cost of capital (10%).

YEAR	(1) DISCOUNTED $\alpha_t \bar{R}_t$	(2) $\bar{R}_t$ DISCOUNTED AT 15%	(3) $\bar{R}_t$ DISCOUNTED AT 10%
Present	$-\$10,000$	$-\$10,000$	$-\$10,000$
1	1,548	1,565	1,636
2	1,384	1,361	1,488
3	1,249	1,184	1,352
4	1,099	1,029	1,229
5	963	895	1,118
6	900	778	1,016
7	841	677	924
8	786	588	840
9	734	512	763
10	686	445	694
11	641	387	631
12	599	336	574
	$\overline{CE} = \$\ 1,430$	$\overline{RAR} = -\$\ 243$	$NPV = \$\ 2,265$

The table shows the value of the cash flows using each of the three approaches. If the certainty equivalent factors are an accurate risk adjustment for this project, it can be seen that the use of a constant risk-adjusted rate of 15% overcompensates for the risk of the project in every year except the first (since the present value using a discount rate of 15% is less than the present values of the $\alpha_t \bar{R}_t$ values). Notice that the difference between these present values is as small as $23 in year 2 and as large as $263 in year 12. It should be stressed that the RAR method, with a constant discount rate, assumes that the risk of the project grows over time; in fact, that it grows at an exponential rate over time, owing to the compounding process associated with the discount factors (since the discount factors are the reciprocals of compound interest factors). However, if the certainty equivalent factors are an accurate risk adjustment for this project, then risk is constant in years 5–12 (evidenced by the constant α_t factor of 0.75) rather than growing exponentially, as implicitly assumed by the RAR method.

Finally, it should be noted by comparing columns 1 and 3 that, for the first 10 years of the project's life, the project is more risky than the firm in general (since the present values using the cost of capital are higher than the discounted $\alpha_t \overline{R}_t$ values), but for the last 2 years the project is less risky than the firm overall (since in years 11 and 12 the discounted $\alpha_t \overline{R}_t$ values are higher than the present values using the cost capital). However, considering the entire life of the project, it is more risky than the firm overall, since $\overline{CE}$ is less than the NPV value found using the appropriate discount rate for projects of average riskiness to the firm (i.e., the 10% cost of capital).

This concludes our discussion of the expected value of the risk-adjusted discount rate distribution. As mentioned, this expected value provides one important piece of information about whether a project being evaluated under conditions of risk is a candidate for acceptance. However, the standard deviation of the distribution provides valuable additional information. Based on the expected value and the standard deviation, the financial manager can determine the probability that the project will achieve a positive risk-adjusted NPV value. Chapter 13 picks up this analysis.

SUMMARY

This chapter discusses the important area of risk analysis in capital budgeting. When the certainty assumption is relaxed, the need arises to examine both a measure of central tendency (i.e., expected return) and a measure of the variability in the distribution of returns (e.g., the standard deviation, coefficient of variation). Further, because of the importance of other goals, trade-offs between them, and risk preferences of decision makers, the maximize expected utility criterion is suggested as being appropriate for decision making under conditions of risk.

The two conventional models to evaluate single projects under conditions of risk —the risk-adjusted discount rate technique and the certainty equivalent method—are introduced and examined in some depth. We illustrated the determination of the expected value for each of these approaches.

The following chapter continues the evaluation of projects under conditions of risk. The remaining important issue that must be explored is: How large is the probability that the project under consideration will increase shareholders' wealth?

QUESTIONS
PROBLEMS

1. A machine with a 4-year life is being replaced with a modern, more efficient piece of equipment with a longer expected life. The equipment will require a payment of $55,000 in the first 30 days of its operation. The expected returns and standard deviation are as follows:

YEAR	EXPECTED RETURNS	STANDARD DEVIATION
1	$14,000	$1,200
2	16,000	1,800
3	18,000	2,000
4	20,000	1,950
5	22,000	3,000

The risk-free rate of return is 5%. The CEC values and the coefficient of variation are as follows for the 5-year period:

COEFFICIENT OF VARIATION	CERTAINTY EQUIVALENT COEFFICIENT				
	YEAR 1	YEAR 2	YEAR 3	YEAR 4	YEAR 5
$v \leq 0.10$	0.92	0.88	0.85	0.80	0.74
$0.10 \leq v \leq 0.25$	0.86	0.82	0.78	0.73	0.69

Determine the expected certainty equivalent value.

2. A boiler manufacturing company uses a certainty equivalent approach in its evaluation of risky investments. Currently, the company is faced with two alternative projects. Project A is Replacement investment—category II; project B is New investment—category II, according to Table 12–1. The expected values of net cash flows for each project and risk-free returns are as follows:

YEAR	A	B	RISK-FREE RETURN
Present	− $40,000	− $50,000	—
1	20,000	20,000	0.05
2	20,000	25,000	0.06
3	20,000	30,000	0.07

Which of the alternatives should be selected?

3. A corporation is considering two projects and will choose one or the other based upon their RAR. The corporation's cost of capital is 14% and the firm estimates that the risk-free rate will be 10%. Project A is a replacement investment—category II. Project B is a new investment—category II. Project A's projected cash flow distribution is as follows:

ORIGINAL COST		CASH FLOWS FOR YEARS 1–6	
PROBABILITY	AMOUNT	PROBABILITY	AMOUNT
0.3	$100,000	0.15	$20,000
0.3	110,000	0.25	25,000
0.4	120,000	0.25	30,000
		0.15	35,000
		0.10	45,000
		0.10	45,000

Project B's projected cash flow distribution is as follows:

ORIGINAL COST		CASH FLOWS FOR YEARS 1–6	
PROBABILITY	AMOUNT	PROBABILITY	AMOUNT
0.5	$225,00	0.25	$50,000
0.2	210,000	0.25	60,000
0.3	200,000	0.15	70,000
		0.15	75,000
		0.10	80,000
		0.10	85,000

Determine the RAR for each project using Table 12–2 for return requirements for investment groups.

4. A company is considering an investment costing $8,000. The investment is such that the size of the inflows will be correlated with the state of the economy. Economists can reliably estimate the following probabilities for the next 3 years.

STATE	PROBABILITIES FOR YEARS 1–3
Recession	0.3
Normal	0.6
Boom	0.1

Company officials can reliably predict the inflows associated with each state of the economy.

STATE	NET CASH INFLOWS
Recession	$2,000
Normal	5,000
Boom	8,000

Assume a cost of capital of 11% and a risk premium of 9%. Compute the risk-adjusted NPV.

5. A corporation has a cost of capital of 12% and a risk-free rate of return of 6% and is considering a replacement project, which has an 8-year expected life. The project will cost approximately $50,000 and will generate cash inflows of $10,000 each year.

   This project is a category II investment (Table 12–1), and the corporation has a hurdle rate of 15%. The corporation also expects that the dispersion of cash flows after year 4 will be relatively constant and that the CECs from the table will be used during the initial period and will be 0.77 thereafter. Determine the project's NPV using the risk-adjusted discount rate and the certainty equivalent method and evaluate the results.

REFERENCES

Ang, James S., and Wilbur G. Lewellen. "Risk Adjustment in Capital Investment Project Evaluations." *Financial Management*, 11 (Summer 1982), 5–14.

Arzac, Enrique R. "Structural Planning Under Controllable Business Risk." *Journal of Finance* (December 1975).

Baldwin, Carliss Y., and Richard S. Ruback. "Inflation, Uncertainty and Investment." *Journal of Finance* (July 1986).

Bar-Yosef, S., and R. Mesznik. "On Some Definitional Problems with the Method of Certainty Equivalents." *Journal of Finance* (December 1977).

Ben-Shahar, Haim, and Frank A. Werner. "Multiperiod Capital Budgeting under Uncertainty: A Suggested Application." *Journal of Financial and Quantitative Analysis*, 12 (December 1977), 859–878.

Beranek, William. "Some New Capital Budgeting Theorems." *Journal of Finance and Quantitative Analysis*, 13 (December 1978), 809–824.

Berg, Claus C. "Individual Decisions Concerning the Allocation of Resources for Projects with Uncertain Consequences." *Management Science Theory* (September 1974).

Bernhard, Richard H. "Risk-Adjusted Values, Timing of Uncertainty Resolution, and the Measurement of Project Worth." *Journal of Financial and Quantitative Analysis* (March 1984).

Bey, Roger P., and J. Clayton Singleton. "Autocorrelated Cash Flows and the Selection of a Portfolio of Capital Assets." *Decision Sciences*, 8 (October 1978), 640–657.

Bierman, Harold Jr., and Jerome E. Hass. "Capital Budgeting Under Uncertainty: A Reformulation." *Journal of Finance* (*March* 1973).

_____, and Warren H. Hausman. "The Resolution of Investment Uncertainty Through Time." *Management Science*, 18 (August 1972), 654–662.

Bildersie, John S. "The Association between a Market-Determined Measure of Risk and Alternative Measures of Risk." *Accounting Review*, 50 (January 1975), 81–98.

Blatt, John M. "Investment Evaluation Under Uncertainty." *Financial Management* (Summer 1979).

Bogue, M., and R. Roll. "Capital Budgeting of Risky Projects with Imperfect Markets for Physical Capital." *Journal of Finance* (May 1974), 601–613.

Bonini, Charles P. "Capital Investment Under Uncertainty with Abandonment Options." *Journal of Financial and Quantitative Analysis* (March 1977), 39–54.

_____. "Comment on Formulating Correlated Cash Flow Streams." *Engineering Economist*, 20 (Spring 1975), 209–214.

_____. "Evaluation of Project Risk in Capital Investments with Abandonment Options." *Research Paper 224*, Stanford Graduate School of Business, 1974.

Brumelle, Shelby L., and Bernhard Schwab. "Capital Budgeting with Uncertain Future Opportunities: A Markovian Approach." *Journal of Financial and Quantitative Analysis* (January 1973).

Buzby, Stephen L. "Extending the Applicability of Probabilistic Management Planning and Control Models." *Accounting Review*, 49 (January 1974), 42–49.

Carter, E. Eugene. *Portfolio Aspects of Corporate Capital Budgeting*. Lexington, Mass.: D.C. Heath & Company, 1974.

Celec, S. E., and R. H. Pettway. "Some Observations on Risk-Adjusted Discount Rates: A Comment." *Journal of Finance* (September 1979).

Chen, A. H., and A. J. Boness. "Effects of Uncertain Inflation on the Investment and Financing Decisions of a Firm." *Journal of Finance*, 30 (May 1975), 469–484.

Chen, Son-Nan, and William T. Moore. "Investment Decisions under Uncertainty: Application of Estimation Risk in the Hillier Approach." *Journal of Financial and Quantitative Analysis* (September 1982).

Cozzolino, John M. "Controlling Risk in Capital Budgeting: A Practical Use of Utility Theory for Measurement and Control of Petroleum Exploration Risk." *The Engineering Economist* (Spring 1980).

Dhingra, Harbans L. "Effects of Estimation Risk on Efficient Portfolios: A Monte Carlo Simulation Study." *Journal of Finance and Accounting* (Summer 1980).

Fama, Eugene F. "Risk-Adjusted Discount Rates and Capital Budgeting under Uncertainty." *Journal of Financial Economics*, 5 (1977), 3–24.

_____. "Components of Investment Performance." *Journal of Finance*, 27 (June 1972), 551–567.

_____. "Efficient Capital Markets: A Review of Theory and Empirical Work." *Journal of Finance*, 25 (May 1970), 333–417.

_____. "Efficient Capital Markets: Restatement of the Theory." *Journal of Finance*, forthcoming.

_____. "Multiperiod Consumption–Investment Decisions." *American Economic Review*, 60 (March 1970), 163–174.

_____. "Risk, Return, and Equilibrium." *Journal of Political Economy*, 79 (January–February 1971), 30–55.

_____. "Risk, Return, and Equilibrium: Some Clarifying Comments." *Journal of Finance*, 23 (March 1968), 29–40.

_____, and James D. MacBeth. "Risk, Return, and Equilibrium: Empirical Tests." *Journal of Political Economy*, 81 (May–June 1973), 607–636.

_____, and Merton H. Miller. *The Theory of Finance*. New York: Holt, Rinehart and Winston, Inc., 1972.

Ferson, Wayne E., Shmuel Kandel, and Robert F. Stambaugh. "Test of Asset Pricing with Time-Varying Expected Risk Premiums and Market Betas." *Journal of Finance* (June 1987).

Findlay, M. Chapman, III, Arthur E. Gooding, and Wallace Q. Weaver, Jr. "On the Relevant Risk for Determining Capital Expenditure Hurdle Rates." *Financial Management*, 5 (Winter 1976), 9–16.

Friedman, M., and L. J. Savage. "Utility Analysis of Choices Involving Risk." *Journal of Political Economy* (August 1948), 279–304.

Gallinger, George W., and Glenn V. Henderson, Jr. "The SML and the Cost of Capital." Research paper, Arizona State University, 1981.

Gehr, Adam K., Jr. "Risk-Adjusted Capital Budgeting Using Arbitrage." *Financial Management*, 10 (Winter 1981), 14–19.

_____. "Risk and Return." *Journal of Finance*, 34 (September 1979), 1027–1030.

Giaccotto, Carmelo. "A Simplified Approach to Risk Analysis in Capital Budgeting with Serially Correlated Cash Flows." research paper, University of Connecticut, Storrs, December 1983.

Gitman, L. J. "Capturing Risk Exposure in the Evaluation of Capital Budgeting Projects." *The Engineering Economist* (Summer 1977).

Gregory, D. D. "Multiplicative Risk Premiums." *Journal of Financial and Quantitative Analysis* (December 1978).

Hanoch, G., and H. Levy. "The Efficiency Analysis of Choices Involving Risk." *Review of Economic Studies* (July 1969).

Harvey, R. K., and A. V. Cabot. "A Decision Theory Approach to Capital Budgeting Under Risk." *Engineering Economist*, 20 (Fall 1974), 37–49.

Haugen, Robert A., and A. James Heins. "Risk and the Rate of Return on Financial Assets." *Journal of Financial and Quantitative Analysis*, 10 (December 1975), 775–784.

Hertz, David B. "Investment Policies That Pay Off." *Harvard Business Review*, 46 (January–February 1968), 96–108.

_____. "Risk Analysis in Capital Investment." *Harvard Business Review*, 42 (January–February 1964), 95–106.

Hirshleifer, J. "Investment Decisions Under Uncertainty: Applications of the State-Preference Approach." *Quarterly Journal of Economics*, 80 (May 1966), 252–277.

_____. *Investment, Interest and Capital*. Englewood Cliffs, N.J.: Prentice Hall, 1970.

Keeley, Robert, and Randolph Westerfield. "A Problem in Probability Distribution Techniques for Capital Budgeting." *Journal of Finance*, 27 (June 1972), 703–709.

Latane, H. A., and Donald L. Tuttle. "Decision Theory and Financial Management." *Journal of Finance* (May 1966).

Levy, Haim, and Marshall Sarnat. "The Portfolio Analysis of Multiperiod Capital Investment under Conditions of Risk." *Engineering Economist* (Fall 1970).

Markowitz, Harry M. "Portfolio Selection." *Journal of Finance* (March 1952).

_____. *Portfolio Selection*. New York: Wiley 1959.

Modigliani, Franco, and Gerald A. Pogue. "An Introduction to Risk and Return." *Financial Analysts Journal*, Part I (March/April 1974), Part II (May/June 1974).

Myers, Stewart C. "The Application of Finance Theory to Public Utility Rate Cases." *Bell Journal of Economics and Management Science*, 3 (Spring 1972), 58–97.

_____. "Procedures for Capital Budgeting Under Uncertainty." *Industrial Management Review*, 9 (Spring 1968), 1–15.

_____. "A Time-State Preference Model of Security Valuation." *Journal of Financial and Quantitative Analysis*, 3 (March 1968), 1–34.

Newhauser, John J., and Jerry A. Viscione. "How Managers Feel About Advanced Capital Budgeting Methods." *Management Review* (September 1973), 16–22.

Pettit, H. Richardson, and Randolph Westerfield. "A Model of Capital Asset Risk." *Journal of Financial and Quantitative Analysis*, 7 (March 1972), 1649–1668.

Pratt, J. W. and J. S. Hammond, III. "Evaluating and Comparing Projects: Simple Detection of False Alarms." *Journal of Finance* (December 1979).

_____. "Risk Aversion in the Small and in the Large." *Econometrica* (January–April 1964).

Robichek, Alexander A., and Stewart C. Myers. "Conceptual Problems in the Use of Risk-Adjusted Discount Rates." *Journal of Finance*, 21 (December 1966), 727–730.

Ross, S. A. "A Simple Approach to the Valuation of Risky Streams." *Journal of Business* (July 1978).

Schall, Lawrence D., and Gary L. Sundem. "Capital Budgeting Methods and Risk: A Further Analysis." *Financial Management*, 9 (Spring 1980), 7–11.

Senbet, L. W., and H. E. Thompson. "The Equivalence of Alternative Mean-Variance Capital Budgeting Models." *Journal of Finance* (May 1978).

Sharpe, William F. "A Simplified Model for Portfolio Analysis." *Management Science* (January 1963).

_____. "Efficient Capital Markets with Risk." Research Paper 71, Stanford Graduate School of Business, 1972.

Spies, Richard R. "The Dynamics of Corporate Capital Budgeting." *Journal of Finance* (June 1974), 829–845.

Van Horne, James C. "The Analysis of Uncertainty Resolution in Capital Budgeting for New Products." *Management Science*, 15 (April 1969), 376–386.

_____. "Capital-Budgeting Decisions Involving Combinations of Risky Investments." *Management Science*, 13 (October 1966), 84–92.

_____. *The Function and Analysis of Capital Market Rates*. Englewood Cliffs, N.J.: Prentice Hall, 1970.

_____ . "Capital Budgeting under Conditions of Uncertainty as to Project Life." *Engineering Economist*, 17 (Spring 1972), 189–199.

Weingartner, H. Martin. "Leasing Asset Lives and Uncertainty: Guides to Decision Making." *Financial Management* (Summer 1987).

Weinwurm, Ernest H. "Utilization of Sophisticated Capital Budgeting Techniques in Industry." *Engineering Economist* (Summer 1974), 271–272.

Zinn, C. D., W. G. Lesso, and B. Motazed. "A Probabilistic Approach to Risk Analysis in Capital Investment Projects." *The Engineering Economist* (Summer 1977).

Advanced Problems in Capital Budgeting Under Conditions of Risk

13

As mentioned in the previous chapter, a complete analysis of a capital project under conditions of risk is best carried out using the following steps:

1 Specify the probability distribution for the cash flows each year over the project's life.
2 Determine the mean and standard deviation of each of these distributions.
3 Based on these results, determine the expected value of the certainty equivalent (CE) or risk-adjusted return (RAR) distribution.
4 Determine the standard deviation of the CE or RAR distribution.
5 Based on the results at steps 3 and 4, make a probability statement about the likelihood that the project will take on a positive CE or RAR value.

We have examined the first three steps listed in Chapter 12. It remains for us in this chapter to illustrate how the standard deviation for CE or RAR is computed and how this measure is used to assess the project's attractiveness.

VARIABILITY IN THE RISK-ADJUSTED DISCOUNT RATE AND CERTAINTY EQUIVALENT PROBABILITY DISTRIBUTIONS

The standard deviation of the RAR or the CE distribution uses as data inputs the standard deviations of each year's cash inflow distribution *and* the degree of correlation between the cash flow distributions over the life of the project. This latter aspect (i.e., the intertemporal correlations between cash flow distributions) plays an important part in determining the magnitude of σ_{RAR} and σ_{CE}, since the interrelationships can either intensify or reduce risk.

To begin our discussion of how to find σ_{RAR} or σ_{CE}, consider the general formula for finding the variance of the sum of three random variables $(\tilde{X}, \tilde{Y}, \tilde{Z})$, where each is multiplied by a constant $(a, b, \text{ and } c, \text{ respectively})$,

$$\text{Var}(a\tilde{X} + b\tilde{Y} + c\tilde{Z}) = a^2\sigma_{\tilde{X}}^2 + b^2\sigma_{\tilde{Y}}^2 + c^2\sigma_{\tilde{Z}}^2$$

$$+ 2ab\rho_{\tilde{X}, \tilde{Y}}\sigma_{\tilde{X}}\sigma_{\tilde{Y}} + 2ac\rho_{\tilde{X}, \tilde{Z}}\sigma_{\tilde{X}}\sigma_{\tilde{Z}}$$

$$+ 2bc\rho_{\tilde{Y}, \tilde{Z}}\sigma_{\tilde{Y}}\sigma_{\tilde{Z}} \qquad (1)$$

where $\sigma_{\tilde{X}}^2$ and $\sigma_{\tilde{X}}$ = the variance and the standard deviation of the random variable $\tilde{X}$, respectively

$\rho_{\tilde{X}, \tilde{Y}}$ = correlation coefficient between the random variables $\tilde{X}$ and $\tilde{Y}$

Notice that the first three terms show the contribution of the three variances, and the last three terms show the contribution of the covariances between all pairs of the three random variables.

To derive the expressions for σ_{RAR} and σ_{CE}, consider that Equation (1) refers to a capital investment project that has a 3-year useful life. Thus, the random variables $\tilde{X}$, $\tilde{Y}$, and $\tilde{Z}$ are the cash inflow distributions of years 1, 2, and 3, respectively; similarly, the constants a, b, and c refer to the discount factors in years 1, 2, and 3, which reflect the time value of money for a given risk-free rate. These discount factors are:

$$\frac{1}{(1 + i)}, \frac{1}{(1 + i)^2}, \text{ and } \frac{1}{(1 + i)^3}$$

respectively, for the risk-free rate i. At this point we consider only two types of cash-flow interdependencies: case I, independent cash flows, and case II, perfectly correlated cash flows.

Case I: Independent Cash Flows

Under this assumption, the cash flows over the life of the project are independent, meaning that successive years' cash flows are not related in any systematic way (i.e., there is a random relationship among cash flows). This condition probably occurs in highly competitive markets devoid of trade names, advertising, and so on, where exogenous forces shape the market demand. Thus, variability in cash flows over the life of the project will be reduced, owing to a canceling out of the cash flows above and below the expected values. If independence is assumed, the correlation ρ_{xy} for all pairs of years in Equation (1) is equal to zero. Hence, the last three covariance terms will drop out and we have

$$\text{Var}(a\tilde{X} + b\tilde{Y} + c\tilde{Z}) = a^2\sigma_{\tilde{X}}^2 + b^2\sigma_{\tilde{Y}}^2 + c^2\sigma_{\tilde{Z}}^2$$

Recall that $\tilde{X}$, $\tilde{Y}$, and $\tilde{Z}$ refer to the cash inflow distributions of years 1, 2, and 3 of a project and that a, b, and c are the discount factors in those three respective years. Hence, calling $\text{Var}(a\tilde{X} + b\tilde{Y} + c\tilde{Z})$ σ_{RAR}^2 or σ_{CE}^2, we arrive at the desired general expression for Case I in Equation (2):

$$\sigma_{\text{RAR}}^2 \text{ or } \sigma_{\text{CE}}^2 = \sum_{t=0}^{n} \frac{\sigma_t^2}{(1+i)^{2t}} \tag{2}$$

It should be noted that the discount factor is raised to the $2t$ power because the values of a, b, and c, which equaled the discount factors

$$\frac{1}{(1+i)}, \frac{1}{(1+i)^2}, \text{ or } \frac{1}{(1+i)^3}$$

were all squared in Equation (1). Of course, if the standard deviation σ_{RAR} or σ_{CE} is desired, we simply take the square root of Equation (2).

Case II: Perfectly Correlated Cash Flows

Under the assumption that cash flows are perfectly correlated, we are positing that given the cash inflow of year 1, all subsequent cash inflows are predetermined, since they will be as many standard deviations above or below their respective means as year 1's cash inflow was. Such a relationship among cash inflows would exist in monopolistically competitive markets, replete with brand names, high-pressure advertising, limited entry, and so on. The variability here will be greater than that found in Case I. This is due to the risk-intensification tendencies of positive correlation, which result from the lack of counteracting variations above and below the means over the life of the project found in the independent cash flow case.

If perfect correlation is assumed, the correlation coefficients $\rho_{\tilde{X}\tilde{Y}}$ for all pairs of years in Equation (1) are equal to $+1$. Hence, Equation (1) becomes

$$\begin{aligned} \text{Var}(a\tilde{X} + b\tilde{Y} + c\tilde{Z}) = {} & a^2\sigma_{\tilde{X}}^2 + b^2\sigma_{\tilde{Y}}^2 + c^2\sigma_{\tilde{Z}}^2 \\ & + 2ab\sigma_{\tilde{X}}\sigma_{\tilde{Y}} + 2ac\sigma_{\tilde{X}}\sigma_{\tilde{Z}} \\ & + 2bc\sigma_{\tilde{Y}}\sigma_{\tilde{Z}} \end{aligned}$$

where the right side can be factored as follows:

$$\text{Var}(a\tilde{X} + b\tilde{Y} + c\tilde{Z}) = (a\sigma_{\tilde{X}} + b\sigma_{\tilde{Y}} + c\sigma_{\tilde{Z}})^2$$

Hence, again calling the left-hand side of this expression σ_{RAR}^2 or σ_{CE}^2 and substituting the usual values for the constants and standard deviations, we arrive at

$$\sigma_{\text{RAR}}^2 \quad \text{or} \quad \sigma_{\text{CE}}^2 = \left[\frac{\sigma_1}{(1+i)} + \frac{\sigma_2}{(1+i)^2} + \frac{\sigma_3}{(1+i)^3} \right]^2$$

For the general project with a useful life of n years, the expression becomes:

$$\sigma_{\text{RAR}}^2 \quad \text{or} \quad \sigma_{\text{CE}}^2 = \left[\sum_{t=0}^{n} \frac{\sigma_t}{(1+i)^t} \right]^2 \tag{3}$$

The use of the two formulas for σ_{CE}^2 (i.e., both for independent cash flows and for perfectly correlated cash flows) is illustrated in Example 1.

EXAMPLE 1

Variance for Perfectly Correlated and Independent Cash Flows

Consider project Alpha, which has an original cost of $200, a 3-year useful life, and cash inflow distributions as follows:

OUTCOME	PERIOD 1 R_{A1}	P_{A1}	PERIOD 2 R_{A2}	P_{A2}	PERIOD 3 R_{A3}	P_{A3}
1	$100	0.10	$ 40	0.10	$ 10	0.10
2	120	0.20	80	0.25	60	0.30
3	140	0.40	120	0.30	100	0.30
4	160	0.20	160	0.25	160	0.20
5	180	0.10	200	0.10	270	0.10

The risk-free rate is 6%.

Compute σ_{CE}^2 under the assumption that (a) cash inflows are independent over Alpha's useful life and (b) cash inflows are perfectly correlated over Alpha's useful life.

SOLUTION: Computing the standard deviations for each of the 3 years, we would find

$$\sigma_1 = \$21.91, \qquad \sigma_2 = \$45.61, \qquad \sigma_3 = \$69.54$$

These three standard deviations are now used to compute σ_{CE}^2.
(a) Assuming independent cash inflows,

$$\sigma_{CE}^2 = \sum_{t=0}^{n} \frac{\sigma_t^2}{(1+i)^{2t}}$$

$$= \frac{(21.91)^2}{(1.06)^2} + \frac{(45.61)^2}{(1.06)^4} + \frac{(69.54)^2}{(1.06)^6}$$

$$= 5,484.07$$

or

$$\sigma_{CE} = \$74.05$$

(b) Assuming perfectly correlated cash inflows,

$$\sigma_{CE}^2 = \left[\sum_{t=0}^{n} \frac{\sigma_t}{(1+i)^t} \right]^2$$

$$= \left[\frac{21.91}{(1.06)} + \frac{45.61}{(1.06)^2} + \frac{69.54}{(1.06)^3} \right]^2$$

$$= (20.67 + 40.59 + 58.39)^2$$

$$= (119.65)^2 = 14,316.1225$$

or

$$\sigma_{CE} = \$119.65$$

Of course, it can be seen that σ_{CE} assuming perfectly correlated cash inflows is significantly greater than σ_{CE} where cash inflows are assumed to be independent. This is due to the risk-intensifying result produced by high positive correlation among the cash flows over the life of the project rather than the canceling out effect of independent (zero-correlation) cash inflows over the project's life.

SENSITIVITY ANALYSIS

The natural reactions of the financial manager to the computation of σ_{CE} under various assumptions might be

1   How can the degree of intertemporal correlation among the cash flows be accurately determined?
2   How can σ_{CE} be used to help evaluate capital projects?

These questions will be examined in turn.

We admit that the degree of intertemporal correlation among the cash inflow distributions over the life of the project is indeed difficult to estimate. However, some comfort can be taken in the fact that σ_{CE} *will take on its maximum value when perfect correlation exists among cash inflow distributions. Further, a somewhat moderate value of σ_{CE} is obtained when it is assumed that cash inflows are independent. It should be noted that σ_{CE} would get smaller if the degree of correlation were allowed to take on negative values and that σ_{CE} would equal zero if it were assumed that the cash inflows were perfectly negatively correlated over the life of the project.* Hence, it is suggested that σ_{CE} be used to evaluate capital projects along the lines of sensitivity analysis, following three steps:

1   σ_{CE} should be computed under the two assumptions of independence and perfect correlation, as demonstrated in Example 1.
2   The risk-return characteristics of the project should be evaluated under the extreme assumption of perfect correlation and the more moderate assumption of independence.
3   Based on its utility curve and its best estimate of the intertemporal correlation, the firm should either reject the proposal or let it stand as a candidate for possible adoption.

The last two steps in the preceding approach point to the answer to the second question posed: How can σ_{CE} be used to help evaluate capital projects? The argument would proceed as follows. If it can be reasonably assumed that each year's cash inflow distribution is normal or approximately normal, the central limit theorem would tell us that the certainty equivalent distribution will be normal or approximately normal with mean $\overline{CE}$ and standard deviation σ_{CE}. The latter distribution can then be used to make probability statements about the certainty equivalent value, taking on any value of interest using the familiar standardized Z-value and tables of the normal distribution (see Appendix A): $Z = (X - \overline{X})/\sigma$. Such probability values are helpful for the firm to evaluate a single project in isolation or to compare several projects. The ultimate decision about project acceptance is determined by the firm's utility function ranking of project attractiveness based on the relevant risk-return information given. An illustration of this situation is found in Example 2.

EXAMPLE 2
Comparison of Two Projects
Using the Certainty Equivalent Method

The firm in Example 1 is also evaluating project Delta, which costs $300 and has cash inflow distributions as follows:

OUTCOME	PERIOD 1 R_{D1}	P_{D1}	PERIOD 2 R_{D2}	P_{D2}	PERIOD 3 R_{D3}	P_{D3}
1	$ 80	0.10	$ 80	0.05	$ 80	0.01
2	100	0.20	100	0.10	100	0.04
3	120	0.40	120	0.15	120	0.10
4	140	0.20	140	0.60	140	0.70
5	160	0.10	160	0.10	160	0.15

The firm assigns the following certainty equivalent factors for the two projects based on their variability in cash flows over their useful lives:

PROJECT ALPHA	PROJECT DELTA
$\alpha_1 = 0.92$	$\alpha_1 = 0.95$
$\alpha_2 = 0.80$	$\alpha_2 = 0.92$
$\alpha_3 = 0.65$	$\alpha_3 = 0.90$

(a) Compute $\overline{CE}$ for both projects.
(b) Compute σ_{CE} for project Delta based on the following assumptions:
  (1) Cash inflows are independent.
  (2) Cash inflows are perfectly correlated.
(c) Compute and explain the coefficient of variation for the certainty equivalent distributions for both projects under both correlation assumptions.
(d) Calling upon the normality assumption, compute the probability that each project will have positive certainty equivalent value, where σ_{CE} is computed under both assumptions of independence and perfect correlation.

SOLUTION: (a) To compute $\overline{CE}$ for each project, we need the expected cash inflow for each of the 3 years.
Project Alpha:

$$\overline{R}_1 = \$100(0.1) + \$120(0.2) + \$140(0.4) + \$160(0.2) + \$180(0.1) = \$140$$

$$\overline{R}_2 = \$40(0.1) + \$80(0.25) + \$120(0.3) + \$160(0.25) + \$200(0.1) = \$120$$

$$\overline{R}_3 = \$10(0.1) + \$60(0.3) + \$100(0.3) + \$160(0.2) + \$270(0.1) = \$108$$

Now, to determine $\overline{CE}$, we multiply the expected cash inflows by their respective certainty equivalent factors and discount at the risk-free rate. Finally, the original costs of projects A and D ($200 and $300, respectively) are substituted into the expression for $\overline{CE}$.

$$\overline{CE}_A = \frac{(0.92)(\$140)}{1.06} + \frac{(0.80)(\$120)}{(1.06)^2} + \frac{(0.65)(\$108)}{(1.06)^3} - \$200$$

$$= \$265.89 - \$200.00 = \$65.89$$

Project Delta:

$$\overline{R}_1 = \$80(0.1) + \$100(0.2) + \$120(0.4) + \$140(0.2) + \$160(0.1) = \$120$$

$$\overline{R}_2 = \$80(0.05) + \$100(0.1) + \$120(0.15) + \$140(0.6) + \$160(0.1) = \$132$$

$$\overline{R}_3 = \$80(0.01) + \$100(0.04) + \$120(0.10) + \$140(0.7) + \$160(0.15) = \$138.80$$

$$\overline{CE}_D = \frac{(0.95)(\$120)}{1.06} + \frac{(0.92)(\$132)}{(1.06)^2} + \frac{(0.90)(\$138.80)}{(1.06)^3} - \$300$$

$$= \$107.55 + \$108.08 + \$104.89 - \$300 = \$20.52$$

(b) Computing σ_{CE} for project Delta we need the following values:

$$\sigma_1 = \$21.90, \qquad \sigma_2 = \$19.39, \qquad \sigma_3 = \$14.09$$

These values were determined using the probability distributions given. The reader should verify these three values.

(1) For independent cash flows:

$$\sigma_{CE}^2 = \frac{(21.90)^2}{(1.06)^2} + \frac{(19.39)^2}{(1.06)^4} + \frac{(14.09)^2}{(1.06)^6}$$

$$= 864.61$$

or

$$\sigma_{CE} = \$29.40$$

(2) For perfectly correlated cash flows:

$$\sigma_{CE}^2 = \left[\frac{21.90}{(1.06)^1} + \frac{19.39}{(1.06)^2} + \frac{14.09}{(1.06)^3} \right]^2$$

$$= (20.66 + 17.26 + 11.83)^2$$

$$= 2475.06$$

or

$$\sigma_{CE} = \$49.75$$

(c) The coefficient of variation can now be computed for each of the two projects. This can be used as a relevant method of comparison because of the size disparity between the two projects:

(1) For independent cash flows,

PROJECT ALPHA	PROJECT DELTA
$\nu = \dfrac{\sigma_{CE}}{CE}$	$\nu = \dfrac{\sigma_{CE}}{CE}$
$= \dfrac{\$74.05}{\$65.89}$	$= \dfrac{\$29.40}{\$20.52}$
$= 1.12$	$= 1.43$

This means that for project Alpha there is 1.12 times as much risk as there is expected return *or* that for every dollar of expected return there is $1.12 of risk, as measured by the standard deviation. For project Delta, the standard deviation is 143% of the expected certainty equivalent return, *or* there is $1.43 of risk for each dollar of expected return. Further, because the two coefficients of variation can be directly compared, project Delta has about 1.3 times as much risk per dollar of expected return as project Alpha.

(2) For perfectly correlated cash flows,

PROJECT ALPHA	PROJECT DELTA
$\nu = \dfrac{\sigma_{CE}}{CE}$	$\nu = \dfrac{\sigma_{CE}}{CE}$
$= \dfrac{\$119.65}{\$65.89}$	$= \dfrac{\$49.75}{\$20.52}$
$= 1.82$	$= 2.42$

Similar interpretations can be attached to these values, as was given. Notice that the relative variability of the two projects has increased proportionately compared with independent cash flows; project Delta's coefficient of variation is still about 1.3 times as great as project Alpha's.

(d) Finally, the probability that each project achieves a positive certainty equivalent factor is determined as follows:

(1) For independent cash flows,

Project Alpha:

$$Z = \frac{0 - \$65.89}{\$74.05} = -0.89 \Rightarrow 0.3133$$

This means that 31.33% of the area under the curve falls between a CE value of 0 and $\overline{CE} = 65.89$. Thus, the probability that project Alpha achieves a positive certainty equivalent value is 0.8133 (0.5000 + 0.3133). It should be noted that the above probability exceeds 0.5000 because $\overline{CE}$ is positive; if $\overline{CE}$ were negative, the probability that the CE value would take on a value greater than zero would be less than 0.5000 and would be quantified by the area in the upper tail of the distribution.

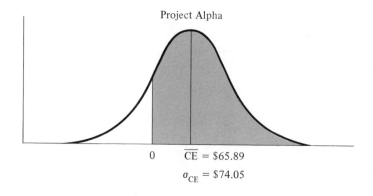

Project Alpha

$0 \qquad \overline{CE} = \$65.89$

$\sigma_{CE} = \$74.05$

Project Delta:

$$Z = \frac{0 - \$20.52}{\$29.40} = -0.698 \Rightarrow 0.2574$$

Thus, the probability that project Delta achieves a positive CE value is 0.7574. Project Delta has almost a 75% chance of achieving a positive CE value, whereas project Alpha has about an 80% chance of doing this *under the assumption that cash flows of the two projects are independent over time.*

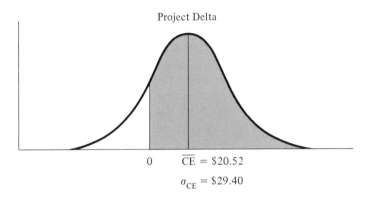

Project Delta

0      $\overline{CE} = \$20.52$

$\sigma_{CE} = \$29.40$

(2) For perfectly correlated cash flows,
Project Alpha:

$$Z = \frac{0 - \$65.89}{\$119.65} = -0.551 \Rightarrow 0.2092$$

$$P\{CE \geq 0 \text{ for project Alpha}\} = 0.7092$$

Project Delta:

$$Z = \frac{0 - \$20.52}{\$49.75} = -0.412 \Rightarrow 0.1598$$

$$P\{CE \geq 0 \text{ for project Delta}\} = 0.6598$$

Under the assumption of perfectly correlated cash flows, the probability of the two projects achieving positive CE values is rather close: 0.7092 for Alpha versus 0.6598 for Delta. Which of these two projects (if either) would meet the firm's criteria for acceptance and what ranking would be assigned to each depends upon the firm's utility function, which quantifies its hierarchy of goals, risk preferences, and attitudes toward risk-return trade-offs. Neither project dominates the other by simultaneously offering a higher expected CE value and a lower σ_{CE}. The measures computed in part (c) of this example plus the probabilities computed in part (d) under the two intertemporal correlation assumptions provide data inputs that help the financial manager rank the two projects and decide which, if either, should be accepted. The ultimate decision depends upon the firm's utility function.

SUMMARY

This chapter and the previous two have examined the area of project evaluation under conditions of risk. We have emphasized the importance of the maximize expected utility criterion.

We examined and illustrated the certainty equivalent method and the risk-adjusted discount rate technique. Both the expected values for these two models and their standard deviations (computed under different assumptions about intertemporal correlations among cash inflow distributions) are computed. Finally, under the assumption that the component cash flow distributions are normal, we demonstrated how probability statements can be made concerning the likelihood that various values are taken on by the random variable measuring certainty equivalent values or risk-adjusted returns.

This chapter concentrates on the evaluation of a single project. Chapter 14 looks at the area of portfolio effects wherein the risk of a combination of projects can be reduced by careful selection to minimize the covariance among all pairs of projects. After that, capital asset pricing theory is examined as a way of integrating this chapter and the following one, which deals with portfolio effects.

QUESTIONS

PROBLEMS

1. Briefly discuss all the ways that utility theory enters into the evaluation of capital projects under conditions of risk.
2. The value of σ_{RAR} or σ_{CE} is dependent upon four variables. Enumerate these variables and discuss whether the relationship between each and σ_{RAR} or σ_{CE} is direct or inverse.
3. Briefly discuss why σ_{RAR} or σ_{CE} takes on a greater value when cash flows are perfectly correlated over the life of the asset compared with when the cash flows are independent over the life of the asset.
4. Briefly discuss how the process of evaluating capital projects differs under conditions of risk from that under conditions of certainty.
5. The Hothouse Corporation is considering project "Woody," the construction of a wood-pruning machine that has the ability to turn entire forests into bundled cords of firewood ready to be delivered to customers.

   The project is anticipated to have an initial cost of $30,000,000, a 3-year useful life, and cash inflow distributions as follows:

	CASH INFLOW PER YEAR (IN MILLIONS)		
PROBABILITY	RW_1	RW_2	RW_3
0.2	$15	$ 8	$20
0.3	20	25	25
0.4	30	40	30
0.1	40	50	35
1.0			

Compute σ_{CE} under the assumption that cash inflows are independent over

Woody's useful life and under the assumption that cash inflows are perfectly correlated over Woody's useful life. Assume that the risk-free rate of return is 6%.

6. A manufacturing company is evaluating two alternative projects. Project A consists of an expansion of the same business by building a new facility at the same location. The total project cost is estimated to be $30,000. Project B consists of an acquisition of another firm selling products unrelated to the company's primary business. The total cost of the project is $40,000. Assume that the risk-free rate is 6%, constant over the life of projects, and that the company considers cash flows for the first 3-year period. The following table shows the cash inflows distribution.

	PROJECT A (CASH FLOW, $000)						PROJECT B (CASH FLOW, $000)					
OUTCOME	RA_1	PA_1	RA_2	PA_2	RA_3	PA_3	OUTCOME	RB_1	PB_1	RB_2	PB_2	RB_3 PB_3
1	10	0.3	15	0.2	10	0.3	1	15	0.2	20	0.3	15 0.2
2	15	0.5	20	0.6	25	0.6	2	20	0.6	25	0.5	30 0.6
3	20	0.2	25	0.2	30	0.1	3	25	0.2	30	0.2	40 0.2

(a) Compute $\overline{CE}$ for both projects.
(b) Compute σ_{CE} for both projects based on the assumptions that cash flows are independent and cash flows are perfectly correlated.
(c) Compute and explain the coefficient of variation of the certainty equivalent distributions for both correlation assumptions.

7. The Energystics Corporation is evaluating two projects. One is the installation of a load shedder, which costs $5,000, including peripheral sensing equipment, and the other, the installation of a 5-ton, high-efficiency air conditioning unit at a cost of $8,000. The energy savings from these two projects are listed in the accompanying table. Distributions are based on the probabilities of future rate increases as set by a local electric company. The risk-free rate in this area is 6%.

Load Shedder

	PERIOD 1		PERIOD 2		PERIOD 3	
RATE INC. (%)	R_{1S}	P_{1S}	R_{1S}	P_{1S}	R_{1S}	P_{1S}
4%	$2,000	0.50	$3,000	0.25	$4,000	0.25
8	4,000	0.25	5,000	0.50	6,000	0.25
12	6,000	0.25	7,000	0.25	8,000	0.50

Air Conditioner

	PERIOD 1		PERIOD 2		PERIOD 3	
RATE INC. (%)	R_{AC}	P_{AC}	R_{AC}	P_{AC}	R_{AC}	P_{AC}
4%	$3,000	0.50	$ 4,000	0.25	$ 5,000	0.25
8	6,000	0.25	7,000	0.50	8,000	0.25
12	9,000	0.25	10,000	0.25	11,000	0.50

Energystics assigns the following certainty equivalent factors for the two projects under consideration based on their variability over the three time periods.

LOAD SHEDDER	AIR CONDITIONER
$\alpha_1 = 0.95$	$\alpha_1 = 0.95$
$\alpha_2 = 0.85$	$\alpha_2 = 0.75$
$\alpha_3 = 0.75$	$\alpha_3 = 0.60$

(a) Compute $\overline{\text{CE}}$ for each project.

(b) Compute σ_{CE} based on independent and perfectly correlated cash flows.

(c) Compute the coefficient of variation for the CE distributions for each project under both correlation assumptions.

(d) Compute the probability that each project will have a positive certainty equivalent value when σ_{CE} is computed under both assumptions of independence and perfect correlation.

8. Using the data from Example 5, perform a sensitivity analysis on the effects of correlation of the cash flows. How did you use this information in deciding on the attractiveness of the project?

9. It is possible for a firm considering two projects under conditions of risk to calculate conflicting decision criteria. For example, Project A could have a higher CE value and a higher σ_{CE} than Project B. Discuss the conditions under which a given firm would correctly choose Project A over Project B.

10. The σ_{CE} value is a function of several variables. Name these variables and discuss whether there is a direct or inverse relationship between each variable and σ_{CE}.

11. Discuss the impact on σ_{CE} as the coefficient of correlation between the annual cash flows (ρ) goes from 0 to $+1$. Similarly as ρ goes from 0 to $+1$, what is the impact on the probability that the CE value will be positive?

REFERENCES

Bernhard, Richard H. "Risk-Adjusted Values, Timing of Uncertainty Resolution, and the Measurement of Project Worth." *Journal of Financial and Quantitative Analysis* (March 1984).

Fama, Eugene F. "Risk-Adjusted Discount Rates and Capital Budgeting under Uncertainty." *Journal of Financial Economics*, 5 (1977), 3–24.

Ferson, Wayne E., Shmuel Kandel, and Robert F. Stambaugh. "Tests of Asset Pricing with Time-Varying Expected Risk Premiums and Market Betas." *Journal of Finance* (June 1987).

Frankfurter, G. M. and T. J. Frecker. "Efficient Portfolios and Superfluous Diversification." *Journal of Financial and Quantitative Analysis* (December 1979).

_____, and Herbert E. Phillips. "Portfolio Selection: An Analytic Approach for Selecting Securities from a Large Universe." *Journal of Financial and Quantitative Analysis* (June 1980).

Fuller, Russell J., and Kim Lang-Hoon. "Inter-Temporal Correlation of Cash Flows and the Risk of Multi-Period Investment Projects." *Journal of Financial and Quantitative Analysis* (December 1980).

Gehr, Adam K., Jr. "Risk-Adjusted Capital Budgeting Using Arbitrage." *Financial Management*, 10 (Winter 1981), 14–19.

Gregory, D. D. "Multiplicative Risk Premiums." *Journal of Financial and Quantitative Analysis* (December 1978).

Hoskins, C. G. "Capital Budgeting Decision Rules for Risky Projects Derived from a Capital Market Model Based on Semivariance." *Engineering Economist* (Summer 1978).

Hsia, Chi-Cheng, and Russell J. Fuller. "Capital Budgeting for Multiperiod Investments with Correlated Cash Flows: A Simplified Approach." Research paper, Washington State University, 1981.

Huang, C. C., I. Vertinsky, and W. T. Ziemba. "On Multiperiod Stochastic Dominance." *Journal of Financial and Quantitative Analysis* (March 1978).

Kudla, Ronald J. "Some Pitfalls in Using Certainty-Equivalents: A Note." *Journal of Business Finance and Accounting* (Summer 1980).

Levy, H., and M. Sarnat. "The Portfolio Analysis of Multiperiod Capital Investment Under Conditions of Risk." *Engineering Economist* (Fall 1970).

Lewellen, W. G. "Some Observations on Risk Adjusted Discount Rates." *Journal of Finance* (September 1977).

_____, and Michael S. Long. "Simulation versus Single-Value Estimates in Capital Expenditure Analysis" *Decision Sciences*, 3 (1973), 19–33.

Lintner, John. "The Aggregation of Investors' Judgments and Preferences in Purely Competitive Security Markets." *Journal of Financial and Quantitative Analysis*, 4 (December 1969), 347–400.

_____. "The Evaluation of Risk Assets and the Selection of Risky Investments in Stock Portfolios and Capital Budgets." *Review of Economics and Statistics*, 47 (February 1965), 13–37.

_____. "Security Prices, Risk and Maximal Gains from Diversification." *Journal of Finance*, 20 (December 1965), 587–616.

Lockett, A. Geoffrey, and Anthony E. Gear. "Multistage Capital Budgeting under Uncertainty." *Journal of Financial and Quantitative Analysis*, 10 (March 1975), 21–36.

Markowitz, Harry M. "Portfolio Selection." *Journal of Finance* (March 1952).

_____. *Portfolio Selection*. New York: Wiley 1959.

Martin, A. D. "Mathematical Programming of Portfolio Selections." *Management Science* (January 1955), 152–166.

Newhauser, John J., and Jerry A. Viscione. "How Managers Feel About Advanced Capital Budgeting Methods." *Management Review* (September 1973), 16–22.

Nielsen, N. C. "The Investment Decision of the Firm Under Uncertainty and the Allocative Efficiency of Capital Markets." *Journal of Finance*, 31 (May 1976), 587–601.

Obel, Borge, and James van der Weide. "On the Decentralized Capital Budgeting Problem under Uncertainty." *Management Science* (September 1979).

Porter, R. B., R. P. Bey, and D. C. Lewis. "The Development of a Mean-Semivariance Approach to Capital Budgeting." *Journal of Financial and Quantitative Analysis* (November 1975).

_____, and _____. "An Evaluation of the Empirical Significance of Optimal Seeking Algorithms in Portfolio Selection." *Journal of Finance* (December 1974).

Schwab, Bernhard. "Conceptual Problems in the Use of Risk-Adjusted Discount Rates with Disaggregated Cash Flows." *Journal of Business Finance and Accounting* (Winter 1978).

_____, and P. Lusztig. "A Note on Abandonment Value and Capital Budgeting." *Journal of Financial and Quantitative Analysis* (September 1970), 377–379.

Stapleton, Richard C. "Portfolio Analysis, Stock Valuation and Capital Budgeting Rules for Risky Projects." *Journal of Finance*, 26 (March 1971), 95–118.

Trueman, Brett. "The Relationship Between the Level of Capital Expenditures and Firm Value." *Journal of Financial and Quantitative Analysis*, (June 1986).

Tuttle, Donald L., and Robert H. Litzenberger. "Leverage, Diversification and Capital Market Effects on a Risk-Adjusted Capital Budgeting Framework." *Journal of Finance*, 23 (June 1968), 427–443.

Zhu, Yu, and Irwin Friend. "The Effects of Different Taxes on Risky and Risk-free Investment and on the Cost of Capital." *Journal of Finance* (July 1986).

CASE STUDY 13-1

Best Foods, Inc. (B)
(Evaluation of capital projects
under conditions of risk and uncertainty)

The CFO and CEO discussion [in Best Foods, Inc. (A), Case 10-1] on the appropriate discount rate to be used in evaluating different capital investment alternatives ended with a mutual agreement that 11% is appropriate when the risk posture of the project is equivalent to the company's overall risk posture.

Three projects were identified for evaluation. The following is the description and relevant data of each of the projects.

PROPOSAL 1: REPLACEMENT OF
THE PACKAGING MACHINERY

This project was proposed by the product manager for the frozen sweet corn product. He is asking for the replacement of the existing packaging machinery with a new and more efficient line. He believes that there is a 50% chance that it will cost $1,250,000, a 30% chance it will cost $1,400,000, and a 20% chance it will cost $1,150,000 to be operational. The existing machinery's market value probability distribution is as follows:

PROBABILITY	MARKET VALUE
0.15	$350,000
0.30	310,000
0.45	285,000
0.10	260,000
1.00	

The new machinery has higher maintenance expenses compared with the old machinery when idle but when fully operational it reduces the packaging costs substantially. Since vegetable crops are seasonal and their availability is subject to unpredictable changes in growing conditions and adverse weather conditions, the product manager estimates the total yearly reductions in packaging costs to have the following probability distribution:

WEATHER CONDITIONS	PROBABILITY	YEARLY COST REDUCTIONS
Excellent	0.25	$325,000
Moderate	0.45	265,000
Bad	0.20	115,000
Disaster	0.10	(30,000)
	1.00	

The new machinery has an estimated life of 12 years with a zero salvage value. Because weather conditions from one year to another are independent, the yearly reductions are not correlated.

PROPOSAL 2: ACQUIRING AMERICAN PRODUCTS, INC.

American Products, Inc., is a manufacturer and distributor of household products and housewares. This company's commitment to the production of quality products gives it a high level of recognition from consumers. Since its establishment in 1981, sales have been increasing steadily at an average compounded growth rate of 21% over the 1981-1986 period. This high sales growth put the corporation under a liquidity crunch, though its return to stockholders was above the average return of the S & P stock index. Best Foods management believes that this company's stock can be purchased from the stockholders at a premium not exceeding 20% of the current market price which is $26.00. Total number of outstanding shares is 107,520.

Best Foods management would alter American Products' dividend policy. All earnings will be retained over a period of ten years and a dividend payout ratio of 50% will be applied thereafter. It is believed that in ten years American Products, Inc., will have grown to its maturity. Then it is estimated that earnings per share will increase 4% annually. The needed data for a preliminary evaluation of this company are the following:

	1981	1982	1983	1984	1985	1986
Earnings per share	$3.08	$3.59	$4.00	$4.43	$4.70	$5.78
Dividends per share	1.65	2.10	2.35	2.65	2.95	3.10
Capital structure	0.95	1.4	1.8	1.6	1.7	1.9

Therefore, the average annual compounded rate of growth in EPS and dividends per share was around 13.5% over the 1981-86 period. Best Foods management believes that there is a 20% chance that this growth rate will be 10% over the coming ten years and a 15% chance instead of 13.5% that it will be 8%.

PROPOSAL 3: FINANCING THE DEVELOPMENT
OF THE PYRETHROIDS INSECTICIDES TECHNOLOGY

The CEO was approached by his old classmate, Mr. Jones, president of National Cyanamid, an established company in the pyrethroid market. Mr. Jones was fighting an unfriendly takeover of his company and could not channel more funds into the R & D department. However, he realized that if he did not pursue the R & D effort to develop the pyrethroids insecticides technology, his company would certainly suffer in the near future. Consequently, he proposed a joint venture agreement with Best Foods.

The CEO of Best Foods, Inc., did not know anything about this industry but found the feasibility study very attractive. In his proposal, Mr. Jones explained that typically a technology advances along an S-curve, with advancement slow initially, then rapid, and finally very slow as the natural limits of the technology are approached. Since that technology is still in its early development, investment at this stage would generate a very high return. For $200,000, Best Foods, Inc., has a good chance of earning more than $1 million.

Besides the high profits potential, the CEO of Best Foods sees in this offer a small start toward diversifying the company. Moreover, he has always thought of Mr. Jones as a man with good business judgment. However, when contemplating the curves and graphs included in the feasibility study presented by Mr. Jones, the CEO was not sure how Mr. Jones could forecast the development of the technology when the core technology has not as yet been discovered. These curves are only forecasts with the uncertainty and inherent risks associated with forecasts. In addition, the CEO was not sure about the reliability or accuracy of the forecasts in determining the inflection points on the S-curve and about the assumption of symmetry of the two halves of the curves.

Mr. Jones explained that it will take at least a year before the technology is developed and probably an additional six months to have the invention in the form of a saleable product. But when this is achieved the technology is expected to have a life of not less than five years, as competitors are far behind in R & D in this area.

QUESTIONS

1. Evaluate these three projects using the different tools of analysis in the evaluation of capital budgeting projects on a LOTUS 1-2-3 template. Conduct a sensitivity analysis where appropriate.
2. Compare the risks involved in the three projects.
3. Would you look for factors other than NPV and risk in making a decision in choosing among these three projects?
4. Recommend a project and justify your recommendation.

Portfolio Effects

14

Chapter 11 provides an overview of decision making under conditions of risk and the importance of utility theory. Chapters 12 and 13 illustrate capital project evaluation for single projects under conditions of risk. As you recall, we determined the risk-adjusted NPV and its standard deviation over the useful life of the project. This chapter shifts the focus of evaluation from individual projects to combinations of projects. Projects that may not be acceptable when considered in isolation might merit acceptance when an optimum *combination* of new and existing projects is sought. This result may occur due to favorable *interaction or portfolio effects* between projects. Thus, we recommend that the firm be viewed as an amalgam of previously accepted projects.

The chapter concentrates initially on portfolios of securities and later applies the principles and techniques to portfolios of capital projects. The chapter draws heavily on the work of Dr. Harry Markowitz, who has been called the father of modern portfolio theory. Every student and practitioner of finance should be familiar with Markowitz's classic works as they have a significant impact on financial decision making under conditions of risk.[1]

The chapter begins by introducing the covariance between a given pair of investments. Next, we present tools for determining the risk and return on portfolios of investments. Finally, we discuss the determination of an optimal portfolio of investments as a preview of Part V, Capital Asset Pricing, and Part VI, Mathematical Programming Applied to the Capital Rationing Problem.

---

[1] See H. Markowitz, "Portfolio Selection," *Journal of Finance* (March 1952), and *Portfolio Selection: Efficient Diversification of Investment* (New York: John Wiley and Sons, Inc., 1959).

PORTFOLIO EFFECTS

Suppose that we consider combinations of possible investments as portfolios. Each investment in the combination has an expected return and risk, the latter measured by its standard deviation. To evaluate different combinations (or budgets) we need an expected return and standard deviation for *each combination*. The expected return, $E(R_p)$, on the portfolio may be computed using Equation (1),

$$E(R_p) = \sum_{j=1}^{N} X_j E(R_j) \tag{1}$$

where X_j = proportion of the total budget allocated to the jth project
$\quad E(R_j)$ = expected rate of return on the jth project

The standard deviation of the budget (σ_p), however, is not simply a weighted average of the project sigmas (σ_j), although these represent one component. Rather, the risk of the budget (σ_p), in addition, reflects the covariances among projects in the combination. *Covariance measures the impact that a pair of securities will have on the portfolio variance due to their interactive effects (i.e., correlation) and their respective standard deviations.* The covariance between two projects (or securities) is the product of three terms: the correlation coefficient and the standard deviations of the two projects, as expressed in Equation (2):

$$Cov_{ij} = \rho_{ij}\sigma_i\sigma_j \tag{2}$$

The reader should recall that the correlation coefficient (ρ_{ij}) measures the nature and strength of the relationship between two securities or two projects. The correlation coefficient can take on values in the following range:

$$-1.0 \leq \rho_{ij} \leq +1.0$$

Note that the covariance will take on the sign of the correlation coefficient (ρ_{ij}) since both standard deviations must be greater than or equal to zero. Thus, the covariance can be positive, negative, or zero, depending on whether the correlation coefficient is positive, negative, or zero, respectively. (The covariance could also be zero if either standard deviation were zero, which would be the case for a risk-free asset.)

1. *Positive covariance* implies that if the cash flows of one project exceed their expected value, the cash flows of the other project in turn are likely to exceed their expected value, and vice versa. Positive covariance intensifies the risk of the combination of assets.

2. *Negative covariance*, by contrast, suggests that if the cash flows of one project exceed their expected value, the cash flows of the other will tend to fall below their expected value, and vice versa. Negative covariance, accordingly, tends to reduce risk significantly in the budget combination.

3. *Zero covariance* (when it results from $\rho_{ij} = 0$) means that the cash flows of the two projects move independently of each other; if the cash flows of one project exceed their expected value, the other project's cash flows are just as likely to exceed as to fall below their expected value. Zero covariance reduces risk in the portfolio.

The standard deviation of the combination is expressed in Equation (3),

$$\sigma_p = \sqrt{\sum_{j=1}^{N} X_j^2 \sigma_j^2 + 2 \sum_{j=1}^{N-1} \sum_{i=j+1}^{N} X_i X_j \, \mathrm{Cov}_{ij}} \tag{3}$$

where i and j represent all projects in the budget, *paired off* for purposes of computing covariance.

The covariance term may be plus (positive covariance), minus (negative covariance), or zero. Obviously, in constructing a portfolio, one would strive *in theory* for a negative covariance sufficient to offset the first term and produce $\sigma_p = 0$. In practice, the returns on capital projects and securities tend to move with the general economy so that negative covariance is seldom obtainable. Generally, the crux of portfolio construction lies in minimizing the degree of positive covariance.

CALCULATING THE COVARIANCE

One approach to computing the covariance considers pairs of observations for the returns on two projects. Deviations of these returns from the respective expected values are multiplied by each other, and then by the joint probability that this pair of returns will occur as shown in Equation (4),

$$\mathrm{Cov}_{ij} = \sum_{t=1}^{N} \left[R_{it} - E(R_i) \right] \left[R_{jt} - E(R_j) \right] P_t \tag{4}$$

where Cov_{ij} = covariance between the ith and jth projects
P_t = joint probability of the paired cash flows for project i and project j
R_{it} = return on the ith project in period t (an element in the probability distribution of returns in project i)
R_{jt} = return on the jth project in period t (an element in the probability distribution of returns in project j)

It should be pointed out that the joint probability, P_t, in Equation (4) can be based on historical experience, an informed subjective estimation, or a simulation of possible outcomes for the two projects under evaluation. Example 1 illustrates the computation of the covariance using Equation (4).

EXAMPLE 1
Expected Value, Standard Deviation, and Portfolio Covariance

Assume that a corporation is evaluating two projects, X and Y. After performing 400 simulation runs showing the interaction of the cash flows generated by the two projects, the manager prepared the following table to summarize the results. This table presents the data necessary to determine the probabilities of various cash flows for each project, as well as the ways in which the two projects interact.

TABLE OF CASH FLOWS GENERATED IN 400 SIMULATION RUNS

| | PROJECT Y | | | |
PROJECT X	$100,000	$250,000	$400,000	TOTAL
$100,000	50	20	5	75
200,000	72	155	3	230
300,000	28	25	42	95
Total	150	200	50	400

Compute the following:

(a) A table of joint and marginal probabilities based on the table of simulation results given.

(b) The expected value and the standard deviation of the cash flow distribution for each of the two projects.

(c) The covariance between the cash flows of projects X and Y using Equation (4) and a contingency table format.

SOLUTION: (a) To facilitate the computations, the contingency table of the number of observations is first converted into joint and marginal probabilities by dividing each entry in the table by 400:

| | PROJECT Y | | | |
PROJECT X	$100,000	$250,000	$400,000	TOTAL
$100,000	0.125	0.0500	0.0125	0.1875
200,000	0.180	0.3875	0.0075	0.5750
300,000	0.070	0.0625	0.1050	0.2375
Total	0.375	0.5000	0.1250	1.0000

(b) To compute the expected cash inflow and the standard deviation for each project, we use the marginal probabilities of each of the three possible outcomes:

Project X:

$$E(R_x) = \$100,000(0.1875) + \$200,000(0.5750) + \$300,000(0.2375)$$
$$= \$18,750 + \$115,000 + \$71,250$$
$$= \$205,000$$

$$\sigma_x = \sqrt{\begin{array}{c}(100,000 - 205,000)^2(0.1875) + (200,000 - 205,000)^2(0.5750) \\ + (300,000 - 205,000)^2(0.2375)\end{array}}$$

$$= \sqrt{2,067,187,500 + 14,375,000 + 2,143,437,500}$$
$$= \$65,000$$

Project Y:

$$E(R_y) = \$100,000(0.375) + \$250,000(0.500) + \$400,000(0.125)$$
$$= \$37,500 + \$125,000 + \$50,000$$
$$= \$212,500$$

$$\sigma_y = \sqrt{\begin{array}{c}(100,000 - 212,500)^2(0.375) + (250,000 - 212,500)^2(0.5) \\ + (400,000 - 212,500)^2(0.125)\end{array}}$$

$$= \sqrt{4,746,093,750 + 703,125,000 + 4,394,531,250}$$
$$= \$99,216$$

(c) Next, we compute the covariance between projects X and Y. We use the joint probabilities in the body of the table and restate the table in a form consistent with Equation (4). We do this by showing each cash flow as a deviation from its respective mean (i.e., subtract $205,000 from each cash flow for project X and $212,500 from each of project Y's cash flows):

	PROJECT Y		
PROJECT X	− $112,500	+ $37,500	+ $187,500
− $105,000	0.1250	0.0500	0.0125
− 5,000	0.1800	0.3875	0.0075
+ 95,000	0.0700	0.0625	0.1050

The covariance is computed by multiplying the respective values for each row and column by the corresponding joint probability, with due regard to the signs.

$$\text{Cov}_{xy} = (-\$105{,}000)(-\$112{,}500)(0.1250) + (-\$5{,}000)(-\$112{,}500)(0.18)$$

$$+ (+\$95{,}000)(-\$112{,}500)(0.07) + (+\$37{,}500)(-\$105{,}000)(0.05)$$

$$+ (+\$37{,}500)(-\$5{,}000)(0.3875) + (+\$37{,}500)(+\$95{,}000)(0.0625)$$

$$+ (+\$187{,}500)(-\$105{,}000)(0.0125) + (+\$187{,}500)(-\$5{,}000)(0.0075)$$

$$+ (+\$187{,}500)(+\$95{,}000)(0.1050)$$

$$= + (\$1{,}476{,}562{,}500) + (\$101{,}250{,}000) + (-\$748{,}125{,}000)$$

$$+ (-\$196{,}875{,}000) + (-\$72{,}656{,}250) + (\$222{,}656{,}250)$$

$$+ (-\$246{,}093{,}750) + (-\$7{,}031{,}250) + (\$1{,}870{,}312{,}500)$$

$$= \$3{,}670{,}781{,}250 - \$1{,}270{,}781{,}250$$

$$= + \$2{,}400{,}000{,}000$$

This calculation shows that the covariance between these two projects is $2.4 billion. This result quantifies the contribution of the interaction between the two projects to the risk of a portfolio of the two projects. We realize that this result is not intuitive so we'll try to bring it into focus.

The contribution of each project to the risk of a portfolio of the two projects is quantified by the variance of the project in question. Thus, project X contributes $4.225 billion ($65,000^2) to the portfolio risk and project Y contributes $9.844 billion ($99,216^2) to the portfolio risk. As mentioned before, the portfolio effects between the two projects are quantified by the covariance. In addition, the covariance computed takes on its maximum value when the correlation coefficient equals $+1$. Had this been the case here, the covariance computed by Equation (2) would equal

$$\text{maximum Cov}_{xy} = \rho_{xy}\sigma_x\sigma_y$$

$$= (+1)(\$65{,}000)(\$99{,}216)$$

$$= + \$6{,}449{,}040{,}000$$

Therefore, we see that the actual covariance of $2.4 billion is far below (only about 37% of) the maximum covariance that could have resulted for these two assets. This "moderate" actual covariance resulted from the fact that the correlation between the two assets is only $+0.372$. Finally, the contribution to the portfolio risk of the interaction effect between the two assets is far below the contribution of either project X ($4.225 billion) or project Y ($9.844 billion) by itself.

Throughout subsequent examples in this chapter, we try to add to your intuitive understanding of the covariance.

A more convenient method of calculating the covariance between two projects makes use of Equation (2):

$$\text{Cov}_{ij} = \rho_{ij}\sigma_i\sigma_j \tag{2}$$

This requires that the correlation coefficient ρ_{ij} be computed directly by regressing the paired cash flows of the two projects under consideration. Since the covariance can be computed using Equation (2), that equation can be substituted directly into Equation (3) to produce Equation (5):

$$\sigma_p = \sqrt{\sum_{j=1}^{N} X_j^2\sigma_j^2 + 2\sum_{j=1}^{N-1}\sum_{i=j+1}^{N} X_i X_j \rho_{ij}\sigma_i\sigma_j} \tag{5}$$

Note in Equation (5) that the standard deviation on a portfolio or combination of assets is the square root of the sum of the weighted variances plus twice the sum of the weighted covariances between all possible pairs of securities or projects. Thus, the covariance plays a critical role in determining the size of the portfolio standard deviation.

To see this computational approach for both Cov_{ij} and σ_p, consider Example 2.

EXAMPLE 2

Portfolio Expected Value and Standard Deviation

A firm desires to evaluate the combination of two projects having the following characteristics as a portfolio:

	R_1	R_2
$E(R_j)$	32%	35%
σ_j	7%	10.7%
X_j	0.5	0.5
ρ_{ij}	-0.32	

Compute $E(R_p)$ and σ_p.

SOLUTION:

$$E(R_p) = \sum_{j=1}^{N} X_j E(R_j)$$

$$= (0.5)(0.32) + (0.5)(0.35)$$

$$= 0.335 \text{ or } 33.5\%$$

and

$$\sigma_p = \sqrt{\sum_{j=1}^{N} X_j^2 \sigma_j^2 + 2\sum_{j=1}^{N-1}\sum_{i=j+1}^{N} (X_i)(X_j)(\rho_{ij})(\sigma_j)(\sigma_i)}$$

$$= \sqrt{(0.5)^2(0.07)^2 + (0.5)^2(0.107)^2 + 2(0.5)(0.5)(-0.32)(0.07)(0.107)}$$

$$= \sqrt{0.001225 + 0.0028623 - 0.0011984}$$

$$= 0.0537, \text{ or } 5.37\%$$

It should be noted that the slightly negative correlation between projects R_1 and R_2 in Example 2 substantially reduces the risk on R_2 through pooling. Hence, while R_2 considered in isolation might be rejected, the combination of R_1 with R_2 could become a more attractive alternative than other combinations.

To summarize the key points in terms of building a portfolio of assets, the crux of the problem lies in balancing σ_j, X_j, and Cov_{ij} to minimize risk for a desired level of return. Since σ_i, σ_j, and ρ_{ij} are fixed for a given pair of projects i and j, finding X_i and X_j to minimize risk becomes of interest to the financial manager building a portfolio of assets.

MINIMUM RISK PORTFOLIOS

Considering two projects i and j, σ_p is minimized if the proportion invested in project i is determined as shown in Equation (6):

$$X_i = \frac{\sigma_j^2 - \text{Cov}_{ij}}{\sigma_i^2 + \sigma_j^2 - 2\,\text{Cov}_{ij}} \tag{6}$$

Equation (6) is derived by differentiating Equation (5) with respect to X_i, setting the derivative equal to zero, and solving for X_i.

Based on our discussion, the following observations or decision rules should provide the financial manager with insight and strategies for diversification in building a portfolio or capital budget. We consider two assets, i and j, but the results can be generalized for a large number of projects.

1   If $\rho_{ij} = 0$, the covariance term in Equation (5) for σ_p drops out and the portfolio's standard deviation is the square root of the weighted sum of the project variances:

$$\sigma_p = \sqrt{\sum_{j=1}^{N} X_j^2 \sigma_j^2}$$

Further, the proportion of project i that should be selected to minimize risk under these conditions (i.e., $\rho_{ij} = 0$) is found using Equation (6), modified as follows:

$$X_i = \frac{\sigma_j^2}{\sigma_i^2 + \sigma_j^2}$$

That is, to minimize risk in the combination, X_i should equal the ratio of the variance of j to the sum of the variances of i and j.

2   If $0 < \rho_{ij} < \sigma_i/\sigma_j$ (where σ_i is the smaller of the two standard deviations), the portfolio standard deviation will be determined using Equation (5), where both the sum of the weighted variances and the weighted positive covariance play a part. However, diversification is still attractive, since σ_p will be smaller than either σ_i or σ_j individually if the proportion invested in X_i is determined using Equation (6).

3   If $\rho_{ij} > \sigma_i/\sigma_j$ (where σ_i is the smaller of the two standard deviations), diversification will not be attractive, since the positive correlation and covariance are too great to reduce σ_p below the smaller standard deviation, σ_i. Hence, to minimize risk, X_i should equal 1.

4   If $\rho_{ij} < 0$, σ_p will be less than the square root of the sum of the weighted variances, owing to the negative weighted covariance. The values for σ_p and X_i are then determined using Equations (5) and (6), respectively.

5   If $\rho_{ij} = -1$, σ_p can be driven to zero by selecting the proper proportions of the two securities or projects whereby the weighted covariance in Equation (5) is equal to the sum of the weighted variances. This proper proportion is found by simplifying Equation (6) for the $\rho_{ij} = -1$ case, as follows:

$$X_i = \frac{\sigma_j}{\sigma_i + \sigma_j}$$

The observations are illustrated in Example 3.

EXAMPLE 3
Portfolio Expected Return and Standard Deviation

Two projects have the following risk-return characteristics:

	P_1	P_2
$E(R_j)$	15%	20%
σ_j	12%	16%

Determine $E(R_p)$ and σ_p for the minimum risk portfolio, where the correlation coefficient between the two projects is (a) 0, (b) 0.20, (c) 0.90, and (d) -1.

SOLUTION: (a) Given that $\rho_{ij} = 0$, the optimal proportion is determined as follows:

$$X_i = \frac{\sigma_j^2}{\sigma_i^2 + \sigma_j^2}$$

$$X_1 = \frac{(0.16)^2}{(0.12)^2 + (0.16)^2}$$

$$= \frac{0.0256}{0.0144 + 0.0256}$$

$$= 0.64$$

Thus, the minimum-risk combination is to invest 0.64 of the portfolio in P_1 and 0.36 in P_2.

Now the expected value and standard deviation of the portfolio may be computed.

$$E(R_p) = 0.64(0.15) + 0.36(0.20)$$
$$= 0.096 + 0.072$$
$$= 0.168, \text{ or } 16.8\%$$

$$\sigma_p = \sqrt{(0.64)^2(0.12)^2 + (0.36)^2(0.16)^2}$$
$$= \sqrt{0.00589824 + 0.00331776}$$
$$= 0.0960, \text{ or } 9.60\%$$

Notice that σ_p is significantly lower than either σ_{p_1} or σ_{p_2}.

(b) Given that $\rho_{ij} = +0.20$, the optimal proportion is determined as follows:

$$X_i = \frac{\sigma_j^2 - \text{Cov}_{ij}}{\sigma_i^2 + \sigma_j^2 - \text{Cov}_{ij}}$$

$$X_1 = \frac{(0.16)^2 - (0.2)(0.12)(0.16)}{(0.12)^2 + (0.16)^2 - 2(+0.2)(0.12)(0.16)}$$

$$= \frac{0.02176}{0.03232}$$

$$= 0.673$$

$$E(R_p) = (0.673)(0.15) + (0.327)(0.20)$$
$$= 0.10095 + 0.0654$$
$$= 0.16635, \text{ or } 16.6\%$$

$$\sigma_p = \sqrt{(0.673)^2(0.12)^2 + (0.327)^2(0.16)^2 + 2(0.673)(0.327)(0.2)(0.12)(0.16)}$$
$$= \sqrt{0.0065221776 + 0.0027373824 + 0.0016901452}$$
$$= 0.10464, \text{ or } 10.5\%$$

Notice that σ_p is still lower than the smaller standard deviation, but that we are investing a greater percent of funds (0.673 versus 0.64) in P_1 than when $\rho_{ij} = 0$. In general, as the correlation becomes more highly positive, more of the funds will be invested in the less risky project. This continues until $\rho_{ij} = \sigma_1/\sigma_2$ (where $\sigma_1 < \sigma_2$), at which point 100% of the available funds are invested in the less risky project.

(c) Given that $\rho_{ij} = +0.90$, by rule 3 we see that $\rho_{ij} = +0.90 > 12\%/16\%$ $= +0.75$, so diversification will not be beneficial, and 100% of the funds should be invested in P_1. Given this degree of correlation, we can demonstrate that even a high percentage invested in P_1 (say, 85% in P_1 and 15% in P_2) will not reduce σ_p below $\sigma_{p_1} = 12\%$:

$$\sigma_p = \sqrt{(0.85)^2(0.12)^2 + (0.15)^2(0.16)^2 + 2(0.85)(0.15)(0.90)(0.12)(0.16)}$$
$$= \sqrt{0.010404 + 0.000576 + 0.0044064}$$
$$= 0.12404, \text{ or } 12.4\%$$

As X_1 increases from 0.85 to 1.00, the σ_p value would continually get smaller, decreasing from 12.404% to 12%.

(d) Given that $\rho_{ij} = -1.0$, we see by rule 5 that the proportion to invest in P_1 is just over 57%:

$$X_1 = \frac{\sigma_2}{\sigma_1 + \sigma_2} = \frac{0.16}{0.12 + 0.16} = 0.571429$$

Having this percent invested in P_1 should drive σ_p to zero:

$$E(R_p) = (0.571429)(0.15) + (0.428571)(0.20)$$
$$= 0.08571435 + 0.0857142$$
$$= 0.17142855 \text{ or } 17.1\%$$

$$\sigma_p = \sqrt{\begin{array}{l}(0.571429)^2(0.12)^2 + (0.428571)^2(0.16)^2 \\ +2(-1)(0.12)(0.16)(0.571429)(0.428571)\end{array}}$$

$$= \sqrt{0.0047020478 + 0.0047020314 - 0.0094040792}$$
$$= 0$$

Based on the results of Example 3, we may draw the following conclusions:

1   As ρ_{ij} decreases from $+1.0$ through σ_1/σ_2 ($\sigma_1 < \sigma_2$), 100% of the funds will be invested in the less risky project.

2   As ρ_{ij} gets smaller, eventually decreasing to -1.0, a smaller and smaller percentage will be invested in the less risky security. This occurs because the interaction between ρ_{ij}, σ_i, σ_j, X_i, and X_j causes σ_p to be minimized as X_i is decreased and X_j increased to capitalize on the favorable covariance effects between the two projects or securities. Figure 14–1 illustrates these facts. As shown in Figure 14–1, the minimum risk percentages invested in P_1 go from 0.673 (point 1 in Figure 14–1) when $\rho_{12} = +0.20$, to 0.64 (point 2 in Figure 14–1) when $\rho_{12} = 0$, to 0.571 (point 3 in Figure 14–1) when $\rho_{12} = -1.0$.

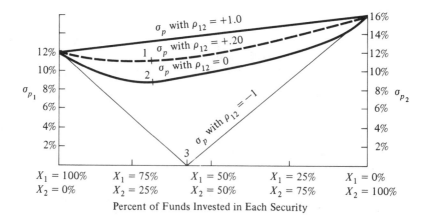

FIGURE 14–1   Portfolio Standard Deviations (σ_p) as the Correlation Coefficient (ρ_{ij}) Varies from +1 to −1

EFFICIENT PORTFOLIOS OR BUDGETS

In earlier chapters, individual projects were ranked by net present value. Since the objective of capital budgeting is to increase the present value of the firm, "rational" management accepted all projects with a positive NPV within the constraints of available capital, and the like. However, this decision rule for individual projects suggests that there does not exist a combination of projects that would be superior to a single investment meeting the criterion. The single project standard ignores the advantage of diversification to improve the quality of earnings through reduction of risk.

When the firm must choose among several capital proposals, a wiser decision rule seeks the combination of projects that maximizes expected present value and minimizes the variance or standard deviation. But experience attests that expected present value and standard deviation generally vary directly, and management can trade off additional risk against additional income. The better decision rule, therefore, stresses the concept of efficient portfolios—those combinations that for any given expected value have a minimum standard deviation (risk) or for any chosen level of risk (standard deviation) have the highest expected return.

Assume that management has a fixed sum to invest and can choose from a number of possible combinations, as illustrated in Figure 14–2. Out of all the combinations obtainable, only some will be efficient. *A combination is inefficient if there exists another portfolio with a higher expected value and a lower standard deviation, a higher expected return and the same standard deviation, or the same expected return and a lower standard deviation.* Eliminating the inefficient portfolios from the set of all possible combinations, the array of efficient portfolios may be plotted as line *AF* in Figure 14–3. Combinations falling below this *efficient frontier* are inefficient: a better return or lower risk or both can always be secured by moving to the frontier. The portfolios above the efficient frontier are unobtainable with the funds and projects available for investment.

Among the efficient set we want to select that combination representing the optimum portfolio (i.e., the combination of risk and return preferred by the investor). The solution lies in the application of utility theory. Figure 14–4 depicts a set of

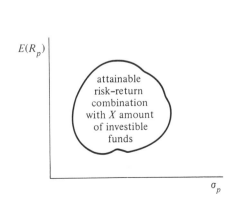

FIGURE 14–2   Attainable Portfolios

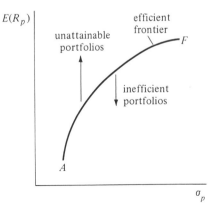

FIGURE 14–3   Efficient Frontier

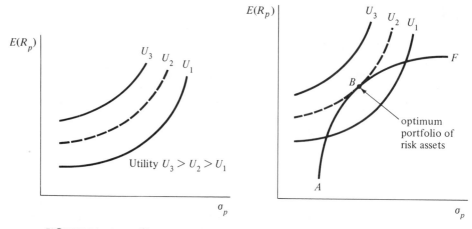

FIGURE 14–4   Utility Isoquants   FIGURE 14–5   Optimal Portfolio

utility isoquants (1, 2, and 3) for a risk-averse decision maker. *Each isoquant plots a series of combinations with different risks and returns which have the same total utility for the investor. On higher utility curves, total utility increases so that total utility $U_3 > U_2 > U_1$.* All combinations of risk and return on curve 2 have the same total utility, but this quantum is larger than the total utility of the combinations on curve 1. *Accordingly, the optimal portfolio for a given investor is found at the tangency point between the efficient frontier and the highest utility isoquant.* This tangency point (B), as shown in Figure 14–5, marks the highest level of satisfaction the investor can attain with the funds available for investment. Other decision makers with unique utility functions would locate their maximum satisfaction at other points of tangency. Each decision maker has his or her own preferred combinations of risky assets (projects or securities).

Let income connote utility and risk, disutility. At the point of equilibrium (B),

$$\frac{\Delta_{utility}}{\Delta_{disutility}} = \frac{\Delta E(R_p)}{\Delta \sigma_p}$$

The equilibrium point is important to the subsequent discussion. Since all portfolios in the efficient set comprise risky assets, the equilibrium point defines the decision maker's preferred combination of risky assets—that combination which dominates all other risky asset packages.

We now address the problem of actually determining the efficient frontier.

DETERMINING THE EFFICIENT FRONTIER

As shown in Figure 14–3, the efficient frontier is a plot of desirable portfolios in risk (σ_p) versus return [$E(R_p)$] space. As you might expect, the efficient frontier is determined by computing σ_p and $E(R_p)$ for a given set of securities as the percentage invested in each security is allowed to vary. By definition, *each portfolio on the efficient frontier has the maximum return for a given level of risk or the minimum risk for a given level of return.* The values for the portfolio risk and return are computed using Equations (3) and (1), respectively.

The shape of the efficient frontier and its location relative to the risk-return axes will vary depending upon the candidate investments under evaluation or changes in the degree of correlation that exists between the investments under evaluation. Example 4 examines the calculation of the risk-return coordinates that yield the plot of the efficient frontier.

EXAMPLE 4
Determination of the Efficient Frontier

Use the following two investments, originally introduced in Example 3:

	P_1	P_2
$E(R_j)$	15%	20%
σ_j	12%	16%

Determine the values for $E(R_p)$ and σ_p for the following values of X_1 and X_2:

X_1	X_2
1.00	0
0.75	0.25
0.50	0.50
0.25	0.75
0	1.00

The following values for ρ_{12} should be used to determine separate efficient frontiers:

$$\rho_{12} = +1.0, \qquad \rho_{12} = +0.20, \qquad \rho_{12} = 0, \qquad \text{and} \qquad \rho_{12} = -1.0$$

Use a tabular format to present the values for $E(R_p)$ and σ_p for the five values of X_1 and X_2 and the four values of ρ_{12}. Finally, plot the four efficient frontiers (one for each value of ρ_{12}) in risk-return space.

SOLUTION: The table of values for $E(R_p)$ and σ_p is as follows:

		$\rho_{12} = +1.0$		$\rho_{12} = +0.20$		$\rho_{12} = 0$		$\rho_{12} = -1.0$	
X_1	X_2	$IE(R_p)$	σ_p	$E(R_p)$	σ_p	$E(R_p)$	σ_p	$E(R_p)$	σ_p
1.0	0	0.15	0.12	0.15	0.12	0.15	0.12	0.15	0.12
0.75	0.25	0.1625	0.13	0.1625	0.1055	0.1625	0.0985	0.1625	0.05
0.50	0.50	0.1750	0.14	0.1750	0.1092	0.1750	0.10	0.1750	0.02
0.25	0.75	0.1875	0.15	0.1875	0.1294	0.1875	0.1237	0.1875	0.09
0	1.0	0.20	0.16	0.20	0.16	0.20	0.16	0.20	0.16

It is instructive to examine this table before we plot the four efficient frontiers. Notice that the values of $E(R_p)$ do not change as ρ_{12} changes. Further, notice that σ_p is an increasing *linear* function only when $\rho_{12} = +1.0$. In the other three cases (i.e., $\rho_{12} = +0.20$,

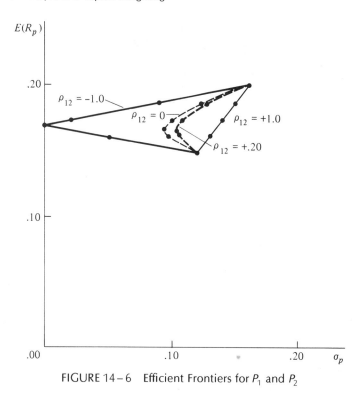

FIGURE 14–6   Efficient Frontiers for P_1 and P_2

$\rho_{12} = 0$, and $\rho_{12} = -1.0$), σ_p is a nonlinear function of X_1 and X_2. The values shown in the given table plus the values for $E(R_p)$ and σ_p computed for the minimum risk portfolios computed in Example 3 enable us to plot the efficient frontiers, as shown in Figure 14–6.

Notice that each of the efficient frontiers starts at the minimum risk portfolio (which was one of the reasons why the minimum risk portfolio is significant) and ends at the maximum risk/maximum return portfolio. Of course, it can be observed pictorially in Figure 14–6 that as ρ_{12} decreases, the value of σ_p decreases, which results in the efficient frontier coming closer to the $E(R_p)$ axis.

PORTFOLIO THEORY AND CAPITAL BUDGETING

Application of the portfolio model to capital budgeting is not without some difficulty. An investment in common stocks is *divisible*; the purchaser acquires units (or shares) each with the same expected return and standard deviation. The efficient frontier is thus a continuous line and the weighting system reflects the percentage of the total investment allocated to one asset or to the amounts of risk and risk-free assets.

Few capital projects divide into homogeneous units with the same expected return and standard deviation. Most projects are lumpy, or *indivisible*. Acceptance means taking the entire project: the whole return and whole standard deviation. The firm cannot buy fractions. It cannot acquire 60% of the return and standard deviation of a project. The continuity of the line between portfolios in Figures 14–3 or 14–6 is due to variations in fractional holdings in a group of divisible projects. For *indivisible projects*, it would not be realistic to join the efficient projects with a continuous line, since fractional projects are not permitted. In constructing portfolios of indivisible projects, therefore, the weighting system is either 0 or 1. The solution in terms of optimum expected return and standard deviation for a portfolio of indivisible projects is most easily reached using integer programming, as illustrated in Chapter 20.

Lower Confidence Limit Criterion

If the number of projects considered is large, the efficient set might involve a substantial number of combinations from which to choose. The use of the lower confidence limit model can reduce the problem to a manageable size. The approach assumes that the investor can state his or her preference in terms of a minimum acceptable return (the lower confidence limit) as opposed to minimizing risk for a given specified return. The lower confidence limit (L) is found using Equation (7),

$$L = E(R_p) - K\sigma_p \tag{7}$$

where K is a constant chosen by the investor and refers to the number of standard deviations in the normal distribution. Thus, the investor (or manager) establishes a floor below which the return on the budget should not fall. Depending on the minimum return stipulated, K may represent, for example, 1, 1.5, 2 standard deviations below the expected return. In other words, the investor, by putting a value on K, establishes a minimum acceptable return on the budget and/or the amount of downside risk she or he willingly bears. If $K = 2$, this means that the manager is willing to accept only a 2.28% probability of the return falling below the minimum acceptable amount. This value is determined by looking up a Z-value of 2 in Appendix A, Table of the Normal Distribution. The table value for a Z-value of 2 is 0.4772. As shown in Figure 14–7, the value of 0.0228 is arrived at by subtracting 0.4772 from 0.5, which is the area under the curve below $E(R_p)$.

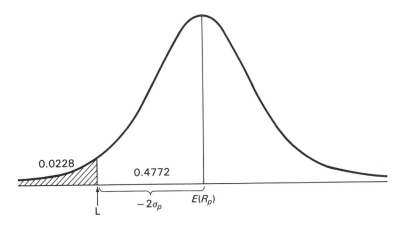

FIGURE 14–7   Illustration of Lower Confidence Limit Criterion

As the minimum acceptable return (L) increases for a given budget, there will be fewer efficient combinations from which to choose. The efficient frontier shrinks as previously efficient portfolios are now considered inefficient. To illustrate the concept, consider Example 5.

EXAMPLE 5

Application of Lower Confidence Limit Criterion

An investor is evaluating the following three portfolios:

PORTFOLIO	$E(R_p)$	σ_p
A	0.22	0.10
B	0.28	0.12
C	0.38	0.14

All three of these portfolios are efficient. Depending upon his or her utility function, the investor might choose any one of the three portfolios. Assume that she or he is only willing to accept a 0.0228 chance of the return falling below L. Determine the value of K that would be assigned and the minimum acceptable returns on the portfolios.

SOLUTION: Assuming a normal distribution, a value of $K = 2$ would include about 95% of the cases. Hence, a K equaling 2 would find only 2.28% of the cases falling below L. (More risk-averse investors would increase the value of K since they would require fewer cases falling below L.) The minimum acceptable returns on the portfolios now become

PORTFOLIO	$E(R_p)$	$-$	$K(\sigma_p)$	$=$	L
A	0.22	$-$	2(0.10)	$=$	0.02
B	0.28	$-$	2(0.12)	$=$	0.04
C	0.38	$-$	2(0.14)	$=$	0.10

Portfolio C now dominates based on the following rule: specify the value of K and choose the portfolio with the highest minimum return, L.

SUMMARY

This chapter explores the important area of portfolio effects in which the focus of the capital investment process shifts from the individual project to that of combinations of projects. The discussion centers on the concept of covariance between pairs of candidate projects that might be included in the capital budget. The computation of the covariance is considered, as well as the determination of the expected return and standard deviation on the portfolio of assets. The area of efficient portfolios is introduced, as is the selection of the optimal efficient portfolio when either exclusively risk assets or a combination of risk and risk-free assets are available to the investor. This chapter serves as a bridge to introduce Chapter 15, which deals with capital asset pricing theory.

1. Empirical studies have derived the following probabilities of the specific outcomes for two projects.

	PROJECT B			
PROJECT A	$250,000	$300,000	$400,000	TOTAL
$50,000	0.1254	0.1073	0.0764	0.3091
75,000	0.0909	0.0673	0.1691	0.3273
90,000	0.1654	0.0618	0.1364	0.3636
Total	0.3817	0.2364	0.3819	

Compute the mean and standard deviation of each project as well as the covariance between the two projects, using the contingency table format.

2. Consider the returns for these four securities:

OBS	SEC 1	SEC 2	SEC 3	SEC 4
1	$ 9	$25	$30	$5
2	10	23	31	6
3	12	22	31	5
4	15	20	32	4
5	16	19	30	2

The correlation coefficients for all combinations of securities are shown here, along with the standard deviations of each security:

$$\rho_{12} = -0.98 \qquad \sigma_1 = 3.05$$

$$\rho_{13} = 0.24 \qquad \sigma_2 = 2.39$$

$$\rho_{14} = -0.85 \qquad \sigma_3 = 0.84$$

$$\rho_{23} = -0.28 \qquad \sigma_4 = 1.52$$

$$\rho_{24} = 0.79$$

$$\rho_{34} = 0.28$$

(a) Compute the covariances for all possible pairs of securities.
(b) Compute the variance of the six two-security portfolios assuming a 50%–50% allocation.

3. Given $\rho_{xy} = 0$ and the following incomplete joint and marginal probability table, calculate the variance of the portfolio of the two securities X and Y in equal proportions. Use the completed table to show that the covariance of the two securities is equal to 0.

JOINT AND MARGINAL PROBABILITIES OF CASH
FLOW GENERATED IN 500 SIMULATION RUNS

PROJECT X	PROJECT Y			
	$100	$200	$300	TOTAL
$150	0.20	———	———	———
200	———	———	0.05	0.20
250	———	———	———	———
Total	0.50	———	———	1.00

Hint: Recall that if two events A and B are independent of each other, $P(A \cap B) = P(A) \cdot P(B)$. Use this hint to fill in all the joint probabilities in the table and then proceed with the solution.

4. RCA is evaluating two securities, which have the following means and standard deviations:

$$E(R_A) = 20\% \qquad E(R_B) = 28\%$$

$$\sigma_A = 10\% \qquad \sigma_B = 14\%$$

RCA feels that the following correlation coefficients could exist between the two securities: (a) $+0.85$, (b) $+0.40$, (c) 0, and (d) -1.0. Determine the minimum-risk portfolios for each of these correlation coefficients, as well as the portfolio return and standard deviation. Selling short is not permitted.

5. For securities A and B and each of the correlation coefficients shown in Problem 4, compute the expected portfolio return and the portfolio standard deviation for the following mixtures:

% IN A	% IN B
100	0
75	25
50	50
25	75
0	100

Also, on the same graph sketch the four efficient frontiers that are generated.

6. A firm is evaluating the following four efficient portfolios:

PORTFOLIO	$E(R_p)$	σ_p
1	0.12	0.04
2	0.24	0.06
3	0.30	0.10
4	0.32	0.12

Determine the optimal portfolio if the firm is willing to accept only a 5% chance that the portfolio return falls below the lower confidence level (L).

REFERENCES

Alexander, G. J. "A Re-evaluation of Alternative Portfolio Selection Models Applied to Common Stocks." *Journal of Financial and Quantitative Analysis* (March 1978).

Barry, C. B., and R. L. Winkler. "Nonstationarity and Portfolio Choice." *Journal of Financial and Quantitative Analysis* (June 1976).

Baum, S., R. C. Carlson, and J. V. Jucker. "Some Problems in Applying the Continuous Portfolio Selection Model to the Discrete Capital Budgeting Problem." *Journal of Financial and Quantitative Analysis* (June 1978).

Bawa, V. S. "Safety-First, Stochastic Dominance, and Optimal Portfolio Choice." *Journal of Financial and Quantitative Analysis* (June 1978).

_____. "Optimal Rules for Ordering Uncertain Prospects." *Journal of Financial Economics* (March 1975).

_____. "Admissible Portfolios for All Individuals." *Journal of Finance* (September 1976).

_____, E. J. Elton, and M. J. Gruber. "Simple Rules for Optimal Portfolio Selection in Stable Paretian Markets." *Journal of Finance* (September 1979).

Blume, Marshall E. "Portfolio Theory. A Step Towards Its Practical Application." *Journal of Business* (April 1970).

_____. "Betas and Their Regression Tendencies." *Journal of Finance*, 30 (June 1975), 785–796.

_____. "On the Assessment of Risk." *Journal of Finance*, 26 (March 1971), 1–10.

Borch, K. *The Economics of Uncertainty.* Princeton, N.J.: Princeton University Press, 1968.

Brealey, R. A. *An Introduction to Risk and Return from Common Stocks.* Cambridge: The M.I.T. Press, 1969.

_____, and S. D. Hodges. "Playing with Portfolios." *Journal of Finance* (March 1975).

Brennan, M. J. "The Optimal Number of Securities in a Risky Asset Portfolio Where There are Fixed Costs of Transacting: Theory and Some Empirical Results." *Journal of Financial and Quantitative Analysis* (September 1975).

_____. "An Approach to the Valuation of Uncertain Income Streams." *Journal of Finance*, 28 (June 1973), 661–674.

Bussey, Lynn E., and G. T. Stevens, Jr. "Formulating Correlated Cash Flow Streams." *Engineering Economist*, 18 (Fall 1972), 1–30.

Chen, A. H. "Portfolio Selection with Stochastic Cash Demand." *Journal of Financial and Quantitative Analysis* (June 1977).

_____, Frank C. Jen, and Stanley Zionts. "The Joint Determination of Portfolio and Transaction Demands for Money." *Journal of Finance* (March 1974).

Cheung, C. Sherman, and Clarence C. Y. Kwan. "A Note on Simple Criteria for Optimal Portfolio Selection." *Journal of Finance* (March 1988).

Cohen, Kalman J., and Edwin J. Elton. "Inter-Temporal Portfolio Analysis Based upon Simulation of Joint Returns." *Management Science*, 14 (September 1967), 5–18.

Dhingra, Harlans L. "Effects of Estimation Risk on Efficient Portfolios: A Monte Carlo Simulation Study." *Journal of Business Finance and Accounting* (Summer 1980).

Dickinson, J. P. "The Reliability of Estimation Procedures in Portfolio Analysis." *Journal of Financial and Quantitative Analysis* (June 1974).

Elton, Edwin, and Martin J. Gruber. "Estimating the Dependence Structure of Share Prices—Implications for Portfolio Selection." *Journal of Finance*, 28 (December 1973), 1203–1232.

_____, _____, and M. W. Padberg. "Simple Criteria for Optimal Portfolio Selection." *Journal of Finance* (December 1976).

_____, _____, and_____. "Simple Criteria for Optimal Portfolio Selection: Tracing out the Efficient Frontier." *Journal of Finance* (March 1978).

_____, and_____. "Earnings Estimates and the Accuracy of Expectational Data." *Management Science*, 18 (April 1972), 409–424.

Eun, Cheol S., and Bruce G. Resnick. "Exchange Rate Uncertainty, Forward Contracts, and International Portfolio Selection." *Journal of Finance* (March 1988).

Evans, Jack, and Stephen H. Archer. "Diversification and the Reduction of Dispersion: An Empirical Analysis." *Journal of Finance*, 23 (December 1968), 761–767.

Falk, Haim, and James A. Heintz. "The Predictability of Relative Risk Over Time." *Journal of Business Finance and Accounting* (Spring 1977).

_____, and_____. "Assessing Industry Risk by Ratio Analysis." *Accounting Review* (October 1975).

Ferson, Wayne E., Shmuel Kandel, and Robert F. Stambaugh. "Tests of Asset Pricing with Time-Varying Expected Risk Premiums and Market Betas." *Journal of Finance* (June 1987).

Fielitz, Bruce D. "Indirect versus Direct Diversification." *Financial Management* (Winter 1974).

Frankfurter, G. M., and T. J. Frecker. "Efficient Portfolios and Superfluous Diversification." *Journal of Financial and Quantitative Analysis* (December 1979).

_____, and Herbert E. Phillips. "Portfolio Selection: An Analytic Approach for Selecting Securities from a Large Universe." *Journal of Financial and Quantitative Analysis* (June 1980).

Friend, I., and M. Blume. "Measurement of Portfolio Performances Under Uncertainty." *American Economic Review* (September 1970), 561–575.

_____, and_____. "The Demand for Risky Assets." *American Economic Review* (December 1975).

Gennotte, Gerard. "Optimal Portfolio Choice under Incomplete Information." *Journal of Finance* (July 1986).

Gonedes, Nicholas J. "A Note on Accounting-Based and Market-Based Estimates of Systematic Risk." *Journal of Financial and Quantitative Analysis*, 10 (June 1975), 355–365.

Grauer, Robert R. "Normality, Solvency, and Portfolio Choice." *Journal of Financial and Quantitative Analysis* (September 1986).

Gressis, N., G. C. Philippatos, and J. Hayya. "Multiperiod Portfolio Analysis and the Inefficiency of the Market Portfolio." *Journal of Finance* (September 1976).

Green, Richard C. "Benchmark Portfolio Inefficiency and Deviations from the Security Market Line." *Journal of Finance* (June 1986).

Hamada, Robert S. "Portfolio Analysis, Market Equilibrium and Corporation Finance." *Journal of Finance*, 24 (March 1969), 13–32.

Hillier, Frederick S. "A Basic Model for Capital Budgeting of Risky Interrelated Projects." *Engineering Economist*, 20 (Fall 1974), 37–49.

Hirshleifer, J. "Efficient Allocation of Capital in an Uncertain World." *American Economic Review*, 54 (May 1964), 77–85.

James J. A. "Portfolio Selection with an Imperfectly Competitive Asset Market." *Journal of Financial and Quantitative Analysis* (December 1976).

Johnson, K. H., and R. C. Burgess. "The Effects of Sample Sizes on the Accuracy of EV and SSD Efficiency Criteria." *Journal of Financial and Quantitative Analysis* (December 1975).

_____, and D. S. Shannon. "A Note on Diversification and the Reduction of Dispersion." *Journal of Financial Economics*, 1 (December 1974), 365–372.

Jorion, Phillippe. "Bayes-Stein Estimation for Portfolio Analyses." *Journal of Financial and Quantitative Analysis* (September 1986).

Joy, O. Maurice, and Jerry O. Bradley. "A Note on Sensitivity Analysis of Rates of Return." *Journal of Finance*, 28 (December 1973), 1255–1261.

Levy, H., and M. Sarnat. "The Portfolio Analysis of Multiperiod Capital Investment Under Conditions of Risk." *Engineering Economist* (Fall 1970).

_____, and _____. "The World Oil Crisis: A Portfolio Interpretation." *Economic Inquiry* (September 1975).

Lewis, Alan L. "A Simple Algorithm for the Portfolio Selection Problem." *Journal of Finance* (March 1988).

Lintner, John. "The Evaluation of Risk Assets and the Selection of Risky Investments in Stock Portfolios and Capital Budgets." *Review of Economics and Statistics*, 47 (February 1965), 13–37.

McInish, Thomas H., and Robert A. Wood. "Adjusting for Beta Bias: An Assessment of Alternate Techniques: A Note." *Journal of Finance* (July 1986).

Nielsen, Lars Tyge. "Portfolio Selection in the Mean-Variance Model: A Note." *Journal of Finance* (December 1987).

_____. "Positively Weighted Frontier Portfolios: A Note." *Journal of Finance* (June 1987).

Pogue, Gerald A. "An Extension of the Markowitz Portfolio Selection Model to Include Variable Transactions Costs, Short Sales, Leverage Policies and Taxes." *Journal of Finance*, 25 (December 1970), 1005–1027.

_____, and Kishore Lall. "Corporate Finance: An Overview." *Sloan Management Review*, 15 (Spring 1974), 19–38.

Schall, Lawrence D. "Asset Valuation, Firm Investment, and Firm Diversification." *Journal of Business*, 45 (January 1972), 11–28.

_____. "Firm Financial Structure and Investment." *Journal of Financial and Quantitative Analysis*, 6 (June 1971), 925–942.

Schlaifer, R. *Probability and Statistics for Business Decisions*. New York: McGraw-Hill Book Company, 1969.

_____. "A Simplified Model for Portfolio Analysis." *Management Science*, 10 (January 1963), 277–293.

Sharpe, William F. "A Simplified Model for Portfolio Analysis." *Management Science* (January 1963).

_____. *Portfolio Analysis and Capital Markets*. New York: McGraw-Hill Book Company, 1970.

_____. *Investments*, 3rd Edition. Englewood Cliffs, N.J.: Prentice-Hall, Inc., 1985.

Shillinglaw, Gordon. "Profit Analysis for Abandonment Decisions," in Ezra Solomon, ed. *The Management of Corporate Capital*. New York: The Free Press, 1959, pp. 269–281.

Stapleton, Richard C. "Portfolio Analysis, Stock Valuation and Capital Budgeting Rules for Risky Projects." *Journal of Finance*, 26 (March 1971), 95–118.

Tehranian, H. "Empirical Studies in Portfolio Performance Using Higher Degrees of Stochastic Dominance." *Journal of Finance* (March 1980).

Tuttle, Donald L., and Robert H. Litzenberger. "Leverage, Diversification and Capital Market Effects on a Risk-Adjusted Capital Budgeting Framework." *Journal of Finance*, 23 (June 1968), 427–443.

Van Horne, James C. "Capital-Budgeting Decisions Involving Combinations of Risky Investments." *Management Science*, 13 (October 1966), 84–92.

Wallingford, B. A. "A Survey and Comparison of Portfolio Selection Models." *Journal of Financial and Quantitative Analysis* (June 1967).

Winkler, Robert L., and Christopher B. Barry. "A Bayesian Model for Portfolio Selection and Revision." *Journal of Finance* (March 1975).

Ziemba, W. T., C. Parkan, and R. Brooks-Hill. "Calculation of Investment Portfolios with Risk Free Borrowing and Lending." *Management Science Application* (October 1974).

Introduction to Capital Asset Pricing

15

In our discussion of portfolio effects, we measured portfolio risk by determining the covariance of each project (or security) with all other projects (or securities) in the combination. The calculations (variances and covariances) for even a small number of projects quickly become voluminous. The number of inputs for a portfolio of N projects equals $N(N + 3)/2$, since we need to consider the expected return and standard deviation for each security and the covariance between all possible pairs of securities. If management were evaluating 12 projects, this approach entails 90 calculations. As N increases in size, the input requirements grow geometrically; witness, that 100 projects would require 5,150 inputs and 200 projects would require 20,300 inputs! In addition, the problem of estimating probabilities and joint probabilities of the cash flows further complicates the application of the portfolio model to capital budgeting. Theoreticians can point to conceptual devices for estimating probabilities, but at this stage of their development, they do not enjoy wide currency among managers.

An alternative approach, employing techniques familiar to financial managers and corporate economists, uses the capital asset pricing model (CAPM).[1] This relates the return of a project (or security) to a broad-based economic indicator of returns on risky assets such as Standard & Poor's 500 Stock Index. The model posits a linear correlation between the returns on the risky asset and the index.

In contrast to the number of calculations demanded by the full variance-covariance portfolio model, the new input requirement is simply $3N + 2$ when using Sharpe's single-index model, expressed as Equation (1) in the next section. For 12 projects, this totals 38 inputs, a reduction of 52; for 100 projects, 302 inputs are

---

[1] For purposes of study of capital asset pricing, we define capital asset as one with a life of more than 1 year, expected to earn an income sufficient to cover the amortization of its acquisition cost and operation expenses plus a net yield commensurate with the time value of money and risk. The term includes long-lived physical assets (plant and equipment) plus claims on such assets (common stocks, bonds, and other securities).

required; for 200 projects, 602, which are reductions of 94% and 97%, respectively, compared with the full variance-covariance model. Moreover, simple linear correlation is a rudimentary technique in statistical analysis and sales forecasting. Thus, business managers and staff specialists have at least a nodding acquaintance with the idea involved. In sum, we shall pursue the same objective—constructing and evaluating portfolios by their expected return and standard deviation—but use market-based data rather than direct comparison of project cash flows. This has the added advantage of stressing the link between the financial manager and the investor. How the investor values the decisions of management determines the present worth of the enterprise.

CAPM has a potential significance in capital budgeting in that:

1   It provides a method of determining the expected or required return of a capital project or security if it can be related to a broad-based economic indicator.
2   It provides an alternative calculation for the cost of capital as discussed in Chapter 16.
3   It can be used in the valuation of the firm and to determine the firm's incremental debt capacity if a project is accepted. Thus, it ties together the investment and financing decisions as well as the valuation process. This application of CAPM is illustrated in Chapter 16.

THE SINGLE-INDEX MODEL

To start the study of CAPM, consider the single-index model developed by Sharpe,[2]

$$\tilde{R}_{jt} = \alpha_j + B_j(\tilde{R}_{mt}) + \tilde{e}_{jt} \tag{1}$$

where $\tilde{R}_{jt}$ = random variable showing the return on asset j (a project or security) in period t
$\tilde{R}_{mt}$ = random variable showing the return on a broad-based market index in period t
α_j, B_j = parameters for asset j (which are developed by regression analysis) which best describe the *average relationship* between the returns $\tilde{R}_{jt}$ and $\tilde{R}_{mt}$
$\tilde{e}_{jt}$ = random error term for asset j in period t

This simple linear regression model determines the parameters α_j and B_j so that an estimate of returns on individual projects (or securities) can be generated using the equation as well as an estimate for the value of the market index. It should be pointed out that because $\tilde{R}_{jt}$ and $\tilde{R}_{mt}$ are both random variables, the simple linear relationship will not be 100% accurate; thus, the random error term $\tilde{e}_{jt}$ measures the difference between the actual returns on project j in period t and those predicted using the regression equation. In regression analysis, the parameters α_j and B_j are determined by the method of least squares, which requires that the random error term $\tilde{e}_{jt}$ will have an expected value of zero and a variance that is a positive, finite constant, Q_j^2, for all values of t (the time variable). In addition to the foregoing assumptions, the following three assumptions are made to arrive at the significant simplifications just discussed:

1   The random error term is uncorrelated with the market index: $\text{Cov}(\tilde{e}_{jt}, \tilde{R}_{mt}) = 0$.
2   The random error terms are not serially correlated over time: $\text{Cov}(\tilde{e}_{jt}, \tilde{e}_{j, t+n}) = 0$ for any value of n.

[2]William F. Sharpe, "A Simplified Model for Portfolio Analysis," *Management Science* (January 1963), 277–293.

3   The random error term for project j is not correlated with any other project's random error term: $\text{Cov}(\tilde{e}_{jt}, \tilde{e}_{it}) = 0$.

Given these assumptions, we can determine the expected value and the variance of Equation (1). These values will be discussed in turn,

$$E(\tilde{R}_{jt}) = E\left[\alpha_j + B_j(\tilde{R}_{mt}) + \tilde{e}_{jt}\right]$$

$$= \alpha_j + B_j\left[E(\tilde{R}_{mt})\right] + E(\tilde{e}_{jt})$$

$$= \alpha_j + B_j\left[E(\tilde{R}_{mt})\right] \tag{2}$$

where $E(\tilde{R}_j)$ and $E(\tilde{R}_m)$ are, respectively, the expected value of the return on project j and the expected value of the return on the market index.

Examining Equation (2) we see that the expected return on project j can be divided into two independent components:

α_j = return on project j due exclusively to its own merits

$B_j\left[E(\tilde{R}_{mt})\right]$ = return on project j associated with the response of project j to changes in the broad-based index of economic activity $\tilde{R}_{mt}$

In ordinary regression analysis, these two components are, respectively, the y-intercept and the slope of the regression line. Both values (α_j, B_j) can be determined using the usual least squares equations. Figure 15–1 shows the relationships. Equations (3)

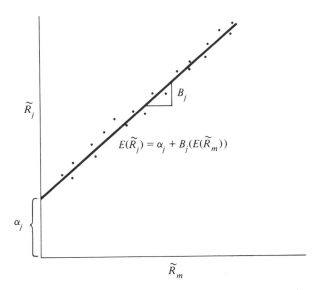

FIGURE 15–1   Simple Linear Regression Equation Relating $\tilde{R}_j$ to $\tilde{R}_m$

and (4) are the least squares equations for α_j and B_j:

$$B_j = \frac{n \sum\limits_{t=1}^{n} \tilde{R}_{mt} \tilde{R}_{jt} - \left(\sum\limits_{t=1}^{n} \tilde{R}_{mt} \right) \left(\sum\limits_{t=1}^{n} \tilde{R}_{jt} \right)}{n \sum\limits_{t=1}^{n} \tilde{R}_{mt}^2 - \left(\sum\limits_{t=1}^{n} \tilde{R}_{mt} \right)^2} \tag{3}$$

$$\alpha_j = E\left(\tilde{R}_j\right) - B_j \left(E\left(\tilde{R}_m\right) \right) \tag{4}$$

Example 1 demonstrates the use of Equations (3) and (4).

EXAMPLE 1
Regression Model

A new project is under consideration. This project is very similar to the project whose returns over a 10-period horizon are shown in the table. The returns on the appropriate market index are also shown.

PERIOD (t)	SIMILAR PROJECT $\tilde{R}_{jt}$	MARKET INDEX $\tilde{R}_{mt}$
1	0.09	0.07
2	0.10	0.09
3	0.10	0.10
4	0.11	0.12
5	0.10	0.11
6	0.11	0.10
7	0.11	0.10
8	0.10	0.09
9	0.09	0.08
10	0.07	0.07

(a) Compute the values for α_j and B_j.
(b) Write and explain the regression equation.

SOLUTION: The following table will be helpful in computing α_j and B_j:

t	$\tilde{R}_{jt}$	$\tilde{R}_{mt}$	$\tilde{R}_{jt}\tilde{R}_{mt}$	$\tilde{R}_{mt}^2$
1	0.09	0.07	0.0063	0.0049
2	0.10	0.09	0.0090	0.0081
3	0.10	0.10	0.0100	0.0100
4	0.11	0.12	0.0132	0.0144
5	0.10	0.11	0.0110	0.0121
6	0.11	0.10	0.0110	0.0100
7	0.11	0.10	0.0110	0.0100
8	0.10	0.09	0.0090	0.0081
9	0.09	0.08	0.0072	0.0064
10	0.07	0.07	0.0049	0.0049
Total	$\sum \tilde{R}_{jt} = 0.98$	$\sum \tilde{R}_{mt} = 0.93$	$\sum \tilde{R}_{jt}\tilde{R}_{mt} = 0.0926$	$\sum \tilde{R}_{mt}^2 = 0.0889$

$$B_j = \frac{n\Sigma \tilde{R}_{mt}\tilde{R}_{jt} - (\Sigma \tilde{R}_{mt})(\Sigma \tilde{R}_{jt})}{n\Sigma \tilde{R}_{mt}^2 - (\Sigma \tilde{R}_{mt})^2}$$

$$= \frac{10(0.0926) - (0.93)(0.98)}{10(0.0889) - (0.93)^2}$$

$$= \frac{0.9260 - 0.9114}{0.8890 - 0.8649}$$

$$= 0.6058$$

$$\alpha_j = E(\tilde{R}_j) - B_j[E(\tilde{R}_m)]$$

$$= 0.098 - (0.6058)(0.093)$$

$$= 0.0417$$

Thus, the regression equation is

$$E(\tilde{R}_j) = \alpha_j + B_j[E(\tilde{R}_m)]$$

$$= 0.0417 + 0.6058[E(\tilde{R}_m)]$$

The regression equation states that the expected return on the project ($E(\tilde{R}_j)$) comprises a basic yield of 4.17% (α_j) plus 60.58% (B_j) of the expected return on the market index [$E(\tilde{R}_m)$].

To complete our discussion of the single-index model, we now turn to Equation (5), which derives the variance of the returns on project j:

$$Var(\tilde{R}_{jt}) = Var[\alpha_j + B_j(\tilde{R}_{mt}) + \tilde{e}_{jt}] \qquad \text{from Equation (1)}$$

$$= Var(\alpha_j) + Var[B_j(\tilde{R}_{mt})] + Var(\tilde{e}_{jt})$$

$$= B_j^2 \sigma_m^2 + Q_j^2 \qquad\qquad\qquad\qquad (5)$$

where σ_m^2 and Q_j^2 are, respectively, the variance on the market index and the variance on the random error term $\tilde{e}_{jt}$.

Notice that the variance shown in Equation (5) stresses the fact that the total risk on project j can be attributed to two distinct types of risk:

1   The risk associated with project j's response to the market index multiplied by the variability in the market index itself: $B_j^2 \sigma_m^2$.

2   The risk associated with the random error term of project j (i.e., due to unexplained causes other than the market index), Q_j^2.

The first of these has come to be known as *systematic risk*. This risk cannot be diversified away since it is the result of variability in the market of risky assets. The latter is known as *unsystematic risk*. It can be diversified away through the selection of other risky assets that are lowly or negatively correlated with the asset in question. Thus, we can speak of partitioning the total risk associated with the returns on project

j into its two components:

$$
\begin{array}{ccc}
\text{total risk} & = \text{systematic risk} & + \text{unsystematic risk} \\
\text{on project } j & \text{(nondiversifiable)} & \text{(diversifiable)} \\
\sigma_{R_j}^2 & = B_j^2\, \sigma_m^2 & + Q_j^2
\end{array}
$$

Several interrelationships are worthy of note. The unsystematic risk on a given project, Q_j^2, is the square of a familiar measure in regression analysis, the standard error of estimate. The *standard error of estimate* is the average amount of error that is made in predicting returns on project j using the regression equation:

$$
Q_j = \sqrt{\frac{\text{variation due to error}}{n-2}}
$$

To explain more fully the numerator of this expression, we will partition the variance in returns on project j in a slightly different way than we did earlier. In regression analysis, the partitioning is as follows:

$$
\begin{array}{ccc}
\text{total variation} & \text{variation} & \text{variation} \\
\text{in returns of} & = \text{explained by} & + \text{due to error} \\
\text{project } j & \text{the regression} & \text{(unexplained} \\
 & \text{equation} & \text{variation)}
\end{array}
$$

$$
\sum_{t=1}^{n} \left(\tilde{R}_{jt} - \overline{R}_j \right)^2 = \sum_{t=1}^{n} \left[E(\tilde{R}_{jt}) - \overline{R}_j \right]^2 + \sum_{t=1}^{n} \left[\tilde{R}_{jt} - E(\tilde{R}_{jt}) \right]^2 \tag{6}
$$

It should be noted that $\tilde{R}_{jt}$ refers to the actual return on project j; $E(\tilde{R}_{jt})$ is the expected value of the return on project j in period t using the regression equation. $\overline{R}_j$ is the expected value for the return on project j. The standard error of estimate is stated more formally as Equation (7):

$$
Q_j = \sqrt{\frac{\Sigma \left[\tilde{R}_{jt} - E(\tilde{R}_{jt}) \right]^2}{n-2}} \tag{7}
$$

Further, there are two final regression statistics of interest. The *coefficient of determination* shows the percentage of the total variation in the dependent variable that is explained by variations in the independent variable. The *coefficient of nondetermination* shows the percentage of the total variation that is left unexplained by the independent variable being used. Of course, the sum of these two coefficients must be 100%. By examining Equation (6), we see that these two statistics may be expressed as shown in Equations (8) and (9):

$$
\text{coefficient of determination} = \rho^2 = \frac{\Sigma \left[E(\tilde{R}_{jt}) - \overline{R}_j \right]^2}{\Sigma \left(\tilde{R}_{jt} - \overline{R}_j \right)^2} \tag{8}
$$

$$
\text{coefficient of nondetermination} = 1 - \rho^2 = \frac{\Sigma \left[\tilde{R}_{jt} - E(\tilde{R}_{jt}) \right]^2}{\Sigma \left(\tilde{R}_{jt} - \overline{R}_j \right)^2} \tag{9}
$$

The coefficient of determination is the square of the correlation coefficient. Thus, this value is also related to the amount of covariance between the project returns and the returns on the market index. The computation of these statistics and their precise interpretation in the terms of our problem are illustrated in Example 2.

EXAMPLE 2

Calculation of Relevant Statistics

For the data shown in Example 1, compute the following.
(a) The standard error of estimate.
(b) The coefficient of determination.
(c) The coefficient of nondetermination.
(d) The variance in the market index.
(e) The variance of the returns on project j.
(f) The correlation coefficient and the covariance between $\tilde{R}_{jt}$ and $\tilde{R}_{mt}$.

SOLUTION: The following table will be helpful in computing the desired statistics:

t	(1) $\tilde{R}_{jt}$	(2) $\tilde{R}_{mt}$	(3) $E(\tilde{R}_{jt})$	(4) $(\tilde{R}_{jt} - \overline{R}_j)^2$	(5) $[\tilde{R}_{jt} - E(\tilde{R}_{jt})]^2$	(6) $[E(\tilde{R}_{jt}) - \overline{R}_j]^2$	(7) $(\tilde{R}_{mt} - \overline{R}_m)^2$
1	0.09	0.07	0.0841	0.000064	0.00003481	0.00019321	0.000529
2	0.10	0.09	0.0962	0.000004	0.00001444	0.00000324	0.000009
3	0.10	0.10	0.1023	0.000004	0.00000529	0.00001849	0.000049
4	0.11	0.12	0.1144	0.000144	0.00001936	0.00026896	0.000729
5	0.10	0.11	0.1083	0.000004	0.00006889	0.00010609	0.000289
6	0.11	0.10	0.1023	0.000144	0.00005929	0.00001849	0.000049
7	0.11	0.10	0.1023	0.000144	0.00005929	0.00001849	0.000049
8	0.10	0.09	0.0962	0.000004	0.00001444	0.00000324	0.000009
9	0.09	0.08	0.0902	0.000064	0.00000004	0.00006084	0.000169
10	0.07	0.07	0.0841	0.000784	0.00019881	0.00019321	0.000529
	$\Sigma\tilde{R}_{jt}$	$\Sigma\tilde{R}_{mt}$	$\Sigma E(\tilde{R}_{jt})$	$\Sigma(\tilde{R}_{jt} - \overline{R}_j)^2$	$\Sigma[\tilde{R}_{jt} - E(\tilde{R}_{jt})]^2$	$\Sigma[E(\tilde{R}_{jt}) - \overline{R}_j]^2$	$\Sigma(\tilde{R}_{mt} - \overline{R}_m)^2$
Total	0.98	0.93	0.9804	0.001360	0.00047466	0.00088426	0.00241

Columns 1 and 2 in the table are the historical observations of $\tilde{R}_{jt}$ and $\tilde{R}_{mt}$, respectively, for the last 10 periods, as shown in Example 1. Column 3 shows the values computed by substituting the values of $\tilde{R}_{mt}$ into the regression equation. Column 4 shows the values for the square of the quantity of the actual $\tilde{R}_{jt}$ minus $\overline{R}_j$ (where $\overline{R}_j = \Sigma\tilde{R}_{jt}/10$ = 0.098). Column 5 is the square of the difference between the actual $\tilde{R}_{jt}$ (column 1) and the predicted value using the regression equation $E(\tilde{R}_{jt})$ shown in column 3. Column 6 is the square of the difference between column 3 and $\overline{R}_j$ = 0.098. Column 7 is the square of the difference between column 2 and $\overline{R}_m = \Sigma\tilde{R}_{mt}/10$ = 0.093. Thus, we see that the

total variation or total sum of squares = 0.00136

variation explained by the regression equation = 0.00088426

variation unexplained by the regression equation = 0.00047466

total variation = explained variation + unexplained variation

0.00136 = 0.00088426 + 0.00047466

0.00136 ≅ 0.00135892

(a) Standard error of estimate:

$$Q_j = \sqrt{\frac{0.00047466}{10-2}} = \sqrt{0.0000593325}$$

$$= 0.007703, \text{ or } 0.7703\%$$

This measure shows that the average amount of error made in predicting the return on project j using the return on the market index and our regression equation $E(\tilde{R}_j) = 0.0417 + 0.6058\,[E(\tilde{R}_m)]$ is 0.7703%. Further, assuming that the variability around the regression line approximates a normal distribution, ± 2 standard errors would include approximately 95% of the variations. Thus, we can be 95% certain that the return on project j would lie within an interval described by the expected return $[E(R_j)]$ plus and minus 1.5406% (2 × 0.7703%).

(b) and (c) Coefficients of determination and nondetermination are:

$$\rho^2 = \frac{0.00088426}{0.001360} = 65\%$$

$$1 - \rho^2 = \frac{0.00047466}{0.001360} = 35\%$$

These two measures show that 65% of the variation in returns on project j is explained by the variation in the market index, while 35% of the variation in returns on project j is due to factors other than the variation in the market index used in the regression equation.

(d) Variance in the market index. This measure is computed using the usual formula for variance:

$$\sigma_m^2 = \frac{\Sigma\left(\tilde{R}_{mt} - \overline{R}_m\right)^2}{n-1} = \frac{0.00241}{10-1}$$

$$= 0.0002677, \text{ or } 0.02677\%$$

The variance in the market index is the average variability in the return on the market index around the mean return.

(e) Variance in returns on project j. This measure can be computed using either the general formula for the variance shown in part (d) or Equation (3):

$$\sigma_{R_j}^2 = \frac{\Sigma\left(\tilde{R}_{jt} - \overline{R}_j\right)^2}{n-1} = \frac{0.001360}{10-1}$$

$$= 0.0001511, \text{ or } 0.01511\%$$

Using Equation (3), we have the following:

$$\text{Var}\left(\tilde{R}_j\right) = \sigma_{R_j}^2 = B_j^2\,\sigma_m^2 + Q_j^2$$

$$= (0.6058)^2(0.0002677) + 0.0000593325$$

$$= 0.0000982441 + 0.0000593325$$

$$= 0.0001576, \text{ or } 0.01576\%$$

The difference between these two figures is due to rounding.

(f) Finally, the correlation coefficient and the covariance between the returns on project j and the market are of interest:

$$\rho = \sqrt{\rho^2} = \text{coefficient of determination} = \sqrt{0.6501911765}$$

$$\rho_{\tilde{R}_j, \tilde{R}_m} = +0.806$$

The covariance is found in the usual manner:

$$\text{Cov}\left(\tilde{R}_j, \tilde{R}_m\right) = \left(\rho_{\tilde{R}_j, \tilde{R}_m}\right)\left(\sigma_{\tilde{R}_j}\right)\left(\sigma_m\right)$$

$$= (+0.806)(0.0126)(0.0164) = 0.0001666$$

Last, it can be shown that B_j has an alternative definition of interest:

$$B_j = \frac{\text{Cov}\left(\tilde{R}_j, \tilde{R}_m\right)}{\sigma_m^2}$$

$$= \frac{0.0001666}{0.0002677}$$

$$= 0.622 \approx 0.6058 \qquad \text{as computed in Example 1}$$

This definition underscores the nature of B_j; it monitors the sensitivity of the project returns to changes in the market index.

To conclude this section, note that the capital asset pricing model, subject to qualification, produces the same information on the project (an expected return, $E(R_j)$, and sigma, σ_j) as that developed from the probability distributions of period cash flows. However, by contrast, the $E(R_j)$ and σ_j from the CAPM model use market data (i.e., the relationship of project returns to a broad-based index). In this regard, the illustrations in Examples 1 and 2 assume that the relationship between the risky asset returns and the appropriate market index described by the beta value will hold for the future or at least the life of the asset. Hence, if the analyst has the expected return on the index over the relevant period, he or she can forecast the expected return, $E(R_j)$, based upon the regression equation. The expected return should also be thought of as a required return given the relationship with the market index of risky asset returns. In the capital budgeting situation, this required return can be compared with an expected return calculated by conventional means (i.e., the expected internal rate of return) and a decision made on the acceptability of the project. Our discussion of the cost of capital in Chapter 16 picks up this theme.

PORTFOLIO PARAMETERS

An important application of CAPM is its use to calculate the risk-return characteristics of portfolios. The portfolio return $E(R_p)$ offers no special problems: a simple weighted average of the expected returns on the individual projects (or securities), as shown in Equation (10):

$$E(R_p) = \sum_{j=1}^{N} X_j E(R_j) \tag{10}$$

where X_j denotes the proportion of the total budget or portfolio invested in the jth project (or security).

In the same manner, the beta value of the portfolio,[3] (B_p), is given by Equation (11):

$$B_p = \sum_{j=1}^{N} X_j B_j \tag{11}$$

However, the measurement of portfolio risk by the CAPM approach provides interesting insights into the construction of portfolios. Recall from Chapter 14 that the Markowitz formulation described portfolio risk as the weighted variance of the individual projects plus twice the sum of the weighted covariances:

$$\sigma_p = \sqrt{\sum_{j=1}^{N} X_j^2 \sigma_j^2 + 2 \sum_{j=1}^{N-1} \sum_{i=j+1}^{N} X_i X_j (\rho_{ij})(\sigma_i)(\sigma_j)}$$

Under CAPM, σ_p, based upon market data, becomes:

$$\sigma_p = \sqrt{B_p^2 \sigma_m^2 + \sum_{j=1}^{N} X_j^2 Q_j^2} \tag{12}$$

Equation (12) recognizes two kinds of risk, similar to those of individual securities already discussed:

1 *Systematic risk* $(B_p^2 \sigma_m^2)$ is that portion of total risk (σ_p) based upon the relationship with the market index $(\bar{R}_m)$. Since all risky assets in the portfolio correlate to some degree with the index of risky assets, the systematic risk is nondiversifiable. No combination of risky assets can eliminate the market risk.

2 *Unsystematic risk* $(\Sigma X_j^2 Q_j^2)$ is that element of total risk (σ_p) responding to forces beyond the market index. If the market discounts all that is known about the risky asset's values, the unsystematic risk measures the variability in the returns due to unanticipated, or random factors. For example, the market may discount all that is known about the production, marketing, and financial strategies of General Motors, yet the price and yield on GM stock will still vary because of unforeseen, randomly occurring events (the energy crisis, technological innovation, political turns, etc.). This is diversifiable risk, and in a properly diversified portfolio, $\sum_{j=1}^{N} X_j^2 Q_j^2$ will *tend to zero*. The reason is as follows: Q_j^2 is the square of the standard error of the estimate or the unexplained variance. As N is increased, the values of X_j^2 become proportionately smaller, so that in the limit the summation approaches zero. Since the limit is never actually reached, the diversifiable risk will only approach zero.

[3]The reader should note that the portfolio beta value is also the beta for the firm as a whole, since the firm is an aggregate of all existing projects.

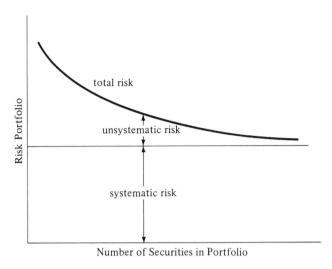

FIGURE 15 – 2   Effects of Diversification on Systematic, Unsystematic, and Total Risk

Figure 15–2 shows how the two risks change as randomly selected securities are added to a portfolio. Empirical studies have shown that with as few as 10 to 15 securities in a portfolio, total risk can be reduced to almost the systematic level.[4]

Example 3 illustrates the calculation of portfolio parameters under CAPM.

EXAMPLE 3

Calculation of Portfolio Parameters Using CAPM

Consider a firm desiring to combine projects Zeta and Delta into a portfolio in the proportions shown in the following table. The procedures described in the previous section have already been applied as have the regression equations developed with the market index:

	PROJECT ZETA	PROJECT DELTA
α_j	0.05	0.02
B_j	0.5	1.5
X_j	0.6	0.4
Q_j	0.0088	0.007

Market index statistics:

$$E\left(\tilde{R}_m\right) = 0.093, \qquad \sigma_m = 0.016$$

[4] See J. Evans and S. H. Archer, "Diversification and the Reduction of Dispersion: An Empirical Analysis," *Journal of Finance* (December 1968), 761–767; and K. H. Johnson and D. S. Shannon, "A Note on Diversification and the Reduction of Dispersion," *Journal of Financial Economics* (December 1974), 365–372.

Compute $E(R_p)$, B_p, and σ_p.

SOLUTION: To compute $E(R_p)$, we must first compute the expected return on each project using Equation (2).

Project Zeta:

$$E(R_Z) = \alpha_Z + B_Z\left(E\left(\tilde{R}_m\right)\right)$$
$$= 0.05 + 0.5(0.093)$$
$$= 0.097$$

Project Delta:

$$E(R_D) = \alpha_D + B_D\left(E\left(\tilde{R}_m\right)\right)$$
$$= 0.02 + 1.5(0.093)$$
$$= 0.16$$

Portfolio expected return:

$$E(R_p) = \Sigma X_j E(R_j)$$
$$= 0.6(0.097) + 0.4(0.16)$$
$$= 0.1222$$

Portfolio beta:

$$B_p = \Sigma X_j B_j$$
$$= 0.6(0.5) + 0.4(1.5)$$
$$= 0.9$$

Portfolio standard deviation:

$$\sigma_p = \sqrt{\left(B_p\right)^2\left(\sigma_{R_m}\right)^2 + \Sigma X_j^2 Q_j^2}$$
$$= \sqrt{(0.9)^2(0.016)^2 + (0.6)^2(0.0088)^2 + (0.4)^2(0.007)^2}$$
$$= \sqrt{0.00020736 + 0.0000278 + 0.00000784}$$
$$= \sqrt{0.000243}$$
$$= 0.0156$$

EFFICIENT FRONTIER UNDER CAPM

CAPM assumes a linear relationship between project returns and the market index. The random error term, Q_j, is assumed to be independent of the index and independent of the random terms for all other projects. As a result of these assumptions, which are not true in general, some part of the variability of $E(R_j)$ is lost. Hence, portfolios constructed by CAPM are less efficient than those constructed using the more elaborate covariance technique. Figure 15–3 compares the approximate character of the index frontier with the efficient frontier found with the covariance technique.

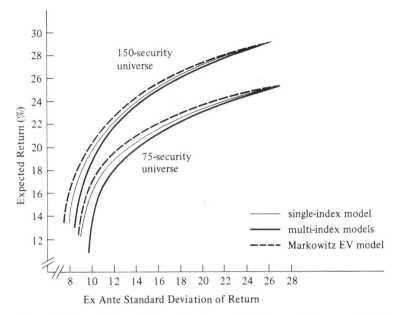

SOURCE: Kalman J. Cohen and Jerry A. Pogue, "An Empirical Evaluation of Alternative Portfolio Selection Models," *The Journal of Business, 40*, no. 2 (April 1967), 179.

FIGURE 15 – 3   Comparison of Efficient Frontiers CAPM Versus Covariance Technique

The proximity of the index frontier to the efficient set derived from the covariances of the cash flows depends on two related considerations:

1   Whether a linear function best describes the dependence of the projects (or securities) on the index. This advises experimentation with higher degree polynomials and transformations.

2   Whether the index selected is the best predictor of changes in the dependent variable j. In turn, this recommends the selection of an index after experimentation with a number of possible choices or the use of multi-index models.

Capital Market Line

For a given investor, the optimum portfolio is located at the tangency between his or her indifference map and the efficient frontier (Figure 15–4) common to all investors. But investors are a diverse group, their utility maps differ, and each might prefer a different point (optimum portfolio) along the common efficient frontier. *The aggregate of these individual investor preferences is represented by the capital market line, as shown in Figure 15–4. For the market to be in equilibrium, the portfolio at M must contain every risky asset in the exact proportion to that asset's fraction of the total market value of all risky assets.* That is, if all investors are holding a part of the same portfolio as their risky asset commitment, this portfolio would have to consist of all risky assets available in the marketplace. The portfolio at M, therefore, with each risky asset weighted by its market value relative to the total market value of all risky

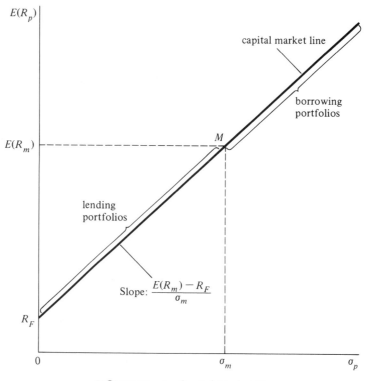

FIGURE 15 – 4   Capital Market Line

assets is termed the *market portfolio*. The formula for the capital market line (CML) is given by Equation (13):

$$E(R_p) = R_F + \frac{E(R_m) - R_F}{\sigma_m} \sigma_p \tag{13}$$

where $E(R_p)$ = expected return on an efficient portfolio
σ_p = standard deviation of returns on portfolio p
R_F = risk-free rate
$E(R_m)$ = expected return on the market portfolio of risky assets
σ_m = standard deviation of the market portfolio

Point R_F on the capital market line describes the return on portfolios composed of risk-free assets (i.e., Treasury bills). Moving up the market line, the investor allocates available funds to portfolios with larger proportions of risky assets. The increased commitment to risky assets increases portfolio returns $[E(R_p)]$. At point M, the investor has all available funds invested in risky assets (the market basket of risky assets). Between points R_F and M, the investor is in a creditor position (i.e., giving up funds in exchange for claims on assets). Beyond point M, the investor begins to leverage his or her portfolio by borrowing at the risk-free rate (R_F) and investing the proceeds to build larger holdings of the market basket of risky securities. Several conclusions can be drawn:

1 The expected return on an efficient portfolio is a linear function of its risk.
2 All efficient portfolios must be on the capital market line.
3 The slope of the line, $[E(R_m) - R_F]/\sigma_m$, is called the *market price of risk* or the *price of risk reduction*.
4 The intercept of the line, R_F, is the *market price of time*, or the time value of money.
5 The relationship does not apply to individual securities or portfolios that are imperfectly diversified. This implies that there is no reward for assuming risk that could be eliminated by proper diversification.
6 All investors *with the market in equilibrium* elect to hold the same portfolio of risky assets (the market portfolio). If, for example, General Motors stock comprised 3% of the total value of all publicly traded stocks, the risk segment of each investor's portfolio should allocate 3% to GM. The dollar size of an investor's portfolio depends on his or her wealth, but the profile of risky assets will be proportionately the same for each investor. Individual risk preferences affect only the allocation of funds within individual portfolios between risky and riskless assets.
7 Because all rational investors share in the market portfolio, each will perceive the riskiness of any given security in terms of its contribution to the riskiness of a fully diversified portfolio (i.e., the market portfolio). Hence, the financial manager needs to define risk in terms of the market portfolio if he or she is to be consistent with the criteria used by investors in valuing securities.
8 Investors increase their returns by changing the proportions of their portfolios (X_j) invested in risky and risk-free securities. Higher risk and return result from increasing the proportion invested in risky assets.

Security Market Line

The capital market line dealt with required return on a portfolio. The security market line (SML) shows the required return on each security in relation to risk. Termed the *market-price-of-risk line*, every security in the market portfolio of risky assets will be priced so that its expected return may be calculated using Equation (14),

$$E(R_j) = R_F + [E(R_m) - R_F] \frac{\text{Cov}(R_j, R_m)}{\sigma_m^2} \tag{14}$$

where $E(R_j)$ designates the required return on a given security.

The required return demanded by investors on a security, therefore, depends on the following four factors:

1 The risk-free rate.
2 The expected return on the market portfolio.
3 The variance on the market portfolio.
4 The covariance of the security's returns with the market portfolio.

The equation for the security market line is graphed in Figure 15–5.

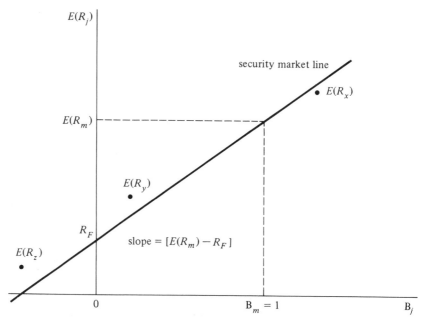

FIGURE 15 – 5   Security Market Line

The SML differs from the CML in two major respects:

1   For the individual security, the risk measure is the covariance instead of the standard deviation. The substitution underscores that the risk of an individual security or firm depends upon its contribution to the risk of the portfolio in which it is placed.

2   The risk of the market portfolio is measured by its variance, not the standard deviation.

If a security had a beta value of 2 [recall that $B_j = \mathrm{Cov}(R_j, R_m)/\sigma_m^2$] and $R_F = 0.06$ and $E(R_m) = 0.10$, then

$$E(R_j) = 0.06 + 2(0.10 - 0.06)$$

$$= 0.14, \text{ or } 14\%$$

A rational, risk-averse investor would not acquire the risky asset unless it promised a return at least equal to 14%. In Figure 15–5, therefore, security X earns a return in excess of the market portfolio [$E(R_m)$] but is not a desirable investment, owing to its strong covariance with market returns; Y has a lower expected return but may be a worthwhile investment, due to its low correlation with the market portfolio; Z, a risky asset, correlates negatively with the market portfolio and hence $E(R_z)$ is less than the risk-free rate and may also be worthy of consideration. *Generally, with the SML drawn as shown in Figure 15–5, returns above the SML are acceptable (i.e., securities Y and Z); below the SML, the amount of risk assumed is not justified by the expected return (i.e., security X)*. An extensive example of CAPM applied to the selection of capital budgeting projects is included in Chapter 16.

SUMMARY

This chapter examines the capital asset pricing model, a new approach that can be beneficially applied to the valuation of risky assets, be they securities or capital projects. Accordingly, this chapter calls upon several concepts and statistics developed in previous chapters on risk analysis and portfolio effects. Examples are used to illustrate the calculations of important new CAPM parameters.

However, financial management is not an abstract science cultivating mathematical models for self-edification. It survives by its ability to function. No matter how sophisticated the mathematical construct, a financial model must ultimately stand or fall on its contribution to the decision-making process. Contribution may take the form of a new insight on some aspect of financial management and/or the provision of a methodology to optimize results. We must now turn to the applicability of CAPM to the strategic decisions involved in long-term asset management.

QUESTIONS

PROBLEMS

1. For the data given for project j and the market index, compute the values for α_j, B_j, and write the regression equation:

PERIOD, t	PROJECT, $R_{jt}(\%)$	MARKET INDEX, $R_{mt}(\%)$
1	9	10
2	8	9
3	8	8
4	10	8
5	11	10

2. For the data given in Problem 1, compute and explain the following:
   (a) The $E(R_{jt})$ value for each R_{mt}.
   (b) The covariance between $\tilde{R}_{jt}$ and $\tilde{R}_{mt}$.
   (c) The correlation coefficient between $\tilde{R}_{jt}$ and $\tilde{R}_{mt}$.
   (d) The standard error of estimate.
   (e) The coefficient of determination.
   (f) The coefficient of nondetermination.

3. For the data given in Problem 1, compute and explain the following:
   (a) The variance of the returns on the market index.
   (b) The variance of the returns on project j.
   (c) The systematic risk on project j.
   (d) The unsystematic risk on project j.

4. The Notos Company is analyzing a project. To facilitate the computation of relevant statistics, the firm has prepared the following tables.

YEAR	$\tilde{R}_{jt}$	$\tilde{R}_{mt}$	$\tilde{R}_{jt}\tilde{R}_{mt}$	$\tilde{R}_{mt}^2$	$E(\tilde{R}_{jt})$
1	0.11	0.10	0.0110	0.0100	0.1086
2	0.12	0.11	0.0132	0.0121	0.1179
3	0.12	0.12	0.0144	0.0144	0.1271
4	0.13	0.11	0.0143	0.0121	0.1179
5	0.10	0.10	0.0100	0.0100	0.1086
Total	0.58	0.54	0.0629	0.0586	0.5801

YEAR	$\tilde{R}_{jt} - \bar{R}_j$	$(\tilde{R}_{jt} - \bar{R}_j)^2$	$\tilde{R}_{jt} - E(\tilde{R}_{jt})$
1	$0.11 - 0.116 = -0.006$	0.000036	$0.11 - 0.1086 = 0.0014$
2	$0.12 - 0.116 = 0.004$	0.000016	$0.12 - 0.1179 = 0.0021$
3	$0.12 - 0.116 = 0.004$	0.000016	$0.12 - 0.1271 = -0.0071$
4	$0.13 - 0.116 = 0.014$	0.000196	$0.13 - 0.1179 = 0.0121$
5	$0.10 - 0.116 = -0.016$	0.000256	$0.10 - 0.1086 = -0.0086$
Total		0.000520	

YEAR	$[\tilde{R}_{jt} - E(\tilde{R}_{jt})]^2$	$E(\tilde{R}_{jt}) - \bar{R}_j$	$[E(\tilde{R}_{jt}) - \bar{R}_j]^2$
1	0.0000020	$0.1086 - 0.116 = -0.0074$	0.00005476
2	0.0000044	$0.1179 - 0.116 = 0.0019$	0.00000361
3	0.0000504	$0.1271 - 0.116 = 0.0111$	0.00012320
4	0.0001464	$0.1179 - 0.116 = 0.0019$	0.00000361
5	0.00007396	$0.1086 - 0.116 = -0.0074$	0.00005476
Total	0.00027716		0.00023994

Compute the following:
(a) α, B.
(b) The covariance between $\tilde{R}_{jt}$ and $\tilde{R}_{mt}$.
(c) The correlation coefficient.
(d) The total risk on $\tilde{R}_{jt}$.
(e) The systematic risk.
(f) The unsystematic risk.
(g) The standard error of estimate.
(h) The coefficient of determination.

5. In 1967, a security of the Dru-White Corporation yielded a return of 4%. For the next 6 years it returned a steady 2% above the prime rate, which was 5% in 1968, 1969, and 1970, and 6% in 1971, 1972, and 1973. In the past 3 years, the stock returned 11%, 12%, and 13%. Our analysts have charted a regression line using the single index model. They tell us that their line explains three-fourths of the total variation in returns of the Dru-White security. If we want 90% certainty, within what limits of the predicted value will the true value lie?

6. Random Investments Corporation is planning to combine two projects into a portfolio. The various statistics are listed for each security and the market index. Compute the expected return on the portfolio, the beta of the portfolio, and the portfolio standard deviation.

	SECURITY A	SECURITY B	
α_j	-0.03	0.04	$E(R_m) = 0.095$
B_j	$+0.75$	$+0.95$	$\sigma_{R_m} = 0.012$
X_j	0.33	0.67	
Q_j	0.0075	0.0025	

7. Consider the following four portfolios and market parameters:

PORTFOLIO	$E(R_p)$	σ_p	
1	0.12	0.04	$R_F = 0.06$
2	0.13	0.06	$E(R_m) = 0.12$
3	0.16	0.10	$\sigma_m = 0.05$
4	0.22	0.12	

Using the capital asset pricing model, determine which of these portfolios have expected rates of return that exceed the required rate of return and thus are underpriced, and those which are overpriced.

8. Starting with the equation for the security market line:

$$E(R_j) = R_F + [E(R_m) - R_F]\frac{\text{Cov}_{jm}}{\sigma_m^2}$$

Derive the equation for the capital market line by recalling that in equilibrium, an efficient portfolio is perfectly correlated with the market (i.e., $\rho_{jm} = +1.0$).

9. A firm is evaluating the following three securities:

j	$E(R_j)$	ρ_{jm}	σ_j
1	0.075	$+0.3$	0.04
2	0.14	$+0.9$	0.09
3	0.12	$+0.2$	0.14

The market parameters are $R_F = 0.07$, $E(R_m) = 0.13$, and $\sigma_m = 0.05$.

(a) Compute the beta coefficients for each of these three securities and explain both the absolute risk of each security and the relative riskiness or volatility of each of the securities compared with the market.

(b) Using the equation for the security market line, determine whether each of these securities falls above or below the security market line (i.e., whether each is overpriced or underpriced).

(c) Briefly discuss why each security is overpriced or underpriced (be precise) and various ways that each could become priced appropriately.

REFERENCES

Alexander, Gordon J., and Norman L. Chervany. "On the Estimation and Stability of Beta." *Journal of Financial and Quantitative Analysis* (March 1980).

Andrews, Victor L. "Sterile Promises in Corporate Capital Theory." *Financial Management*, 8 (Winter 1979), 7–11.

Barry, C. B. "Effects of Uncertain and Non-Stationary Parameters upon Capital Market Equilibrium Conditions." *Journal of Financial and Quantitative Analysis* (September 1978).

Beja, Avraham, and Barry Goldman. "On the Dynamic Behavior of Prices in Disequilibrium." *The Journal of Finance* (May 1980).

Ben-Horim, Moshe, and Haim Levy. "Total Risk, Diversifiable Risk: A Pedagogic Note." *Journal of Financial and Quantitative Analysis* (June 1980).

Bierman, Harold, Jr., and Warren H. Hausman. "The Resolution of Investment Uncertainty Through Time." *Management Science*, 18 (August 1972), 654–662.

Black, F., M. C. Jensen, and M. Scholes. "The Capital Asset Pricing Model: Some Empirical Tests," in M. C. Jensen, ed. *Studies in the Theory of Capital Markets*. New York: Praeger Publishers, Inc., 1972.

_____. "Capital Market Equilibrium with Restricted Borrowing." *Journal of Business* (1972).

Blume, M. E. "Betas and Their Regression Tendencies: Some Further Evidence." *Journal of Finance* (March 1979).

_____. "On the Assessment of Risk." *Journal of Finance*, 26 (March 1971), 1–10.

_____, and Irwin Friend. "A New Look at the Capital-Asset Pricing Model." *Journal of Finance*, 28 (March 1973), 19–34.

_____, and Z. Bodie. "Common Stocks as a Hedge Against Inflation." *Journal of Finance*, 31 (May 1976), 459–470.

Bos, T., and P. Newbold. "An Empirical Investigation of the Possibility of Stochastic Systematic Risk in the Market Model." *Journal of Business* (January 1984).

_____, S. J. Kretlow, and J. H. Oakes. "The Capital Asset Pricing Model under Certainty." *Review of Business and Economic Research* (Fall 1978).

Bower, Richard S., and Donald Lessard. "An Operational Approach to Risk-Screening." *Journal of Finance*, 28 (May 1973), 321–337.

Boyer, Marcel, Sverre Storoy, and Thore Sten. "Equilibrium in Linear Capital Market Networks." *Journal of Finance* (December 1975).

Breeden, D. T. "An Intertemporal Asset Pricing Model with Stochastic Consumption and Investment Opportunities." *Journal of Financial Economics* (June 1979).

Brennan, Michael J. "Taxes, Market Valuation and Corporate Finance Policy." *National Tax Journal*, 23 (1970).

Brenner, Menachem, and Seymour Smidt. "Asset Characteristics and Systematic Risk." *Financial Management* (Winter 1978).

Brito, N. O. "Marketability Restrictions and the Valuation of Capital Assets under Uncertainty." *Journal of Finance* (September 1977).

Brown, S. L. "Autocorrelation, Market Imperfections, and the CAPM." *Journal of Financial and Quantitative Analysis* (December 1979).

Casabona, Patrick A., and Ashok Vora. "The Bias of Conventional Risk Premiums in Empirical Tests of the Capital Asset Pricing Model." *Financial Management*, 11 (Summer 1982), 90–95.

Chen, A. H., E. H. Kim, and S. J. Kon. "Cash Demand, Liquidation Costs and Capital Market Equilibrium under Uncertainty." *Journal of Financial Economics* (September 1975).

Cheng, Pao L., and Robert R. Grauer. "An Alternative Test of the Capital Asset Pricing Model." *American Economic Review* (September 1980).

Dybig, Phillip H. "Short Sale Restrictions and Kinks on the Mean Variance Frontier." *Journal of Finance* (March 1984).

Elton, Edwin J., and Martin J. Gruber. "Non-Standard CAPMs and the Market Portfolio." *Journal of Finance* (July 1984).

Epstein, Larry G., and Stuart M. Turnbull. "Capital Asset Prices and the Temporal Resolution of Uncertainty." *Journal of Finance* (June 1980).

Evans, Jack, and Stephen H. Archer. "Diversification and the Reduction of Dispersion: An Empirical Analysis." *Journal of Finance*, 23 (December 1968), 761–767.

Everett, James E., and Bernhard Schwab. "On the Proper Adjustment for Risk Through Discount Rates in a Mean-Variance Framework." *Financial Management* (Summer 1979).

Fabozzi, F. J., and J. C. Francis. "Beta as a Random Coefficient." *Journal of Financial and Quantitative Analysis* (March 1978).

Fabry, Jaak, and Willy van Grembergen. "Further Evidence on the Stationarity of Betas and Errors in their Estimates." *Journal of Banking and Finance* (October 1978).

Fama, Eugene F. "Components of Investment Performance." *Journal of Finance*, 27 (June 1972), 551–567.

_____. "Efficient Capital Markets: A Review of Theory and Empirical Work." *Journal of Finance*, 25 (May 1970), 333–417.

_____. "Efficient Capital Markets: Restatement of the Theory." *Journal of Finance*, forthcoming.

_____. "Multiperiod Consumption–Investment Decision." *American Economic Review*, 60 (March 1970), 163–174.

_____. "Risk, Return, and Equilibrium." *Journal of Political Economy*, 79 (January–February 1971), 30–55.

_____. "Risk, Return, and Equilibrium: Some Clarifying Comments." *Journal of Finance*, 23 (March 1968), 29–40.

_____, and James D. MacBeth. "Risk, Return, and Equilibrium: Empirical Tests." *Journal of Political Economy*, 81 (May–June 1973), 607–636.

_____, and Merton H. Miller. *The Theory of Finance*. New York: Holt, Rinehart and Winston, Inc., 1972.

_____, Lawrence Fisher, Michael Jensen, and Richard Roll. "The Adjustment of Stock Prices to New Information." *International Economic Review* (February 1969).

Foster, G. "Asset Pricing Models: Further Tests." *Journal of Financial and Quantitative Analysis* (March 1978).

Frankfurter, G. M. "The Effect of 'Market Indexes' on the Ex-Post Performance of the Sharpe Portfolio Selection Model." *Journal of Finance* (June 1976).

Friend, Irwin, and Randolph Westerfield. "Co-Skewedness and Capital Asset Pricing." *Journal of Finance* (September 1980).

_____, and _____. "Risk and Capital Asset Prices." *Journal of Banking and Finance*, forthcoming.

Friend, L., R. Westerfield, and M. Granito. "New Evidence on the Capital Asset Pricing Model." *Journal of Finance* (June 1978).

Gennotte, Gerard. "Optimal Portfolio Choice under Incomplete Information." *Journal of Finance* (July 1986).

Goldberg, M. A., and A. Vora. "Bivariate Spectral Analysis of the Capital Asset Pricing Model." *Journal of Financial and Quantitative Analysis* (September 1978).

Grauer, R. R. "Generalized Two Parameter Asset Pricing Models: Some Empirical Evidence." *Journal of Financial Economics* (March 1978).

Green, Richard C. "Benchmark Portfolio Inefficiency and Deviations from the Security Market Line." *Journal of Finance* (June 1986).

Haley, Charles W., and Lawrence D. Schall. *The Theory of Financial Decision*. New York: McGraw-Hill Book Company, 1973, Chaps. 5–7.

Hamada, Robert S. "Multiperiod Capital Asset Prices in an Efficient and Perfect Market: A Valuation or Present Value Model Under Two Parameter Uncertainty." Unpublished manuscript, University of Chicago, 1972.

Harris, Richard G. "A General Equilibrium Analysis of the Capital Asset Pricing Model." *Journal of Financial and Quantitative Analysis* (March 1980).

Hays, Patrick A., and David E. Upton. "A Shifting Regimes Approach to the Stationarity of the Market Model Parameters of Individual Securities." *Journal of Financial and Quantitative Analysis* (September 1986).

Heaney, W. John, and Pao L. Cheng. "Continuous Maturity Diversification of Default Free Bond Portfolios and a Generalization of Efficient Diversification." *Journal of Finance* (September 1984).

Hill, Ned C., and Bernell K. Stone. "Accounting Betas, Systematic Operating Risk, and Financial Leverage: A Risk-Composition Approach to the Determinants of Systematic Risk." *Journal of Financial and Quantitative Analysis* (September 1980).

Hillier, Frederick S. "A Basic Model for Capital Budgeting of Risky Interrelated Projects." *Engineering Economist*, 17 (October–November 1971), 1–30.

_____. "The Derivation of Probabilistic Information for the Evaluation of Risky Investments." *Management Science*, 9 (April 1963), 443–457.

Hirshleifer, Jack. "Investment Decisions Under Uncertainty: Applications of the State-Preference Approach." *Quarterly Journal of Economics*, 80 (May 1966), 252–277.

_____. *Investment, Interest and Capital*. Englewood Cliffs, N.J.: Prentice Hall, 1970.

Jarrow, Robert, and Eric R. Rosenfeld. "Jump Risks and the Intertemporal Capital Asset Pricing Model." *Journal of Business* (July 1984).

Jensen, Michael C., ed. *Studies in the Theory of Capital Markets*. New York: Praeger Publishers, 1972.

_____. "Risk, the Pricing of Capital Assets and the Evaluation of Investment Portfolios." *Journal of Business*, 42 (April 1969), 167–247.

Jobson, J. D., and Bob Korkie. "On the Jensen Measure and Marginal Improvements in Portfolio Performance: A Note." *Journal of Finance* (March 1984).

Johnson, K. H., and D. S. Shannon. "A Note on Diversification and the Reduction of Dispersion." *Journal of Financial Economics*, 1 (December 1974), 365–372.

Jones-Lee, M. W., and D. S. Poskitt. "An Existence Proof for Equilibrium in a Capital Asset Market." *Journal of Business Finance and Accounting* (Autumn 1975).

Kazemi, Hossein B. "An Alternative Testable Form of Consumption CAPM." *Journal of Finance* (March 1988).

Kraus, Alan, and Robert H. Litzenberger. "Market Equilibrium in a Multiperiod State Preference Model with Logarithmic Utility." *Journal of Finance* (December 1975).

Levy, H. "Another Look at the Capital Asset Pricing Model." *Quarterly Review of Business and Economics* (Summer 1984).

_____. "The Capital Asset Pricing Model: Theory and Empiricism." *Economic Journal* (March 1983).

Levy, Haim. "Measuring Risk and Performance Over Alternative Investment Horizons." *Financial Analysts Journal* (March–April 1984).

_____, and Marshall Sarnat. "The Portfolio Analysis of Multiperiod Capital Investment Under Conditions of Risk." *Engineering Economist*, 16 (Fall 1970), 1–19.

_____. "The CAPM and Beta in an Imperfect Market." *Journal of Portfolio Management* (Winter 1980).

Lewellen, Wilbur G., Ronald C. Lease, and Gary G. Schlarbaum. "Portfolio Design and Portfolio Performance: The Individual Investor." *Journal of Economics and Business* (Spring/Summer 1980).

Lin, Winston T., and Frank C. Jen. "Consumption, Investment, Market Price of Risk, and the Risk-Free Rate." *Journal of Financial and Quantitative Analysis* (December 1980).

Lintner, John. "The Valuation of Risk Assets and the Selection of Risky Investments in Stock Portfolios and Capital Budgets." *Review of Economics and Statistics* (February 1965), 13–37.

_____. "Security Prices, Risk and Maximal Gains from Diversification." *Journal of Finance*, 20 (December 1965), 587–616.

_____. "The Aggregation of Investors' Judgements and Preferences in Purely Competitive Security Markets." *Journal of Financial and Quantitative Analysis*, 4 (December 1969), 347–400.

Litzenberger, Robert H., and Alan P. Budd. "Corporate Investment Criteria and the Valuation of Risk Assets." *Journal of Financial and Quantitative Analysis* (December 1970).

_____, and O. M. Joy. "Target Rates of Return and Corporate Asset and Liability Structure under Uncertainty." *Journal of Financial and Quantitative Analysis* (March 1971).

Logue, D. E., and L. J. Merville. "Financial Policy and Market Expectations." *Financial Management* (Summer 1972), 37–44.

Markowitz, H. "Portfolio Selection." *Journal of Finance* (March 1952), 77–91.

Merton, Robert C. "Capital Budgeting in the Capital Asset Pricing Model." Unpublished note, 1973.

_____. "An Intertemporal Capital Asset Pricing Model." *Econometrica*, 45, 5 (September 1973), 867–887.

McEntire, Paul L. "Portfolio Theory for Independent Assets." *Management Science* (August 1984).

Milne, Frank, and Clifford Smith, Jr. "Capital Asset Pricing with Proportional Transaction Costs." *Journal of Financial and Quantitative Analysis* (June 1980).

Modigliani, Franco, and Gerald A. Pogue. "An Introduction to Risk and Return." *Financial Analysts Journal*, 30 (March–April 1974), 68–80; and (May–June 1974), 69–86.

_____, and R. Cohn . "Inflation, Rational Valuation and the Market." *Financial Analysts Journal*, 35 (March–April 1979), 24–44.

Myers, Stewart C., and Stuart M. Turnbull. "Capital Budgeting and the Capital Asset Pricing Model: Good News and Bad News." *Journal of Finance*, 32 (May 1977), 321–332.

Perold, Andre F. "Large-Scale Portfolio Optimization." *Management Science* (October 1984).

Perrakis, Stylianos. "Capital Budgeting and Timing Uncertainty Within the Capital Asset Pricing Model." *Financial Management* (Autumn 1979).

Pogue, Gerald A. "An Extension of the Markowitz Portfolio Selection Model to Include Variable Transaction Costs, Short Sales, Leverage Policies and Taxes." *Journal of Finance*, 25 (December 1970), 1005–1027.

Rabinovitch, R., and J. Owen. "Nonhomogeneous Expectations and Information in the Capital Asset Market." *Journal of Finance* (May 1979).

Rendleman, Richard J. Jr. "Ranking Errors in CAPM Capital Budgeting Applications." *Financial Management* (Winter 1978).

Robichek, Alexander A., and Stewart C. Myers. "Conceptual Problems in the Use of Risk-Adjusted Discount Rates." *Journal of Finance*, 21 (December 1966), 727–730.

Roenfeldt, R. L., G. L. Griepentrof, and C. C. Pflaum. "Further Evidence on the Stationarity of Beta Coefficients." *Journal of Financial and Quantitative Analysis* (March 1978).

Roll, Richard. "Ambiguity When Performance is Measured by the Securities Market Line." *Journal of Finance*, 33 (September 1978), 1051–1069.

_____, and Marcus C. Bogue. "Capital Budgeting of Risky Projects with Imperfect Markets for Physical Capital." *Journal of Finance*, 29 (May 1974), 606–612.

Ross, S. A. "The Capital Asset Pricing Model (CAPM), Short-Sale Restrictions and Related Issues." *Journal of Finance* (March 1977).

_____. "The Current Status of the Capital Asset Pricing Model (CAPM)." *Journal of Finance* (June 1978).

Schlaifer, R. "A Simplified Model for Portfolio Analysis." *Management Science*, 10 (January 1963), 277–293.

Scott, E., and S. Brown. "Biased Estimators and Unstable Betas." *Journal of Finance* (March 1980).

Shanken, Jay. "Testing Portfolio Efficiency When the Zero-Beta Rate is Unknown: A Note." *Journal of Finance* (July 1986).

Sharpe, William F. "Capital Asset Prices: A Theory of Market Equilibrium under Conditions of Risk." *Journal of Finance*, 19 (September 1964), 425–442.

_____. "Efficient Capital Markets with Risk." Research Paper 71, Stanford Graduate School of Business, 1972.

_____. *Portfolio Analysis and Capital Markets*. New York: McGraw-Hill Book Company, 1970.

_____, and Guy M. Cooper. "Risk-Return Classes of New York Stock Exchange Common Stocks." *Financial Analysts Journal*, 28 (March–April 1972), 46–54.

Tobin, James. "Liquidity Preference as Behavior Towards Risk." *Review of Economic Studies*, 25 (February 1958), 65–86.

Trauring, M. "A Capital Asset Pricing Model with Investors' Taxes and Three Categories of Investment Income." *Journal of Financial and Quantitative Analysis* (September 1979).

Tuttle, Donald L., and Robert H. Litzenberger. "Leverage, Diversification and Capital Market Effects on a Risk-Adjusted Capital Budgeting Framework." *Journal of Finance*, 23 (June 1968), 427–443.

Van Horne, James C. "The Analysis of Uncertainty Resolution in Capital Budgeting for New Projects." *Management Science*, 15 (April 1969), 376–386.

_____. "Capital Budgeting Decisions Involving Combinations of Risky Investments." *Management Science*, 13 (October 1966), 84–92.

_____. *The Function and Analysis of Capital Market Rates*. Englewood Cliffs, N.J.: Prentice Hall, 1970.

Weston, J. Fred. "Developments in Finance Theory." *Financial Management*, 10 (Summer 1981), 5–22.

_____. "Investment Decisions Using the Capital Asset Pricing Model." *Financial Management* (Spring 1973).

Capital Asset Pricing, Project Selection, and the Cost of Capital

16

Chapter 10 described the marginal cost of capital as a weighted average cost of the next dollar of debt and equity for the firm. It reflects the risk posture of the firm or the average risk implicit in all previously accepted capital projects. Consequently, the marginal cost of capital would not be likely to represent the risk associated with future capital projects and would have to be adjusted before being used to estimate the net present value of a proposed project. Our previous discussion noted several methods of risk adjustment. The capital asset pricing model (CAPM) constitutes yet another technique of project evaluation.

CAPM IN PROJECT EVALUATION

One potential difficulty that may be encountered with the application of conventional methods for risk adjustment is a rise, or ratcheting upward, in the firm's cost of capital. This could come about by accepting projects having risk postures in excess of the firm's risk complexion and thereby increasing the firm's risk posture. If this were to happen, the firm's marginal cost of capital would increase to reflect the firm's new risk structure. If, however, the conventional methods were correctly applied, the firm would also accept projects having a lower risk complexion than the firm overall, and the ratcheting effect should not take place. Put another way, the average cost of capital represents a strategic rate that management strives to earn on the totality of the operation. Management accepts some projects with higher and others with lower risk-return levels, but the average risk-return posture approximates that embodied in the marginal cost of capital.

The capital asset pricing model can also be used to calculate a market-based hurdle rate, risk-adjusted to the project under evaluation. The methodology relates a project's expected returns to an index representing a broad-based measure of economic activity. In Table 16–1, a project's expected return, $E(R_j)$, and the expected

Table 16-1 Illustration of Project Evaluation Using CAPM

Table A

STATE OF THE ECONOMY	P_s	R_m	R_a	R_b	R_c	R_d
Revival (S_1)	0.20	20%	15%	40%	15%	10%
Prosperity (S_2)	0.50	30	20	30	40	15
Recession (S_3)	0.20	6	13	0	0	− 6
Depression (S_4)	0.10	0	3	− 30	0	− 3
	1.00					

Table B

STATE OF THE ECONOMY	P_s	R_m	$P_s \times R_m$	$[R_m - E(R_m)]$	$[R_m - E(R_m)]^2$	$[R_m - E(R_m)]^2 P_s$
S_1	0.20	0.20	0.040	+ 0.002	0.000004	0.0000008
S_2	0.50	0.30	0.150	+ 0.098	0.009604	0.0048020
S_3	0.20	0.06	0.012	− 0.142	0.020164	0.0040328
S_4	0.10	0.00	0.000	− 0.202	0.040804	0.0040804
		$E(R_m) = 0.202$				$\sigma_m^2 = 0.0129160$
						$\sigma_m = 0.1136485$

Table C*

STATE OF THE ECONOMY	P_s	R_a	$P_s \times R_a$	$d_a = R_a - E(R_a)$	$d_m = R_m - E(R_m)$	$d_a d_m$	$d_a d_m P_s$
S_1	0.20	0.15	0.030	− 0.009	− 0.002	+ 0.000018	+ 0.0000036
S_2	0.50	0.20	0.100	+ 0.041	+ 0.098	+ 0.004018	+ 0.0020090
S_3	0.20	0.13	0.026	− 0.029	− 0.142	+ 0.004118	+ 0.0008236
S_4	0.10	0.03	0.003	− 0.129	− 0.202	+ 0.026058	+ 0.0026058
		$E(R_a) = 0.159$				$\text{Cov}(R_a, R_m) = + 0.005442$	

$$B_a = \frac{\text{Cov}(R_a, R_m)}{\sigma_m^2} = \frac{0.005442}{0.012916} = 0.421$$

Table D

$E(R_a) = 0.159$	$\text{Cov}(R_a, R_m) = + 0.005442$	$B_a = 0.421$
$E(R_b) = 0.20$	$\text{Cov}(R_b, R_m) = + 0.020620$	$B_b = 1.596$
$E(R_c) = 0.23$	$\text{Cov}(R_c, R_m) = + 0.019543$	$B_c = 1.513$
$E(R_d) = 0.08$	$\text{Cov}(R_d, R_m) = + 0.009620$	$B_d = 0.745$

*The notation d_a and d_m is used to represent the deviation of the return for each state of the economy from the expected return of project a and the market, respectively. Mathematically, $d_a = R_a - E(R_a)$ and $d_m = R_m - E(R_m)$, as shown in columns 4 and 5 of Table C.

return on the index, $E(R_m)$, are computed based upon different states of the economy and their respective probability of occurrence.

In Table A of Table 16–1, the returns from the index, R_m, and four projects (a, b, c, and d) are shown for four possible states of the economy. The probability of each state of the economy is denoted by P_s. All the forecasted returns (R_m, R_a, R_b, R_c, and R_d) and probabilities in Table A represent estimates for single periods for each of the projects and the market index. Estimates may be the result of projections from historical data or simulation. The data in Table A are the results of economic forecasts.

Table B is a summary of the calculations needed to obtain the expected return, variance, and standard deviation for the market index. Note that the estimated returns for the market index, R_m, are expressed in decimal form in Table B rather than as percentages as in Table A. The results show that the expected return on the market index is 20.2%, with a standard deviation of 11.36%.

Table C derives the necessary inputs to determine the required return from investment a, consistent with its risk characteristics. The results for all four projects are shown in Table D. The required return as determined using Equation (1) is compared with the project's expected return, which is the weighted average of the estimated returns of each of the possible states of the economy. If the expected return equals or exceeds the required return, the project is accepted; otherwise, it is rejected,

$$R_j^0 = R_F + \left[E(R_m) - R_F \right] B_j \qquad (1)$$

where R_j^0 = required return from project j

R_F = risk-free rate of return

$E(R_m)$ = expected return on the market index

B_j = beta factor for project j, which is defined in Equation (2):

$$B_j = \frac{\text{Cov}(R_j, R_m)}{\sigma_m^2} \qquad (2)$$

where $\text{Cov}(R_j, R_m)$ = covariance between the returns on project j and the returns on the market index

σ_m^2 = variance of the market index

Based on the inputs of Table D, it is possible to compute the required return for each project, R_j^0, employing Equation (1). In our computations we will assume that the risk-free rate of return, R_F, is 8%:

	R_j^0	$E(R_j)$
$R_a^0 = 0.08 + (0.202 - 0.08)$	$0.421 = 13.14\%$	15.9%
$R_b^0 = 0.08 + (0.202 - 0.08)$	$1.596 = 27.47\%$	20%
$R_c^0 = 0.08 + (0.202 - 0.08)$	$1.513 = 26.46\%$	23%
$R_d^0 = 0.08 + (0.202 - 0.08)$	$0.745 = 17.09\%$	8%

Using the CAPM approach, only project a would be accepted, since its expected return exceeds its required return. Each of the other three projects has an expected return that is less than its required return.

Figure 16–1 shows where each project falls relative to the market price of risk line (i.e., the security market line, SML). Only project a lies above the SML, indicating that it offers a rate of return sufficient to compensate for its risk. The other three projects lie below the SML since their returns are not sufficient to cover the market-related risk.

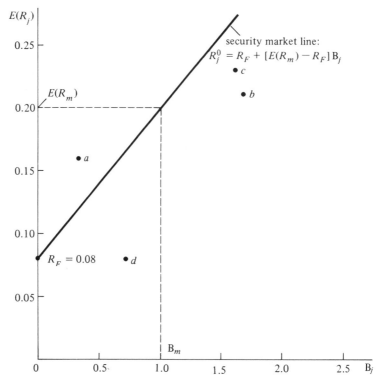

FIGURE 16-1   Project Selection Using Capital Asset Pricing

Several aspects of the capital asset pricing approach just illustrated warrant attention:

1   The possible states of the economy over the life-span of the projects must be forecasted. It should be noted that intermediate- and long-term forecasting as commonly practiced by business firms have larger variances than do short-term projections.

2   The probabilities related to different states of the economy can be derived from historical data on cyclical behavior and/or by simulation.

3   Based upon these variables, the forecaster can project returns on the broad-based market index. It will suffice that the market index consists of assets comparable with or meaningfully related to the projects studied. Alternatively, the analysis could have employed historical data on the relationship between similar projects and the market index to calculate beta.

4   The forecasted returns of the index and the projects are correlated to derive the beta on each project. Managers seek projects such as project a, with returns in excess of the levels required by the risk-return market relation illustrated in Figure 16–1. When such projects are added to the firm's portfolio, the expected returns on the firm's common stock (represented by its price) will be higher than those of the market line.

5   In practical implementation, the success of the method hinges on the stability of beta. Empirical evidence points to instability when only a few time periods are utilized in the calculation, but the variance in beta tends to decrease as the number of time periods increases.

This raises the issue of whether beta is a viable statistic in the evaluation of shorter-term capital projects.

6   Myers and Turnbull suggest that the real determinants of beta are more complicated than the preceding illustration would imply.[1] Beta, they stress, depends on the link between forecasted errors for cash flow and those for the market return, the growth trend in cash flows, asset life, the pattern of expected cash flows over time, and the procedure by which investors forecast asset cash flows. Given the Myers-Turnbull caveats, beta becomes extremely difficult to measure accurately. Moreover, the calculated beta generally will lead to biased hurdle rates in the presence of strong growth opportunities for the firm.

7   CAPM provides an alternative approach for estimating the firm's cost of equity capital. If we know the beta of the firm, B_p, then the cost of common stock equity capital can be defined using Equation (3):

$$K_e = R_F + \big[E(R_m) - R_F \big] B_p \qquad (3)$$

Equation (3) may be used to determine the firm's cost of equity capital in place of the dividend-valuation model derived in Chapter 3 and discussed in Chapter 10.

8   The project's acceptance or rejection is a function of the investment's own systematic risk. Thus, since the contribution of the project to the firm's variance of equity rate does not affect the accept or reject decision given by the security market line, diversification can be ignored in capital budgeting decisions. Each project is evaluated on its own merits without reference to the firm's existing investments.

COST OF CAPITAL, DEBT CAPACITY, AND THE CAPITAL BUDGETING DECISION

The CAPM, in a capital budgeting context, provides the decision maker with a risk-adjusted hurdle rate specific to the project evaluated and an alternative methodology for computing the cost of capital. It follows that CAPM relates immediately to the valuation process discussed earlier in this chapter. Hence, in looking at a project, it is pertinent to assess the value of the project based upon systematic risk and—with that knowledge—to estimate the debt-carrying capacity of the proposed acquisitions. Martin and Scott make a valuable contribution to the analysis of these questions.[2]

Based upon the work of Modigliani and Miller,[3] Martin and Scott define the value of the firm, as well as any asset, to comprise the present value of an uncertain income stream (EBIT) plus the present value of a certain stream of tax savings generated by debt, as shown in Equation (4),

$$V = \frac{\text{EBIT}(1 - t)}{K_e} + \frac{D(K_d)(t)}{K_d} \qquad (4)$$

[1]S. C. Myers and S. M. Turnbull, "Capital Budgeting and Asset Pricing Model: Good News and Bad News," *The Journal of Finance* (May 1977), 321–333. Also see comments on this article by R. S. Hamada, "Discussion," *The Journal of Finance* (May 1977), 333–336.

[2]See John D. Martin and David F. Scott, Jr. "Debt Capacity and the Capital Budgeting Decision," *Financial Management* (Summer 1976), 7–14.

[3]Franco Modigliani and Merton Miller, "Corporate Income Taxes and the Cost of Capital: A Correction," *The American Economic Review* (June 1963), 433–443.

where t = marginal tax rate on the firm or the project

D = market value of debt in firm's capital structure

K_d = rate at which the market capitalizes a certain stream of tax savings generated by debt

K_e = rate at which the market capitalizes the expected after-tax returns of an unlevered (debt-free) company with the same EBIT and risk posture

V = value of the firm (V_F) or value of the project (V_P), depending on the purpose of the analysis

Equation (4) facilitates the incorporation of added information bearing on the acceptance of the project.

Also, K_e is calculated using Equation (3), as modified by substituting B_0 for B_p in Equation (5):

$$K_e = R_F + \left[E(R_m) - R_F \right] B_0 \qquad (5)$$

The value B_0 represents the beta coefficient of an unlevered stream of income (EBIT) of the same size and risk level. It is *approximated* using Equation (6),

$$B_0 = B_p \frac{S}{S_0 - MTS} \qquad (6)$$

where B_p = beta of the firm's common stock assuming its current levered position

S = market value of the firm's equity shares in period $t = 1$

S_0 = market value of the firm's equity, debt and preferred in period $t = 1$

MTS = market value of the tax shelter on the outstanding debt for the preceding period as defined in Equation (7)

For example, assume the following information relative to a firm before the acceptance of a capital project:[4]

EBIT = \$95,000	$K_d = 0.10$	$S = \$23,800$
$D = \$17,000$	$t = 0.5$	$S_0 = \$40,800$
$E(R_m) = 0.15$	$R_F = 0.06$	$B_p = 2.41$

Then we may determine the following:

1   *Market value of tax shelter*:

$$MTS = \frac{D(K_d)(t)}{K_d} \qquad (7)$$

where D = current amount of outstanding debt

K_d = pretax average cost of outstanding debt

$$MTS = \frac{\$17,000(0.10)(0.5)}{0.10} = \$8,500$$

---

[4]The following example is adapted from Martin and Scott, "Debt Capacity."

2   *Beta value of the unencumbered cash flow:*

$$B_0 = B_p \frac{S}{S_0 - MTS}$$

$$= 2.41 \frac{\$23,800}{\$40,800 - \$8,500} = 2.41 \frac{\$23,800}{\$32,300} = 1.78$$

3   *Unlevered cost of equity:*

$$K_e = R_F + \left[E(R_m) - R_F \right] B_0$$
$$= 0.06 + (0.15 - 0.06)1.78$$
$$= 0.22 \text{ or } 22\%$$

4   *Value of firm before acceptance of the project* (V_F):

$$V_F = \frac{EBIT(1 - t)}{K_e} + \frac{D(K_d)(t)}{K_d}$$

$$= \frac{\$95,000(1 - 0.5)}{0.22} + \frac{17,000(0.10)(0.5)}{0.10}$$

$$= \$215,909.09 + \$8,500$$
$$= \$224,409.09$$

5   *Firm's average cost of capital before acceptance of the project:*

$$K = \frac{EBIT(1 - t)}{V_F} \tag{8}$$

where K = firm's average cost of capital before acceptance of the project
  t = firm's marginal tax rate
  V_F = value of the firm before acceptance of the project

Applying Equation (8), we have the following:

$$K = \frac{\$95,000(1 - 0.5)}{\$224,409.09} = 0.21, \text{ or } 21\%$$

Debt capacity is here defined as the risk of insolvency resulting from the use of financial leverage, that is, the risk that the unencumbered cash flows will be less than or equal to zero. The unencumbered cash flows may be found using Equation (9):

$$C = EBIT + \text{depreciation} - \left(I + \frac{SF}{1 - t} \right) \tag{9}$$

where C = unencumbered cash flow prior to the acceptance of the project
  I = annual interest expense prior to the acceptance of the project
  SF = sinking-fund payments or principal payments required under existing debt agreements

If C is assumed to be normally distributed with an expected value of $E(C)$ and standard deviation σ_C, the risk of insolvency is defined by the probability statement, Equation (10):

$$P(C \leq 0) = P\left[E(C) - Z\sigma_C \leq 0\right] \tag{10}$$

where Z is the ratio of $E(C)/\sigma_C$ corresponding to the number of standard deviations that the firm's expected unencumbered cash flow $E(C)$ lies away from zero. In short, we have a probability distribution of unencumbered cash flows. Assume for the firm in our illustration that $E(C) = \$100,000$ and $\sigma_C = \$78,125$; then the Z-value is determined as follows:

$$Z = \frac{\$100,000}{\$78,125} = 1.28$$

Reading from the normal table in Appendix A, 1.28 corresponds to approximately a 10% risk of insolvency.

Shifting the focus to the capital project that the firm is considering, assume that the project has an unencumbered cash flow $E(P)$ of \$10,000 and a σ_P of \$7,800. The coefficient of correlation between the cash flows of the firm and the project is 0.80. What does acceptance of the project add to the debt capacity of the firm? Using the Markowitz portfolio model described in Chapter 14, standard deviation of the firm's unencumbered cash flows after acceptance of the project is determined using Equation (11):

$$\sigma_{FC} = \left[\sigma_C^2 + \sigma_P^2 + 2(\rho)(\sigma_C)(\sigma_P)\right]^{1/2} \tag{11}$$

where σ_{FC} = standard deviation of the firm's unencumbered cash flows after the acceptance of the project

σ_C^2 = variance of the firm's unencumbered cash flows prior to acceptance of the project

σ_P^2 = variance of project's unencumbered cash flows

ρ = correlation coefficient between the firm's unencumbered cash flows and those of the new project

Using the information for the firm and project just discussed and applying Equation (11) results in the following:

$$\sigma_{FC} = \left[(\$78,125)^2 + (\$7,800)^2 + 2(0.80)(\$78,125)(\$7,800)\right]^{1/2}$$
$$= \$84,495$$

The expected unencumbered cash flows of the firm now total \$110,000 (\$100,000 originally plus \$10,000 on the new project). To find the risk of insolvency we again employ the normal distribution:

$$Z = \frac{\$110,000}{\$84,495} = 1.3$$

A Z-value of 1.3 corresponds to a probability of 0.0968; that is, acceptance of the project has reduced the risk of insolvency from 10% to 9.68%.

6   *Computation of additional debt capacity.* The acceptance of a new project may affect the capacity of the firm to utilize additional debt while retaining its original risk of insolvency. To determine the *debt service* that may be added, we employ Equation (12),

$$Z = \frac{E(C') - d}{\sigma_{FC}} \tag{12}$$

where $E(C') =$ expected unencumbered cash flow after acceptance of the project
$d =$ added debt service that can be carried at the 10% risk level

Applying Equation (12) to our example, where $Z = 1.28$, yields the following:

$$1.28 = \frac{\$110,000 - d}{\$84,495}$$

$$d = \$1,846$$

Since $K_d = 10\%$, \$1,846 of added *debt service* translates to an \$18,460 increment in debt capacity (\$1,846/0.10).

7   *Value of firm after acceptance of the project* (V_{FC}). To compute the value of the firm after acceptance of the project, we use Equation (4), where the EBIT value is the new $E(C')$ value less depreciation on the new project and the value of D is the original debt plus the incremental debt capacity determined in step 6. For our example, the calculations are as follows, assuming a new value for EBIT of \$105,000 after acceptance of the project.

$$V_{FC} = \frac{EBIT(1 - t)}{K_e} + \frac{D(K_d)(t)}{K_d}$$

$$= \frac{\$105,000(1 - 0.5)}{0.22} + \frac{\$35,460(0.10)(0.5)}{0.10}$$

$$= \$238,636.36 + \$17,730$$

$$= \$256,366.36 \tag{4}$$

The increase in the value of the firm is \$31,957.27 (\$256,366.36 less the value of the firm before acceptance, \$224,409.09).

8   *Average cost of capital after acceptance of the project.*

$$K_{FC} = \frac{EBIT(1 - t)}{V_{FC}} \tag{13}$$

where $K_{FC} =$ firm's average cost of capital after acceptance of the project
$V_{FC} =$ value of the firm after acceptance of the project

Applying Equation (13) results in the following:

$$K_{FC} = \frac{\$105,000(1 - 0.5)}{\$256,366.36}$$

$$= 0.20$$

We have now come full cycle with CAPM, using it as follows:

1   As an alternative in the computation of the cost of equity.
2   As a hurdle rate in the selection of capital projects.
3   In combination with the Modigliani-Miller tax model, as a technique for valuing the firm and determining its debt capacity.
4   To determine the firm's average cost of capital.

The Martin-Scott formulation, to recapitulate, defines debt capacity by the level-of-insolvency risk. They demonstrate how the risk of insolvency might be reduced by the acceptance of *one additional capital project*. Whenever the risk of insolvency is reduced, the firm increases its absolute debt capacity. If the project is accepted and the incremental debt capacity is utilized the value of the firm is enhanced.

The Martin-Scott model states that the impact of a project on the firm's expected level of cash flow is *additive*, that is, equal to the level of annual before tax cash flows expected from the acceptance of the project. However, the crucial point is that the impact of the project on the *variability* of the firm's cash flow is not additive. Variability depends upon the correlation between the expected cash flows of the firm and the project—the portfolio effect. The portfolio effect, in turn, depends upon the characteristics of the firm and the project. Consequently, the same project can affect the valuations of two firms in different ways.

We should also take note of the practical difficulties in applying the Martin-Scott model. One obstacle centers on the calculation of B_0 (the beta coefficient of a debt-free stream of income) from the estimate of the market value of the firm's capital structure less the market value of the tax shelter, as shown in Equations (6) and (7). The problem is one of homogeneity in firm characteristics over the period used in estimating B_0. A period long enough to attain stability in the value of B_0 will likely involve capital budgeting decisions which will effect changes in the capital structure and risk posture of the firm.

On this note, others have added further caveats to the application of the Martin-Scott model. Conine, for example, asserts that the integration of the Modigliani-Miller tax model and CAPM implicitly assumes the firm issues riskless debt and is not compatible with the issuance of risky corporate debt. He presents a methodology to correct this inconsistency between theory and practice.[5] Gahlon and Stover, on the other hand, stress the restrictiveness of illustrating the theory by assuming only one project is acceptable. A capital budget generally comprises several projects of different size and variability. In this case, the model must consider the correlation of cash flows *between* the firm and the individual projects, as well as the sizes and correlation *among* the project cash flows. The objective lies in selecting that combination of projects which maximizes the increase in the value of the firm while keeping the probability of insolvency at some target level. Otherwise, it is possible that two projects might win acceptance when analyzed independently but in combination might actually decrease the value of the firm.[6]

SUMMARY

In this chapter we take the theoretical conceptions of capital asset pricing developed in Chapter 15 and apply them to financial management considerations, such as the

[5]Thomas E. Conine, Jr., "Debt Capacity and the Capital Budgeting Decision: A Comment," *Financial Management* (Spring 1980), 20–22.

[6]James M. Gahlon and Roger D. Stover, "Debt Capacity and the Capital Budgeting Decision: A Caveat," *Financial Management* (Winter 1979), 55–59.

evaluation of capital projects, the value of the firm before and after acceptance of one or more capital projects, the impact of the capital budget on the firm's debt capacity, determination of the firm's cost of equity capital and average cost of capital. Few would disagree that this constitutes a substantial array of topics—all revolving around the calculation of essentially a single statistic: beta. Manifestly, the application of CAPM to financial management has profound implications for the practice of corporate finance and the supporting securities industry. But capital asset pricing is not without its critics, and it is to these arguments we must now turn.

QUESTIONS

PROBLEMS

1. The Capital Asset Pricing Corporation is evaluating three projects, which have various returns based on the states of nature shown:

STATE OF NATURE	PROBABILITY	MARKET RETURNS	PROJECT RETURNS P_1	P_2	P_3
1	0.1	− 0.10	− 0.30	− 0.15	0.00
2	0.2	0.00	− 0.10	− 0.05	0.04
3	0.3	0.05	0.15	0.04	0.08
4	0.2	0.09	0.25	0.10	0.09
5	0.2	0.12	0.35	0.15	0.10

(a) Compute the expected returns for each project, as well as the expected return and standard deviation for the market, based on the probability distributions given.

(b) Compute the covariance between each project and the market.

(c) Compute the beta for each project.

(d) Compute the required rate of return for each project based on the capital asset pricing model, assuming that the risk-free rate is 3%.

(e) Discuss which of the projects are candidates for acceptance and why.

2. If the CAP Corporation's average marginal cost of capital were 12% and it evaluated the projects by the internal rate of return method, how would its project selections differ?

3. Safetynet, Inc., management is risk averse and sets the return required on capital projects as

$$R_j = R_F + b \times \sigma(R_j)$$

where R_F is the risk-free interest rate and b is a penalty per unit of risk. Management defines risk in terms of standard deviation of returns. The following two projects are under consideration:

PROJECT	$E(R_j)$	$\sigma(R_j)$	COST	LIFE
X	0.12	0.025	2,000	∞
Y	0.20	0.070	2,000	∞

The risk-free rate is 8%, and b is 2.0

(a) Evaluate projects X and Y individually, and decide whether to accept or reject.

(b) Assume the projects are independent (i.e., uncorrelated) and evaluate the portfolio combination of X plus Y. Is the portfolio acceptable? Explain.

(c) Assume the firm already possesses a single capital project, X, and will evaluate Y as an additional investment. Is Y acceptable? Explain.

4. Cavaliere Company has joined the "beta revolution" and believes capital projects ought to be evaluated using measures of systematic risk, as defined by modern portfolio theory. The security market line is estimated as

$$R_j = R_f + B_j(R_m - R_f)$$
$$= 0.08 + B_j(0.16 - 0.08)$$
$$= 0.08 + 0.08B_j$$

where R_f is the risk-free rate, R_m is the return expected on the general market index, and B_j is a measure of the nondiversifiable risk of a project's cash flows. Two 1-year projects, S and T, are

PROJECT	B_j	$E(R_j)$	$\sigma(R_j)$
S	0.4	0.12	0.025
T	1.6	0.20	0.070

(a) Evaluate projects S and T individually, and decide whether to accept or reject.

(b) Evaluate the portfolio combination of S plus T. Is the combination acceptable? Explain.

(c) Assume the firm already possesses a single capital project and will evaluate T as an additional investment. Is T acceptable? Explain.

5. What are uses or applications of the capital asset pricing model as discussed in this chapter?

6. Parton Inc. is evaluating the three projects shown below, which have returns dependent on the states of nature given:

STATE OF NATURE	PROBABILITY	MARKET RETURNS	PROJECT RETURNS P1	P2	P3
1	.4	− .15	− .10	− .25	− .225
2	.3	0	0	− .10	.05
3	.2	.08	.053	.14	.12
4	.1	.20	.13	.20	.30

(a) Compute the expected return for each project, as well as the expected return and standard deviation for the market, based on the probability distributions shown.

(b) Compute the covariance between each project and the market.

(c) Compute the correlation coefficient between each project and the market.

(d) Compute the beta for each project.

(e) Compute the required rate of return for each project based on the capital asset pricing model, assuming that the risk-free rate is 3%.

(f) Discuss the acceptability of the projects.

(g) If Parton's average marginal cost of capital were 10% and it evaluated the projects by the internal rate of return method, how would its project selections differ?

7. In writing the capital budgeting procedures manual for Big Corporation, you must recommend investment evaluation techniques for choosing projects. Discuss which procedures you would recommend. Be sure to consider the following: 1) the size of the project, 2) the cost of using sophisticated techniques (training employees, preparing analyses, etc.), 3) the advantages and disadvantages of the methods, 4) other factors you consider important.

8. Discuss the role of taxation on project selection. (*Hint:* Consider the cost of capital in a tax-free world vs. the cost of capital in a world where taxes do exist.)

REFERENCES

Ang, James, and Thomas Schwarz. "Risk Aversion and Information Structure: An Experimental Study of Price Variability in the Securities Markets." *Journal of Finance* (July 1985).

Ashley, Richard A., and Douglas M. Patterson. "A Nonparametric Distribution-Free Test for Serial Independence on Stock Returns." *Journal of Financial and Quantitative Analysis* (June 1986).

Balachandran, Bala V., Nandu J. Nagarajan, and Alfred Rappaport. "Threshold Margins for Creating Economic Value." *Financial Management* (Spring 1986).

Bernhard, Richard H. "Risk-Adjusted Values, Timing of Uncertainty Resolution, and the Measurement of Project Worth." *Journal of Financial and Quantitative Analysis* (March 1984).

Bos, T., and P. Newbold. "An Empirical Investigation of the Possibility of Stochastic Systematic Risk in the Market Model." *Journal of Business* (January 1984).

Brigham, Eugene F., Dilip Shome, and Steve R. Vinson. "The Risk Premium Approach to Measuring a Utility Cost of Equity." *Financial Management* (Spring 1985).

Brito, N. O. "Marketability Restrictions and the Valuation of Capital Assets under Uncertainty." *Journal of Finance* (September 1977).

Brown, S. L. "Autocorrelation, Market Imperfections, and the CAPM." *Journal of Financial and Quantitative Analysis* (December 1979).

Cheung, C. Sherman, and Clarence C. Y. Kwan. "A Note on Simple Criteria for Optimal Portfolio Selection." *Journal of Finance* (March 1988).

Cho, D. Chinhyong, Edwin J. Elton, and Martin J. Gruber. "On the Robustness of the Roll and Ross Arbitrage Pricing Theory." *Journal of Financial and Quantitative Analysis* (March 1984).

Conine, Thomas E., Jr. "Debt Capacity and the Capital Budgeting Decision: A Comment." *Financial Management*, 9 (Spring 1980), 20–22.

_____, and Maurry Tamarkin. "Implications of Skewness in Returns for Utilities: Cost of Equity Capital." *Financial Management* (Winter 1985).

Crockett, Jean, and Irwin Friend. "Capital Budgeting and Stock Valuation Comment." *American Economic Review* (March 1967).

Crum, Roy L., and Keqian Bi. "An Observation on Estimating the Systematic Risk of an Industry Segment." *Financial Management* (Spring 1988).

Dybig, Phillip H. "Short Sale Restrictions and Kinks on the Mean Variance Frontier." *Journal of Finance* (March 1984).

Elton, Edwin J., and Martin J. Gruber. "Non-standard CAPM's and the Market Portfolio." *Journal of Finance* (July 1984).

Elton, Edwin J., Martin J. Gruber, and Seth Grossman. "Discrete Expectational Data and Portfolio Performance." *Journal of Finance* (July 1986).

Epstein, Larry G., and Stuart M. Turnbull. "Capital Asset Prices and the Temporal Resolution of Uncertainty." *Journal of Finance* (June 1980).

Eun, Cheol S., and Bruce G. Resnick. "Exchange Rate Uncertainty, Forward Contracts, and International Portfolio Selection." *Journal of Finance* (March 1988).

Evans, Jack, and Stephen H. Archer. "Diversification and the Reduction of Dispersion: An Empirical Analysis." *Journal of Finance*, 23 (December 1968), 761–767.

Franke, Günter. "Conditions for Myopic Valuation and Serial Independence of the Market Excess Return in Discrete Time Models." *Journal of Finance* (June 1984).

Frankfurter, G. M. "The Effect of 'Market Indexes' on the Ex-Post Performance of the Sharpe Portfolio Selection Model." *Journal of Finance* (June 1976).

Gahlon, James M., and D. Roger Stover. "Debt Capacity and the Capital Budgeting Decision: A Caveat." *Financial Management*, 8 (Winter 1979), 55–59.

Gennotte, Gerard. "Optimal Portfolio Choice under Incomplete Information." *Journal of Finance* (July 1986).

Heaney, W. John, and Pao L. Cheng. "Continuous Maturity Diversification of Default Free Bond Portfolios and a Generalization of Efficient Diversification." *Journal of Finance* (September 1984).

Hillier, Frederick S. "A Basic Model for Capital Budgeting of Risky Interrelated Projects." *Engineering Economist*, 17 (October–November 1971), 1–30.

Huffman, Gregory W. "Adjustment Costs and Capital Asset Pricing." *Journal of Finance* (July 1985).

Kazemi, Hossein B. "An Alternative Testable Form of Consumption CAPM." *Journal of Finance* (March 1988).

Lakonishak, J., and A. C. Shapiro. "Stock Returns, Beta, Variance and Size: An Empirical Analysis." *Financial Analysts Journal* (July–August 1984).

Levy, H. "Another Look at the Capital Asset Pricing Model." *Quarterly Review of Business and Economics* (Summer 1984).

Levy, Haim. "Measuring Risk and Performance over Alternative Investment Horizons." *Financial Analysts Journal* (March–April 1984).

Lewis, Alan L. "A Simple Algorithm for the Portfolio Selection Problem." *Journal of Finance* (March 1988).

Linke, Charles M., and J. Kenton Zumwalt. "The Irrelevance of Compounding Frequency in Determining a Utility's Cost of Equity." *Financial Management* (Autumn, 1987).

Scott, Louis O. "The Stationarity of the Conditional Mean of Real Rates of Return on Common Stocks: An Empirical Investigation." *Journal of Financial and Quantitative Analysis* (June 1984).

Shanken, Jay. "On the Exclusion of Assets from Tests of the Mean Variance, Efficiency of the Market Portfolio: An Extension." *Journal of Finance* (June 1986).

Siegel, Jeremy J. "The Application of the DCF Methodology for Determining the Cost of Equity Capital." *Financial Management* (Spring 1985).

Simonds, Richard R., Lynn Roy La Motte, and Archer McWhorter, Jr. "Testing for Non-stationarity of Market Risk: An Exact Test and Power Considerations." *Journal of Financial and Quantitative Analysis* (June 1986).

Torkay, Albert, Gabriel Hawawini, and Pierre Michel. "Seasonality in the Risk-Return Relationship: Some International Evidence." *Journal of Finance* (March 1987).

Treobald, Michael, and Vera Price. "Seasonality Estimation in Thin Markets." *Journal of Finance* (June 1984).

Treynor, J. L. "Value and Systematic Risk." Unpublished manuscript.

van zijl, Tony. "Risk Decomposition: Variance on Standard Deviation—A Reexamination and Extension." *Journal of Financial and Quantitative Analysis* (June 1987).

CASE STUDY 16-1

Locklow Aircraft Co.

(CAPM and debt capacity)

Locklow Aircraft is considering the introduction of a new fuel-efficient airliner. The present financial condition of Locklow shows the following:

$$\text{EBIT} = \$190,000 \qquad K_d = 0.15 \qquad S = \$23,800$$

$$D = \$34,000 \qquad t = 0.52 \qquad S_0 = 40,800$$

$$E(R_m) = 0.30 \qquad R_f = 0.10 \qquad B_p = 2.00$$

$$E(C) = \$500,000 \qquad \sigma = \$78,125 \qquad \sigma_p = \$7,800$$

The project has an unencumbered cash flow of $50,000 with a standard deviation of $5,000. The coefficient of correlation between the cash flows of the firm and the project is 0.60, and debt is carried at a 10% risk level.

QUESTIONS

1. Before acceptance of the project, determine
   (i)   Market value of the tax shelter.
   (ii) Beta value of the unencumbered cash flow.
   (iii) Unlevered cost of equity.
   (iv) Value of the firm before acceptance of the project.
   (v)   Average cost of capital before acceptance of the project.
2. After acceptance of the project, determine
   (i)   The firm's additional debt capacity.
   (ii) Value of the firm after acceptance of the project.
   (iii) Average cost of capital after acceptance of the project.

CASE STUDY 16-2

B-W Corporation
(CAPM)

B-W Corporation was founded in 1918 and continues as a major supplier to the automotive industry. It has also diversified extensively into the following major product and service groups: automotive; chemicals and plastics; financial services; industrial products; and protective services.

Over the past decade, as the economic environment has been changing, B-W Corporation has been restructuring itself in a steady evolution that aims at increasing value to its shareholders. Through the 1970s and 1980s, the company divested non-mainstream operations with cumulative assets of more than $1 billion, entering new areas of endeavor and building them into major operations.

In 1986, the York air conditioning operation that had been part of the company for 30 years was spun off to the shareholders, and B-W acquired C-X Corporation in the field of information technology. Management announced its intention to sell two of the six groups, industrial products and financial services. It was argued that the operations of the industrial products group were unconnected to any other aspect of the company, and that it should do better under the umbrella of more related businesses. Similar considerations applied to the financial services group. There was a question as to whether B-W could supply the capital needed to keep financial services a major player without depleting resources needed to build up operations which better integrated the unique capabilities of the group into their own operations.

The 1986 annual report of B-W reinforced this same orientation of management. The shareholders' letter explained that fifteen years ago, B-W was a loose blend of dozens of divisions and hundreds of major products. It had been rebuilt steadily for greater coherence and strength. The company's strategy called for continued, but controlled, diversification, balanced between manufacturing and services. Management still believed in diversification but wanted to focus on fewer businesses that individually offered opportunity to build value.

A major stockholder of B-W Corporation, Mr. Jones, was pleased to read the above in the annual report. The seemingly long-term orientation of management and also its recognition of the social and legal charters of the company were also regarded positively by Mr. Jones. However, he was not sure whether the process by which management reached a decision on divesting old business, acquiring existing ones, or building new ones was appropriate.

Mr. Jones knows that the evaluation of alternative investments requires knowledge of reliable information about both the economic potential and the possible dangers of each. The evaluation and prediction of returns has become very sophisticated in recent years but forecasting annual cash flows is not enough since the value of an investment depends on the timing of the cash flows and the risk of its expected return. He sees in the capital asset pricing model a vehicle for quantifying risk and linking it with expected returns on a company's equity.

QUESTIONS

1. By defining the risk of the company as the volatility of shareholders' returns and estimating this volatility by using the changes in B-W's stock price over time relative to the price volatility of the stock market as a whole (that is, by running a simple regression model where the shareholders' return is a linear function of the market return, $R_j = \alpha_j + B_j R_M + e_j$), use the quarterly data shown in the following table to examine the effect of risk on the returns to shareholders. Interpret α_j and B_j.

Quarterly Rates of Return on the Market and B-W Common Stock

YEAR	QUARTER	MARKET RATE OF RETURN	B-W RATE OF RETURN
1983	1st	− 6%	− 10%
	2nd	0	− 3
	3rd	5	15
	4th	9	25
1984	1st	12	35
	2nd	6	20
	3rd	1	5
	4th	− 3	− 9
1985	1st	− 5	− 6
	2nd	7	4
	3rd	8	10
	4th	12	19
1986	1st	− 2	0
	2nd	− 4	4
	3rd	0	8
	4th	8	9
1987	1st	13	20
	2nd	17	25
	3rd	14	17
	4th	12	19

2. Determine whether the risk measured in Question 1 is appropriate to the generated returns. Obviously neither risk nor return alone tells the whole story about value.

3. Since B-W is a diversified company, the causes of good or poor performance should be found at the level of the business unit. Consequently, one should compare the risk and return of each subsidiary with those of the company as a whole in order to understand the unit's contribution to the company's overall risk and return. However, since these subsidiaries are not publicly traded, what framework can you develop and apply in order to compare the contribution of each unit to the company's overall risk and return? Using your framework, can you get the beta of the whole company by relying on the estimated betas of the individual business units? Can you determine which businesses the company should sell off and which it should keep?

A Critique of
the Capital Asset Pricing Model

17

The Capital Asset Pricing Model (CAPM) provides a comprehensive theory of finance linking the decisions of financial managers to the risk-return expectations of investors. Although it amplifies Markowitz's seminal work on portfolio selection and traces its roots to the economist's theory of choice, CAPM takes the ultimate step in the progress of finance from a descriptive-institutional discipline to the deductive-empirical scientific method.

Nevertheless, the scientific method is a restless device. Each advance in knowledge unearths new insights and opens the door to refinements and/or new theoretical constructs. Application ineluctably lags behind the output of research, making the latter prone to the perils of faddism.[1] Happily, in finance, the penalties of unfettered inquiry are self-limiting, for theory ultimately must be validated by better decision making in firms and in security markets. Such caveats condition our critique of the CAPM.

ASSUMPTIONS OF CAPITAL ASSET PRICING

It is trite but essential to observe that no theory is better than the assumptions upon which it rests. These should bear some relevance, albeit imperfect, to the realities of the phenomenon explained. CAPM rests upon two sets of assumptions:

1 *Assumptions about investor behavior*:
   a. Investors are risk averse. They expect to be rewarded for assuming risk.
   b. Acting rationally, investors choose only efficient portfolios: the largest return, $E(R_p)$, for a given level of risk, σ_p, or the lowest risk, σ_p, for a specified return $E(R_p)$.

---

[1]Victor L. Andrews, "Sterile Promises in Corporate Capital Theory," *Financial Management*, 8, no. 4 (Winter 1979), 7–11.

   c. As a corollary, investors optimize their portfolio combinations by efficient diversification.

   d. Investors have the same time horizon regarding the risk-return payoff on risk assets. They strive to maximize the single-period expected utility of terminal wealth.

   e. All investors share the same estimates of the expected return and risk $[E(R_p)$, σ_p, and $\text{Cov}(R_p, R_m)]$ for all risk assets traded.

2   *Assumptions about the market:*

   a. All investors can borrow or lend in unlimited amounts at the risk-free rate (R_F).

   b. There are no taxes or transaction costs.

   c. Information is freely available to all investors.

   d. All assets are perfectly divisible and perfectly liquid (i.e., marketable at the going price).

   e. The cost of insolvency or bankruptcy is zero.

CAPM, in effect, says that the market is efficient, that it quickly discounts all publicly available information. Some proponents go further and affirm that the market has discounted all information, public and otherwise, on a security. This, in turn, leads to the *random walk hypothesis*, which states that changes in stock prices cannot be predicted on the basis of past price movements. Hence, historical data on market price changes will not enable the trader to earn above-normal, risk-adjusted returns. The best strategy then lies in buying into the market portfolio and sitting tight. The strategy assures that the investor always does as well as the market, and he or she cannot beat the market in any event.

In this respect, when CAPM is applied to the problem of evaluating capital projects, the user must bear in mind that investments in securities versus plant and equipment are not completely analogous. Securities are *divisible* assets; fractional shares can be rounded to integer amounts in constructing a portfolio. Each share of a given stock has the same expected return and systematic risk. On the other hand, capital projects are generally indivisible—accepted or rejected in toto. The choice is all or nothing. Fractional acceptance is not a viable alternative. The efficient frontier for a set of capital projects consequently becomes a sequence of corner points, which can be connected only artificially to form a continuous frontier (Figure 17–1).

The assumption of zero bankruptcy or insolvency cost is manifestly suspect. Under real-world conditions, assets of a bankrupt firm are sold at distress prices and accompanied by selling costs, legal fees, and other opportunity costs of a cumbersome legal system. Reality tells us the assets of the bankrupt will not be sold at their economic values with any residual value distributed to the shareholders. Under these circumstances, investors are not able to diversify their risks as CAPM presumes.

Moreover, the probability of a firm's financial collapse depends upon total risk (defined by Markowitz), not on systematic risk per se. Accordingly, when bankruptcy costs are significant and potential, the financial manager may be well advised to formulate the capital budget with an eye on total risk and not to focus simply on systematic risk. This implies a degree of risk aversion greater than that which would maximize shareholders' wealth under CAPM.[2] In short, the manager should be confident that the risk of insolvency is sufficiently low before evaluating investment alternatives on the basis of systematic risk alone.

Similarly, if investors in fact have different borrowing or lending rates or different expectations and time horizons and if transaction costs do exist and informa-

---

[2]James C. Van Horne, *Financial Management and Policy* (Englewood Cliffs, N.J.: Prentice Hall, 1983), pp. 208–209.

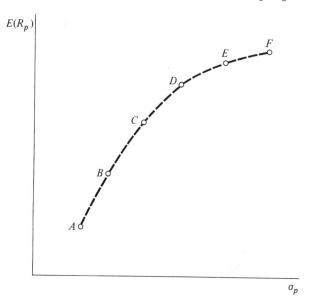

FIGURE 17–1   Efficient Frontier: Capital Projects

tion is not available without cost, then there will not be a single capital market line nor one best market portfolio. This, too, imparts added significance to residual risk.

Finally, when we affirm that the stock market discounts all available information, we must bear in mind the market does not record information in the manner of a computer. Rather, it registers the reactions of the participants to the received news. These reactions may be rational in terms of the participants' perspectives, but rationality does not equate with infallibility. Judged by hindsight, the security markets have not been outstandingly successful as indicators of economic activity or of industry and company performance.

SOME OPERATIONAL PROBLEMS

Stability of Beta

Alpha (α_j) and beta (B_j) describe an average relationship between the behavior of the security and market index existing in some prior period and *assumed to hold for the future*. Although the parametric values can be updated annually or quarterly, the model fundamentally relies on past performances, capturing the influences on the market at the time of calculation. Is the beta computed from historical data a good surrogate for the true beta reflecting investors' estimates of the stock's future volatility? If so, the financial manager has a significant new tool to assist his or her deliberations aimed at maximizing shareholders' wealth or the present value of the enterprise.

Some recent surveys indicate that the historically computed beta closely approximates the true, contemporary beta. Blume,[3] for example, showed that the beta of

[3]Marshall E. Blume, "On the Assessment of Risk," *Journal of Finance*, 26 (March 1971), 1–10.

a firm:

1   Is fairly stable over time.
2   Can be forecasted accurately from historical data.
3   Generally tends over a long time span, 1926–1968 in his study, to unity, the beta of the market as a whole.

Logue and Merville found that beta values bear a significant correlation to the firm's financial policies expressed in liquidity ratios, leverage measures, dividend payments, and profitability.[4]

Not all the evidence is positive. In another investigation, Levy examined the weekly returns for over 500 stocks on the New York Stock Exchange over the period December 30, 1960, through December 18, 1970 (520 weeks) to establish stationary data for betas over 52-week, 26-week, and 13-week forecast periods for stock portfolios ranging from 1, 5, 10, 25, and 50 stocks per portfolio.[5] Levy concluded that:

1   Average betas are reasonably predictable for large portfolios, less predictable for smaller portfolios, and quite unpredictable for individual securities.
2   Forecasts are clearly better over longer periods than over shorter periods.
3   Although predictability improves as the forecast period lengthens, the relative improvement tends to be less for larger portfolios.
4   For portfolios of 25 stocks or more over forecast intervals of 26 weeks and longer, historical betas seem to be fairly good and stable indicators of future risk.

Levitz's study supported Levy's conclusions.[6] He showed that for individual stocks the correlation of historical and actual betas was extremely poor (i.e., 0.55 for the test period). However, for portfolios—even those with as few as 10 stocks—statistically significant correlations were obtained, in some instances up to 0.90. He states:

For individual stocks the historical beta coefficient is not an accurate predictor of future relative volatility, although it may provide a "best-guess" estimate.

There is doubt, too, about the interpretation of alpha. Alpha, the y-intercept of the regression line, indicates the rate of return produced, on the average, by the investment independent of the market. Stocks with high alphas tend to have lower betas, and vice versa. Wells notes that one means of obtaining above-average performance lies in selecting a stock with a positive alpha.[7] When one stock has a higher (lower) return than another stock with the same beta, it has done better (worse) against the market than its beta would have predicted, and this is said to be

---

[4]Dennis E. Logue and Larry J. Merville, "Financial Policy and Market Expectations," *Financial Management* (Summer 1972), 37–44.

[5]R. A. Levy, "On the Short-Term Stationarity of Beta Coefficients," *Financial Analysts Journal* (November–December 1971), 55–62.

[6]G. D. Levitz, *A Study of the Usefulness of Beta Analysis in the Management of Common Stock Portfolios* (New York: Brown Brothers, Harriman & Co., 1972).

[7]C. Wells, "The Beta Revolution: Learning to Live with Risk," *Institutional Investor* (September 1971), 21–64.

due to its alpha factor or the residual, nonmarket influences unique to each stock. Alpha mirrors influences from the industry, such as technological breakthroughs, management shifts, merger prospects, and so on. However, more research is needed to assess the full significance of alpha.

Identifying the Market Portfolio

Addressing himself to the problems of application in CAPM, Roll shows that the operational equations are not testable unless the exact composition of the true market portfolio is known and used. Furthermore, if the true market portfolio were indeed known, the only hypothesis that could be tested by the security market line is the efficiency of the market portfolio.

Using proxies—such as the Standard & Poor's 500 Stock Index or the New York Stock Exchange Index—does not solve the problem. If the proxy index is not efficient, the CAPM relationship does not hold. Conversely, if the proxy index is efficient, this does not establish that the true market portfolio is also efficient since the composition of the true market portfolio is unknown.[8]

It is likely, of course, that most feasible proxy portfolios are highly correlated with one another as well as with the true market portfolio. The correlation may exist whether or not the portfolios are mean-variance efficient. The condition would seemingly support the viewpoint of some CAPM advocates that the exact composition of the true market portfolio and its surrogates is unimportant in practice. However, Weston notes that

> Small differences from the true market portfolios, however, can cause substantial biases in the measurement of risk and expected return . . . . Until the total market portfolio containing all assets is known and measured, ambiguities in the tests of the asset pricing models and of security investment performance will remain.[9]

The validation problem is further complicated by allowing for different borrowing and lending rates, different expectations and time horizons, the presence of transactions cost, and other lapses from the assumptions of CAPM that abort the possibility of a single-security market line and a single market portfolio. But tests for efficiency presuppose identification of the relevant market portfolio as well as its composition. In short, not only have we not identified the composition of the true market portfolio, but also we do not know whether such a portfolio can operationally exist at all.

Market Efficiency

When security market performance is compared against the criterion of efficiency, troublesome anomalies surface. For example, common stocks constitute claims on real assets. Ex ante, we should reasonably expect stocks to provide a hedge against inflation. Investigation indicates otherwise. Bodie found that, in the United

[8]Richard Roll, "Ambiguity When Performance Is Measured by the Securities Market Line," *The Journal of Finance*, (September 1978), 1051–1069.

[9]J. Fred Weston, "Developments in Finance Theory," *Financial Management*, 10, no. 2 (Summer, 1981), 5–22.

States during the period 1953–1972, common stocks failed to serve as a hedge against either anticipated or unanticipated inflation.[10]

In an attempt to explain the failure of common stocks to perform as inflation hedges, Modigliani and Cohn hypothesized that inflation had a negative effect on value due to its impact on accounting-determined profits. The market, in turn, committed two basic valuation errors:

1   It failed to realize that in a period of inflation part of the interest expense is not truly an interest expense but rather a repayment of real principal.

2   It tended to capitalize long-run profits not at a real rate of interest but at a rate that varied with the nominal interest rate.[11] Cohn and Lessard demonstrated that this phenomenon was not restricted to U.S. markets.[12]

Another anomaly appears when portfolios are formed on the basis of firm size. Banz, and later Reinganum, demonstrated that small firms systematically experienced average rates of return nearly 20% per year greater than those of large firms, even after accounting for differences in estimated betas. An adequately specified model of equilibrium should eliminate persistent abnormal returns.[13]

In evaluating the market's performance against the criterion of efficiency, several caveats must be borne in mind. First, the statistical tests of efficiency are essentially tests of the *joint* hypotheses of the validity of the regression model (CAPM) *and* of market efficiency. Whenever the assumptions of the model do not accord with reality, the "lapses" of the market may be traceable to the model and not to market inefficiency per se. Second, the notion of efficiency itself has evolved from stronger and more rigid notions of efficiency to weaker specifications since the introduction of CAPM. It is vital to define the level of efficiency expected from the market before assessing market performance. Third, the market prices of securities (common stocks) respond to the risk-return calculations of traders. How is return measured—by accounting numbers or cash flow? Accounting earnings are subject to a variety of options (regarding depreciation, inventory valuation, bad-debt allowances, and so on), which significantly affect earnings after taxes. Furthermore, accounting returns represent a mixture of present and past values because the firm's balance sheet comprises a heterogeneous conglomeration of assets and liabilities acquired or incurred at different price levels. Cash flow is the better statistic to employ in measuring return, but it is complicated to measure given the information available to investors. Nor are cash flow ambiguities diminished by resorting to the device of adding depreciation back to accounting earnings—a shorthand method frequently favored by security analysts and finance researchers. The conclusion is manifest: if the measurement of earnings is flawed, then the calculations of the required return (R_j) and the beta (B_j) are misleading. Market efficiency cannot be tested by the use of flawed data, no matter how sophisticated the mathematical construct.

[10] Z. Bodie, "Common Stocks as a Hedge Against Inflation," *The Journal of Finance*, 31, no. 2 (May 1976), 459–470.

[11] F. Modigliani and R. Cohn, "Inflation, Rational Valuation and the Market," *Financial Analysts Journal*, 35, no. 2 (March–April 1979), 24–44.

[12] Richard A. Cohn and Donald R. Lessard, "The Effect of Inflation on Stock Prices: International Evidence," *The Journal of Finance*, 36, no. 2 (May 1981), 277–289.

[13] Cited in Marc R. Reinganum, "The Arbitrage Pricing Theory: Some Empirical Results," *The Journal of Finance*, 36, no. 2 (May 1981), 313–321.

Multiperiod Investments

In common stock investment, CAPM relates the cash flows of the investment to the returns on the market portfolio of risky assets as shown in Equation (1):

$$R_j^0 = R_F + B_j \left[E(R_m) - R_F \right] \qquad (1)$$

where R_j^0 = required return on the investment
R_F = risk-free rate of return
$E(R_m)$ = expected return on the market portfolio

Return is defined as the price at the end of the period less the price at the beginning of the period plus dividends received divided by the price at the beginning of the period. The returns on the stock and on the market portfolio are both single-period returns—monthly, quarterly, or annually—are identical in content, and are directly comparable.

However, the use of CAPM in a capital budgeting context raises questions on the comparability of the measured returns. Capital projects are evaluated using an IRR (internal rate of return) or NPV (net present value). Each involves the discounting of cash flows over several time periods. Therefore, the return on the market portfolio in CAPM (a single-period return) is not comparable to IRR (a multiperiod measurement). Also, the content of the two returns differ. The return on the market portfolio (R_m) combines dividend inflows and changes in the market price of securities for the period involved. Cash flows of a capital project do not incorporate changes in the market price of the initial investment, but may include a final residual value.[14]

In Chapter 16, we partially address the problem of multiperiod returns in CAPM for capital budgeting utilizing a basic model proposed by Weston.[15] This allows for the computation of returns on both the project and the market portfolio period by period. If we go a step farther and include the residual values of the initial investment at the end of each period, the criterion of comparable returns is met.

This can be done in either of two ways. First, the firm could take an already accepted project similar to the one under consideration and compare its rate of return (R_{jt}) with the return on the market portfolio (R_{mt}) for the same time frame. From this historical data, a beta value can be calculated and applied to the new project. The approach assumes that the future will repeat the past—that is, the project and market portfolio cash flow patterns will be substantially unchanged. There is here an implicit forecast of no change—a robust assumption to put forth in a dynamic economy. Second, the firm could face the forecasting problem directly and compute an expected return on the project $[E(R_{jt})]$ and the market $[E(R_{mt})]$. From these projections, the firm can calculate beta (B_j) in order to determine the required return $[R_j^0]$ on the capital expenditure proposed. The approach requires the application of long-term forecasting techniques to project cash flows, the return on the market portfolio of risk securities, and the risk-free rate of return. The forecast problem is made explicit, but

[14] Richard S. Bower and Donald R. Lessard, "An Operational Approach to Risk-Screening," *The Journal of Finance*, 28, no. 2 (May 1973), 321–337.

[15] J. Fred Weston, "Investment Decisions Using the Capital Asset Pricing Model," *Financial Management*, 2, no. 1 (Spring 1973), 25–33.

the task is not eased. Suffice it to say, the error factor in business forecasting tends to increase with the passage of time, and it is particularly difficult to forecast interest rates or the performance of the security markets over an extended time frame. On the other hand, the beta obtained is future oriented rather than being the product of historical relationships.

EXAMPLE 1

Assume a 10-year project with the following data:

(1)	(2)	(3)	(4)	(5)
				EXPECTED RETURN ON MARKET PORT-
		EXPECTED RESIDUAL	EXPECTED CASH	
PERIOD (t)	INVESTMENT	VALUE, $E(S_t)$	FLOW, $E(C_t)$	FOLIO, $E(R_{mt})$
0	$200,000			
1		$180,000	$40,000	0.20
2		160,000	30,000	0.15
3		140,000	35,000	0.10
4		120,000	45,000	0.20
5		100,000	50,000	0.22
6		80,000	45,000	0.25
7		70,000	40,000	0.20
8		50,000	35,000	0.18
9		25,000	30,000	0.17
10		5,000	25,000	0.15
				$E(R_m) = \overline{\overline{0.182}}$

The risk-free rate of return is $R_F = 12\%$. Should the project be accepted?

SOLUTION:

Part I:

The expected return for the project in each period is calculated using Equation (2):

$$E(R_{jt}) = \frac{E(S_t) - E(S_{t-1}) + E(C_t)}{E(S_{t-1})} \qquad (2)$$

where $E(S_t)$ = the expected residual value at the end of period t
$\quad\;\; E(C_t)$ = the expected cash flow for period t
For period 1, this becomes

$$E(R_{j1}) = \frac{(\$180,000 - \$200,000) + \$40,000}{\$200,000}$$

$$= \frac{-\$20,000 + \$40,000}{\$200,000} = 0.10$$

We calculate $E(R_{jt})$ in this way to make it comparable to the return on the market portfolio,

$$E(R_{mt}) = \frac{(P_t - P_{t-1}) + D_t}{P_{t-1}} \qquad (3)$$

Table 18-1   Multiperiod Analysis of Projected Expected Returns $[E(R_{jt})]$

(1) PERIOD	(2) INVESTMENT	(3) EXPECTED RESIDUAL VALUE AT END OF EACH PERIOD, $E(S_t)$	(4) EXPECTED CASH FLOW, $E(C_t)$	(5) EXPECTED RETURNS, $E(R_{jt}) = \dfrac{E(S_t) + E(C_t) - E(S_{t-1})}{E(S_{t-1})}$
0	$200,000			
1		$180,000	$40,000	0.100
2		160,000	30,000	0.056
3		140,000	35,000	0.094
4		120,000	45,000	0.178
5		100,000	50,000	0.250
6		80,000	45,000	0.250
7		70,000	40,000	0.375
8		50,000	35,000	0.215
9		25,000	30,000	0.100
10		5,000	25,000	0.200
			$E(R_j) =$	0.182

where P_t = value of portfolio at the end of period t
P_{t-1} = value of portfolio at the end of period $t - 1$.
D_t = dividends for period t

Table 18-1 summarizes the results of the calculations for $E(R_{jt})$ and $E(R_j)$.

Part II:
Determine the beta value of the project in relation to the expected return on the market portfolio using linear-regression analysis:

$$E(R_j) = \alpha_j + B_j(E(R_m)) \tag{4}$$

Using the least squares method, the value of beta is calculated to be 1.24. Therefore, for the project under consideration, the required return—using Equation (1)—becomes

$$R_j^0 = R_F + B_j\left[E(R_m) - R_F\right] = 0.12 + 1.24(0.182 - 0.12)$$

$$= 0.197, \text{ or } 19.7\% \tag{5}$$

The required return on the project, R_j^0 can be used in either of two ways:

1. *Comparison with the expected return on the project* $E(R_j)$. If the project's required return exceeds the expected returns, $R_j^0 > E(R_j)$, then the project is rejected. The return on the project is not commensurate with the risk accepted. Conversely, if $R_j^0 < E(R_j)$, the project merits favorable consideration inasmuch as the return compensates for the risk. In our illustration, because $R_j^0 > E(R_j)$ (0.197 > 0.182), the firm should reject the project.

2. *As the discount rate in computing the NPV for the project.*

(1) PERIOD (t)	(2) CASH FLOW	(3) DISCOUNT FACTORS AT 19.7%	(4) PRESENT VALUE (2 × 3)
1	$40,000	0.8354	$33,416
2	30,000	0.6979	20,937
3	35,000	0.5831	20,408
4	45,000	0.4871	21,920
5	50,000	0.4069	20,345
6	45,000	0.3399	15,296
7	40,000	0.2840	11,360
8	35,000	0.2373	8,305
9	30,000	0.1983	5,949
10	25,000	0.1656	4,140
		Total present value	$162,076
		Investment (t_0)	200,000
		Net present value	($37,924)

The project has a negative net present value and would normally be rejected.

SUMMARY

It is the nature of hypothesis testing in finance that the jury is always out. More research has to be done on CAPM, as well as on arbitrage pricing theory (APT) and other multivariable models. CAPM, an inheritance from economic theory, must concentrate on the composition of the market portfolio. Until the question of the composition of the market portfolio is resolved, it will not be possible to test the efficiency of the market or of investor portfolios. There is also the problem of circular reasoning, in that the CAPM assumes the market is efficient and then proceeds to employ the CAPM construct in testing the efficiency of the market. We cannot have it both ways.

The time element presents another complicating factor in the real-world application of CAPM. CAPM, conceived by Sharpe, is a single-period, single-factor equilibrium model in the tradition of static economic analysis. Intertemporal analysis (dynamic analysis), as we have seen, is handled more by expediency than by conformity with the full array of restrictive assumptions underlying CAPM. Perhaps the solution to this particular conundrum is to look at the disequilibria models prevalent in modern economic theory.

On the other hand, APT, for instance, has a long road ahead before it will enter the discussions of corporate management. If multifactor models are per se more desirable, the APT adherents have yet to specify the several factors.

This returns us to our starting point that CAPM remains the only comprehensive theory of finance that does enjoy some real-world application. Such limited acceptance is perhaps traceable to the capability of the model to describe tendencies

—albeit imperfectly—that apparently hold up even when the assumptions are not fully met. As in scientific investigation, it is sometimes possible to predict results without fully knowing all the causes.

QUESTIONS

PROBLEMS

1. What does the assumption of rationality mean?

2. Is information freely available to all investors? Does it really matter that all investors have equal access to security information for the market to be efficient?

3. Why are capital projects generally indivisible?

4. Summarize the problem of intertemporal cash flows when CAPM is applied to capital budgeting. How does the CAPM model in Chapter 16 (Equations 1 and 2) differ from the model in this chapter?

5. The Avant Garde Corporation is evaluating three projects:

	CASH FLOWS		
PERIOD (t)	P_1	P_2	P_3
0	− $1,000	− $1,000	− $1,000
1	600	250	100
2	300	200	140
3	150	140	180
4	250	150	100
5	350	200	100

The residual values for each project by period are

	RESIDUAL VALUES		
PERIOD (t)	P_1	P_2	P_3
0	$1,000	$1,000	$1,000
1	500	700	900
2	300	300	800
3	100	300	850
4	100	300	1,000
5	100	300	1,200

(a) Compute the expected cash flow and the expected return for each project.

(b) Compute the beta for each project. The market returns, $E(R_{mt})$, are

PERIOD	$E(R_{mt})$
1	0.20
2	0.13
3	0.18
4	0.25
5	0.20

(c) Compute the required return R_j^0 on each project assuming a risk-free rate (R_F) of 0.12.

(d) Which projects would be accepted and why?

6. Review the two sets of assumptions underlying the CAPM. Do you believe they are approximately realistic? What effect would each of the assumptions, if completely invalid, have on the CAPM? That is, how sensitive are the conclusions of the CAPM to its assumptions?

7. What might cause B to change? What effects might a variable B have on a firm's capital budgeting process? How would you, as a financial manager, incorporate varying B values into your project analysis?

8. Assume a 3-year project with the following data:

PERIOD (t)	INVESTMENT	EXPECTED RESIDUAL VALUE $E(S_t)$	EXPECTED CASH FLOW $E(C_t)$	EXPECTED RETURN ON MARKET PORTFOLIO $E(R_{mt})$
0	$50,000			
1		$40,000	$20,000	0.18
2		$32,000	$25,000	0.16
3		$25,600	$30,000	0.14

The risk-free rate of return is $R_F = 6\%$. Assume that B is varying and cannot be calculated using linear regression. You forecast the following values for B:

PERIOD (t)	EXPECTED B $E(B_t)$
1	1.30
2	1.20
3	1.15

Should the project be accepted? Justify your decision. (Hint: Use the geometric average of R to approximate a required rate of return.)

9. Assume a 5-year project with the following data:

PERIOD (t)	INVESTMENT	EXPECTED RESIDUAL VALUE $E(S_t)$	EXPECTED CASH FLOW (C_t)	EXPECTED RETURN ON MARKET PORTFOLIO $E(R_{mt})$
0	$75,000			
1		$45,000	$20,000	.14
2		$27,000	$18,000	.13
3		$16,200	$16,000	.125
4		$ 9,720	$14,000	.12
5		$ 5,800	$12,000	.11

Assume further that the risk-free rate and B will vary over the 5-year project as follows:

PERIOD (t)	R_{Ft}	B_t
1	.04	1.2
2	.04	1.1
3	.05	1.2
4	.06	1.2
5	.06	1.3

Should the project be accepted? (See hint from question 8.)

REFERENCES

Alexander, Gordon J., and Norman L. Chervany. "On the Estimation and Stability of Beta." *Journal of Financial and Quantitative Analysis* (March 1980).

Barry, C. B. "Effects of Uncertain and Non-Stationary Parameters upon Capital Market Equilibrium Conditions." *Journal of Financial and Quantitative Analysis* (September 1978).

Black, F., M. C. Jensen, and M. Scholes. "The Capital Asset Pricing Model: Some Empirical Tests," in M. C. Jensen, ed. *Studies in the Theory of Capital Markets*. New York: Praeger Publishers, Inc., 1972.

Brenner, Menachem, and Seymour Smidt. "Asset Characteristics and Systematic Risk." *Financial Management* (Winter 1978).

Casabona, Patrick A., and Ashok Vora. "The Bias of Conventional Risk Premiums in Empirical Tests of the Capital Asset Pricing Model." *Financial Management*, 11 (Summer 1982), 90–95.

Chen, A. H., E. H. Kim, and S. J. Kon. "Cash Demand, Liquidation Costs and Capital Market Equilibrium under Uncertainty." *Journal of Financial Economics* (September 1975).

Cheng, Pao L., and Robert R. Grauer. "An Alternative Test of the Capital Asset Pricing Model." *American Economic Review* (September 1980).

Elton, Edwin J., and Martin J. Gruber. "Non-Standard CAPMs and the Market Portfolio." *Journal of Finance* (July 1984).

Foster, G. "Asset Pricing Models: Further Tests." *Journal of Financial and Quantitative Analysis* (March 1978).

Friend, Irwin, and Randolph Westerfield. "Co-Skewedness and Capital Asset Pricing." *Journal of Finance* (September 1980).

Friend, L., R. Westerfield, and M. Granito. "New Evidence on the Capital Asset Pricing Model." *Journal of Finance* (June 1978).

Harris, Richard G. "A General Equilibrium Analysis of the Capital Asset Pricing Model." *Journal of Financial and Quantitative Analysis* (March 1980).

Jahankhani, A. "E-V and E-S Capital Asset Pricing Models: Some Empirical Tests." *Journal of Financial and Quantitative Analysis* (September 1976).

Jarrow, Robert, and Eric R. Rosenfeld. "Jump Risks and the Intertemporal Capital Asset Pricing Model." *Journal of Business* (July 1984).

Jones-Lee, M. W., and D. S. Poskitt. "An Existence Proof for Equilibrium in a Capital Asset Market." *Journal of Business Finance and Accounting* (Autumn 1975).

Kazemi, Hosseim B. "An Alternative Testable Form of Consumption CAPM." *Journal of Finance* (March 1988).

Lee, C. F., and F. C. Jen. "Effects of Measurement Errors on Systematic Risk and Performance Measure of a Portfolio." *Journal of Finance and Quantitative Analysis* (June 1978).

Levitz, G. D. *A Study of the Usefulness of Beta Analysis in the Management of Common Stock Portfolios*. New York: Brown Brothers, Harriman & Co., 1972.

Levy, H. "The Capital Asset Pricing Model: Theory and Empiricism." *The Economic Journal* (March 1983).

_____. "Another Look at the Capital Asset Pricing Model." *Quarterly Review of Business and Economics* (Summer 1984).

Lintner, John. "The Valuation of Risk Assets and the Selection of Risky Investments in Stock Portfolios and Capital Budgets." *Review of Economics and Statistics* (February 1965), 13–37.

Merton, Robert C. "Capital Budgeting in the Capital Asset Pricing Model." Unpublished note, 1973.

Mossin, Jan. "Equilibrium in a Capital Asset Market." *Econometrica*, 34, 4 (October 1966), 768–783.

Myers, Stewart C., and Stuart M. Turnbull. "Capital Budgeting and the Capital Asset Pricing Model: Good News and Bad News." *Journal of Finance*, 32 (May 1977), 321–332.

Nielson, N. C. "The Investment Decision of the Firm under Uncertainty and the Allocative Efficiency of Capital Markets." *Journal of Finance* (May 1976).

Rendleman, Richard J. Jr. "Ranking Errors in CAPM Capital Budgeting Applications." *Financial Management* (Winter 1978).

Roenfeldt, R. L., G. L. Griepentrof, and C. C. Pflaum. "Further Evidence on the Stationarity of Beta Coefficients." *Journal of Financial and Quantitative Analysis* (March 1978).

Roll, Richard. "Ambiguity When Performance Is Measured by the Securities Market Line." *Journal of Finance*, 33 (September 1978), 1051–1069.

Ross, S. A. "The Capital Asset Pricing Model (CAPM), Short-Sale Restrictions and Related Issues." *Journal of Finance* (March 1977).

Scott, E., and S. Brown. "Biased Estimators and Unstable Betas." *Journal of Finance* (March 1980).

Sharpe, William F. "Capital Asset Prices: A Theory of Market Equilibrium under Conditions of Risk." *Journal of Finance*, 19 (September 1964), 425–442.

Simonds, Richard R., Lynn Roy La Motte, and Archer McWhorter, Jr. "Testing for Non-stationarity of Market Risk: An Exact Test and Power Considerations." *Journal of Financial and Quantitative Analysis* (June 1986).

Stapleton, Richard C. "Portfolio Analysis, Stock Valuation and Capital Budgeting Decision Rules for Risky Projects." *Journal of Finance* (March 1971).

Trauring, M. "A Capital Asset Pricing Model with Investors' Taxes and Three Categories of Investment Income." *Journal of Financial and Quantitative Analysis* (September 1979).

Tuttle, Donald L., and Robert H. Litzenberger. "Leverage, Diversification and Capital Market Effects on a Risk-Adjusted Capital Budgeting Framework." *Journal of Finance*, 23 (June 1968), 427–443.

Van Horne, James C. "The Analysis of Uncertainty Resolution in Capital Budgeting for New

Projects." *Management Science*, 15 (April 1969), 376–386.

_____. *The Function and Analysis of Capital Market Rates*. Englewood Cliffs, N.J.: Prentice Hall, 1970.

Weston, J. Fred. "Investment Decisions Using the Capital Asset Pricing Model." *Financial Management* (Spring 1973).

CASE STUDY 17-1

Chance Gardner Corp.

(Multiperiod CAPM)

The Chance Gardner Corporation is evaluating four projects:

	CASH FLOWS			
PERIOD (t)	$P1$	$P2$	$P3$	$P4$
0	− $1000	− $1000	− $1000	− $1000
1	700	600	800	750
2	400	500	300	350
3	200	300	250	350
4	350	300	400	350
5	150	100	150	200

The residual values for each project by period are:

	RESIDUAL VALUES			
PERIOD (t)	$P1$	$P2$	$P3$	$P4$
0	$1000	$1000	$1000	$1000
1	870	910	900	1000
2	760	850	825	1000
3	660	800	760	500
4	580	770	715	200
5	500	750	675	100

QUESTIONS

1.   Compute the expected return for each project.

2. Compute β for each project. The market returns $E(R_{mt})$ are:

PERIOD (t)	$E(R_{mt})$
1	.15
2	.14
3	.15
4	.13
5	.14

3. Compute the required return R on each project, assuming a risk-free rate (R_F) of 0.08.

4. Which projects would be accepted? Why?

Introduction to Mathematical Programming

18

Mathematical programming (MP) models are a set of techniques in the broader fields of operations research or management science. These fields utilize quantitative models to describe various business, industrial, or governmental problem settings to gather information, obtain greater insight, and evaluate various decision alternatives. In our definition of mathematical programming, we used the term "quantitative models," which deserves further elaboration. Quantitative models are descriptive representations of a real problem setting using mathematical equations. Such models are constructed to obtain information and insight about a problem setting more quickly and in a less costly and less disruptive way than by experimenting directly on the actual system. These models are, therefore, abstractions of the real system; that is, they try to capture only the most critical elements and relationships that exist in the real system; otherwise, it would be as difficult, time consuming, and costly to analyze the model as it would be to analyze the real system. Because quantitative models are usually rather involved, a "solution algorithm" must generally be used to solve the model. This is merely a step-by-step process that guarantees reaching the correct solution to the model formulation.

The complexity of real systems, as well as hidden interrelationships among system components, makes it advantageous for the analyst to perform "sensitivity analysis" on the solution obtained. Sensitivity analysis is a process whereby the analyst determines how significantly the solution to the problem will change if various assumptions are modified in the model. This process points to the characteristics of the system that are most critical and require most attention in the management control area. Sensitivity analysis generally leads to changes in the model representation that may require re-solving the model to obtain information on the new solution. The results of the sensitivity analysis become inputs to the decision-making process wherein additional quantitative and qualitative factors (not reflected in the original model) which differentiate the various alternatives are taken into account before the "best" alternative is selected for implementation into the real system. Periodically

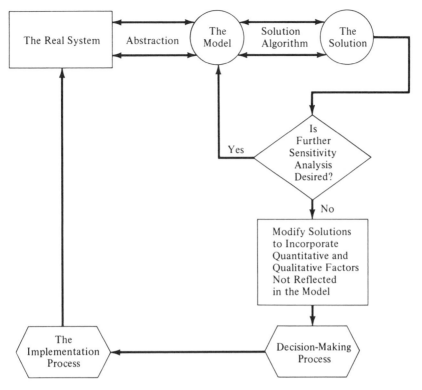

FIGURE 18–1   Model-Building and Decision-Making Process

after this implementation, feedback is obtained to determine how well the system is functioning so that timely corrective action can be taken, if necessary. This model-building and decision-making process is summarized in Figure 18–1.

To begin our discussion of MP models, we must define a number of terms. There are two major categories of equations that are used in MP models:

1   The objective function describes the goal or objective the decision maker desires to achieve.
2   Constraint equations describe any limitations on resources, restrictions imposed by the environment within which the system functions, or managerial policies that the firm desires to observe.

The basic approach of MP models is to optimize the objective function while simultaneously satisfying all the constraint equations that limit the activities of the decision maker. In formulating both the objective function and the constraint equations used in MP models, two types of variables are used:

1   *Input parameters* are values specified by the decision maker to describe characteristics of the system.
2   *Decision variables* will be determined by the model as a part of achieving the optimal solution.

As a brief illustration of these definitions, consider a firm manufacturing and selling two products (X and Y) and desiring to determine that product mix that will maximize total dollar profit. The firm estimates that the unit profit figures are $6 and $18, respectively. The objective function to maximize profit for this firm would therefore be expressed as follows:

$$\text{maximize profit} = \$6X + \$18Y$$

In this objective function the two values $6 and $18 are the *input parameters* since management had to specify these values pertaining to their two products. The variables X and Y, which designate the number of units of product X and the number of units of product Y that should be produced, are *decision variables* since the model will determine their values so as to maximize profits.

CATEGORIES OF MATHEMATICAL PROGRAMMING MODELS

Within the general class of models referred to as *mathematical programming*, there are several specific models that can be applied to problem settings, depending on the assumptions made about the problem being analyzed and the interrelationships among system components. Several categories of mathematical programming models are shown in Table 18–1. Each utilizes different types of equations in the objective function or constraint equations and/or permits different assumptions about the input parameters: either these values are assumed to be known with certainty or they are assumed to be known only by means of a probability distribution (i.e., conditions of risk exist). *Herein lie the major strengths of mathematical programming models: they are optimization models (i.e., they find the best possible solution for a given problem representation), and they can accurately describe virtually any real-world system assuming that either conditions of certainty or risk exist.* Hence, MP models provide a powerful tool for the decision maker.

Table 18–1   Categories of Mathematical Programming Models

CONDITIONS OF CERTAINTY	CONDITIONS OF RISK*
1. Linear programming (LP)	1. Stochastic LP (SLP)
	LP under uncertainty (LPUU)
	Chance-constrained programming (CCP)
2. Integer programming (IP)	2. IP under uncertainty (IPUU)
3. Goal programming (GP)	3. Stochastic GP (SGP)
4. Nonlinear programming (NLP)	4. NLP under uncertainty (NLPUU)
Quadratic programming (QP)	QP under uncertainty (QPUU)
5. Dynamic programming (DP)	5. DP under uncertainty (DPUU)

*Based on our definitions of risk and uncertainty in Chapter 11, the models listed technically assume conditions of risk, while in the literature they are frequently referred to in terms of *uncertainty*.

The use of the basic *linear programming (LP)* model, which we will discuss in more detail in the following section, requires three assumptions:

1 The input parameters are known with certainty.
2 Both the objective function and the constraint equations can be accurately described using linear equations.
3 The decision variables are continuous (i.e., they can take on any value).

Linear programming is the most widely known and used MP model because it represents problems with reasonable accuracy utilizing linear equations that may be solved easily with computerized solution algorithms.

If the assumption of certainty is relaxed, the decision maker may select among three alternative methods available for handling conditions of risk in a linear programming setting:

1 *Stochastic LP* is a two-stage decision process wherein stage 1 decisions are fixed and random events are generated; then the stage 2 decisions are determined to optimize the objective function given the stage 1 decisions and the random events.
2 *LP under uncertainty* is also a two-stage decision process wherein stage 1 decisions are fixed and random events are generated; then stage 2 decisions are determined to minimize the penalty assessed for violation of any of the constraints caused by the random events that were encountered.
3 *Chance-constrained programming* attempts to maximize the expected return or minimize the variance of returns, where, owing to the stochastic nature of the input parameters, the constraint equations are required to hold only with some probability less than 1.

Integer programming (IP) relaxes the third assumption required by the LP model, namely, that the decision variables must be continuous. IP allows the decision variables to take on integer values. This seemingly small change in the LP model greatly increases solution time as compared with the corresponding LP problem but permits the solution of large classes of problems wherein the decision variables must take on integer values. IP under uncertainty is analogous to LP under uncertainty.

Goal programming (GP) is a powerful and interesting extension of LP, wherein a hierarchy of multiple objectives is incorporated into the model; thus, the objective function becomes multidimensional. GP provides an effective operational methodology to maximize expected utility as discussed in Chapter 12. Stochastic GP is analogous to stochastic LP and is treated in a similar manner.

Nonlinear programming (NLP) is an MP model wherein either or both the objective function and the constraint equations must be described using nonlinear equations. NLP is frequently used to solve problems involving curvilinear cost functions.

Quadratic programming is a special type of nonlinear programming model wherein the only nonlinearity is in the objective function. QP models are significantly easier to solve than NLP models because there is no general way to solve the latter type of problem. Again, the "risk" setting merely necessitates incorporating the probability distributions of the input parameters.

Dynamic programming (DP) is a useful method of optimizing a system over time. In addition, DP may be used to divide large decision problems into a sequence of smaller, interrelated decision problems wherein recursive equations are used to describe the flow of decisions and the state of the system. Recursive equations relate adjacently indexed variables of a set so that if we know the value of one variable, we can determine the value of the next one. DP under uncertainty assumes that new information is acquired as the decision maker moves through time and that this information is used to update system parameters and to aid in the sequential decision process.

This brief introduction to the various MP models is designed to give an overview rather than specific details of each model. Several of the models will be examined in more depth in this and the following chapters. Extensive research has been undertaken in the area of mathematical programming applied to various problem areas in finance, as evidenced by the entries cited in the selected bibliography. The interested reader is encouraged to seek out such references.

LINEAR PROGRAMMING

Because of the widespread use and importance of linear programming, it is examined in greater detail in this section. In our initial discussion of LP, three major assumptions underlying its use were cited. These assumptions imply various other aspects of LP models, which are delineated in Table 18-2. In our discussion of other MP models, we noted that several of the assumptions required for LP can be relaxed to establish models that more closely describe the real-world decision settings faced by the analyst.

Table 18-2   Assumptions of Linear Programming Models

The major assumptions of linear programming models are as follows:

1. The objective of the system under analysis and all its relevant resource limitations, restrictions, and requirements can be accurately described using *linear equations*. That is, the objective function and all constraint equations must be linear.

2. Conditions of *certainty* exist. All the model's parameters (i.e., the objective function coefficients, the technical coefficients in the constraints, and the right-hand side values in the constraints) are known precisely and are not subject to variation.

3. All decision variables are restricted to *nonnegative* values.

4. Only a *single objective* is optimized.

5. The decision variables are considered to be continuous rather than discrete. This is known as the *divisibility* assumption.

6. Resources available are *homogeneous*. Example: If 10 hours of direct labor are available, each of these hours is just as productive as any other and can be used equally well on any activity that requires direct labor.

7. *Proportionality* exists. This means that if it is desired to increase the activity level of any decision variable, proportionately greater amounts of each resource are required. The linearity assumption implies proportionality.

8. All parameters of the model are *unaffected* by changes in methods used, level of utilization, economies of scale, and so on. Again, the linearity assumption implies this.

9. The system is *additive* in nature: the whole is equal to the sum of the parts. The effectiveness of the system equals the sum of each system component's effectiveness. The total resources utilized equal the sum of the resources used on each activity variable.

10. *Independence* exists throughout the system. This means there is no interaction among decision variables, resources available, or different operations performed.

For example, the LP assumption of certainty can be relaxed by utilizing SLP, LPUU, or CCP; the limitation of a single objective function can be overcome by using GP; and the need for continuous rather than discrete variables may be relaxed by using IP. Of course, each of these enrichments to the basic LP model necessitates greater input requirements, as well as more computer time and memory to solve the model. It should be stressed that the LP model, although it has shortcomings, is a reasonable starting point for many practical decision problems. Thus, the methodology of LP problem solving deserves study.

The basic approach to LP problem solving proceeds through the following stages:

Stage 1   Formulate the problem in the LP framework. This requires specification of input parameters and decision variables, the objective function, and all relevant constraint equations. The latter two sets of equations must all be linear in nature.

Stage 2   Solve the problem using either a graphical approach, the simplex method, or a computer-based solution algorithm.

Stage 3   Interpret the optimal solution which is expressed in terms of an alternative decision point within the feasible solution domain.

Stage 4   Perform a detailed sensitivity analysis on the optimal solution to determine ranges for each of the input parameters wherein the optimal solution remains valid.

To illustrate stages 1 and 2, consider the graphical LP solution demonstrated in Example 1.

EXAMPLE 1

Graphical Solution to LP Problem

A firm manufactures and sells two grades of leather wallets, standard and deluxe. Two resources are constrained for the coming week: production time (80 hours are available) and process and shipping time (1,000 wallets can be shipped during the coming week regardless of which of the two types of wallets make up the order). The firm has sufficient raw materials, working capital, and other resources to support any desired product mix. Further, the firm can sell any number of units of either type of wallet at the going market price. However, the firm wants to produce a minimum of 400 units of its deluxe wallet in order to satisfy the demands of its prime customers for this type of wallet. Management has been provided with the following financial and production data:

WALLET TYPE	PRODUCTION TIME (HR)	SELLING PRICE
Standard	0.05	$ 7.00
Deluxe	0.1	10.00

Production time is estimated to cost the firm $40 per hour. Shipping and processing costs are estimated to be $3 per unit. Management desires to select the product mix that will maximize the total dollar contribution needed to cover fixed costs and generate profits. Formulate this problem using the LP model and solve it graphically.

SOLUTION: To formulate this problem using the LP model, the following decision variables must be defined:

X_1 = number of units of the *standard* wallet to be produced
X_2 = number of units of the *deluxe* wallet to be produced

To specify the objective function, variable cost per unit must be determined for each product so that this amount can be subtracted from the selling price per unit to determine the contribution margin per unit:

	STANDARD	DELUXE
Selling price per unit	$7.00	$10.00
Variable production cost per unit	− 2.00	− 4.00
Variable shipping cost per unit	− 3.00	− 3.00
Contribution margin per unit	$2.00	$ 3.00

The LP formulation is as follows:

$$\text{maximize total dollar contribution} = \$2X_1 + \$3X_2$$

subject to

production capacity	$0.05X_1 + 0.10X_2 \leq 80$ hours
shipping capacity	$1X_1 + 1X_2 \leq 1{,}000$ units
minimum requirements	$X_2 \geq 400$ units
nonnegativity condition	$X_1, X_2 \geq 0$

The graphical solution is shown in Figure 18–2 and the method of arriving at the optimal solution is described below.

As shown in Figure 18–2, the area labeled *feasible region* consists of all possible X_1- and X_2-values that simultaneously satisfy all the constraint equations. Not all of these possible combinations must be evaluated to determine the optimal solution because we have a helpful theorem in LP which states that the optimal solution can only occur at an *extreme point* of the feasible region (i.e., at the intersection of two or more constraints or a constraint and either axis) or possibly along a boundary between two extreme points. There are two methods of determining the optimal solution in the graphical approach:

1 The objective function could be graphed at successively higher values moving farther away from the origin; the optimal solution is reached when the objective function line is as far away from the origin as possible but still touching the feasible region—the point or boundary where the objective function is tangent to the feasible region is the optimal solution.

2 The coordinates for each extreme point are determined either graphically or algebraically and these values are substituted into the objective function, with the results being tabulated as shown in the insert to Figure 18–2; the extreme point with the largest value of the objective function is the optimal solution.

As shown in Figure 18–2, the objective function is maximized at point B (400 standard and 600 deluxe wallets), where it equals $2,600. Since the objective function decreases as we move toward either point A or C, the optimal solution is only at point B rather than along either boundary. If the value of the objective function at *either* point A or C had also been $2,600, then any combination of X_1 and X_2 along the relevant boundary AB or BC would represent an optimal solution to the problem.

Whenever there are more than two decision variables, or if there are numerous constraint equations, the graphical LP method is of limited value. Hence, it becomes

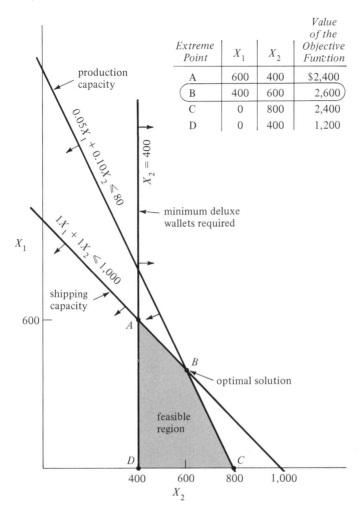

Extreme Point	X_1	X_2	Value of the Objective Function
A	600	400	$2,400
B	400	600	2,600
C	0	800	2,400
D	0	400	1,200

FIGURE 18–2

necessary to resort to an algebraic technique to arrive at the optimal solution. One of the most widely used techniques of solving LP problems is the *simplex method*, developed by George B. Dantzig[1] in the 1940s.

Several new definitions are necessary to understand the simplex method. First, the approach requires that all the constraint equations be converted to strict equalities if they are less-than-or-equal-to ($\leq$) or greater-than-or-equal-to ($\geq$) constraints in the original formulation of the problem. This requires that a unique *slack variable* be added to each "less than or equal to constraint" to convert it into a strict equality. Similarly, a unique *surplus variable* must be subtracted from each "greater-than-or-equal-to constraint" to convert it into a strict equality.

[1]George B. Dantzig, *Linear Programming and Extensions* (Princeton, N.J.: Princeton University Press, 1963).

As mentioned, packaged computer algorithms can be used to perform all the LP problem calculations. An LP package available to users of IBM computers is referred to as the MPSX software package. Similar LP packages are available to users of other computers. Such packaged programs facilitate a capitalization on the speed and accuracy of the computer to handle the tedious calculations required by the simplex method. The reader can obtain documentation detailing the use and interpretation of any such software package.

INTERPRETATION OF THE OPTIMAL LP SOLUTION

At this juncture, we assume readers are able to formulate and solve LP problems (the first two stages in the problem solution listed are complete). The last two stages will be illustrated using computer printouts from the MPSX packaged LP program. Stage 3 entails a complete interpretation of the optimal solution, including the "shadow prices." *Shadow prices show how much the decision maker would be willing to pay to acquire one unit of each resource that is constrained in the problem.* Stage 4 is the sensitivity analysis of the optimal solution, which determines by how much each input parameter could change and leave the optimal solution unchanged in any significant way.

Interpretation of the optimal solution and the discussion of shadow prices is demonstrated in Example 2.

EXAMPLE 2
Interpretation of the Optimal Solution: Shadow Prices

Using the information provided in Example 1 and the optimal solution given, completely interpret the optimal solution.

SOLUTION: We are given the following optimal solution:

BASIC VARIABLES	X_1	X_2	S_1	S_2	R_1	RHS
X_1	1	0	-20	2	0	400
X_2	0	1	20	-1	0	600
R_1	0	0	20	-1	1	200
Objective function	0	0	20	1	0	\$2,600

As can be seen, the basic variables are X_1, X_2, and R_1. These variables have a value of 1 in one of the rows and zeros everywhere else in the column for that variable. These variables are basic in the row where the 1 appears, which means that they take on the value shown on the right-hand side (RHS) in the table. Thus, $X_1 = 400$, $X_2 = 600$, and $R_1 = 200$. The value of the objective function is shown in the objective function row on the right-hand side (\$2,600).

The two variables whose columns do not have a 1 in one row and zeros everywhere else in the column (i.e., S_1 and S_2) are nonbasic variables and hence take on values of zero in the optimal solution.

It is easy to demonstrate that these values satisfy the original constraints by substituting the values into the constraint equations.

production capacity
$$\begin{cases} 0.05X_1 & +0.10X_2 & +S_1 = 80 \\ 0.05(400) & +0.10(600) & +0 = 80 \\ 20 & +60 & +0 = 80 \end{cases}$$

shipping capacity
$$\begin{cases} 1X_1 & +1X_2 & +S_2 = 1{,}000 \\ 400 & +600 & +0 = 1{,}000 \end{cases}$$

minimum requirement for X_2
$$\begin{cases} X_2 - R_1 & = 400 \\ 600 - 200 & = 400 \end{cases}$$

The values shown in the objective function row under the slack and surplus variables have special significance. They are the *shadow prices* and, *for slack variables, show the amount by which the value of the objective function would increase* (in a maximization problem) *if the original right-hand side value associated with the slack variable were increased by 1 unit. For surplus variables, the shadow prices show the amount by which the objective function would increase if the original right-hand side value associated with the surplus variable were decreased by 1 unit.* Thus, the shadow prices show the maximum amount that the decision maker would be willing to pay to acquire 1 additional unit of a resource (for slack variables) or to have a requirement relaxed by 1 unit (for surplus variables). In this example, the shadow price for S_1 = $20.00, for S_2 = $1.00, while it is $0 for R_1. This means that the firm would be willing to pay up to a maximum of $20.00 (in addition to the current variable production cost of $40.00 per hour) to acquire 1 hour of added production time and $1.00 (in addition to the variable shipping cost of $3 per unit) to acquire 1 unit of added shipping capacity. To verify that these shadow prices are correct, consider a customer's order for 10 additional deluxe wallets. If the shadow prices are paid in addition to the current variables costs, the marginal revenue will just equal the marginal cost and the marginal profit will be zero. If the variable inputs can be obtained at a cost less than the shadow prices, profit will increase.

incremental contribution margin from the new order	incremental cost of filling new order if maximum shadow prices are paid to acquire = additional resources	
	production capacity:	
	10 units × 0.10 hr/unit × $20/hr	= $20
10 units at $3	shipping capacity:	
	10 units × $1/unit	= $10
$30 =		$30

It should be stressed that shadow prices are incremental in nature; that is, they indicate the maximum additional amount that the firm would be willing to pay over and above the current prices paid for needed resources. To demonstrate this for this example, refer back to Example 1 to get the selling price per unit of the deluxe wallet and the variable cost per hour of production capacity as well as the variable cost per unit of shipping capacity. These values are, respectively, $10 per unit, $40 per hour, and $3 per unit. It is now shown that marginal revenue equals marginal cost for the new order of 10 wallets:

marginal revenue =	marginal cost of filling new order if maximum shadow prices are paid (in addition to current cost) to acquire additional resources	
	production capacity:	
	10 units × 0.10 hr/unit × $60/hr	= $ 60
10 units at $10	shipping capacity:	
	10 units ×$4/unit	= $ 40
$100 =		$100

Notice that the variable costs of $60 per hour and $4 per unit for production capacity and shipping capacity, respectively, are the sum of current costs (i.e., $40 per hour and $3 per unit, respectively) plus the incremental shadow prices (i.e., $20 per hour and $1 per unit, respectively).

The shadow price for R_1 is zero because R_1 is a basic variable in the optimal solution which means that this constraint was not binding. That is, we exceeded the 400-unit minimum requirement for deluxe wallets by 200 units, so we would not be willing to pay anything to get this minimum requirement reduced. A similar interpretation would be given to a slack variable that was basic in the optimal solution. That is, since the constraint was not binding, not all the resource originally available was utilized in the optimal solution. Thus, the firm would not be willing to pay anything to obtain additional units of the resource, because these units would just add to the already existing excess in the optimal solution.

The shadow prices discussed in Example 2 remain valid only within the specific range of additional units that the firm could acquire. In addition, questions often arise concerning the impact of changes in original values of input parameters on the optimal solution. Both these areas may be addressed using the important tool referred to as *sensitivity analysis*.

SENSITIVITY ANALYSIS

Prudent financial management requires a determination of how sensitive the preferred alternative is to forecasting errors for the model's data inputs. The LP model is no exception. As mentioned earlier, sensitivity analysis in LP modeling ascertains how much of a change would be required in the input parameters for there to be a significant change in the optimal solution found by the model.

Sensitivity analysis can be performed either on the original right-hand side values for each of the constraint equations or on the objective function coefficients for each decision variable. *In sensitivity analysis, on the right-hand side, Δ^+ and Δ^- are the amounts by which the original right-hand side value could increase or decrease, respectively, without changing the basic variables in the optimal solution. In sensitivity analysis, on the objective function coefficients, Δ^+ and Δ^- are the amounts by which the objective function coefficient could increase or decrease, respectively, without changing the optimal solution.* Notice the difference in the statements made concerning the two types of sensitivity analysis. With respect to the right-hand side values, we talked about leaving the same basic variables in the optimal solution but that the optimal values for each basic variable would change with any change of a right-hand side value of a binding constraint. For objective function coefficients, we talked about the range within which the *optimal solution* (both the basic variables and their specific values) would remain unchanged. For all these input parameters, a range can be determined as specified in Equations (1) and (2):

$$\text{upper limit} = \text{original value plus } \Delta^+ \tag{1}$$

$$\text{lower limit} = \text{original value less } \Delta^- \tag{2}$$

We first undertake a sensitivity analysis of the right-hand side values.

For slack variables that are basic variables in the optimal solution,

$$\Delta_{S_j}^{+} = \infty \tag{3}$$

and

$$\Delta_{S_j}^{-} = \text{amount of this resource still available in the optimal solution} \tag{4}$$

These two values are consistent with the discussion just presented. If there is some quantity of a resource still available in the optimal solution (i.e., the definition of slack variable being "basic" in the optimal solution), then if we had more of it originally, we would merely have more of it left over in the optimal solution. This would be true for any increase in the original amount available; hence, the value of Δ^{+} is infinite. On the other hand, we could decrease the original amount available only by the amount left over in the optimal solution, since to decrease it by an amount greater than this would lead to a different optimal solution.

For surplus variables that are basic variables in the optimal solution,

$$\Delta_{R_j}^{+} = \text{value of this basic variable in the optimal solution} \tag{5}$$

$$\Delta_{R_j}^{-} = \infty \tag{6}$$

These values should be clear based on the discussion relating to the complements of surplus variables (i.e., slack variables).

The same values for nonbasic variables in the optimal solution require computations based on the tableau from the optimal solution. *Thus, for slack or surplus variables that are nonbasic in the optimal solution,*

$$\Delta_{R_j}^{+} \text{ or } \Delta_{S_j}^{+} = \min \left| \frac{b_i}{a_{ij} < 0} \right| \tag{7}$$

$$\Delta_{R_j}^{-} \text{ or } \Delta_{S_j}^{-} = \min \left\{ \frac{b_i}{a_{ij} > 0} \right\} \tag{8}$$

where b_i = right-hand side value in row i of the optimal solution

a_{ij} = coefficient in column j (i.e., the column of slack or surplus variable j) and row i

S_j = slack variable in column j which is associated with the original resource that we are interested in changing

R_j = surplus variable in column j which is associated with the original resource that we are interested in changing

To perform sensitivity analysis on the optimal solution shown in Example 2, for example, consider slack variable S_1, which is nonbasic in the optimal solution; we look up and down in column S_1 for values that are negative. For each one that is found, divide its corresponding right-hand side value by the a_{ij} value and take the absolute value. Among the resulting values, select the smallest; this value is Δ^{+}. Repeat the process looking for positive values in the column S_1 in order to compute Δ^{-}.

Finally, we look at sensitivity analysis on the objective function coefficients for a maximization problem. Of course, we perform this analysis on decision variables in the problem which can either be basic or nonbasic in the optimal solution.

For decision variables that are nonbasic in the optimal solution,

$$\Delta^+_{X_k} = \text{value of the shadow price for this decision variable in the optimal solution} \qquad (9)$$

$$\Delta^-_{X_k} = \infty \qquad (10)$$

If a decision variable is nonbasic in the optimal solution, the values found using Equations (9) and (10) should indicate that the decision variable was not attractive enough to enter the solution. Hence, it will remain unattractive if its objective function coefficient is decreased by any amount (i.e., $\Delta^- = \infty$). Furthermore, the shadow price in the optimal solution shows the amount by which the objective function would decrease if a nonbasic variable were forced into solution. Thus, the objective function coefficient would have to increase by more than its shadow price to make the nonbasic variable in question attractive (i.e., $\Delta^+ =$ shadow price in the optimal solution).

For decision variables that are basic in the optimal solution,

$$\Delta^+_{X_k} = \min \left| \frac{C_j}{a_{ij} < 0} \right| \qquad (11)$$

$$\Delta^-_{X_k} = \min \left\{ \frac{C_j}{a_{ij} > 0} \right\} \qquad (12)$$

where C_j = value in the objective function row of the optimal tableau in column j
$\quad a_{ij}$ = coefficient in row i (i.e., the row in the optimal tableau where X_k is basic) and column j
$\quad X_k$ = decision variable k of interest which is basic in row i of the optimal tableau

To perform sensitivity analysis on the optimal solution shown in Example 2, for example, consider decision variable X_2, which is basic in row 2 of the optimal tableau; we would look across row 2 for negative a_{ij} values. For each one that is found, divide C_j (i.e., the value in the objective function row of the tableau) for that column by a_{ij} and take the absolute value. Among the resulting values, select the smallest: this is $\Delta^+_{X_2}$. The process would then be repeated looking for positive a_{ij} values in row 2 in order to compute $\Delta^-_{X_2}$.

All these computations are for *maximization problems*. To compute the Δ^+ and Δ^- values for *minimization problems*, the identities of the two values are interchanged; that is, Equations (9) and (11) become the appropriate formulas for Δ^- and Equations (10) and (12) are used to compute Δ^+.

Example 3 illustrates the computation of Δ^+ and Δ^- values.

EXAMPLE 3

Sensitivity Analysis

Perform a complete sensitivity analysis on the following optimal solution:

BASIC VARIABLES	X_1	X_2	S_1	S_2	R_1	RHS
X_1	1	0	-20	2	0	400
X_2	0	1	20	-1	0	600
R_1	0	0	20	-1	1	200
Objective function	0	0	20	1	0	$2,600

SOLUTION: Sensitivity analysis will first be performed on the original right-hand side values. Recall that in the original problem we had the following resources available and minimum requirements:

$$\text{production capacity} \leq 80 \text{ hours}$$
$$\text{shipping and processing capacity} \leq 1{,}000 \text{ units}$$
$$\text{minimum requirement for deluxe wallets} \geq 400 \text{ units}$$

Slack variables S_1 and S_2 correspond to the production and shipping capacity constraints, respectively; surplus variable R_1 corresponds to the minimum requirement for deluxe wallets. Thus, these columns in the tableau are relevant for sensitivity analysis on the original right-hand side values for the three constraints.

Since R_1 is a basic variable in the optimal solution, we examine it first. Since R_1 is a surplus variable that is basic in the optimal solution, its Δ^+ and Δ^- values are found using Equations (5) and (6).

$$\Delta_{R_1}^+ = 200, \text{ the value of } R_1 \text{ in the optimal solution}$$

$$\Delta_{R_2}^- = \infty$$

The range of possible values that the minimum requirement for deluxe wallets could take on using Equations (1) and (2) is as follows:

$$\text{range} \begin{cases} \text{upper limit} = \text{original amount plus } \Delta^+ = 400 + 200 = 600 \\ \text{lower limit} = \text{original amount minus } \Delta^- = 400 - \infty = -\infty \end{cases}$$

Hence, if our minimum requirement were any value less than 600 units of the deluxe wallet, we would have the same optimal basis that we presently have.

The two capacity constraints have slack variables that are nonbasic. Therefore, performance of a sensitivity analysis using Equations (7) and (8) yields the following results:

$$\Delta_{S_1}^+ = \min \left| \frac{400}{-20} \right| = 20 \text{ hours}$$

$$\Delta_{S_1}^- = \min \left\{ \frac{600}{20}, \frac{200}{0.20} \right\} = \min(30, 10) = 10 \text{ hours}$$

Thus, if the actual production capacity falls anywhere in the range of 70 hours (80 − 10 hours) to 100 hours (80 + 20 hours), we have the same optimal basis as we do currently (X_1, X_2, R_1), and new optimal values for the variables can be determined by performing calculations on the optimal tableau.

In addition, the shadow price of $20 per hour of production capacity remains valid as long as the firm does not attempt to purchase more than 20 additional hours ($\Delta_{S_1}^+$) of production capacity or to sell more than 10 hours ($\Delta_{S_1}^-$) at that price. Outside this range there is a new shadow price, indicating the value of each production hour to the firm. Thus, there is a close and important relationship between shadow prices and the values of Δ^+ and Δ^- determined in sensitivity analysis.

For S_2, the sensitivity analysis yields the following results:

$$\Delta_{S_2}^+ = \min\left| \frac{600}{-1}, \frac{200}{-1} \right| = 200 \text{ units}$$

$$\Delta_{S_2}^- = \min\left\{ \frac{400}{2} \right\} = 200 \text{ units}$$

Thus, if the actual shipping capacity falls anywhere in the range of 800 units (1,000 − 200) to 1,200 units (1,000 + 200), we again have the same optimal basis and do not have to re-solve the problem to determine the optimal solution. The same comments hold true for the shadow price of $1 for each unit of shipping capacity remaining valid only within the range 800 to 1,200 units.

To perform sensitivity analysis on the original objective function coefficients for the two decision variables, which are both basic in the optimal solution, we use Equations (11) and (12):

$$\Delta_{X_1}^+ = \min\left| \frac{\$20}{-20} \right| = \$1.00$$

$$\Delta_{X_1}^- = \min\left\{ \frac{\$1}{2} \right\} = \$0.50$$

If the profit coefficient for standard wallets falls anywhere between $3.00 ($2.00 + $1.00) and $1.50 ($2.00 − $0.50), we have the same optimal solution. Similarly, for deluxe wallets,

$$\Delta_{X_2}^+ = \min\left| \frac{\$1}{-1} \right| = \$1.00$$

$$\Delta_{X_2}^- = \min\left\{ \frac{\$20}{20} \right\} = \$1.00$$

If the profit coefficient for deluxe wallets falls anywhere between $4.00 ($3.00 + $1.00) and $2.00 ($3.00 − $1.00), we have the same optimal solution as before.

Up to this point we have been saying that, within the ranges for right-hand side values which are determined by means of sensitivity analysis, the optimal basis would remain unchanged. Further, it was mentioned that the new optimal values for each of the basic variables could be determined by looking at the optimal tableau rather than having to re-solve the complete problem. We now explore how this is done.

Whenever a specific right-hand side value in the original problem is changed to take on some other value within its sensitivity range limits, the column of its slack variable becomes the relevant column to use in the optimal tableau in order to determine the new optimal value for each basic variable. The new optimal values are computed using Equation (13),

$$\begin{matrix} \text{new optimal value} \\ \text{of basic variable } i \end{matrix} = \begin{matrix} \text{current optimal} \\ \text{value of basic} \\ \text{variable } i \end{matrix} + (a_{ij}) \begin{pmatrix} \text{change in original} \\ \text{right-hand side value} \end{pmatrix} \quad (13)$$

where a_{ij} is the value in the current optimal tableau in row i and in column j which is the column of the slack or surplus variable associated with the right-hand side value that is being changed. Note that the "change in original right-hand side value" shown in Equation (13) has *both* a magnitude (numerical value) and a direction (sign) that must be incorporated into the calculations.

Example 4 illustrates the use of Equation (13).

EXAMPLE 4
Optimal Solution Using Sensitivity Range Limits

Find the new optimal solution in our example problem if the number of *production hours* is actually (a) 105 hours, (b) 72 hours.

SOLUTION: (a) If the actual number of production hours is 105 hours, the problem has to be re-solved to obtain the new optimal solution because the value 105 hours falls outside the range of 70 to 100 hours determined by sensitivity analysis in Example 3.

It should be noted that if we attempt to use Equation (13) to find the value of X_1 for the change up to 105 hours, the result is

$$X_1 = 400 \text{ units} + (-20)(+25 \text{ hr}) = -100 \text{ units}$$

which is of course *infeasible* since the nonnegativity constraint would be violated.

(b) Since 72 hours does fall within the range of 70 to 100 hours, we can proceed with calculations as follows:

$$\begin{matrix} \text{new optimal} \\ \text{value of basic variable} \end{matrix} = \begin{matrix} \text{current} \\ \text{optimal value} \end{matrix} + \begin{pmatrix} a_{ij} \\ \text{value} \end{pmatrix} \begin{pmatrix} \text{change in} \\ \text{production capacity} \end{pmatrix}$$

$$X_1 = 400 \text{ units} + (-20)(-8 \text{ hr}) = 560 \text{ units}$$
$$X_2 = 600 \text{ units} + (+20)(-8 \text{ hr}) = 440 \text{ units}$$
$$R_1 = 200 \text{ units} + (+20)(-8 \text{ hr}) = 40 \text{ units}$$

$$\text{new profit} = \text{original profit} + (\text{shadow price}) \begin{pmatrix} \text{change in} \\ \text{production capacity} \end{pmatrix}$$

$$= \$2,600 + (+\$20)(-8 \text{ hr})$$
$$= \$2,440$$

The new profit can also be computed by multiplying the number of units of each product by its respective contribution margin and totaling.

DUALITY THEORY

Another important area related to linear programming problem formulation and solution is referred to as *duality theory*. Corresponding to every maximization LP problem, usually called the *primal problem*, there is a closely related minimization problem called the *dual problem*. From our point of view, the major attractiveness of duality theory lies in the interesting economic interpretation of the dual problem and the insight that the dual problem provides for extensions of LP, mainly to integer linear programming.

The following properties of duality are the most important:

1   The primal problem is generally a maximization problem, which has less-than-or-equal-to constraint equations.

2   The dual problem is generally a minimization problem, which has greater-than-or-equal-to constraint equations.

3   The dual of the dual is the primal.

4   The decision variables in the dual correspond to constraint equations in the primal, and vice versa. Thus, if there are n decision variables and m constraint equations in the primal problem, there will be m decision variables and n constraint equations in the dual.

5   An optimal solution to the dual exists only when the primal has an optimal solution, and vice versa. Further, the optimal value of the objective function must be the same for the primal and the dual.

6   By examining the optimal tableau of the primal problem we can also determine the optimal values for the dual variables, since they are the shadow prices associated with each of the slack and surplus variables.

Formulation of the dual problem for the problem that has been used throughout the chapter is demonstrated in Example 5.

EXAMPLE 5
Formulation of the Dual

Formulate the dual for the problem in Example 1.

SOLUTION: Recall the primal problem formulated in Example 1:

$$\text{maximize } \$2X_1 + \$3X_2$$

subject to the following constraints:

$$0.05X_1 + 0.10X_2 \le 80 \text{ hours production capacity}$$

$$1X_1 + 1X_2 \le 1,000 \text{ units shipping capacity}$$

$$1X_2 \ge 400 \text{ units minimum requirements for deluxe wallets}$$

$$X_1, X_2 \ge 0$$

where X_1 = the number of standard wallets to be produced
      X_2 = the number of deluxe wallets to be produced

The dual problem is as follows:

$$\text{minimize } 80\,u_1 + 1000\,u_2 - 400\,u_3$$

subject to the following constraints:

$$0.05\,u_1 + 1\,u_2 + 0\,u_3 \geq \$2 \text{ profit for } X_1$$

$$0.10\,u_1 + 1\,u_2 - 1\,u_3 \geq \$3 \text{ profit for } X_2$$

$$u_1, u_2, u_3 \geq 0$$

where u_1 = the imputed price that the firm would be willing to pay per hour of production capacity

u_2 = the imputed price that the firm would be willing to pay per unit of shipping capacity

u_3 = the imputed price that the firm would be willing to pay per unit of minimum requirement for the deluxe wallet

The primal and dual forms in Example 5 are closely related to each other, as stated previously. The dual problem seeks to find the *smallest imputed prices (u_1, u_2, and u_3) that should be associated with the firm's resources available or requirements on activities (80 hours of production capacity, 1,000 units of shipping capacity, and a minimum requirement to produce 400 units of the deluxe wallet) subject to the requirement that these prices completely account for the profit generated per unit of each product.*

It should also be pointed out that the *decision variables* in the primal problem refer to the number of units of each product that should be produced while the slack variables refer to the quantity of excess resources available. In the dual problem, the decision variables are the imputed prices (or accounting values) associated with each of the resources that will be used to produce the various products, and the surplus variables show the excess of the imputed costs of a unit of output of a given product over its profit per unit. These interpretations of the description, based on the characteristics of duality, are expanded here:

1   The optimal production, which is found in the primal problem, determines the total profits generated and the quantity of excess resources still available.

2   The optimal price per unit for each resource is found in the dual, which generates the same total dollar value as was found in the primal.

3   The optimal price (found in the dual) for any resource of which there is an excess amount still available given the optimal production (found in the primal) will be zero.

4   Given the optimal prices found in the dual, any product whose profit does not equal the opportunity cost of the resources required to produce one unit will not be produced in the optimal product mix found in the primal problem.

In the next chapter, we demonstrate that the dual problem has a very important interpretation in the capital budgeting problem setting.

The optimal solution to the dual is closely related to the optimal solution of the primal problem. This is shown in Example 6.

EXAMPLE 6

Solution of the Dual

Find the optimal solution to the dual problem formulated in Example 5 and compare it with the optimal primal solution.

SOLUTION: The optimal primal solution, as developed in Example 2, is

BASIC VARIABLES	X_1	X_2	S_1	S_2	R_1	RHS
X_1	1	0	-20	2	0	400
X_2	0	1	20	-1	0	600
R_1	0	0	20	-1	1	200
Objective function	0	0	20	1	0	$2,600

The optimal solution to the dual is

BASIC VARIABLES	u_1	u_2	u_3	R_2	R_3	RHS
u_2	0	1	1	-2	1	1
u_1	1	0	-20	20	-20	20
Objective function	0	0	200	400	600	$2,600

The optimal primal solution indicates that 400 standard and 600 deluxe wallets should be produced. This is 200 units over the minimum requirement of 400 deluxe wallets and generates $2,600 of profit. All of the production capacity originally available (80 hours), as well as the shipping capacity (1,000 units) originally available, have been consumed by the optimal production plan, since the associated slack variables, S_1 and S_2, respectively, are nonbasic in the optimal solution. The shadow prices for these two resources show that the firm would be willing to pay up to a maximum of $20 to acquire one additional hour of production capacity and up to $1.00 to purchase one additional unit of shipping capacity.

The optimal dual solution shows that the optimal prices (u_1, u_2, and u_3) for the three resources or activities (production capacity, shipping capacity, and minimum production requirement of deluxe wallets) are $20, $1, and 0, respectively. Of course, these optimal values are exactly the shadow prices associated with the corresponding slack and surplus variables in the primal due to the interrelationships between the primal and dual formulations discussed earlier. The optimal value of the objective function for the dual is also $2,600. The two surplus variables R_2 and R_3 are *nonbasic* in the optimal solution. This means that, given the optimal values to be paid for the resources needed (u_1, u_2, and u_3) to produce products X_1 and X_2, the dollar profit generated by these two products is exactly accounted for.

The shadow prices in the optimal dual solution indicate the following:

1   The objective function would increase by $200 if u_3 were forced into solution at a value of 1.

2   The objective function would increase by $400 ($R_2$) if the right-hand side value for constraint 1 were increased by 1 unit (i.e., if the dollar profit for product X_1 were increased from $2 to $3).

3 The objective function would increase by \$600 (R_3) if the right-hand side value for constraint 2 were increased by 1 unit (i.e., if the dollar profit for product X_2 were increased from \$3 to \$4). Sensitivity analysis would be performed on the dual in exactly the same way as it was done on the primal.

SUMMARY

This chapter surveys the rather broad field of mathematical programming with an eye toward the use of this powerful class of management science models in the capital budgeting area. Model building is discussed in general, as well as in the specific area of mathematical programming. Various mathematical programming models are introduced to handle problems under the assumption that either conditions of certainty or risk are present in the decision setting.

Linear programming is treated in depth because of the importance of this technique, its widespread use, and the reliance of more advanced techniques on the LP formulation and solution. Problem formulation, graphical and computerized solution approaches, and sensitivity analysis are all discussed and illustrated with examples. Finally, the important area of duality is examined to show the interesting interrelationships and important economic interpretations of the primal-dual LP problems.

The material in this chapter forms a basis for the following two chapters. The strengths of mathematical programming techniques are examined as tools to assist the financial manager in evaluating capital investment alternatives and to integrate investment decisions with financing and dividend decisions.

QUESTIONS
──────────
PROBLEMS

1. The Datamax Company has recently become enthralled with linear programming and wants to utilize it in determining the optimal product mix for its two product lines. The relevant information about its products is as follows:

	PRODUCT X	PRODUCT Y
Selling price	\$16.00	\$23.00
Standard material cost	1.50	2.25
Standard labor cost	6.00	8.00
Standard machine time cost	4.50	5.25
Standard shipping cost	1.00	1.00
Maximum demand	None	500 units
Minimum requirements	100 units	None

In addition, Datamax has several resource constraints that cannot be violated:

Raw material constraint	1,000 units at \$1.50 standard cost
Labor hours constraint	1,200 hours at \$4.00 standard cost
Machine hours constraint	2,800 hours at \$1.50 standard cost
Shipping capacity constraint	650 units at \$1.00 standard cost

Formulate this linear-programming problem and solve it using the graphical technique.

2. Find the optimal solution to Problem 1 using the simplex method or a packaged LP algorithm.

3. Perform a sensitivity analysis on the right-hand side values for the solution arrived at in Problem 2.

4. Perform a sensitivity analysis on the objective function coefficients for the solution arrived at in Problem 2.

5. Formulate the dual LP problem for Problem 1. Solve it using the simplex method or a packaged LP algorithm.

6. A sophisticated farmer uses LP to determine the amount of various crops to plant. She has 1,000 acres of land on which she can grow corn, wheat, or soybeans. Each acre of corn costs $100 for preparation, requires 7 worker-days of labor, and yields a profit of $30. Each acre of wheat costs $120 for preparation, requires 10 worker-days of labor, and yields $40 in profit. Finally, soybeans cost $70 to prepare the land, require 8 worker-days, and yield a $20 profit. If the farmer has $100,000 available for preparation expenses, has 8,000 worker-days of labor available, and wants to maximize profit, her LP formulation would be

$$\text{maximize } 30X_1 + 40X_2 + 20X_3$$

subject to

$$100X_1 + 120X_2 + 70X_3 + S_1 = 100{,}000$$
$$7X_1 + 10X_2 + 8X_3 + S_2 = 8{,}000$$
$$X_1 + X_2 + X_3 + S_3 = 1{,}000$$
$$X_i, S_i \geq 0 \qquad i = 1, 2, 3$$

Solve this problem using the simplex method or a packaged LP algorithm.

7. The optimal LP solution to Problem 6 is as follows:

	X_1	X_2	X_3	S_1	S_2	S_3	RHS
	0	1	1.9375	-0.04375	0.625	0	625
	1	0	-1.625	0.0625	-0.75	0	250
	0	0	0.6875	-0.01875	0.125	1	125
Z	0	0	8.75	0.1250	2.50	0	32,500

Answer the following questions about the optimal solution.

(a) What is the optimal amount of each of the three crops that should be planted?

(b) What is the dollar profit generated by the optimal planting? Show a proof that this figure is correct.

(c) Are there any excess resources given the optimal planting? Demonstrate that this is correct by plugging the optimal values for X_1, X_2, and X_3 into the constraint equations.

(d) How much would the farmer be willing to pay for an additional dollar of capital? An additional worker-day of labor? An additional acre of land?

(e) Demonstrate that the answers given for part (d) are correct assuming that the farmer wants to plant 10 more acres of wheat.

(f) What is the meaning of the value in row Z and column X_3?

(g) Demonstrate that the value mentioned in part (f) is correct by computing the cost of planting an acre of X_3 using the shadow prices shown in the optimal tableau.

8. For the optimal solution given in Problem 7, perform a sensitivity analysis on the right-hand side values.

9. For the optimal solution given in Problem 7, perform a sensitivity analysis on the objective function coefficients.

10. For the optimal solution given in Problem 7, find the new optimal solution if the original labor availability was 8,100 worker-days (i.e., what would be the new values for each of the basic variables if there were originally 8,100 worker-days of labor available?).

11. For the optimal solution shown in Problem 7, find the new optimal solution if the original amount of capital available was $104,000.

REFERENCES

Beale, E. M. L. *Mathematical Programming in Practice*. Pitman, 1968.

Booth, G. Geoffrey, and Peter E. Koveos. "A Programming Model for Bank Hedging Decisions." *Journal of Financial Research* (August 1986).

Boquist, John A., and William T. Moore. "Estimating the Systematic Risk of an Industry Segment: A Mathematical Programming Approach." *Financial Management* (Winter 1983).

Charnes, A., and W. W. Cooper. *Management Models and Industrial Applications of Linear Programming*, Vols. I and II. New York: John Wiley & Sons, Inc., 1961.

Dantzig, G. B. *Linear Programming and Extensions*. Princeton, N.J.: Princeton University Press, 1963.

Dorfman, R., P. A. Samuelson, and R. M. Solow. *Linear Programming and Economic Analysis*. New York: McGraw-Hill Book Company, 1958.

Gale, D. *The Theory of Linear Economic Models*. New York: McGraw-Hill Book Company, 1960.

Gass, S. I. *Linear Programming: Methods and Applications*, 3rd ed. New York: McGraw-Hill Book Company, 1969.

Karlin, S. *Mathematical Methods and Theory in Games, Programming and Economics*, Vol. 1. Reading, Mass.: Addison-Wesley Publishing Co., Inc. 1959.

Koopmans, T. C., ed. *Activity Analysis of Production and Allocation, Proceeding of a Conference*. New York: John Wiley & Sons, Inc. 1951.

Kuhn, H. W., and A. W. Tucker, eds. *Linear Inequalities and Related Systems*. Princeton, N.J.: Princeton University Press, 1956.

Ladson, L. *Optimization Theory for Large Systems*. New York: Macmillan Publishing Co., Inc., 1970.

Orchard-Hays, W. *Advanced Linear-Programming Computing Techniques*. New York: McGraw-Hill Book Company, 1968.

Perold, Andre F. "Large-Scale Portfolio Optimizations." *Management Science* (October 1984).

Stowe, John D. "An Integer Programming Solution for the Optimal Credit Investigation/Credit Granting Sequence." *Financial Management* (Summer 1985).

Zionts, S. *Linear and Integer Programming*. Englewood Cliffs, N.J.: Prentice Hall, 1974.

Multiperiod Analysis Under Conditions of Certainty: Linear Programming

19

This chapter examines the application of linear programming (LP) to the capital budgeting problem where capital is rationed and other human and material resources are limited. Under these conditions, the firm must evaluate portfolios of projects which simultaneously satisfy all constraints on the problem setting. From this group of "feasible portfolios of capital projects," the firm should select the one that maximizes the aggregate net present value.

In addition to examining the formulation of the capital rationing problem using LP, this chapter illustrates the interpretation of the optimal LP solution so that the information can be translated into effective financial decisions. Finally, the important areas of shadow price interpretation and the performance of sensitivity analysis on the optimal solution are discussed in depth. These latter tools provide a wealth of information for financial managers.

The sophisticated mathematical programming techniques to be discussed in the next few chapters have become increasingly popular and diverse. Table 19-1 reports results of surveys on the use of sophisticated techniques.

HISTORICAL PERSPECTIVE

In 1955, Lorie and Savage discussed the shortcomings of various methods of analysis, especially the internal rate of return method, when capital is rationed.[1] They presented examples demonstrating

1   Problems that develop because multiple projects under consideration are not independent.
2   Problems that develop when capital is rationed in more than a single time period.

[1] J. H. Lorie and L. J. Savage, "Three Problems in Rationing Capital." *The Journal of Business*, (October 1955), 229–239.

Table 19–1 Use of Sophisticated Capital Budgeting Techniques
(percentage of respondents using each technique)

	AUTHOR AND YEAR						
	KLAMMER			WESTON	KIM AND FARRAGHER	PETTY AND BOWLIN	KIM AND FARRAGHER
TECHNIQUE	1959	1964	1970	1973	1975	1976	1979
Decision Theory	3%	4%	9%		10%		12%
Mathematical Programming	1	3	4		11		13
Game Theory		2	3		6	25%	7
Pert/CPM	4	13	28	14%	19		23
LP	5	8	17	21	12	25	18
GP					6	8	7
Nonlinear Programming				8		3	
Dynamic Programming				4		2	
Simulation				29		34	

SOURCE: Klammer, T., "Empirical Evidence of the Adoption of Sophisticated Capital Budgeting Techniques," *Journal of Business* (July 1972); Frederick C. Weston, Jr., "Operations Research Techniques Relevant to Corporate Planning Function Practices: An Investigative Look," *Academy of Management Journal* (September 1973); J. W. Petty and O. D. Bowlin, "The Financial Manager and Quantitative Decision Models," *Financial Management* (Winter 1976); S. H. Kim and E. J. Farragher, "Current Capital Budgeting Practices," *Management Accounting* (June 1981).

3 Problems that develop when analyzing projects that have both cash inflows and outflows dispersed over their lives.

They overcome the first and third problems by utilizing the net present value approach rather than the internal rate of return. They *attempted* to overcome the second problem. A breakdown in their approach opened the way for the subsequent research that applied mathematical programming to the capital rationing problem area.

Charnes, Cooper, and Miller[2] and Weingartner[3] were the pioneers who concentrated on Lorie and Savage's second problem of capital rationing and its resolution. These authors demonstrated that Lorie and Savage's generalized multipliers do not exist for all types of capital rationing problems, that an optimal solution is not guaranteed using the multipliers, and that the transformed problem using the approach may not be equivalent to the original problem. Charnes, Cooper, and Miller formulated an LP model to assist the firm in allocating funds among competing uses considering both operating decisions and financial planning. Weingartner's outstanding work formulates the capital rationing problem first as an LP, then as an IP (integer programming) model. His work also provided valuable insights concerning the shadow prices and dual variables for the integer programming formulation.

Since these pioneering works, there have been many advances in the area of mathematical programming applied to the capital budgeting problem. The major

[2]A. Charnes, W. W. Cooper, and M. H. Miller, "An Application of Linear Programming to Financial Budgeting and the Cost of Funds." *The Journal of Business* (January 1959), 20–46.

[3]H. Martin Weingartner, *Mathematical Programming and the Analysis of Capital Budgeting Problems* (Englewood Cliffs, N.J.: Prentice Hall, 1963).

extensions have either sought to integrate other financial decision areas with the capital budgeting decision, relaxed the single goal assumption of LP and IP, or attempted to handle the capital rationing problem under conditions of risk. The focus of Chapters 19 and 20 will be to survey the important areas of linear, integer, and goal programming as they apply to the capital rationing problem.

MOTIVATION FOR THE USE OF MATHEMATICAL PROGRAMMING

As we have pointed out, it can be demonstrated that (under the assumptions enumerated in Chapter 4) the selection of that set of projects that maximizes the net present value will simultaneously maximize shareholders' wealth or shareholders' utility. However, as argued in Chapter 8, when capital is rationed in one or more periods, no longer should we merely rank projects according to their net present values and just continue to select them in order until the budgets are exhausted. This is due to disparities in the original costs of projects under consideration, which may find that several projects with smaller original costs have a greater combined net present value than one larger project. Hence, what must be done is to find the combination of *projects that will maximize net present value while not violating any relevant constraints*. As the number of projects and/or the number of years in the planning horizon increase, the number of feasible combinations of projects grows exponentially. Thus, it becomes advantageous to call upon a set of models such as mathematical programming, which does not require the explicit evaluation of each feasible combination and which can be solved within modest computer time and memory requirements (even for very large problems). Mathematical programming models are powerful in that they are optimization techniques (i.e., they find the best possible solution to a given problem representation) and they can be used to provide an accurate representation for virtually any real-world problem setting. Numerous computerized solution algorithms are available through every computer manufacturer; thus, even small firms can afford to call upon mathematical programming techniques to facilitate the decision-making process in the capital budgeting area as well as other problem areas.

LINEAR-PROGRAMMING REPRESENTATION OF THE CAPITAL RATIONING PROBLEM

Based on the introduction to linear programming provided by Chapter 18, we can proceed directly to the formulation of the capital rationing problem using the LP model,

$$\text{maximize NPV} = \sum_{j=1}^{N} b_j X_j \tag{1}$$

subject to

$$\sum_{j=1}^{N} C_{jt} X_j \le K_t \qquad t = 1, 2, \dots, T \tag{2}$$

$$X_j \le 1 \tag{3}$$

$$X_j \ge 0 \tag{4}$$

where X_j = percent of project j that is accepted
      b_j = net present value of project j over its useful life
      C_{jt} = cash outflow required by project j in year t
      K_t = budget availability in year t
      N = the number of projects under evaluation

This formulation merely states that the firm wants to select the set of projects that maximizes the net present value without violating any of the budget constraints.

In addition, the following aspects of the LP formulation for the capital rationing problem should be noted after referring to the general assumptions of LP models listed in Table 18–2:

1   The X_j decision variables are assumed to be continuous; that is, partial projects are allowed in the LP formulation.

2   Equation (3) is used to show an upper limit for each project; that is, it is required that each project have a maximum value of 1.00 or that it is accepted 100% (there is only one project of each type available). This upper limit does not create problems under conditions where multiple projects of the same type can be accepted. In such cases, we just define a new decision variable for each time that the project could be accepted.

3   It is assumed that all the input parameters— b_j, C_{jt}, K_t —are known with certainty.

4   The b_j parameter shows the net present value of project j over its useful life, where all cash flows are discounted at the cost of capital, which is known with certainty.

5   The values of C_{jt} in the budget constraints are not discounted back to year 0 since the budget funds available (K_t) are expressed in year t's dollars.

To illustrate the general approach, consider the following classic example.

EXAMPLE 1

Lorie-Savage Nine-Project Problem

The following nine-project, two-period problem was originally considered by Lorie and Savage. Later, it was used by Weingartner to illustrate the use of LP to represent the capital rationing problem:

PROJECT	NPV_j	C_{1j} = CASH OUTFLOW IN PERIOD 1	C_{2j} = CASH OUTFLOW IN PERIOD 2
1	$14	$12	$ 3
2	17	54	7
3	17	6	6
4	15	6	2
5	40	30	35
6	12	6	6
7	14	48	4
8	10	36	3
9	12	18	3

Budget available: $\Sigma C_{1j}X_j \leq \$50$; $\Sigma C_{2j}X_j \leq \$20$

Formulate this problem as an LP problem. In the formulation, define and incorporate a slack variable for each "less than" constraint. Solve the problem using a packaged LP solution algorithm. Finally, interpret the optimal solution for management.

SOLUTION: The LP formulation is as follows:

$$\text{maximize NPV} = 14X_1 + 17X_2 + 17X_3 + 15X_4 + 40X_5$$
$$+ 12X_6 + 14X_7 + 10X_8 + 12X_9$$

subject to

$$12X_1 + 54X_2 + 6X_3 + 6X_4 + 30X_5 + 6X_6 + 48X_7$$
$$+ 36X_8 + 18X_9 + S_1 = 50 \quad \text{budget constraint year 1}$$

$$3X_1 + 7X_2 + 6X_3 + 2X_4 + 35X_5 + 6X_6 + 4X_7$$
$$+ 3X_8 + 3X_9 + S_2 = 20 \quad \text{budget constraint year 2}$$

$$
\left.
\begin{array}{lll}
X_1 + S_3 = 1 & X_4 + S_6 = 1 & X_7 + S_9 = 1 \\[4pt]
X_2 + S_4 = 1 & X_5 + S_7 = 1 & X_8 + S_{10} = 1 \\[4pt]
X_3 + S_5 = 1 & X_6 + S_8 = 1 & X_9 + S_{11} = 1
\end{array}
\right\}
\begin{array}{l}
\text{upper limits on} \\
\text{project acceptance}
\end{array}
$$

$$X_j, S_i \geq 0 \quad i = 1, 2, \ldots, 11; \quad j = 1, 2, \ldots, 9 \quad \text{nonnegativity constraint}$$

The following aspects should be pointed out concerning this formulation.

The general approach taken in this example is similar to that shown in Equations (1)–(4). However, slack variables have been added to each less-than constraint so that a fuller interpretation can be given to the optimal solution. Slack variables S_1 and S_2 represent, respectively, the number of budget dollars in years 1 and 2 that remain unallocated to any of the nine projects under evaluation. Slack variables S_3 through S_{11} represent the percentage of projects 1 through 9, respectively, that are not accepted by the firm—the sum of X_j and its corresponding slack variable S_{j+2} must equal 1.00 or 100% since the entire project must be either accepted or not accepted. The optimal LP solution, obtained from IBM's MPSX package, is shown in Table 19–2.

Interpreting the optimal solution, we see that the basic variables; that is, the variables that are equal to a positive value in the optimal solution, are $X_1, X_3, X_4, X_6, X_7, X_9, S_4, S_7, S_8, S_9, S_{10}$, which are equal to their corresponding values on the right-hand side of the optimal tableau (i.e., $X_1 = 1.0$, $X_3 = 1.0$, $X_4 = 1.0$, $X_6 = 0.969697$, and so on). Any of the variables in the problem that are not listed as basic variables are, in fact, nonbasic variables in the optimal solution, which means that they are equal to zero. Thus, $X_2 = X_5 = X_8 = 0$, which shows that these three projects should be completely rejected; in addition, $S_1 = S_2 = 0$, shows that the entire budget allotment of $50 in year 1 and $20 in year 2 has been spent on the six projects that have been designated for acceptance; further, $S_3 = S_5 = S_6 = S_{11} = 0$, since the projects corresponding to these slack variables (i.e., X_1, X_3, X_4, X_9) have been 100% accepted. To summarize, projects 1, 3, 4, and 9 have been fully accepted; 97% of project 6 is accepted; and only 4.5% of project 7 is accepted. These projects require the use of the entire budget in both years and generate the maximum objective function value of $70.273, which is the net present value of the accepted projects.

The examples that follow interpret the shadow prices in row Z of the optimal tableau, as well as perform sensitivity analysis on the optimal solution.

Of course, it could be asked: Do the partial projects in our LP solution to Example 1 really make sense? The answer is maybe. The preceding LP solution,

Table 19–2 Optimal Tableau for LP Formulation of Lorie-Savage Nine-Project Problem

BASIC VARIABLES	X_1	X_2	X_3	X_4	X_5	X_6	X_7	X_8	X_9	S_1	S_2	S_3	S_4	S_5	S_6	S_7	S_8	S_9	S_{10}	S_{11}	RHS
X_1	1.0																				1.00
X_3			1.0																		1.00
X_4				1.0																	1.00
X_6		0.455			5.91	1.0				−0.015	0.1818	−0.364		−1.0	−0.273					−0.273	0.969697
X_7		1.068			−0.114		1.0	0.75		0.023	−0.023	−0.205			−0.091					−0.341	0.045455
X_9									1.0												1.00
S_4		1.0											1.0								1.00
S_7					1.0											1.0					1.00
S_8		−0.455			−5.91			−0.75		0.015	−0.1818	0.364		1.0	0.273		1.0			0.273	0.030303
S_9		−1.068			0.114			1.0		−0.023	0.023	0.205			0.091			1.0		0.341	0.954545
S_{10}																			1.0		1.00
Z		3.41			29.32			0.50		0.1364	1.864	6.77		5.0	10.45					3.95	70.273

354

which was determined using only tenths of a second of computer time, does provide considerable insight into the nine projects under evaluation. The fully accepted projects (1, 3, 4, and 9) are clearly very attractive to the firm. On the other hand, the partially accepted projects (6 and 7) were the last two to be brought into the firm's portfolio. These partial projects would be feasible only if the firm could find a partner or the other party interested in entering a joint venture to undertake the project in question. Recall that the use of LP to handle the capital rationing problem means that partial projects cannot be excluded from the optimal solution.

The LP formulation of the capital rationing problem is significantly easier to solve than the integer programming formulation (discussed in Chapter 20), wherein no partial projects are allowed. Integer programming problems can take up to 100 times longer to solve on the computer than the equivalent LP formulation. This fact, plus the realization that firms may be considering thousands of projects for possible adoption, definitely makes it advantageous to call upon the LP formulation at least as a first approximation to determine the optimal portfolio of projects.

OTHER CONSTRAINED RESOURCES

Example 1 included as less-than constraints only the budget limitation in 2 years and the upper limit on the acceptance of any project. Linear programming models can incorporate numerous other constraints which show other limited resources, legal requirements, managerial policies, and requirements imposed by the environment. Example 2 illustrates several of these constraints.

EXAMPLE 2
Modified Lorie-Savage Problem

Consider a firm that is evaluating the same nine projects as in Example 1, but with limitations imposed on working capital requirements for all projects ($25) over their useful lives, managerial supervision of the projects (120 hours), and a legal requirement for water purity control. (The firm feels that EPA will not bother it if it achieves at least 10 water purity control points in the projects it accepts.)

PROJECT	NPV_j	C_{1j} = CASH OUTFLOW IN PERIOD 1	C_{2j} = CASH OUTFLOW IN PERIOD 2
1	$14	$12	$ 3
2	17	54	7
3	17	6	6
4	15	6	2
5	40	30	35
6	12	6	6
7	14	48	4
8	10	36	3
9	12	18	3
Budget available:		$\Sigma C_{1j} X_j \leq \$50;$	$\Sigma C_{2j} X_j \leq \$20$

PROJECT	W_j = WORKING CAPITAL REQUIREMENT	M_j = MANAGERIAL SUPERVISION IN HOURS	P_j = WATER PURITY CONTROL IN POINTS
1	$ 5	20	1.2
2	11	80	6.3
3	7	18	2.7
4	4	14	2.2
5	8	88	8.8
6	5	16	2.0
7	12	74	5.7
8	9	60	5.9
9	6	28	3.2
Other constraints:	$\Sigma X_j W_j \leq \$25$;	$\Sigma X_j M_j \leq 120$;	$\Sigma X_j P_j \geq 10$

Formulate and solve this problem as an LP and interpret the optimal solution.
SOLUTION: The formulation is as follows:

$$\text{maximize NPV} = 14X_1 + 17X_2 + 17X_3 + 15X_4 + 40X_5$$
$$+ 12X_6 + 14X_7 + 10X_8 + 12X_9$$

subject to

$$12X_1 + 54X_2 + 6X_3 + 6X_4 + 30X_5 + 6X_6$$
$$+ 48X_7 + 36X_8 + 18X_9 + S_1 = 50 \quad \text{budget year 1}$$
$$3X_1 + 7X_2 + 6X_3 + 2X_4 + 35X_5 + 6X_6$$
$$+ 4X_7 + 3X_8 + 3X_9 + S_2 = 20 \quad \text{budget year 2}$$

$$\left.\begin{array}{lll} X_1 + S_3 = 1 & X_4 + S_6 = 1 & X_7 + S_9 = 1 \\[4pt] X_2 + S_4 = 1 & X_5 + S_7 = 1 & X_8 + S_{10} = 1 \\[4pt] X_3 + S_5 = 1 & X_6 + S_8 = 1 & X_9 + S_{11} = 1 \end{array}\right\} \begin{array}{l} \text{upper limits} \\ \text{on project acceptance} \end{array}$$

$$5X_1 + 11X_2 + 7X_3 + 4X_4 + 8X_5 + 5X_6$$
$$+ 12X_7 + 9X_8 + 6X_9 + S_{12} = 25 \quad \text{working capital}$$
$$20X_1 + 80X_2 + 18X_3 + 14X_4 + 88X_5 + 16X_6$$
$$+ 74X_7 + 60X_8 + 28X_9 + S_{13} = 120 \quad \text{management supervision}$$
$$1.2X_1 + 6.3X_2 + 2.7X_3 + 2.2X_4 + 8.8X_5 + 2.0X_6$$
$$+ 5.7X_7 + 5.9X_8 + 3.2X_9 - R_1 = 10 \quad \text{water purity control}$$

$$X_j, S_i, R_1 \geq 0 \quad j = 1, \ldots, 9; \quad i = 1, 2, \ldots, 13$$

Notice that this formulation is exactly the same as the formulation in Example 1 except for the last three constraints, which show the new limited resources (working capital and management supervision) and a restriction imposed by legal authorities outside the firm (water pollution control). The new slack variables S_{12} and S_{13} show, respectively, the number of unused working capital dollars of the 25 originally available and the number of unallocated hours of management supervision among the 120 hours originally available. There is another new variable (R_1) in the last constraint, which is a "surplus variable," showing the number of water purity control points that accepted projects score above the minimum level of 10 specified by management. The optimal solution to this formulation is shown in Table 19–3.

The optimal solution shows a number of changes resulting from the additional constraints. As can be noticed from the tableau, projects 1, 3, 4, and 9 are fully accepted. Two projects are partially accepted—5 and 6—and are accepted 9.45% and 44.88%, respectively. There are excess budget dollars in year 1 (slack variable S_1) in the amount of $2.472, as well as excess hours of management supervision (slack variable S_{13}) in the amount of 24.5 hours. The accepted projects used the entire budget in year 2 and the entire working capital availability (slack variables S_2 and S_{12} are not among the basic variables and hence are equal to zero), while they generated an excess number of water purity points (1.029) over the minimum level of 10 as shown by the surplus variable R_1 being basic in the optimal solution. The new value of the objective function is $67.165, which is down from $70.273 in Example 1 because the current problem has additional constraints that must be met.

Next, we consider the interpretation of shadow prices.

INTERPRETATION OF SHADOW PRICES

As pointed out in Chapter 18, a complete analysis of the optimal solution is a critically important step in the effective use of linear programming models. This post-optimality analysis consists of interpretation of the shadow prices and the performance of sensitivity analysis. Shadow prices are shown in the optimal LP tableau in the "Z" or last row.

In the LP formulation of the capital rationing problem, there are three sets of shadow prices:

1   The shadow price associated with each of the limited resources in the problem
2   The shadow price associated with each accepted project
3   The shadow price associated with each rejected project

Each of these sets are adjusted in turn.

Shadow Prices for Limited Resources

Each of the constraints for resource limitations or environmental restrictions in the capital rationing problem has a unique slack or surplus variable associated with it. Each of these slack or surplus variables will have a corresponding shadow price in the optimal LP solution.

The following general principles will hold relative to these shadow prices:

1   For all slack or surplus variables that are *basic* in the optimal solution, the corresponding shadow price will be *zero*.

Table 19–3 Optimal Solution to Modified Lorie-Savage Nine-Project Problem

BASIC VARIABLES	X_1	X_2	X_3	X_4	X_5	X_6	X_7	X_8	X_9	S_1	S_2	S_3	S_4	S_5	S_6	S_7	S_8	S_9	S_{10}	S_{11}	S_{12}	S_{13}	R_1	RHS
X_1	1.0																							1.00
X_3			1.0																					1.00
X_4				1.0																				1.00
X_5		−0.244			1.0		−0.409	−0.307			0.0394	0.118		0.0945	0.110					0.165	−0.0472			0.094488
X_6		2.59				1.0	3.055	2.291			−0.063	−1.189		−1.55	−0.976					−1.46	0.276			0.448819
X_9									1.0															1.00
S_1		45.78					41.95	31.46		1.0	−0.803	−8.41		0.472	−3.45					−14.17	−0.236			2.472441
S_4		1.0											1.0											1.00
S_7		0.244					0.409	0.307			−0.0394	−0.118		−0.0945	−0.110	1.0				−0.165	0.0472			0.905512
S_8		−2.59					−3.055	−2.291			0.063	1.189		1.55	0.976		1.0			1.46	−0.276			0.551181
S_9							1.0											1.0						1.00
S_{10}								1.0											1.0					1.00
S_{13}		60.03					61.15	50.36			−2.46	−11.37		−1.496	−8.08					−19.12	−0.252	1.0		24.50394
R_1		−3.27					−3.19	−4.02			0.220	0.139		0.429	1.22					1.73	0.135		1.0	1.029134
Z		4.323					6.283	5.213			0.819	4.46		2.165	7.693					1.039	1.417			67.165

358

2 For all slack or surplus variables that are *nonbasic* in the optimal solution, the corresponding shadow price will be a *positive value.*

There are two meanings associated with the shadow prices for these slack and surplus variables:

1 The shadow price shows the *maximum amount that the firm would be willing to pay*
a. To acquire one additional unit of the resource in question.
b. To relax the restriction on the firm by one unit.

2 The shadow price shows the amount by which the *objective function will increase* if the firm acquires one more unit of the resource in question or relaxes the restriction on the firm by one unit.

An illustration will help to clarify this discussion.

EXAMPLE 3
Interpretation of Resource Shadow Prices

For the optimal solution to Example 2 shown in Table 19–3, interpret the shadow prices for:

1 The four limited resources in the problem—capital budget in years 1 and 2 (S_1 and S_2), working capital funds (S_{12}), and management supervision (S_{13}).

2 The operating restrictions on the minimum number of water purity control points which must be generated by the capital program (R_1).

SOLUTION: The reader will notice slack variables S_1 and S_{13} and surplus variable R_1 are basic variables in the optimal solution, since there are \$2.472 of the first year's capital budget (S_1) still remaining, 24.5 hours of management supervision time (S_{13}) available, and the desired level of 10 water purity control points established by management has been exceeded by 1.029 points (R_1).

Hence, the shadow price for each of these variables is zero, since the firm would be unwilling to purchase any additional units of these resources (first year's capital budget or hours for supervision of projects by management) or to pay anything to reduce the original 10-unit lower limit for the desired level of water purity control points of accepted projects. If any of these corresponding right-hand side values were changed (resources increased or minimum requirements decreased), the objective function would not increase, since the other constraints are binding on the optimal solution. The binding constraints are the ones that would have to be altered. Since the objective function would not increase, the firm would not be willing to pay anything for any of these changes because the end result would only be that more of these resources would be left over in the optimal solution.

On the other hand, variables S_2 and S_{12} are nonbasic variables in the optimal solution, which means that their corresponding resources (budget dollars in year 2 and working capital funds, respectively) are completely exhausted in the optimal solution. The shadow price for S_2 is 0.819, which means that the firm would be willing to pay up to a maximum of 81.9% interest on new capital that could be raised in year 2 (a somewhat significant cost of capital) because the objective function would increase by this amount (0.819) for each dollar of additional budget that could be obtained. Similarly, the shadow price for additional working capital (S_{12}) is \$1.417, which means that the objective function would increase by this amount for each dollar over the original \$25 available.

Part of post-optimality analysis related to shadow price interpretation is the determination of how the optimal solution would change if the firm acquired additional units of some resource. Equation (13) in Chapter 18 shows how the decision maker would determine the new optimal value for each basic variable if additional units of some resource were required. It should be mentioned that the limits determined in sensitivity analysis (covered in the next section) must be observed in the analysis using Equation (13). That is, Equation (13) will only provide correct results if the number of additional units acquired is less than Δ^+ for the slack variable in question.

As additional units of some resource are acquired, the analysis using Equation (13) proceeds by using the a_{ij} values in the column of the optimal tableau of the slack variable for the resource which is being acquired. For example, if the firm in Example 2 were going to acquire additional budget dollars in year 2, the column for slack variable S_2 in Table 19–3 would be used in Equation (13). Looking at the S_2 column in Table 19–3, we see that the only two projects which would be affected if we acquired additional budget dollars in year 2 would be the two partial projects (5 and 6). Let's turn next to Example 4, which verifies the accuracy of the shadow price for S_2 and shows how the optimal solution would change as additional budget dollars in year 2 are acquired.

EXAMPLE 4

Post-optimality Analysis

Using the optimal solution obtained in Example 2, which is shown in Table 19–3,

1   Determine the contributions of projects 5 and 6 to the value of the objective function.
2   If the firm acquired $2 of additional budget in year 2, determine the new percentage accepted of projects 5 and 6, using Equation (13) from Chapter 18, and the new value of the objective function generated by these two projects.
3   Verify the shadow price for slack variable S_2 by dividing the change in the value of the objective function by the number of new year 2 budget dollars acquired.

SOLUTION: 1. Currently, the contribution of these two projects to the objective function is the percentage accepted of each multiplied by the objective function coefficient for the respective project:

	% ACCEPTED		NPV OBJECTIVE FUNCTION COEFFICIENT		CONTRIBUTION TO VALUE OF OBJECTIVE FUNCTION
Project 5	(0.094488)	$\times$	$40	=	$3.77952
Project 6	(0.448819)	$\times$	$12	=	5.385828
					$9.165348

2. and 3. Consider now that we could obtain $2 of additional budget in year 2. The way that we determine the impact that this would have on each basic variable in the optimal

solution is by looking up the column for S_2 in the optimal tableau. Notice that the coefficients in the row for X_5 and X_6 are 0.0394 and -0.063, respectively. This means that additional dollars in year 2 would *increase the percentage purchased of project 5* (by 3.94% for each dollar) and *decrease the percentage of project 6 purchased* (by 6.3% for each dollar). Thus, the new percentage of each project accepted if we had \$2 additional in year 2 would be:

	CURRENT PERCENT ACCEPTED		CHANGE PER DOLLAR		CHANGE IN DOLLARS		NEW PERCENT ACCEPTED		NPV OBJECTIVE FUNCTION COEFFICIENT		CONTRIBUTION TO VALUE OF OBJECTIVE FUNCTION
Project 5	0.094488	+	(0.0394)	×	(+\$2)	=	0.173288	×	\$40	=	\$ 6.93152
Project 6	0.448819	+	(− 0.063)	×	(+\$2)	=	0.322819	×	12	=	3.873828
											\$10.805348
				Less current contribution to value of objective function							9.165348
				Increase in value of objective function							\$1.640000
				Divided by \$ change in year 2							÷ 2
				Increase in objective function value per dollar change						=	\$0.82 ≈ \$0.819 Shadow price

This last step verified that S_2's shadow price was valid. The shadow prices for each of the other resources in Example 2 could be verified in a similar fashion. It should be emphasized again that the analysis requires that the change in the resource not exceed Δ^+ or Δ^- for increases or decreases in the resource, respectively.

Shadow Prices for Accepted and Rejected Projects

In the LP formulation of the capital budgeting problem, *there are shadow prices associated with both accepted and rejected projects. These values enable the decision maker to rank all projects according to their relative attractiveness* (as will be demonstrated in the next example). For *accepted projects*, the shadow prices are found under the *slack variables* (S_k) for the following constraints:

$$X_j + S_k = 1$$

Conceptually, the shadow prices for accepted projects show the amount by which the project's NPV exceeds the implicit cost associated with using the resources which are required to accept the project.

Mathematically, the shadow price for each accepted project can be determined using the following equation:

$$\gamma_j = b_j - \sum_{t=1}^{T} \rho_t^* C_{jt} \tag{5}$$

where γ_j = shadow price associated with accepted project j (shown under the slack variable associated with project j)

b_j = net present value for project j shown in the objective function

ρ_t^* = shadow price in the optimal solution associated with each resource t which is required to accept a project (shown under the slack variable associated with the corresponding resource)

C_{jt} = quantity of resource of type t required by project j (shown in the constraints of the LP formulation)

The shadow prices γ_j usually will give a ranking for the projects which differs from that given by any of the simple models such as payback, NPV, IRR, or the profitability index. Such differences in ranking will exist because the latter models look at the projects independently and without any resource limitations. On the other hand, *the LP shadow prices show interrelationships among projects* as they compete against each other for the firm's limited resources; these shadow prices incorporate the information contained in the project's NPV as well the implicit cost associated with using the firm's limited resources.

In addition to the shadow prices for accepted projects, the optimal LP solution has shadow prices for rejected projects. Conceptually, the shadow price for rejected project j shows the amount by which the implicit cost associated with using the resources required for project j exceeds project j's NPV.

Mathematically, the shadow price for each rejected project is found using the following equation,

$$\mu_j = \sum_{t=1}^{T} \rho_t^* C_{jt} - b_j \tag{6}$$

where μ_j is the shadow price associated with rejected project j (shown in the objective function row in the column for X_j). The μ_j *value shows the amount by which the objective function would decrease if the firm were forced to accept the unattractive project j.* If such projects were accepted, this would mean that the scarce capital budget dollars would be used in a suboptimal way, since the opportunity cost associated with the cash outflows $(\Sigma \rho_t^* C_{jt})$ exceeds the present value of the benefits generated by the project. It should be mentioned that the μ_j values must be zero *for all projects that are accepted (including partially accepted projects) because the benefits of these projects must justify the cash outlays in the various periods of the planning horizon (C_{jt}) when they are evaluated at the implied cost of capital (ρ_{jt}^*) when the budgets each year are used in an optimal way.*

The next example illustrates the computation of these shadow prices and explains their significance.

EXAMPLE 5
Interpreting Project Shadow Prices

For the optimal solution to Example 2 shown in Table 19–3,

1 Determine the rank order of accepted projects.
2 Verify the value of project 1's shadow price using Equation (5).

3 Determine the rank order of rejected projects.

4 Verify the value of project 8's shadow price using Equation (6).

SOLUTION: 1. The rank order of the accepted projects which also shows the order in which projects were accepted into the optimal portfolio is:

$$\text{Project 4:} \quad \gamma_4 = 7.693$$

$$\text{Project 1:} \quad \gamma_1 = 4.46$$

$$\text{Project 3:} \quad \gamma_3 = 2.165$$

$$\text{Project 9:} \quad \gamma_9 = 1.039$$

$$\left.\begin{array}{l}\text{Project 5:} \quad \gamma_5 = 0 \\ \text{Project 6:} \quad \gamma_6 = 0\end{array}\right\} \quad \text{partially accepted or marginal projects}$$

2. The shadow price for project 1 is verified as follows:

$$\gamma_1 = b_1 - \sum_{t=1} \rho_t^* C_{1t}$$

$$= 14 - \left[\underbrace{(0)(12)}_{\substack{\text{NPV}}} + \underbrace{(0.819)(3)}_{\text{budget 1}} + \underbrace{(1.417)(5)}_{\text{budget 2}} + \underbrace{(0)(20)}_{\substack{\text{working}\\\text{capital}}} + \underbrace{(0)(1.2)}_{\substack{\text{management}\\\text{supervision}}} \underbrace{}_{\substack{\text{water purity}\\\text{control}}} \right]$$

$$= 14 - (2.457 + 7.085) = \underline{\underline{4.458}}$$

3. The shadow prices under X_2, X_7, and X_8 (the three rejected projects) show the amount by which the objective function would decrease if we were forced to accept one of these three projects. Thus, these values give a ranking of the rejected projects; the smaller the shadow price, the less objectionable it would be to be forced to accept the project.

PROJECT	SHADOW PRICE
2	$4.323
8	5.213
7	6.283

4. Using Equation (6), we can show how the shadow price for project 8 is verified as follows:

$$\mu_8 = \sum_{t=1}^{T} \rho_t^* C_{8t} - b_8$$

$$= \underbrace{(0)(36)}_{} + \underbrace{(0.819)(3)}_{\text{budget 1}} + \underbrace{(1.417)(9)}_{\text{budget 2}} + \underbrace{}_{\substack{\text{working}\\\text{capital}}} + \underbrace{(0)(60)}_{\substack{\text{management}\\\text{supervision}}} + \underbrace{(0)(5.9)}_{\substack{\text{water purity}\\\text{control}}} - \underbrace{10}_{\text{NPV}}$$

$$= 0 + 2.457 + 12.753 + 0 + 0 - 10 = \underline{\underline{\$5.21}}$$

SENSITIVITY ANALYSIS ON THE OPTIMAL SOLUTION

Throughout the text, we have emphasized the vital importance of carrying out sensitivity analysis to determine the impact of changes in input values on the decisions made by financial managers. In the LP formulation of the capital rationing problem, sensitivity analysis is usually performed on:

1   The original right-hand side values for each resource constraint.

2   The original NPV values for each project shown in the LP objective function.

Sensitivity analysis on the original resource availabilities determines a Δ^+ and Δ^- value as shown in Chapter 18 in Equations (1) through (8). In the capital rationing problem, the Δ^+ value shows the maximum additional amount of each resource which can be acquired and still have the same optimal portfolio of projects. The Δ^- value shows the maximum amount of each resource which the firm can give up and still have the same optimal portfolio of projects. The Δ^+ and Δ^- values specify the range for each resource wherein the procedure illustrated in Example 4 can be used to find the new optimal solution from the present optimal solution. This range also shows the limits for each resource wherein the shadow price for that resource will remain valid. Variations of a resource beyond the range determined by Δ^+ and Δ^- will require that the problem be re-solved completely. Furthermore, beyond the range, the shadow prices for any resource no longer specify a correct value.

For instance, Example 3 mentions that the shadow price for budget dollars in year 2 is 0.819; that is, we are willing to pay a rate of interest of 81.9% to obtain additional budget dollars in year 2. However, we would not be willing to pay this rate indefinitely. In fact, we would only be willing to pay such a high rate until:

1   One of the other resources still available (i.e., budget dollars in year 1, or managerial supervision time) became exhausted because of the acquisition of an additional portion of a partial project enabled by the new budget dollars obtained for year 2.

2   A partially accepted project became completely accepted through the new budget dollars obtained for year 2.

3   A partially accepted project became completely rejected since funds were removed from it as new budget dollars were obtained for year 2.

Notice that the occurrence of any of these conditions would change the basis of the optimal solution or make it infeasible. Thus, the values of Δ^+ and Δ^- for each input parameter will be the smallest of 1, 2, or 3. Sensitivity analysis is now completed in Example 6 by means of the computation of all Δ^+ and Δ^- values for the original resource availabilities.

EXAMPLE 6

Sensitivity Analysis on Resource Availabilities

Compute and interpret all Δ^+ and Δ^- values for the optimal solution shown in Example 2 using the approach outlined in Equations (1) through (8) in Chapter 18.

SOLUTION: We notice that slack variables S_1 and S_{13}, as well as surplus variable R_1, are basic variables in the optimal solution. Hence, using the approach shown in Chapter 18, we find that:

$$\Delta_{S_1}^+ = \infty \qquad \Delta_{S_{13}}^+ = \infty \qquad \Delta_{R_1}^+ = 1.029$$

$$\Delta_{S_1}^- = 2.472 \qquad \Delta_{S_{13}}^- = 24.504 \qquad \Delta_{R_1}^- = \infty$$

The values imply that we would have the same basis in the optimal solution (i.e., the same set of optimal projects will be accepted and the same resources will still be available) as long as each of the following resources takes on values within the respective ranges:

$$\begin{array}{ll} \text{budget} \\ \text{in year 1} \end{array} \left\{ \begin{array}{l} \text{upper limit} = \infty = 50 + \infty \\ \text{lower limit} = \$47.528 = 50 - 2.472 \end{array} \right.$$

$$\begin{array}{ll} \text{management} \\ \text{supervision} \end{array} \left\{ \begin{array}{l} \text{upper limit} = \infty = 120 + \infty \\ \text{lower limit} = 95.496 \text{ hr} = 120 - 24.504 \end{array} \right.$$

$$\begin{array}{ll} \text{water purity} \\ \text{control} \end{array} \left\{ \begin{array}{l} \text{upper limit} = 11.029 = 10 + 1.209 \\ \text{lower limit} = -\infty = 10 - \infty \end{array} \right.$$

The other two slack variables of interest are the nonbasic variables associated with the budget dollars in year 2 (S_2) and working capital (S_{12}). Using the approach shown in Equations (7) and (8) in Chapter 18 to compute Δ^+ and Δ^- for nonbasic variables,

$$\Delta^+ = \min \left| \frac{b_i}{a_{ij} < 0} \right| \qquad \Delta^- = \min \left(\frac{b_i}{a_{ij} > 0} \right)$$

we find

$$\Delta_{S_2}^+ = \min \left(\left| \frac{0.448819}{-0.063} \right|, \left| \frac{2.472441}{-0.803} \right|, \left| \frac{0.905512}{-0.039} \right|, \left| \frac{24.50394}{-2.46} \right| \right)$$

$$= \min(7.124, 3.079, 23.218, 9.96)$$

$$= \underline{\underline{3.079}}$$

It is interesting to note that each of the foregoing ratios has an economic meaning in terms of the capital rationing problem addressed in Example 2. Specifically, the first ratio is related to project 6 which can be observed by looking back at Table 19–3. In the optimal solution, project 6 is accepted 44.8819%. With each additional dollar of budget in year 2 which is acquired by the firm, 6.3% less of project 6 will be accepted (because the coefficient in the X_6 row and the S_2 column is -0.063, as shown in the denominator of the first ratio). Thus, as the firm acquired $7.124 additional budget dollars in year 2 (i.e., the result shown on the second line of the calculation of $\Delta_{S_2}^+$), project 6 would no longer be accepted in the optimal portfolio of assets. Similarly, the second ratio refers to slack variable S_1 which has a value in the optimal solution of $2.472441. Each additional unit of budget in year 2 which is acquired reduces the amount of extra budget dollars in year 1 by $0.803 (this coefficient is shown in the S_2 column and the S_1 row in Table 19–3). Thus, as the firm acquires $3.079 additional budget dollars in year 2, the value of S_1 will go to zero. If the firm tried to acquire more than $3.079 budget dollars in year 2, S_1 would become negative which would violate the nonnegativity constraint in the LP formulation. Each of the other ratios can be interpreted in a similar fashion.

Finally, we would have to select the minimum ratio in determining the value of $\Delta_{S_2}^+$ because the minimum ratio indicates the first variable which would violate a constraint in the LP formulation.

We now continue the calculations for the remaining Δ^+ and Δ^- values. Each of the ratios and the final results can be interpreted in a similar manner as $\Delta_{S_2}^+$. We find:

$$\Delta_{S_2}^- = \min\left(\frac{0.094488}{0.0394}, \frac{0.551181}{0.063}, \frac{1.029134}{0.220} \right)$$

$$= \min(2.398, 8.749, 4.678)$$

$$= \underline{\underline{2.398}}$$

$$\Delta_{S_{12}}^+ = \min\left(\left| \frac{0.094488}{-0.0472} \right|, \left| \frac{2.472441}{-0.236} \right|, \left| \frac{0.551181}{-0.276} \right|, \left| \frac{24.50394}{-0.252} \right| \right)$$

$$= \underline{\underline{1.997}}$$

$$\Delta_{S_{12}}^- = \min\left(\frac{0.448819}{0.276}, \frac{0.905512}{0.047}, \frac{1.029134}{0.135} \right)$$

$$= \underline{\underline{1.626}}$$

Thus, the ranges wherein the optimal basis will remain unchanged are

$$\text{budget in} \left\{ \begin{array}{l} \text{upper limit} = \$23.079 = \$20 + 3.079 \\ \text{lower limit} = \$17.602 = \$20 - 2.398 \end{array} \right.$$
$$\text{year 2}$$

$$\text{working} \left\{ \begin{array}{l} \text{upper limit} = \$26.997 = \$25 + 1.997 \\ \text{lower limit} = \$23.374 = \$25 - 1.626 \end{array} \right.$$
$$\text{capital}$$

Again, the ranges show the possible changes wherein the shadow prices would remain valid. For example, we would only be willing to pay the interest cost of 81.9% for additional budget dollars in year 2 until we acquired $3.079. Beyond that level, the problem would have to be completely re-solved, because we would get a new optimal set of projects. A similar interpretation can be put on each of the other shadow prices and ranges.

The final area of sensitivity analysis is performed on the NPV values for each project shown in the LP objective function. This sensitivity analysis determines Δ^+ and Δ^- values as introduced in Chapter 18 in Equations (9) through (12). In the capital rationing problem, the Δ^+ value shows the amount by which a rejected or partially accepted project's NPV would have to increase before the project would be fully accepted into the firm's optimal portfolio of projects. Conversely, the Δ^- value shows the amount by which a fully accepted project's NPV could decrease before the project was in jeopardy of no longer being in the firm's optimal portfolio of projects.

Of course, the firm must be more concerned about projects which have small Δ^- values either in an absolute sense or relative to their original NPV values. Such projects require greater attention by management because of the possibility that these projects should be excluded from the optimal portfolio if actual cash flows drop even nominally from the forecasted values.

The next example illustrates the calculation of Δ^+ and Δ^- values and also discusses the implications of the results for financial managers.

EXAMPLE 7

Sensitivity Analysis on NPV Values

Compute and interpret all Δ^+ and Δ^- values for the project NPVs based on the optimal solution in Example 2 using the methodology outlined in Equations (9) through (12) in Chapter 18.

SOLUTION: We begin by determining the Δ^+ and Δ^- values for the rejected projects (i.e., nonbasic projects in the optimal solution shown in Table 19–3) using Equations (9) and (10) in Chapter 18:

$$\Delta^+_{X_2} = 4.323 \qquad \Delta^+_{X_7} = 6.283 \qquad \Delta^+_{X_8} = 5.213$$

$$\Delta^-_{X_2} = \infty \qquad \Delta^-_{X_7} = \infty \qquad \Delta^-_{X_8} = \infty$$

These values show that if the objective function coefficient for any rejected project were reduced by any amount, the project would still be rejected. Further, the objective function coefficients would have to be increased by the amount of their shadow prices to make the rejected projects start to become attractive.

For any of the completely accepted projects (i.e., $X_j = 1.00$), the value for Δ^+ and Δ^- are determined in a straightforward manner:

	X_1	X_3	X_4	X_9
$\Delta^+_{X_j}$	∞	∞	∞	∞
$\Delta^-_{X_j}$	4.46	2.165	7.693	1.039
NPV_j	14	17	15	12

This table shows that the objective function coefficient for any completely accepted project j could be increased by any amount or decreased up to the value of the shadow price γ_j and the project would still be attractive enough to accept.

It should be noted that project 9 has the smallest Δ^- value both in absolute amount and as a percentage of the original NPV. Project 9's NPV would have to decline by only $1.039 or 8.67% of its original amount before it would no longer be fully accepted. Project 3 has the second smallest Δ^- value of $2.165 or 12.74% of the original NPV value. Both these projects warrant monitoring by management in terms of how accurate the original cash flow estimates are.

Turning finally to the two partial projects, we apply Equations (11) and (12) in Chapter 18:

$$\Delta^+ = \min\left|\frac{C_j}{a_{ij} < 0}\right|$$

$$\Delta^- = \min\left(\frac{C_j}{a_{ij} > 0}\right)$$

$$\Delta^+_{X_5} = \min\left(\left|\frac{4.323}{-0.244}\right|, \left|\frac{6.283}{-0.409}\right|, \left|\frac{5.213}{-0.307}\right|, \left|\frac{1.417}{-0.0472}\right|\right)$$

$$= \min(17.717, 15.362, 16.980, 30.02)$$

$$= \underline{\underline{15.362}}$$

$$\Delta^-_{X_5} = \min\left(\frac{0.819}{0.0394}, \frac{4.46}{0.118}, \frac{2.165}{0.0945}, \frac{7.693}{0.110}, \frac{1.039}{0.165}\right)$$

$$= \min(20.787, 37.797, 22.91, 69.936, 6.297)$$

$$= \underline{\underline{6.297}}$$

$$\Delta^+_{X_6} = \min\left(\left|\frac{0.819}{-0.063}\right|, \left|\frac{4.46}{-1.189}\right|, \left|\frac{2.165}{-1.55}\right|, \left|\frac{7.693}{-0.976}\right|, \left|\frac{1.039}{-1.46}\right|\right)$$

$$= \min(13.000, 3.751, 1.397, 7.882, 0.712)$$

$$= \underline{\underline{0.712}}$$

$$\Delta^-_{X_6} = \min\left(\frac{4.323}{2.59}, \frac{6.283}{3.055}, \frac{5.213}{2.291}, \frac{1.417}{0.276}\right)$$

$$= \min(1.669, 2.057, 2.275, 5.134)$$

$$= \underline{\underline{1.669}}$$

Thus, as can be seen from the Δ^- values, project 6 is much more vulnerable to elimination from the optimal portfolio due to declines in cash flows or NPV than is project 5. Again, management should review the cash flow estimates for project 6 to make sure they are based on sound assumptions because relatively minor decreases could render project 6 unattractive even as a partial project.

In concluding this section on sensitivity analysis, it should be stressed that the Δ^+ and Δ^- values for the objective function coefficients are critically important in that these coefficients may have significant biases because of the assumptions of LP and the capital budgeting problem setting. That is, the objective function coefficients are calculated by discounting both cash inflows and outflows that are assumed to be known with certainty, where the discounting is done at a rate that is also assumed to be known with certainty. Thus, even small percentage changes in these inputs can cause large changes in the objective function coefficients, which could easily throw them outside the range wherein the optimal set of projects would remain unaffected. These facts have noteworthy managerial implications for accuracy in forecasting cash flows, accuracy in estimating future costs of capital, optimal project selection, and managerial control activities.

THE DUAL LP FORMULATION
FOR THE CAPITAL BUDGETING PROBLEM

As discussed in Chapter 18, the dual LP formulation has important implications for the financial manager. Namely, the dual formulation and its optimal solution provide valuable information for both planning and control functions in the capital budgeting decision process; the solution contributes to both coordination of activities and motivation of decision makers in decentralized organizations.

The dual formulation of the capital budgeting problem is constructed in the same manner, as discussed in Chapter 18. That is, there will be a dual decision variable associated with each constraint in the primal problem, and there will be a constraint equation associated with each project in the primal problem. Further, these dual variables will be found in exactly the way that the shadow prices in the primal problem were computed (as illustrated in the previous section).

The general dual formulation that corresponds to the primal formulation in Equations (1) through (4) is

$$\text{minimize} \sum_{t=1}^{T} \rho_t K_t + \sum_{j=1}^{N} \gamma_j \tag{7}$$

subject to

$$\sum_{t=1}^{T} \rho_t C_{jt} + \gamma_j \geq b_j \quad j = 1, 2, \dots, N \tag{8}$$

$$\rho_t, \gamma_j \geq 0 \quad t = 1, 2, \dots, T; \; j = 1, 2, \dots, N \tag{9}$$

where ρ_t = dual decision variable which represents the cost associated with each resource of type t

γ_j = dual decision variable associated with project j which shows the excess of its net present value (b_j) over its required use of resources (C_{jt}) when the latter are "costed out" at the appropriate rate ρ_t for each resource t

It should be noted that constraint Equation (8) is used in rearranged fashion to compute the values of the shadow prices γ_j and μ_j in the optimal primal solution as shown by Equations (5) and (6). Of course, this is another illustration of our discussion in Chapter 18 concerning the close relationship between the primal and dual LP problems and their optimal solutions.

It is only necessary to solve *either* the primal or the dual problem because the optimal solution for either contains all the information that is in the other. The only difference is the economic interpretation that is given the optimal values of the variables. The correspondence is interesting and helpful in arriving at a complete interpretation and can lend assistance in solving problems more efficiently.

PROGRAMMING AND THE COST OF CAPITAL: A CONTROVERSY

Before we leave the area of linear programming to look at two interesting and powerful extensions (integer programming and goal programming), a noteworthy controversy relative to the appropriate LP formulation should be mentioned. Weingartner's pioneering work,[4] which saw him formulate the primal and the dual LP capital budgeting problem along the lines that we have illustrated, was not without its detractors. Baumol and Quandt[5] contend that the primal problem as formulated by Weingartner runs afoul due to the "Hirshleifer paradox."[6] A simple statement of the paradox is: Under capital rationing, *the appropriate discount* rate to use in determining the net present values of projects under consideration cannot be determined until the optimal set of projects is determined, so that the size of the capital budget is ascertained as well as the sources of the subsequent financing and hence the cost of capital (or the appropriate discount rate to use in calculating NPVs). However, we contend that this is *not* a paradox at all, but rather a simultaneous problem wherein the firm should concurrently determine, through an iterative mathematical programming process, *both the optimal set of capital projects and the optimal financing package, using its associated marginal cost of capital in the discounting process.*

Nevertheless, Baumol and Quandt suggest a formulation that maximizes the utility of the dollars withdrawn from the firm by the owners for their consumption over the planning horizon. Weingartner[7] counters that this is not an operational approach; it assumes that all shareholders have the same linear utility preferences for consumption, it requires the assignment of utility values in advance of information about withdrawal possibilities, and it makes the period-by-period utilities independent of one another. He then proposes a more operational model, which maximizes the

[4] Weingartner, *Mathematical Programming*.

[5] W. J. Baumol and R. E. Quandt. "Investment and Discount Rates Under Capital Rationing—A Programming Approach." *The Economic Journal* (June 1965), 317–329.

[6] J. Hirshleifer, "On the Theory of Optimal Investment Decisions," *The Journal of Political Economy* (August 1958), 329–352.

[7] H. Martin Weingartner, "Criteria for Programming Investment Project Selection," *Journal of Industrial Economics* (November 1966), 65–76.

dividends to be paid in a terminal year, where throughout the planning horizon dividends are nondecreasing and can be required to achieve a specified annual growth rate. Over the past decade, several other authors have jumped into the controversy, each suggesting his own reformulation. The interested reader should consult the appropriate references at the end of the chapter.

SUMMARY

This chapter examines the application of linear programming to the capital rationing problem. The optimal solution indicates the portfolio of projects that maximizes NPV. In addition, the optimal tableau provides valuable information for financial managers in the form of shadow prices and for the performance of sensitivity analysis. Currently, LP is becoming more and more widely used in capital budgeting applications even by medium-sized and small firms. The increasing availability of LP software packages and minicomputers or microcomputers should bring about even greater use of the powerful LP model in capital investment decisions.

The following chapter examines two extensions of LP—integer programming and goal programming. These models enable direct incorporation of additional practical considerations of the capital rationing problem.

QUESTIONS
PROBLEMS

1. The LP Company is considering the adoption of 10 projects that require varied budget commitments over the next 3 years. In addition, the projects have different work forces, managerial supervision, and machine-hour requirements. The table shows the relevant data:

		WORK FORCE	MANAGEMENT	MACHINE	BUDGET		
PROJECTS	NPV	REQUIREMENTS	SUPERVISION	HOURS	YEAR 1	YEAR 2	YEAR 3
X_1	$10	5	1	50	$2	$1	$3
X_2	20	2	1	20	3	2	4
X_3	35	20	1	10	5	4	2
X_4	45	25	3	30	1	3	2
X_5	60	10	1	15	6	2	5
X_6	75	7	2	16	3	1	2
X_7	15	12	1	18	4	5	1
X_8	50	15	1	22	5	3	3
X_9	90	30	4	35	7	4	2
X_{10}	55	3	1	45	2	1	1
Constraints:		$K_1 \leq 70$	$K_2 \leq 8$	$K_3 \leq 150$	$K_4 \leq 20$	$K_5 \leq 15$	$K_6 \leq 20$

Formulate this as an LP problem and solve it using the simplex method or a packaged LP algorithm.

2. The Hyperspace Company is evaluating 12 projects which have cash outflow requirements and NPVs as shown in the following table:

PROJECTS	NPV	CASH OUTFLOWS		
		YEAR 1	YEAR 2	YEAR 3
X_1	$19.31	$100	$ 0	$ 0
X_2	52.68	100	0	0
X_3	43.21	100	0	0
X_4	32.29	100	0	0
X_5	57.50	100	60	60
X_6	112.82	200	0	0
X_7	7.30	150	0	0
X_8	13.71	100	0	0
X_9	47.90	150	75	75
X_{10}	57.35	50	100	175
X_{11}	204.06	100	150	100
X_{12}	18.26	0	100	0

Constraints: $K_1 \leq 1000$ $K_2 \leq 400$ $K_3 \leq 300$

Formulate this as an LP problem to maximize NPV and solve it using the simplex method or a packaged LP algorithm.

3. Formulate the Hyperspace Company problem (Problem 2) as an LP to maximize the present value of the cash inflows and solve it using the simplex method or a packaged LP algorithm. Hyperspace's cost of capital is 6%.

4. For the optimal solution to Problem 1,
   (a) Completely interpret the optimal solution by enumerating projects to be accepted and rejected, ranking all projects, and computing the shadow prices.
   (b) Perform a complete sensitivity analysis.

5. For the optimal solution to Problem 2,
   (a) Completely interpret the optimal solution by enumerating projects to be accepted and rejected, ranking all projects, and computing the shadow prices for budget constraints.
   (b) Is the ranking the accepted projects the same as a simple ranking of the projects by their NPVs? If these rankings differ, why do they, and computing which ranking is more relevant?
   (c) Perform a complete sensitivity analysis.

6. The optimal solution to Problem 3 is shown on the following pages. For this optimal solution,
   (a) Completely interpret the optimal solution by enumerating projects to be accepted and rejected, ranking all projects, and computing the shadow prices for budget constraints. [*Caution*: Be careful in interpreting the shadow prices.]
   (b) Is the ranking of the accepted projects the same as a simple ranking by their present value of cash inflows or by their NVPs? If these rankings differ, why do they, and which ranking is more relevant to the Hyperspace Company?
   (c) Perform a complete sensitivity analysis.

Optimal Solution for Problem 3

Basic Variables	X1	X2	X3	X4	X5	X6	X7	X8	X9	X10	X11	X12	S1	S2	S3	S4	S5	S6	S7	S8	S9	S10	S11	S12	S13	S14	S15	RHS
X_1	1.0																											1.0000
X_2		1.0																										1.0000
X_3			1.0																									1.0000
X_4				1.0																								1.0000
X_6						1.0																						1.0000
X_7							1.0		0.857				0.0067		−0.0019	−0.667	−0.667	−0.667	−0.667	−0.552	−1.33		−0.667			−0.476		0.4000
X_8								1.0	0.429						0.0057					−0.343						−0.571		1.0000
X_{10}										1.0													1.0					0.8000
X_{11}											1.0															1.0		1.0000
X_{12}												1.0																1.0000
X_5					1.0																							10.0000
S_2									32.14				−0.0067	1.0	−0.571					−25.71						−92.86	−100.	0.6000
S_{10}									−0.857						0.0019	0.667	0.667	0.667	0.667	0.552	1.33	1.0	0.667			0.476		1.0000
S_{12}																								1.0				1.0000
S_{13}									−0.429						−0.0057					0.343					1.0	0.571		0.2000
Objective function									92.625				1.0467		1.7467	14.44	47.81	38.34	27.42	58.35	103.09		8.843			255.38	112.56	2237.71

REFERENCES

Bhaskar, Krish. "Linear Programming and Capital Budgeting: The Financing Problem." *Journal of Business Finance and Accounting* (Summer 1978).

Bradley, Stephen, and Sherwood C. Frey, Jr. "Equivalent Mathematical Programming Models of Pure Capital Rationing." *Journal of Financial and Quantitative Analysis*, 13 (June 1978), 345–361.

Carleton, W. T. "Linear Programming and Capital Budgeting Models: A New Interpretation." *Journal of Finance* (December 1969), 825–833.

Chen, Son-Nan, and William T. Moore. "Multi-Period Asset Pricing: The Effects of Uncertain Inflation." *Financial Review* (May 1984).

Dantzig, G. B. *Linear Programming and Extensions*. Princeton, N.J.: Princeton University Press, 1963.

Dorfman, R., P. A. Samuelson, and R. M. Solow. *Linear Programming and Economic Analysis*. New York: McGraw-Hill Book Company, 1958.

Freeland, J. R., and M. J. Rosenblatt. "An Analysis of Linear Programming Formulations for the Capital Rationing Problem." *Engineering Economist* (Fall 1978).

Gale, D. *The Theory of Linear Economic Models*. New York: McGraw-Hill Book Company, 1960.

Gass, S. I. *Linear Programming: Methods and Applications*, 3rd ed. New York: McGraw-Hill Book Company, 1969.

Kuhn, H. W., and A. W. Tucker, eds. *Linear Inequalities and Related Systems*. Princeton, N.J.: Princeton University Press, 1956.

Lusztig, P., and B. Schwab. "A Note on the Application of Linear Programming to Capital Budgeting." *Journal of Financial and Quantitative Analysis*, 3 (December 1968), 427–431.

McClain, J. O. "Linear Programming Is a Shrinking Watermelon and Optimality Is a Black Hole." *Interfaces*, 10 (June 1980), 106–107.

Orchard-Hays, W. *Advanced Linear-Programming Computing Techniques*. New York: McGraw-Hill Book Company, 1968.

Perold, Andre F. "Large-Scale Portfolio Optimization." *Management Science* (October 1984).

Rychel, Dwight F. "Capital Budgeting with Mixed Integer Linear Programming: An Application." *Financial Management*, 6 (Winter 1977), 11–19.

Zionts, S. *Linear and Integer Programming*. Englewood Cliffs, N.J.: Prentice-Hall, 1974.

Multiperiod Analysis Under Conditions of Certainty: Integer and Goal Programming

20

The previous chapter examined the use of LP (linear programming) to represent the capital budgeting problem under capital rationing. This chapter presents two powerful extensions of LP that provide financial managers with additional flexibility in handling the complexities often encountered in practice. Specifically, this chapter explores the use of integer programming (IP) and goal programming (GP) to determine optimal portfolios of capital projects.

Parallel to the development in the previous chapter, the present chapter guides the reader through the major stages in using IP and GP models for the capital rationing problem:

Stage 1 Formulate the problem in the correct format by specifying the input parameters, the decision variables, the objective function, and all relevant constraint equations (including goal constraints in GP).

Stage 2 Solve the problem by using a computer software package appropriate for the model under study.

Stage 3 Completely interpret the economic meaning of the optimal solution for management so that effective financial decision making is facilitated.

Stage 4 Perform a complete sensitivity analysis on the optimal solution so that additional insights can be provided to management.

All four stages are vitally important in order to capitalize on the capabilities of the IP and GP models to the fullest extent. The advances in computer technology should enable more widespread use of the powerful and flexible models examined in this chapter. However, careful financial analysis, correct model formulation and interpretation, and overall informed use of the models are necessary to help prevent meaningless results.

INTEGER PROGRAMMING APPLIED
TO THE CAPITAL BUDGETING PROBLEM

In his pioneering work *Mathematical Programming and the Analysis of Capital Budgeting Problems*, Weingartner suggested an integer programming approach to the capital budgeting problem in addition to the LP models discussed in Chapter 19. The main reasons for the use of IP in the capital budgeting setting are as follows:

1 Difficulties imposed by the acceptance of partial projects in LP are eliminated, since IP requires that projects be either completely accepted or rejected.

2 All the project interdependencies discussed in Chapter 7 can be formally included in the constraints of the IP, while the same is not true for LP due to the possibility of accepting partial projects.

The general IP formulation for the capital budgeting problem is:

$$\text{maximize NPV} = \sum_{j=1}^{N} b_j X_j \tag{1}$$

subject to

$$\sum_{j=1}^{N} C_{jt} X_j \le K_t \qquad t = 1, 2, \ldots, T \tag{2}$$

$$X_j = \{0, 1\} \qquad j = 1, 2, \ldots, N \tag{3}$$

Notice that the only change in the formulation compared with the primal LP formulation shown in Equations (1) through (4) in Chapter 19 is that Equation (3), which is the zero-one condition of IP, guarantees that each project is completely accepted ($X_j = 1$) or that it is rejected ($X_j = 0$).

The second attractive feature of IP mentioned deserves elaboration. In using the simple capital budgeting models (NPV, IRR, PI), it is assumed that all the investment projects are independent (i.e., that project cash flows are not related to each other and do not influence or change one another if various projects are accepted). In using IP, virtually any project dependencies can be incorporated into the model by means of the special constraints discussed next.

Project Interrelationships

The three types of project dependencies defined in Chapter 7—mutually exclusive, prerequisite, and complementary projects—can be handled in a straightforward manner. Each will be discussed in turn.

Recall that *mutually exclusive* projects are defined as a set of projects wherein the acceptance of one project in the set precludes the simultaneous acceptance of any other project in the set. The existence of such a set of projects is incorporated in an IP model by the following constraint,

$$\sum_{j \in J} X_j \le 1 \tag{4}$$

where J = set of mutually exclusive projects under consideration
    $j \in J$ = project j is an element of the set of mutually exclusive projects J

Note that the constraint states that *at most* one project from set J can be accepted; this means that the firm can choose not to accept any project from set J. On the other hand, if it is necessary to select one project from the set, constraint (4) would appear as a strict equality:

$$\sum_{j \in J} X_j = 1 \tag{5}$$

Another important application of this constraint is the situation wherein a firm is considering the possibility of delaying a project for one or more years. For example, consider project X, which has the following characteristics:

TIME	CASH FLOWS PROJECT X
0	− $100
1	+ 75
2	+ 75
3	+ 75

The NPV of this project at 10% is $86.51. If the firm wants to determine whether it is desirable to delay project X either 1 or 2 years, the following two new projects, X′ and X″, respectively, can be defined:

TIME	CASH FLOWS PROJECT X′	PROJECT X″
0	$ 0	$ 0
1	− 100	0
2	+ 75	− 100
3	+ 75	+ 75
4	+ 75	+ 75
5		+ 75

The NPVs (with a cost of capital of 10%) that would be included in the objective function for projects X′ and X″, respectively, are $78.66 and $71.50. These values differ from the NPV of project X because of the 1- and 2-year delays in the cash flows, which necessitate multiplying project X's NPV by $1/1.10$ to arrive at the NPV for X′ and by $1/(1.10)^2$ to arrive at the NPV for X″. Of course, the $100 cash outflow would be shown in the budget constraint for year 0 for project X, year 1 for project X′, and year 2 for project X″. Finally, to show that at most one of these three versions of project X can be accepted, the following constraint is included in the IP formulation:

$$X + X' + X'' \leq 1$$

Prerequisite (or contingent) projects are two or more projects wherein the acceptance of one project necessitates the prior acceptance of some other project(s). For example, if project A cannot be accepted unless project Z is accepted, we would say that project Z is a prerequisite project for acceptance of project A; alternatively, we could also say that acceptance of project A is contingent upon the acceptance of project Z. Again, the representation of this contingency relationship in IP is immediate,

$$X_A \leq X_Z \tag{6}$$

where X_A and X_Z are decision variables denoting projects A and Z. Note in Equation

(6) that if project A is accepted (i.e., $X_A = 1$), then, necessarily, project Z must be accepted. However, project Z may be accepted on its own and project A rejected. Of course, there are many possible variations to constraints (4), (5), and (6), as shown in Example 1.

EXAMPLE 1

Project Interrelationship Constraints in IP

Formulate the appropriate IP constraints for each of the following cases:

(a) Two projects (6 and 8) are mutually exclusive and a third project (16) is contingent upon the acceptance of *either* project 6 or 8.

(b) Project 10 cannot be accepted unless both project 7 and project 9 are accepted.

(c) In the set of projects 1, 2, 3, 4, and 5, at most three can be accepted; furthermore, for project 11 to be accepted, at least two projects from the foregoing set must be accepted, and for project 14 to be accepted, three projects from the foregoing set must be undertaken.

SOLUTION: (a) Two constraints are required to capture the conditions specified, one for the mutually exclusive relationship between projects 6 and 8 and the second for the contingency relationship between 16 and projects 6 and 8:

$$X_6 + X_8 \leq 1$$
$$X_{16} \leq X_6 + X_8$$

(b) Only one constraint similar to Equation (6) is required to express this contingency:

$$2X_{10} \leq X_7 + X_9$$

We see that the only way project 10 can be accepted is for the constraint to hold as an equality. This means that both sides will equal 2, which necessitates the acceptance of both $X_7 + X_9$.

(c) Three constraints are necessary to relate these conditions: one for the acceptance of at most three projects from the first set and one each for the contingency between projects 11 and 14 and the first set:

$$X_1 + X_2 + X_3 + X_4 + X_5 \leq 3$$
$$2X_{11} \leq X_1 + X_2 + X_3 + X_4 + X_5$$
$$3X_{14} \leq X_1 + X_2 + X_3 + X_4 + X_5$$

The final type of project interrelationship is that of *complementary projects*, wherein the acceptance of one project enhances the cash flows of one or more other projects. This synergistic effect is reflected in an IP formulation by using the strategy outlined next.

Step 1 Define a new decision variable which represents the acceptance of the complementary project.

Step 2 Incorporate the new decision variable for the complementary project into the objective function and all relevant constraints. The coefficients for the new decision variable in the objective function and the constraints will be determined by the facts of the situation at hand (i.e., the magnitude of the cost savings and other benefits associated with the acceptance of the combined project).

Step 3 Write a constraint similar to Equation (4) for mutually exclusive projects that precludes the acceptance of either or both of the individual projects and the complementary project.

A brief illustration will be helpful. Consider that we have two complementary projects, 7 and 8. Either of these projects may be accepted in isolation. However, if both are accepted simultaneously,

(a) The cost will be reduced by, say, 10%.

(b) The net cash inflow will be increased by, for example, 15%.

To handle the problem, a new project (call it 78) would be constructed having a cost equal to 90% of the cost of project 7 plus project 8 and net cash inflows equal to 115% of those of project 7 plus project 8. In addition, we would need the following constraint to preclude acceptance of both projects 7 and 8 as well as 78, because the latter is the composite project consisting of the two former projects:

$$X_7 + X_8 + X_{78} \leq 1$$

It should be mentioned that with complementary projects we have a more strict definition for the single projects which make up the complementary set. Namely, in the foregoing example, X_7 will equal zero if project 7 by itself is rejected; X_7 will equal one if project 7 is accepted by itself and project 8 is rejected. The decision variable X_8 is given a comparable interpretation. The decision variable X_{78} will equal one if the joint project 7 and 8 is accepted; if $X_{78} = 1$, then $X_7 = X_8 = 0$. The decision variable X_{78} will equal zero if the joint project 7 and 8 is rejected, in which case X_7 or X_8 (but not both) could equal one or both X_7 and X_8 could equal zero.

To conclude this section, we turn to a comprehensive example of the flexibility of IP in representing the capital budgeting problem.

EXAMPLE 2
Complete IP Formulation

Consider the following 15 projects:

	CASH OUTFLOWS			
PROJECT	C_{1j}	C_{2j}	C_{3j}	NPV
1	$40	$80	$ 0	$24
2	50	65	5	38
3	45	55	10	40
4	60	48	8	44
5	68	42	0	20
6	75	52	20	64
7	38	90	14	27
8	24	40	70	48
9	12	66	20	18
10	6	88	17	29
11	0	72	60	32
12	0	50	80	38
13	0	34	56	25
14	0	22	76	18
15	0	12	104	28

Budget constraints: $\Sigma C_{1j}X_j \leq \$300;$

$\Sigma C_{2j}X_j \leq \$540;$

$\Sigma C_{3j}X_j \leq \$380$

The following project interrelationships exist:

1 Of the set of projects 3, 4, and 8, at most two can be accepted.
2 Projects 5 and 9 are mutually exclusive, but one of the two must be accepted.
3 Project 6 cannot be accepted unless both projects 1 and 14 are accepted.
4 Project 1 can be delayed 1 year—the same cash outflows will be required, but the NPV will drop to $22.
5 Projects 2 and 3 and projects 10 and 13 can be combined into complementary or composite projects wherein total cash outflows will be reduced by 10% and NPV increased by 12% compared with the total of the separate projects.
6 At least one of the two composite projects above must be accepted.

Required:
(a) Define the new decision variables needed for the problem.
(b) Formulate the problem as an IP.

SOLUTION: (a) The new decision variables required in addition to X_1 through X_{15} for the original 15 projects are as follows:

X_{16} is a decision variable to denote the delay of project 1 for 1 year

X_{17} is a decision variable to denote the acceptance of the composite of projects 2 and 3

X_{18} is a decision variable to denote the acceptance of the composite of projects 10 and 13

(b) The IP formulation for this problem is as follows:

$$\text{maximize NPV} = 24X_1 + 38X_2 + 40X_3 + 44X_4 + 20X_5$$
$$+ 64X_6 + 27X_7 + 48X_8 + 18X_9 + 29X_{10}$$
$$+ 32X_{11} + 38X_{12} + 25X_{13} + 18X_{14} + 28X_{15}$$
$$+ 22X_{16} + 87.36X_{17} + 60.48X_{18} \qquad \text{(a)}$$

subject to

$$40X_1 + 50X_2 + 45X_3 + 60_4 + 68X_5$$
$$+ 75X_6 + 38X_7 + 24X_8 + 12X_9 + 6X_{10}$$
$$+ 85.5X_{17} + 5.4X_{18} \qquad \leq 300 \qquad \text{(b)}$$

$$80X_1 + 65X_2 + 55X_3 + 48X_4 + 42X_5$$
$$+ 52X_6 + 90X_7 + 40X_8 + 66X_9 + 88X_{10}$$
$$+ 72X_{11} + 50X_{12} + 34X_{13} + 22X_{14} + 12X_{15}$$
$$+ 40X_{16} + 108X_{17} + 109.8X_{18} \qquad \leq 540 \qquad \text{(c)}$$

$$5X_2 + 10X_3 + 8X_4 + 20X_6 + 14X_7$$
$$+ 70X_8 + 20X_9 + 17X_{10} + 60X_{11} + 80X_{12}$$
$$+ 56X_{13} + 76X_{14} + 104X_{15} + 80X_{16} + 13.5X_{17}$$
$$+ 65.7X_{18} \qquad \leq 380 \qquad \text{(d)}$$

$$X_3 + X_4 + X_8 \leq 2 \tag{e}$$

$$X_5 + X_9 = 1 \tag{f}$$

$$\left.\begin{array}{l} 2X_6 \leq X_1 + X_{14} \\ 2X_6 \leq X_{16} + X_{14} \end{array}\right\} \begin{array}{l} \text{either constraint (g) or} \\ \text{(h) must be satisfied} \end{array} \quad \begin{array}{l} \text{(g)} \\ \text{(h)} \end{array}$$

$$X_1 + X_{16} \leq 1 \tag{i}$$

$$X_2 + X_3 + X_{17} \leq 1 \tag{j}$$

$$X_{10} + X_{13} + X_{18} \leq 1 \tag{k}$$

$$X_{17} + X_{18} \geq 1 \tag{l}$$

$$X_i = \{0, 1\} \quad i = 1, 2, \ldots, 18 \tag{m}$$

A few comments should be made concerning this formulation. In expression (a), the objective function, the coefficients for X_1 through X_{16} were given in the problem description, the coefficient for X_{17} equals 1.12 times (38 + 40), or 87.36, to show the 12% increase in NPV over the benefits generated by projects 2 and 3 separately. The coefficient for X_{18} is arrived at in a similar fashion. Equations (b), (c), and (d) are the budget constraints for years 1, 2, and 3, respectively. The coefficients for projects 1 through 15 are straightforward; the coefficients for X_{16} are those of X_1 delayed by 1 year; for X_{17} and X_{18} the coefficients are 90% of the sum of the coefficients for the respective pairs of projects.

Equation (e) shows that no more than two of projects 3, 4, and 8 can be accepted. Equation (f) shows that either project 5 or project 9 must be accepted but that both cannot be accepted, because they are mutually exclusive; the strict equality sign conveys that one of the two must be accepted (i.e., either $X_5 = 1$ or $X_9 = .1$). Equations (g) and (h) show that for project 6 to be accepted, *either* project 1 and project 14 must be accepted [Equation (g)] or project 1 delayed by 1 year (i.e., project 16) and project 14 must be accepted [Equation (h)]; it is assumed here that project 1 delayed by 1 year still satisfies the requirement that both project 1 and project 14 are accepted. Notice also that even if one of these combinations of projects 1 and 14 is accepted, project 6 can either be accepted or rejected because of the $\leq$ inequality. Further, if desired, equations (g) and (h) can be combined to arrive at a single constraint which must be satisfied: $2X_6 \leq X_1 + X_{14} + X_{16}$.

Equation (i) shows that *only one* of the two projects 1 or 16 (i.e., project 1 delayed by 1 year) *can be accepted*; if we wanted to force acceptance of one of these two, a strict equality would replace the $\leq$ sign. Equations (j) and (k) convey that with the two composite projects, at most one of the individual projects or the composite project can be accepted. Equation (1) indicates that either one or both of the composite projects must be accepted. Equation (m) states IP's usual (0, 1) requirement.

Clearly, the ability to include the various types of constraints for project interrelationships adds to the realism of the problem representation using IP as compared with LP (which encounters difficulty handling such constraints). Furthermore, the existence of partial projects in the optimal LP solution raises questions about how realistic the problem representation is. However, before we conclude our discussion of IP, the shortcomings of IP should be mentioned. The first is concerned with the significant increase in computer solution time and memory requirements for IP problems compared with LP problems. The second is that shadow prices do not exist and sensitivity analysis cannot be performed in IP.

One aspect of IP solution times that causes some concern is that IP problems can take hundreds of times longer to solve compared with LP solutions for the same size problem. In addition, computer memory requirements can be prohibitive for large-scale problems. Today there is virtually no problem which is too large to solve as an LP. But, clearly, this is not the case as far as IP problems go. In addition, the solution time for IP problems grows exponentially with the number of projects, owing to the combinatorial nature of the problem. One baffling aspect of IP solution times is their variability. Often, smaller problems (in terms of number of constraints and number of decision variables) can take longer to solve than larger problems. Further, very minor changes in the problem (even with the same number of constraints and decision variables) can significantly increase solution times. No single solution approach works best on all types of IP problems. However, given this somewhat bleak picture, Geoffrion and Nauss cite progress that is being made on several fronts in developing more efficient solution algorithms.[1]

The second shortcoming of IP formulations and solutions is perhaps more devastating: meaningful shadow prices (which show the marginal change in the value of the objective function for an incremental change in the right-hand sides of various constraints) are not available in IP. That is, many of the constraints on IP problems that are not binding on the optimal integer solution will be assigned shadow prices of zero, which indicates that these resources are "free goods." In reality, this is not true since the objective function would clearly decrease if the availability of such resources were decreased.

Baumol, who was one of the pioneers in the area of dual variables in IP (see his article with Gomory[2]), summarizes the problem of shadow prices in IP quite well:

However, we must be careful here—the preceding interpretation amounts to our thinking of these dual prices as the marginal revenue of these inputs. In the integer programming case, this concept runs into difficulties. In integer programming, inputs clearly must be thought of as coming in *indivisible units*. For that reason we cannot speak, e.g., of the marginal profit contribution of a small change in input, i.e., we must deal with $\Delta R/\Delta X$ rather than dR/dX (as we do in LP) where ΔX is an indivisible unit of input X and R is total profit. But a dual price represents dR/dX, which may change over the range of a *unit change in X*, and hence it may well give an *incorrect evaluation* of the marginal revenue of input X. [emphasis added][3]

Thus, the IP model, in trying to handle the problem of indivisibilities, runs into problems itself because the feasible region consists only of points that have integer values for all decision variables. This same problem of "gaps in the feasible region" is the culprit in creating both of the problems cited: computer time required to solve IP problems and difficulties in interpreting the shadow prices in IP. On the brighter side, Geoffrion and Nauss cite progress also on this latter problem area in their exceptional paper on parametric and post-optimality analysis in IP.[4]

This concludes our discussion of IP. We now turn to goal programming, which is another powerful extension of LP in handling the capital budgeting problem.

[1] A. M. Geoffrion and R. Nauss, "Parametric and Post-Optimality Analysis in Integer Linear Programming," *Management Science* (January 1977), 453–466.

[2] R. E. Gomory and W. J. Baumol, "Integer Programming and Pricing," *Econometrica* (September 1960), 521–550.

[3] W. J. Baumol, *Economic Theory and Operations Analysis*, 2nd ed. (Englewood Cliffs, N.J.: Prentice Hall, 1965), 165–166.

[4] Geoffrion and Nauss, "Parametric and Post-Optimality Analysis."

GOAL PROGRAMMING APPLIED
TO THE CAPITAL BUDGETING PROBLEM[5]

Throughout the text, we point out that the primary goal of financial management is the maximization of shareholders' wealth. Given the ever-present complexities, this is a rather tall order, since it is not always obvious how to maximize shareholders' wealth in an operational manner. Thus, it seems logical that progress toward this global goal will be facilitated if it is disaggregated into various subgoals, the rationale being that as the subgoals are achieved, definite strides will be made in the direction of shareholder wealth maximization. It was demonstrated in Chapter 7 that under conditions of certainty and perfect capital markets, the selection of the set of capital projects that maximizes NPV will guarantee maximization of shareholders' wealth or utility.[6]

However, if capital market imperfections exist (such as capital rationing, differences in lending and borrowing rates, and so on), then the maximization of NPV *may very well not* lead to the maximization of shareholders' wealth. In addition, observation plus empirical studies have demonstrated that investors and managers are interested in and motivated by several objectives. The following are representative of the more significant: growth and stability of earnings and dividends per share; growth in sales, market share, and total assets; growth and stability of reported earnings or accounting profit (as argued by the Lerner and Rappaport article[7]); favorable use of financial leverage; diversification to reduce variability in earnings; and return on sales, equity, and operating assets. Thus, only a model that incorporates multiple criteria or objectives can be a robust, yet operational, representation of the pluralistic decision environment found in real-world capital budgeting problem setting. Goal programming is such a multicriteria model in that it allows the establishment of a hierarchy of multiple objectives with diverse penalties associated with deviations from different goals. A brief survey of GP is presented prior to its application to the capital budgeting problem.

Goal programming was originally proposed in 1961 by Charnes and Cooper.[8] The technique has been expanded and popularized by the more recent works of Ijiri,[9] Lee,[10] and Ignizio.[11] The approach is an extension of linear programming wherein the usual "unidimensional" objective function (i.e., the optimization of a single measure of effectiveness) is transformed into a "multidimensional" criterion (i.e., the deviations

[5]This section draws on the paper by A. Fourcans and T. J. Hindelang, "The Incorporation of Multiple Goals in the Selection of Capital Investments," presented at the 1973 Financial Management Association Convention, Atlanta, Ga., October 1973.

[6]See also I. Fisher, *The Theory of Interest* (New York: Macmillan Publishing Co., 1930), and J. Hirshleifer, "On the Theory of Optimal Investment Decisions," *The Journal of Political Economy* (August 1958), 329–352.

[7]E. M. Lerner and A. Rappaport, "Limit DCF in Capital Budgeting," *Harvard Business Review* (September–October 1968), 133–138.

[8]A. Charnes and W. W. Cooper, *Management Models and Industrial Applications of Linear Programming*, Vols. I and II (New York: John Wiley and Sons, Inc., 1961).

[9]Y. Ijiri, *Management Goals and Accounting for Control* (Amsterdam: North-Holland Publishing Co., 1965).

[10]S. M. Lee, *Goal Programming for Decision Analysis* (Philadelphia: Auerbach Publishing Co., 1972).

[11]J. P. Ignizio, *Goal Programming and Extensions* (Lexington, Mass.: Lexington Books, 1976).

from several goals are minimized according to a priority ranking scheme). The priority structure specifies a hierarchy of multiple goals wherein the highest-order goals are striven for first. Only after the optimal level of priority 1 goals has been achieved will priority 2 goals be considered, and so on. In addition, the relative importance of two or more goals at any priority level is shown by the weights assigned to each. The model is flexible enough to handle conflicting objectives, situations wherein only underachievement or overachievement of a goal is penalized, and conditions where the decision maker seeks to come as close as possible to a desired target. Thus, GP offers an operational method of approximating a decision maker's utility curve that does not require the derivation of a family of utility functions in a multidimensional space. GP requires the assignment of ordinal priorities to the respective goals, with relative weights required by any goals placed on the same priority level. The optimal trade-off among goals on the same or different priority levels can be established through various interactive approaches or through sensitivity analysis, which will be discussed shortly.[12]

In formulating decision problems using the goal programming format, three major components are required:

1   The usual *economic constraints* of LP, which are also called *hard constraints*, in that they cannot be violated since they represent resource limitations or restrictions imposed by the decision environment.

2   The *goal constraints*, which are also called *soft constraints* because they represent managerial policies and desired levels of various objectives which are being sought by the decision maker.

3   The *objective function*, which minimizes the weighted deviations from the desired levels of the various objectives according to a specified priority ranking.

Each of these components deserves elaboration. The economic constraints in GP are exactly like the constraints in LP problems. Thus, such constraints still require the usual slack or surplus variables. On the other hand, goal constraints are most conveniently specified as strict equalities that contain *two deviational variables*, represented as d_i^+ and d_i^-, which indicate that the desired level of goal i is either overachieved or underachieved, respectively. Of course, one of the two deviational variables will always be zero and the other will equal the magnitude of the deviation from the desired goal level; if the desired goal level is exactly met, both deviational variables will equal zero. The deviational variables are the mechanism that is used to tie the goal constraints into the objective function. That is, the appropriate deviational variable(s) for each goal is (are) placed in the objective function, depending upon the desired action for that goal. For example, if it is desired to achieve a minimum level of net income, the only deviational variable required in the objective function is d^-; on the other hand, if the decision maker does not want to exceed a cost goal, the only deviational variable required in the objective function is d^+ since only exceeding the cost goal should be penalized.

[12]See J. S. Dyer, "Interactive Goal Programming," *Management Science*, 19, no. 1 (September 1972), 62–70; J. S. Dyer, "A Time-Sharing Computer Program for the Solution of the Multiple Criteria Problem," *Management Science*, 19, no. 12 (August 1973), 1379–1383; and A. Geoffrion, J. S. Dyer, and A. Feinberg, "An Interactive Approach for Multi-Criterion Optimization with an Application to the Operation of an Academic Department," *Management Science*, 19, no. 3 (November 1972), 357–368.

Table 20−1   Appropriate Objective Function Terms in Goal Programming

DESIRED ACTION	OBJECTIVE FUNCTION TERM
Achieve a minimum level of some goal	minimize d^-
Do not exceed a specified level of some goal	minimize d^+
Come as close as possible to a specified goal level	minimize $(d^+ + d^-)$
Maximize the value achieved relative to a given goal level	minimize $(d^- - d^+)$
Minimize the value achieved relative to a given goal level	minimize $(d^+ - d^-)$

More complex actions relative to goals require the use of both deviational variables. If the decision maker wants to come as close as possible to some goal level, then both overachieving and undershooting the goal are penalized; hence, the objective function term is minimize $(d^+ + d^-)$. If the decision maker desires to maximize net income and has established an achievable minimum level of net income as referred to earlier, the maximization is carried out in two steps—first achieving the minimum level and then overshooting the minimum by the greatest possible amount; hence, the objective function term is minimize $(d^- - d^+)$. It should be noted that we want to maximize d^+ but recall that the overall objective function is being minimized, which means that we minimize $-d^+$ to obtain the same result. Finally, if the decision maker wants to minimize the cost referred to earlier and has established a maximum level, the appropriate objective function term is minimize $(d^+ - d^-)$ using the same logic traced out for the maximization case. This discussion is summarized in Table 20–1 for convenient reference.

To represent the objective function in a GP problem formally, the following three aspects must be specified:

1   The *priority level* on which the goal is placed, which indicates the ordinal ranking scheme whereby the goals will be optimized.

2   The *relative weight* assigned to each goal when there are two or more goals on the same priority level; this weighting indicates the relative importance of the goals.

3   The *relevant deviational variable(s)*, which should be penalized with respect to each goal and which is (are) dependent upon the desired action.

The priority level is shown by P_i, where the subscript i designates the level—the smaller the value of i, the more important is the goal. Further, it should be noted that there is an *absolute dominance* among the priority levels; that is, priority 2 goals will only be considered after all goals on priority level 1 are optimized as far as possible. Furthermore, nothing on priority level 2 can act to the detriment of the goals on priority level 1, and similarly for all lower-priority levels. Because of the absolute dominance among priority levels, trade-offs are not allowed between different priority levels. Placing two or more goals on the same priority level does allow trade-offs between or among these goals. The trade-offs are designated by the relative weights assigned; the higher the relative weight, the more important is the goal.

Goal programming formulations can be used to optimize over a planning horizon consisting of many time periods. Goals can be established for the entire horizon or for various subperiods within the horizon. GP can handle deterministic or stochastic problem settings. The GP model discussed in this chapter is a multiperiod goal program where conditions of certainty are assumed.

It should be mentioned that GP models in their fullest context should be viewed as an *iterative process*. A set of priorities and relative weights are assigned to the various goals and the optimal solution is obtained. Next, based on the degree of consensus among management concerning the original priorities and weights, and to gain insight into trade-offs among goals, a *sensitivity analysis* should be performed to see the impact that varying priorities and weights has on the optimal values of decision variables. The less significant the impact on the decision variables, the less effort management has to expend in arriving at a consensus to specify the precise priority structure. Using the sensitivity information, the trade-off question can also be addressed based on management perceptions, risk posture, and preferences.

GP models are solved in the same fashion as LP models. Very simple problems with only two decision variables can be solved by a graphical procedure. More complex problems can be solved using the simplex method of GP[13] or, preferably, using computerized algorithms.[14] The solution of GP problems can be visualized as follows. The original feasible region of the problem is bounded by the economic (hard) constraints, which cannot be violated. The highest-priority goal(s) is (are) examined first; we try to drive the appropriate deviational variables for all priority 1 goals to zero. This results in a reduction in the size of the feasible region as we move on to priority 2 goals. Thus, each lower-priority level will have a successively smaller feasible region in as much as any portion of the region previously eliminated cannot be reexamined, owing to the absolute dominance relationship of higher-priority levels over all successively lower priority levels.

As we move from one priority level to the next lower one, the relevant feasible region can be a region, a plane, a line, or a single point in n-dimensional space, where n is the number of decision variables in the problem. Of course, the priority structure assigned to the goals will determine the order in which various regions will be cut off from the feasible region, and hence the optimal solution can differ significantly as different priority structures are utilized (including relative weights) for any given problem. This is why we stressed the importance of the iterative approach to GP problems through sensitivity analysis. Of course, once the feasible solution consists of only a single point, there is no way that we can move from that point on any lower priority level; thus, it must be the optimal solution. For this reason, it is recommended that high-priority goals be stated as *achieving minimum levels* of various goals or *not exceeding a maximum level*, rather than to maximize or minimize, because the latter alternatives will drive the decision maker to a single point in the feasible region. Maximization or minimization operations can be carried out on low priority levels once all other relevant goals have been achieved.

We now illustrate the formulation and graphical solution of a simple two-project capital budgeting problem using a GP model.

----

[13]See Lee, *Goal Programming*, Chap. 5; S. M. Lee, *Linear Optimization for Management* (New York: Petrocelli/Charter Publishers, Inc., 1976), Chap. 7; and Ignizio, *Goal Programming*, Chap. 4.

[14]See Ignizio, *Goal Programming*, Chaps. 3, 5, and 6, where FORTRAN programs are presented for integer GP and nonlinear GP problems.

EXAMPLE 3

Two-Project GP Formulation

Consider that a firm is evaluating two projects with the following characteristics:

| | ECONOMIC CONSTRAINTS | | | | MANAGERIAL GOALS | | | |
| | CASH OUTFLOW | CASH OUTFLOW | MANAGEMENT | | NET INCOME | NET INCOME | NET INCOME |
PROJECT	YEAR 1	YEAR 2	SUPERVISION	NPV	YEAR 1	YEAR 2	YEAR 3
1	$25	$20	5 units	$14	$10	$11	$12
2	40	15	16	60	4	7	11
Amount available	30	20	10 units				
Desired goals levels				Maximum	$6	$8	$10

This firm has a strict limitation on the funds that can be utilized for capital expenditures in years 1 and 2, as well as on the amount of time available for the management supervision of new projects (the amount of each of these resources available is shown); hence, there are three economic or hard constraints. Furthermore, partial projects can be accepted, but only one complete project of each type is available; cash outflows occur at the beginning of the period, while the subsequent cash inflows that generate net income cannot be used to finance the current year's or any later year's cash outflows. Four managerial goals have been established: net income in each of the first three years of the planning horizon and NPV over the entire planning horizon. The firm wants to maximize NPV but will accomplish this in two stages: on priority level 1, the firm wants to achieve a minimum NPV level of 20, and on the last priority level, the firm wants to maximize NPV. On priority levels 2, 3, and 4, the firm wants to achieve the minimum levels of net income in years 1, 2, and 3 specified.

Formulate this as a GP problem and solve it using the graphical method.

SOLUTION: First, the problem is formulated as a GP. The objective function shown below will be optimized subject to the economic and goal constraints shown first:

Economic constraints:

$$25X_1 \qquad +40X_2 \qquad \leq 30 \qquad \text{budget in year 1}$$

$$20X_1 \qquad +15X_2 \qquad \leq 20 \qquad \text{budget in year 2}$$

$$5X_1 \qquad +16X_2 \qquad \leq 10 \qquad \text{management supervision}$$

$$X_1 \qquad\qquad\qquad \leq 1 \qquad \text{upper limits on}$$

$$\qquad\qquad X_2 \qquad \leq 1 \qquad\quad \text{project acceptance}$$

$$X_i, d_j^+, d_j^- \geq 0 \quad i = 1, 2; \ j = 1, 2, 3, 4 \qquad \text{nonnegativity}$$

$$P_k \gg P_{k+1} \ \text{for all} \ k \qquad\qquad \text{absolute dominance}$$

$$\text{between priority levels}$$

Goal constraints:

$$10X_1 + 4X_2 + d_1^- - d_1^+ = 6 \qquad \text{net income year 1}$$
$$11X_1 + 7X_2 + d_2^- - d_2^+ = 8 \qquad \text{net income year 2}$$
$$12X_1 + 11X_2 + d_3^- - d_3^+ = 10 \qquad \text{net income year 3}$$
$$14X_1 + 60X_2 + d_4^- - d_4^+ = 20 \qquad \text{NPV}$$

Objective function:

$$\text{Minimum weighted deviations} = P_1 d_4^- + P_2 d_1^- + P_3 d_2^- + P_4 d_3^- + P_5(d_4^- - d_4^+)$$

Note in the preceding formulation that the goal levels for each of the four goals are those specified by management as the minimum levels that it wants to achieve. Recall also that the firm wants to achieve the maximum level of NPV. As we discussed, we will maximize NPV by first achieving the minimum level of 20 and then overachieving this level by as much as possible. The objective function term for priority level 5 is consistent with Table 20–1 and enables the firm to maximize NPV.

The problem is solved using the graphical method by drawing the lines representing all the economic constraints; these boundaries form the initial feasible region shown:

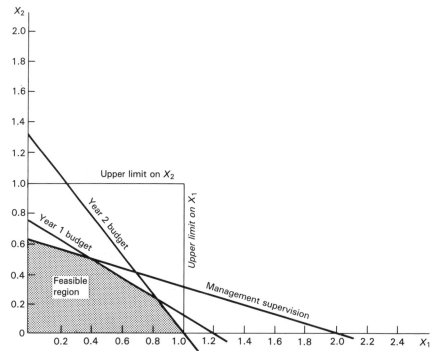

In diagrams (a) through (e), the four goal constraints are plotted and the region representing the deviation to be penalized has been eliminated as we move to the next lower priority level.

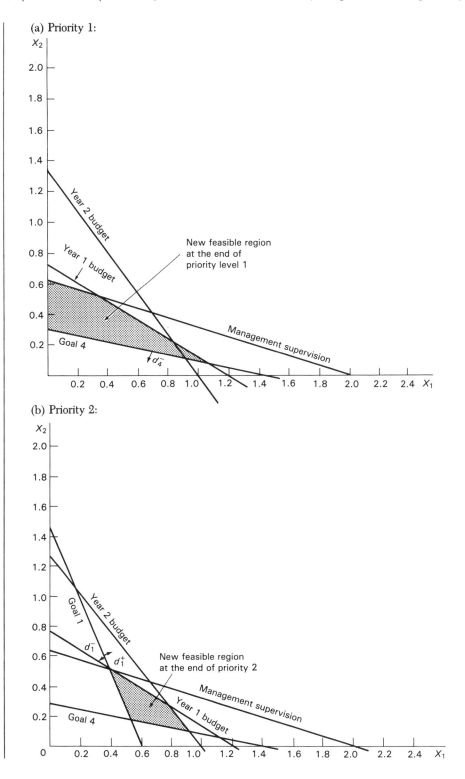

(a) Priority 1:

(b) Priority 2:

(c) Priority 3:

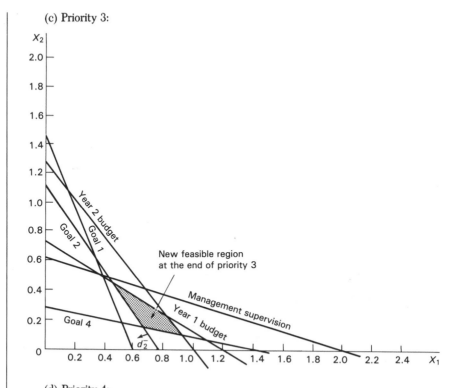

(d) Priority 4:

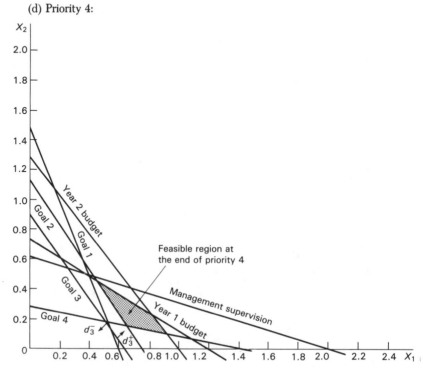

Notice that we have the same feasible region at the end of priority 4 that we had at the end of priority 3, since goal 3 is dominated by goal 2. Therefore, if we achieve goal 2, we will automatically achieve goal 3.

(e) Priority 5: Here we maximize NPV by first graphing goal 4, which has an NPV value of $20, then moving as far above the line for the NPV goal as possible leads to the optimal solution of $X_1 = 0.415$ and $X_2 = 0.49$.

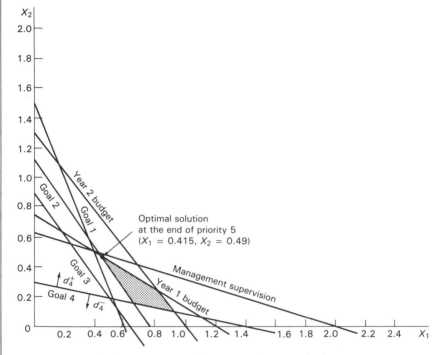

This optimal solution is quite different from the optimal solution obtained by simply maximizing NPV (i.e., to accept 0.625 of project 2 and nothing of project 1). The table summarizes the goal levels achieved by the LP and GP optimal solutions:

GOAL	OPTIMAL LP SOLUTION $X_1 = 0$ AND $X_2 = 0.625$	OPTIMAL GP SOLUTION $X_1 = 0.415$ AND $X_2 = 0.49$
Net income year 1	$2.5	$6.11
Net income year 2	4.375	8.00
Net income year 3	6.875	10.37
NPV	37.5	35.21

As can be seen, the GP optimal solution generates a net income level in year 1 that is 2.4 times that generated by the optimal LP solution. In years 2 and 3, the optimal GP solution generates net income levels that are 1.8 and 1.5 times the respective net income levels for the optimal LP solution. The price paid for the achievement of these three short-run goals is 2.29 units of NPV. Most financial managers would be willing to sacrifice such a small amount of long-run profitability to achieve the more stable and consistent short-run growth in profitability provided by the GP optimal solution. These results demonstrate the power of a multiobjective model such as GP.

Our next illustration of the use of GP in the capital budgeting setting will show how sensitivity analysis provides valuable information for management in addressing issues concerning trade-offs among their goals. To also be able to compare the results obtained here with the LP solution, we refer to the Lorie-Savage problem shown in Example 1, Chapter 19.

EXAMPLE 4

GP Formulation and Solution of the Lorie-Savage Problem

The same firm that was evaluating the nine projects under the conditions described in Example 1, Chapter 19, now believes that the NPV objective should be supplemented with four other goals which reflect the short-run attractiveness of the projects. Specifically, the firm feels that stability and growth in sales as well as net income are very important vehicles to assist the firm in maximizing shareholders' wealth.[15]

The table shows the contribution that each of the projects will make to net income and sales growth in the next 2 years.

	NET INCOME		SALES GROWTH	
PROJECT	YEAR 1	YEAR 2	YEAR 1	YEAR 2
1	$2.0	$4.0	0.02	0.03
2	2.0	4.2	0.01	0.03
3	1.6	2.5	0.02	0.02
4	1.2	2.8	0.01	0.02
5	3.0	5.0	0.03	0.04
6	1.1	1.4	0.01	0.01
7	1.5	3.0	0.01	0.02
8	1.2	1.8	0.01	0.015
9	1.3	2.4	0.01	0.018

The firm wants to achieve net income levels of 8 and 16, respectively, in years 1 and 2, and sales growth of 0.08 in each year as well as to maximize NPV.

(a) In addition to the information just presented, use the basic data on the nine projects from Example 1 in Chapter 19 to formulate all the economic and goal constraints for this problem.

(b) The firm is interested in evaluating two objective functions to determine the impact on the optimal set of projects:

1 Place the net income goals on priority 1, the sale goals on priority 2, and the NPV goal on priority 3; on the first two priority levels, the year 1 goals should be weighted twice as much as the year 2 goals.

2 Place all five goals on priority level 1, but assign relative weights of 10 for net income in year 1, 2 for net income in year 2, 5 for sales growth in year 1, and 2 for sales growth in year 2, and 1 for NPV.

Formulate these two objective functions.

(c) After setting the target levels for net income and sales growth, the firm feels it may be overoptimistic. Thus, the levels are revised to 7 and 12 in years 1 and 2, respectively, for net income and 0.07 in each year for sales growth. How will this affect the formulation in part (a)?

---

[15]A similar type of analysis was performed by C. A. Hawkins and R. A. Adams, "A Goal Programming Model for Capital Budgeting," *Financial Management* (Spring 1974), 52–57.

(d) If a computerized GP algorithm is available, obtain the optimal solutions for the two objective functions in part (b) and for the changes in the target levels mentioned in part (c). Briefly discuss differences in the optimal sets of projects. If a computerized algorithm is not available using the optimal solutions shown, briefly discuss the differences in the optimal sets of projects.

SOLUTION: (a) The GP formulation is as follows:

Economic constraints:

$$12X_1 + 54X_2 + 6X_3 + 6X_4 + 30X_5$$
$$+ 6X_6 + 48X_7 + 36X_8 + 18X_9 + S_1 = 50 \quad \text{budget constraint year 1}$$

$$3X_1 + 7X_2 + 6X_3 + 2X_4 + 35X_5$$
$$+ 6X_6 + 4X_7 + 3X_8 + 3X_9 + S_2 \quad = 20 \quad \text{budget constraint year 2}$$

$$
\left.
\begin{array}{lll}
X_1 + S_3 = 1 & X_4 + S_6 = 1 & X_7 + S_9 = 1 \\
X_2 + S_4 = 1 & X_5 + S_7 = 1 & X_8 + S_{10} = 1 \\
X_3 + S_5 = 1 & X_6 + S_8 = 1 & X_9 + S_{11} = 1
\end{array}
\right\}
\begin{array}{l}
\text{upper limits on} \\
\text{project acceptance}
\end{array}
$$

$$
X_j, S_i, d_h^+, d_h^- \geq 0
\left.
\begin{array}{l}
j = 1, 2, \ldots, 9 \\
i = 1, 2, \ldots, 11 \\
h = 1, 2, \ldots, 5
\end{array}
\right\}
\text{nonnegativity constraint}
$$

$$P_k \gg P_{k+1} \qquad \text{for all } k \qquad \begin{array}{l} \text{absolute dominance} \\ \text{between priority} \\ \text{levels} \end{array}$$

Goal constraints:

$$2X_1 + 2X_2 + 1.6X_3 + 1.2X_4 + 3X_5 + 1.1X_6$$
$$+ 1.5X_7 + 1.2X_8 + 1.3X_9 + d_1^- - d_1^+ = 8 \qquad \text{net income year 1}$$

$$4X_1 + 4.2X_2 + 2.5X_3 + 2.8X_4 + 5X_5 + 1.4X_6$$
$$+ 3X_7 + 1.8X_8 + 2.4X_9 + d_2^- - d_2^+ = 16 \qquad \text{net income year 2}$$

$$0.02X_1 + 0.01X_2 + 0.02X_3 + 0.01X_4 + 0.03X_5 + 0.01X_6$$
$$+ 0.01X_7 + 0.01X_8 + 0.01X_9 + d_3^- - d_3^+ = 0.08 \qquad \text{sales growth year 1}$$

$$0.03X_1 + 0.03X_2 + 0.02X_3 + 0.02X_4 + 0.04X_5 + 0.01X_6$$
$$+ 0.02X_7 + 0.015X_8 + 0.018X_9 + d_4^- - d_4^+ = 0.08 \qquad \text{sales growth year 2}$$

$$14X_1 + 17X_2 + 17X_3 + 15X_4 + 40X_5 + 12X_6$$
$$+ 14X_7 + 10X_8 + 12X_9 + d_5^- - d_5^+ = 40 \qquad \text{NPV}$$

Notice again that the goal level for NPV is an arbitrary achievable value.

(b) The two objective functions are as follows:

1   Minimize weighted deviations $= P_1(2d_1^- + d_2^-) + P_2(2d_3^- + d_4^-) + P_3(d_5^- - d_5^+)$.
2   Minimize weighted deviations $= P_1(10d_1^- + 2d_2^- + 5d_3^- + 2d_4^- + d_5^- - d_5^+)$.

(c) The only changes that will be necessitated by the desired changes in the target goal levels are that the right-hand sides of goals one through four become 7, 12, 0.07, and 0.07, respectively.

(d) The optimal solutions for the two objective functions and the two different sets of goal levels are shown below:

Objective function 1 and goal values of 8, 16, 0.08, and 0.08:

PROJECT ACCEPTANCE	GOAL LEVELS ACHIEVED	
$X_1 = 1.0000$	7.231	Net income year 1
$X_2 = 0.0426$		
$X_3 = 1.0000$	13.209	Net income year 2
$X_4 = 1.0000$		
$X_5 = 0.0000$	0.0699	Sales growth year 1
$X_6 = 0.9504$		
$X_7 = 0.0000$	0.0988	Sales growth year 2
$X_8 = 0.0000$		
$X_9 = 1.0000$	70.129	NPV

Objective function 2 and goal values 8, 16, 0.08, and 0.08:

PROJECT ACCEPTANCE	GOAL LEVELS ACHIEVED	
$X_1 = 1.0000$	7.235	Net income year 1
$X_2 = 0.0000$		
$X_3 = 1.0000$	13.194	Net income year 2
$X_4 = 1.0000$		
$X_5 = 0.0000$	0.0702	Sales growth year 1
$X_6 = 0.9697$		
$X_7 = 0.0455$	0.0986	Sales growth year 2
$X_8 = 0.0000$		
$X_9 = 1.0000$	70.273	NPV

Objective function 1 and goal values 7, 12, 0.07, and 0.07:

PROJECT ACCEPTANCE	GOAL LEVELS ACHIEVED	
$X_1 = 1.0000$	7.252	Net income year 1
$X_2 = 0.0000$		
$X_3 = 1.0000$	13.215	Net income year 2
$X_4 = 1.0000$		
$X_5 = 0.0000$	0.0703	Sales growth year 1
$X_6 = 0.9858$		
$X_7 = 0.0451$	0.0988	Sales growth year 2
$X_8 = 0.0000$		
$X_9 = 1.0000$	70.273	NPV

Objective function 2 and goal values 7, 12, 0.07, and 0.07:

PROJECT ACCEPTANCE	GOAL LEVELS ACHIEVED	
$X_1 = 1.0000$	7.252	Net income year 1
$X_2 = 0.0000$		
$X_3 = 1.0000$	13.215	Net income year 2
$X_4 = 1.0000$		
$X_5 = 0.0000$	0.0703	Sales growth year 1
$X_6 = 0.9858$		
$X_7 = 0.0451$	0.0988	Sales growth year 2
$X_8 = 0.0000$		
$X_9 = 1.0000$	70.273	NPV

The optimal solutions above were obtained using the GP algorithm from Ignizio.[16]

As will be recalled, the optimal LP solution showed 100% acceptance of projects 1, 3, 4, and 9 as well as 97% acceptance of project 6 and 4.5% acceptance of project 7, which generated an NPV level of $70.273. All the GP solutions above also accept 100% of projects 1, 3, 4, and 9. The only difference among the solutions is in the area of the partially accepted projects. With the original goal levels and priority structure, we find that projects 2 and 6 were partially accepted. Project 2 enters into the solution because of its contribution to the achievement of the new goals in the GP formulation. The other three GP solutions are virtually the same as the LP optimal solution. Greater variation in the optimal solutions would probably have been found if more projects were under evaluation and/or a greater diversity of goals were included in the formulation.

Our final illustration is a GP model; it is a global capital investment model that considers both replacement alternatives and new investment projects wherein multiple goals are sought and conditions of capital rationing exist. The model is comprehensive in that it integrates the capital investment, financing, and dividend decisions of firms into a single optimization approach. New financing for the firm, which can take the form of either debt or equity, is incorporated into the model. In addition, cash inflows generated during the planning horizon by projects that are accepted as well as by replacements that are made are taken into consideration. This comprehensive GP formulation and the accompanying example represent a more typical capital investment problem faced by medium-sized firms. The GP model and existing computerized algorithms can easily handle such awesome-looking problems.

A COMPREHENSIVE GP MODEL

The Goals

The GP model illustrated here includes six goals which are of significant importance to firms in evaluating the selection of new capital projects, the optimal timing of equipment replacements, and the best way to finance such capital commit-

[16] Ignizio, *Goal Programming*.

ments:

1   Attainment of a minimum yearly level of net income generated by the new investments (both new projects and replacements).
2   Achievement of a minimum desired annual growth in the productivity of operating assets (both for new projects and equipment replacement decisions).
3   Achievement of a minimum desired level of earnings per dollar of stockholders' equity each year (a surrogate goal for earnings per share).
4   Minimization of the deviation from a financial leverage goal at the end of the planning horizon.
5   Attainment of a minimum desired growth rate in total assets over the planning horizon.
6   Maximization of the net present value of accepted projects given that the budget constraints and the goals are satisfied as far as possible.

Other goals could be added to the list, but it is felt that these six represent the most important criteria that firms use in evaluating new capital investment and replacement decisions.

Table 20–2 gives the mathematical representation of the six goals, using the symbols defined in Table 20–3. A brief rationale is now presented for the inclusion of each of the goals in the model.

The net income goal was included because both investors and managers have an objective of stable and steadily rising earnings. Such earnings are achieved only through judicious capital investments and equipment replacement decisions over time. Thus, this goal for each year of the planning horizon can be summarized as follows:

$$
\begin{array}{l}
\text{net income} \\
\text{from ongoing} \\
\text{operations}
\end{array}
+
\begin{array}{l}
\text{net income} \\
\text{generated by} \\
\text{new investment} \\
\text{projects}
\end{array}
+
\begin{array}{l}
\text{net income} \\
\text{generated by} \\
\text{equipment} \\
\text{replacement} \\
\text{projects}
\end{array}
-
\begin{array}{l}
\text{after-tax} \\
\text{interest} \\
\text{cost}
\end{array}
=
\begin{array}{l}
\text{management's} \\
\text{net income} \\
\text{goal each year}
\end{array}
$$

Productivity increases over the planning horizon are another relevant area of concern in making new capital commitments, especially equipment replacement decisions. Hence, how attractive a particular capital investment is can be measured in part by how much it increases productivity compared with current operations. The goal of achieving the minimum productivity increase established by management merely adds together the productivity growth per dollar invested in equipment replacements and new capital projects.

Earnings per share is one of the most closely watched statistics by investors and managers. Of course, this figure is based directly upon the level of net income (discussed in the first goal) but also implicitly reflects the way that new capital investments (both new projects and equipment replacements) are financed (debt versus equity) and the dividend policy utilized by the firm. Thus, the next two goals—earnings per dollar of equity and leverage—incorporate two important dimensions used to judge how well a firm is doing in its profitability endeavors and its search for an optimal capital structure. The earnings per dollar of equity goal (which is a surrogate for earnings per share) adds net income of ongoing operations to the net income generated by new capital investments (after deducting interest charges on debt). This result is compared with management's target return per dollar of stockholders' equity to determine the quality of capital investment alternatives undertaken.

ble 20 – 2   Goal Constraints of the Model

Net income:	$e_j + \sum_{i \in n_1} a_{ij}X_{ij} + \sum_{i \in n_2} \bar{a}_{ij}Y_{ij} - (1 - t)I_j - d_{1j}^+ + d_{1j}^- = p_j$ $j = 1, 2, \ldots, T$
Productivity:	$\sum_{j=1}^{T} \sum_{i \in n_1} r_{ij}X_{ij} + \sum_{j=1}^{T} \sum_{i \in n_2} \bar{r}_{ij}Y_{ij} - d_2^+ + d_2^- = U$
Earnings/dollar equity:	$e_j + \sum_{i \in n_1} a_{ij}X_{ij} + \sum_{i \in n_2} \bar{a}_{ij}Y_{ij} - (1 - t)I_j - q_j\left(E_0 + \sum_{k=1}^{j-1} E_k\right)$ $- d_{3j}^+ + d_{3j}^- = 0 \qquad j = 1, 2, \ldots, T$
Leverage:	$E_0 + \sum_{j=1}^{T} E_j + \sum_{j=1}^{T} e_j + \sum_{j=1}^{T} \sum_{i \in n_1} a_{ij}X_{ij} + \sum_{j=1}^{T} \sum_{i \in n_2} \bar{a}_{ij}Y_{ij} - \sum_{j=1}^{T} (1 - t)I_j$ $- \sum_{j=1}^{T} V_j\left(E_0 + \sum_{k=1}^{j-1} E_k\right) - S\left(D_0 + \sum_{j=1}^{T} D_j\right) - d_4^+ + d_4^- = 0$
Growth rate in assets:	$\sum_{j=1}^{T} \sum_{i \in n_1} BV_{ij}^T X_{ij} + \sum_{j=1}^{T} \sum_{i \in n_2} \overline{BV}_{ij}^T Y_{ij} - gA_0 - d_5^+ + d_5^- = 0$
Net present value:	$\sum_{j=0}^{T} \sum_{i \in n_1} \frac{1}{(1 + k)^j}(b_{ij}X_{ij} - C_{ij}X_{ij} + W_T)$ $+ \sum_{j=0}^{T} \sum_{i \in n_2} \frac{1}{(1 + k)^j}(\bar{b}_{ij}Y_{ij} - \overline{C}_{ij}Y_{ij} + \overline{W}_T) - d_6^+ + d_6^- = 0$

The financial leverage goal can be expressed as follows:

$$\frac{\text{total equity issued} + \begin{array}{c}\text{net income generated}\\\text{by the firm's new}\\\text{investments and}\\\text{replacement projects}\end{array} - \text{dividends paid}}{\text{total debt incurred}} = \begin{array}{c}\text{management's}\\\text{leverage goal}\end{array}$$

Therefore, through these two goals the model integrates the important investment, financing, and dividend policy dimensions of the capital budgeting and equipment replacement decisions.

Growth rate in assets is a natural consideration in allocating capital among competing alternatives, because such growth contributes to the intrinsic value of the firm and its potential for stable and rising earnings. This goal is simply

$$\frac{\begin{array}{c}\text{book value of}\\\text{new capital investments}\\\text{at end of planning horizon}\end{array} + \begin{array}{c}\text{book value of}\\\text{equipment replacements}\\\text{at end of planning horizon}\end{array}}{\begin{array}{c}\text{book value of initial assets at the}\\\text{beginning of the planning horizon}\end{array}} = \begin{array}{c}\text{management's}\\\text{desired growth}\\\text{rate in assets}\\\text{over the plan-}\\\text{ning horizon}\end{array}$$

Finally, the introduction of capital market imperfections weakens the validity of NPV as a *unique* criterion of investment evaluation. However, in conjunction with the goals cited, definite strides are taken toward the maximization of shareholders' wealth.

Table 20–3 Glossary of Symbols in Alphabetical Order

A_0 = book value of total operating assets at time zero

a_{ij} = net income generated by project i in year j

$\bar{a}_{ij}$ = net income generated by the replacement of machine i in period j

b_{ij} = net cash inflow generated by project i in year j

$\bar{b}_{ij}$ = net cash inflow generated by replacement of machine i in period j

BV_{ij}^{T} = book value in year T of project i acquired in year j

$\overline{BV}_{ij}^{T}$ = book value in year T of replacement of machine i in period j

C_{ij} = cash outflow required for project i in year j

$\bar{C}_{ij}$ = cash outflow required to replace machine i in period j

D_0 = dollar amount of long-term debt outstanding at time zero

D_j = dollar amount of long-term debt acquired during year j

D_j^* = upper limit of the dollar amount of debt funds that can be acquired in year j

E_0 = dollar amount of equity outstanding at time zero

E_j = dollar amount of equity acquired during year j

E_j^* = upper limit of the dollar amount of equity funds that can be acquired in year j

e_j = dollar amount of net income generated by ongoing operations in year j

g = desired growth rate in assets over the planning horizon

I_0 = dollar amount of interest paid on long-term debt outstanding in year zero

I_j = dollar amount of interest paid on long-term debt outstanding in year j

i_j = percent interest rate paid on long-term debt in year j

k = firm's cost of capital to be used in discounting cash flows

n_1 = class of accepted projects in year j

n_2 = class of machine replacements undertaken in year j

n_1^* = class of accepted projects that have cash flows beyond the end of the planning horizon T

n_2^* = class of machine replacements that have cash flows beyond the end of the planning horizon T

p_j = net income goal in year j

q_j = earnings per dollar of equity goal in year j

r_{ij} = productivity growth per dollar invested achieved by accepting project i in year j

$\bar{r}_{ij}$ = productivity growth per dollar invested achieved by replacing machine i in year j

S = leverage goal to be achieved by the end of the planning horizon

t = corporate tax rate

U = productivity growth goal to be achieved by the end of the planning horizon

V_j = percentage of dividends per dollar of equity to be paid in year j

X_{ij} = decision variable representing project i in period j

Y_{ij} = decision variable representing the replacement of machine i in period j

Hence, new investments and replacement decisions will be evaluated in terms of the first five goals. Then the feasible set of capital commitments that maximizes NPV will be undertaken. This goal adds the NPV of new investment projects to the NPV of equipment replacement alternatives.

The Economic Constraints

Table 20–4 shows the economic constraints of the model. The interest expense constraint states that the dollar interest will be the amount of interest on debt outstanding at the beginning of the planning horizon plus the interest on new debt

Table 20–4   Economic Constraints of the Model

Interest expense:	$I_j = I_0 + \displaystyle\sum_{k=1}^{j-1} i_k D_k \quad j = 1, 2, \dots, T$
Budget:	$\displaystyle\sum_{i \in n_1} C_{ij} X_{ij} + \sum_{i \in n_2} \bar{C}_{ij} Y_{ij} \le D_j + E_j + e_j + \sum_{k=1}^{j-1} \sum_{i \in n_1} a_{ik} X_{ik}$
	$+ \displaystyle\sum_{k=1}^{j-1} \sum_{i \in n_2} \bar{a}_{ik} Y_{ik} - (1-t) I_j - V_j \left(E_0 + \sum_{k=1}^{j-1} E_k \right) \quad j = 1, 2, \dots, T$
Horizon value:	$W_T = \displaystyle\sum_{j=T+1}^{J} \sum_{i \in n_1^*} \frac{1}{(1-k)^{j-T}} (b_{ij} X_{ij} - C_{ij} X_{ij});$
	$\overline{W}_T = \displaystyle\sum_{j=T+1}^{J} \sum_{i \in n_2^*} \frac{1}{(1+k)^{j-T}} (\bar{b}_{ij} Y_{ij} - \bar{C}_{ij} Y_{ij})$
Upper limits:	$D_j \le D_j^* \quad E_j \le E_j^* \quad j = 1, 2, \dots, T$
Mutually exclusive replacements:	$\displaystyle\sum_{j=1}^{T} Y_{ij} \le 1 \quad i = 1, 2, \dots, N$
Mutually exclusive projects:	$\displaystyle\sum_{i \in C} X_{ij} \le 1 \quad$ where C is a class of mutually exclusive projects in any year j
Decision variables:	$X_{ij} = \begin{cases} 1 & \text{if project is accepted in year } j \\ 0 & \text{otherwise} \end{cases}$
	$Y_{ij} = \begin{cases} 1 & \text{if machine } i \text{ is replaced in year } j \\ 0 & \text{otherwise} \end{cases}$
Nonnegativity:	$d_{ij}^+, d_{ij}^-, D_j, E_j \ge 0 \quad j = 1, 2, \dots, T \quad i = 1, 2, \dots, 6$

issued. It is assumed that no long-term debt matures or is retired during the planning horizon. The next constraint is the all-important budget constraint, which states that new funds committed to projects in any year cannot exceed the amount of new debt issued plus the amount of new equity issued plus the internally generated funds (i.e., ongoing operations of the firm plus cash inflows generated by new projects and replacements undertaken to date) less interest and dividend payments. These first two economic constraints are tied into the net income, leverage, and earnings per dollar of equity goals. Such interrelationships are needed to achieve the following important dimensions: (1) the integration of the investment, financing, and dividend policy aspects of the capital budgeting and equipment replacement decision areas; and (2) the optimal timing of changes in the firm's capital structure based on the cost and availability of funds in the capital markets, the firm's leverage goal, the attractiveness of new projects and replacements, and the portfolio of assets accepted to date in the planning horizon.

   The next two constraints show the values of the discounted cash inflows less outflows for all accepted projects and replacements, respectively, which occur beyond the end of the planning horizon. These two values are used in the net present value goal. Upper limits are shown for the amount of new debt and new equity that can be issued each year to reflect market or self-imposed limits on the amount of external financing that the firm can undertake.

Finally, two constraints are shown which incorporate the fact that replacements of existing assets are mutually exclusive (i.e., if a given asset is replaced in year 1, the same original asset cannot be replaced in any other year of the planning horizon) and that new capital projects can be mutually exclusive (i.e., if one project is accepted, then any other project in the mutually exclusive set may not be accepted). Other project interdependencies discussed in the section on integer programming could also be incorporated in the model. The usual zero-one conditions are imposed on the decision variables for both new projects and replacements. The nonnegativity requirement is placed on deviational variables and the debt and equity decision variables.

The Objective Function

The model's objective function consists of minimizing the appropriate deviations $(d^+, d^-,$ or both) from the multiple goals according to the priority scheme established by the firm. Thus, for the first three goals and goal 5, only the d^- deviation will be penalized, since a minimum level of these goals is sought; for goal 4, both the d^+ and d^- deviations are important, because we seek to come as close as possible to the leverage goal that is established; and finally, we penalize $(d^- - d^+)$ for goal 6 because we are seeking to maximize the NPV of accepted investments. For each of the six goals a priority level must be specified which shows its ordinal importance in the firm's hierarchy of objectives.

Owing to the flexibility of goal programming, a firm can tailor the model to its own hierarchy of goals and its own circumstances. For illustrative purposes, suppose that a corporation under consideration is concerned about the market price of its stock, since it finds equity issues a favorable way to obtain new financing for capital acquisitions. It also maintains that its image as a growth firm is very important. Given these conditions, the firm finds the following priority structure appropriate:

Priority 1 (P_1)   The achievement of a minimum earnings per dollar of equity and the achievement of a minimum level of annual net income.

Priority 2 (P_2)   The attainment of a specified growth in productivity of operating assets and a desired growth rate in assets over the planning horizon.

Priority 3 (P_3)   Coming as close as possible to the firm's desired leverage goal at the end of the planning horizon.

Priority 4 (P_4)   The maximization of the NPV of all accepted projects and replacements.

In addition, the firm decides that on the first priority level the earnings per dollar of equity goal is three times as important as the net income goal; on the second priority level, the growth rate in assets is thought to be twice as important as the productivity growth goal.

This hierarchy is expressed mathematically by the following objective function:

$$\text{minimize weighted deviations} = 3P_1 \sum_{j=1}^{T} d_{3j}^- + P_1 \sum_{j=1}^{T} d_{1j}^- + 2P_2 d_5^- + P_2 d_2^-$$

$$+ P_3\left(d_4^+ + d_4^-\right) + P_4\left(d_6^- - d_6^+\right)$$

We now illustrate this comprehensive formulation with a numerical example.

EXAMPLE 5

Comprehensive 28-Project Example

The table on pages 402–403 presents cash flow data for 28 investment proposals. The data are adapted from test problems originally presented by Weingartner.[17] The projects have varying initial investments, cash flow patterns, and useful lives of 7 to 26 years. The planning horizon of interest was 10 years. To simplify matters slightly, the productivity goal will not be considered nor will the integer requirements on project acceptance or project interrelationship constraints. The desired levels of the various goals are also given at the bottom of the table, together with other input parameters for the model. The optimal solution and goal achievements are presented and discussed in the paragraphs that follow.

SOLUTION: The following table shows the optimal solution and goal achievements.

Model Solution

	GOAL ATTAINMENT			AMOUNT	AMOUNT OF
	EARNINGS PER			BORROWED	STOCK ISSUED
YEAR	DOLLAR OF EQUITY	PROFIT			
1				$200.00	$500.00
2	Achieved	Achieved,	$p = \$404.00$		500.00
3	Achieved	Not achieved,	$p = 333.75$		183.18
4	Achieved	Achieved,	$p = 572.27$		
5	Achieved	Achieved,	$p = 513.33$		
6	Achieved	Achieved,	$p = 454.00$		
7	Achieved	Not achieved,	$p = 336.71$		
8	Achieved	Not achieved,	$p = 248.60$		
9	Achieved	Not achieved,	$p = 206.33$		
10	Achieved	Not achieved,	$p = 106.66$	200.00	

Leverage at the end of the planning horizon	Growth rate in assets	Net present value of accepted projects (at 6%)
$\dfrac{\text{common stock}}{\text{debt}} = 283\%$	111%	$381.30

Accepted Projects

PROJECT	PROPORTION ACCEPTED	PROJECT	PROPORTION ACCEPTED
1	1.00	17	1.00
2	1.00	18	1.00
3	1.00	19	1.00
4	1.00	20	1.00
5	0.092	21	1.00
6	1.00	22	1.00
7	0.948	23	1.00
13	0.559	25	1.00
15	1.00	28	1.00

[17]H. Martin Weingartner, *Mathematical Programming and the Analysis of Capital Budgeting Problems* (Englewood Cliffs, N.J.: Prentice Hall, 1963), pp. 180–181.

Input Values and Goals

PROJECT NUMBER	YEARS										
	1	2	3	4	5	6	7	8	9	10	11
	CASH FLOWS (DOLLARS)										
1	− $100	$ 20	$ 20	$ 20	$ 19	$ 19	$ 18	$16	$14	$11	$ 6
2	− 100	20	18	18	18	18	14	14	14	14	14
3	− 100	15	15	15	15	15	13	13	13	13	13
4	− 100	20	6	11	7	16	5	14	18	3	20
5	− 100	− 60	− 60	80	74	66	56	44	30	14	
6	− 200	25	25	25	25	25	25	25	25	25	25
7	− 150	20	20	20	20	20	20	20	20	20	20
8	− 100	20	18	16	14	12	10	4	− 20	20	18
9	− 150	− 75	− 75	60	60	55	50	44	38	36	35
10	− 50	− 100	− 175	50	55	60	65	60	50	40	30
11	− 100	− 150	− 100	10	20	30	40	60	60	60	60
12	− 250	45	45	40	30	25	20	15	10 −	40	40
13	− 75	− 75	− 40	40	40	40	35	35	30	25	15
14	− 180	20	12	16	13	11	19	17	12	15	19
15	− 275	40	45	45	40	35	30	25	20	15	− 75
16	− 140	20	20	18	16	14	11	8	− 25	18	18
17		− 100	18	17	15	12	8	− 10	18	17	15
18		− 85	20	20	16	15	13	10	7	3	
19		− 270	− 100	125	115	105	80	60	35	25	15
20		− 200	60	40	30	15	− 25	− 25	50	40	30
21		− 355	60	70	80	70	55	40	25	15	5
22			− 150	25	25	30	35	30	25	20	15
23							− 80	20	20	20	19
24								− 95	− 60	47	42
25								− 50	10	10	9
26									− 60 −	30 −	10
27										− 175	50
28										− 40	15

Net income generated by existing assets (e_j)	$400	360	320	280	240	200	160	120	80	40
Profit targets (p_j) (3% increase per year)	$404	416	428	441	454	468	482	496	511	
Earnings per dollar of equity goal (q_j)	3%	3%	3%	4%	4%	4%	5%	5%	5%	

Growth rate in assets goal (G) 90% over the planning horizon

Leverage goal (S) $\dfrac{\text{equity}}{\text{debt}} = 250\%$ over the planning horizon

Upper bound on borrowing $200 every year

Upper bound on equity issue $500 every year

Cost of borrowing 5% every year

Depreciation method Straight line over the life of each project

Existing assets $2000

Existing debt $ 300

Existing equity $ 800

Tax rate 50% every year

						YEARS									
12	13	14	15	16	17	18	19	20	21	22	23	24	25	26	NPV OF PROJECTS AT $k = 6\%$
						CASH FLOWS (DOLLARS)									
−$8															$19.31
10	$10	$10	$10	$10	$6	$6	$6	$6	$6						52.68
11	11	11	11	11	9	9	9	9	9						43.21
2	22	8	10	18	6	9	14	24							32.29
															57.50
25	25	25	25	25	25	25	25	25	25	$25	$25	$25	$25	$25	112.82
20															7.30
	16	14	12	10	4										13.71
34	33	30	25	17	9										47.90
20	10	−25	50	41	35	25	15	5							57.35
60	60	60	60	60	60	60	60	60	60	60	60	60	60	60	204.06
32	25	19	14	10	7	5									− 8.77
5															6.02
13	14	17	20	14	11	15	17	12							− 9.90
35	30	25	20	15	10	5									− 17.27
16	13	10	6	−25	16	16	14	11	8	5	2				− 9.33
12	8	−10	18	17	15	12	8								18.26
															0.25
10															73.10
20	10														− 12.90
															− 13.52
10	5														42.16
17	14	10	6	2											15.08
37	31	24	18	13	9	6	4	3							17.12
7	4	−14	9	9	8	6	3	−16	8	8	4				− 1.97
45	34	25	16	12	8	−20	21	16	12	9	7	5	3		20.92
45	35	25	10	−60	45	35	25	10							− 0.64
13	9	7	5	2											2.22

It is interesting to analyze the achievement of the various goals. The earnings per dollar of equity goal is achieved each year in the planning horizon, while the profit targets exhibit a more erratic behavior. These goals are generally attained in the first 6 years (except in year 3), but the low magnitude of the cash throw-offs generated by existing operations prevents their achievement in the final years of the planning horizon.

Borrowing occurs in the very first and the last year of the planning period. Of course, the large outlays at the beginning of the horizon trigger the $200 borrowing in year 1. The bond issue of the last year, however, takes place so as to bring the leverage ratio closer to the desired target. In spite of this final borrowing, the leverage goal is overshot by a nonnegligible amount (283% for equity/debt).

The limit on the new stock issued is operative for the first 2 years, whereas only $183.18 is raised in the third year. Again, the firm would enter the stock market to meet the charges associated with the capital outlays of the first periods.

The accepted projects allow the firm to maintain a very comfortable growth in assets (111%), somewhat over the 90% desired level. Finally, the net present value of the portfolio of accepted projects is equal to $381.30.

It is also instructive to analyze the values of the deviational variables—d^+ and d^-—for each goal. Since the earnings per dollar of equity goal was achieved in each year, d^-_{3j} was equal to zero for each year, and d^+_{3j} would equal the excess of the percentage returns over the goals shown in the table of input values and goals. Similarly, for each year that the net income goal was achieved, the d_{1j}^- term would equal zero, which means that there would be no penalty in the objective function and that d_{1j}^+ would equal the excess of actual profits over the goal established. For example, in year 4, the net income goal was 428 and the actual level was 572.27; thus, the goal was achieved, $d_{14}^- = 0$, and $d_{14}^+ = 144.27$ (572.27 − 428.00). An analogous interpretation can be provided for the deviational variables for the other three goals. As in the previous example, sensitivity analysis could be performed to determine the impact on the optimal projects and goal achievement as the priority structure is changed.

SUMMARY

This chapter explores in depth the advanced models of mathematical programming applied to the capital budgeting problem under conditions of certainty. We examine the areas of integer linear programming and goal programming. Both approaches provide a powerful methodology to determine the optimal set of projects under various conditions and consider several types of constraints or restrictions. Chapter 21 explores mathematical programming models under conditions of risk.

QUESTIONS
——————
PROBLEMS

1. Firm XYZ has 10 projects with the following characteristics. Projects 1, 3, and 5 are mutually exclusive. For project 6 to be accepted, project 3 must also be accepted. Of projects 2, 4, 7, and 10, at least two must be accepted; however, project 7 cannot be accepted unless projects 8 and 9 are also accepted. If projects 5 and 9 are accepted together, their cost in combination is only 90% of the cost of the two individual projects. Finally, the firm feels that it must undertake at least 5 of the 10 proposed projects to maintain stable employment levels. Formulate the appropriate IP constraints for firm XYZ.

2. Firm TUB is evaluating the following 10 projects:

| PROJECT | CASH OUTFLOWS | | | NPV |
	YEAR 1	YEAR 2	YEAR 3	
X_1	$250	$200	$100	$60
X_2	300	250	150	80
X_3	275	250	175	55
X_4	225	225	50	50
X_5	150	250	150	25
X_6	400	150	0	100
X_7	200	150	100	90
X_8	350	50	25	40
X_9	250	100	150	75
X_{10}	175	175	175	75
Budget constraints:	$K_1 \leq \$2,000$	$K_2 \leq \$1,500$	$K_3 \leq \$1,000$	

The following interrelationships exist between the projects:

(a) Only X_6 or X_7 can be accepted; not both.
(b) If X_6 is accepted, X_2 cannot be accepted.

(c)   If X_7 is accepted, X_8 must be accepted.

(d) X_9 and X_{10} are mutually exclusive, but one must be accepted.

(e)   If projects 2 and 4 are accepted in combination, 120% of the NPV will be generated and the cost will only be 85% of the combined cash outflows for the two projects separately.

Formulate this problem as an integer LP.

3. Acme Market is considering five new supermarkets, which have the following characteristics:

PROJECT CHARACTERISTICS	PROJECTS				
	1	2	3	4	5
Cash outflow year 1	$10,000	0	$14,000	$30,000	$12,000
Cash outflow year 2	20,000	$18,000	10,000	15,000	0
Cash inflow year 1	8,000	0	5,000	3,000	4,000
Cash inflow year 2	12,000	8,000	6,000	18,000	20,000
Net income year 1	5,000	12,000	3,000	2,500	− 2,000
Net income year 2	10,000	6,000	5,000	14,000	16,000
Profitability index	1.4	1.8	0.6	1.2	0.9
Salvage value year 10	$ 4,000	$ 0	$ 3,000	$ 2,000	$ 1,000

Acme has a budget constraint of $50,000 in year 1 and $40,000 in year 2. Any unused funds in year 1 can be invested in Treasury bills at 6% and carried over into year 2. In addition, of the benefits received from accepted projects, 60% will be required for operating expenses or dividends; the remainder can be used for reinvestment in other projects. Acme's cost of capital is 10%. The projects require cash outflows only in year 1 or 2 or both. Among the five supermarkets, several interrelationships must be taken into account:

(a)   Either project 1 or project 4 must be accepted.

(b)   If project 2 is accepted, project 3 must also be accepted.

(c)   Project 1 cannot be accepted unless project 5 is also accepted.

(d)   Of the set of projects 1, 2, and 4, at most two may be accepted.

The firm has established the following goals:

Priority 1:   Achieve a minimum net income of $15,000 in year 1.

Priority 2:   Weight 2—maximize NPV of accepted projects.

Weight 1—come as close as possible to a net income goal of $20,000 in year 2.

Formulate this problem as an integer GP. [*Hint*: All cash outflows are shown in the table, but all cash inflows are not. Thus, determine the NPV for each project by using the profitability index and the discounted cash outflows for each project.]

REFERENCES

Ashton, D. J., and D. R. Atkins. "Multicriteria Programming for Financial Planning." *Journal of Operational Research Society*, 30 (March 1979), 259–270.

Baumol, W. J., and R. E. Quandt. "Investment and Discount Rates under Capital Rationing—A Programming Approach." *Economic Journal*, 75 (June 1965), 317–329.

Beale, E. M. L. *Mathematical Programming in Practice.* Pitman, 1968.

Bey, R. P., and R. B. Porter. "An Evaluation of Capital Budgeting Portfolio Models Using Simulated Data." *Engineering Economics* (Fall 1977).

Bradley, Stephen, and Sherwood C. Frey, Jr. "Equivalent Mathematical Programming Models of Pure Capital Rationing." *Journal of Financial and Quantitative Analysis,* 13 (June 1978), 345–361.

Burton, R. M., and W. W. Damon. "On the Existence of a Cost of Capital under Pure Capital Rationing." *Journal of Finance* (September 1974).

Charnes, A., and W. W. Cooper. *Management Models and Industrial Applications of Linear Programming,* Vols. I and II. New York: John Wiley & Sons, Inc., 1961.

Cheng, Pal L., and John P. Shelton. "A Contribution to the Theory of Capital Budgeting—The Multi-Investment Case." *Journal of Finance* (December 1963).

Ederington, L. H., and W. R. Henry. "On Costs of Capital in Programming Approaches to Capital Budgeting." *Journal of Financial and Quantitative Analysis* (December 1979).

Elton, Edwin J. "Capital Rationing and External Discount Rates." *Journal of Finance* (June 1970), 573–584.

—————, and Martin J. Gruber. *Finance as a Dynamic Process.* Englewood Cliffs, N.J.: Prentice-Hall, 1975.

Fama, Eugene E., and Merton H. Miller. *The Theory of Finance.* New York: Holt, Rinehart and Winston, Inc., 1972.

Fandel, G., and T. Cal, eds. *Multiple Criteria Decision Making Theory and Application.* New York: Springer-Verlag, 1980.

Fogler, H. Russell. "Ranking Techniques and Capital Rationing." *Accounting Review,* 47 (January 1972), 134–143.

Fourcans, A., and Thomas J. Hindelang. "The Incorporation of Multiple Goals in the Selection of Capital Investments." Paper presented at Financial Management Association Meeting, October 1973.

Goldberger, Juval, and Jacob Paroush. "Capital Budgeting of Interdependent Projects." *Management Science* (July 1977).

Haley, Charles W. "Taxes, the Cost of Capital and the Firm's Investment Decisions." *Journal of Finance,* 26 (September 1971), 901–918.

Hawkins, Clark A., and Richard A. Adams. "A Goal Programming Model for Capital Budgeting." *Financial Management,* 3 (Spring 1974), 52–57.

Hemming, T. *Multiobjective Decision Making under Certainty.* Stockholm: Economic Research Institute, Stockholm School of Economics, 1978.

Hughes, John S., and Wilbur G. Lewellen. "Programming Solutions to Capital Rationing Problems." *Journal of Business Finance and Accounting* (Winter 1974).

Ignizio, James P. "An Approach to the Capital Budgeting Problem with Multiple Objectives." *Engineering Economist,* 21 (Summer 1976), 259–272.

—————. *Goal Programming and Extensions.* Lexington, Mass.: Lexington Books, 1977.

Ijiri, Y. *Management Goals and Accounting for Control.* Amsterdam: North-Holland Publishing Co., 1965.

Karlin S. *Mathematical Methods and Theory in Games, Programming and Economics,* I. Reading, Mass.: Addison-Wesley Publishing Co., Inc. 1977.

Keown, Arthur J., and John D. Martin. "Capital Budgeting in the Public Sector: A Zero-One Goal Programming Approach." *Financial Management,* 7 (Summer 1978), 21–27.

—————, and —————. "An Integer Goal Programming Model for Capital Budgeting in Hospitals." *Financial Management,* 5 (Autumn 1976), 28–35.

Koopmans, T. C., ed. *Activity Analysis of Production and Allocation, Proceeding of a Conference*. New York: John Wiley & Sons, Inc., 1951.

Krainer, Robert E. "A Neglected Issue in Capital Rationing—The Asset Demand for Money." *Journal of Finance* (December 1966).

Lee, Sang M. *Goal Programming for Decision Analysis*. Philadelphia: Auerbach Publishing Co., 1972.

Lerner, Eugene M., and Alfred Rappaport. "Limit DCF in Capital Budgeting." *Harvard Business Review*, 46 (July–August 1968), 133–139.

Lorie, J. H., and L. J. Savage. "Three Problems in Rationing Capital." *Journal of Business*, 28, 4 (October 1955), 229–239.

Manne, A. S. "Optimal Dividend and Investment Policies for a Self-Financing Business Enterprise." *Management Science*, 15, 3 (November 1968), 119–129.

Mao, J. C. T. *Quantitative Analysis of Financial Decisions*. New York: Macmillan Publishing Co., Inc. 1969, 266–280.

Martin, A. D. "Mathematical Programming of Portfolio Selections." *Management Science*, (January 1955), 152–166.

Merville, L. J., and L. A. Tavis. "A Generalized Model for Capital Investment." *Journal of Finance*, 28, 1 (March 1973), 109–118.

Moag, J. S., and E. M. Lerner. "Capital Budgeting Decisions under Imperfect Market Conditions." *Journal of Finance*, 25 (June 1970), 613–621.

Myers, Stewart C. "Interactions of Corporate Financing and Investment Decisions—Implications for Capital Budgeting." *Journal of Finance*, 29 (March 1974), 1–26.

_____, and Gerald A. Pogue. "A Programming Approach to Corporate Financial Management." *Journal of Finance* (May 1974).

Ophir, T. "Optimum Capital Budgeting Lessons of a Linear Programming Formulation." Research No. 6, The Hebrew University, Israel.

Peterson, D. E., and R. B. Haydon. *A Quantitative Framework for Financial Management*. Homewood, Ill.: Richard D. Irwin, Inc., 1969, 404–434.

_____, and D. J. Laughhunn. "Capital Expenditure Programming and Some Alternative Approaches to Risk." *Management Science*, 17 (January 1971), 320–336.

Petty, J. William, David F. Scott, Jr., and Monroe M. Bird. "The Capital Expenditure Decision-Making Process of Large Corporations." *Engineering Economist*, 20 (Spring 1975), 159–172.

Rychel, Dwight F. "Capital Budgeting with Mixed Integer Linear Programming: An Application." *Financial Management*, 6 (Winter 1977), 11–19.

Sealey, C. W., Jr. "Financial Planning with Multiple Objectives." *Financial Management*, 7 (Winter 1978), 17–23.

_____. "Utility Maximization and Programming Models for Capital Budgeting." *Journal of Business Finance and Accounting* (Autumn 1978).

Spies, Richard R. "The Dynamics of Corporate Capital Budgeting." *Journal of Finance* (June 1974).

Teichroew, Daniel, Alexander A. Robichek, and Michael Montalbano. "An Analysis of Criteria for Investment and Financing Decisions under Certainty." *Management Science*, 12 (November 1965), 151–179.

Wacht, Richard F., and David T. Whitford. "A Goal Programming Model for Capital Investment Analysis in Nonprofit Hospitals." *Financial Management*, 5 (Summer 1976), 37–47.

Whitmore, G. A., and L. R. Amey. "Capital Budgeting under Rationing: Comments on the Lusztig and Schwab Procedure." *Journal of Financial and Quantitative Analysis*, 8 (January 1973), 127–135.

Weingartner, H. Martin. "Capital Budgeting of Interrelated Projects: Survey and Synthesis." *Management Science*, 12 (March 1966), 485–516.

_____. "Capital Rationing: n Authors in Search of a Plot." *Journal of Finance*, 32 (December 1977), 1403–1431.

_____. *Mathematical Programming and the Analysis of Capital Budgeting Problems.* Englewood Cliffs, N.J.: Prentice-Hall, 1963.

_____. "The Excess Present Value Index—A Theoretical Basis and Critique." *Journal of Accounting Research*, 1 (Autumn 1963), 213–224.

Multiperiod Analysis Under Conditions of Risk

21

In Chapters 19 and 20 we explored the important models in the area of mathematical programming under conditions of certainty. Such models enable the decision maker to select the set of projects that maximizes net present value or (in the case of goal programming) and achieves a hierarchy of multiple goals. Such models also enable the decision maker to consider more realistic and complex problem settings than those handled by the simple models covered in Chapters 5–8. This chapter parallels the previous two in that it introduces sophisticated approaches for handling conditions of risk in the capital budgeting problem. The new models surveyed here will enrich the simple risk models handled in Chapters 12, 13, and 14 by determining the set of projects that will maximize expected shareholder utility under the complex conditions of multiperiod uncertainty. The important area of Monte Carlo simulation is surveyed first and then applied to the capital budgeting problem. Next, the most helpful mathematical programming models under conditions of risk are discussed and their applications in capital budgeting are illustrated.

MONTE CARLO SIMULATION

Monte Carlo simulation is a flexible and useful operations research technique that can handle any finite problem whose structure and logic can be specified. *Simulation* is the imitation of a real-world system by using a mathematical model which captures the critical operating characteristics of the system as it moves through time encountering random events. Groff and Muth identify three major uses for simulation models:[1]

1   To determine improved operating conditions (i.e., systems design).

[1]G. K. Groff and J. F. Muth, *Operations Management: Analysis for Decisions* (Homewood, Ill.: Richard D. Irwin, Inc., 1972), pp. 369–370.

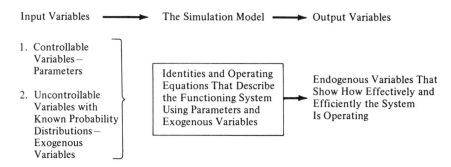

FIGURE 21–1   Schematic of a Simulation Model

2   To demonstrate how a proposed change in policy will work and/or how the new policy compares with existing policies (i.e., systems analysis or sensitivity analysis).

3   To train operating personnel to make better decisions, to react to emergencies in a more efficient and effective manner, and to utilize different kinds of information (i.e., simulation games and heuristic programming).

Figure 21–1 shows a schematic of a simulation model composed of the following four major elements:

1   *Parameters*, which are input variables specified by the decision maker which will be held constant over all simulation runs.

2   *Exogenous variables*, which are input variables outside the control of the decision maker which are subject to random variation—hence, the decision maker must specify a probability distribution to describe possible events that may occur and their associated likelihood of occurrence.

3   *Endogenous variables*, which are output or performance variables describing the operations of the system and how effectively the system achieves various goals as it encounters the random events mentioned above.

4   *Identities and operating equations*, which are mathematical expressions making up the heart of the simulation model by showing how the endogenous variables are functionally related to the parameters and exogenous variables.

A flow chart for a general simulation model is shown in Figure 21–2. The focus of the simulation is to develop empirical distributions for each endogenous variable to describe how efficiently and effectively the system operated during the 500 or 1,000 sampling trials that represent various combinations of random events encountered. As shown in Figure 21–2, the simulation progresses as follows. The parameters of the model are initialized and the probability distributions for each exogenous variable are read in; the simulation itself consists of the DO loop, which will be executed the number of times the user specifies (i.e., MAX is a parameter set by the decision maker to show how many trials are desired wherein system behavior will be studied). On each simulation run, a value is generated for each exogenous variable by randomly selecting from its input probability distribution. Based on these randomly generated values and the values of the parameters, a value is computed for each endogenous variable using the appropriate identity or operating equation. Each simulation run

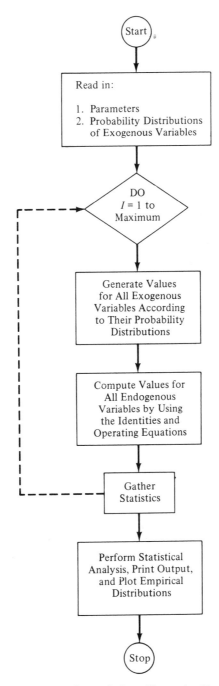

FIGURE 21-2   General Flow Chart of a Simulation

provides one sampling observation for each endogenous variable, and when these observations are aggregated for all simulation runs, the analyst has an empirical distribution from which the usual statistics can be computed and probability statements made about the likelihood of the endogenous variable taking on a value within any given range. Based on the empirical distributions and their statistics which are printed out after the completion of all simulation runs (as well as other such distributions arrived at through prior simulations performed using other values for the parameters, etc.), decisions are made.

A very good survey of the simulation technique appears in Groff and Muth.[2] In addition, Naylor et al. and Shannon[3] provide an extensive treatment of simulation studies, as well as an in-depth discussion of several applications.

Monte Carlo simulation has a number of significant advantages over comparable analytical techniques for handling conditions of risk. First, simulation can handle problems that may have the following characteristics:

1 Numerous exogenous random variables that are each described by a unique probability distribution.
2 Any number of system interrelationships among variables.
3 Identities or operating equations taking on nonlinear, differential, or integral equation forms.

Virtually any analytical or optimization technique would have severe difficulties in handling such problems, if they could be handled at all. Second, sensitivity analysis can be performed in a straightforward manner so that the impact on the system can be pinpointed as parameters or the probability distribution for any combination of exogenous variables is varied. Third, even though simulation models are powerful and flexible, the cost of carrying out simulation runs is relatively small and simulation programs can be modified easily to reflect new structure and relationships in the system under study. However, simulation models (like any decision facilitating model) have their limitations:

1 Input requirements can often put great demands on the decision maker.
2 Valid specification of system variables and interrelationships in the simulation model require a rather extensive understanding of the logical and mathematical properties (many of which can be hidden or nonobvious) of the real system under analysis.
3 Experimental design requires careful attention by the analyst so that the simulation model can be verified and so that it provides output that is as free of error and as informative as possible.

SIMULATION APPLIED TO CAPITAL BUDGETING

One of the first authors to recommend that simulation be used in evaluating capital expenditures was David B. Hertz in his famous 1964 *Harvard Business Review* article.[4] Hertz, a consultant with McKinsey and Co., Inc., described the approach

---

[2]Ibid., Chap. 12.

[3]T. H. Naylor, J. L. Balintfy, D. S. Burdick, and K. Chu, *Computer Simulation Techniques* (New York: John Wiley and Sons, Inc., 1966); and R. E. Shannon, *System Simulation: The Art and Science* (Englewood Cliffs, N.J.: Prentice Hall, 1975).

[4]David B. Hertz, "Risk Analysis in Capital Investment," *Harvard Business Review* (January–February 1964), 95–106.

that his firm utilized to assist an industrial chemical producer who was evaluating a $10 million expansion of its processing plant that would have a 10-year service life. The simulation approach that was used had nine input variables:

Variables for investment cost analysis:

1   Original investment required.
2   Useful life of the facility.
3   Residual value of the investment.

Variables related to revenue generated by the investment:

4   Selling price of the product.
5   Size of the market.
6   Annual growth rate in the size of the market.
7   Share of the market captured by the firm.

Variables related to the operating costs associated with the investment:

8   Variable operating costs per unit of output.
9   Fixed operating costs per year.

The flow chart used by Hertz is shown in Figure 21–3. As can be seen, simulation encounters no difficulties in handling exogenous variables with any desired shape or moments (i.e., mean, variance, skewness, or kurtosis—the first four moments of the probability distribution). It is important to note that the probability distributions must be assessed by management so that they reflect the statistical dependence that exists between various combinations of variables: selling price and size of the market, size of the market and market growth rate, the trade-off between fixed and variable operating costs, and so on. Hertz does not discuss the exact methodology he used to accomplish the task but, as indicated, building interrelationships between variables into the model is one of the rather important aspects of simulation and requires careful attention by management and staff experts involved in building the simulation model.

Interpretation of the information about endogenous variables which is printed out and/or plotted by the computer at the end of the desired number of simulation runs is another essential phase of the overall simulation process. Of course, this output information usually provides valuable data that management uses to compare the risk-return characteristics of investment alternatives under consideration and to select the alternative that offers the maximum expected utility. To illustrate these ideas, consider Figure 21–4, again from the Hertz article. The figure shows the rate of return on two hypothetical alternatives (A versus B) that could be competing designs for the new plant addition in the chemical firm mentioned earlier. The differences are based on the degree of automation. The latter alternative has a higher intensity of capital equipment. The former requires the same dollar investment because more and better facilities to accommodate greater numbers of workers are necessitated by the nature of the less automated plant. As can be seen, alternative B has both a higher expected return and a greater risk, owing to the increased variability in its returns as compared with alternative A. Management should use this information, as well as similar results

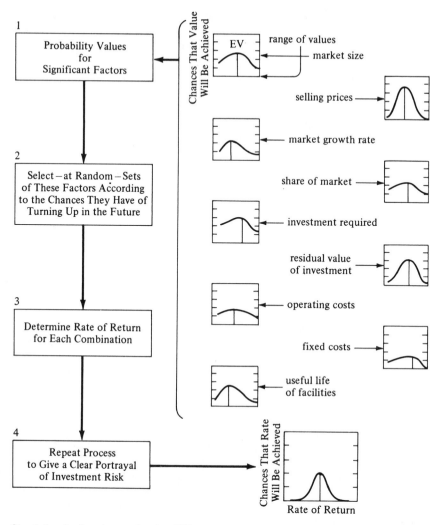

Simulation for investment planning. EV = expected value =average, or the "one best estimate."

SOURCE: David B. Hertz, "Risk Analysis in Capital Investment," *Harvard Business Review* (January–February 1964), 105. Copyright © 1963 by the President and Fellows of Harvard College; all rights reserved.

FIGURE 21 – 3   Flow Chart Used in Hertz Simulation Model

on other endogenous variables, to select the alternative that is preferred given the firm's utility function.

To summarize our discussion and illustrate the components of a simulation model, introduced in the previous section, we will now formally define the parameters, exogenous variables, endogenous variables, and the identities and operating equations for the capital budgeting problem setting using Example 1.

SELECTED STATISTICS

	INVESTMENT A	INVESTMENT B
Amount of investment	$10,000,000	$10,000,000
Life of investment (years)	10	10
Expected annual net cash inflow	$1,300,000	$1,400,000
Variability of cash inflow		
1 chance in 50 of being *greater* than	$1,700,000	$3,400,000
1 chance in 50 of being *less than**	$900,000	($600,000)
Expected return on investment	5.0%	6.8%
Variability of return on investment		
1 chance in 50 of being *greater* than	7.0%	5.5%
1 chance in 50 of being *less than**	3.0%	(4.0%)
Risk of investment		
Chances of a loss	Negligible	1 in 10
Expected size of loss		$200,000

*In the case of negative figures (indicated by parentheses), *less than* means *worse than*.

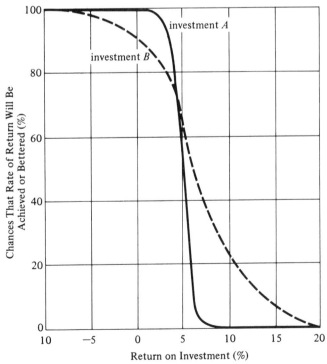

FIGURE 21–4 Comparison of Two Investment Opportunities

EXAMPLE 1

Formulation of Simulation Model for Capital Budgeting Problem

For the general capital budgeting problem discussed in this section, formulate a simulation model by specifying the parameters, exogenous variables, endogenous variables, identities, and operating equations. A flow chart should also be drawn. It can be assumed that the selling price of the product is controlled by the firm and thus is not subject to uncertainty and that the risk-free rate will remain constant over the life of the project. Further, the firm will evaluate any projects under consideration by determining its net income after taxes each year, net cash flows each year, net present value over the life of the project, internal rate of return, and payback period.

SOLUTION: The simulation model with the required components is presented in the table:

General Capital Budgeting Simulation Model

Parameters:

$$SP_t = \text{unit selling price in year } t$$

$$DR_t = \text{depreciation rate for year } t$$

$$i = \text{risk-free rate}$$

$$MAX = \text{total number of simulation runs to be performed}$$

Exogenous variables (Stochastic variables with known probability distribution):

$$MG_t = \text{market growth rate during year } t$$

$$MS_t = \text{market size in number of units in year } t$$

$$SM_t = \text{share of the market in year } t$$

$$INV = \text{initial investment required by the project}$$

$$N = \text{useful life of the investment}$$

$$FC_t = \text{total operating fixed costs in year } t$$

$$VC_t = \text{variable operating costs per unit in year } t$$

$$OC_t = \text{other project related costs in year } t$$

$$TR_t = \text{tax rate in year } t$$

Endogenous variables (Performance variables computed by using identities and operating equations):

$$USAL_t = \text{unit sales generated by the project in year } t$$

$$REV_t = \text{total revenue generated by the project in year } t$$

DEP_t = depreciation on the project in period t

TVC_t = total variable costs associated with the project in year t

TC_t = total costs associated with the project in year t

$NIAT_t$ = net income after tax generated by the project in year t

NCI_t = net cash inflow generated by the project in year t

BV_t = book value of the project at the end of year t

NPV_m = net present value for the investment on the mth simulation run

IRR_m = internal rate of return for the investment on the mth simulation run

$PAYB_m$ = payback period for the investment on the mth simulation run

Identities and operating equations:

$$BV_0 = INV$$

$$DEP_t = (DR_t)(BV_{t-1})$$

$$BV_t = BV_{t-1} - DEP_t$$

$$MS_t = (MS_{t-1})(1 + MG_{t-1}) \text{ for } t = 2, 3, 4, \ldots$$

$$USAL_t = (MS_t)(SM_t)$$

$$REV_t = (USAL_t)(SP_t)$$

$$TVC_t = (VC_t)(USAL_t)$$

$$TC_t = TVC_t + FC_t + OC_t + DEP_t$$

$$TAX_t = TR_t(REV_t - TC_t)$$

$$NIAT_t = REV_t - TC_t - TAX_t$$

$$NCI_t = NIAT_t + DEP_t$$

$$NPV_m = \sum_{t=1}^{N} \frac{NCI_t}{(1+i)^t} + \frac{BV_n}{(1+i)^n} - INV$$

IRR_m = rate r such that

$$\sum_{t=1}^{N} \frac{NCI_t}{(1+r)^t} + \frac{BV_n}{(1+r)^n} - INV = 0$$

$PAYB_m$ = payback period is the value K such that

$$\sum_{t=1}^{K} NCI_t = INV$$

A flow chart showing how the foregoing model would operate appears in Figure 21–5.

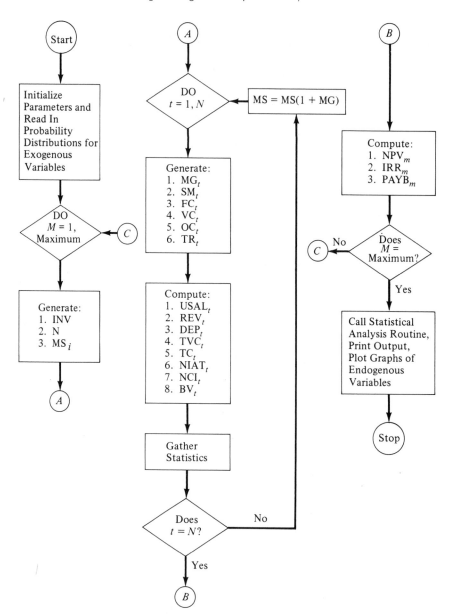

FIGURE 21–5   Flow Chart For Capital Budgeting Simulation

The general model can be enriched or reduced in terms of the number of variables based on the firm's needs. The approach used in Example 1 is straightforward and conventional except for the computation of NPV on each simulation run. It should be noticed that the risk-free rate (rather than the cost of capital or a risk-adjusted discount rate) is used to compute NPV, since the discounting process within a simulation model must reflect discounting only for futurity or the time value of money and not for the specific riskiness of the project under consideration. The degree of risk of the investment project is ascertained in the simulation runs themselves and will be reflected in all the empirical distributions of the endogenous variables. To discount the cash flows of the project at a rate in excess of the risk-free rate would burden the project with an improper double adjustment for uncertainty.[5] Thus, all that is required is to discount the cash flows at the risk-free rate to arrive at an empirical NPV distribution that contains valuable information regarding both the expected value and the risk associated with the project under consideration.

Any large-scale simulation would, of course, be performed on a computer since a minimum of 500 to 1,000 simulation runs are required to achieve stability in the results, and because there are usually many factors to monitor, as can be seen in Example 1. However, to provide insight concerning the operation of the simulation technique, the next example demonstrates a very simple hand simulation.

EXAMPLE 2
Capital Budgeting Simulation Experiment

The Monte Carlo Company is evaluating an investment proposal which has uncertainty associated with the three important aspects: the original cost, the useful life, and the annual net cash inflows. The three probability distributions for these variables are

ORIGINAL COST		USEFUL LIFE		ANNUAL NET CASH INFLOWS	
VALUE	PROBABILITY	VALUE	PROBABILITY	VALUE	PROBABILITY
$60,000	0.3	5 yr	0.4	$10,000	0.1
70,000	0.6	6 yr	0.4	15,000	0.3
90,000	0.1	7 yr	0.2	20,000	0.4
				25,000	0.2

The firm wants to perform five simulation runs of this project's life. The firm's cost of capital is 15% and the risk-free rate is 6%; for simplicity it is assumed that these two values are known for certain and will remain constant over the life of the project.

Determine the NPV, IRR, and payback period for each of the five simulation runs.

SOLUTION: To perform the desired simulation runs by hand, a random number table would be required. An excerpt from the RAND table which shows random numbers

[5]See W. G. Lewellen and M. S. Long, "Simulation vs. Single-Value Estimates in Capital Expenditure Analysis," *Decision Sciences*, 3, no. 4 (October 1972), 22 ff.

uniformly distributed between zero and 1 is presented next. From this table we can randomly generate values from each of the three discrete probability distributions shown.

Table of Random Digits

09656	96657	64842	49222	49506	10145	48455	23505	90430	04180
24712	55799	60857	73479	33581	17360	30406	05842	72044	90764
07202	96341	23699	76171	79126	04512	15426	15980	88898	09658
84575	46820	54083	43918	46989	05379	70682	43081	66171	38942
38144	87037	46626	70529	27918	34191	98668	33482	43998	75733
48048	56349	01986	29814	69800	91609	65374	22928	09704	59343
41936	58566	31276	19952	01352	18834	99596	09302	20087	19063
73391	94006	03822	81845	76158	41352	40596	14325	27020	17546
57580	08954	73554	28698	29022	11568	35668	59906	39557	27217
92646	41113	91411	56215	69302	86419	61224	41936	56939	27816
07118	12707	35622	81485	73354	49800	60805	05648	28898	60933
57842	57831	24130	75408	83784	64307	91620	40810	06539	70387
65078	44981	81009	33697	98324	46928	34198	96032	98426	77488
04294	96120	67629	55265	26248	40602	25566	12520	89785	93932
48381	06807	43775	09708	73199	53406	02910	83292	59249	18597
00459	62045	19249	67095	22752	24636	16965	91836	00582	46721
38824	81681	33323	64086	55970	04849	24819	20749	51711	86173
91465	22232	02907	01050	07121	53536	71070	26916	47620	01619
50874	00807	77751	73952	03073	69063	16894	85570	81746	07568
26644	75871	15618	50310	72610	66205	82640	86205	73453	90232

The simulation process is now undertaken. To generate random numbers from the table, we would just start anywhere at random in the table, reading any pair of adjacent columns, since we need a two-digit random number and read either down the column or across the row. For this example we simply use the first two columns in the table and start at the top with the number 09 and then read down the column. In addition, the foregoing three probability distributions should be cumulated to facilitate running the simulation.

ORIGINAL COST			USEFUL LIFE			ANNUAL NET CASH INFLOWS		
VALUE	PROB.	CUM. PROB.	VALUE	PROB.	CUM. PROB.	VALUE	PROB.	CUM. PROB.
$60,000	0.3	0.30	5 yr	0.4	0.40	$10,000	0.1	0.10
70,000	0.6	0.90	6 yr	0.4	0.80	15,000	0.3	0.40
90,000	0.1	1.00	7 yr	0.2	1.00	20,000	0.4	0.80
						25,000	0.2	1.00

Thus, we can immediately see that the original cost of the project will be $60,000 if the two-digit random number generated is between 00 and 30; the cost will be $70,000 if the random number generated is between 30 and 90; the cost will be $90,000 if the random number generated is between 90 and 99. This methodology carries over to the other two distributions.

The five simulations are now performed and the results are tabulated:

Simulation Results

	ORIGINAL COST		USEFUL LIFE		ANNUAL CASH FLOWS				
RUN	R.N.	VALUE	R.N.	VALUE	R.N.	VALUE	NPV	IRR	PAYBACK
1	09	$60,000	24	5 yr	07	$10,000	− $17,876.36	Negative	None
2	84	70,000	38	5 yr	48	20,000	14,247.28	13.12%	3.5 yr
3	41	70,000	73	6 yr	57	20,000	28,346.48	18.00%	3.5 yr
4	92	90,000	07	5 yr	57	20,000	5,752.72	3.55%	4.5 yr
5	65	70,000	04	5 yr	48	20,000	14,247.28	13.12%	3.5 yr

Recall that the NPV is computed using the risk-free rate of 6%. Of course, this simulation is greatly simplified, but it should provide the general flavor of the approach. Notice that there is substantial variability in the results due to the small number of exogenous variables, their discrete distributions, and the small number of simulation runs performed.

The basic simulation approach has been extended in several directions. Some of the more interesting are now discussed briefly, with references given so that the interested reader can explore them further.

Kryzanowski, Lusztig, and Schwab discuss the application of a Hertz-type simulation model to a plant expansion decision by a natural resource firm.[6] Thuesen describes the use of simulation by the Georgia Power Company in performing risk analysis in the evaluation of nuclear versus fossil-fuel power plants.[7] Philippatos and Mastai present a model designed to assist a wholesaler of nondurable goods in evaluating a proposed computer-controlled automated warehouse.[8] Chambers and Mullick present a simulation model that they designed and used at Corning Glass Works to evaluate five alternative manufacturing facilities in various foreign countries for one of their major product lines.[9] Fourcans and Hindelang formulate a general two-stage simulation model wherein both the subsidiary and the parent company of a multinational firm can evaluate and rank investment opportunities considering both project-related and critical international variables as well as various interrelationships among these variables.[10]

Cohen and Elton suggest that simulation is an efficient way of determining the elements of the variance-covariance matrix required to evaluate joint returns on a

[6]L. Kryzanowski, P. Lusztig, and B. Schwab, "Monte Carlo Simulation and Capital Expenditure Decisions—A Case Study," *The Engineering Economist*, 18 (Fall 1972), 31–48.

[7]G. J. Thuesen, "Nuclear vs. Fossil Power Plants: Evolution of Economic Evaluation Techniques," *The Engineering Economist*, (Fall 1975), 21–38.

[8]G. C. Philippatos and A. J. Mastai, "Investment in an Automated Warehouse: A Monte Carlo Simulation and Post-Optimality Analysis," *Proceedings of the 1971 Conference on Systems, Networks and Computers*, January 1971, Mexico City; also see G. C. Philippatos, *Financial Management: Theory and Techniques* (San Francisco: Holden-Day, Inc., 1973), Chap. 21.

[9]J. C. Chambers and S. K. Mullick, "Investment Decision Making in a Multinational Enterprise," *Management Accounting* (August 1971).

[10]A. Fourcans and T. J. Hindelang, "A Simulation Approach to Capital Budgeting for the Multinational Firm," presented to the *1976 Financial Management Association Conference*, October 1976. Montreal, Canada; also see Appendix 26A of this text.

portfolio of capital budgeting projects under evaluation.[11] Salazar and Sen develop a simulation model which they combined with Weingartner's linear programming model. Their simulation incorporates two types of uncertainty: environmental uncertainty based on what future economic, social, and competitive conditions may be, and cash flow uncertainty, wherein only the shape and parameters of a probability distribution are specified.[12] Their approach generates efficient portfolios of projects which are ranked as a function of differing environmental conditions and/or managerial preferences toward risk and return. Finally, Carter suggests an interactive simulation model wherein all projects under consideration are simulated jointly in order to derive covariances among the projects.[13] Based on this simulation, the expected return and variance of various portfolios are computed and managers can obtain further information on any desired portfolio to make the final selection.

Our overview of the simulation methodology, plus the survey of the direction of simulation research, will be helpful in the following section, which introduces the complex area of mathematical programming under conditions of risk.

MATHEMATICAL PROGRAMMING UNDER RISK

This section surveys the application of mathematical programming models under conditions of risk to the capital budgeting problem. Table 18–1 identified the five categories of mathematical programming models under conditions of risk:

1   Stochastic linear programming (SLP)
    Linear programming under uncertainty (LPUU)
    Chance-constrained programming (CCP)
2   Integer programming under uncertainty (IPUU)
3   Stochastic goal programming (SGP)
4   Nonlinear programming under uncertainty (NLPUU)
    Quadratic programming under uncertainty (QPUU)
5   Dynamic programming under uncertainty (DPUU)

Among these approaches, the major applications in the capital budgeting area have been in stochastic LP, chance-constrained programming, and quadratic programming under uncertainty. A brief overview of each of these models, as well as the significance of their application within the field of capital investment will be presented.

Stochastic Linear Programming

Stochastic LP is a method of handling conditions of risk similar to Monte Carlo simulation already discussed. In SLP, a linear programming model replaces the

[11]K. J. Cohen and E. J. Elton, "Intertemporal Portfolio Analysis Based on Simulation of Joint Returns," *Management Science*, 14 (September 1967), 5–18.

[12]R. C. Salazar and S. K. Sen. "A Simulation Model of Capital Budgeting Under Uncertainty," *Management Science*, 15 (December 1968), 161–179.

[13]E. E. Carter, *Portfolio Aspects of Corporate Capital Budgeting* (Lexington, Mass.: Lexington Books, 1974).

identities and operating equations of the simulation model and the two-stage process proceeds as follows. In stage 1, we first set a number of decision variables and consider that they will be fixed (just like parameters in a simulation model) for all subsequent observations of random events. In stage 2, random events are generated and these values plus the parameters from stage 1 are substituted into the LP model. The LP is solved, which provides one empirical observation of the optimal value of the LP objective function and the optimal values of the decision variables. Next, we go back and repeat the process of generating random events and solving LP problems some desired number of times, thereby deriving a complete empirical distribution for the LP objective function. Finally, we compare this empirical distribution with other empirical distributions determined using different stage 1 decisions to ascertain that set of stage 1 decisions which optimizes the decision maker's utility function.

The major SLP approach to capital budgeting is attributed to Salazar and Sen.[14] To provide greater insight into their approach and to further describe SLP, several figures from their article are presented. Salazar and Sen incorporate two kinds of uncertainty into their model: uncertainty related to significant economic and competitive variables which are likely to affect project cash flows and uncertainty related to the cash flows of the projects under consideration based on these variables. Salazar and Sen handle the first type of uncertainty by a tree diagram (similar to that introduced in Chapter 11) shown in Figure 21–6. Notice that there are 12 branches in the tree diagram with their respective joint probabilities of occurrence shown on the far right of the tree; the derivation of those probabilities is based on the table below the tree. In the SLP framework, the 12 branches in this tree diagram are considered as stage 1 decisions to be fixed; for each branch in the tree, cash flows for each project under consideration are randomly generated and then plugged into the LP model. To elaborate, consider the flow chart used by Salazar and Sen, which is shown in Figure 21–7. The first processing box in the flow chart randomly selects a branch from the tree shown in Figure 21–6. Next, the time counter, t, is set to 1 and then the project counter, j, is also set to 1. The two DO loops randomly generate the cash flows for all projects (up to $j = 15$—all 15 projects under consideration) over all time periods (up to $t = 21$—the planning horizon of the model). These random cash flows are plugged into the model's LP algorithm (which would be similar to the models discussed in Chapter 20) and the optimal set of projects, and the optimal objective function value is obtained. We then check to see if we have performed the desired number of simulations (S^*). If not, we go back and randomly select another branch from the tree diagram in Figure 21–6 and repeat the simulation and LP solution again. When all simulation runs have been performed, the empirical LP objective function results are plotted on the risk-return axes.[15] Given this summary of the results, management can decide which portfolio of assets optimizes its utility function. This approach is a flexible and powerful combination of mathematical programming and the simulation technique.

Chance-Constrained Programming

The next major category which has seen capital budgeting applications is that of *chance-constrained programming*. The approach of CCP is to maximize the expected

---

[14] Salazar and Sen, "A Simulation Model."
[15] Ibid., p. 173.

Structure of the Model

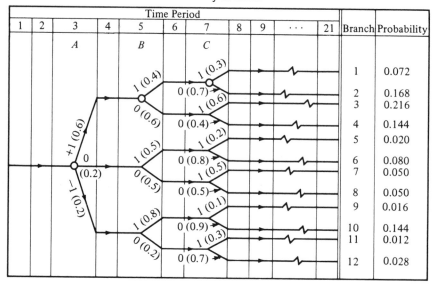

											Branch	Probability
											1	0.072
											2	0.168
											3	0.216
											4	0.144
											5	0.020
											6	0.080
											7	0.050
											8	0.050
											9	0.016
											10	0.144
											11	0.012
											12	0.028

Interpretation of Chance Nodes

VARIABLE		TIME	ENVIRONMENTAL STATE		PROBABILITY OF
NAME	SYMBOL	PERIOD	NAME	SYMBOL	OCCURRENCE
GNP	A	3	Rises	+1	0.6
			No change	0	0.2
			Falls	−1	0.2
(Competitor's price— our price)	B	5	(0 or +)	1	0.4
			(−)	0	0.6
Introduction of new product by competitor	C	7	Yes	1	0.3
			No	0	0.7

Structure of the Model Interpretation of Chance Nodes

VARIABLE		TIME	ENVIRONMENTAL STATE		PROBABILITY OF
NAME	SYMBOL	PERIOD	NAME	SYMBOL	OCCURRENCE
GNP	A	3	Rises	+1	0.6
			No change	0	0.2
			Falls	−1	0.2
(Competitor's price— our price)	B	5	(0 or +)	1	0.4
			(−)	0	0.6
Introduction of new product by competitor	C	7	Yes	1	0.3
			No	0	0.7

SOURCE: R. C. Salazar and S. K. Sen, "A Simulation Model of Capital Budgeting Under Uncertainty," *Management Science*, 15 (December 1968), 165.

FIGURE 21–6   Tree Diagram Used by Salazar and Sen

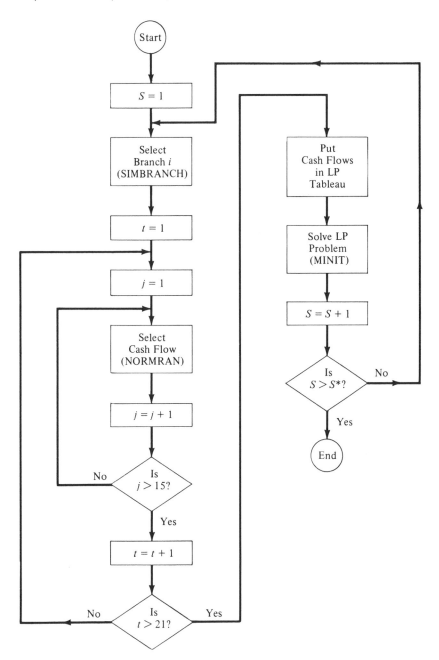

SOURCE: R. C. Salazar and S. K. Sen, "A Simulation Model of Capital Budgeting Under Uncertainty," *Management Science*, 15 (December 1968), 169.

FIGURE 21–7   Macro Flow Chart of System Program

value of the objective function subject to economic constraints that are allowed to be violated some given percentage of the time due to random variations in the system. Chance constraints are arrived at as follows, with the usual constraints of LP:

$$\sum_{j=1}^{N} a_{ij}X_j \leq b_i$$

Owing to randomness in either the a_{ij} coefficients or the b_i right-hand side values, we show that the economic constraints do not have to be satisfied all the time by associating a probability or chance constraint statement with each economic constraint,

$$P\left\{ \sum_{j=1}^{N} a_{ij}X_j \leq b_i \right\} \geq \alpha_i$$

where P = probability

α_i = minimum probability that the decision maker is willing to accept that a given constraint is satisfied

If $\alpha_i = 0.90$, for example, this would mean that the decision maker requires that the economic constraint be satisfied at least 90% of the time and that he or she is willing to allow $\Sigma a_{ij}X_j$ to exceed b_i up to 10% of the time.

The solution methodology for CCP problems requires that the *deterministic equivalent* be derived for all chance constraints by taking into account the shape and parameters of the probability distributions for all random variables, as well as the degree of correlation between all pairs of random variables. This derivation usually results in nonlinear equations, which greatly threatens the feasibility of solving all but the smallest problems. Difficulties in problem solution escalate rapidly as the size of the problem grows or as the distributions of random variables describing the system depart from normality. The finding of these "deterministic equivalents" is beyond our scope, but the interested reader is referred to Charnes and Cooper[16] or Taha.[17]

Three significant contributions have been made in the area of CCP applied to capital budgeting. The earliest work was due to Naslund.[18] The expected horizon value of the firm was maximized subject to probabilistic constraints on financing alternatives that could be violated some fraction of the time. He considered both perfect and imperfect capital markets. Naslund's work extended Weingartner's (covered extensively in Chapter 19) to the risk area.

The second contribution was an article in 1967 by Byrne, Charnes, Cooper, and Kortenek.[19] Their model incorporated probabilistic payback and liquidity constraints

[16]A. Charnes and W. W. Cooper, "Deterministic Equivalents for Optimizing and Satisficing Under Chance Constraints," *Operations Research*, 11 (January 1963), 18–39.

[17]H. A. Taha, *Operations Research: An Introduction* (New York: Macmillan Publishing Co., 1971), pp. 649–653.

[18]B. Naslund, "A Model for Capital Budgeting Under Risk," *Journal of Business*, 39 (April 1966), 257–271.

[19]R. Byrne, A. Charnes, W. W. Cooper, and K. Kortenek, "A Chance-Constrained Programming Approach to Capital Budgeting," *Journal of Financial and Quantitative Analysis*, 2 (December 1967), 339–364.

as well as requirements for the firm's posture at the end of the planning horizon. Using the deterministic equivalents, the authors were able to derive a numerical solution for a small three-period, four-project example. They also presented strategies for doing sensitivity analysis on the results. Because of the unresolved difficulty of solving large CCP problems, the same four authors recommended two alternative solution techniques based on assumptions that project cash flows could be closely approximated by discrete probability distributions.[20] The second article of the pair developed an integer LP model to approximate the nonlinear CCP model (for which no efficient solution technique exists).

The final major model was formulated by Hillier when he maximized the expected utility of the shareholders at the end of the planning horizon subject to probabilistic constraints on the net cash flows in each period, as well as cumulative net cash flows in each period over the planning horizon.[21] The author suggested two solution techniques:

1 An approximate LP model based on the deterministic equivalents for the chance constraints.
2 An exact branch-and-bound algorithm that he developed for handling continuous zero-one chance-constrained programming problems.[22]

To illustrate the CCP formulations and the results of finding the deterministic equivalent for chance constraints, consider the model suggested by Naslund.[23] His model consisted of the objective function plus the chance constraints,

$$\text{maximize } E\left(\sum_{j=1}^{N} A_j X_j + V_T - W_T \right)$$

subject to

$$P\left(\sum_{j=1}^{N} a_{1j} X_j + V_1 - W_1 \le D_1 \right) \ge \alpha_1$$

$$P\left(\sum_{i=1}^{t} \sum_{j=1}^{N} a_{ij} X_j - \sum_{i=1}^{t-1} V_i r + \sum_{i=1}^{t-1} W_i r + V_t - W_t \le \sum_{i=1}^{t} D_i \right) \ge \alpha_t$$

$$t = 2, 3, \dots, T$$

$$0 \le X_j \le 1 \quad V_t, W_t \ge 0$$

where E = expected value operator
    P = probability of the expression within the parentheses
    A_j = horizon value at time T of all cash flows subsequent to the horizon associated with project j
    X_j = fraction of project j accepted

[20] R. Byrne, A. Charnes, W. W. Cooper, and K. Kortenek, "A Discrete Probability Chance Constrained Capital Budgeting Model—I and II," *Opsearch*, 6 (December 1969), 171–198, 226–261.

[21] F. S. Hillier, *The Evaluation of Risky Interrelated Investments* (Amsterdam: North-Holland Publishing Co., 1969); also F. S. Hillier, "A Basic Model for Capital Budgeting of Risky Interrelated Investments," *The Engineering Economist*, 17, no. 1, 1–30.

[22] F. S. Hillier, "Chance-Constrained Programming with Zero-One or Bounded Continuous Decision Variables," *Management Science*, 14, (September 1967), 34–57.

[23] Naslund, "A Model for Capital Budgeting," pp. 258–261.

V_t = amount of money lent in period t at interest rate r

W_t = amount of money borrowed in period t at interest rate r

a_{tj} = cash flows associated with project j in time period t—positive signs for this variable are associated with cash outflows while negative signs are associated with cash inflows

D_t = cash flow generated by other activities than the investment projects that we are going to consider

α_t = probability required the constraint within the parentheses hold

In the formulation, the following variables can be considered random: a_{tj}, A_j, D_i. Owing to this randomness, the constraints within the parentheses may not always be satisfied, but the decision maker requires that they be satisfied at least α_t percent of time. Thus, the formulation maximizes the expected value of the horizon value of all accepted projects plus money lent, minus money borrowed at the horizon date, T. This maximization is carried out subject to a budget limitation expressed as a chance constraint in each period over the planning horizon. The constraint for period 1 states that the amount spent on new projects ($\Sigma a_{ij}X_j$) plus the amount of funds lent (V_1) less the amount of funds borrowed (W_1) cannot exceed the cash flows generated by operations (D_1). The probabilistic constraint in each subsequent period considers cumulative cash inflows and outflows on all projects ($\Sigma\Sigma a_{ij}X_j$), the cumulative amount of interest received on funds lent up to the present period ($\Sigma V_i r$), the cumulative amount of interest paid on borrowed funds up to the present period ($\Sigma W_i r$), and the cumulative cash inflow from operations (ΣD_i). The constraint states that cumulative net cash outflows for all projects up to the period minus cumulative interest earned plus cumulative interest paid plus the amount lent less the amount borrowed cannot exceed cumulative cash inflow from operations. Finally, we have the nonnegativity constraint and the upper limit on project acceptance. As indicated, to solve this problem the deterministic equivalent must be taken considering the random variables that are present. Naslund[24] assumed that the only random variables were the a_{tj}, which he further assumed were normally distributed with means U_{tj} and variances σ_{tj}^2 and further that all these variables were independent of one another. Given these assumptions, the deterministic equivalent that Naslund derived is

$$\text{maximize} \sum_{j=1}^{N} A_j X_j + V_T - W_T$$

subject to

$$\sum_{j=1}^{N} U_{1j}X_j + V_1 - W_1 + \sqrt{\sum_{j=1}^{N} \sigma_{1j}^2 X_j^2}\, F^{-1}(\alpha_1) \leq D_1$$

$$\sum_{i=1}^{t}\sum_{j=1}^{N} U_{ij}X_j - \sum_{i=1}^{t-1} V_i r + \sum_{i=1}^{t-1} W_i r + V_t - W_t$$

$$+ \sqrt{\sum_{j=1}^{N} \sigma_{tj}^2 X_j^2}\, F^{-1}(\alpha_t) \leq \sum_{i=1}^{t} D_i \qquad t = 2,3,\ldots,T$$

$$0 \leq X_j \leq 1 \qquad V_t, W_t \geq 0$$

[24] Ibid., p. 261.

where F^{-1} is the inverse cumulative density function associated with the random variables a_{tj}. As can be seen, all the constraints are nonlinear in the decision variables X_j because of the square root of the sum of the variances times X_j squared. Of course, these nonlinearities in the constraints cause significant problems in solving the formulation, since there is no general way of solving nonlinear programming problems. The approximation methods just discussed provide assistance in solving CCP problems. We now turn to a discussion of one final mathematical programming model under risk.

Quadratic Programming

Quadratic programming is the mathematical programming model wherein a nonlinear objective function is optimized subject to linear constraints. This model is far easier to solve than the nonlinear programming model, because the feasible region is convex. The convexity assures that a local optimal solution is also the global optimal solution. This greatly facilitates the optimization process, since the feasible region for a nonlinear model is not necessarily convex.

The earliest QP model in the capital budgeting area is attributed to Farrar,[25] who in 1962 extended the work of Markowitz (who used QP in portfolio selection) and Weingartner (who did pioneering work in the capital budgeting area) by reflecting both the project's expected net present value (NPV) and the variance of the NPVs in the objective function. The general QP formulation recommended by Farrar is as follows,

$$\text{maximize } Z = \sum_{j=1}^{N} X_j U_j - A \sum_{i=1}^{N} \sum_{j=1}^{N} X_i X_j \sigma_{ij}$$

subject to

$$\sum_{j=1}^{N} X_j = 1$$

$$X_j \geq 0$$

where X_j = proportion of the total budget invested in project j
  U_j = expected NPV of project j
  A = stockholders' average coefficient of risk aversion
  σ_{ij} = covariance between the NPV of project i and project j—when $i = j$, this is the variance of project j

Note that the objective function seeks to maximize shareholders' expected utility, since it reflects both the mean and variance of all possible portfolios of projects plus the average coefficient of risk aversion. Thus, the trade-offs between risk and return are incorporated, as are the interactions between all possible pairs of investments projects.

[25] D. F. Farrar, *The Investment Decision Under Uncertainty* (Englewood Cliffs, N.J.: Prentice Hall, 1962).

One problem with this formulation is that the decision variables are continuous (i.e., $X_j \geq 0$) and that the decision variables are stated in the portfolio convention of percent of the budget availability (in a single period) to be invested in each project. To overcome these difficulties it was necessary to arrive at an integer quadratic programming algorithm that could efficiently handle realistic-sized problems. Such a development was forthcoming when Mao and Wallingford[26] extended a previous integer LP branch-and-bound algorithm developed by Lawler and Bell.[27] They reported promising computational results showing that problems with 15 projects and 15 constraints were solved in less than 1 second of computer time. Of course, the variance-covariance matrix grows exponentially with the number of projects under evaluation.

The most recent quadratic programming capital budgeting model was developed by Thompson in a capital asset pricing context.[28] He formulated a single-period model which handles competitive and complementary projects where the market value is determined by the capital asset pricing model. However, he concluded his article with a word of caution:[29]

> The programming approach has been shown to deal effectively with multiperiod problems. Its credentials are strong. The capital asset pricing model, however, deals with a single period. Developing a multiperiod approach to capital budgeting using a multiperiod capital asset pricing model appears more formidable.

This concludes the discussion of QP, which provides the decision maker with assistance in capturing the covariance between projects and between projects and the ongoing operations of the firm.

SUMMARY

This chapter presents an overview of sophisticated approaches for handling conditions of risk in a multiperiod setting. The first approach introduced is that of Monte Carlo simulation—a powerful and flexible approach to handling the capital budgeting problem. Next, the mathematical programming models under risk of stochastic LP, chance-constrained programming, and quadratic programming are surveyed and illustrated. These techniques provide valuable assistance to financial managers as they wrestle with capital budgeting problems under conditions of risk.

QUESTIONS
───────────
PROBLEMS

1. Discuss the strengths and weaknesses of Monte Carlo simulation in decision making under conditions of risk.
2. Discuss the major components of a Monte Carlo simulation model and illustrate these in the capital budgeting problem setting.

[26]J. C. T. Mao and B. A. Wallingford, "An Extension of Lawler and Bell's Method of Discrete Optimization," *Management Science* (October 1968), 51–61.

[27]E. E. Lawler and M. D. Bell, "A Method for Solving Discrete Optimization Problems," *Operations Research* (November–December 1966), 1098–1112.

[28]H. E. Thompson, "Mathematical Programming, The Capital Asset Pricing Model, and Capital Budgeting of Interrelated Projects," *The Journal of Finance*, 31, no. 1 (March 1976), 125–131.

[29]Ibid., p. 130.

3. Discuss the strengths and weaknesses of stochastic LP, chance-constrained programming, and quadratic programming for handling the capital budgeting problem under conditions of risk.

4. For the Monte Carlo Company shown in Example 2:
   (a) Using the probability distributions shown in Example 2 and assuming independence in the cash flows over time, compute the expected NPV and the standard deviation for this distribution over the life of the project.
   (b) Assuming normality, compute the probability that the NPV will be positive as well as the probability that it will exceed $10,000.
   (c) Perform 10 simulation runs for the project shown in Example 2 and compute the mean NPV and the standard deviation of this distribution.
   (d) Assuming normality, compute the probability that the NPV will be positive as well as the probability that it will exceed $10,000, based on the results of your 10 simulation runs in part (c). Compare these results with those obtained in part (b) and comment on any differences (i.e., Why do the differences arise? Which probabilities are more reliable? etc.).

5. The Wee Producem Company is deciding whether to introduce a new product on the market. At the present time it has two decisions to make: the overall decision of whether to introduce the product with additional production costs of $15,000,000 versus dropping the project and simply suffering the loss of the $2,500,000 already invested, or to do further market research at a cost of $1,500,000 and then make the introduction decision (with the same costs as above). Wee Producem estimates that the market research group will assign a probability of 0.7 that the product will be introduced. Because of the unusual nature of the product, only two final outcomes are possible: outcome A derives $40,000,000 profit while outcome B derives a $5,000,000 loss. The present estimated likelihood of outcome A is 0.6 and 0.4 for outcome B.

   Determine the optimal strategy by using a decision tree to compare the expected returns of the different possible strategies.

REFERENCES

Agrawal, Anup, and Gershon N. Mandelker. "Managerial Incentives and Corporate Investment and Financing Decisions." *Journal of Finance* (September 1987).

Balachandran, Bala V., Nandu J. Nagarajan, and Alfred Rappaport. "Threshold Margins for Creating Economic Value." *Financial Management* (Spring 1986).

Bernhard, Richard H. "Mathematical Programming Models for Capital Budgeting—A Survey, Generalization, and Critique." *Journal of Financial and Quantitative Analysis*, 4 (June 1969), 111–158.

Byrne, R., A. Charnes, W. W. Cooper, and K. Kortenek. "A Chance-Constrained Programming Approach to Capital Budgeting." *Journal of Financial and Quantitative Analysis*, 2 (December 1967), 339–364.

_____, A. Charnes, W. W. Cooper, and K. Kortenek. "A Discrete Probability Chance Constrained Capital Budgeting Model-I and II." *Opsearch*, 6 (December 1969), 171–198, 226–261.

Carter, E. E. *Portfolio Aspects of Corporate Capital Budgeting*. Lexington, Mass.: Lexington Books, 1974.

Chambers, J. C., and S. K. Mullick. "Investment Decision Making in a Multinational Enterprise." *Management Accounting* (August 1971).

Charnes, A., and W. W. Cooper. "Deterministic Equivalents for Optimizing and Satisficing under Chance Constraints." *Operations Research*, 11 (January 1963), 18–39.

Cohen, K. J., and E. J. Elton. "Intertemporal Portfolio Analysis Based on Simulation of Joint Returns." *Management Science*, 14 (September 1967), 5–18.

Farrer, D. F. *The Investment Decision under Uncertainty*. Englewood Cliffs, N.J.: Prentice-Hall, 1962.

Fourcans, A., and T. J. Hindelang. "A Simulation Approach to Capital Budgeting for the Multinational Firm." Paper presented to the 1976 Financial Management Association Conference, Montreal, Canada, October 1976.

Harrington, Diana R. "Stock Prices, Beta and Strategic Planning." *Harvard Business Review* (May–June 1983).

Haugen, Robert A., and Lemma W. Serbet. "Bankruptcy and Agency Costs: Their Significance to the Theory of Optimal Capital Structure." *Journal of Financial and Quantitative Analysis* (March 1988).

Hertz, David B. "Investment Policies That Pay Off." *Harvard Business Review*, 46 (January–February 1968), 96–108.

_____. "Risk Analysis in Capital Investment." *Harvard Business Review*, 42 (January–February 1964), 95–106.

Hespos, Richard F., and Paul A. Strassmann. "Stochastic Decision Trees for the Analysis of Investment Decisions." *Management Science*, 11 (August 1965), 244–259.

Hillier, Frederick S. "A Basic Model for Capital Budgeting of Risky Interrelated Projects." *Engineering Economist*, 20 (Fall 1974), 37–49.

_____. "Chance-Constrained Programming with 0–1 or Bounded Continuous Decision Variables." *Management Science*, 14 (September 1967), 34–57.

_____. "The Derivation of Probabilistic Information for the Evaluation of Risky Investments." *Management Science*, 9 (April 1963), 443–457.

_____. *The Evaluation of Risky Interrelated Investments*. Amsterdam: North-Holland Publishing Co., 1969.

Jones, E. Phillip, Scott P. Mason, and Eric Rosenfeld. "Contingent Claims Analysis of Corporate Capital Structures: An Empirical Investigation." *Journal of Finance* (July 1984).

Kroll, Y., H. Levy, and H. M. Markowitz. "Mean-Variance Versus Direct Utility Maximization." *Journal of Finance* (March 1984).

Kryzanowski, Lawrence, Peter Lusztig, and Bernhard Schwab. "Monte Carlo Simulation and Capital Expenditure Decisions—A Case Study." *Engineering Economist*, 18 (Fall 1972), 31–48.

Lewellen, Wilbur G., and Michael S. Long. "Simulation Versus Single-Value Estimates in Capital Expenditure Analysis." *Decision Sciences*, 3 (1973), 19–33.

Lockett, A. Geoffrey, and Anthony E. Gear. "Multistage Capital Budgeting under Uncertainty." *Journal of Financial and Quantitative Analysis*, 10 (March 1975), 21–36.

MacMinn, Richard D. "Forward Markets, Stock Markets, and the Theory of the Firm." *Journal of Finance* (December 1987).

Magee, J. F. "How to Use Decision Trees in Capital Investment." *Harvard Business Review*, 42 (September–October 1964), 79–96.

Mandelker, Gershon, and S. Ghon Rhee. "The Impact of the Degrees of Operating and Financial Leverage on Systematic Risk of Common Stock." *Journal of Financial and Quantitative Analysis* (March 1984).

McConnell, John J., and Chris J. Muscarello. "Capitalized Value, Growth Opportunities and Corporate Capital Expenditures Announcements." Research paper, Purdue University, Lafayette, Ind., January 4, 1984.

Miller, Robert E., and Michael H. Morris. "Multiproduct C-V-P Analysis and Uncertainty: A Linear Programming Approach." *Journal of Business Finance and Accounting* (Winter 1985).

Myers, S. C. "Procedures for Capital Budgeting under Uncertainty." *Industrial Management Review*, 9 (Spring 1968), 1–15.

Naslund, B. "A Model for Capital Budgeting under Risk." *Journal of Business*, 39 (April 1966), 257–271.

_____, and A. Whinston. "A Model of Multi-Period Investment under Uncertainty." *Management Science*, 9 (January 1962), 184–200.

Naylor, T. H., J. L. Balintfy, D. S. Burdick, and K. Chu. *Computer Simulation Techniques.* New York: John Wiley & Sons, Inc., 1966.

Ofer, Aharon R., and Daniel R. Siegel. "Corporate Financial Policy, Information, and Market Expectations: An Empirical Investigation of Dividends." *Journal of Finance* (September 1987).

Philippatos, G. C. *Financial Management: Theory and Techniques.* San Francisco: Holden-Day, Inc., 1973, Chap. 21.

Robichek, Alexander A. "Interpreting the Results of Risk Analysis." *Journal of Finance*, 30 (December 1975), 1384–1386.

Salazar, R. C., and S. K. Sen. "A Simulation Model of Capital Budgeting under Uncertainty." *Management Science*, 15 (December 1968), 161–179.

Schall, Laurence D. "Taxes, Inflation and Corporate Financial Policy." *Journal of Finance* (March 1984).

Shannon, R. E. *System Simulation: The Art and Science.* Englewood Cliffs, N.J.: Prentice-Hall, 1975.

Sick, Gordon. "Multiperiod Risky Project Valuation: A Mean-Covariance Certainty Equivalent Approach." research paper, University of Alberta, Edmonton, May 1984.

Sundem, Gary L. "Evaluating Capital Budgeting Models in Simulated Environments." *Journal of Finance*, 30 (September 1975), 977–992.

Thanassoulis, E. "Selecting a Suitable Solution Method for a Multi-Objective Programming Capital Budgeting Problem." *Journal of Business Finance and Accounting* (Autumn 1985).

Thompson, H. E. "Mathematical Programming, the Capital Asset Pricing Model and Capital Budgeting of Interrelated Projects." *Journal of Finance*, 31, 1 (March 1976), 125–131.

Thuesen, G. J. "Nuclear vs. Fossil Power Plants: Evolution of Economic Evaluation Techniques." *Engineering Economist*, 21 (Fall 1975), 21–38.

Trueman, Brett. "The Relationship between the Level of Capital Expenditures and Firm Value." *Journal of Financial and Quantitative Analysis* (June 1986).

Williams, Joseph. "Perquisites, Risk, and Capital Structure." *Journal of Finance* (March 1987).

_____, and A. J. Mastai. "Investment in an Automated Warehouse: A Monte Carlo Simulation and Post-Optimality Analysis." *Proceedings of the 1971 Conference on Systems, Networks and Computers*, Mexico City, January 1971.

Wilson, Robert B. "Investment Analysis under Uncertainty." *Management Science*, 15 (August 1969), 650–664.

Strategic Planning for Capital Investment Decisions[*]

22.

Previous chapters have thoroughly examined the technical aspects of evaluating investment projects. This examination included estimation of cash flows, alternative calculations for the cost of capital used in discounting these cash flows, and the evaluation of mutually exclusive projects using different criteria. An implicit assumption throughout the earlier presentation is that the firm has a substantial range of investment opportunities available for consideration. However, little guidance has been given regarding how these profitable opportunities are actually found. Strategic planning assists managers in accomplishing this challenging task. Once identified, these opportunities should be considered in the context of the firm's existing assets (assets in place) and in relation to future options which could be created through the adoption of these investment opportunities (growth options). In other words, these opportunities should be analyzed in the context of how they interface with the firm's strategic objectives.

It is often taken for granted that a firm always has the ability to develop investment opportunities with positive net present values (NPVs). This may be based on the belief that most investments considered by a firm stem from existing operations in an attempt to improve the firm's productive efficiency, for example, through the use of more cost-effective equipment. Although this belief has its merit, not all projects are of this engineering type, that is, replacement projects related to existing assets. Investment opportunities available for consideration are classified as either mandatory or discretionary. Mandatory investment opportunities are those replacement investment projects that help the firm to improve its productive capabilities and cash flows as they relate to the current line of business. Discretionary investment opportunities, on the other hand, are future investment options that represent the potential for new growth in related or different product lines.

Mandatory investment opportunities are relatively easy to search for and to identify given the familiarity and experience of management with current operations.

*The authors express their deep appreciation to Dr. George P. Tsetsekos, Drexel University, for his contributions in writing this chapter. Dr. Tsetsekos wrote this chapter while serving on the Finance Faculty of the Kogod College of Business Administration, The American University, Washington, D.C.

The evaluation of these projects can easily be performed with the discounted cash flow (DCF) techniques extensively discussed in the literature. However, the evaluation of discretionary investment opportunities requires a different set of analytical techniques which are dictated by strategic considerations. This is because discretionary opportunities reflect the aspirations or goals of management and represent options for new direction of the organization which are difficult to evaluate with the conventional (DCF) techniques, primarily because of the nature and risks involved in these cash flows. In addition, investments related to growth opportunities must fit into an overall strategic plan for the firm which considers these opportunities together with existing assets. Although projects evaluated in isolation might be found to have positive NPVs, there is no assurance that when evaluated as a set of projects they will generate maximum market value for the firm.

It is obvious that managers need to develop qualitative means of identifying those investment opportunities that will generate positive NPVs on an ex ante basis. Moreover, managers must consider the possibility that some investment opportunities might generate future options to the firm whose realization would provide substantial economic rents to shareholders. Strategic planning addresses some of these managerial issues and assists managers in the development of an investment strategy for the identification and evaluation of growth opportunities.

In this chapter, we emphasize the analytical techniques and conceptual models used in the evaluation of investments that are considered discretionary and are related to the firm's growth opportunities. It is suggested that the strategic planning approach presented here is compatible with the capital budgeting techniques that have been presented earlier. It is further suggested that the strategic planning techniques presented complement the analysis of the capital budgeting problem faced by an organization. We can think of the analysis of the capital budgeting problem as a two-stage process. In the first stage, the firm identifies growth opportunities through the use of strategic planning techniques, and in the second stage, the more precise technical calculations take place. For example, after an opportunity has been identified through the strategic planning process, quantitative DCF techniques can offer more precise information on the level of windfalls that might result from the investment opportunity.

This chapter is organized as follows. The first section discusses the essence of strategic planning, advocating that strategic planning focuses on the search for investment projects that have positive NPVs. The second section considers the concepts applied in identifying those market imperfections that result in excess economic rents, thereby identifying projects that will increase the firm's value. The third section introduces tools and techniques to be used in the more precise identification and selection of projects that produce high NPVs. The fourth section deals with issues of risk in strategic planning and the market value assessment of investment strategies that are implemented on the basis of strategic planning.

THE ESSENCE OF STRATEGIC PLANNING IN CAPITAL INVESTMENTS

Strategic planning allows managers to search in a systematic and structured way for investment opportunities that are compatible with the firm's internal financial resources and capabilities. The search for these opportunities should consider the firm's ability to adapt to changes in the external competitive environment while at the same time deploying its internal capital resources. The ability of the firm to adapt is considered an active response to changes in competitive market conditions. As a result of continuous adaptation, the firm can deploy its capital resources by acquiring productive assets that are worth more than they cost, thereby increasing shareholders' wealth.

Strategic planning, therefore, is a process by which managers systematically develop alternative scenarios for investing in various projects. While there may be important subgoals, when we examine strategic planning in conjunction with the firm's investment decisions, the ultimate goal is to increase shareholders' wealth. The increase in shareholders' wealth is reflected in the enhancement of the economic value of the assets acquired by the firm. Economic value is enhanced only when the current market price of the assets, measured by the present value of future income generated by these assets, is greater than the purchasing price of the same assets.

It is recognized that the selection of investment projects with good growth opportunities will enhance the firm's economic value. However, the economic value of a growth opportunity is relatively difficult to determine precisely since the realization of benefits depends upon future competitive market conditions which are not easily predictable. In this context, investments in growth opportunities are considered strategic in that they require precommitment of capital resources with unknown consequences. As a result, the choice of a project related to a growth opportunity is discretionary and is analyzed through the strategic planning process, which emphasizes the firm's ability to deal with the competitive environment.

Strategic planning, however, goes beyond the simple identification of growth opportunities and how they will behave in relation to the firm's competitive environment. Effective strategic planning not only looks at the interface between the firm's external environment and its internal resources, but also looks at three other considerations of substantial importance to the survival of the firm. The *first* is the potential interaction of growth opportunities with the firm's existing assets, and their possible complementarities and synergies, that is, the cross-sectional relationships between growth investment projects and existing assets. The *second* consideration deals with the examination of the degree of relatedness of current growth opportunities with future opportunities; that is, it deals with time-series relationships of investments made today with growth opportunities that may be generated tomorrow because of the investments made today. The *third* consideration deals with the incorporation of risk analysis in the identification of investment opportunities; that is, investment opportunities are examined in the context of the risk profile and the risk-return trade-offs of the organization. Therefore, the strategic planning process examines potential interactions among existing assets, growth opportunities, and future investment options, as well as how all these assets interface with the risk profile of the firm.

The scope of strategic analysis presented cannot be considered myopic. Rather, it is a comprehensive and integrative approach that we suggest will result in decisions that will improve the economic value of the firm and, consequently, shareholders' wealth. Finally, strategic planning complements the analysis of capital budgeting expenditures by providing a conceptual framework for the search for positive NPV projects.

Investment opportunities are valuable to the firm to the extent that they generate economic rents. The following section discusses concepts applied to identification of those market imperfections that result in excess economic rents, thereby identifying projects that will increase the firm's value.

MARKET IMPERFECTIONS GENERATING EXCESS ECONOMIC RETURNS (RENTS)

Net present values are related to those investments that can generate excess returns, that is, returns above the cost of capital or required return to shareholders. It is important to recognize that in a perfectly competitive environment, excess returns cannot be derived from allocating capital to the acquisition of real assets. Perfect competition, which is characterized by undifferentiated products and costless entry, drives the price of goods produced on the basis of the assets used to the point where marginal costs are equal to marginal revenues. Thus, perfect competition ensures fair returns from investments in growth opportunities, or returns that are commensurate with the amount of risk assumed. In other words, excess returns cannot be realized. To obtain excess returns and, consequently, positive NPVs from an investment, some market imperfections must exist, creating a less than perfectly competitive environment for the firm.

Imperfections are the direct result of distinct advantages that some firms have over others. This implies that excess returns can be obtained from those investments that are directly related to those specific competitive advantages. However, excess returns obtained from investments are transitory, because they attract competitors, thus bringing prices to the level where marginal costs are equal to marginal benefits. At this point the NPV of the investment is equal to zero. This leads to the conclusion that for a firm to obtain long-term excess returns, it should invest in those projects or growth opportunities that *create* and *maintain* distinct advantages over competitors. A clear understanding of the nature of market imperfections and how they relate to competitive advantages is essential in identifying those growth opportunities that increase the firm's value. Investments structured in a way that exploit these advantages can generate excess returns and, most likely, will result in positive NPVs. Porter[1] and Shapiro[2] have suggested that the following investment opportunities, among others, can generate specific competitive advantages for a firm:

1   *Investments with high capital requirements.* Investments in research and development, production, and distribution require large initial outlays of capital, thus discouraging competitors from entering the market by creating conditions that are difficult to duplicate or mimic at lower costs. These conditions generate barriers for competitors who would like to enter the market, thereby increasing the potential that the investment made will result in high excess returns in the long term. In addition, investments with high capital requirements typically result in sizable cost reductions for the firm by substantially reducing the cost per unit of investment, thus generating another disadvantage for competitors seeking to enter the market. Therefore, investments requiring large initial outlays of capital and offering economies of scale discourage competitors from entering the market and increase the possibility that these investments will create value to the firm.

2   *Investments related to the development of a differentiated product.* Products or services that can be differentiated on the basis of quality, uniqueness, and so on, can generate excess returns to the firm in the long term. The competitive advantage is gained through market segmentation and product position, which will result in the capturing of all potential consumers. Investments directed at product differentiation require large capital outlays in advertising and specialized

---

[1]M. Porter, *Competitive Strategy* (New York: Free Press, 1980).

[2]A. C. Shapiro, "Corporate Strategy and the Capital Budgeting Decision," *Midland Corporate Finance Journal*, 3 (Spring 1985), 22–36.

marketing skills, creating another barrier to entry for competitors. Therefore, investments that take advantage of product differentiation will generate excess returns for the firm.

3 *Investments which gain access to distribution channels.* Distribution channels are essential to increased volume of sales and, therefore, contribute to the profitability of the firm. Investments designed to create distribution channels that can penetrate a market establish a competitive advantage for the firm. A well-functioning distribution channel guarantees prompt and efficient service to customers, resulting in a continuous advantage over competitors. It follows that a distribution channel acquired through investments is an asset for the firm. New entrants into the market would be placed in a disadvantageous position, since penetration of the distribution channel almost certainly would imply reductions in future income through price cuts or other costly promotional methods.

4 *Investments related to government regulations.* Government regulations, such as those imposing import restrictions, occupational safety and health standards, environmental controls and tax regulations, provide natural barriers to competition. The reason for this is that already established firms in some industries find prohibitive government regulations a barrier to expanding their resources, while other newly established firms or those in the process of being established have the benefit of considering these restrictions in their production plans. To the extent that costs can be kept to a minimum, investment projects designed to exploit advantages of government-imposed restrictions are profitable and, therefore, increase the firm's value. For example, because of trade restrictions, an investment in the production of a good that is considered an import substitution will generate conditions of profitability.

5 *Investments related to the exploitation of cost advantages.* Cost advantages, other than those related to economies of scale, include location, favorable access to raw materials, proprietary technology, and control of prices for raw materials. Those firms that take such cost advantages into account operate in a more efficient manner which is reflected in better use of raw materials, improved production methods, declining costs, and higher-quality products. In essence, a cost advantage for one firm is a cost disadvantage for the competing firm which views it as a barrier to entry. Therefore, investments designed with the objective of creating a clear cost advantage over competitors will generally generate excess returns and improve the firm's value.

These considerations lead to the conclusion that investment opportunities that exploit any of the foregoing competitive advantages most likely will result in positive NPVs for the firm. More precise identification of these opportunities takes place through the use of some conceptual and analytical tools which are used in strategic planning.

TOOLS USED IN IDENTIFYING INVESTMENT OPPORTUNITIES

With increased firm value as the objective, the use of strategic planning tools in the search for profitable opportunities is crucial. The importance of these tools lies in their diagnostic ability to position the firm vis-à-vis its competitors and identify the necessary actions that need to be taken to maintain the firm's competitive advantage. In a complex and dynamic environment, positioning the firm in relation to its competitors helps managers to assess the firm's strengths and weaknesses, thereby separating the important issues from those that are unimportant. This focus assists managers in identifying those opportunities that will enhance the firm's market value by integrating the firm's internal resources with the external competitive environment. Therefore, the benefits of these tools is based on their capacity to offer a comprehensive framework which synthesizes and integrates the direction of future decisions so that profitable opportunities are exploited for the benefit of shareholders.

Of all decisions that must be made, of primary importance to the firm's value are decisions related to investment opportunities. By taking into account interactions between existing internal resources and the external competitive environment, strategic planning tools offer recommendations regarding the appropriate allocation of capital in an organization. In more general terms, these tools transform the shareholder's need for excess returns into a series of investment action programs which, once implemented, will ultimately enhance the firm's market value. In addition, by providing an objective assessment of the firm's internal financial capabilities, the use of these tools results in the adoption of investment plans which are compatible with the firm's budgetary constraints.

The tools most applicable for strategic planning are presented in the following section. Although there is no single tool that can be applied to all situations, the frameworks offered by the tools presented provide structure to the search for investment growth opportunities and insights into the firm's competitive environment. The life-cycle approach, the experience curve, and the growth-share matrix (the portfolio approach) will be discussed.

The Life-Cycle Approach

All products evolve through stages of development that are characterized by the product life cycle. This approach has been recognized as a valuable tool for describing the dynamic evolution of products, firms, and industries. This evolution has distinct stages associated with the product's sales volume, a four-phase cycle known as pioneering, expansion, maturity, and decline. The intuitive logic of the life cycle is based on the observation that for each product there is a sequence of events from birth to decline and that the process reflects the outcome of competitive market conditions that exert an impact on the sales volume of the firm. Although there are some direct implications related to the sales levels and growth rates, there are also implications related to investment requirements, risk, and profitability which are of primary interest. Benton Gup[3] has analyzed these and other issues. The important distinct features of the life-cycle approach are the following:

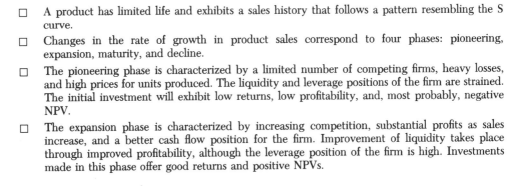

□ A product has limited life and exhibits a sales history that follows a pattern resembling the S curve.

□ Changes in the rate of growth in product sales correspond to four phases: pioneering, expansion, maturity, and decline.

□ The pioneering phase is characterized by a limited number of competing firms, heavy losses, and high prices for units produced. The liquidity and leverage positions of the firm are strained. The initial investment will exhibit low returns, low profitability, and, most probably, negative NPV.

□ The expansion phase is characterized by increasing competition, substantial profits as sales increase, and a better cash flow position for the firm. Improvement of liquidity takes place through improved profitability, although the leverage position of the firm is high. Investments made in this phase offer good returns and positive NPVs.

[3] B. E. Gup, *Guide to Strategic Planning* (New York: McGraw-Hill Book Company, 1980).

☐ The maturity stage is characterized by a decreasing rate in profitability because of no additional demand for the product and a decline in the price per unit. The firm's liquidity has improved substantially, and leverage has decreased primarily because of financing through equity rather than through debt. In this phase, there is a reservoir of available funds (excess cash flows). The investments made in this phase are relatively small replacement-type investments and offer good returns and high NPVs to the firm.

☐ The decline phase is characterized by declining prices of the product which reduce the firm's profitability. Although the firm's liquidity is maintained at good levels and the leverage position of the firm is low, there are no excess cash flows available for future investments.

Figure 22-1 presents a typical life-cycle diagram for a firm. For each of the phases, the profitability, liquidity, and cash flow position are shown.

The life-cycle approach, therefore, serves as a tool that describes the distinct evolutionary phases of a new product. Each phase presents different investment opportunities that exhibit specific cash flow characteristics. For example, while the

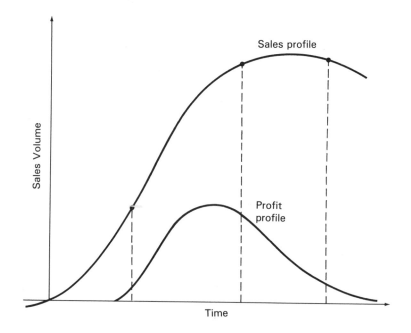

Phase				
	Pioneering	Growth	Maturity	Decline
Liquidity	Low	Low improving	Improving	High
Profits	Negative	Improving	Decreasing	Decreasing
Leverage	High	High	Decreasing	Low
Cash flows	Small (losses)	High and rising	Large and positive	Declining
Sales	Low	Rapidly rising	Slowing	Declining

FIGURE 22-1   Typical Life-Cycle

pioneering phase requires large investments with cash flows that are risky and quite small, the maturity phase requires investments that are usually smaller with more or less predictable cash flows. The application of conventional discounted cash flow techniques in each of the phases will result in myopic and biased recommendations regarding the adoption of a project, especially in the pioneering phase.

It is important to recognize that the firm enters into a series of investment arrangements that link today's investments with tomorrow's opportunities. Investing in a new product with even a negative NPV at the pioneering phase may allow the firm to enter a market which will be profitable at the growth and maturity phases. In other words, the pioneering phase investment has future investment options attached to it and is chosen for its future value-creating opportunities. While DCF techniques capture future income, they do not capture the value of future investment options. The alternative, the simple forecasting of cash flows derived from future phases and then the discounting to the present, is also an inappropriate way of dealing with the correct evaluation of investment projects, because future cash flows are realized only if the firm exercises its option to continue the projects.

Although the life-cycle approach describes the normal cycle for a new project, its ability to predict the various phases accurately is questionable. Some products skip stages and others do not have predictable lengths of time for a particular phase. In addition, the duration of the cycle depends upon the product. There are circumstances in which the firm lengthens this duration by making a new investment in a differentiated product. These considerations reinforce our concern about applying DCF techniques in the evaluation of projects that exhibit life-cycle characteristics. Although DCF techniques are helpful in evaluating projects in the second to fourth life cycle stages, their value diminishes if the project under consideration is at the pioneering phase or if its cash flows depend largely on future growth options.

The Experience Curve

While the life cycle describes the dynamic evolution of the sales of products, the experience curve offers an analysis of the cost behavior of products which is the result of competitive interactions among firms. The firm's ability to operate under conditions of low costs enhances its performance and improves its value by increasing efficiency. From this point of view, the cost structure of a firm plays a central role in its long-term survival and profitability. Investments related to the reduction of costs, therefore, are essential to the accomplishment of this goal. A tool used in planning for such investments is the experience curve.

The experience curve provides a relationship between accumulated volume of production and changes in total production costs. The message provided here is simple: as experience increases with production, costs decline. Accumulated volume of production refers to the total number of units delivered from the beginning of production activity and should not be confused with the annual production rate. Total production costs are not only those related to direct manufacturing costs, such as production methods and tools, but also indirect costs such as those dealing with product design, material utilization, and inventories. The concept of total production costs, therefore, is related to the organization as a whole, not just specifically to the production function. Figure 22-2 shows how costs are reduced with accumulated production. Costs per unit have been calculated on a present value basis; that is, they have been deflated. The experience curve in Figure 22-2 is called an "80% experience

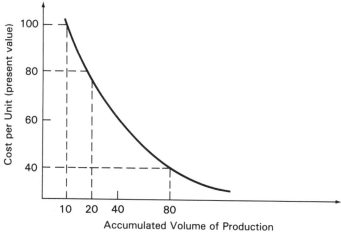

FIGURE 22-2   An 80% Experience Curve

curve" because costs decline by 20% for each doubling of accumulated volume. If the same relationship (Figure 22-3) is presented on log-log scale, a linear relationship between total costs and accumulated volume is derived.

Cost reduction through operations is the result of a number of factors whose impact contributes in a systematic way to this decline. These factors are:

☐ *Learning effects.* Due to continuous performance of repetitive tasks, labor skills improve, and, as a result, productivity is enhanced. In addition, experience in production leads to redesign of tasks and specialization in task performance, which contribute to increased productivity and cost savings.

☐ *Technological improvements.* With increased volume, new production techniques and processes might be introduced that result in higher productivity and substantial cost reductions for the

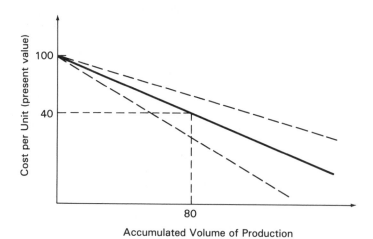

FIGURE 22-3   An 80% Experience Curve on a Log-Log Scale

firm. For example, more efficient utilization of resources through improved technologies can contribute to the reduction of costs. Automation is an example of such an improvement.

☐   *Economies of scale.* Economies of scale occur when added capacity reduces cost per unit produced. This concept is known as a rule of "60%–80%," which implies that if manufacturing capacity doubles, the investment required to meet this capacity increases only by $2 \exp(n)$, where n varies between 60% and 80%. In other words, for a 100% increase in capacity, the corresponding increase in investment is between 52% and 74%. Economies of scale are the direct result of the availability of efficient processes for high-volume production, the necessity to adopt large-scale production because of the indivisibility of resources, and the integration of business activities that are justified only for large-scale operations.

One direct implication derived from the application of the experience curve is that the firm with the largest market share in an industry enjoys cost leadership because of the number of units produced. This advantage can be maintained through continuous investments in capacity and operations. Thus, through experience curve effects, such a firm would have the lowest cost among competitors, a position that perpetuates the firm's competitive advantage. Investment opportunities resulting in the establishment of a high market share are those related to one or all of the cost reduction factors discussed, such as those dealing with product and process improvements, including better utilization of resources, design of more efficient product distribution processes, and the like.

Evaluation of these investment opportunities is not as straightforward as is suggested through the use of DCF techniques, primarily because future benefits or cash flows are not easily determined. These investment opportunities are not considered in the same light as replacement projects because they are designed to increase the firm's productive capacity and scale of operations. By increasing the scale of operations, the firm's ability to respond in a flexible way to shifts in the external environment and new competitive market conditions is reduced considerably. Therefore, the risk attached to these investments is quite different from the risk associated with replacement projects. These considerations complicate cash flow calculations and impair the ability of DCF techniques to offer clear recommendations on acceptance of such projects. It is suggested, therefore, that investments made because of the implicit assumption of experience curve effects have strategic implications and are discretionary in nature.

The Growth-Share Matrix

Another tool widely used in strategic planning is the growth-share matrix. Its foundation is based on a more general concept developed in portfolio planning that advocates that a diversified firm which operates with many autonomous units (business units) manages those business units in a way that resembles a portfolio of securities. That is, depending upon some predetermined key dimensions, business units are judged for inclusion in the portfolio, an increase in holdings, or a decrease in holdings. Although there are many different dimensions upon which each business unit is judged, the most common dimensions employed are the growth of the market in which the firm competes and the relative market share that the firm holds in the particular market. The portfolio mode, which uses these two distinct dimensions and offers recommendations for the firm regarding future strategic moves, is called the growth-share matrix.

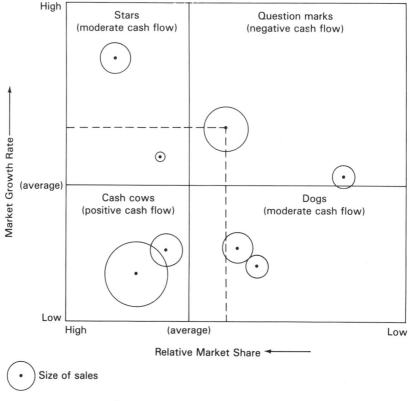

FIGURE 22-4   The Growth-Share Matrix

The premise of the growth-share matrix in strategic planning is twofold. First, it offers an assessment of the present position of the firm in relation to competitors. Second, it suggests strategic movements according to the attractiveness of the market for each business unit which are compatible with the firm's ability to compete. By addressing these two issues, the growth-share matrix is a valuable tool in identifying profitable investment opportunities, as well as in choosing strategic movements that are consistent with the firm's objectives for profitability and value.

The basic dimensions of the growth-share matrix are drawn in Figure 22-4. The first dimension, the growth rate, is expressed as

$$\text{market growth rate} = \frac{\text{market sales year } t - \text{market sales year } t - 1}{\text{market sales year } t - 1} \times 100$$

It is used as an indicator of the degree of market attractiveness for each of the business units and as a surrogate for profitability. The higher the growth rate of the market in which the business unit competes, the more attractive it is to the business unit. The second dimension, the (relative) market share, is expressed as follows:

$$\text{market share (relative)} = \frac{\text{business unit's sales year } t}{\text{leading competitor's sales year } t}$$

It serves as a proxy for the internal strength of each business unit. It represents how many times the sales of a unit is related to the sales of the leading competitors. In Figure 22-4, the market growth rate is expressed in percentages, while the market share is expressed in numbers and is plotted on a log scale. Each unit is placed in the matrix according to its market growth rate and market share. Circles indicate the size of the business unit's sales.

This procedure of positioning business units according to market growth rate and market share assists the manager in deciding which units should receive resources, which units should have resources withheld, and which units should be resource generators. Therefore, the growth-share matrix addresses the critical elements of the investment decision by identifying those opportunities that need funding for future growth. Assuming that there is capital rationing, those units that have growth potential and good market share positioning (referred to as "stars") are considered profitable opportunities and, consequently, receive cash resources for investments. On the other hand, those units that have low market shares and belong to a market with low rates of growth (referred to as "dogs" or "cash traps") are considered unattractive and weak businesses. Consequently, investments in these units should be avoided since there is no profit potential. The necessary capital resources required for investments usually do not come from the capital market but, rather, from those units that have the ability to generate cash flows (referred to as "cash cows") even though their market growth potential is limited.

Essentially, a key implication of the growth-share matrix is that the internal allocation of resources with cross-financing among units helps the firm to achieve a competitive and profitable position in the market in the long run. It is suggested that this approach will create two important conditions: (1) a proper *balance* of the firm's assets, in the sense that the firm can achieve a symmetry among units with regard to growth and cash resources, and (2) a precise *structural integration* of various units, in the sense that the investment decision is centralized. To the extent that these conditions are compatible with shareholders' wealth maximization, the growth-share matrix offers helpful prescriptions for the selection of investment opportunities in the organization.

Investment opportunities can be identified for each of the four classifications in the growth-share matrix. For example, if an investment is considered in the "star" category, it would be a category of increasing capacity which would result in better product prices due to cost reductions through accumulated volume. An investment in the "cash cow" category would be a replacement project or a marketing program that would increase its cash flow potential. It is interesting to note that the investment sizes and the profitability potential might be different. For example, while investments required in the "star" category are quite large, with low net cash flow generating ability, investments in the "cash cow" category are low, with highly positive net cash flows. Therefore, myopic evaluation of each of the projects in these classification categories, or evaluation of these projects in isolation without consideration of potential interaction effects among projects, might create problems. These interactions effects are the result of cash flow interdependencies and, in particular, cross-section and time-series relationships among project cash flows which, again, are not easily captured in the DCF calculations. One problem is related to the potential suboptimality of the total capital budget. Although projects selected on a "piecemeal" basis using DCF techniques might create value to the firm individually, when interaction effects are considered, the resulting total capital budget may not be optimal in terms of market value.

The problem in evaluating projects using DCF techniques in the growth-share planning framework is not limited to the fact that these cash flows may exhibit interdependence or synergistic effects. In addition, some of the projects, in particular those in the "star" category, are high-growth projects whose cash flows are not easily quantifiable in view of the fact that the realization of these cash flows depends upon future competitive market developments. Also, some of the projects have future options whose values, as was discussed in the previous sections, are not captured directly through the DCF techniques.

Such problems occur when the investment decision process for the identification of projects that have positive NPVs starts from the bottom of the organization and proceeds to the top. This approach may miss some strategic dimensions important to the firm's long-term competitive adaptability. The top-down approach (that is, a strategic planning approach that uses the growth-share matrix) offers a framework for the identification of those projects that create conditions of competitive advantage for the firm.

The three approaches just presented are some of the strategic planning models available for consideration and adoption by managers. As stated earlier, although there is no single model that solves all the planning problems for all firms, it is clear that different important strategic dimensions (i.e., scale effects, growth, market share) should be considered for the development of an investment strategy that maximizes shareholders' wealth. In this respect, the DCF calculations are instrumental in supporting or rejecting the recommendations derived through the strategic planning process. In other words, it is suggested that DCF techniques provide the necessary final check for the acceptance of projects that fit into the firm's overall strategic plan.

RISK AND MARKET VALUE ASSESSMENT OF AN INVESTMENT STRATEGY

Strategic planning tools are used in designing the firm's investment strategy for the purpose of maximizing shareholders' wealth. Such a design would be incomplete without consideration of elements of risk. In addition, an investment decision made as a result of comprehensive and sound strategic planning should be evaluated to determine whether, in fact, the ultimate objective of the maximization of shareholders' wealth was accomplished. In this section, we will briefly discuss how consideration of risk enters into the strategic planning process and how the success or failure of an investment decision can be evaluated.

Issues of Risk in Strategic Planning

Strategic planning is not a process through which an organization eliminates or avoids risk. To the contrary, strategic planning, as suggested by Hertz and Thomas,[4] helps managers in the identification and assessment of risks. Identification of risks involves the development, in descriptive terms, of an understanding of the key variables which might have an impact on future income derived from investment opportunities. Risk assessment involves the measurement of risk in more precise

---

[4]D. Hertz, and H. Thomas, *Risk Analysis and Its Applications* (New York: John Wiley, 1983).

quantitative terms, such as standard deviation or variance of expected cash flows. The CAPM could be used in strategic planning for the estimation of those risks that are consistent with market-related risks.

In identifying risks, the manager considers those market or environmental factors that might have an impact on the future cash flows of an investment. Movement of factors which are due to general market conditions can have an impact on investment cash flows. Some of the factor movements are *anticipated*, while others are *unanticipated*. Anticipated factor movements are taken into account by managers in their investment decisions. Unanticipated factor movements, however, are difficult to predict and, therefore, constitute a major concern. Managers cannot accurately predict the movement of unanticipated factors or the magnitude of unexpected changes of those factors that affect investment cash flows. Although knowledge of these parameters is helpful, since the competitive environment changes in a dynamic fashion, what is more important is the knowledge of the intertemporal volatility of these factors, that is, factor risks.

In designing an investment strategy, simply knowing the factor risks is not sufficient. It is true that all firms are affected by the same market forces in a systematic way; that is, all firms are influenced by the same set of factor risks. However, the degree of impact varies across firms depending on the firm's exposure to individual factor risks. This is because shifts of some factors exert a greater impact on investment cash flows than do others. For example, unanticipated changes in oil prices will have more impact on an oil exploration investment than on a consumer electronics investment. Therefore, an important consideration is the identification of those factors that exert an influence on investment cash flows and the degree of the firm's exposure to those factors. Tsetsekos[5] suggested a useful framework for risk analysis in strategic planning. The framework considers the coupling of the firm's external competitive forces with its internal financial capabilities. It is suggested that managers make two sequential planning decisions. The first, the *risk specialization planning decision*, involves the selection of the number of factor uncertainties that affect investment cash flows. The second, the *risk concentration planning decision*, involves the choice of the degree of exposure to an already-specified number of factor risks. These planning decisions emphasize the link between the firm's value and the risks of those factors that most influence the pattern of the firm's cash flow.

While identification of risks is an important consideration in strategic planning, risk evaluation is equally important. Quantitative measures of risk can be developed on the basis of subjective or objective probability distributions. The actual evaluation of risks, however, takes place through the use of a screening process which allows managers to classify projects into different risk classes. An approach suggested by Bauer[6] could be used for evaluating the risk associated with alternative investment opportunities identified through the strategic planning process.

In Figure 22-5, investments under consideration are classified into four risk class groups depending upon their risk (measured by expected cash flow variability) and their return (measured by the expected return on investment (ROI)). Two other

---

[5]G. Tsetsekos, "Financial Strategy and the Firm's Value," paper presented at the Financial Management Association Meeting, Denver, Colo., October 11, 1985; also see his "A Multifactor Model for Strategic Planning," Working paper, American University, Washington D.C., August 1986.

[6]E. E. Bauer, "Meaningful Risk and Return Criteria for Strategic Investment Decisions." *Mergers and Acquisitions* (Winter 1981), 5–17.

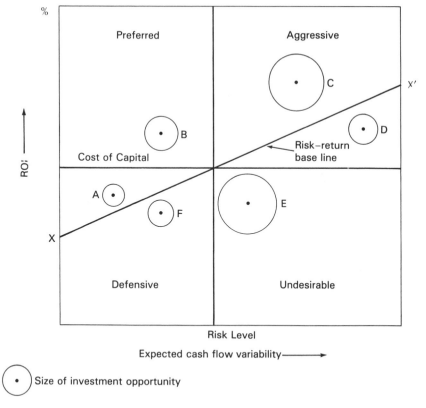

FIGURE 22-5   Considerations of Risk in Strategic Planning

variables are also important for this classification: the cost of capital and variability of cash flows of the firm under consideration. This approach produces the risk class categories of investments that are labeled as preferred, aggressive, defensive, and undesirable. In addition, the line XX' in Figure 22-5, called the risk-return base line, expresses the combinations of risk and return of alternative investments that the firm experiences. The risk-return base line resembles the CAPM line.

By considering the interdependence of risk and return in an investment opportunity, the manager's attention is concentrated on those projects that are above the risk-return base line. For example, projects A, B, and C should be considered for adoption, while projects D, E, and F should be considered for rejection. This screening approach produces investment alternatives that are consistent with the firm's risk profile, yet are the result of a strategic planning process which searches for value-creating opportunities. Therefore, the outcome of this analysis most probably will enhance shareholders' wealth.

Market Value Assessment

A criterion which is widely accepted can be applied to the assessment of the contribution of an investment strategy to the maximization of shareholders' wealth.

This criterion is related to the ratio of market value to book value (MV/BV) of the firm's assets before and after the investment in a growth opportunity. It is regarded as an approximation of an economic ratio referred to as Tobin's q, after the economist James Tobin.[7] (Tobin's q is the ratio of market value of the firm's assets over the estimated replacement costs of these assets. Tobin argued that the firm has an incentive to invest in the acquisition of more assets only when assets are worth more than they cost to be replaced, that is, when $q > 1$. Conversely when $q < 1$, the firm stops investing in new assets.)

The criterion of MV/BV casts some light on how capital markets react to investments in growth opportunities. The market value variable measures the expected incremental benefits received from the new investment as reflected in the equity prices of the firm. On the other hand, the book value variable measures, on an historical basis, the value of the resources contributed by shareholders for the investment decision. Through the acquisition of assets, the book value of these resources is reflected in the book value of the firm's assets. Some important implications are derived depending on whether the ratio MV/BV is greater than 1 or less than 1. If the MV/BV exceeds 1, the firm's economic value is enhanced through investment and, therefore, shareholders' wealth increases. This is because the market value of expected benefits derived from the investment exceeds the costs of the committed resources by shareholders. On the other hand, if the MV/BV is less than 1, the investment undertaken by the firm decreases the firm's economic value, and, as a result, shareholders' wealth is decreased. A MV/BV ratio greater than 1 derived from an investment is consistent with the NPV > 0.

The enhancement of the economic value of the firm through an investment opportunity, as reflected in the ratio of MV/BV, should be translated into actual excess returns to shareholders. Fruhan[8] has suggested that a value-creating opportunity is reflected in the positive spread (ROE $-$ k), where ROE is the return on equity and k is the firm's cost of capital calculated through the CAPM. An MV/BV ratio greater than 1 is reflected in a positive spread. Figure 22-6 shows the direct relationship between excess equity returns, measured by the spread (ROE $-$ k) and MV/BV ratio. For firm A, the worthiness of an investment would be reflected in a high MV/BV and positive spread. Those firms, such as B or C, that do not generate wealth to shareholders through investment decisions have low MV/BV ratios and negative spreads.

SUMMARY

Strategic planning is a structured and organized way of identifying those discretionary investment opportunities that will enhance the firm's value. Through the strategic planning process, opportunities can be created to exploit market imperfections to the competitive advantage of the firm. Investment decisions targeted at creating and maintaining competitive advantages, such as economies of scale, differentiated prod-

---

[7]James Tobin, "A General Equilibrium Approach to Monetary Theory," *Journal of Money, Credit, and Banking*, Vol. 1 (February 1969), 15–29.

[8]W. Fruhan, *Financial Strategy: Studies in the Creation, Transfer, and Destruction of Shareholders' Wealth* (Homewood, Ill.: Richard D. Irwin, Inc., 1979).

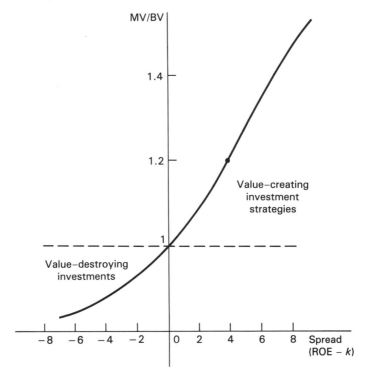

FIGURE 22-6   The MV/BV Assessment Criterion of an Investment Strategy

ucts, unique distribution channels, and government regulation incentives most probably will generate excess returns to shareholders.

The search for these opportunities, however, must recognize the potential interaction effects among existing assets, growth opportunities, and future investment options. The life-cycle approach, the experience curve, and the growth-share matrix are strategic planning tools used to analyze these interactions. These tools emphasize the linkages between the firm's internal resources and its competitive environment. An additional consideration that must be recognized in the search for and analysis of profitable investment opportunities is the element of risk. Risk factors that might have an impact on investment cash flows should be identified and the degree of impact caused by the firm's exposure to individual factor risks should be determined. In addition, risk characteristics of investment opportunities should be evaluated to produce those investment alternatives that are consistent with the firm's risk profile.

To evaluate the success or failure of an investment strategy, the market value-to-book value ratio must be calculated. Successful strategic planning leads to MV/BV ratios which are greater than 1 and give positive spreads (ROE − k).

Strategic planning should be viewed as the first phase in the analysis of capital budgeting problems. For an organization that practices top-down decision making, strategic planning offers a process through which economically sound investment opportunities can be identified. In the second phase, the capital budgeting techniques presented in previous chapters of this book can be applied to arrive at more precise calculations of the net benefits that will accrue to shareholders, that is, the net present value of investment projects. The second phase, therefore, offers the necessary evaluation tools to be used by a financial manager who is concerned with the correct estimation of costs and benefits of an investment.

1. Why is strategic planning necessary in capital budgeting?
2. Are the DCF techniques for capital budgeting incompatible with the strategic planning approach?
3. What categories of investment projects generate positive NPVs?
4. Describe the applicability of the experience curve in analyzing investment proposals.
5. Describe how the share growth matrix is used in analyzing investment proposals.
6. How is risk introduced in strategic planning for capital investments?

REFERENCES

Ackoff, R. L. *A Concept of Corporate Planning*. New York: Wiley-Interscience, 1970.

Alberts, W. W., and J. M. McTaggart. "Value Based Strategic Investment Planning." *Interfaces*, 14 (January–February 1984), 138–151.

Andrews, K. R. *The Concept of Corporate Strategy*. Homewood, Ill.: Dow Jones-Irwin, 1971.

Ang, J. S. "A Graphical Presentation of an Integrated Capital Budgeting Model." *Engineering Economist* (Winter 1978).

Ansoff, I. H. *Corporate Strategy*. New York: McGraw-Hill, 1965.

Boardman, E. A., and N. E. Carruthers. "A Note on the Use of the CAPM as a Strategic Planning Tool." *Management Science*, 31 (December 1985), 1589–1592.

Caves, R. "Economic Analysis and the Quest for Competitive Advantage." *American Economic Review* (May 1984), 127–132.

_____. "Industrial Organization, Corporate Strategy and Structure." *Journal of Economic Literature* (March 1980), 64–92.

Chandler, A. D. *Strategy and Structure*. Cambridge, Mass.: MIT Press, 1962.

Durand, David. "Comprehensiveness in Capital Budgeting." *Financial Management*, 10 (Winter 1981), 7–14.

Grabowski, Henry G., and Dennis C. Mueller. "Managerial and Stockholder Welfare Models of Firm Expenditures." *Review of Economics and Statistics*, 54 (February 1972), 9–24.

Grossman, S. J., and J. E. Stiglitz. "On Value Maximization and Alternative Objectives of the Firm." *Journal of Finance*, 32 (May 1977), 389–415.

Haspeslagh, P. "Portfolio Planning: Uses and Limits." *Harvard Business Review* (January 1982), 58–73.

Hax, A. *Readings on Strategic Management*. Cambridge, Mass.: Ballinger, 1984.

Henderson, B. D. *Henderson on Corporate Strategy*. Cambridge, Mass.: Abt, 1979.

_____. *The Product Portfolio*, No. 66. Boston: The Boston Consulting Group, 1970.

Hill, Lawrence W. "The Growth of the Corporate Finance Function." *Financial Executive*, 44 (July 1976), 36–43.

Hofer, C. W., and D. Schendel. *Strategy Formulation: Analytical Concepts*, St. Paul, Minn.: West, 1978.

Lee, Sang M., and A. J. Lerro. "Capital Budgeting for Multiple Objectives." *Financial Management* (Spring 1974).

Levy, Haim, and Marshall Sarnat. "A Pedagogic Note on Alternative Formulations of the Goal of the Firm." *Journal of Business*, 50 (October 1977), 526–528.

Lorange, P. *Corporate Planning*. Englewood Cliffs, N.J.: Prentice Hall, 1980.

————, and R. Vancil. *Strategic Planning Systems*. Englewood Cliffs, N.J.: Prentice Hall, 1977.

Masson, Robert Tempest. "Executive Motivations, Earnings, and Consequent Equity Performance." *Journal of Political Economy*, 79 (November–December 1971), 1278–1292.

Myers, S. *Modern Developments in Financial Management*. Hinsdale, Ill.: Dryden Press, 1976.

Naylor, T. H., and F. Tapon. "The Capital Asset Pricing Model: An Evaluation of Its Potential as a Strategic Planning Tool." *Management Science*, 28 (October 1982), 1166–1173.

————, and C. Thomas. *Optimization Models for Strategic Planning*, Amsterdam: North-Holland, 1984.

Pinches, G. "Myopia, Capital Budgeting and Decision Making," *Financial Management*, 11, (Autumn 1982), 6–19.

Pogue, G. A., and K. Lall. "Corporate Finance: An Overview." *Sloan Management Review* (Spring 1974), 19–38.

Rumelt, R. *Strategy, Structure and Economic Performance*. Cambridge, Mass.: Harvard Business School, 1974.

Schandel, D. and C. Hofer, *Strategic Management: A New View of Business Policy and Planning*. Boston: Little, Brown, 1979.

Simkowitz, Michael A., and Charles P. Jones. "A Note on the Simultaneous Nature of Finance Methodology." *Journal of Finance*, 27 (March 1972), 103–108.

Steiner, G. *Strategic Planning*. New York: Free Press, 1979.

Business Combinations and Divestitures

23

The acquisition of one corporation by another qualifies as a capital budgeting decision inasmuch as the project involves the alternative usage of investable funds. Corporate acquisitions, accordingly, stand or fall by the same criteria applied to all discretionary capital expenditures. Consistent with the assumptions of financial management, the presumed objective of a combination is to enhance the present worth of the joint enterprise and thereby improve the wealth position of the common stockholders, as measured by the market value of their shares.

The measure of a successful acquisition rests upon the market value of the acquiring firm's stock. If the market value has increased, the increment in post-combination market value over the preacquisition values denotes the synergistic effects of the combination. The gain or loss to any one group of shareholders naturally depends upon the exchange ratios, as will be discussed in a following section. Because market values trade off risk and return, synergism results only if:

1   The combination increases earnings for the same level of risk.
2   The combination reduces risk while maintaining the same level of earnings.
3   Earnings and risk are both changed to improve the risk-return combination.

Equally proportionate increases in earnings and risk do not raise market values, although the financial statements may show higher earnings per share. The combination has merely moved up the security market line.

Synergism is not easy to obtain and is even more difficult to measure when achieved. The criterion assumes a linear relationship between market returns and risk (i.e. that the market is efficient). Time is also a factor. *Synergistic effects rarely appear in the fiscal period following the combination, and it may be many periods in the future before the full benefits of the combination are realized.* In the meantime, the acquiring firm may have entered upon other combinations and the national economy may have moved from one plateau to another. Under these circumstances, it becomes almost impossible to quantify precisely the synergistic effects of a single combination.

ACQUISITION AND DIVESTITURE STRATEGIES

Whether a firm undertakes a single merger or pursues a policy of continued expansion by combination, it will enhance the probability of a successful venture by articulating an acquisition strategy. This should represent a precise statement of the goal to be achieved by the business combination(s). Typical goals of firms deciding to enter the acquisitions market include diversification of the product line, economies-of-scale through increased size, increased market share, updating of managerial skills, organization of research and development facilities, control of resources essential to the production process, and so forth. While common to many combinations, these objectives are by no means a definitive list of acquisition goals.

An acquisition strategy must also address the issue of divestiture, that is, selling off a division or subsidiary which is not performing as expected. For example, when Lockheed Aircraft terminated its production of civilian airliners, the price of the corporation's stock increased after the announcement. Prudent divestment can generate positive synergism by improving the risk-return posture.

Acquisitions and divestitures are not separate types of transactions. Rather, they are related on several counts. Both types of transactions seek to increase the market value of the common shares. For example, a company—for whatever reason—may be worth more broken up than retained as a single entity. This was the solution proposed for the Allegis Corporation, the holding company for United Airlines and several of its travel-oriented subsidiaries. Second, one man's acquisition is frequently another man's divestiture. For example, Beatrice, Inc., sold International Playtex, Inc., to a management group in a leveraged buyout deal (LBO). Third, both acquisitions and divestitures have been increasing in recent years. The number of acquisitions increased from 1,361 in 1963 to 3,336 in 1986, a rise of 145%. The average value of an acquisition was $28.8 million in 1968 and $117.9 million in 1986. Divestitures, on the other hand, climbed from 191 in 1965 to 1,259 in 1986, an increase of 559%. The average purchase price rose from $45.6 million in 1981 to $110.4 million in 1986. Finally, both acquisitions and divestitures are part of a broad restructuring movement in American business.

Restructuring

W. T. Grimm & Co. describes the urge to restructure as follows:

U.S. corporations reevaluated both the composition of their business mix and the profitability of individual units. Armed with a renewed emphasis on efficiency, tighter control and product quality, companies proceeded to divest slow growing cash-draining and unrelated business units and, in turn, to refocus on businesses their managements know best.

Actually, restructuring to enhance the market value of the common shares can take different forms:

1   *Financial restructuring.* If the financial structure can be revised to lower the cost of capital (Chapter 10), the result will, all things being equal, increase the value of the common shares and lessen the probability of a takeover attempt.

2 *Divestitures.* If a company is not earning its anticipated return (or at least its cost of capital) from a subsidiary, the subsidiary should be considered a candidate for divestiture. The issue then is when to divest. In this respect, the abandonment model (discussed in Chapter 25) is an appropriate methodology for analysis.

3 *Investment.* Restructuring may take the form of rationalizing the production process by procurement of new technology or state-of-the-art plant and equipment. Facilities can be acquired by direct investment or leasing of new plant and equipment. The techniques of capital budgeting, covered in previous chapters, can make a worthy contribution to the selection of an optimal alternative.

4 *Human resources.* Restructuring may also constitute a reallocation of the human input to production. American management has been criticized as being desk bound, paper rather than product oriented, overstaffed with middle managers, and suffering from long-term myopia. Different but severe criticisms have been paid to American labor. Whether true or not, these adverse descriptions spill over to the sociopolitical arena in its educational and industrial policy decisions.

Has the restructuring of American industry which began with the "Fourth Merger Wave" in 1980 strengthened the ability of U.S. products to compete internationally? At this point, the statistics are scanty. However, Ennus Bengsma of McKinsey & Co., writing in *The Wall Street Journal* (February 12, 1988) notes

In a study of 16 transactions completed between 1977 and 1986 in the U.S. paper and forest products industries, McKinsey found that only 16% of the $6.5 billion in additional value generated in these deals could be attributed to finance-driven changes, such as increased leverage. The remainder—84%—stemmed from operating changes.

Bengsma suggests that bigness per se may not be as important as in previous decades; that scale advantages in R & D, production, distribution, access to capital, and recruitment are rapidly diminishing; that the value of horizontal and vertical integration can be undercut by changes in market structure. Citing the steel industry, he notes the new rule: own those assets that enable you to create value; control the others. Thus, "just the cost of being a large diversified enterprise is starting to outweigh the benefits of scale and energy."

The following questions, therefore, are pertinent to the firm contemplating a merger or divestiture:

1 Is internal or external expansion the preferable alternative?
2 What is the direction of expansion?
3 What is the legal form of expansion?
4 What are the appropriate accounting options to structure the combination?
5 What tax options will minimize the tax liabilities of the parties?
6 Is the combination liable to antitrust action?

The responses to these inquiries must be integrated into a comprehensive plan for intercorporate investments. They are discussed sequentially in the following sections.

INTERNAL VERSUS EXTERNAL EXPANSION

A firm may expand either internally or externally. Thus far in our discussion of the capital investment process, we have limited our examination to the former, so it is valuable at this juncture to enumerate the primary advantages and disadvantages of internal expansion. This will provide a benchmark for comparison as we examine external expansion.

Internal expansion enjoys the following advantages:

1   The valuation process of expansion by combination is avoided.
2   There are fewer accounting and tax problems to resolve.
3   The problem of minority stockholders does not arise.
4   Subject to some qualification, the situation may diminish the likelihood of unfavorable antitrust action.
5   The firm has the opportunity to acquire new facilities designed and located specially to meet its operational requirements, and, as a corollary, management has the opportunity to entrench the firm as a low-cost producer.

The disadvantages inherent to internal expansion also warrant close consideration:

1   The availability of funds (retained earnings or issuance of new securities) limits the scope of the expansion programs.
2   The disbursal of funds to acquire new assets may drain liquidity.
3   The tempo of expansion depends upon the construction period or lead times of the assets concerned.

Alternatively, if the firm expands by combination, it will enjoy other advantages:

1   The funds available for expansion may be supplemented by the issuance of securities so that more expansion can be accomplished for the same dollar outlay and, as a corollary, to the extent the combination is financed by the exchange of securities, liquidity is conserved.
2   The firm secures additional facilities at once.
3   The acquisition may reduce the number of competitors or otherwise improve market control.
4   If the transaction meets IRS criteria, it may qualify as a tax-deferred exchange.
5   The combination may be the vehicle for recruiting new managerial talent.

Disadvantages associated with combination include the following:

1   The process of negotiation encompasses valuation problems, choice of accounting methodology and tax treatment, and the question of minority interests.
2   All things equal, the situation carries a higher probability of antitrust prosecution.
3   Depending upon the terms of exchange, the transaction may create a substantial tax liability for the selling corporation.
4   The acquiring firm may have to invest additional funds to integrate the facilities into its operational pattern.
5   The success of the combination depends upon the ability of management to mesh in a single operation two previously independent organizations. *The human equation in this regard presents a substantial challenge.*

Of the two approaches, internal expansion predominates, but expansion by combination is more common as asset size increases.

DIRECTION OF EXPANSION

The achievement of synergistic effects depends upon the economic substance of the combination, that is, the earnings potential and risk posture of the joint enterprise. In terms of economic substance there are five basic classes of combinations:

1   *Vertical combination.* The acquiring firm expands backward toward sources of supply or forward toward market outlets. The United States Steel Corporation, for example, sought a completely integrated system from the raw material stage to the finished product. More recent illustrations of vertical combination include the acquisition of Conoco by DuPont (1981) and Pillsbury's acquisition of Burger King (1978). *Potentially, vertical combinations can stabilize the supply and/or demand schedules of the acquiring company, reduce inventories, facilitate production planning, and economize on working capital investment.*

2   *Horizontal combination.* This entails the amalgamation of competing firms at the same stage of the industrial process. Examples include the 1973 Coca-Cola Bottling acquisition of Franzia Brothers Winery and McDonnell's acquisition of Douglas Aircraft Company (1967). *In addition to reducing the degree of competition, horizontal combinations offer the prospect of eliminating duplicate facilities and operations,* reducing the investment in working capital, a broadened product line, and better market control.

3   *Product extension.* This strategy unites companies which are functionally related in production and/or distribution but sell products that do not compete directly with one another. Examples include Sperry-Rand's acquisition of Univac (RCA) and American Express Company's acquisition of Shearson Loeb Rhoades (both in 1981).

4   *Market extension.* Mergers in this category add to the product market served by the acquiring firm; that is, the acquiring and acquired firms manufacture the same product but sell it in different geographic markets. Dairy, beer, cement, and oil producers are the most common source of market extension combinations.

5   *Conglomerate combination.* The conglomerate combines firms in different lines of endeavor. General Dynamics, for example, spans such diverse operations as aerospace manufacture, surface and subsurface marine vehicles, rubber and tire manufacture, and communications. *Among so diversified a collection of outputs, it seems difficult to envision operating economies, although risk pooling may reduce financing charges. On the other hand, the market value of the whole enterprise may increase through reducing the variance in total revenues by including firms that covary unequally with fluctuations in general business activity, by increasing capacity to leverage the capital structure, and by improving substandard earnings of the component units.*

It is easier to enumerate the theoretical advantages of different combinations than it is to achieve them in practice. Larger size does not invariably equate with greater efficiency. Problems of managerial effectiveness afflict all organizations, but they grow disproportionately with size. Paperwork proliferates, and bureaucratic red tape discourages initiative. Moreover, the advantages of specialization can be lost with integration. Studies by the Federal Trade Commission and independent bodies suggest that the largest firms in an industry are not always the lowest-cost producers.

The particular direction of expansion varies with the circumstance of the day and the evolution of industry. Vertical and horizontal combinations dominated the scene in the nineteenth and the first half of the twentieth centuries. The 1950s saw the emergence of the conglomerate movement, which reached significant proportions in the 1960s.

Specifically, in 1966, 10.5% of the combinations were horizontal; 10.5%, vertical; 1.3%, market extension; 53.9%, product extension; and 24%, pure conglomerates. By

1980, horizontal and vertical combinations each accounted for 5.2% of the combinations; market extension types, 2.1%; product extension combinations, 42.3%; and the pure conglomerate, 45.4%. The shift in the type of business combination is dramatically highlighted by the statistic that 89.8% of the combinations presently fall under the conglomerate category.

In general, merger activity tends to rise and fall with stock prices and exhibits a close average lead or lag with business-cycle upturns and downturns. However, we cannot say that changes in the capital markets *cause* merger activity to increase or decrease or that the ups and downs of the business cycle have a similar effect. Neither can we say that changes in merger activity initiate corresponding movements in stock prices or business conditions. We can safely say that the state of the capital markets and business conditions set a stage favorable or unfavorable to merger activity. How or whether merger activity responds to these macrovariables depends upon the myriad factors which condition a particular merger—motivations of management, trends in technology, the long-term outlook for the industry or product line, and so forth.

LEGAL FORMS OF COMBINATION

Interrelated with the economic objective of expansion is the legal form of the combination. Economic objectives influence management structure (e.g., centralized versus decentralized management) and particular legal forms facilitate one or the other type of management structures. *Specifically, the form of combination impacts on the time required to effect the combination, the ease of financing, the degree of management control, the flexibility of the organization, the degree of permanence in the arrangement, and the tax liability of the enterprise.* The principal forms of combination—purchase of assets, mergers and consolidations, and formation of holding companies—are discussed in the paragraphs that follow.

Purchase of Assets

As the term implies, the acquiring firm may purchase all or some of the seller's assets and assume all, some, or none of his liabilities. For example, the sale of the RCA computer division to Sperry-Univac falls into this category. The procedure has several advantages:

1 The sale may not require the approval of the selling corporation's stockholders. Unless the sale changes the character of the seller's business (the sale of goodwill or property forming an integral part of the business), the transaction would not require the consent of the stockholders.

2 In contrast to the merger approach described next, purchase of assets has an inherent flexibility. The acquiring corporation may purchase only those facilities pertinent to its operations and may or may not assume any liabilities. Consideration may take the form of cash, securities, or a combination thereof.

3 Tax shields may be created if the sale results in a capital loss to the seller.

4 The acquiring corporation does not inherit the personnel or management problems of the selling firm.

The disadvantages associated with the purchase of assets also warrant close attention:

1   If the sale requires the consent of the shareholders, the usual problems of minority rights arise. Creditors, however, cannot object in the absence of fraud, and their liens follow the property subject to the attachment.
2   If the selling firm realizes a large gain, substantial tax liabilities may be involved.
3   Some state laws mandate the approval of the seller's stockholders when the buyer purchases the assets by issuing stock in exchange for assets.

Merger and Consolidation

Technically speaking, in a merger, the acquiring firm assumes all the assets and liabilities of the seller and the latter is dissolved. Consolidation involves forming a new corporation which assumes the assets and liabilities of two or more selling corporations. The latter are then dissolved. The reader should bear in mind, however, that the term *merger* in *popular usage* describes all business combinations.

By way of illustration, in 1954, the Nash Corporation, renamed American Motors Corporation, acquired by *merger* the Hudson Motor Car Company. Hudson shareholders received 2 American Motors shares for every 3 Hudson shares. Nash stock exchanged share for share. In 1967, a new company, McDonnell Douglas Corporation, was formed to *consolidate* the McDonnell and Douglas corporations. Douglas shareholders received 1 share of the new firm's common for each Douglas share. McDonnell shares were swapped on a one-to-one ratio.

Some advantages of the merger or consolidation include the following:

1   Taxes on intercorporate dividends may be eliminated.
2   Financial reporting is simplified by elimination of consolidated financial statements.
3   Centralization of authority is facilitated.
4   The tax expense of maintaining separate corporate entities is eliminated.
5   It may be possible to effect a merger or consolidation as a tax-free exchange.

Disadvantages must also be considered:

1   There may be some loss of goodwill. When a small company combines with a significantly larger firm, circumstances dictate the dissolution of the smaller organization. This may result in loss of some goodwill.
2   The arrangement is inflexible. The acquiring corporation must assume all the assets and liabilities of the seller, including those of only peripheral importance.
3   Stockholders of both corporations must assent to the combination. Dissenting stockholders may demand an appraisal of their holdings and payment in cash. Dissenters may also sue to test compliance with the legal formalities stipulated by state law.
4   Negotiators must wrestle with the question of valuation, choice of accounting method, and the tax status of the selling firm's shareholders.
5   The perennial managerial problem of blending two previously distinct organizations remains. The Penn Central combination is a prime example.

Holding Company

Generally speaking, any corporation that invests in the stock of another firm constitutes a holding company. Holding companies function in all fields of business but are common to public utilities and banking, where legal restrictions set geographic limits on the establishment of new facilities. Within the study of capital investment, we are concerned with two objectives of a holding company: investment and control. Control might signify majority ownership of the outstanding shares, but often, especially if the subsidiary is a large corporation with scattered stock ownership, the investor may secure *de facto* control with relatively few shares, perhaps only 20% of the outstanding stock.

There are two functional types of holding companies: pure holding companies and holding-operating companies. The former have no operating functions. The assets consist solely of holdings in subsidiary stocks, bonds, and loans, while the chief sources of income are the dividends, interest, and fees earned from providing services to the subsidiary units. The United States Steel Corporation and American Home Products were formed *initially* with the prime purpose of acquiring stocks in operating companies. The latter represents a mixed form. General Motors, organized initially as a pure holding company, was reorganized as an operating company by converting the subsidiary corporations into GM divisions. However, the company still retains subsidiary investments in General Motors Acceptance Corporation and various foreign affiliates.

Several factors recommend the holding company:

1   It is not necessary to secure the consent of stockholders of the subsidiary corporations, and the need to pay off dissenters does not arise.

2   The parent acquires a going concern intact without loss of goodwill; if cash is paid to purchase subsidiary stock, a sum far less than the net value of the subsidiary's assets need be invested to acquire control. The parent has only to gain sufficient outstanding shares to ensure control, and where the subsidiaries have large blocks of long-term debt outstanding, this can represent a small portion of the total assets brought under control. The pyramiding of debt leverages the parent's investment.

3   The parent need not assume the liabilities of the subsidiary corporations.

4   It may make possible a combination of enterprises which legislation would not permit under a single corporate roof. By the late 1960s, virtually all the nation's larger commercial banks converted their corporate structures to holding company form to enable them to undertake such diverse functions as data processing, insurance, mutual fund sales, investment advisory services, and leasing. As banks they could not participate in these activities.

5   The holding company organizational form facilitates decentralized operations over state and international boundaries.

Several factors that detract from the holding company organization must be considered:

1   The structure may prove unstable. If the subsidiary fails to pay dividends on its preferred or misses an interest payment, the parent's investment may be lost or its control jeopardized.

2   The income tax laws work to the disadvantage of the holding company. If the holding company owns less than 80% of the subsidiary's stock, it must pay a 15% tax on dividends received from the subsidiary. This creates three tiers of taxation: the operating company on the original income earned, the parent holding company in receipt of dividends from the operating

company, and the holding company's stockholders on the dividends they receive from the parent.

3   Maintaining separate corporate entities duplicates expenses: franchise taxes, annual meetings, officers' salaries, and so on.

4   Minority interests of the subsidiary corporations can prove troublesome. The minority is there to challenge intercorporate transfers, accounting methods, inventory control, or practices that appear to "exploit" the subsidiary corporations.

5   Because of historical abuses, the holding company device is regulated by the SEC under the Public Utility Holding Company Act of 1937 and the ICC under the Interstate Commerce Act.

To recapitulate, *an acquisition strategy should first define the economic substance of the combination, that is, whether the objective is to increase revenues, achieve operating economies, diversify, readjust the financial structure, or reduce the risk of ultimate failure.*[1] This will largely determine whether the combination is best accomplished by internal financing or by acquisition. It will also influence the management structure: the degree of centralization and the arrangement of line and staff functions.

Economic substance also influences the choice of accounting methodology; that is, the accounting system should record the nature of the economic event taking place. It should record the economic substance of the transaction on a basis that permits comparison of precombination and postcombination results and facilitate the prediction of future performance. At any rate, this represents the theory. In practice, the choice of accounting methodology—purchase or pooling—has become the source of much argumentation, and the suspicion persists that some recent combinations would not have taken place except for the accounting options available. Since the choice of accounting methodology can affect earnings per share, the accounting numbers figure prominently in an acquisition strategy.

THE ACCOUNTING DECISION

Copeland and Wojdak stated the essence of the accounting decision in business combinations:[2]

The manipulative quality of the purchase-pooling decision rule derives from the fact that acquired assets may be valued differently under the two methods. If a merger is accounted for as a purchase, acquired assets are recorded at the fair value of the consideration given by the acquiring company; however, under the pooling method they are valued at their pre-acquisition book values.... *The method that minimizes asset values usually maximizes profits.* [emphasis added]

[1] The reader will correctly observe that the statement oversimplifies the problem of motivation underlying merger activity. Mixed motives may predominate, the parties of interest having different objectives in fostering the combination. In some instances, the predominant objective may look to speculative gains from rising market prices or the issuance of new securities. The lurid details of "big killings" decorate business history books. Yet, if the combination survives, it must serve an economic purpose, and indeed without some ostensible economic rationale, the stock market would probably not react positively to the announcement of the combination.

[2] Ronald M. Copeland and Joseph F. Wojdak, "Income Manipulation and the Purchase-Pooling Choice," *Journal of Accounting Research* (Autumn 1969), 188–195.

Minimizing asset values on the books reduces future charges against income. Hence, if book values exceed market values, the decision rule dictates a purchase treatment. When this condition is reversed, the pooling of interest is the appropriate treatment. But two assumptions underlie the rule: management seeks to maximize future accounting incomes, and accounting numbers determine the market value of the common shares (i.e., the value of the combination).[3]

Empirical evidence supports the first assumption. Gagnon investigated a sample of 500 mergers from New York Stock Exchange listing applications for the period 1955–1958.[4] He found approximately 51% followed the proposed decision rule. Copeland and Wojdak showed a much higher incidence of maximizing behavior in the period 1966–1967.[5] They concluded that

> There has been a trend toward pooling since 1958 . . . and the results strongly support the hypothesis that firms record mergers by the method that maximizes reported income.

A study by Anderson and Louderback covered the period 1967–1974.[6] They found about 86% of the surveyed firms followed the decision rule. Their findings seemingly lend support to an observation of Wyatt:[7]

> Accounting for a combination is commonly decided in advance of consummation of the transaction. That is, *the accounting treatment is one of the variables that must be firmed up before the final prize (in terms of exchange ratios) is determined.* [emphasis added]

The accounting methodology is an important element in the overall acquisition strategy. It affects such factors as the earnings per share, asset values, and retained earnings of the combination. The major accounting options available in business combinations are purchase or pooling.

Purchase

Accounting Principles Board (APB) Opinion No. 16 defines a purchase as a "business combination of two or more corporations in which an important part of the ownership interests in the acquired corporation or corporations is eliminated." The notion is one of discontinuity in voting participation, financial structure, and accountability. The characteristics of a purchase transaction follow from the definition:

1 The acquiring corporation views the transaction as an investment; that is, if the value of the consideration (cash and/or securities) exceeds the *appraised* value of the assets acquired, the excess may be recorded as goodwill. APB Opinion No. 16 requires that the portion of the excess recorded as goodwill be amortized against earnings over some reasonable period. The charge

---

[3] Ibid.

[4] Jean-Marie Gagnon, "Purchase v. Pooling-of-Interests: The Search for a Predictor," *Empirical Research in Accounting: Selected Studies,* 1969. Supplement to *Journal of Accounting Research,* pp. 187–204.

[5] Ronald M. Copeland and Joseph F. Wojdak, "Income Manipulation and the Purchase-Pooling Choice," *Journal of Accounting Research* (Autumn 1969), 188–195.

[6] John C. Anderson and Joseph G. Louderback III, "Income Manipulation and Purchase-Pooling: Some Additional Results," *Journal of Accounting Research* (Autumn 1975), 338–343.

[7] Arthur R. Wyatt, "Discussion of Purchase v. Pooling-of-Interests: The Search for a Predictor," *Empirical Research in Accounting: Selected Studies,* 1967. Supplement to *Journal of Accounting Research,* pp. 187–204.

against earnings, on the other hand, while lowering accounting net income, does not qualify as a tax deduction. Other things being equal, taxable income exceeds accounting income.

2   The surviving firm records the acquired assets at their cost (i.e., current value), not the book value to the selling corporation. A new basis of accountability is established, possibly resulting in higher depreciation charges against income with consequent effects on earnings after taxes.

3   Consideration may take the form of debt securities, stock, and/or cash. Securities issued by the acquiring corporation are deemed to have been issued at current market values. Debt securities and cash are frequently used to reduce the participation of the acquired firm's shareholders in the management of the surviving corporation. As a corollary, if the surviving corporation had acquired its own voting stock (treasury stock) in contemplation of the combination, the transaction must be recorded as a purchase.

4   The selling corporation's liabilities become the obligations of the surviving firm. However, the seller's retained earnings are not added to those of the surviving firm. *Purchase accounting, in effect, capitalizes the retained earnings of the seller.* The basic notion is that one company cannot increase its retained earnings by buying another company.

As contrasted to pooling, purchasing suffers several disadvantages which can prove to be fatal impediments to a management seeking to demonstrate quickly the wisdom of the combination:

1   Given the presence of goodwill and/or a higher basis of accountability on depreciable assets, net income will be lower than if the transaction were consummated as a pooling.

2   There are negotiation problems. If the consideration includes cash, the seller may incur substantial taxable gains and demand a higher price to offset the tax bite. Or the acquiring firm may wish to allocate the purchase price to assets that may be amortized to reduce taxable income while the seller may seek to allocate the purchase price against assets that reduce taxable gains. The objectives may be in juxtaposition.

3   The investor corporation requires earnings projections on the seller under a variety of purchase terms. This implies an understanding of the accounting methods adopted by the seller in calculating net income and an estimate of the current value of the seller's assets.

An important limitation of the purchase option should be mentioned at this point. *Under purchase, the acquiring corporation includes all of the seller's assets and liabilities in its consolidated statement, no matter when during the fiscal period the transaction was consummated. However, on the consolidated income statement, it picks up only the income of the seller applicable to the period between the transaction date and the end of the fiscal period.*

The choice between purchase or pooling depends upon the state of the economy, the earning capacity of the combining firms, their financial structures, and the objectives of the ownership interests. In general, focusing only on the accounting numbers, purchase is the choice if the book value of the acquired assets exceeds fair market value and the effective yield on the financing used is less than the return on assets for the acquired company. This situation tends to be more prevalent in a period of declining business activity. Conversely, in a period of expansion, market values tend to exceed book values and pooling may seem the attractive option.

Pooling

APB Opinion No. 16 describes pooling as a business combination in which the holders of substantially all the ownership interest in the constituent corporations become the owners of a single corporation that owns the assets and businesses of the constituent corporation. Continuity of voting participation and operation is the core of a pooling arrangement. Some specific features of this accounting treatment include:

1   The acquisition is not viewed as an investment; rather, the two predecessor corporations combine into a single entity.
2   The original accounts (assets and liabilities) are carried over to the combined entity at book values. The transaction does not create a new basis of accountability or generate goodwill.
3   A pooling must be accomplished by an exchange of voting stock between previously independent companies. Bond and preferred stocks that alter the structure of ownership may not form part of the consideration. For the same reason, cash is ruled out along with Treasury stock acquired in contemplation of the merger.
4   Since assets and liabilities carry over at book values, the retained earnings of the seller corporation carry over to the combination.
5   On the same premises, the minority interest is left untouched by the pooling of the majority interests.

The *stated* capital of the pooled companies may be greater or less than the total capital of the individual units. If it is greater, the excess is deducted first from the total of any other contributed capital and then from the consolidated retained earnings. If it is less, the difference is reported on the consolidated balance sheet as excess over par.

Distinct advantages can accrue to management through executing a pooling of interests:

1   The transaction may qualify as a tax-free exchange if it also meets Internal Revenue criteria.
2   The transaction does not drain liquid assets or increase the debt/equity ratio of the combination.
3   All things equal, pooling results in a higher net income due to the absence of goodwill and no change in the basis of accountability.
4   Regardless of market values, the postcombination entity bears responsibility only for the dollar amounts that existed prior to the combination. Hence, if synergism results, pooling can create "instant growth" in earnings. As a general rule, pooling is desirable if the assets of the acquired company at book are undervalued in relation to actual or potential earning power.
5   Retention of retained earnings may permit the combination to write off any deficit on the books of the acquiring firm.
6   In contrast to the purchase transaction, the combination may pick up not only the assets and liabilities of the constituents but also their *full income* irrespective of the transaction date—even after the close of the fiscal year or before the auditors arrive.

The advantages to pooling are easily demonstrated in a situation where all variables are constant except for the choice of accounting method. The real world, on the other hand, affords few instances for such simple laboratory comparisons. Instead, the relative advantage to pooling will depend upon the specific terms of the combination: the asset values, type and amounts of consideration, presence of goodwill, and so on. Earnings per share could be higher under purchase accounting depending upon the consideration mix and asset values. This complicates the researchers' problem of assessing whether security markets ignore accounting numbers in pricing the common shares of a business combination. The accounting effects may be clouded by the presence of other variables.

In summary, pooling sees nothing of significance in the event. Assets are the same as prior to the combination and the management structure remains mostly untouched. Hence, the accounting record should leave the relationships undisturbed and the market value of the shares issued to effect the combination is of no consequence for the accounting entries. Conversely, a significant change in voting rights or the sale of a substantial portion of the business suggests a purchase transaction.

Accounting Methodology and Security Prices

Combination by purchase or pooling of interests can result in significant differences in earnings per share. Do security prices reflect these differences? Will the market price of the common shares be higher if the combination is effected as a pooling rather than a purchase? Does the accounting treatment convey important information to the user of financial statements? To this point, we have assumed that managements believe in the importance of accounting numbers in shaping security prices. They are not alone. It is also widely believed by business writers that stockholders of companies using pooling make abnormal gains from higher stock prices as a direct consequence of reporting relatively higher earnings.

For example, Copeland and Wojdak sampled 169 poolings[8] and estimated that earnings were overstated by 3% to 98.15%. Lintner agrees that companies which manipulate accounting numbers in mergers successfully mislead shareholders and raise the aggregate value of the combination even in a perfect securities market.[9] Mosich gives a theoretical estimate of a 60% increase in stock price of a typical merging company, choosing pooling instead of purchase accounting.[10]

On the significance of the accounting treatment for the user of financial statements, the FASB surveyed analysts using financial statements in making investment and credit decisions.[11] Most respondents expressed a greater need for appropriate disclosures about a combination rather than preference for a particular accounting method. With better disclosure, the analyst can adjust the statement amounts to reflect the economic and financial impact of the combination. Burton surveyed 210 financial analysts and found them evenly split as to whether purchase or pooling presented data more meaningfully.[12] Yet a survey of 64 financial analysts by Bullard showed a marked preference for purchase accounting.[13] In general, these and

[8] Ronald M. Copeland and Joseph F. Wojdak, "Valuation of Unrecorded Goodwill in Merger-Minded Firms," *Financial Analysts Journal* (September–October 1969), 57–62.

[9] J. Lintner, "Expectations, Mergers and Equilibrium in Purely Competitive Securities Markets," *American Economic Review* (1971), 101–111.

[10] A. N. Mosich, "Impact of Merger Accounting on Post-Merger Financial Reports," *Management Accounting* (December 1965).

[11] Financial Accounting Standards Board, *Accounting for Business Combinations and Purchased Intangibles* (August 19, 1976), 36–40.

[12] John C. Burton, *Accounting for Business Combinations* (New York: Financial Executives Research Foundation, 1970).

[13] Ruth Harper Bullard, "The Effect of Accounting for Combinations on Investor Decisions," The University of Texas at Austin, August 1972.

other surveys show no unanimity among users of financial statements regarding a preference for a particular accounting treatment, nor do they provide much information about why users of financial statements prefer a particular accounting treatment. Implicitly, however, the evidence points to a general conclusion; namely, analysts are alert to the effect on earnings of recording the combination as a purchase or pooling. It would seem they would allow for these effects in evaluating the combination.

Recent studies, looking at the informational content of alternative accounting methods and their effects on stock prices, seem to confirm the conclusion. These studies report that accounting manipulations not accompanied by real economic impacts (cash flows) have no statistically significant effects on stock prices. Apparently, the presence of alternative sources of information on corporate performance enables investors to look beyond the accounting numbers in assessing equity securities. Therefore, if the market is efficient, it will respond to the real economic consequences of the combination. Kaplan and Roll, Sunder, and Ball all report that differences in accounting methodology have no statistically significant effect on security prices, and accounting data are unimportant relative to the aggregate supply of information.

But the evidence leaves much room for reasonable doubt, and so the argument will continue unabated. It will take more substantial evidence than is currently available to convince businessmen that accounting strategy has neutral effects on the market value of the combination.

Tax Options

Accounting advantages may not harmonize with preferred tax treatments. An acquisition strategy to optimize tax benefits for the acquiring corporation may result in a lower earnings per share. For example, a cash transaction treated as a *taxable exchange* and a *purchase* may generate higher tax shields and increased cash flow but carry a lower earnings per share, owing to added depreciation charges and the amortization of goodwill. To complicate the issue further, the criteria for a tax-free exchange and pooling differ. Hence, it is sometimes possible to treat the acquisition as taxable to obtain depreciation tax shields and for accounting purposes as a pooling to secure higher earnings per share.

Tax strategies conflict and the tax objectives of the buyer and seller may not coincide. Tax objectives depend upon a comparison of the purchase price for the property acquired and the seller's tax basis on the stock or other assets sold. Where the purchase price is less than the tax cost, the seller will likely opt for a taxable transaction. Conversely, if the purchase price exceeds the tax cost, the seller more often seeks a tax-free transaction. The buyer, on the other hand, would aim at a tax-free exchange in the first instance and a taxable exchange in the second case. Then, too, the tax position of the shareholders may differ from the tax position of their corporation so that what is good for one may not under all circumstances meet the interests of the other. The issue arises depending on whether the corporation is disposing of assets or its stockholders are selling their shares in a takeover situation.

Buyer and seller may also disagree over the allocation of the purchase price in a taxable transaction. The buyer strives to allocate the purchase price to depreciable property in order to capture the tax shields. The seller, on the other hand, seeks to allocate the purchase price to assets that qualify for capital gains or to those assets where the tax basis approximates or exceeds their purchase cost. The seller will also resist the allocations to inventories, since gains on inventory investment are taxable as ordinary income.

Finally, a tax-free exchange does not imply forgiveness, only deferral. The seller does not pay a tax at the time he or she exchanges his or her stock for shares in the acquiring corporation. Instead, the tax basis of the original shares becomes the basis of the new shares, and the seller pays a tax calculated on this basis when he or she *subsequently* disposes of the new shares. In short, no tax is payable at the time of the stock swap. Further, if the seller wills the shares to his or her estate, they are valued in the estate on the basis of their worth at time of death, and the entire capital gain is thus avoided. The latter arrangement at best gives the seller a vicarious satisfaction— wherever he or she may be.

IDENTIFYING TAKEOVER OPPORTUNITIES

The articulation of an acquisition strategy (covering economic substance, accounting methodology, and tax objectives, as well as the pertinent options under the security and antitrust regulations) sets the stage for the process of identifying a potential merger partner. No matter what the particular techniques employed (and each practitioner has his or her own angle) selection requires a forecast of future earnings and assessment of risk. There are two fundamental approaches: present value analysis and capital asset pricing.

Present Value Analysis

When present value analysis is used, the earnings of the acquired firm are projected and discounted at the investor's cost of capital to obtain a theoretical market price on the shares of the investee corporation. This is compared with the actual market price to determine the net present value of the investment.

Assume that Alpha, Inc., is considering the acquisition of 100% of Delta's voting shares. Alpha's cost of capital is 10%. Delta has maintained a constant payout ratio with the current dividend at $1 per share. Earnings are expected to grow at 9% annually. Delta's shares currently sell at $52. The *theoretical price* of Delta's shares, using the dividend valuation model from Chapter 10, is:

$$D_1 = D_0(1 + g) = \$1.00(1.09)$$

$$= \$1.09 \tag{1}$$

$$P_0 = \frac{D_1}{K - g} = \frac{\$1.09}{0.10 - 0.09} = \$109$$

Because the theoretical price exceeds the market price (or cost of the investment) of $52, the NPV equals $57 per share. The situation, accordingly, warrants further investigation of Delta.

The NPV approach has several shortcomings. The analysis assumes that the acquired corporation will do as well after the combination as before (i.e., in the case of Delta, it will at least maintain the 9% growth rate). More important, if the acquired company is large relative to the size of the investor, the acquisition will likely change the risk-return characteristics of the surviving firm. This alters its cost of capital and upsets the calculation of NPV. Also, unless NPV is put on an expected value basis and the variance and covariances calculated, the method does not specifically assess the risk posture of the combination (i.e., the portfolio effects). Thus, the analysis at best provides only a point of departure for further investigation of a merger candidate.

Capital Asset Pricing

The NPV approach has the advantage of using concepts familiar to everyday financial practices. The CAPM (capital asset pricing model), however, enjoys theoretical superiority.[14] Following the procedures of Chapter 16, CAPM employs the security market line or the market price of risk as the hurdle rate in identifying a potential merger partner. A required return is calculated, $E(R_j^0) = R_F + [E(R_m) - R_F](B_j)$ and compared with an expected return, $E(R_j)$, calculated independently. If the expected return exceeds the required return, $E(R_j) > E(R_j^0)$, the acquiring firm has a potential merger partner. In this case $E(R_j)$ lies above the security market line.

In Table 23–1 we have assumed four possible states of the economy with related probabilities (P_s), and rates of return for the market index (R_m) and the potential merger partner (R_j). These rates of return depict the performance of the market index and the acquiring firm over the past business cycles (which are expected to hold for the future), or they may be projections of future performance allowing for deviations from past behavior. Either approach may be used. Note in Table 23–1 that the required rate of return $E(R_j^0) = 16.3\%$ exceeds the expected return $E(R_j) = 14.5\%$, so j would not qualify as a desirable merger partner.

The contribution of the acquired firm to the combination's variance-of-equity rate does not affect the accept or reject decision based upon the market price of risk, so diversification (the reduction of the variance) can be ignored. In the absence of synergy, $E(R_j^0) = E(R_j)$, each potential merger partner can be evaluated without reference to the firm's existing risk-return characteristics. CAPM simply assumes that the acquiring firm will always seek merger partners having estimated returns at least commensurate with their risk posture.

All the same, the application of portfolio theory to the firm and to its acquisitions/divestitures to an extent represents a leap of faith. For practical purposes, securities can be treated as *divisible assets* in arriving at a portfolio decision; fractional shares can then be rounded to integer amounts with little damage to the optimal solution. On the other hand, few capital projects are insignificant relative to the total capital budget; likewise for each project, the decision is to accept or reject in total (0–1 decision). Fractional acceptance (except in joint ventures) is not an option. We cannot speak of small changes in the portfolio weights, since the acquisition or divestiture of a business unit may alter very considerably the entire weighting system. The result is a suboptimal solution. However, integer programming is often useful in designing capital project portfolios (see Chapter 20), since the analyses can be structured to compensate for the 0–1 nature of the decision.

---

[14]Subject to the restrictive assumptions discussed in Chapter 17.

Table 23–1   Selecting a Merger Partner by CAPM

STATES OF THE ECONOMY	P_S	R_m	R_j
Revival (S_1)	0.20	0.10	0.15
Prosperity (S_2)	0.50	0.15	0.20
Recession (S_3)	0.20	0.08	0.06
Depression (S_4)	0.10	0.06	0.03
	1.00		

Market Parameters

	P_S	R_m	$(P_S)(R_m)$	$R_m - E(R_m)$	$[R_m - E(R_m)]^2$	$[R_m - E(R_m)]^2 P_S$
S_1	0.20	0.10	0.020	-0.017	0.000289	0.0000578
S_2	0.50	0.15	0.075	$+0.033$	0.001089	0.0005445
S_3	0.20	0.08	0.016	-0.037	0.001369	0.0002738
S_4	0.10	0.06	0.006	-0.057	0.003249	0.0003249
			$E(R_m) = 0.117$		$\sigma_m^2 = 0.0012010$	

Cov $R_j R_m$

	P_S	R_j	$(P_S)(R_j)$	$d_j = R_j - E(R_j)$	$d_m = R_m - E(R_m)$	$d_j d_m$	$d_j d_m P_S$
S_1	0.20	0.15	0.030	$+0.005$	-0.017	-0.000085	-0.0000170
S_2	0.50	0.20	0.100	$+0.055$	$+0.033$	$+0.001815$	$+0.0009075$
S_3	0.20	0.06	0.012	-0.085	-0.037	$+0.003145$	$+0.0006290$
S_4	0.10	0.03	0.003	-0.115	-0.057	$+0.006555$	$+0.0006555$
			$E(R_j) = 0.145$			$\text{Cov}(R_j, R_m) = 0.0021750$	

Assume a 6% risk-free rate (R_F). Then:

$$B_j = \frac{\text{Cov}(R_j, R_m)}{\sigma_m^2} = \frac{0.0021745}{0.0012010} = 1.81$$

Therefore,

$$E(R_j^0) = R_F + [E(R_m) - R_F]B_j \qquad (2)$$
$$= 0.06 + (0.117 - 0.06)1.81$$
$$= 0.163$$

The Bargaining Area

After identifying the merger target, the implementation of an acquisition strategy requires identification of a bargaining area: maximum and minimum exchange ratios acceptable to the shareholders of the acquiring and acquired firms. For this purpose, the model developed by Larson and Gonedes offers a useful framework.[15]

[15] Kermit D. Larson and Nicholas J. Gonedes, "Business Combinations: An Exchange Ratio Determination Model," *The Accounting Review* (October 1969), 720–728.

This model assumes the following:

1   The objective of the combination is to enhance the market value of the common shares.
2   The shareholders will not approve of the combination unless it promises to maintain or increase their wealth position measured by the market value of their holdings.
3   The price-earnings (P/E) ratio of the shares captures the risk-return characteristics of the merging firms. In other words, market price trades off risk and return.
4   The shares are publicly traded.
5   No synergism will eventuate in the first year of merger.
6   Bargaining is a condition of bilateral monopoly: one buyer of the shares and one seller.

The Larson-Gonedes model requires the calculation of several components:

1   *Pre-combination wealth position of the firms.* This represents the market value of a common share 6 months to 1 year before the announcement of any merger. The objective is to establish the value of the equity shares uneffected by news of an impending combination:
a. *Wealth of acquiring company* (W_A):

$$W_A = (P/E_A)(EPS_A) \qquad (3)$$

b. *Wealth of acquired company* (W_B):

$$W_B = (P/E_B)(EPS_B)$$

2   *Post-combination wealth position.* This refers to the value of a common share (W_{AB}) after the combination or merger,

$$W_{AB} = (\Theta)(Y_A + Y_B) \times \frac{1}{S_A + (ER)S_B} \qquad (4)$$

where Θ = the expected P/E ratio after the combination
Y = total earnings of each entity for latest period prior to combination or first period earnings of the entity after the combination
S_A = number of pre-combination shares of acquiring company
S_B = number of pre-combination shares of acquired company
ER = exchange ratio to affect the combination

Note that for any given value of Θ, there is a corresponding exchange ratio.

3   *Wealth position of acquiring shareholders, post-combination.* The shareholders of the acquiring firm (A) will approve the combination if they *expect*

$$W_{AB} \geq W_A \qquad (5)$$

That is, the market value of their common shares will be equal to or greater than the pre-combination value. In other words, they anticipate the benefits of synergism.

4   *Wealth position of the acquired shareholders, post-combination.* The shareholders of the acquired firm (B) will approve the combination if they *expect*

$$W_{AB} \geq \left(\frac{1}{ER}\right)W_B \qquad (6)$$

where

$$\text{ER} = \frac{W_B}{W_A} \tag{7}$$

The same rationale for approval of the combination applies to the acquired shareholders.

5   Bargaining area.

a. *Maximum exchange ratio.* The maximum exchange ratio acceptable to the shareholders of the acquiring company (ER_A) is that which leaves their wealth position unchanged ($W_{AB} = W_A$). A higher exchange ratio transfers wealth to the shareholders of the acquired company. It follows that the acquiring company will bargain for a lower exchange ratio.

$$\text{ER}_A = \frac{(\Theta)(Y_A + Y_B) - (P/E_A)(Y_A)}{(P/E_A)(Y_A)(1/S_A)(S_B)} \tag{8}$$

ER_A will increase at a constant rate as Θ increases (see Figure 23–1).

b. *Minimum exchange ratio.* This designates the minimum number of shares of company A acceptable to the acquired shareholders (ER_B) that will leave their wealth position unchanged: $W_{AB} = (1/\text{ER})W_B$. A lower exchange ratio would transfer wealth to the shareholders of the acquiring company. Hence, the acquired company will bargain for a higher exchange ratio.

$$\text{ER}_B = \frac{(P/E_B)(Y_B/S_B)(S_A)}{(\Theta)(Y_A + Y_B) - (P/E_B)(Y_B)} \tag{9}$$

The minimum exchange ratio varies inversely with theta (see Figure 23–1).

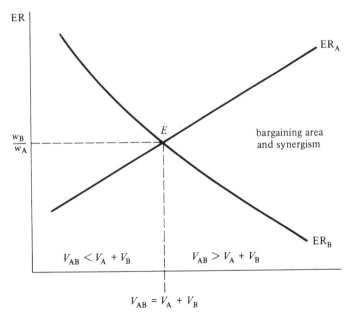

FIGURE 23-1 Business Combinations Bargaining Area

In Figure 23–1, the bargaining area is bounded by $\mathrm{ER_A}$–E–$\mathrm{ER_B}$. Here, the market value of the combination (V_{AB}) exceeds the pre-combination values of the separate entities $(V_A$ and $V_B)$, thereby creating synergism. To the left of the equilibrium, E, no merger would take place because both sets of shareholders would be less well off. At E, their wealth positions remain unchanged; the exchange ratio equals the ratio of the market prices of the common shares for A and B; and Θ equals an average of the P/E ratios of A and B weighted by their total earnings, Y_A and Y_B.

EXAMPLE 1

Larson-Gonedes Model

Assume Air-Frames, Inc. is negotiating a marger with Windom Engines, Inc. The comparative data on the two corporations is as follows:

	AIR-FRAMES, INC. (A)	WINDOM ENGINES, INC. (B)
Earnings per share	$2.87	$1.65
Dividends	$1.8	$1.00
Growth rate	6%	7%
Book value per share	$26.50	$33
Market value per share	$43	$52
Shares outstanding	3 million	1 million
P/E	15	31.5
Total earnings (Y)	$8,610,000	$1,650,000
Total value of equity	$129,000,000	$52,000,000

Projected P/E of combination $(\Theta) = 25$

(a) Should the shareholders of both corporations approve the merger?

(b) What are the minimum and maximum exchange ratios for acquiring and acquired corporations?

(c) What is the total synergism projected? If the actual exchange ratio agreed upon is 1.2 A for 1 B, how is the synergism divided?

SOLUTION: (a) First, find the pre-combination wealth position [Equation (3)]:

$$\text{Air Frames, Inc.} \quad W_A = (15)(2.87) = \$43.05$$

$$\text{Windom Engines, Inc.} \quad W_B = (31.5)(1.65) = \$51.98$$

Then, find the post-combination wealth position [Equation (4)]:

$$W_{AB} = (25)(\$8,610,000 + \$1,650,000) \times \frac{1}{3,000,000 + (1.2)1,000,000}$$

$$= \$256,500,000 \times \frac{1}{4,200,000}$$

$$= \$61.07$$

The wealth position of Air-Frame shareholders [Equation (5)] is

$$\$61.07 > \$43$$

Air-Frame shareholders should vote for merger.

The wealth position of Windom Engines shareholders [Equation (6)] is

$$\$61.07 > \frac{1}{1.2} \times \$52$$

$$\$61.07 > \$43.33$$

Windom shareholders should vote for the merger.

(b) The maximum exchange ratio [Equation (8)] is

$$ER_A = \frac{(25)(\$8,610,000 + \$1,650,000) - (15)(\$8,610,000)}{(15)(8,610,000)(1/3,000,000)(1,000,000)}$$

$$= \frac{\$256,500,000 - \$129,150,000}{\$129,150,000 \times 1,000,000/3,000,000}$$

$$= \frac{\$127,350,000}{43,050,000}$$

$$= 2.96 \text{ shares}$$

The minimum exchange ratio [Equation (9)] is

$$ER_B = \frac{(31.5)(\$1,650,000/1,000,000)(3,000,000)}{(25)(\$8,610,000 + \$1,650,000) - (31.5)(\$1,650,000)}$$

$$= \frac{\$155,925,000}{\$256,500,000 - \$51,975,000}$$

$$= \frac{\$155,925,000}{\$204,525,000}$$

$$= 0.76 \text{ shares}$$

(c) To find synergism, assuming an actual exchange rate of 1.2 A = 1 B, use the following:

Post-combination value of common shares [Equation (4)]:
$$\$61.07 \times 4,200,000 = \qquad\qquad \$256,494,000$$
Pre-combination value of common shares:

Air-Frames, Inc.	$43 × 3,000,000 = $129,000,000	
Windom Engines, Inc.	$52 × 1,000,000 = 52,000,000	181,000,000
Total synergism		$75,494,000

less

Amount to Air-Frames holders
$$\$61.07 - \$43 \times 3,000,000 \qquad = 54,210,000$$
Amount to Windom holders $\qquad\qquad\qquad\qquad\qquad \$21,284,000$

If the actual exchange ratio equals the ratio of market prices for the acquired and acquiring companies $(ER = MV_B/MV_A)$, then the synergism will be divided proportionately; that is, the parties retain their same relative wealth positions as before the merger. If the actual exchange ratio exceeds the ratio of market values, then the shareholders of the acquired company do proportionately better; they have gained relatively. If the actual exchange ratio is less than the ratio of market values, the shareholders

> of the acquiring company gain relatively. These conclusions follow from the bargaining strategies derived from Equations (8) and (9).

Within the bargaining area, the final exchange ratio may depend upon a balance of factors representing the strengths and weaknesses of the firms in light of the merger objectives. These include the following:

1 *Liquidity.* In the McDonnell-Douglas merger, for example, Douglas had important contracts but had working-capital problems. McDonnell had the liquidity to rectify the deficiency, and this became an important element in effecting the combination. It is worth recalling that the primary cause of business failures in the 1970s among larger firms was inadequate working capital.

2 *Strategic assets.* One firm may possess facilities, patents, and other special assets that enhance its bargaining power.

3 *Management capabilities.* If one firm possesses a particularly strong management team, it may figure prominently in assessing the future prospects of the combination.

4 *Tax-loss carryovers.* In a tax-free exchange, tax losses carry over to the acquiring corporation, but the principal purpose of the acquisition cannot look to the tax benefits. Assuming a legitimate business objective, tax-loss carryovers are attractive where the acquiring firm has income against which deductions may be applied. In a taxable exchange, the loss remains with the selling firm and may be applied against the gain from the sale of assets.

5 *Reproduction cost.* In a period of sustained inflation, it may be more economical to acquire assets through combination than by new construction. The factor may motivate mergers where the acquisition of fixed assets determines the objectives of expansion.

6 *Investment value.* Where the merger involves combination with a newly organized firm and/or the promotion of a new process, the amount of cash actually paid into the newcomer (investment value) may influence the exchange rate.

7 *Market value.* Probably the most common determinant of the final exchange ratio is the relative market value of the combined firms' shares. It is also the most logical element. If there exists an active market in the shares and if the market is efficient, the market will discount all that is known about the future prospects of the firms and reflect it in the market value of the shares.

8 *Book values.* Where conservative accounting practices have been followed, book values offer the advantage of convenience and speed in negotiation.

The reader may add other factors, such as earnings per share, and dividend payout ratios. Suffice it to say, as the negotiations swing toward higher or lower exchange ratios, wealth is transferred from one group of shareholders to the other.

SUMMARY

A comprehensive merger theory has been slow in evolving. This is not surprising because business combinations spring from different motivations and cover a time frame concomitant with the evolution of capitalism. Moreover, the available studies consider different time periods, employ dissimilar sample selection criteria, use disparate techniques in measuring the "effects" of business combinations, and apply varying statistical techniques in assessing results. The chameleon policies of government, which may channel business combinations in less than economically optimal directions, compound these problems. For example, Weston points out that the 1950 amendments to Section 7 of the Clayton Act enabled regulatory authorities virtually to abort horizontal and vertical mergers in which one of the parties has 10% or more of the defined market area. This change in the institutional structure contributed to the rising tide of conglomerate mergers.[16]

All the same, a survey of the modern literature (1960–1988) underscores the following characteristics of acquired firms:

- ☐ They have a cost of capital higher than other firms in their industry. Merger lowers the cost of capital, thus facilitating investment in the acquired firms operations.
- ☐ They are situated in an industry with favorable growth and profit opportunities. The acquiring firm has more funds than capital projects to absorb them. Investment opportunities are relatively more favorable in the acquired firm's industry than the acquiring firm's industry.
- ☐ They have organizational and/or managerial capital of value in the upcoming combination.
- ☐ They have lower P/E ratios and lower financial leverage than acquiring firms.
- ☐ Their shareholders experience significant positive wealth effects from the market reaction to news of the combination or the tender offer.

QUESTIONS
PROBLEMS

1. Briefly discuss the elements of the acquisition decision.
2. What are the shortcomings of a present value analysis in the acquisition decision?
3. Discuss how CAPM would be used in the acquisition decision and when it would point to an attractive merger.
4. Return to Air-Frames, Inc. Air-Frames has another merger opportunity with General Aviation. The latter has the following financial profile:

Earnings per share	$4.20
Annual dividend	$3.50
Growth rate	1%
Book value per share	$55
Market value per share	$41
Shares Outstanding	2,000,000
P/E ratio	9.76
Total earnings	$8,400,000
Total value	$82,000,000
Projected P/E (Θ)	13
Proposed actual exchange ratio	0.95 A = 1 B

Determine each of the following.
(a) Pre-combination wealth position.
(b) Post-combination wealth position.
(c) Maximum and minimum exchange ratios.
(d) The amount and division of total synergism.

[16]J. Fred Weston, "Developments in Finance Theory," *Financial Management* (Summer, 1981), 5–22.

(e) Air-Frames has decided to evaluate General Aviation using the CAPM approach:

STATE OF THE ECONOMY	P_S	R_m	GENERAL AVIATION (R_j)
Revival (S_1)	0.20	0.20	0.15
Prosperity (S_2)	0.50	0.30	0.20
Recession (S_3)	0.20	0.16	0.09
Depression (S_4)	0.10	0.12	0.05

The risk-free rate is 10%. Is General Aviation worth consideration as a takeover prospect?

REFERENCES

AICPA, Inc. *Accounting for Business Combinations*. Chicago: Commerce Clearing House, 1973.

Alberts, William W., and Segall, Joel E. *The Corporate Merger*. Chicago: University of Chicago Press, 1966.

Alexanda, Gordon J., P. George Benson, and Elizabeth W. Gunderson. "Asset Redeployment: Trans World Corporations Spinoff of TWA." *Financial Management* (Summer 1986).

Backman, Jules. "An Economist Looks at Accounting for Business Combination." *Financial Analysts Journal* (July–August 1970), 39–48.

Bagley, Edward R. *Beyond the Conglomerates: The Impact of the Supercorporations on the Future Life and Business*. New York: AMACOM, 1975.

Bock, Betty. *Antitrust Issues in Conglomerate Acquisitions: Tracking a Moving Target*. New York: National Industrial Conference Board, 1969.

Bradley, James W., and Donald H. Korn. *Acquisition and Corporate Development*. Lexington, Mass.: Lexington Books, 1981, 64.

Brown, Keith C., and Michael V. Raymond. "Risk Arbitrage and the Prediction of Successful Corporate Takeovers." *Financial Management* (Autumn 1986).

Brozen, Yale. *Mergers in Perspective*. Washington D.C.: American Enterprise Institute for Public Policy Research, 1982.

Clayton, Ronnie J., and William Beranek. "Disassociation and Legal Combinations." *Financial Management* (Summer 1985).

Comiskey, Eugene E., Ruth Ann McEwen, and Charles W. Mulford. "A Test of Pro Forma Consolidation of Finance Subsidiaries." *Financial Management* (Autumn 1987).

Committee of Experts on Restrictive Business Practices. *Mergers and Competitive Policy: A Report*. Paris: Organization for Economic Co-operation and Development, 1974.

Gahlon, James M., and Roger D. Stover. "Diversification, Financial Leverage and Conglomerate Systematic Risk." *Journal of Financial and Quantitative Analysis* (December 1979).

Grammarino, Ronald M., and Robert L. Heinkel. "A Model of Dynamic Takeover Behavior." *Journal of Finance* (June 1986).

Higgins, Robert C. "Sustainable Growth under Inflation." *Financial Management*, 10 (Autumn 1981), 36–40.

Keenan, Michael, and Lawrence J. White. *Mergers and Acquisitions*. Lexington, Mass.: D. C. Heath and Co., 1982.

Kemp, Bernard A. *Understanding Merger Activity*. New York: New York University, 1969.

Klein, April. "The Timing and Substance of Divestiture Announcements: Individual, Simultaneous and Cumulative Effects." *Journal of Finance* (July 1986).

Knortz, Herbert C. "The Realities of Business Combinations." *Financial Analysts Journal* (July–August 1970), 28–32.

Lewellen, Wilbur G. "A Pure Financial Rationale for the Conglomerate Merger." *Journal of Finance* (May 1971), 532–533.

Linowes, David F. *Managing Growth Through Acquisitions*. New York: AMA, 1968.

Little, Arthur D., Inc. *Mergers and Acquisitions*. Cambridge, Mass.: 1963.

Mase, Myles La Grange. *Management Problems of Corporate Acquisitions*. Cambridge, Mass.: Harvard University Press, 1962.

_____, and George C. Montgomery. *Management Problems of Corporate Acquisitions*. (Massachusetts: Division of Research, 1971).

Mason, R. Hal, and Maurice B. Gondzwaard. "Performance of Conglomerate Firms: A Portfolio Approach." *Journal of Finance*, 31 (March 1976), 39–48.

Mautz, R. K. *Financial Reporting By Diversified Companies*. New York: Financial Executives Research Foundation, 1968.

McCord, Jim, and Robert J. Oziel. *Conglomerates & Cogenerics*. New York: Practicing Law Institute, 1970.

Meyers, Gustavus. *History of Great American Fortunes*. New York: Random House, 1936.

Mueller, Dennis C. "The Effects of Conglomerate Mergers: A Survey of Empirical Evidence." *Journal of Banking and Finance*. I: 339 (1977).

Mueller, Willard F. "Conglomerates: A Nonindustry," in Walter Adams, *The Structure of American Industry*. New York: Macmillan Publishing Co., Inc., 1982.

Nelson, Ralph Lowell. *Merger Movements in American Industry*. Princeton, N.J.: Princeton University Press, 1959.

Pettway, Richard H., and Jack W. Trifto. "Do Banks Overbuy When Acquiring Failed Banks?" *Financial Management* (Summer 1985).

Reich, Robert B. "Making Industrial Policy." *Foreign Affairs* (Spring 1982).

Renshaw, Edward F. "The Theory of Financial Leverage and Conglomerate Mergers." *California Management Review* (Fall 1968).

Report of the Federal Trade Commission on the Merger Movement, 1968.

Roy, Asim. "Partial Acquisition Strategies for Business Combinations." *Financial Management* (Summer 1985).

Salter, Malcolm S., and Wolf A. Weinhold. *Diversification Through Acquisition*. New York: The Free Press, 1979.

Townsend, Harry. *Scale, Innovation, Merger and Monopoly*. Oxford: Pergamon Press, 1968.

Welcome to Our Conglomerate—You're Fired! New York: Delacorte Press, 1971.

Weston, J. Fred, and S. K. Monsinghka. "Tests of the Efficiency Performance of Conglomerate Firms." *Journal of Finance* (September 1971), 919–936.

Wyatt, Arthur R. *A Critical Study of Accounting for Business Combinations*. New York: AICPA, 1963.

_____. "Inequities in Accounting for Business Combinations." *Financial Executive* (December 1972), 28–35.

_____, and Donald E. Kieso. *Business Combinations: Planning and Action*. Scranton, Pa.: International Textbook Company, 1969.

CASE STUDY 23-1

Fort Howard – Maryland Cup Combination

In the 1983 annual report of Fort Howard Paper Co., the president, Paul J. Schierl, said, "Without question, the highlight of the year was our acquisition of Maryland Cup which was finalized on August 31, 1983. As a result of that acquisition, our total sales will more than double on an annualized basis. The acquisition also pushed employment to near the 15,000 mark and significantly increased the number of manufacturing facilities." He added, "Domestic Maryland Cup operations include manufacturing plants and warehouse facilities which are strategically located throughout the operations in the United Kingdom and The Netherlands as well as joint ventures in Japan and Canada."

THE ACQUIRING COMPANY — FORT HOWARD PAPER

Fort Howard Paper Company manufacturers a broad line of disposable paper products, including table napkins, towels, toilet tissue in roll and interfold form, industrial and automotive wipers, and boxed facial tissues. The acquisition of Maryland Cup Corporation in August 1983 expanded the company's product line to disposable food and beverage service products, including paper and plastic plates, cups, bowls, and drinking straws; ice cream cones; plastic tableware; and containers for use in packaging food and dairy products. The acquisition included a line of container filling equipment for use by dairies and other food processors.

Fort Howard sells a large majority of products through paper wholesalers and central purchasing activities. Fort Howard's sanitary tissue products for home use are sold under the brand names Mardi Gras, So-Dri, Page, Edon, Dolly Madison, and Soft 'n Gentle. The company also creates and prints logos, commercial messages, and designs on paper napkins and placemats for its commercial customers. Food and beverage service products are sold under the brand names Sweetheart, Guildware, Appeal, and Elegant.

The company's products are distributed throughout the United States to commercial, institutional, and industrial customers by a trained sales force. Tissue products and food service items for household use are sold to accounts which include major food store chains, mass merchandisers and wholesale grocers. These products are sold by the company's salaried sales force and by brokers. Fort Howard manufactures tissue products in the United Kingdom. Food and beverage service products are also manufactured in both the United Kingdom and the Netherlands. In early 1982, the company acquired an 80% stock ownership interest in Sterling International's United Kingdom subsidiaries.

Fort Howard manufactures paper rolls for sale to both domestic and foreign purchasers. The company also owns a wastepaper dealer based in New York, the principal business of which is the purchase and sale of recyclable wastepaper, primarily on the East Coast.

Fort Howard believes it is one of the leading producers of disposables for the food service and dairy industry and is one of the largest suppliers of disposable paper products to the industrial, commercial, and institutional markets. All of the geographic markets in which the company sells its products are extremely competitive, and the company's products compete directly with those of other major manufacturers, a number of which are larger and have greater resources than the company. Most of the time, customers look principally toward price, quality, distribution, and service as factors when considering purchasing products from the company.

THE ACQUIRED COMPANY — MARYLAND CUP CO.

Maryland Cup Co. is engaged in the manufacture and distribution of a variety of food service wares, including plates, cups, bowls, and drinking and dairy products. To aid in packaging its products, the company developed versatile equipment for container filling of ice cream and other products for the dairy and food industries. The company's products are also packaged for home use.

All the company's items are single-service, disposable products with similar markets and methods of distribution. The major item of the company's products are sold through wholesale distributing channels, the vending, dairy and food industries, institutional feeding markets (hospitals, nursing homes, schools and colleges, plants and offices) and leisure-time concessionaires, fast-food chains, and independent restaurants, and to consumers for home use through supermarkets and other retailers. The company markets its products throughout the United States and in certain foreign countries. The company is the leading producer of disposable products, such as paper and plastic cups, containers, disposable tableware, and ice cream cones, for the food service and dairy industries. Other single-service disposables represent a minor phase of total volume including drinking straws and toothpicks. Its principal trademarks are Sweetheart, Guildware, and Eat-it-All.

Between 1980 and 1982, the company increased its expenditures on research and development from $1,700,000 to $2,800,000. Maryland Cup has 10,000 employees, of which about 600 persons are in sales and sales-related activities. The company considers the business seasonal in the sense that its major sales and earnings are realized during the third and fourth quarters from April through September, when warmer temperatures create greater demand for single-service containers for food and beverage consumption.

THE MERGER AGREEMENT

The merger agreement provides for the merger of Maryland Cup into Acquisition, Inc., a wholly owned subsidiary of Fort Howard. Each Maryland Cup stockholder will receive either $52 in cash or 0.85 of one Fort Howard common share for each share of Maryland common owned. Approximately 49% of the outstanding Maryland Cup common shares will receive $52 per share in cash, and approximately 51% of the outstanding Maryland Cup common shares will be converted into Fort Howard common shares.

The separate corporate existence of Maryland Cup will be terminated. Acquisition, Inc., as the surviving corporation, will succeed to all of Maryland Cup's assets and liabilities. Acquisition's name will then be changed to Maryland Cup Corporation.

Statistical Data on Fort Howard and Maryland Cup, December 31, 1982

	FORT HOWARD	MARYLAND CUP
EPS	$3.43	$3.10
Dividend growth rate	18.7%	10%
Book value per share	$16.40	$24.19
Market price per share	$55	$49.13
Number of shares	26,733,000	10,638,915
P/E	16.03	15.85
Total earnings	$92,400,000	$31,744,000
Weighted average cost of capital	15%	

Based on your analysis of the Fort Howard–Maryland Cup combination, comment on the following:

1   Is the combination an internal or external form of expansion?
2   What is the direction of the combination?
3   What is the legal form of the combination?
4   How was the transaction treated for accounting purposes?
5   Was this a taxable or tax deferred reorganization? If the latter, which type?
6   Using NPV analysis, determine if Fort Howard properly identified Maryland Cup as a target worthy of investigation.
7   Assuming the projected P/E is achieved, did the combination result in a post-acquisition synergism? If so, how was it divided between the shareholders of Fort Howard and Maryland Cup?

Sustainable Growth

24

Strategic planning pertains to the establishment of goals and the progress of the firm in moving toward the defined targets. In periods of expanding economic activity, typical goals include increased market penetration through modification of product lines, additions to plant and equipment, added research and development spending, updating management training and personnel administration, the achievement of an optimal financial structure to minimize the cost of capital, and so forth. Many of these topics, the reader will observe, form the subject matter of capital budgeting—and not by coincidence. *Important components of the strategic plan are given concrete expression by the capital budget and the supporting decisions made in formulating a capital budget.*

Strategic planning does not relate solely to the balmy days of prosperity. Mistakes are made in the planning process that become sorely obvious during economic retrenchment. The strategic plan in a recession environment may stress retreat from indefensible positions and reductions in cost of operations to restore profit margins. The decision to abandon a project or subsidiary relies upon the same techniques of capital budgeting as those required by the initial evaluation of investment opportunities. In addition, decisions such as lease or own, lease or sell, refunding of corporate debt, buying the firm's stock on the open market also relate to strategic planning but utilize capital budgeting evaluation techniques in execution.

Viable strategic planning demands a balanced relationship among the defined goals. If imbalances appear in the implementation, then some goals are necessarily compromised. This chapter centers on the problem of balancing growth (or shrinkage) in assets with other established financial policies enunciated in the strategic plan.

SUSTAINABLE GROWTH (STABLE PRICES)

In a strategic planning context, the question of an appropriate growth rate over a defined long-term period takes the form: What rate of growth is sustainable with regard to established financial policies? Specifically, given the firm's target dividend-payout ratio and capital structure (long-term debt to equity), what percentage increase in sales can be maintained without necessitating a change in financial policy?[1] If sales grow at a higher rate, the firm can exercise a combination of options: increase debt, reduce dividend payout, improve operating performance to increase profit margins, or issue equity securities. Except for improved operating efficiency, each option alters established financial policies.[2]

For purposes of initial discussion, let us assume the following:

1   The depreciation is adequate to recapture the value of existing assets.

2   The profit margin (P) on new sales (ΔS) corresponds to that of existing sales (S).

3   The firm has an established financial structure goal (L) without the sale of new common stock.

4   The firm has an established dividend payout rate (D); thus, the target retention ratio is $1 - D$.

5   New fixed assets at book values (F) represent a stated proportion of the change in physical volume of output (real sales).

6   New current assets (C) are a stated proportion of sales in nominal dollars.

7   The initial level of sales at the beginning of the period is represented by S and the change in sales during the period by ΔS.

8   The ratio of *total* assets to net sales is denoted by T; the ratio is constant for new and existing sales.

9   The firm will rely on retained earnings for equity financing—no new common stock is to be issued.

Assuming a stable price level for the moment as well as all of the symbols just defined, the sustainable growth rate (g^*) becomes

$$g^* = \frac{\Delta S}{S} = \frac{P(1 - D)(1 + L)}{T - P(1 - D)(1 + L)} \tag{1}$$

Equation (1) is illustrated in Example 1.

---

[1] The reader will recall the distinction between *capital structure* (long-term debt to equity) and *financial structure* (total debt to equity).

[2] The discussion is based upon the following articles: Robert C. Higgins, "How Much Growth Can a Firm Afford?" *Financial Management* (Fall 1977), and "Sustainable Growth in an Inflationary Environment," *Financial Management* (Autumn 1981); and Dana Johnson, "The Behavior of Financial Structure and Sustainable Growth in an Inflationary Environment," *Financial Management* (Autumn 1981).

EXAMPLE 1

Micro-Industries, Inc.

Micro-Industries, Inc.
Balance Sheet
December 31, 198X

ASSETS	$	%	LIABILITIES AND EQUITIES	$	%
Cash	$10,000	0.12	Accounts payable	$ 5,000	0.06
Inventory	15,000	0.18	Bonds payable	30,000	0.35
Equipment	80,000	0.94	Capital stock (7,500 shares)	30,000	0.35
Less: Accumulated					
depreciation	20,000	− 0.24	Retained earnings	20,000	0.24
	$85,000	1.00		$85,000	1.00

Micro-Industries, Inc.
Income Statement
December 31, 198X

Sales	$30,000	(10,000 units at $3.00)
Less: cost of sales	8,000	
Gross profit	$22,000	
Less: selling and administrative expenses	11,000	
Net operating income (EBIT)	$11,000	
Less: interest (10%) on debt	3,500	
Earnings before taxes (EBT)	$ 7,500	

Profit margin $(P) = 0.25$
Earnings per share (EPS) = $75,00/7,500 = $1.00 before taxes
Dividend payout ratio $(D) = 33\%$, or $1.00 × 0.33 = 33¢ per share
Retention ratio $= 1 − D = 1 − 0.33 = 0.67$, or 67%
Total assets/sales ratio $(T) = \$85,000/\$30,000 = 2.833$
Financial structure objective $(L) = D/E = \$35,000/\$50,000 = 0.70$
Price trend $(J) = + 10\%$ (revival); 10% (recession)
Current assets/current sales $(C) = \$25,000/\$30,000 = 0.833$
Fixed assets/sales $(F) = \$80,000/\$30,000 = 2.67$

What is the sustainable rate of growth for Micro-Industries?

SOLUTION:

$$g^* = \frac{0.25(1 − 0.33)(1 + 0.70)}{2.83 − 0.25(1 − 0.33)(1 + 0.70)}$$

$$= \frac{0.28475}{2.83 − 0.28475} \tag{2}$$

$$= 0.111875, \text{ or } \approx 11.2\%$$

Since assets must equal liabilities plus equity, growth-induced assets must be financed by new debt and/or an increase in retained earnings. Unless the actual growth level rate (g) equals the sustainable growth rate (g^*), the profit margin, dividend-payout ratio, debt/equity ratio, or total assets/sales ratio must change or the firm will be compelled to issue new equities.

Thus, the optimal growth level is not simply the product of accepting all investments with a positive NPV or an IRR greater than or equal to K. Management may have to reflect explicitly upon the implications of higher growth rates and the revision of financial policies through lower dividend payout, increased leveraging, or sale of equities. These decisions have both financial and managerial control implications.

SUSTAINABLE GROWTH (RISING PRICE TREND)

Allowing for the effect of a rising price trend revises Equation (1) as follows:

$$g_R^* = \frac{(1 + J)P(1 - D)(1 + L) - JC}{(1 + J)C + F - (1 + J)P(1 - D)(1 + L)} \tag{3}$$

Equation (3) is illustrated in the following example.

EXAMPLE 2
Micro-Industries Extended

Use the same data on Micro-Industries, but now take a 10% rate of price increase into account. What is the real sustainable growth rate (g_R^*)?

SOLUTION: Calling on Equation (3), we find:

$$
\begin{aligned}
g_R^* &= \frac{(1 + 0.10)0.25(1 - 0.33)(1 + 0.70) - (0.10)(0.833)}{(1 + 0.10)0.833 + 2.67 - (1 + 0.10)0.25(1 - 0.33)(1 + 0.70)} \\
&= \frac{0.313225 - 0.0833}{3.5863 - 0.313225} \\
&= \frac{0.229925}{3.273075} \\
&= 0.0702473, \text{ or } 7\%
\end{aligned}
\tag{4}
$$

Overall, *given the assumptions of the model*, an upward trend in prices acts to reduce real sustainable growth unless offset by operating efficiencies. In the extreme case, inflation-induced increases in retained earnings and borrowing are more than offset by required increases in working capital investment. Higgins[3] estimates, for example, that real sustainable growth declines by 2.2% for every 5% increase in the rate of inflation. He further notes,

To the extent that depreciation is insufficient to maintain the value of assets... sustainable growth is reduced.... If newly acquired assets are more profitable than existing

[3]Higgins, "Sustainable Growth under Inflation."

assets in the sense of producing sales with a higher profit margin, offering a more rapid depreciation rate or generating more sales per dollar of assets ... sustainable growth will rise.

Similarly sustainable growth (g^*) can rise if the firm intensifies asset utilization by reducing the assets required to support a given level of sales. Otherwise, the firm can restore its sustainable rate of growth (g^*) in an inflationary environment subject to the stipulated assumptions only by altering accepted financial policies (reducing dividend payout, increasing leverage, sale of new equity shares). All things considered, therefore, inflation has inimical effects on the sustainable rate of growth (g^*). A sustainable growth rate different from g^* is inconsistent with established financial targets.

Johnson qualified the original Higgins model and the presumption of a constant *financial* structure. The former hinged the discussion on the rate of sustainable growth using a constant *capital* structure [long-term debt to equity ratio (L_L)]. Based upon Higgins's assumptions, Johnson shows that total uses of funds are composed of the change in total nominal current assets, $[(S + \Delta S)(1 + J) - S]C$, plus new nominal fixed assets, $(\Delta S)F$. Sources of funds equal the increase in nominal debt plus retained earnings, $(S + \Delta S)(1 + J)P(1 - D)(1 + L)$. The real sustainable rate of growth (g_R) as restated by Johnson[4] using the Higgins assumptions becomes:

$$g_R = \frac{(1 + J)Y - JC}{F - (1 + g)Y + C(1 + J)} \tag{5}$$

where

$$Y = P(1 - D)(1 + L)$$

EXAMPLE 3

Using the data on Micro-Industries, determine the sustainable rate of growth by applying Equation (5).

SOLUTION:

$$Y = 0.25(1 - 0.33)(1 + 0.70)$$

$$= 0.28475$$

Then,

$$g_R = \frac{(1 + 0.10).28475 - (0.10)(0.833)}{2.67 - (1 + 0.10)0.28475 + 0.833(1 + 0.10)}$$

$$= \frac{0.229925}{2.67 - 0.313225 + 0.9163} \tag{6}$$

$$= \frac{0.229925}{3.273075}$$

$$= 0.0702473, \text{ or } 7\%$$

[4] Johnson, "The Behavior of Financial Structure."

> This agrees with Higgins' results from Equation (4) based upon a constant financial structure. However, Johnson by focusing on capital structure (long-term debt to equity) allows working capital to float with nominal sales.

The revised real sustainable rate of growth thus takes the form

$$g_R = \frac{\Delta S}{S} = \frac{Y(1 + J) - WJ}{F - (1 + J)Y + W(1 + J)} \tag{7}$$

where $Y = P(1 - D)(1 + L_L)$

W = the ratio of nominal net working capital to nominal sales

EXAMPLE 4

> Assume the same data used in the preceding examples except that the long-term debt to equity ratio (L_L) equals 0.60; and the ratio of net working capital to nominal sales (W) equals 0.67. What is the real sustainable growth based upon a constant *capital* structure?
>
> SOLUTION:
>
> $$Y = 0.25(1 - 0.33)(1 + 0.60)$$
> $$= 0.268$$
>
> Then,
>
> $$
> \begin{aligned}
> g_R &= \frac{0.268(1 + 0.10) - (0.67)(0.10)}{2.67 - (1 + 0.10)0.268 + 0.67(1 + 0.10)} \\[2mm]
> &= \frac{0.2948 - 0.067}{2.67 - 0.2948 + 0.737} \\[2mm]
> &= \frac{0.2278}{3.1122} \\[2mm]
> &= 0.0731958, \text{ or } 7.3\%
> \end{aligned} \tag{8}
> $$

Comparison of Equations (5) and (7) indicates that the incremental price-induced financing for current assets is partially offset by the price-adjusted rise in current liabilities. Thus, with a constant capital structure the real sustainable rate of growth is higher than that attainable were the firm to adhere to an established financial structure. In both cases (a target financial structure or a target capital structure), the sustainable rate is lower than that attainable under conditions of price stability. The reason for the latter phenomenon lies in the assumption that management uses historical-cost financial statements in describing the optimal financial or capital structures and in setting up target ratios. It follows that in the face of persistent inflation, management can maintain a stable capital structure over time only by using a constant dollar debt/equity ratio or a ratio based upon market values.

Bear in mind our conclusions apply to any generalized upward trend in prices. Inflation (see Chapter 9) is a special, albeit extreme, case of an upward movement in prices.

SUSTAINABLE GROWTH (DOWNWARD TREND IN PRICES)

This section addresses the questions raised as the price level turns downward from equilibrium, depicted in Equations (3) and (4). A priori, one would expect a slowdown in the rate of real sustainable growth. Applying Equation (3) for a *fixed financial structure*, we have

$$
\begin{aligned}
g_R^* &= \frac{(1 - 0.10)0.25(1 - 0.33)(1 + 0.70) - (-0.10)(0.833)}{(1 - 0.10)0.833 + 2.67 - (1 - 0.10)0.25(1 - 0.33)(1 + 0.70)} \\
&= \frac{0.256275 - (-0.0833)}{3.4197 - 0.256275} \\
&= \frac{0.339575}{3.163425} \\
&= 0.1073441, \text{ or } 10.7\%
\end{aligned}
\tag{9}
$$

For a constant capital structure, applying Equation (7), we have

$$
\begin{aligned}
g_R &= \frac{0.268(1 - 0.10) - (0.67)(0.10)}{2.67 - (1 - 0.10)0.268 + 0.67(1 - 0.10)} \\
&= \frac{0.2412 - 0.067}{2.67 - 0.2412 + 0.603} \\
&= \frac{0.1742}{3.0318} \\
&= 0.0574576, \text{ or } 5.7\%
\end{aligned}
\tag{10}
$$

Based upon the Johnson formulation [Equation (7)], the real sustainable growth rate drops to zero with a 28% decline in the price level and shows a negative rate at 30%. Improved productivity can wholly or partially offset declining growth rates by enhancing profit margins. Otherwise, the situation dictates a defensive strategy of building liquidity, reducing leverage or increasing dividend payouts in the presence of capital in excess of investment opportunities.

ESTABLISHING FINANCIAL POLICY IN RELATION TO A TARGET GROWTH RATE

Obviously, the preceding equations can be employed to solve for any unknown value, as illustrated in the following example.

EXAMPLE 5

Suppose that Micro-Industries, assuming a stable price level, establishes a target growth rate of 11.2% for the period covered by its strategic plan. What D/E is compatible with the stated objective?

SOLUTION: Using the original Higgins model expressed in Equation (1), we have

$$g^* = \frac{P(1 - D)(1 + L)}{T - P(1 - D)(1 + L)}$$

$$11.2 = \frac{0.25(1 - 0.33)(1 + L)}{2.83 - 0.25(1 - 0.33)(1 + L)} \tag{11}$$

$$11.2 = \frac{0.1675(1 + L)}{2.83 - 0.1675(1 + L)}$$

Let $(1 + L) = X$. Then,

$$11.2 = \frac{0.1675(X)}{2.83 - 0.1675(X)}$$

Let $Y = 0.1675(X)$:

$$0.112(2.83 - Y) = Y$$
$$0.112 \times 2.83 = Y + 0.112Y$$
$$0.112 \times 2.83 = 1.112Y$$
$$Y = \frac{0.112 \times 2.83}{1.112}$$
$$= 0.285$$

Then,

$$X = \frac{Y}{0.1675}$$
$$X = \frac{0.285}{0.1675}$$
$$X = 1.7$$

Since $X = (1 + L)$, $L = X - 1 = 1.7 - 1 = 0.70$. The D/E ratio consistent with the targeted growth rate is 0.70.

In like manner, Micro-Industries might test the compatibility of other variables, such as the dividend payout policy, total assets to sales, profit margin on sales. The testing procedure can also incorporate projected price trends by using Equation (3). If we assume that the targeted growth rate is primarily dependent on capital budget items, then the manipulation of Equation (1) relates the significance of the capital budget for other key planning variables. The Johnson models can, of course, be similarly utilized, as is now demonstrated.

EXAMPLE 6

Posing the same question for Micro-Industries as raised in Example 5, determine g_R using Equation (7).

SOLUTION:

$$g_R = \frac{Y(1 + J) - WJ}{F - (1 + J)Y + W(1 + J)}$$

where $Y = P(1 - D)(1 + L_L)$.

If we insert the disaggregated value of Y into the primary equation, g_R becomes:

$$g_R = \frac{[P(1 - D)(1 + L_L)](1 + J) - WJ}{F - (1 + J)[P(1 - D)(1 + L_L)] + W(1 + J)}$$

$$0.073 = \frac{[0.25(1 - 0.33)(1 + L_L)](1 + 0.10) - (0.67)(0.10)}{2.67 - (1 + 0.10)[0.25(1 - 0.33)(1 + L_L)] + 0.67(1 + 0.10)} \tag{12}$$

$$0.073 = \frac{[0.1675(1 + L_L)](1.1) - 0.067}{2.67 - (1.1)[0.1675(1 + L_L)] + 0.737}$$

Let $X = (1 + L_L)$. Then,

$$0.073 = \frac{[0.1675(X)](1.1) - 0.067}{2.67 - (1.1)[0.1675(X)] + 0.737}$$

If $Z = 0.1675(X)$,

$$0.073 = \frac{Z(1.1) - 0.067}{2.67 - Z(1.1) + 0.737}$$

$$0.073(2.67 - 1.1Z + 0.737) = 1.1Z - 0.067$$

$$0.19491 - 0.0803Z + 0.053801 = 1.1Z - 0.067$$

$$0.19491 + 0.053801 + 0.067 = 1.1Z + 0.0803Z$$

$$0.315711 = 1.1803Z$$

$$0.2674836 = Z$$

Accordingly,

$$Z = 0.1675(X)0.2674836 = 0.1675(X)$$

$$X = 1.596917 \approx 1.6$$

$$X = (1 + L_L) = 1.6 = (1 + L_L)L_L = 0.60.$$

A long-term debt/equity ratio of 0.60 is compatible with a growth rate of 7.3%.

Sustainable Growth Based upon Cash Flow

The Higgins and Johnson models measure sustainable growth based upon accrual accounting information. Accrual accounting statements comprise an amalgam of values taken at different price levels and embody varying degrees of liquidity. Thus, in the models examined, the sustainable growth rate is determined by the historical values of the account distribution to take place at a price level which may be higher or lower than the average implicit in the distribution. The historical values on the balance sheet, for example, cycle through the income statement affecting the key variable in the growth models—the profit margin (P). *Moreover, the accretion in retained earnings—$P(1 - D)$—may be impounded in nonliquid assets or assets not currently producing income and not immediately available to finance growth in sales.* Conversely, the growth calculation may be understated by charges against income that do not represent cash payments.

It is the objective of cash flow analysis to adjust the conventional statements to show the cash available for investment (cash from operations, cash from net debt and equity transactions, change in working capital) and the cash required for investment (cash outlays for plant and equipment, merger acquisitions, dividends, etc.). The bottom line, therefore, is the change in cash and temporary investments. Thus, cash flow analysis does not abandon the traditional accounting information system. Rather, it builds on the information in the balance sheet and income statements to picture another aspect of the firm's situation, the Statement of Changes in Financial Position.

In other words, it is not appropriate simply to add back accruals and noncash charges and call the product "cash flow." An all too common practice among practitioners is to add back depreciation expense to net income (EAT) to secure the firm's "cash flow." Gombola and Ketz stress that financial analysts "employing net-income plus depreciation should be warned that this measure is not a measure of cash flow, but rather a measure of profitability." They distinguish between working capital from operations and cash flow from operations. Table 24–1 illustrates the Gombola-Ketz adjustments to secure cash flow from operations.

It should be obvious that to project sustainable growth from the financial statements of the firm requires a model of greater complexity and a knowledgeable financial analyst to make the judgment calls on the content and calculations of the component variables. The complexity of the models and requisite experienced judgment of the analyst are traceable to the marked diversity between industries and firms within the same industry.

Casting the notion of sustainable growth in a cash flow context also broadens the question raised by the sustainable growth models of Higgins and Johnson. These accounting-based models asked the question: "What rate of growth in sales can be maintained over the following period without the need to alter the existing financial (or capital) structure?" By contrast, the cash flow models *explicitly* ask the question: "What is the sustainable growth rate in sales which can be maintained from resources required to finance the working capital and capital budgets of the firm?" The latter represents a drawdown on financial resources (outflows) which may not be offset by inflows in the same or following period.

The accounting growth models are derived from the basic accounting equation: assets = liabilities + equity. The cash flow approach states that the firm is in equilibrium when the funds available for investment (FAI) = funds required for investment (FRI). FRI links directly to the working and capital budgets of the firm.

Govindarajan and Shank Model

Govindarajan and Shank (G & S) speak to the "maximum growth in sales that a firm can sustain" and advocate that statistic as an important element in cash sufficiency planning. The firm is in equilibrium when cash "generated from operations plus the debt the internal funds are assumed to support just equals the funds required

Table 24–1   Computation of Cash Flow

I   *Working Capital from Operations (WCO).* WCO is equal to net income plus or minus the following items:

ADDITIONS

1. Depreciation expenses, depletion expenses, amortization of intangibles, and deferred charges.
2. Amortization of discount on bonds payable.
3. Amortization of premium on bond investments.
4. Additions to deferred investment tax credits.
5. Increase in deferred income taxes payable.
6. Pro-rata share of reported losses in excess of cash dividends recognized from unconsolidated stock investments under the equity method.
7. Minority interest in consolidated subsidiaries' net income
8. Losses from nonoperating items.

SUBTRACTIONS

1. Amortization of deferred credits.
2. Amortization of premium on bonds payable.
3. Amortization of discount on bond investments.
4. Amortization of deferred investment tax credits.
5. Decrease in deferred income taxes payable.
6. Pro-rata share of reported income in excess of cash dividends recognized from unconsolidated stock investment under the equity method.
7. Minority interest in consolidated subsidiaries' net loss.
8. Gains from nonoperating items.

II   *Cash Flow from Operations (CFO).* CFO is equal to WCO plus or minus the following:

ADDITIONS

1. Decrease in trade accounts and notes receivable.
2. Decrease in inventory.
3. Decrease in prepaid expenses.
4. Increase in trade accounts and notes payable.
5. Increase in accrued liabilities.

SUBTRACTIONS

1. Increase in trade accounts and notes receivable.
2. Increase in inventory.
3. Increase in prepaid expenses.
4. Decrease in trade accounts and notes payable.
5. Decrease in accrued liabilities.

SOURCE: Michael J. Gombola and J. Edward Ketz, "A Note on Cash Flow and Classification Patterns of Financial Ratios," *The Accounting Review* (January 1983).

to support the incremental sales and to maintain the existing productive capacity."[5] Thus,

$$g^* = \frac{\text{FPO} + (\text{FPO} \times R) - M}{(F + U_A + W + M - \text{FPO}) - (\text{FPO} \times R)} \tag{13}$$

where FPO = funds provided by operations $= (P - i)(1 - T)(1 - D) + D_p$

   P = earnings before interest and taxes (EBIT)/net sales

   i = interest expense/net sales

   D_p = depreciation expense/net sales

   M = maintenance expense/net sales

   W = change in working capital/change in net sales

   F = fixed asset investment rate =
      (construction activity + capitalized interest + acquisitions)/net sales

   U_A = investment in nonoperational assets/EAT
      (this variable is a modification of the G & S model to allow for capital investments in progress and not as yet producing a positive cash flow)

   T = income tax rate = tax expense/earnings before taxes (EBT)

   D = dividend rate = dividends paid/earnings after taxes (EAT)

   R = change in long-term and intermediate debt/cash retained by company
      [cash retained by company = working capital provided by operations
      + change in working capital (includes cash and temporary investments)
      − dividends paid]

The following example illustrates the application of the G & S model.

EXAMPLE 7

In 1985, the financial statements of Anheuser-Busch Corporation showed the following data (millions of dollars):

EBIT	$873.9
Interest expense	93.4
EBT	$780.5
Income tax expense	$336.8
EAT	443.7
Depreciation and amortization	236.1
Dividends	129.7
Funds provided by operations (FPO)	550.7
Issuance of long-term debt	157.9
Reduction of long-term debt	136.4
Maintenance expense	0
Fixed asset purchases	601.0

[5]V. Govindarajan and John K. Shank, "Cash Sufficiency: Missing Link in Strategic Planning," *Corporate Accounting*, Winter 1984.

Capitalized interest	$37.2
Acquisitions	0
Divestitures	0
Increase (decrease) in working capital	47.4
Increase (decrease) in cash	91.0
Common stock issued	0
Other cash retained by company	0
Investment in nonoperational assets	288.9
Net sales (1985)	7,686.0
Net sales (1984)	7,159.0

Therefore, the following values result which will be used to determine g_c^*:

$$
\begin{aligned}
P &= \$873.9/\$7,686 & &= 0.1137 \\
T &= \$336.8/\$780.5 & &= 0.4315 \\
D &= \$129.7/\$443.7 & &= 0.2923 \\
D_p &= \$236.1/\$7,686.0 & &= 0.0307 \\
i &= \$93.4/\$7,686.0 & &= 0.0122 \\
M & & &= 0 \\
W &= \$47.4/\$7,686 - \$7,159 \text{ or} & & \\
&\quad \$47.4/\$527 & &= 0.0900 \\
R &= \$21.5/\$559.4 & &= 0.0384 \\
&\quad \text{(cash retained by company} & &= \\
&\quad \text{funds provided by operations} & &= \$550.7 \\
&\quad + \text{change in working capital} & &= \$138.4 \\
&\quad - \text{dividends paid)} & &= \$129.7 \\
F &= \$01 + \$37.2/\$7,686.0 & &= 0.08303 \\
U_A &= \$228.9/\$443.7 & &= 0.65112
\end{aligned}
$$

Determine g_c^*.

SOLUTION: First we find FPO by substituting the appropriate values into Equation (14):

$$
\text{FPO} = (P - i)(1 - T)(1 - D) + D_p \tag{14}
$$

$$
= (0.1137 - 0.0122)(1 - 0.4315)(1 - 0.2923) + 0.0307
$$

$$
= (0.1015)(0.5685)(0.7077) + 0.0307
$$

$$
= 0.071536
$$

Next, we use Equation (13) to determine g_c^*:

$$
g_c^* = \frac{\text{FPO} + (\text{FPO} \times R) - M}{(F + U_A + W + M - \text{FPO}) - (\text{FPO} \times R)}
$$

$$g_c^* = \frac{0.071536 + (0.071536 \times 0.0384) - 0}{(0.08303 + 0.65112 + 0.0900 + 0 - 0.071536) - (0.071536 \times 0.0384)}$$

$$= \frac{0.07428298}{(0.752614) - (0.00274698)}$$

$$= \frac{0.07428298}{0.74986702}$$

$$= 0.09906154, \text{ or } 10\%$$

Typical of financial models, the G & S model is not without caveats. Note:

1   The format assumes that to support each dollar of extra sales, an extra investment in plant and equipment would be required. This would be a valid assumption only if the company were operating at capacity. If the company were operating at less than capacity, the extra investment in plant and equipment would be zero.

2   The model establishes a linear relationship between sales and other variables such as maintenance, EBIT, depreciation, working capital, and interest expense. Actually these relationships are not constant from period to period or from one sales level to another. In other words, the relationship need not be linear. We know, for example, that in many industries up to some point, average variable cost will decrease as sales increase and turn upward forming a "U"-shaped curve. These troubles, of course, can be mitigated by constructing pro forma financial statements for the following period and from these estimating the component values required by the model.

3   The model is sensitive to changes in the firm's cash or debt position which are not reflected in *sales generating* fixed asset purchases or acquisitions. A similar situation arises when a firm accumulates excess cash and temporary investments from internal operations and/or debt not intended for operational employment. Defense against takeover moves represents a case in point.

The G & S model does illustrate the relationship between sustainable growth and the size and method of financing the capital budget. If the firm cannot raise additional funds by debt or stock financing—if it must rely on retained earnings for required funds—then it may have to trade off the present value of current earnings against the expected gains accruing from the capital budget. Stated differently, the capital budget is not simply the product of accepting projects until NPV = 0 or IRR = k_{mc}. In the presence of fixed resources, this could unduly penalize current operations. Under these conditions, the firm must investigate the opportunity costs of shifting resources from current to future operations or vice versa.

In keeping with the conceptual framework of financial management, we may think of the firm achieving an equilibrium between current sales (financed by net working capital and operational fixed assets) and future benefits (represented by the capital budget) when the present value of current sales equals the present value of the capital budget. Given the opportunity costs and benefits in deploying assets between current and future operations, k_{mc} would appear to be the appropriate discount rate in arriving at the respective present values. However, the selection of a discount rate is always a matter of some argument in financial management, and the reader should not take our use of k_{mc} as the final word on the subject. The advantage to this conception, on the other hand, is that it forces management to view the firm as a whole, with an eye on the present and future; the capital budget is no longer an exercise in future expectations without regard to its impact on current operations.

VALUATION

Of course, in developing the financial component of the strategic plan, management attempts to make decisions that maximize the market value of the firm. The market price of long-term debt and common stock reflects the quality of decisions made on the capital budget, the debt/equity ratio, the target growth rate, and the other variables displayed in the preceding formulas. To illustrate, let us again use the Higgins model and the Micro-Industries data.

EXAMPLE 8

Micro-Industries has a financial structure composed of 37.5% long-term debt and 62.5% equity at book values. This structure is sustainable at a target growth rate of 11.2%. If Micro bonds sell at 80 and the P/E ratio is 8, what is the market value of the firm? Micro has a combined marginal tax rate (federal and state) of 50% and has 3,750 common shares outstanding.

SOLUTION: *I:* This approach assumes that business risk and financial risk influence value (see Chapter 10). The method allows for the inclusion of income tax effects (see Table 8-1). Increased leveraging, therefore, will (up to some point) lower the average cost of capital and raise the value of the firm.

Net operating income (EBIT)	$11,000
Interest (10%)	3,500
Earnings before taxes (EBT)	$ 7,500
Taxes (0.50)	3,750
Earnings after taxes (EAT)	$ 3,750
Market value of common stock:	
EPS (after-tax) × P/E ratio	
× no. of shares = $1.00 × 8 × 3,750 =	$30,000
Market value of debt:	
30 bonds × $800	24,000
Market value of firm	$54,000

COST OF CAPITAL AT MARKET WEIGHTS:	AFTER-TAX COST	WEIGHT	TOTAL
$\text{Debt} = \dfrac{\$3,500}{24,000}(1 - 0.50)$	0.0729	0.375	0.0273
$\text{Equity} = \dfrac{\$7,500}{30,000}(1 - 0.50)$	0.125	0.625	0.0781
Weighted average cost of capital (K)			0.1054

SOLUTION: *II:* This alternative method of valuation assumes that the cost of capital (K) is influenced only by business risk, with the financial risk discounted against the market worth of the common stock.

EBIT $(1 - 0.50) = \$11,000 \times 0.50$ $ 5,500

Cost of capital $(K) = 0.1054$

Market value of the firm:

$$\frac{\$5,500}{0.1054} = \$52,182$$

Market value of debt   24,000

Market value of common $28,182

Cost of equity (K)

$$\frac{\$3,750}{\$28,182} = 0.133$$

In both solutions, the short-term debt ($5,000) was omitted. This was done on the assumption that the short-term debt carried no interest charge and offered no discount for prompt payment. Inclusion of the short-term debt would increase both solutions by $5,000.

SUMMARY

This chapter has underscored the interrelatedness of the financial elements that enter the articulation of the firm's strategic planning. The capital budget in greater or lesser degree affects the target growth rate. The latter, in turn, relates to specific levels of debt and equity financing, earnings retention, profit margins, productivity, and price trends. The sum of these factors influences the market value of the firm. The essence of strategic planning in the financial area is to balance these elements to achieve an optimal growth rate and a related financial structure which will maximize the market value of the firm.

Financial theory dictates that the firm strive toward an optimal financial structure: that combination of debt and equity which minimizes the weighted average marginal cost of capital. This figure reflects the average risk posture of the firm and the reinvestment rate on retained cash flows. It is a rate which in conjunction with a given level of operating income maximizes the market value of the firm.

The optimal marginal cost of capital is not, as we have seen, a static calculation. It corresponds to the dynamic business and financial risks of the enterprise and to broad trends moving through the economic environment. In particular, with relation to the formulation of a strategic plan, a target growth rate implies a compatible set of established financial policies. Growth rates above and below the target rate eventually impel alterations in the financial or capital structure. Only by keeping the two in balance can a sustainable growth be realized.

In this respect, we should not equate growth with rising prices and slow down with falling prices. The firm's profit margin reflects trends in prices, production costs, and quantities. Cost-price movements are rarely synchronized. Fixed costs by definition lag behind price-level adjustments. A firm selling in a competitive market but buying in a monopolisticly-competitive market might find its profit margin under pressure, although the prices show an upward trend. Conversely, declining prices may not adversely impact profit margins if management can improve the firm's output per worker-hour.

The reader will recognize that the chapter does not refer to portfolio effects or the capital asset pricing model in a strategic planning context. Problems of required return and systematic risk and the effect of a capital project on debt capacity manifestly have an important role in the specifics of strategic planning. These topics are covered extensively in Chapters 15 through 17, and the reader should easily relate them to the present theme.

QUESTIONS
PROBLEMS

1. Assume a dividend payout ratio of 40% and the following financial statements for Aloc Industries.

Aloc Industries
December 31, 198X
Balance Sheet

ASSETS		LIABILITIES AND EQUITY	
Cash	$ 22,000	Current liabilities	$ 6,000
Accounts receivable	40,000	Long-term debt	12,000
Inventory	10,000	Capital stock	50,000
Fixed assets	41,000	Retained earnings	45,000
	$113,000		$113,000

Aloc Industries
December 31, 198X
Income Statement

Sales	$122,000
Less: Cost of sales	65,000
Gross profit	$ 57,000
Less: Selling and administrative expenses	22,000
Net operating income	$ 35,000
Less: Interest on long-term debt	$ 1,500
Earnings before taxes	$ 33,500

(a) Assume a stable price level.
  (i) Determine the sustainable rate of growth under each.
    (a) Fixed financial structure.
    (b) Fixed capital structure.
  (ii) How might Aloc improve upon the sustainable rate of growth?
(b) Assume a rising price level of 20%.
  (i) Determine the *real* sustainable rate of growth under each.
    (a) Fixed financial structure.
    (b) Fixed capital structure.
  (ii) How might Aloc improve upon the *real* sustainable rate of growth?
(c) Assume a decline in prices of 25%.
  (i) Determine the *real* sustainable rate of growth under each.
    (a) Fixed financial structure.
    (b) Fixed capital structure.
  (ii) How might Aloc improve upon the *real* sustainable rate of growth?

2. What are the deficiencies of computing financial ratios and establishing financial policies based upon book values? How might this be overcome with regard to the establishment of financial policies?

3. If Aloc Industries sets a target growth rate of 25%, how will this objective affect the financial structure and the capital structure?

4. If, all other things equal. Aloc Industries reduces its cost of sales from $65,000 to $45,000, how will the change affect the sustainable growth rate?

5. Based upon the discussion in this chapter, which factors should Aloc Industries bear in mind when adding new capital projects to the existing mix in formulating the firm's strategic plan?

6. How would you modify the Higgins and Johnson type models to include the Gombola-Ketz adjustments?

7. Assume the following data:

ABC Co., Inc.
December 31, 19XX
Balance Sheet

ASSETS		%	LIABILITIES & EQUITIES		%
Cash	$2,000	.16	Accounts Payable	$3,000	.24
Inventory	5,000	.40	Bonds Payable	2,600	.21
Equipment	7,000	.56	Capital Stock	900	.07
Less: acc. dep.	(1,500)	(.12)	(600 shares)		
	$12,500	1.00	Retained Earnings	6,000	.48
				$12,500	1.00

ABC Co., Inc.
December 31, 19XX
Income Statement

Sales	$35,375
Less: Cost of Sales	11,200
Gross Profit	24,175
Less: SGA expenses	11,500
EBIT	12,675
Less: Interest (10% on debt)	560
EBT	$12,115

The current year's dividends were $6.75 per share, the current financial structure is considered optimal, and the price trend is: +12% (revival), −11% (recession). What is the sustainable growth rate for ABC Co., Inc.?

8. Referring to Example 1, Micro-Industries would like to adjust its dividend payout ratio to support a 12% sustainable rate of growth. What will the new dividend payout ratio be? If Micro-Industries were not willing to adjust its dividend payout ratio, how else might it support a 12% growth rate?

REFERENCES

Herring, Richard J., and Prashant Vankuche. "Growth Opportunities and Risk-Taking by Financial Intermediaries." *Journal of Finance* (July 1987).

Higgins, R. C. "How Much Growth Can a Firm Afford?" *Financial Management* (Fall 1977).

Holbrook, Steward H. *The Age of Moguls.* New York: Doubleday, 1954.

O'Brien, Thomas J., and Paul A. Vanderkeiden. "Empirical Measurement of Operating Leverage for Growing Firms." *Financial Management* (Summer 1987).

Yagil, Joseph. "Growth, Risk and the Yield on Common Stocks in the Context of the Dividend-Growth Model." *Journal of Business Finance and Accounting* (Summer 1986).

CASE STUDY 24-1

RJR Nabisco, Inc.

The following are the financial statements of RJR Nabisco, Inc.

RJR Nabisco, Inc.
Consolidated Statements of Earnings and Earnings Retained
for the Years Ended December 31, 1984–1986
(dollars in millions except per share amounts)

	1986	1985*	1984
Net sales[†]	$15,978	$12,388	$8,903
Costs and expenses			
Cost of products sold[†]	8,383	6,423	4,648
Selling, advertising, administrative,			
and general expenses	5,117	3,885	2,721
Earnings from continuing operations	2,478	2,080	1,534
Interest and debt expense (net of capitalized			
amounts of $71, $67 and $29, respectively	(574)	(351)	(182)
Other income (expense), net	13	60	127
Earnings from continuing operations before			
provision for income taxes	1,917	1,789	1,479
Provision for income taxes	837	813	671
Net earnings from continuing operations	1,080	976	808
Net earnings from discontinued operations	23	25	127
Gain (loss) on sale of discontinued			
operations, net of taxes	(39)	—	275
Net earnings	1,064	1,001	1,210
Less: Preferred dividends	102	91	56
Net earnings applicable to common stock	962	910	1,154
Earnings retained at beginning of year	4,357	4,034	4,461
Less: Cash dividends on common stock	378	357	360
Distribution of Sea-Land stock	—	—	540
Retirement of company's stocks	109	230	681
Earnings retained at end of year	$ 4,832	$ 4,357	$4,034

Net earnings per common share			
Continuing operations	$3.90	$3.50	$2.68
Discontinued operations	(0.07)	0.10	1.43
	$3.83	$3.60	$4.11
Average number of common shares			
outstanding (in thousands)	251,073	252,941	280,938

*The 1985 amounts include the operations of Nabisco Brands, Inc. from July 2, 1985.
†Excludes excise taxes of $3,557, $3,062, and $3,059 for 1986, 1985, and 1984, respectively.

RJR Nabisco, Inc.
Consolidated Balance Sheets
December 31, 1985 – 1986
(dollars in millions)

	1986	1985
Current assets		
Cash and short-term investments	$ 863	$ 582
Accounts and notes receivable		
(less allowances of $77 and $86, respectively)	1,931	1,913
Inventories	2,986	3,184
Prepaid expenses	154	119
Total current assets	5,934	5,798
Property, plant and equipment, at cost	6,925	5,887
Less: Depreciation and amortization	1,413	1,059
Net property, plant, and equipment	5,512	4,828
Trademarks, goodwill, and other intangibles	4,875	4,609
Other assets and deferred charges	698	647
Net assets of discontinued operations	—	$ 791
	$17,019	$16,673
Liabilities and Stockholder's Equity		
Current liabilities		
Notes payable	$ 520	$ 647
Accounts payable and accrued accounts	3,126	2,917
Current maturities of long-term debt	425	166
Income taxes accrued	248	220
Total current liabilities	$4,319	$3,950
Long-term debt	4,844	4,839
Other noncurrent liabilities	1,489	806
Deferred income taxes	760	695
Commitments and contingencies		
Redeemable preferred stocks, net	291	1,587
Common stockholders' equity		
Common stock, net		
(250,394,933 shares outstanding)	236	247
Paid-in capital	320	332
Cumulative translation adjustments	(76)	(140)
Earnings retained	4,832	4,357
Total common stockholders' equity	5,312	4,796
	$17,019	$16,673

RJR Nabisco, Inc.
Consolidated Statements of Changes in Financial Position
For the Years Ended December 31, 1984 – 1986
(dollars in millions)

	1986	1985	1984
Funds provided by continuing operations			
Net sales	$15,978	$12,388	$8,903
Less: Operating costs and expenses which required the outlay of working capital	14,011	10,842	7,726
Total funds provided by continuing operations	1,967	1,546	1,177
Funds required by continuing operations			
Change in working capital resulting from operations	(67)	(48)	(6)
Capital expenditures	1,047	972	655
Miscellaneous acquisitions	—	28	274
Miscellaneous dispositions of businesses	(376)	—	—
Disposals of property, plant, and equipment	(64)	(60)	(27)
Cash dividends	480	448	416
Cumulative translation adjustments	(31)	15	39
Other	170	256	99
Total funds required by continuing operations	1,159	1,611	1,450
Net funds provided (required) by continuing operations	808	(65)	(273)
Funds provided (required) by financing transactions			
Net change in current notes payable*	(127)	432	(31)
Issuance of long-term debt	1,125	3,339	51
Retirements of long-term debt	(909)	(537)	(35)
Issuance of company stock	41	1,241	11
Repurchases of company stock	(1,469)	(403)	(877)
Net funds provided (required) by financing transactions	(1,339)	4.072	(881)
Net change in funds related to discontinued operations	812	(76)	2,115
Net funds required for acquisition of Nabisco Brands, Inc.	—	(4,672)	—
Increase (decrease) in cash and short-term investments	281	(741)	961
Analysis of change in working capital resulting from operations*:			
Funds required (provided) by the change in:			
Accounts and notes receivable	18	136	439
Inventories	(198)	(16)	(202)
Prepaid expenses	35	14	10
Accounts payable and accrued accounts	(195)	(457)	(203)
Income taxes accrued	273	275	(50)
Change in working capital resulting from operations	(67)	(48)	(6)

*Does not include Nabisco Brands, Inc., amounts at date of acquisition (see Note 1) or items related to discontinued operations.

Assuming an anticipated increase in the price level of 3.5%, calculate the sustainable growth of RJR Nabisco using

(a) the Higgins model;

(b) the Johnson model;

(c) the G & S cash model of sustainable growth.

CASE STUDY 24-2

National Products, Inc.

(Strategic planning)

National Products, Inc., is a leading manufacturer and marketer of prescription drugs and medical supplies, packaged medicines, food products, and household products and housewares. The company's brands have achieved a high level of recognition from health care professionals and consumers and many are the largest selling in their respective categories. The company's commitment to the development of quality products, along with an emphasis on aggressive marketing and strict financial controls, has enabled the company to record consistent growth in sales, earnings, and dividends for the thirty-fourth consecutive year. Net sales grew from $1,784 million in 1973 to $4,926 million in 1986, an average yearly compounded growth rate of 8.13%. Net income climbed from $199 million in 1973 to $779 million in 1986, an average yearly compounded growth rate of 11.10%, and net income per common share grew steadily from $1.25 in 1973 to $5.18 in 1986. Dividends per common share grew from $0.625 in 1973 to $3.10 in 1986. Finally, the return on the average stockholder's equity rose steadily from 29.0% in 1973 to 33.3% in 1986.

An analysis of the company's financial statements reveals a constantly high liquidity position and a low financial leverage. The ratio of current assets to current liabilities was never below 2.85 to 1 during the period 1973–1986 with an average of 3.13 to 1. The total debt (short- and long-term) to equity ratio never exceeded 88% during the period 1973–1986 with an average of 56%. Management has always had a policy of maintaining a solid financial position.

In its annual meeting to discuss strategy, the Board of Directors of National Products was satisfied with the continuous prosperity of the company but paid attention to the relatively low levels of sales growth rates during the last four years (1983–1986) and thus geared the strategy of the company to focus on three basic areas:

☐ New products. Through internal research and development, licensing and joint venture agreements.

☐ New businesses. Acquisitions should play a role in the company's growth, providing new product lines which can be improved and sold through the company's strong marketing organizations.

☐ Greater efficiencies. Continued emphasis on achieving greater efficiency in the company's operations, including combining the marketing and distribution channels in the company's non-U.S. consumer products businesses and several consolidation moves.

This strategy will, it is believed, boost the sales growth rate while maintaining the consistent growth in earnings and dividends and the excellent financial standing of the company. By developing new products that are expected to become stars (using the Boston Consulting Group concept) the excellent future financial performance of the company is guaranteed.

However, Mr. Schmidt, the chief financial officer at National Products, noticed during his review of the financial statements of the company for the last thirty-four years, a tendency for the debt-to-equity ratio to rise along with a rise in the sales growth rate and to decline along with a decline in the sales growth rate. Table 1, covering the period 1981–1986, supports this discovery.

Table 1

	1986	1985	1984	1983	1982	1981
Total debt-to-equity ratio	75%	46%	45%	35%	88%	56%
Actual sales growth rate	5.16	4.44	4.96	7.57	14.44	10.33

Mr. Schmidt was also concerned about another issue. He noticed that the debt-to-equity ratio has been rising for the last four years, which is not desirable according to the policies of the company. He was wondering why is it that since the company is outperforming most U.S. firms in terms of growth and profitability, it is gradually moving to higher levels of financial leverage and hence to a higher risk exposure. The issuance of new equity to bring the debt-to-equity ratio down was obviously not the answer, since this would depress the financial gains of the common stockholders in terms of the dividend growth rate and return on the average stockholder's equity, and ultimately the market value of the firm.

Mr. Schmidt found the answer he needed by reviewing the performance of Hewlett-Packard over the period 1950–57, in which it grew at an annual compound growth rate of 43% without the acquisition of outside capital and while maintaining firm control of its finances. HP used a valuable financial model called the *sustainable rate of growth in sales* or the affordable rate of growth. The sustainable growth rate is that maximum annual sales growth rate that a firm can maintain over a defined period of time without altering its financial policies. By assuming that a firm's sales can grow only as fast as its assets and that the company has a target debt-to-equity ratio, the sustainable growth rate would be the retention ratio multiplied by the return on equity of the company. Accordingly, the sustainable growth rate of National Products should be 12.5%, calculated by multiplying the 40% retention ratio of the company by the average rate of return on the stockholders' equity.

Mr. Schmidt is convinced of the importance of this concept, since every strategic plan will ultimately be represented by and brought down to some financial measures and the availability of funds to carry a certain plan will be a major concern. However, he was not sure that the above model would be an accurate way to measure that rate. Why is it that despite the fact that the actual compounded sales growth rate of National Products is below the calculated sustainable growth rate, the debt-to-equity ratio has risen during the last three years?

Consequently, Mr. Schmidt sought other models for the sustainable growth rate calculation. Four models were identified, each having different underlying assumptions. These are the following:

1   *Robert Higgins' Model*[1]

$$g^* = \frac{P(1 - D)(1 + L)}{T - P(1 - D)(1 + L)}$$

where g^* = the sustainable growth rate in sales
P = the after-tax profit margin on new and existing sales
D = the target dividend payout ratio
L = the target total debt-to-equity ratio
T = the ratio of total assets to net sales on new and existing sales

2   *Dana Johnson's Model*[2]

$$g^* = \frac{P(1 - D)(1 + L_L)(1 + j) - C_j}{F - P(1 - D)(1 + L_L)(1 + j) + C(1 + j)}$$

where g^* = real sustainable growth rate in sales
P = after-tax profit margin on new and existing sales
D = target dividend payout ratio
L_L = target capital structure
j = uniform rate of inflation
C = ratio of nominal net working capital nominal sales
F = ratio of nominal fixed assets to nominal sales

3   *Peter Eisemann's Model*[3]

$$g^* = \frac{P(1 - D)}{T - L' - P(1 - D)}$$

where P = after-tax profit margin on new and existing sales
D = target dividend payout ratio
T = total assets-to-sales ratio
L' = spontaneous debt-to-sales ratio

Here the assumption of a target financial structure is taken a step further. Only spontaneous liabilities are allowed to grow at the same rate as sales, without increasing other sources of debt.

4   *Govindarajan and Shank's Model*[4]

$$g^* = \frac{[P(1 - D) + A](1 + L_R) - M}{E + W + M - [P(1 - D) + A](1 + L_R)}$$

[1]Robert Higgins, "How Much Growth Can a Firm Afford?" *Financial Management* (Fall 1977), 7–15.

[2]Dana Johnson, "The Behavior of Financial Structure and Sustainable Growth in an Inflationary Environment," *Financial Management* (Autumn 1981), 30–35.

[3]Peter Eisemann, "Another Look at Sustainable Growth," *The Journal of Commercial Bank Lending* (October 1984), 47–51.

[4]V. Govindarajan and J. K. Shank, "Cash Sufficiency: The Missing Link in Strategic Planning," *Corporate Accounting*, 2, no. 1 (Winter 1984).

where P = after-tax profit margin on new and existing sales
D = target dividend payout ratio
A = amortization, depletion, and depreciation charges as a percent of sales
L_R = target debt to retained earnings ratio
M = maintenance expense as a percent of sales
E = plant and equipment to sales ratio
W = working capital to sales ratio

QUESTIONS

1. Calculate the sustainable growth rate for National Products, Inc., using all four models.
2. Evaluate each model in terms of the viability of its underlying assumptions—whether it captures any change in the financial position of the company, its reliability, and its managerial usefulness.
3. As long as the company is profitable and has "star" products, does it really need to examine these models? Would not each product sustain itself in terms of liquid funds required for its production and sale?
4. Can the cash budget be an alternative to the abovementioned models? Compare them.
5. Present a new model that overcomes the weaknesses of the abovementioned models. Justify its superiority. Apply it to National Products, Inc.

Monitoring and Controlling
the Capital Budgeting Process

25

We have stressed the quantitative formulation of the capital budget and supporting theoretical concepts. However, the budgeting process is not an abstraction from reality; it takes place in an organization with all its attendant problems of human relations, ambitions, and political maneuvering. Some individuals may have pet projects—attachments resulting perhaps from many hard hours of detailed analysis. Others may oppose a proposal out of fear that it will shift the corporate power structure to their discomfort or evoke unemployment. The cynical quickly learn that any project can be made to look good or bad by comparing it against a sufficiently poor or strong alternative. It is for top management to monitor the process to assure that all possible alternatives have been arrayed so that a reasonably sound budget may be constructed. This chapter touches on a few of the cautionary points in the management of the capital budget. These include the following important truths:

1 Capital budgeting necessitates forecasting.
2 It is vitally important to review and control implemented projects.
3 Not all capital projects succeed.
4 The process of evaluating proposed capital projects must be cost justified.

CAPITAL BUDGETING NECESSITATES FORECASTING

Capital budgeting speaks of *future revenues* and *expenses*, yet textbooks tend to ignore the process of how these estimates are derived. Capital budgets are forecasts of varying duration and uncertainty usually based on significant assumptions.

In theory, an assumption is an explicit statement about the expected performance of the economy, industry, or the firm; the likelihood of disruptive events (strikes, new technology, or other unusual occurrences); and the consistency of or

506

Table 25 – 1   Quality of Published Assumptions: Recent U.S. Examples

---

1 Sales are based on the average monthly sales for the 17-month period ended September 30, 19—, and have been adjusted to reflect anticipated increases in demand as expected by the company.

2 Cost of sales . . . reflect unit cost changes in relation to increased sales volume and other factors anticipated by the company.

3 Operating expenses . . . assume no changes for inflation or otherwise during the life of the project. General operating expenses for . . . and . . . are based on assumptions of partial occupancy.

4 Cross revenues . . . are based on past trends and current charges adjusted for managerial policies contemplated for the proposed expanded facilities and anticipated price-level changes in the future.

5 Historically the . . . rates have been increased to absorb the rising costs of health-care services and accordingly have maintained a satisfactory margin of income over expenses. It is the opinion of . . . management that this trend will continue.

6 The mix of furniture to be rented has been assumed and a weighted average computed. This resulting theoretical set costs $509.40 and rents for $41.20 per month.

7 Although salaries and other costs will increase in the future, advertising costs should decrease at the assumed level of activity per store. For this reason, total expenses are assumed to remain constant.

8 Our outlook for continued rapid growth . . . is based on expansion of the boat and motorcycle trailer market, increasing market penetration, expanded geographical distribution, the introduction of new products, and, of course, the past record of the company.

9 We expect . . . to have another good year in 19—; but operating projections are less reliable than in some other . . . operations . . . . This projection is based on the expectation that a new labor agreement will be successfully negotiated . . . and that appropriate rate increases will be granted.

Source: Published annual reports of various U.S. corporations.

changes in accounting policy. Typically omitted from assumptions such as those stated in Table 25–1 are those implicit in the choice of a forecast methodology. All forecasting techniques specify a distinctive link between future revenues and various determining factors. These are *technical* assumptions that relate to the statistical model used in projecting the future.

Few companies employ a purely quantitative model to forecast revenues and expenses, but a growing number of companies make some use of quantitative projection methods. The choice of methodology is decidely a matter of judgment and involves assumptions concerning the relevant variables and their interrelationships. Different statistical techniques, applied to the same data base, can yield different forecasts. The same technique may yield divergent results for different time spans or if other explanatory variables are included (Table 25–2). Naturally, management will modify its forecasting procedures to obtain estimates with a reliability appropriate to the circumstances of the business.

Statistical models are not perfect predictors and the variance from actual sales will in part be attributable to the particular assumptions of the model. Too often these assumptions lack explicit statement; more often, they would not be understood by top

Table 25–2   Some Assumptions Underlying Forecasting Models

---

1 The conditions in the past which generated the observed data will persist into the future. In the concept of stationarity, the future becomes an extension of the past, and historical simulation is the standard method for validation of the model. Yet many of the changes affecting business activity spring from discontinuities and by definition are either unpredicted or unpredictable.

2 As a corollary, models generally respond to novel circumstances slowly. Rates of change are often too rapid for models to accommodate—the reaction time of the model is too slow. However, even in a stable situation, the time required to collect data, process data, and provide output to the decision maker may conflict with the time schedule of budget formulation.

3 A further corollary: if the data base is flawed—if it contains inadequate, inaccurate, or irrelevant historical information—the past may be as obscure as the future. The model cannot rise above the quality of the input data.

4 In the case of noncausal models, the variable is a function of time.

5 The evolution of the variables is completely systematic and hence predictable.

6 Except where qualified by the introduction of weights, all previous observations yield the same amount of information about the likely value of the next observation.

7 Causal models assume that the average relationship calculated between dependent and independent variable(s) will hold for the future. The task of defining these relationships is a formidable one during period of accelerated change. Models of simple static systems are easy to construct, but their naivete will likely trap the user. On the other hand, models of complex and dynamic systems require painstaking efforts and *may* improve the precision of the projections—albeit with a higher price tag for the information.

8 Unless sales and cost data are considered to be random and normally distributed, the models do not provide a statistical basis for establishing the probability of error or confidence interval estimates. In the absence of the normality presumption, practice resorts to establishing ranges based upon past deviations between actual and project results such that one can be reasonably certain the next period's projection will fall within the established limits. Statistically speaking, however, the assumption that future deviations will fall within the defined range is at best tenuous.

---

management even if stated in elementary terms. The truth we seek here is that the technical assumptions combined with the effects of leverage can convert a small variance in gross revenues into an acceptable variance in net operating revenues of the project.

Planning assumptions relate to market and production strategies as well as erratic events (for example, outcome of litigation) and, perhaps, the intuitive adjustments of top officers. In this respect, production strategies merit special comment. The bridge that leads from project revenues to net operating revenues in a given period is distinct from the external link of revenues (or savings) to the market. Revenue projections only initiate the analysis of the project, for management has considerable latitude in responding to the market environment. It may, for example, alter the product mix, adjust production schedules, modify inventory policies, or regulate discretionary expenditures. Consequently, any single projected (or most probable) revenue level can translate into a broad range of net operating cash flows.

Prime cost projections assume reliable estimates of factor prices and efficiencies in production, variable overheads may be allocated to product lines by statistical formulas and management judgment, discretionary fixed costs may actually be revised throughout the budget period, programmed fixed costs (such as supervisory salaries or financial charges) share the uncertainties of interest rate changes and similar variations in specific price levels. Other illustrations could be introduced, but the list is sufficient to emphasize the uncertainties of forecasting project earnings and stresses the variety of assumptions, environmental and internal, buttressing net cash flow estimates.

There exists a group of standard assumptions, akin to the "going concern" principle in financial accounting, which are vital to appraisal of the forecast, yet merit explicit mention only by exception. Unless alerted to the contrary, the reader of a financial forecast (or capital budget) properly assumes that the firm's accounting statements are prepared in a manner consistent with the applicable accounting principles adopted by the firm in the annual report.[1] Similarly, the composition of top corporate management, the continuing availability of normal sources of supply, and reasonable stability of the tax environment, are implied unless the user is informed to the contrary.

Each forecasting and budgeting system should be uniquely designed to meet the objectives of the company. Successful forecasting commences with close collaboration among executives, other internal users of forecasted data, and systems consultants. Collaboration begins with three basic questions:

1   What is the purpose of the forecast? How is it to be used? The desired accuracy and power of the techniques chosen will largely hinge on the answers.

2   What are the staff requirements to implement the forecasting system? For example, personnel capacities vary according to the detail and accuracy required. For primarily quantitative approaches, forecasters should be competent in research techniques, in application of mathematical-statistical models, and in computer usage. On the other hand, judgmental methods call upon personnel in marketing who have long association with the industry. Best results require a blending of both types.

3   What, if any, additional facilities or services are needed to inaugurate the forecasting-budgeting space and equipment, access to computer capability, library resources, and subscriptions to external data sources?

Because information, personnel, and facilities have price tags attached, the forecast-budget system must relate to the realistic needs of the business and balance the tangible values of better information against the costs of acquiring the data. In some situations, simple techniques and few organizational shifts may well accomplish the purpose.

Viewed as an integrated system, the forecast of project cash benefits and costs represents the first step in the preparation of a comprehensive capital budget. The budget will be no better than the soundness of the forecasting techniques employed.

---

[1] Although capital budgeting is on a cash flow basis, as we note, management must consider the impact of the capital budget on the firm's conventional accounting statements (see Chapters 19–20). A capital budget that may qualify on an NPV basis may have severe adverse effects in the short term on the accounting statements, and this management may not choose to accept.

Business forecasting, short or long term, is a field unto itself. However, the astute financial manager will always inquire as to how the budget estimates were prepared.

REVIEW AND CONTROL OF CAPITAL INVESTMENT PROJECTS

The capital budgeting process does not terminate with the selection of a set of projects that the firm believes will provide maximum benefits without violating any of its resource constraints. Rather, sound financial management demands that the firm carefully monitor project implementation as well as perform postcompletion audits on major projects.

The review and control of capital expenditures can be divided into two major categories:

1   The review and control of projects in the process of being implemented. These are called *in-progress* projects. This review and control entails auditing the cash outflows related to the acquisition of the project. This process results in information of cost underruns or overruns.

2   The review and control of projects as they are used in the firm's operations. This entails auditing the benefits generated by the project, as well as the operating expenses incurred as the project is used. The goal is to determine the cash flows generated over the life of the project.

Much effort is expended in evaluating capital projects to select those projects that *should be* most beneficial in helping the organization to achieve its goals. Once a set of projects has been selected, management may assume that the projects will be implemented in an optimal fashion. Of course, this is rarely the case. Witness the constantly recurring cost overruns, as well as timing delays, in efforts to carry out any large-scale capital project. Thus, it is necessary to exert strict control on in-progress projects.

There are two parts to the process of controlling in-progress capital projects. First is the establishment of internal accounting control procedures to accumulate all relevant project-related costs. Second is the use of periodic progress reports that gauge actual expenditures against estimates and provide explanations for significant variances that occur. The timing of the reports may be on a regular calendar basis (such as monthly) and/or keyed to critical events in the acquisition process. The latter would be especially useful if network methods for project scheduling such as PERT or CPM are employed.

The first step specified usually sees the establishment of control accounts for each in-progress capital project. These control accounts are charged with all relevant expenditures, which are further categorized into those items that will be capitalized and those that will be expensed in the current year. These accounts reflect both out-of-pocket payments for materials, labor, overhead, outside purchases, and subcontracts, as well as relevant allocated expenses.

The segregation of costs on a project-by-project basis facilitates the control process because appropriate attention can be given to projects as they approach various completion points and/or a cost-overrun status. Further, the use of *responsibility accounting procedures* is also beneficial since control centers that are held accountable for any given project must be notified when cost overruns are imminent so that proper control measures can be implemented.

The use of regular progress reports as projects are being implemented provides several benefits for an organization. First, such timely information presents advance warning to management of potential future difficulties in time for corrective action to be taken. Second, these reports provide a basis for data input to the cash-budgeting process. Third, these reports provide insight to management on projects that could require additional expenditures due to inflation and other unforeseen causes. Fourth, as part of the control process, these reports provide the basis for comparing cumulative actual expenditures with budgeted amounts so that variances can be computed and explanations provided for significant unfavorable variances.

Such procedures should provide valuable assistance to firms in the control of in-progress capital projects. Next, we turn to the postcompletion audit of capital projects.

POSTCOMPLETION AUDITS OF CAPITAL PROJECTS

It is essential for firms to review and control capital projects once they are in use. This is necessary in order to compare their actual benefits with their forecasted benefits, to compare actual operating costs with forecasted operating costs, and to take timely corrective action, if necessary.

Several additional benefits accrue to firms that use postcompletion audits. First, the audits provide an on-the-scene verification of the profitability or savings generated by the project. The audit attempts to isolate the effects of the project under study as far as possible. The auditor, as part of his or her investigation, should seek out reasons why projects turned out either significantly more or significantly less profitable than projected on either an absolute dollar or a percentage basis. In arriving at these results, as much detail as practicable should be provided rather than arbitrarily aggregating different cost or benefit categories; the latter technique could obscure relevant offsetting changes.

Second, divisions and managers are more likely to act in their own (as well as the organization's) best interests relative to the implementation and operation of new capital projects if they realize that postcompletion audits will be performed and that they will be held accountable for the results. The feedback provided to responsible managers should help them to improve their future estimation of costs and benefits, as well as provide insight about effective operating strategies for new capital projects. Organizations should stress that postcompletion audits are not designed to censure managers, but rather to help them improve their forecasting and operating activities.

Next, the postcompletion audit is beneficial in identifying the causes of difficulties in project implementation and/or operation. The variances of actual results from projected results raise questions that demand explanation and point to possible areas where breakdowns may have occurred. The insight provided here will often suggest corrective action that should be taken or point to alternative courses of action (including the possibility of project abandonment) that should be explored.

Finally, the results obtained through postcompletion audits provide managers of divisions—as well as the members of the capital budgeting review committee—with information that should be helpful in evaluating similar projects in the future. Audits enable organizations to learn from past successes and difficulties so that their operations will be more effective and efficient in the future.

Given these benefits, questions arise concerning who should perform and review postcompletion audits, which projects should be the subject of such audits, and how the process should be carried out.

Ideally, the postcompletion audit should be performed by an independent and unbiased individual, preferably from the internal audit staff or the corporate controller's staff. This will increase the chances that an objective evaluation will be performed.

The postcompletion audit should be reviewed by the manager of the department or division that proposed the project so that he or she can see the results and obtain helpful feedback for operating decisions and future proposals. The manager who recommended the project will usually be one of the major resource persons that the auditor utilizes in preparing the audit since the manager will be one of the more informed individuals concerning the reasons for variances of actual results from projections.

The postcompletion audit should be reviewed by everyone in the project-approval process, including the group or individual that actually approved the project in question. This will facilitate the learning process among key individuals in terms of future proposals.

Clearly, not all capital projects deserve the time, resources, and effort required to perform a postcompletion audit. Most firms perform audits on very large outlay projects or those of special significance to management. In addition, corporate and division managers can often select projects for audit that are of interest or concern in order to gauge results and/or locate difficulties. Finally, a number of projects may be selected randomly at each division in order to provide feedback to local and corporate management.

Pflomm derived an extensive list of data frequently included on postcompletion audits by the 346 manufacturing firms that participated in his Conference Board study.[2] The following information was usually included:

- Number of the approved appropriation request.
- Location that requested the appropriation.
- Description of the item(s) purchased.
- Purpose of the project.
- Amount authorized.
- Amount actually expended.
- Estimated savings and/or return on investment.
- Actual savings or return.
- Reasons for variations.
- Signatures of those who prepared and/or reviewed the postaudit.

In addition, Pflomm identified the following supplemental information that he often found included in the postcompletion audit:[3]

- Estimated versus actual project completion dates with explanations of delays.
- Explanation of project cost overruns.

[2]Norman E. Pflomm, *Managing Capital Expenditures* (New York: The Conference Board, 1963), pp. 83–84.
[3]Ibid.

☐   Action taken to correct deficiencies.

☐   Future prospects for currently failing projects.

☐   Details of equipment performance.

☐   Comments on the adequacy of local accounting records needed for making a postaudit.

We consider the review and control of accepted projects as a vitally important link in the overall management of capital expenditures. All too often, organizations downplay or disregard entirely this essential step in obtaining feedback and taking corrective action. To facilitate the initiation of postcompletion audits in organizations, we include an appendix to this chapter which shows two helpful exhibits: 1) a comprehensive checklist and evaluation form developed by a food products firm and 2) a standard postcompletion audit form. These exhibits were originally published in The Conference Board report by Pflomm and are reprinted with permission.[4] It is to be hoped that this appendix will provide guidance for firms seeking to implement or modify their postcompletion audit systems.

THE ABANDONMENT DECISION
UNDER CONDITIONS OF RISK

The abandonment option was initially explored in Chapter 6. In intervening chapters we discussed various factors that create uncertainty relative to a project's actual costs and benefits. The following list is indicative of some of these major factors: problems in forecasting future cash flows, problems in estimating inflation rates, interest rates, and future tax rates, difficulties in estimating variability in the project's returns over its life, and difficulties in accurately assessing portfolio effects among projects. This chapter examines the necessity of monitoring accepted projects to see if they are "on track." The abandonment option constitutes one of the alternatives open to management in constructing the capital budget.

Managing the capital budget of a corporation must be a dynamic process. Capital investments cannot be viewed as a commitment until the end of the project's life. Since changes in the attractiveness of projects or even entire divisions or subsidiaries can occur, regular periodic reappraisals of investments must be undertaken to determine whether the value of continuing the endeavor exceeds the cost of abandoning it. Since managing the capital budget is usually a rationing problem, a company cannot afford to tie up funds in investments that are below acceptable standards. Managing the capital budget must be viewed as a continuing process of optimally allocating available funds. Thus, this process must include the reevaluation of projects already undertaken.

When investment opportunities are initially considered, key variables are identified and assumptions are made to arrive at some choice. As time passes, changes can occur that could affect these key variables. Assumptions made initially may prove incorrect, or perhaps some additional unforeseen new investment opportunities may arise. *Failure to abandon projects that are no longer desirable could be very costly. By the same reasoning, failure to abandon projects that could make funds available for substantially better investment opportunities might also be costly from an opportunity*

---

[4] Ibid., pp. 90–94.

Period 1		Period 2		Period 3		Cash-Flow Sequence Number	Probability of Sequence (in 64ths)
Cash Flow	Probability	Cash Flow	Conditional Probability	Cash Flow	Conditional Probability		
$1,000	0.25	0	0.25	−$1,000	0.25	1	1/64
				− 500	0.50	2	2/64
				0	0.25	3	1/64
		$ 500	0.50	− 500	0.25	4	2/64
				0	0.50	5	4/64
				500	0.25	6	2/64
		1,000	0.25	0	0.25	7	1/64
				1,000	0.50	8	2/64
				2,000	0.25	9	1/64
2,000	0.50	1,000	0.25	0	0.25	10	2/64
				1,000	0.50	11	4/64
				2,000	0.25	12	2/64
		2,000	0.50	1,000	0.25	13	4/64
				2,000	0.50	14	8/64
				3,000	0.25	15	4/64
		3,000	0.25	2,000	0.25	16	2/64
				3,000	0.50	17	4/64
				4,000	0.25	18	2/64
3,000	0.25	2,000	0.25	1,000	0.25	19	1/64
				2,000	0.50	20	2/64
				3,000	0.25	21	1/64
		3,000	0.50	2,000	0.25	22	2/64
				3,000	0.50	23	4/64
				4,000	0.25	24	2/64
		3,500	0.25	3,000	0.25	25	1/64
				3,500	0.50	26	2/64
				4,000	0.25	27	1/64

Abandonment value
at end of period:
$3,000 $1,900   0

FIGURE 25–1   Expected Future Cash Flows for Project A

standpoint. Therefore, the prudent financial manager must incorporate abandonment values (at various points throughout the life of the project) into the analysis for capital project evaluation and selection.

The most widely cited work in the abandonment area under conditions of changing risk posture is that due to Robichek and Van Horne,[5] in which they recommend the use of decision trees and simulation to handle abandonment values. To illustrate the use of decision trees, consider Figure 25–1, which shows the cash flows for project A over its 3-year useful life.[6] Note that Figure 25–1 has the same design as the tree diagrams for single projects, which are discussed in Chapter 11. However, the presence of the abandonment option (which is shown at the bottom of the figure) necessitates that a decision tree approach be taken at each point in time

[5]A. A. Robichek and J. C. Van Horne, "Abandonment Value and Capital Budgeting," *Journal of Finance*, 22, no. 4 (December 1967), 577–590.

[6]This example originally appeared in ibid., pp. 579–582.

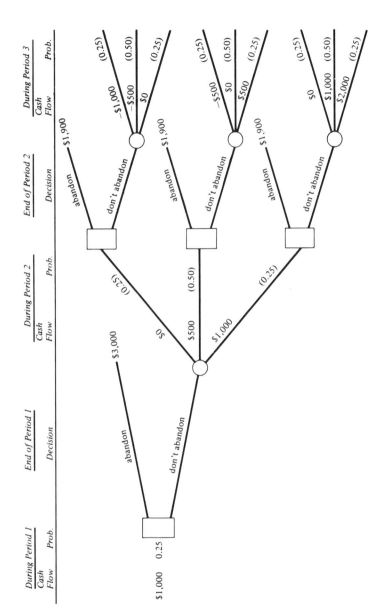

FIGURE 25 – 2   Partial Decision Tree for Project A

where this option exists to evaluate whether or not the project should be abandoned. Figure 25–2 shows a small part of the decision tree that would be necessary to evaluate abandoning project A. If the cash flow in period 1 was $1,000, to decide whether the project should be abandoned at the end of period 1, the entire tree in the exhibit must be folded back. We know that the value of the project, if abandoned at the end of period 1, is $3,000, but we must compute the value of the decision alternative "don't abandon." This necessitates evaluation of all subsequent states of nature and decision alternatives which emanate from this branch, in order to compare the expected values of these two alternatives. The procedure then is to select the alternative at each decision node which maximizes the expected present value of future benefits. For the "abandon" alternative, the expected present value is merely the expected value of the abandonment value probability distribution; whereas for the "don't abandon" alternative, we would have to compute the present value of all future cash flows whether they be from keeping the project or abandoning it later. This process is illustrated in Example 1.

EXAMPLE 1

Abandonment Values at End of Period 2

     For each of the cash flow sequences shown in Figure 25–3 determine whether it would be better to abandon or retain at the end of year 2. Assume that all cash flows have already been discounted for time.

SOLUTION: For each of the branches shown in the decision tree, the value of not abandoning is found by summing the product of the year 3 cash flows multiplied by its respective probability of occurrence. The decision is made by comparing this value to the abandonment value of $1,900.

PERIOD 1 FLOW	PERIOD 2 FLOW	VALUE OF NOT ABANDONING AT END OF PERIOD 2	DECISION
$1,000	$ 0	– $ 500	Abandon
1,000	500	0	Abandon
1,000	1,000	1,000	Abandon
2,000	1,000	1,000	Abandon
2,000	2,000	2,000	Don't abandon
2,000	3,000	3,000	Don't abandon
3,000	2,000	2,000	Don't abandon
3,000	3,000	3,000	Don't abandon
3,000	3,500	3,500	Don't abandon

Thus, the partially folded back decision tree would appear as in Figure 25–3. Note that the branch of the less desirable alternative at the end of period 2 has been marked with a pair of parallel lines.

Example 1 is continued in Example 2, where we evaluate abandonment at the end of period 1. To evaluate the alternative of abandoning or not at the end of period 1, we would fold back the tree to the end of period 1. The value of not abandoning is determined by adding the value of the optimal decision at the end of period 2 (found

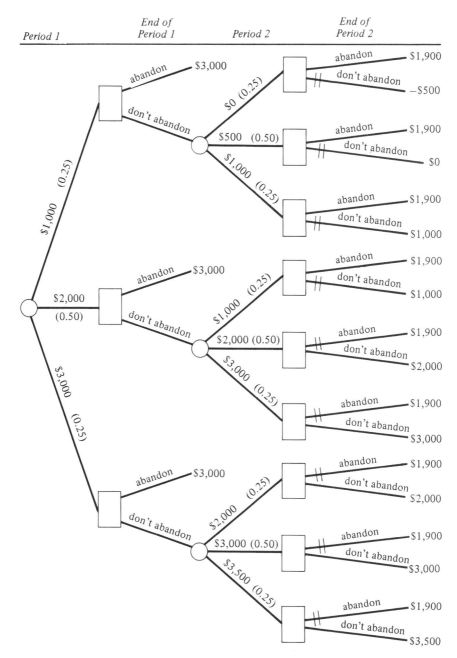

FIGURE 25 – 3   Partial Decision Tree

in Example 1) to the cash flows in period 2 and then multiplying by the respective probability of occurrence and summing over all events, shown in Example 2.

EXAMPLE 2

Abandonment Decisions at the End of Period 1

For each of the possible cash flows of project A that can occur in period 1, compute the expected value of not abandoning and determine the optimal decision (abandon or not) at that point in time.

SOLUTION: For each of the three possible cash flows in period 1, the value of not abandoning project A is found by multiplying column 4 by column 5 in the following table:

(1) PERIOD 1 CASH FLOW	(2) PERIOD 2 CASH FLOW	(3) VALUE OF OPTIMAL DECISION AT END OF PERIOD 2	(4) SUM OF (2) AND (3)	(5) PROBABILITY OF EVENT	(6) VALUE OF NOT ABANDONING AT THE END OF PERIOD 1
$1,000	$ 0 500 1,000	$1,900 1,900 1,900	$1,900 2,400 2,900	0.25 0.50 0.25	$ 475 1,200 725 $2,400
2,000	1,000 2,000 3,000	1,900 2,000 3,000	2,900 4,000 6,000	0.25 0.50 0.25	725 2,000 1,500 $4,225
3,000	2,000 3,000 3,500	2,000 3,000 3,500	4,000 6,000 7,000	0.25 0.50 0.25	1,000 3,000 1,750 $5,750

The decision tree folded back to the end of period 2 is shown in Figure 25–4. Thus, the optimal decision at the end of period 1 would be to abandon project A if the cash flow in period 1 was $1,000; however, if the cash flow in period 1 was either $2,000 or $3,000, the optimal decision would be to continue to hold project A (i.e., do not abandon).

Summarizing the results of Examples 1 and 2 by referring to the two decision trees drawn, we see that: (1) if the period 1 cash flow was $1,000, project A should be abandoned at the end of period 1; (2) if the period 1 cash flow was $2,000, the project should be held for the second period and abandoned at the end of the second period *only if* the period 2 cash flow was $1,000 (if the period 2 cash flow was either $2,000 or $3,000, the project should be held for period 3; (3) if the period 1 cash flow was $3,000, the project should be held for its entire useful life. Following these decision rules, the firm will optimally hold or abandon project A over its life.

The examples demonstrate that the abandonment option increases the expected NPV of the project compared with the same project without the alternative of abandoning at various points throughout its useful life. In addition, the abandonment

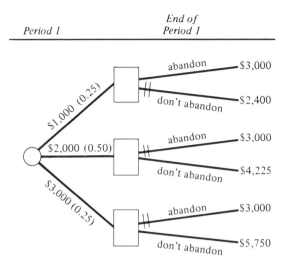

FIGURE 25 – 4   Partial Decision Tree

option has a desirable impact on both the absolute and relative risk of the project, as well as on the skewness in the distribution of the NPV values over the project's useful life. These characteristics are demonstrated in Example 3.

EXAMPLE 3

Impact of Abandonment on Project Risk

Consider project B, which has a 2-year useful life, an original cost of $400,000, and possible cash inflows as follows:

Cash Flows of Project B
(in thousand of dollars)

PERIOD 1		PERIOD 2		
CASH FLOW	PROBABILITY	CASH FLOW	CONDITIONAL PROBABILITY	CASH-FLOW SEQUENCE
$300	0.3	$250	0.30	1
		300	0.50	2
		350	0.20	3
400	0.4	300	0.30	4
		400	0.50	5
		500	0.20	6
500	0.3	400	0.30	7
		500	0.40	8
		600	0.30	9

The firm's cost of capital is 12% and the undiscounted cash flows tabulated above would lead to an expected NPV of $271,000 as follows:

CASH FLOW SEQUENCE	TOTAL PRESENT VALUE OF CASH FLOW (THOUSANDS)	SEQUENCE PROBABILITY	EXPECTED VALUE (THOUSANDS)
1	$467	0.09	$ 42
2	507	0.15	76
3	547	0.06	33
4	596	0.12	72
5	676	0.20	135
6	756	0.08	60
7	765	0.09	69
8	845	0.12	101
9	925	0.09	83
		1.00	$671

Expected present value = $671,000

Initial investment = 400,000

Expected net present value = $271,000

In addition, calculation of the variance, semivariance, measure of skewness, and coefficient of variation for project B shown below uses the techniques developed in Chapters 11 and 12.

CASH FLOW SEQUENCE	NPV OF SEQUENCE	EXPECTED NPV	SEQUENCE DEVIATION	$\left(\begin{array}{c}\text{SEQUENCE}\\\text{DEVIATION}\end{array}\right)^2$	SEQUENCE × PROBABILITY	= RESULT
1	$ 67	$271	− $204	41,616	0.09	$3,745
2	107	271	− 164	26,896	0.15	4,034
3	147	271	− 124	15,376	0.06	923
4	196	271	− 75	5,625	0.12	675
5	276	271	+ 5	25	0.20	5
6	356	271	+ 85	7,225	0.08	578
7	365	271	+ 94	8,836	0.09	795
8	445	271	+ 174	30,276	0.12	3,633
9	525	271	+ 254	64,516	0.09	5,806
					1.00	$20,194

$$\text{Variance} = V_B = 20{,}194$$

$$\text{Standard deviation} = \sigma_B = \sqrt{20{,}194} = \$142$$

$$\text{Semivariance} = SV_B = 9{,}377$$

$$\text{Measure of skewness} = \frac{V_B}{2SV_B} = 1.077$$

$$\text{Coefficient of variation} = \frac{\sigma_B}{E(X_B)} = 0.524$$

Now, consider that the firm has the option to abandon project B at the end of year 1 for $280,000. Compute the expected NPV, the standard deviation, variance, semivariance, measure of skewness, and coefficient of variation given the abandonment option and show that these measures dominate their counterparts given that the abandonment option did not exist.

SOLUTION: Given the possible cash inflows in periods 1 and 2 and their associated probabilities as shown in the first table, the expected present values of the second period's cash inflows are computed in the following table:

CASH FLOW SEQUENCE	CASH FLOW	PRESENT* VALUE	CONDITIONAL PROBABILITY	EXPECTED PRESENT VALUE
1	$250	$199	0.3	$ 60
2	300	239	0.5	120
3	350	279	0.2	56
			Branch total	$236
4	$300	$239	0.3	72
5	400	319	0.5	160
6	500	399	0.2	80
			Branch total	$312
7	$400	$319	0.3	96
8	500	399	0.4	160
9	600	478	0.3	143
			Branch total	$399
		Present value of salvage $(0.8929)(\$280) = \$250$		

*PV factor = 0.7972.

If a cash inflow of $300 occurs in period 1, project B is expected to be abandoned for $280 at the end of period 1. Cash flow sequences 1 to 3 are reduced to one sequence with a present value of $518 (i.e., $300 + $280)(0.8929). In all other cases, the project is held for year 2 rather than abandoned. The following table computes the expected NPV with the abandonment option:

CASH FLOW SEQUENCE	TOTAL PRESENT VALUE OF CASH FLOW	SEQUENCE PROBABILITY	EXPECTED VALUE
1–3	$518	0.3	$155
4	596	0.12	72
5	676	0.20	135
6	756	0.08	60
7	765	0.09	69
8	845	0.12	101
9	925	0.09	83
		1.00	$675

Expected present value = $675

Initial investment = 400

Expected net present value = $275

Given these calculations, we now compute the measures of risk and skewness for the abandonment option:

CASH FLOW SEQUENCE	NPV OF SEQUENCE	EXPECTED NPV	SEQUENCE DEVIATION	$\left(\dfrac{\text{SEQUENCE}}{\text{DEVIATION}}\right)^2$	SEQUENCE × PROBABILITY	= RESULTS
1–3	$118	$275	− $157	24,649	0.3	$7,395
4	196	275	− 79	6,241	0.12	749
5	276	275	+ 1	1	0.20	0
6	356	275	+ 81	6,561	0.08	525
7	365	275	+ 10	8,100	0.09	729
8	445	275	+ 170	28,900	0.12	3,468
9	525	275	+ 250	62,500	0.09	5,625
					1.00	$18,491

$$\text{Variance} = V_B = 18{,}491$$

$$\text{Standard deviation} = \sigma_B = \sqrt{18{,}491} = \$136$$

$$\text{Semivariance} = SV_B = 8{,}144$$

$$\text{Measure of skewness} = V_B/2SV_B = 1.135$$

$$\text{Coefficient of variation} = \frac{\sigma_B}{E(X_B)} = 0.495$$

Finally, the following table compares project B with and without the abandonment option, as well as the percentage changes in each of the computed statistics.

NET PRESENT VALUE	WITHOUT ABANDONMENT	WITH ABANDONMENT	PERCENT CHANGE
Expected value	$271	$275	+ 1.5
Standard deviation	$142	$136	− 4.2
Skewness	1.077	1.135	+ 5.4
Coefficient of variation	0.524	0.495	− 5.5

As shown, all the measures of risk and skewness move in a favorable direction as the abandonment option is included. Notice that the standard deviation has decreased by 4.2% and the relative size of the standard deviation to the expected return has decreased by a significant 5.5%. Further, the measure of skewness has increased 5.4%, to 1.135. Since the skewness value is greater than 1 and larger than before, the distribution is more skewed to the right than previously. A distribution more skewed to the right has a lower downside risk. Thus, the risk of *cash flows below the expected value is reduced.*

Reflecting on the results of Example 3, it should be stressed that the abandonment option will not always have the impact on project risk and return obtained in that problem (i.e., project risk was reduced and project return was increased). On the contrary, project risk could increase if the expected abandonment values were sufficiently large and/or project return could decrease if abandonment variances were sufficiently small. Thus, the abandonment option in its most general form should be handled by using the utility maximization criterion based upon the investor's risk-return preferences.[7]

As can clearly be seen from Examples 1, 2, and 3, the calculations can quickly become tedious as the number of periods increases, or the number of possible cash flows each period increases, or if the abandonment value is known only by a probability distribution. Thus, Robichek and Van Horne recommended and illustrated the use of the Monte Carlo simulation under such conditions.[8] The simulation model to handle the abandonment problem is a straightforward extension of the models discussed in Chapter 2. In addition, the interested reader is referred to the appendix in the Robichek and Van Horne article,[9] where the authors give a brief description of the simulation model they used.

Finally, Bonini formulated a dynamic programming model that finds the optimal abandonment strategy under both conditions of certainty and uncertainty.[10] The approach can also be viewed as an analytic extension of the Hillier formulation for quantifying project risk[11] where the abandonment option exists. The interested reader should consult this reference.

This section should be closed with a word of caution. Capital budgeting projects should be monitored, and it may become advantageous to terminate some. However, the abandonment decision must stand the test of maximizing shareholders' wealth. It is often extremely difficult to estimate the costs and benefits of abandoning large capital projects which may necessitate closing down or selling off a product line or division. Such changes involve disentangling accounting and tax effects, managerial reassignments, work force dislocations, customer relations problems, community and societal impacts, and so on. Thus, the process can entail very long lead times, perhaps spanning a decade. The proper timing of abandonment and the attendant dislocations affect the ultimate decision and modify the structures of theory.

COST JUSTIFYING CAPITAL BUDGETING

Capital budgeting must be monitored by management for yet another reason: it can be expensive in manpower, time, and facilities. The sophistication of the process naturally varies with the size of the firm and the importance of the projects under consideration. Also, the techniques we have discussed can be applied to a wide variety of project types: plant and equipment, lease versus buy analysis, refunding proposals, advertising expenditures, research and development projects, and abandonment issues. So many and varied are the applications that, at the outset, management must establish a cutoff point; that is, spending proposals below a certain amount will be treated as simple expenditure items. Above this amount, the budgeting process will take over.

---

[7]The authors thank Dr. Arthur C. M. Clarke for pointing out these aspects in a book review on the first edition of this text which was published in *The Engineering Economist*.

[8]Robichek and Van Horne, "Abandonment Value," pp. 582–584.

[9]Ibid., pp. 588–589.

[10]C. P. Bonini, "Capital Investment Under Uncertainty with Abandonment Options," *Journal of Financial and Quantitative Analysis*, 12, no. 1 (March 1977), 39–54.

[11]F. S. Hillier, "The Derivation of Probabilistic Information for the Evaluation of Risky Investment," *Management Science*, 9, no. 3 (April 1963), 443–457.

The objective is to establish a cost-effective budgeting procedure. This is fostered by following up on projects to assure that the desired return is realized, abandoning projects that fail the test, and limiting the budgeting process to projects of a size appropriate to the analytical techniques applied. The latter, it should be noted, is not the most common sin of the U.S. financial management; rather the converse—spending large sums without appropriate analysis.

Nonetheless, one can appropriately raise the question of whether firms using the more sophisticated discounted cash flow methods show enhanced profitability compared to those which adhere to older rules of thumb. The evidence is uncertain on the point and the analysis difficult, owing to the presence of so many variables intruding on the firm's profitability other than the capital budgeting decision. Yet we can cite some research on the topic. George A. Christy, for example, matched earnings per share of his surveyed companies against the capital budgeting techniques employed. Christy found no significant relationship between profitability and the methodology of long-range asset management.[12]

By contrast, Suk H. Kim at the University of Detroit surveyed 114 machinery companies and related their average earnings per share to several variables: the degree of sophistication in capital budgeting, size of the firm, capital intensity, degree of risk, and debt ratio. Kim found a positive relationship between profitability and the budgeting technique when the latter is considered as a broad process involving the added variables ignored in the Christy study.[13]

SUMMARY

In this chapter we stress the importance of financial forecasting (both short run and long run) in the capital budgeting decision-making process. An overview of major assumptions and strategies in financial forecasting is presented.

Next, the very important area of the review and evaluation of previously accepted capital projects is addressed. The impact of the abandonment option on the attractiveness of investment proposals is measured and illustrated by examples. The optimal time to abandon a project is that period which leads to a maximization of the NPV considering both the present value of project cash inflows and the present value of the abandonment value. Under conditions of changing risk, it is shown that the abandonment option can increase the expected NPV, decrease both the absolute and relative risk of the project, and increase the positive skewness of the project (which reduces the downside risk of the project).

Finally, the importance of cost-effective capital project evaluation is stressed so that firms avoid committing major dollar amounts without appropriate analysis.

QUESTIONS

PROBLEMS

1. Discuss the importance of capital budgeting to a firm's overall strategic planning and the interrelationships between capital budgeting and the functional areas of finance, production, personnel, marketing, and accounting.

[12]George A. Christy, *Capital Budgeting: Current Practices and Their Efficiency* (Eugene: Bureau of Economic Research, University of Oregon, 1966).

[13]Suk H. Kim, "Capital Budgeting Practices in Large Corporations and Their Impact on Overall Profitability," *Baylor Business Studies* (January 1979), 49–66.

2. Discuss the importance of forecasting to capital budgeting and the importance of taking cognizance of the assumptions underlying forecasting models in use.

3. List at least three reasons why capital investment projects may have to be abandoned before the end of their useful lives in order to maximize shareholders' wealth.

4. The Ridgway Company is evaluating a capital project that it feels has quite a bit of uncertainty associated with it. Namely, the firm feels that the following probabilities should be assigned to various cash flows and abandonment values (which are all considered to be independent):

		PERIOD				
	PROB.	0	1	2	3	4
Cash	0.2	− $14,000	+$10,000	+$ 9,000	+$ 8,000	+$ 7,000
flows	0.5	− 20,000	+ 12,000	+ 14,000	+ 15,000	+ 16,000
	0.3	− 22,000	+ 13,000	+ 15,000	+ 17,000	+ 19,000
Abandonment	0.3		+ 10,000	+ 7,000	+ 6,000	+ 4,000
values	0.6		+ 11,000	+ 9,000	+ 7,000	+ 5,000
	0.1		+ 12,000	+ 11,000	+ 8,000	+ 6,000

The firm's cost of capital is 12%, and this project is considered to be of average riskiness to the firm. Because of the independence between successive years' cash flows and between these flows and the abandonment values, expected values can be used to determine the NPV and the optimal time to abandon. Compute the following.

(a) The expected NPV if the project is held to the end of its useful life.

(b) The optimal time to abandon the project, which is determined by maximizing the expected value of NPV^m.

5. Jones Brothers, Inc., is considering investing in a new machine to package cough drops. The machine has a potential useful life of 3 years, with a possibility of abandonment at the end of year 1 or 2. The possible cash flows, abandonment values, and their associated probabilities are as follows:

Year 1		Year 2		Year 3	
Cash Flow	Prob.	Cash Flow	Prob.	Cash Flow	Prob.
				$ 8,000	0.3
		$ 6,000	0.2	10,000	0.3
$4,000	0.4	7,000	0.4	12,000	0.4
		8,000	0.4	13,000	0.3
				15,000	0.3
				10,000	0.2
		8,000	0.2	11,000	0.4
9,000	0.6	11,000	0.6	13,000	0.4
		12,000	0.2	15,000	0.2
				16,000	0.4

AT THE END OF YEAR 1:		AT THE END OF YEAR 2:	
VALUE	PROBABILITY	VALUE	PROBABILITY
$16,000	0.2	$10,000	0.3
18,000	0.7	12,000	0.6
19,000	0.1	14,000	0.1

Jones Brothers' required rate of return for this project is 14%.

(a) Draw the complete decision tree, which represents the decision alternatives available to the firm at various points through time.

(b) For each of the possible cash flows during year 2, determine whether the project should be abandoned at the end of year 2.

(c) For each of the cash flows during year 1, determine whether the project should be abandoned at the end of year 1.

(d) Summarize your results in parts (b) and (c) concerning what the firm should do in both years for all possible cash flows that could occur (i.e., make a recommendation to Jones Brothers about whether it should hold or abandon the asset for each possible cash flow).

(e) Assuming that the project cost is $20,000, compute the expected NPV, σ_{NPV}, semivariance, measure of skewness, and coefficient of variation for the project without the abandonment option.

(f) Compute all of the measures mentioned in part (e) but this time with the abandonment option.

REFERENCES

Anderson, Leslie P., Vergil V. Miller, and Donald L. Thompson. *The Finance Function.* Scranton, Pa.: International Textbook Company, 1971.

Ang, J. S. "A Graphical Presentation of an Integrated Capital Budgeting Model." *Engineering Economist* (Winter 1978).

Brill, Martin. *An Approach to Risk Analysis in the Evaluation of Capital Ventures.* Philadelphia: Drexel Institute of Technology, 1966.

Branch, Ben. "Corporate Objectives and Market Performance." *Financial Management*, 2 (Summer 1973), 24–29.

De Alessi, Louis. "Private Property and Dispersion of Ownership in Large Corporations." *Journal of Finance*, 28 (September 1973), 839–851.

Elliott, J. W. "Control, Size, Growth, and Financial Performance in the Firm." *Journal of Financial and Quantitative Analysis*, 7 (January 1972), 1309–1320.

Grossman, S. J., and J. E. Stiglitz. "On Value Maximization and Alternative Objectives of the Firm." *Journal of Finance*, 32 (May 1977), 389–415.

Levy, Haim, and Marshall Sarnat. "A Pedagogic Note on Alternative Formulations of the Goal of the Firm." *Journal of Business*, 50 (October 1977), 526–528.

Petty, J. W., D. F. Scott, Jr., and M. M. Bird. "The Capital Expenditure Decision-Making Process of Large Corporations." *Engineering Economist* (Spring 1975).

APPENDIX: POSTCOMPLETION AUDIT CHECKLISTS

FIGURE 25A-1

<u>CAPITAL PROJECT FINANCIAL EVALUATION AUDIT CHECKLIST</u>

Division -
Project -

	Payback Years	Return on Funds Employed 5 Years	Return on Funds Employed 10 Years	Total New Funds 5-Yr. Average	Total New Funds 10-Yr. Average

Original Request -

Latest Estimate/Actual -

General Comments -

Audit Performed by -
Date of Audit -

Item	Points To Be Checked	Yes Sat.	No Un-sat.	Un-nec.	Remarks/ Reference
Funds Employed					
1. Cash	A. Was total computed according to formula?				
2. Receivables	A. Compare Latest Estimate or Actual to total reported in original submission for:				
	1. Reasonableness of absolute amount.				
	2. Relationship to Net Sales.				
	3. Obtain reason for significant differences.				
	B. Compare relationship to Net Sales for this project to the relationship for the division in total.				
	C. Check Distribution Sales and Service allocations.				
3. Inventories	A. Compare Latest Estimate or Actual to total reported in original submission for:				
	1. Reasonableness of absolute amount.				
	2. Inventory turnover (cost of goods sold + inventory). (a) Also compare to Divisional Turnover.				
	3. Obtain reason for significant differences.				
	B. Is total shown incremental to this project?				
	1. Check division's allocation of inventory to this project.				
	2. Check levels of inventory for this product both before and after this project.				
4. Prepaid and Deferred Expense	A. Compare Latest Estimate or Actual to total reported in original submission for:				
	1. Reasonableness of absolute amount.				
	2. Relationship to expense items in Profit and Loss (marketing, etc.).				
	3. Obtain reasons for significant differences.				

Item	Points To Be Checked	Yes Sat.	No Un-sat.	Un-nec.	Remarks/ Reference
	B. Check division's computations.	_____			
	C. Check books of account for years where actual figures are available.	_____			
5. Current Liabilities	A. Compare Latest Estimate or Actual to total reported in original submission for:				
	1. Reasonableness of absolute amount.	_____			
	2. Obtain reason for significant differences.	_____			
	B. Check division's computation.	_____			
	1. Has 50% of tax expense been included?	_____			
6. Total Working Funds	A. Verify arithmetical accuracy of total (lines 1 through 4, less line 5).	_____			
7. Land	A. Compare Latest Estimate or Actual to total reported in original submission for:				
	1. Reasonableness of absolute amount.	_____			
	2. Obtain reasons for significant variation.	_____			
	B. Trace amount capitalized to:				
	1. Original purchase records.	_____			
	2. Engineering reports.	_____			
	3. Check year-end workpapers.	_____			
8. Buildings	A. Compare Latest Estimate or Actual to total reported in original submission for:				
	1. Reasonableness of absolute amount.	_____			
	2. Obtain reasons for significant variation.	_____			
	B. Trace amount capitalized from Construction Work in Progress into fixed asset account.	_____			
	1. Spot check invoices in vendor's files.	_____			
	2. Check engineering final close-out report.	_____			
	3. Check year-end workpapers.	_____			
	C. Does total shown in first year plus first-year depreciation equal amount in original request?	_____			
	D. Verify reasonableness of depreciation method:				
	1. Is method used acceptable?	_____			
	2. Is estimated life of asset reasonable?	_____			

Item	Points To Be Checked	Yes Sat.	No Un- sat.	Un- nec.	Remarks/ Reference
9. Manufacturing and Engineering	A. Compare Latest Estimate or Actual to total reported in original submission for:				
	1. Reasonableness of absolute amount.			_____	
	2. Obtain reasons for significant variation.			_____	
	B. Trace amount capitalized.			_____	
	1. Check engineering reports.			_____	
	2. Check vendors' invoices.			_____	
	3. Check year-end workpapers.			_____	
	C. Does total shown in first year plus first-year depreciation equal amount in original request?			_____	
	D. Verify reasonableness of depreciation method:			_____	
	1. Is method used acceptable?			_____	
	2. Is estimated life of asset reasonable?			_____	
10. Total Engr'g.	A. Compare Latest Estimate or Actual to total reported in original submission for:				
	1. Reasonableness of absolute amount.			_____	
	2. Obtain reasons for significant variation.			_____	
	B. Check total to Engineering Report on Project.				
11. Other (Explain)	A. Compare Latest Estimate or Actual to total reported in original submission for:				
	1. Reasonableness of absolute amount.			_____	
	2. Obtain reasons for significant variation.				
12. Expense (After Taxes)	A. Compare Latest Estimate or Actual to total reported in original submission for:	_____			
	1. Reasonableness of absolute amount.			_____	
	2. Check to total expense amount included on Appropriation Request.			_____	
	3. Obtain reasons for significant differences.				
	B. Verify that total has been repeated for all years.			_____	
13. Total Capital Funds	A. Verify arithmetical accuracy of total (add lines 7 through 12).			_____	
14. Tot. New Funds	A. Verify arithmetical accuracy of total (lines 6 plus 13).			_____	
15. Cumulative Depreciation	A. Determine that line 15 equals cumulative annual depreciation shown on line 32. (The accuracy of line 32 will be determined later.)			_____	

Item	Points To Be Checked	Yes Sat.	No Un- sat.	Un- nec.	Remarks/ Reference
16. Cum. Net Profit & Depreciation	A. Determine that this line is identical to line 34. (The accuracy of line 34 will be determined later.)		_____		
17. New Funds to Repay	A. Determine that this line equals line 14 plus line 15 minus line 16 for each year.		_____		
	B. Verify accuracy of payback calculation (shown on top of form).				
	1. Determine the number of years with a figure on line 17. This is the number of full years to repay that is to be listed on the first line in payback calculation above.		_____		
	2. Determine the part year (second line above) by dividing the figure on line 17 in the last full year to repay column, by the total on line 33 in the succeeding year.		_____		
	3. The sum of these items will determine the total years to repay.		_____		
Profit and Loss Projection					
18. Gross Sales	A. Compare Latest Estimate or Actual to total reported in original submission for:				
	1. Reasonableness of absolute amount.		_____		
	2. Obtain reasons for differences.		_____		
	B. Determine whether sales were incremental to this project:				
	1. Check reasonableness and accuracy of division's calculations.		_____		
	(a) Where appropriate, check production records and convert output to sales dollars.		_____		
	2. If not a new product, determine capacity of previously existing facilities and subtract this from total sales for product, which should give incremental sales.		_____		
19. Deductions	A. Compare Deductions from Gross Sales in this Profit and Loss projection to the historical and planned rate for:				
	1. The total division, and		_____		
	2. The total product Profit and Loss, and		_____		
	3. Obtain reasons for any significant variations.		_____		
	4. Check divisional allocation to this project.		_____		

Item	Points To Be Checked	Yes Sat.	No Un- sat.	Un- nec.	Remarks/ Reference
20. Net Sales	A. Verify arithmetical accuracy (line 18 less line 19).	_____			
21. Cost of Goods Sold	A. Check division's computation.	_____			
& 22. Gross Profit	1. Review cost records before and after capital project, thereby ascertaining savings.	_____			
	B. Compare the Gross Profit rate in this Profit and Loss projection to the historical and planned rate for:				
	1. The original submission, and	_____			
	2. The total division, and	_____			
	3. The total product Profit and Loss, and	_____			
	4. If a new product, to any similar products.	_____			
	5. Obtain explanations of significant variations.	_____			
23. Advertising	A. Check division's computation.	_____			
	B. Compare as a % of Net Sales to the historical and planned rate for:				
	1. The original submission, and	_____			
	2. The total division, and	_____			
	3. The total product Profit and Loss, and	_____			
	4. If a new product, compare to similar products when possible, and	_____			
	5. Observe trends in rate and absolute amounts,	_____			
	6. Obtain explanations of any significant variations.	_____			
24. Selling	A. Check division's computation.	_____			
	B. Compare as a % of Net Sales to the historical and planned rate for:				
	1. The original submission, and	_____			
	2. The total division, and	_____			
	3. The total product Profit and Loss, and	_____			
	4. If a new product, compare to similar products when possible, and	_____			
	5. Observe trends in rate and absolute amounts,	_____			
	6. Obtain explanations of any significant variations.	_____			

Item	Points To Be Checked	Yes Sat.	No Un-sat.	Un-nec.	Remarks/ Reference
25. General and Administrative	A. Check division's computation.	_____			
	B. Compare as a % of Net Sales to the historical and planned rate for:				
	1. The original submission, and	_____			
	2. The total division, and				
	3. The total product Profit and Loss, and	_____			
	4. If a new product, compare to similar products when possible, and	_____			
	5. Observe trends in rate and absolute amounts,	_____			
	6. Obtain explanations of any significant variations.	_____			
26. Research	A. Check division's computation.	_____			
	B. Compare as a % of Net Sales to the historical and planned rate for:				
	1. The original submission, and	_____			
	2. The total division, and	_____			
	3. The total product Profit and Loss, and	_____			
	4. If a new product, compare to similar products when possible, and	_____			
	5. Observe trends in rate and absolute amounts,	_____			
	6. Obtain explanations of any significant variations.	_____			
27. Other	A. Division should satisfactorily explain totals included on this line. Auditor should take steps necessary to satisfy himself of reasonableness and accuracy of these totals.	_____			
28. Adjustment	A. Division should satisfactorily explain totals included on this line. Auditor should take steps necessary to satisfy himself of reasonableness and accuracy of these totals.	_____			
29. Profit Before Taxes	A. Verify arithmetical accuracy.	_____			
30. Taxes	A. Verify that proper tax rate has been used.	_____			
31. Net Profit	A. Verify arithmetical accuracy.	_____			
32. Annual Depreciation	A. Determine reasonableness of totals (see Items 8D and 9D).	_____			
33. Annual Net Profit & Depreciation	A. Verify arithmetical accuracy (lines 31 plus 32).	_____			

Item	Points To Be Checked	Yes Sat.	No Un-sat.	Un-nec.	Remarks/Reference
34. Cumulative Net Profit and Depreciation	A. Verify arithmetical accuracy (should equal the cumulative total of line 33).		_____		
5-and 10-Year Averages	A. Verify arithmetical accuracy of all 5- and 10-year average figures shown.		_____		
Return on Funds	A. Verify that correct 5- and 10-year average figures have been brought up to Return on Funds section in the upper right-hand corner of the form.		_____		
	B. Confirm Return on Funds calculations for both the 5- and 10-year periods.		_____		

FUNDS EMPLOYED AND PROFIT AND LOSS PROJECTIONS

XYZ DIVISION	CHICAGO, ILLINOIS LOCATION	Project "A" PROJECT TITLE	PROJECT NO. 11	SUPPLEMENT NO. —

RETURN OF NEW FUNDS EMPLOYED

PAY BACK YEARS FROM DATE OF COMPLETION
Number Of Full Years To Pay Back — 4.0 YEARS
Part Year Calculation — .5 YEARS
Total Years To Pay Back — 4.5 YEARS

RETURN ON NEW FUNDS EMPLOYED

A—Average Funds Employed—Line 14
B—Profit Before Taxes—Line 32
C—Calculated Return—B ÷ A

	Five-Yr. Average	Ten-Yr. Average
A	$ 2,902	$ 2,447
B	$ 1,228	$ 1,828
C	42.3 %	74.7 %

Funds Employed	Gross Cost	1st Yr.	2nd Yr.	3rd Yr.	4th Yr.	5th Yr.	5-Yr. Avg.	6th Year	7th Year	8th Year	9th Year	10th Year	10-Yr. Avg.
1 Cash		290	222	209	215	221	232	233	239	251	263	276	242
2 Receivables		338	287	296	304	312	307	329	338	355	372	388	332
3 Inventories		766	651	670	689	709	697	747	766	804	843	881	753
4. Prepaid and Deferred Expenses		12	10	11	11	11	11	12	12	13	13	14	12
5 Current Liabilities		(121)	191	502	520	543	327	581	603	643	682	721	487
6 Total Working Funds (1 thru 4-5)		1,527	979	684	699	710	920	740	752	780	809	838	852
7 Land	100	100	100	100	100	100	100	100	100	100	100	100	100
8 Buildings	1,000	976	928	881	835	790	882	747	705	664	624	586	774
9 Machinery & Equipment	1,240	1,166	1,024	891	768	655	900	552	459	376	302	238	643
10 Engineering	100	94	82	71	61	51	72	42	34	27	21	16	50
11 Other (Explain)	—	—	—	—	—	—	—	—	—	—	—	—	—
12 Expense (After Taxes)	60	28	28	28	28	28	28	28	28	28	28	28	28
13 Total Capital Funds (7 Thru 12)		2,364	2,162	1,971	1,792	1,624	1,982	1,469	1,326	1,195	1,075	968	1,595
14 Total New Funds (6 + 13)		3,891	3,141	2,655	2,491	2,334	2,902	2,209	2,078	1,975	1,884	1,806	2,447
15 Cum. Depreciation On 8 Thru 11		104	306	497	676	844		999	1,142	1,273	1,393	1,500	
16 Cum. Net Profit & Deprec. (Line 37)		(108)	430	1,503	2,597	3,718		4,895	6,099	7,360	8,679	10,053	
17 New Funds To Repay (14 + 15-16)		4,103	3,017	1,649	570	—		—	—	—	—	—	—

FIGURE 25A–2 Postcompletion Audit Form for Capital Projects

Profit and Loss Projection	1st Yr.	2nd Yr.	3rd Yr.	4th Yr.	5th Yr.	5-Yr. Avg.	6th Year	7th Year	8th Year	9th Year	10th Year	10-Yr. Avg.
18 Unit Volume	2,000	1,700	1,750	1,800	1,850	1,820	1,950	2,000	2,100	2,200	2,300	1,965
19 Gross Sales	7,426	6,312	6,498	6,683	6,869	6,758	7,240	7,426	7,797	8,169	8,540	7,296
20 Deductions	670	570	586	603	620	610	653	670	704	737	771	658
21 Net Sales	6,756	5,742	5,912	6,080	6,249	6,148	6,587	6,756	7,093	7,432	7,769	6,638
22 Cost of Goods Sold	3,210	2,901	2,957	3,011	3,066	3,029	3,196	3,251	3,382	3,512	3,642	3,213
23 Gross Profit	3,546	2,841	2,955	3,069	3,183	3,119	3,391	3,505	3,711	3,920	4,127	3,425
24 G.P. % Net Sales	52.5	49.5	50.0	50.5	50.9	50.7	51.5	51.9	52.3	52.7	53.1	51.6
25 Advertising	3,358	1,725	649	661	669	1,413	719	747	799	838	887	1,105
26 Selling	300	300	300	300	300	300	320	320	320	340	350	315
27 General & Administrative	65	65	65	75	80	70	80	80	85	85	85	77
28 Research	130	20	20	20	20	42	10	10	10	10	10	26
29 Start-up Costs	135					27						14
30 Other (Explain)	2	1	1	3	1	2	1	2	1	1	2	1
31 Adjustment (Explain)	10	12	35	55	75	37	77	79	81	83	85	59
32 Profit Before Taxes	(454)	718	1,885	1,955	2,038	1,228	2,184	2,267	2,415	2,563	2,708	1,828
33 Taxes—Federal & State Income	(242)	382	1,003	1,040	1,085	653	1,162	1,206	1,285	1,364	1,441	973
34 Net Profit	(212)	336	882	915	953	575	1,022	1,061	1,130	1,199	1,267	855
35 Annual Depreciation	104	202	191	179	168	169	155	143	131	120	107	150
36 An. Net Profit & Deprec. (34 + 35)	(108)	538	1,073	1,094	1,121	744	1,177	1,204	1,261	1,319	1,374	1,005
37 Cum. Net Profit & Depreciation	(108)	430	1,503	2,597	3,718		4,895	6,099	7,360	8,679	10,053	

Capital Budgeting
for the Multinational Firm

26

The somewhat complicated evaluations of investment opportunities in national settings are rendered extremely complex in less familiar international environments. Capital budgeting theory does not change, but the application is bedeviled by varying institutional environments (differing governmental systems, tax laws, import and export regulations, etc.). In essence, capital budgeting in an international environment demands not only a grasp of theoretical concepts covered earlier in this text, but also an intimate knowledge of local economic conditions and customs. Figure 26–1 gives an overall view of the unique variables attendant upon capital budgeting in an international setting.

In spite of the growing importance of the subject matter, the great number of variables and the uncertainty of their nature seems to deter model builders. This fact is unfortunate because the rapid growth in the number of multinational corporations and the difficulty of their decision settings necessitate sophisticated tools of analysis. Monte Carlo simulation, introduced in Chapter 21, is extended in the appendix to this chapter and has great potential for handling the complex multinational capital investment decisions. It can incorporate the interdependence of the large number of variables in the decision process and makes it possible to visualize the dynamics of business decisions in complex settings. Furthermore, the peculiarities of international risk can be efficiently introduced through simulation into the capital investment decision area.

Multinational corporations follow a variety of capital budgeting practices. As with domestic corporations, multinational corporations practice diverse capital budgeting techniques. Table 26–1 shows the results of four surveys of multinational firms. As can be seen, multinational companies (MNC) use IRR more extensively than any other technique. The NPV method and payback are distant second and third place evaluation techniques. Table 26–2 shows how MNCs determine the discount rates utilized. The predominant approach is to use the weighted-average cost of capital (WACC) based on either just local or local and overseas financing.

Finally MNCs can adjust for risk either through discount rates or cash flows. Table 26–3 reports on techniques used by the firms. It does not appear that very sophisticated methods are in widespread use by MNCs.

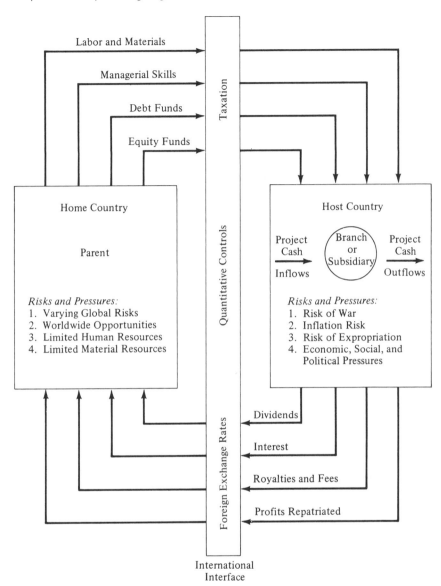

FIGURE 26 – 1   Multinational Capital Budgeting Environment

CAPITAL BUDGETING PROCESS

The capital budgeting objective for the multinational corporation (MNC) is the same as for a domestic firm: to maximize the firm's value as expressed in terms of the market price of the common shares. Therefore, for any proposed project to be attractive, firms insist that the discounted cash inflows exceed the discounted outflows where the discount rate reflects the risk associated with the project under evaluation.

Table 26–1   Primary Capital Budgeting Techniques Employed by Multinational Corporations (Percentage of Respondents Using Each Technique)

TECHNIQUE	AUTHOR AND YEAR			
	OBLAK AND HELM 1980	KIM, CRICK, AND FARRAGHER 1981	BAVISHI* 1981	STANLEY AND BLOCK 1984
Payback	10%	12%	76%	5%
Accounting Rate of Return	14	14		11
Net Present Value	14	9	40	17
Internal Rate of Return	60	62	69	65
Profitability Index		3	10	

*Includes primary and secondary use.

Table 26–2   Method Used to Determine Discount Rate Used by Multinational Corporations (Percentage of Respondents Using Each Method)

TECHNIQUE	AUTHOR AND YEAR		
	OBLAK AND HELM 1980	KIM, CRICK, AND FARRAGHER 1981	BAVISHI 1981
Subjectively vary WACC	40%	20%	30%
Cost of Funds Applied	4		
Local (Foreign) WACC	44	45	27
Local (Foreign) Prime Rate	4	10	
Other	8	25	
WACC for both domestic and overseas financing			43

The capital budgeting process for an MNC typically involves the following activities:

1   Identification of cash flows generated by the proposed project.
2   Identification of flows available for repatriation to the MNC.
3   Conversion of cash flows by means of exchange rates.
4   Adjustments to compensate for financial risks, including sensitivity analysis.
5   Selection of a minimum rate of return.
6   Calculation of investment profitability, including sensitivity analysis.
7   Acceptance or rejection of the proposed investment.

Table 26-3   Cash Flow Risk Adjustment Techniques Used by Multinational Corporations (Percentage of Respondents Using Each Technique)

	AUTHOR AND YEAR	
TECHNIQUE	OBLAK AND HELM 1980	KIM, CRICK, AND FARRAGHER 1981
Adjust Cash Flow	7%	
Adjust Cost of Capital in Present Value	14	
Adjust Payback Period	13	16%
Adjust Acctng. Rate of Return	19	10
Borrow Locally	22	22
Insure	9	13
No distinction	11	9
Other	5	5
Certainty Equivalent		11
Risk-Adjusted Discount Rate		14

Identification of Cash Flows Generated by the Project

The MNC first concentrates its analysis on the cash flows generated by the project. A budget statement is prepared which provides estimates for the project cash inflows and cash outflows over the designated evaluation period. Generally, an investment will be analyzed over a limited period of time (10 years is typical) rather than making an attempt to forecast flows indefinitely.

The initial *cash outflows* required by the project can be identified as the costs to acquire the land and fixed assets associated with the project. Attendant with all new investments are many other start-up costs that should be considered. Such costs include selling expenses, legal expenses, initial inventories, administrative and manufacturing staffing costs, and financing costs for debt and equity. For the most part these costs can be classified as the initial working capital and organizational costs.

Furthermore, the MNC must anticipate additional investments beyond its initial commitment. In reality, original investments are usually followed by a succession of further investments, some of which may be involuntary. If a project is started within a country which provides tariff protections for fledgling industries, it may be necessary to expand operations after tariffs are removed in order to compete with foreign markets. Moreover, some countries disallow total repatriation of cash flows, thereby making reinvestment mandatory. Finally, the new venture may be set up with a large debt structure, which will require the reinvestment of profits to provide greater "financial strength."

The cash flows represent typical operating revenues and expenses. First, the MNC develops a demand forecast from such factors as historical demand, alternative sources of products, general population growth, ease of entry into the industry by competitors, and the feasibility of serving nearby markets. From this forecast the sales projections over the project period are derived.

Second, the MNC forecasts its expected expenditures for operating the subsidiary and the fees or charges that it would expect to receive from the subsidiary. These forecasts can usually be obtained from the historical data of similar ventures. Such forecasting techniques as *percentage of sales* or *simple linear regression* can be applied to the historical data to obtain reasonable estimates of the necessary expenditures.

Next, the MNC reviews the tax structure of the host country, including the income taxes, indirect taxes, and tax treaties enforced by local authorities. From these data, the estimated tax requirements can be projected.

The estimated sales, less the estimated expenses, will yield the after-tax profits from operations. These profits plus any depreciation write-offs will give the cash inflows from operations.

Identification of Cash Flows Available for Repatriation

The MNC would like to maximize the utility of the project cash throw-offs on a worldwide basis. The MNC may wish to reinvest the cash in other subsidiaries, pay dividends, pay debt obligations, or invest in new ventures. The profits from any project would have little value if the MNC could not use the cash throw-offs for these alternatives.

In essence, the MNC must determine which of the cash throw-offs it will be allowed to convert into other currencies for transfer elsewhere. The MNC must examine the existing laws pertaining to such subsidiary remittances as profits from operations, management and technical fees, royalties, loans, and dividends. Moreover, a study of exchange controls in the past would be advisable to ascertain which remittances are more frequently restricted. Once the available cash flows for the MNC worldwide network have been identified, the budgeted statement for the parent may be prepared.

All anticipated remittances from the subsidiary will necessitate transactions in the foreign exchange markets. Thus, it is important that the cash flows be represented in the currencies of the two countries involved. This conversion will allow the MNC to visualize the effects of currency values and exchange rates.

Conversion of Cash Flows Using Exchange Rates

Two interrelated risks faced by the MNC are (1) the risk associated with different rates of inflation in the host country of the subsidiary versus the home country of the parent company and (2) the risk associated with unanticipated changes in foreign exchange rates over the life of the project under evaluation. As mentioned earlier, repatriated cash flows must be converted to the parent's currency using the foreign exchange market. However, it is also necessary to address the two risks just mentioned. Recent research by Dufey[1] and Shapiro[2] has indicated that the primary determinant of an MNC's exposure to these two risks is a function of whether the subsidiary is (1) engaged in business whose nature is purely domestic, competing with

[1]Gunter Dufey, "Corporate Finance and Exchange Rate Variations," *Financial Management* (Summer 1972), 51–57.

[2]Alan C. Shapiro, "Exchange Rate Changes, Inflation and the Value of the Multinational Corporation," *Journal of Finance* (May 1975), 485–502.

imported goods, or by-and-large export oriented; and/or (2) dependent for its inputs to the production process on nontraded domestic goods and services, traded inputs, or imported raw materials. In addition to these factors, the MNC has the opportunity to hedge against inflation and foreign exchange risks.

The management of foreign exchange risk is beyond our scope here; however the interested reader is referred to several recent, comprehensive works in this area.[3] Clearly, the impact of inflation and foreign exchange risks impose new complexities on the capital budgeting decision process. However, the MNC should enter into a foreign direct investment decision with its eyes open and with formal policies and strategies for coping with the additional risks. In addition, our recommended approach calls upon the use of sensitivity analysis to determine the variables that most critically impact the project under evaluation and the degree of variation that would jeopardize the project's viability.

Required Rates of Return and Adjustments for Risk

Before assigning a required rate of return to a particular project, it is necessary for an MNC to be certain that all risks peculiar to international activities have been defined and incorporated into total analysis. We have briefly discussed the international financial risks that might confront the MNC and have cited references for strategies to minimize losses. We also mentioned that analysis of foreign tax laws and repatriation policies would assist in the proper allocation of remittances for the purpose of making funds available to the worldwide network. However, all these strategies are operational in nature and do not assist in determining the profitability of a project when evaluating the decision to invest.

A highly recommended approach for risk adjustment suggests that an MNC perform a sensitivity analysis of the factors that would influence the profitability of a project. This implies an analysis of the risks, estimating their possible changes, and applying these changes to the elements of the prepared budget data. Not only will this method serve to incorporate the variable risks, but also it will educate responsible persons about the inherent risks and will facilitate anticipation of such risks during initial project evaluation.

Some of the possible sensitivity adjustments are as follows:

1   If inflation is expected in the near future, increased domestic prices could reduce domestic demands.

2   If devaluation is expected, increased foreign prices could increase domestic demands.

3   Expected inflation would increase the operating costs.

4   Expected inflation would increase asset replacement costs. If revaluation is allowed, increased depreciation write-offs would occur.

[3]See L. L. Jacque, "Management of Foreign Exchange Risk: A Review Article," *Journal of International Business Studies* (Spring/Summer 1981), 81–101; David K. Eiteman and Arthur I. Stonehill, *Multinational Business Finance*, 2nd ed. (Reading, Mass.: Addison-Wesley Publishing Company, 1979), Chapters 2, 3, and 4; Rita M. Rodriguez and E. Eugene Carter, *International Financial Management*, 2nd ed. (Englewood Cliffs, N.J.: Prentice Hall, 1979), Chapters 5–9; L. L. Jacque, *Management of Foreign Exchange Risk: Theory and Praxis* (Lexington, Mass.: D. C. Heath, Inc., 1978).

5   The new subsidiary may cause undue contraction of sales for existing subsidiaries. An estimated value for these losses could be included in the cash outflows for the project.

6   The budget statement should be scheduled over the 10-year period, showing the expected annual flows. Realistically, the project will show a series of uneven cash flows with decreasing accuracy further ahead in the 10-year projection span.

7   Conversion of the budget elements using different exchange rates is important because the many transactions involving foreign exchange are quite often subject to different duties, tariffs, or other special exchange restrictions. One single rate may not represent the estimate range adequately.

8   Imposition of exchange controls not currently in effect (but commonly enforced) could be injected into the statement.

As can be readily concluded, the objective of a sensitivity analysis is to anticipate as many contingencies as possible, thereby increasing the accuracy of the project's expected returns. Feeling reasonably confident that the budgeted statement has considered all risks, the MNC may now direct its attention to the project's required rate of return.

In the case of evaluating one separate investment opportunity, it is necessary to establish a minimum rate of return to be used as a cutoff point when deciding to accept or reject the investment. The most commonly accepted minimum rate used by firms has been their risk-adjusted cost of capital. For an MNC, this rate would represent its worldwide cost of acquiring additional funds adjusted to reflect project-specific risk. This rate is defined as the rate of return that must be realized to maintain the corporation's current stock price.

If an MNC perceives that greater risks are inherent in a particular investment, it may adjust for risk in a manner such as illustrated in Chapter 13. It could be perceived that the effects of inflation or exchange controls are also predictable, thus justifying an additional adjustment for risk.

Measuring the Profitability of the Investment

As intimated, the MNC is greatly concerned about its ability to recover its initial investment. This concern exists because the effects of inflation and exchange controls could ultimately restrict the repatriation of funds or greatly reduce the value of funds received. Consequently, discounted cash flow techniques for measuring profitability are highly recommended.

In essence, the attractiveness of any investment is based on the ability of its eventual cash inflows to exceed its required cash outflows. However, monies received in future years would be worth less in terms of purchasing power, owing to either inflation or devaluations. To measure the real value of future cash inflows, these inflows should be expressed in constant (current) values equivalent to the values of the outflows in the earlier years. If the inflows then exceed the outflows, the investment will contribute to maximizing the dollar value of the firm in present values.

It is the primary objective of discounted cash flow techniques to provide for the time value of money by expressing future flows in terms of present value. One final factor for imputing cash inflows has been introduced and that is to assign a terminal value to the project. It is expected that the assets of the subsidiary will have a salable value at the end of the designated period, either as an ongoing concern or through liquidation. In addition, this approach can be called upon to handle compensation received by the MNC in the event that expropriation takes place.

Following our preference for the net present value (NPV) model, we recommend that MNCs evaluate the attractiveness of projects using Equation (1):

$$\text{NPV} = \sum_{t=0}^{T-1} \frac{\overline{R}_t}{(1 + r')^t} + \frac{\overline{\text{TINF}}_T}{(1 + r')^T} - I_o \tag{1}$$

where $\overline{R}_t$ = the parent company's expected (after-tax, after-exchange-rate adjustment) net cash flow in period t

$\overline{\text{TINF}}_T$ = the expected (after-tax, after-exchange-rate adjustment) terminal net cash inflow to the parent company when either expropriation takes place or the end of the planning period occurs

r' = the risk-adjusted discount rate appropriate for the project under evaluation

I_o = the initial (after-tax, after-exchange-rate adjustment) cash outflow required by the parent company to acquire the asset.

Equation (1) provides a mechanism to evaluate most projects under evaluation by the MNC. In addition, the various sensitivity adjustments recommended earlier can be easily implemented using Equation (1).

Where the firm is evaluating projects with a very high initial investment or with a high degree of uncertainty given the host country environment, the methodology presented in the appendix to this chapter, "A Simulation-Based Multinational Capital Budgeting Approach," is justified. This latter approach provides a more powerful methodology to handle risky conditions faced by the MNC.

Acceptance of Investment

Referring to the previous premises, for an investment to be acceptable, the NPV value must be positive when the cash flows are discounted at the risk-adjusted rate appropriate for the project under evaluation. Again this risk-adjusted rate is a function of the MNC's cost of capital, as well as the environmental risk that exists for a project of this type in the host country of the subsidiary.

Furthermore, the acceptance of a proposed investment does not necessarily imply that it will be implemented. Acceptance merely includes the investment with other accepted investment opportunities. The accepted investment must now appear more attractive than the others to be fully implemented. Finally, the investment's performance will continually be reviewed after implementation. If performance is poor, abandonment procedures may be considered.

COST OF CAPITAL

Risk differences cause the cost of funds from a particular source to be higher than the risk-free rate and account for the possibility of loss and prospect of gain. It is also apparent that the type of funding chosen affects fees, flotation costs, rates of interest paid, and indirect costs, such as minimum balance deposits required. However, it is important to note that for multinational corporations the risk or degree of variability for all the preceding factors differs with the host country involved. The differences relate to inflation rates, possible changes in regulations of the MNC, balance of payments, variability in labor costs, and political changes. It is for this reason that subsidiary costs of capital should be examined for the effect on the companywide cost of capital.

The cost of borrowing is expected to vary because of business risk, financial structure, variability of earnings, company size, money market conditions, and other variables. The cost and availability of funds in the international capital markets adds another dimension.

Effective interest rates in different national money markets vary considerably, and because, in general, bond yields are lower in the United States, a cost differential on long-term borrowing exists. This is further widened by security flotation costs also being higher outside the United States. Interest rates in underdeveloped countries are usually much higher than in developed countries because of smaller local savings; capital flight, which reduces local fund supplies; continuous inflation; and higher business risk.

A study that compares the cost of equity capital of U.S. multinational firms and their domestic counterparts looks at the possibility of higher risk for business operations abroad and the implication that the cost of capital would automatically be higher because of the entry into foreign markets.[4] By using a version of the dividend valuation model over 28 quarters, a sample of 110 companies from the *Fortune* 500 was used to evaluate cost of equity capital. The multinational firms on the list were compared with their domestic counterparts on that list, using the paired-difference test to detect statistically significant differences. Seven industries were studied: nonferrous metals, fabricated metals products, electrical machinery, other machinery, petroleum refining, chemical and allied products, food products, and companies without distinction by industry. Of the seven distinct industries, only the chemical and allied products industry showed noticeably higher costs of equity capital for multinational firms. Interestingly, the oil and nonferrous metals industries have both been prone to expropriation by foreign governments. Kohers states that by making distinct differences in the capitalization rates of companies in different industries and not necessarily by domestic or MNC status, investors appear to clearly differentiate investment risks and opportunities among industries. They do not tend to discriminate unfairly against foreign operations in their appraisal of common stock investment values. From these findings it is concluded that by becoming involved in foreign business activities a company does not automatically raise its cost of capital.

The cost of short-term and medium-term funds, as mentioned earlier, now becomes a matter of operating most profitably (and prudently) while in compliance with FASB no. 8 (to be discussed momentarily). Minimization of dollar investment exposure to currency devaluation leads to scheduled repatriation of dollars by dividend payments and maximum efficient utilization of local funding sources by constant comparison of short-term rates for various instruments such as overdrafts, notes, and so on. When borrowing becomes difficult as a result of the general lack of availability of funds and retention of dividends becomes necessary to augment working capital, forward hedging is an alternative to protect investments and its cost can be considered as a cost of funds. Ordinarily, forward cover against the fall of currency, especially in a developing country, is expensive and considered prohibitive.

---

[4]Theodore Kohers, "The Effect of Multinational Operations on the Cost of Equity Capital: An Empirical Study," *Management International Review* (1975).

It is quite apparent from the preceding discussion in this section that risk may not be perceived as greater for a multinational firm than for a domestic company, but it definitely can take many more forms. It follows that a decision to commit capital internationally deserves careful analysis. Techniques to effectively determine the worth of a capital expenditure proposal have been the subject of many books and papers. Brill surveyed the range of techniques in practice and presented an approach to treat subjective data that possesses certain desirable properties:[5]

1   It summarizes relevant investment decision information in a single figure.
2   It is useful for all types of proposals.
3   It permits appraisal in terms of a single set of standards.
4   It provides an easily computed index.
5   It is easily understood.
6   It is adjustable to allow for ranges of uncertainty.

A shortcoming of discounted cash flow calculations is that the discount rates are often adjusted with "not totally rational" values for risk. These values are arrived at by conventional approaches to risk analysis, which include sensitivity studies, adjustments to venture worth criteria, and the *three-level estimate* method. In sensitivity studies, the effects of unit changes in the many parameters governing the profitability of a contemplated venture are determined to establish which parameters are most significant. Management must subjectively evaluate the relevance of the variables, because the likelihood of their deviations is unknown. Adjustments to venture worth criteria to reflect levels of risk are based on the theory that the risk incurred is related to the rewards expected. Results can be inconsistent, and recognition of risk in computing cash flows is more effective. In the three-level estimate approach, optimistic, pessimistic and most likely cases are developed and intuitively assigned probabilities of occurrence. The analysis is treated as decision under risk to arrive at an expected value of investment worth for venture analysis. The subjectivity of the probability designations, in addition to the omission of the dimension of variability, leads to rejection of this approach in risk analysis for investments as well as project management.

The limitations of the techniques discussed above are better overcome by more advanced techniques that develop distributions of return through Monte Carlo simulation (see the appendix to this chapter). To overcome the requirement for knowledge of the distribution of each variable in the analysis, Brill proposes a method utilizing reasonable estimates of the parameter distributions, thereby validly incorporating the risk dimension in venture analysis.[6] The technique relies on the assumptions that venture analysis variables can be described by a beta distribution with ranges usually reliably obtained from experts representing a 95% confidence interval. Although still subjective owing to the very nature of the task of prediction, the method is rational and useful and meets the guidelines presented earlier. Major banks readily volunteer expertise and information on domestic and international banking and financial matters as part of their marketing approach to attract new customers.

---

[5]Martin Brill, *An Approach to Risk Analysis in the Evaluation of Capital Ventures* (Philadelphia: Drexel Institute of Technology, 1966).
   [6]Ibid.

Such expertise, combined with a firm's knowledge of its own business, could well be applied in the simulation approach.

REPATRIATION VERSUS REINVESTMENT OF PROFITS

The decision process of whether to repatriate dividends or reinvest in the foreign subsidiary requires examination beyond the original commitment in terms of what is needed to protect or strengthen the original investment. This is, of course, based heavily on the reassessment of the subsidiary's market position for an extended period of time, nominally 10 years, and the related investment alternatives.[7] Considerations generally include ultimate remittability of the required investment expenditures. Rather than measure returns only in terms of the local currency, inflows available to the investor are a key consideration. Inflation and money valuation forecasts play an important part in the long-range reinvestment plan. As indicated by recent moves of Japanese and German manufacturers to build plants in the United States, this country holds a favored position in the struggle against inflationary effects. For this reason, United States–based MNCs will also lean toward expansion and improvement of domestic plants while maintaining sales and service branches overseas.

The important judgment in formulating and screening alternatives is to determine whether each alternative will remain attractive if host country restrictions become more stringent.

Another factor that influences the remittance decision and, therefore, the reinvestment decision of many multinational companies is taxation. Tax objectives vary and can reflect varying emphasis among companies. Firms that are most tax conscious will make every attempt to minimize the corporations' total tax burden and give this consideration higher priority than any others in the investment decision. This would come about by modeling the tax situation after the other project-related details and projections are evaluated. Alternatively, the tax burden might be given equal weight with one or two other factors, such as the risk of leaving funds abroad or the subsidiary's requirements for funds. The latter point is considered in relation to the availability and cost of funds locally.

Some companies consider paying taxes to the United States on repatriated dividends a fact of doing business, and no effort is made to delay or avoid this obligation. However, they do try to avoid penalty taxes for paying too high or too low a dividend, as might occur in Germany.[8] A few corporations, because of the minimal amounts involved, assign a low level of importance to any tax consideration relative to foreign dividends.

Foreign dividends established to suit the corporate plan regarding taxes, reinvestment, or dividends to stockholders are only one part of the total fund remittance framework. Other mechanisms include management fees, technical service fees, royalties, interest on parent loans, principal repayments on such loans, license fees, commissions on exports, and payments for merchandise obtained from the parent.[9] Basic decisions regarding fund remittances are centralized, with the goal of maximiz-

[7]David B. Zenoff and Jack Zwick, *International Financial Management* (Englewood Cliffs, N.J.: Prentice Hall, 1969), pp. 148, 149.

[8]Ibid., p. 415.

[9]See Eiteman and Stonehill, *Multinational Business Finance*, p. 308.

ing corporate worldwide placement of funds. Perception of the overall needs of the entire corporate network and availability of the necessary financial data can only occur at a central office. As indicated earlier, the corporate prerogative to control and dispense funds can be affected by the policy of a host country. This is increasingly evident for all forms of fund remittance, including pricing, as active surveillance of invoices by customs agents is conducted.

STATEMENTS NO. 8 AND NO. 52
OF THE FINANCIAL ACCOUNTING STANDARDS BOARD

The foreign-investment decision setting is clouded by the existence of FASB rulings on foreign exchange translation of the financial statements of an MNC's subsidiaries. FASB statement no. 8, "Accounting for the Translation of Foreign Currency Transactions and Foreign Currency Financial Statements," was implemented January 1, 1976. The mandatory guidelines of FASB statement no. 8 (and its successor, FASB-52) had three major effects:

1 It required that foreign transactions be handled using both a current rate and a historical rate; the former is used for real assets carried at market value, cash, accounts receivable, and *all* liabilities; the latter is used for all real assets carried at original cost.

2 It required that all foreign exchange gains and losses be reflected in net income *during the period* in which the change in the exchange rate occurred.

3 The use of reserve accounts and the distinction between realized and unrealized foreign exchange gains and losses were eliminated.

In viewing the impact of FASB no. 8; it is important to identify three types of exposure faced by the MNC: (1) translation exposure, (2) transaction exposure, and (3) economic exposure. Translation exposure is the exposure of an MNC to foreign-exchange loss as the net assets of its foreign subsidiary are translated into the home-country currency. Transaction exposure is the exposure of an MNC to foreign-exchange loss due to a contractual obligation of its foreign subsidiary to deliver goods or services in the future. Economic exposure is the risk of loss to the MNC due to the long-term impact of foreign-exchange fluctuations on the valuation of the corporation. The FASB statements address only the first two of these exposures, while the third is also of significant importance to multinational firms.

FASB no. 8 was a highly controversial accounting standard because reported income showed great volatility due to the requirement that all translation gains and losses had to be shown in the current income statement. FASB no. 8 was replaced by FASB no. 52, "Foreign Currency Translation," in December 1981. FASB no. 52 imposes two major changes: (1) a mandatory use of an all-current rate method and (2) a differing treatment for transaction and translation gains and losses. The first revision eliminates the use of historical exchange rates in translating financial statements. The second revision would charge only *transaction* gains and losses to current income, whereas *translation* gains and losses would be handled in a manner akin to charging these to a stockholders' equity reserve account. Financial managers should be aware of the existence of such rulings by the FASB and they should incorporate the impact of such rulings into the capital project evaluation process.

SUMMARY

This chapter surveys the important area of capital budgeting for the multinational firm. The new dimensions and variables present in the international environment are outlined and discussed. A seven-step approach is suggested to evaluate and select capital projects for the multinational firm. The important area of the cost of capital for the multinational firm is discussed next. Following this, repatriation versus reinvestment of profits is addressed, since this trade-off is an important phase in the strategic planning area for the multinational firm. Finally, the impact of FASB no. 8 and FASB no. 52 was outlined.

The appendix that follows illustrates many of the techniques and concepts discussed in the chapter by showing a Monte Carlo simulation model for capital budgeting for the multinational firm.

QUESTIONS
PROBLEMS

1. Discuss at least four major risks that multinational firms face in their capital budgeting activities.
2. Outline a general approach to capital budgeting for the multinational firm.
3. Discuss several "operating strategies" that multinational firms can use to reduce foreign exchange risks.
4. Discuss several strategies that can be implemented to reduce the impact of inflation on the multinational firm.
5. Mention several characteristics that could point to greater risk of expropriation for the multinational firm.
6. Based on the simulation model presented in the appendix:
   (a) Outline the suggested two-stage approach for capital investment evaluation by the multinational firm.
   (b) For both the parent company and the subsidiary, list the major cash inflows and outflows.
   (c) List the major "endogenous variables" that will be used to evaluate the rank capital projects.
   (d) Discuss why both the parent company and the subsidiary will utilize their respective risk-free rates in conjunction with the simulation.
   (e) Discuss how sensitivity analysis would be performed in conjunction with the simulation and why this is important.

REFERENCES

Alexander, Gordon J., Cheol S. Eun, and S. Janakiramana. "Asset Pricing and Dual Listing on Foreign Capital Markets: A Note." *Journal of Finance* (March 1987).

Anvari M. "Efficient Scheduling of Cross-Border Cash Transfers." *Financial Management* (Summer 1986).

Bodurtha, James N., Jr., and Georges R. Courtadon. "Efficiency Tests of the Foreign Currency Options Market." *Journal of Finance* (July 1986).

Carter, E. Eugene, and Rita M. Rodriguez. *International Financial Management*, 2nd ed. Englewood Cliffs, N.J.: Prentice Hall, 1979.

Corkay, Albert, Gabriel Hawawini, and Pierre Michel. "Seasonality in the Risk-Return Relationship: Some International Evidence." *Journal of Finance* (March 1987).

Einzig, P. *Foreign Exchange Crises*. New York: Macmillan Publishing Co., Inc., 1970.

Eun, Cheol S., and Bruce G. Resnick. "Exchange Rate Uncertainty, Forward Contracts, and International Portfolio Selection." *Journal of Finance* (March 1988).

Feierabend, I. "Conflict, Crisis, and Collision: A Study of International Stability." *Psychology Today* (May 1968).

Finnerty, John D. "Zero Coupon Bond Arbitrage: An Illustration of the Regulatory Dialectic at Work." *Financial Management* (Winter 1985).

Flood, Eugene, J., and Donald R. Lessard. "On the Measurement of Operating Exposure to Exchange Rates: A Conceptual Approach." *Financial Management* (Spring 1986).

Grauer, Robert R., and Nils H. Hakansson. "Gains from International Diversification: 1968–85 Returns on Portfolios of Stocks and Bonds." *Journal of Finance* (July 1987).

Hodder, James E. "Evaluation of Manufacturing Investments: A Comparison of U.S. and Japanese Practices." *Financial Management* (Spring 1986).

Howe, John S. and Kathryn Kelm. "The Stock Price Impacts of Overseas Listings." *Financial Management* (Autumn 1987).

Huang, Roger D. "Expectations of Exchange Rates and Differential Inflation Rates: Further Evidence on Purchasing Power Parity in Efficient Markets." *Journal of Finance* (March 1987).

Kaufold, Howard, and Michael Smerlock. "Managing Corporate Exchange and Interest Rate Exposure." *Financial Management* (Autumn 1986).

Kester, W. Carl. "Capital and Ownership Structure: A Comparison of United States and Japanese Manufacturing Corporations." *Financial Management* (Spring 1986).

Kidwell, David S., M. Wayne Marr, and G. Rodney Thompson. "Eurodollar Bonds: Alternative Financing for U.S. Companies." *Financial Management* (Winter 1985).

Koveos, Peter, and Bruce Seifert. "Purchasing Power Parity and Black Markets." *Financial Management* (Autumn 1985).

Mauriel, J. J. "Evaluation and Control of Overseas Operations." *Management Accounting* (May 1969), 35–39.

Misawa, Mitsuru. "Financing Japanese Investments in the United States: Case Studies of a Large and a Medium-Sized Firm." *Financial Management* (Winter 1985).

Peterson, David R., and Alan L. Tucker. "Implied Spot Rates as Predictors of Currency Returns: A Note." *Journal of Finance* (March 1988).

Robbins, Sidney M., and Robert B. Stobaugh. *Money in the Multinational Enterprise*. New York: Basic Books, Inc., 1973.

Rutenberg, David P. "Maneuvering Liquid Assets in a Multinational Company." *Management Science* (June 1970).

Shapiro, Alan C. "Capital Budgeting for the Multinational Corporation." *Financial Management* (Spring, 1978), 7–16.

_____. *Multinational Financial Management*. Boston: Allyn and Bacon, Inc., 1988.

_____. "Currency Risk and Country Risk in International Banking." *Journal of Finance* (July 1985).

Shastri, Kuldeep, and Kiskore Tandon. "Valuation of Foreign Currency Options: Some Empirical Tests." *Journal of Financial and Quantitative Analysis* (June 1986).

Singer, H. W. *International Development: Growth and Change*. New York: McGraw-Hill Book Company, 1964.

So, Jacky C. "The Distribution of Foreign Exchange Price Changes: Trading Day Effects and Risk Measurement—A Comment." *Journal of Finance* (March 1987).

Solnik, Bruno. "Using Financial Prices to Test Exchange Rate Models: A Note." *Journal of Finance* (March 1987).

Stobaugh, R. B. "How to Analyze Foreign Investment Climates." *Harvard Business Review* (September–October 1969), 100–108.

_____. *Multinational Financial Management*. Boston: Allyn & Bacon, Inc., 1982.

Stonehill, Arthur D., and Leonard Nathanson. "Capital Budgeting and the Multinational Corporation." *California Management Review* (Summer 1968).

Sweeney, Richard J. "Beating the Foreign Exchange Market." *Journal of Finance* (July 1986).

Tho, D. Chinhyung, Cheol S. Eun, and Lemma W. Sinbeat. "International Arbitrage Pricing Theory. An Empirical Investigation." *Journal of Finance* (June 1986).

Wolff, Christian C. "Forward Foreign Exchange Rates, Expected Spot Rates, and Premia: A Signal Extraction Approach." *Journal of Finance* (June 1987).

Zenoff, David B., and Jack Zwick. *International Financial Management*. Englewood Cliffs, N.J.: Prentice Hall, 1969.

_____. *International Financial Management*. Boston: Warren, Gorham, and Lamont, 1979.

APPENDIX:
SIMULATION-BASED MULTINATIONAL
CAPITAL BUDGETING APPROACH[10]

This appendix outlines a Monte Carlo simulation model for multinational capital budgeting. The model has been made as general as possible while not sacrificing ease of understanding and use. To provide adequate information and a flexible analysis, a two-stage simulation is recommended. First, each investment opportunity is evaluated in a uninational setting by the subsidiary proposing it. If it passes the first screening, it is then analyzed from the parent's point of view. This joint evaluation is of paramount importance. Indeed, a plant built in a foreign country can be a very profitable investment in itself, but currency devaluations, tax differentials, and/or quantitative controls can make it significantly less attractive to the parent company. The proposed model handles the cases where the parent is considering a joint venture as well as a 100% participation.

The model provides an operational, theoretically sound, and mathematically powerful capital project ranking methodology wherein project uncertainty as well as environmental uncertainty (including all major international variables) are incorporated into the analysis. Based on this ranking of investment proposals (consisting of empirical risk-return characteristics for several relevant evaluation criteria), both the subsidiary and parent can select the set of projects that best meets their risk-return preferences, financing availabilities, and objectives for synergy considering interactions between current operations and new projects. The model's two-stage simulation approach utilizing all relevant international variables is consistent with prior research in the international capital budgeting area. The model focuses well on the behavioral theory of the MNC postulated by Stonehill and Nathanson,[11] wherein they suggest an independent financial evaluation of projects by both the parent and subsidiary.

_____

[10] The model presented in this appendix is based on André Fourcans and Thomas J. Hindelang, "Capital Budgeting for the Multinational Firm: A Simulation Approach," paper presented at The Financial Management Association Conference, October, 1975.

[11] A. I. Stonehill and L. Nathanson, "Capital Budgeting and the Multinational Corporation," *California Management Review* (Summer 1968), 39–54.

Further, the model avoids the serious disadvantages cited by the authors that prevail when a risk-adjusted discount rate is used to reflect political and foreign exchange uncertainties. Last, the model provides helpful information in implementing the "uncertainty absorption" program suggested by the authors, as well as in arriving at an operational approach for charging each period with the cost of such a program. The model capitalizes on the strengths of the most sophisticated approach recommended by Stobaugh[12] in analyzing foreign investment climates, namely, that of risk analysis, wherein the full range of international uncertainty and variable interactions are incorporated rather than just the "optimistic," "most likely," and "pessimistic" estimates. In addition, the recommended model is not burdened with the assumption of independence of variables as are some models.[13] Finally, the model addresses the important cultural, economic, and political aspects of the capital investment decision setting that Mauriel[14] points to as differentiating uninational from multinational operations.

Subsidiary Simulation

The subsidiary's evaluation of a given investment proposal utilizes mainly the direct project costs and revenues discussed immediately above. The analysis uses a uninational framework and considers the parent mainly as a source of funds to finance accepted projects. Furthermore, in order not to unduly complicate matters, it is assumed that the subsidiary only sells and buys inside the host country (this assumption could be relaxed, if desired).

The technical details of this stage of the simulation are presented in three illustrations. Table 26A–1 lists the relevant cash inflows and outflows for the subsidiary. Table 26A–2 defines the variables (both exogenous and endogenous) and formulates the identities of the simulation model. Figure 26A–1 shows a flow chart of this part of the simulation.

As we can see from Table 26A–2, the main endogenous variables that determine an investment proposal's attractiveness are the total revenue, total costs, net income after taxes, and net cash inflow each year. From these measures the payback, NPV, and IRR are computed for each simulated observation of the proposal's useful life.

Table 26A – 1   Subsidiary Cash Flows

INFLOWS	OUTFLOWS
Revenue from sales	Initial outlay
Salvage value	Financing costs
	Operating costs
	Host country taxes

---

[12]R. B. Stobaugh, "How to Analyze Foreign Investment Climates," *Harvard Business Review* (September–October 1969), 100–108.

[13]J. Chambers and S. Mullick, "Investment Decision Making in a Multinational Enterprise," *Management Accounting*, (August 1971), 44–59.

[14]J. J. Mauriel, "Evaluation and Control of Overseas Operations," *Management Accounting* (May 1969), 35–39.

Table 26A – 2 Variables of the Subsidiary Simulation Model

PARAMETERS

SP_t	= selling price per unit in year t
KS	= subsidiary risk-free rate
DR_t	= depreciation rate for year t
MAX	= total number of simulation runs to be considered

EXOGENOUS VARIABLES

Stochastic variables with known probability distributions:

MG_t	= market growth rate for each year t
MS_t	= initial market size in number of units
SM_t	= share of the market for each year t
INV	= initial investment required by the proposal
N	= useful life of investment
FC_t	= total operating fixed costs in year t
VC_t	= variable operating costs per unit in year t
IC_t	= interest cost associated with the project in year t
OC_t	= other project related costs in year t
WC_t	= working-capital needs of the project in year t
TR_t	= tax rate for host country tax on project returns in year t
IR_t	= rate of inflation in year t
WAR_t	= probability that a war will break out in the host country during year t
$LWAR_t$	= % of loss suffered by the firm if a war occurs in year t
EX_t	= probability that expropriation will take place in host country in year t
LEX_t	= % of loss suffered by the firm if expropriation takes place in host country during year t

ENDOGENOUS VARIABLES

$USAL_t$	= unit sales generated by the proposal in year t
REV_t	= total revenue generated by the proposal in year t
TC_t	= total costs associated with the project in year t
TAX_t	= host country tax on taxable income generated by project in year t
$NIAT_t$	= net income after host country tax generated by project in year t
NCI_t	= net cash inflow generated by project in year t
BV_t	= book value of the project at the end of year t
SV_t	= salvage value of the project at the end of year t
$TINF_n$	= terminal inflow if expropriation or war occurs during year n
$PAYB_m$	= payback period for the investment on the mth simulation run
NPV_m	= net present value for the investment on the mth simulation run
IRR_m	= discounted rate of return for the investment on the mth simulation run

IDENTITIES AND OPERATING EQUATIONS

BV_0	$= INV$	
DEP_t	$= (DR_t)(BV_{t-1})$	
BV_t	$= BV_{t-1} - DEP_t$	
MS_t	$= (MS_{t-1})(1 + MG_{t-1})$	$t = 2, 3, \ldots, N$
$USAL_t$	$= (MS_t)(SM_t)$	$t = 1, 2, \ldots, N$
REV_t	$= (SP_t)(USAL_t)$	$t = 1, 2, \ldots, N$
TVC_t	$= (VC_t)(USAL_t)$	$t = 1, 2, \ldots, N$
TC_t	$= TVC_t + FC_t + OC_t + DEP_t$	$t = 1, 2, \ldots, N$

$$
\begin{array}{lll}
\text{TAX}_t &= (\text{TR}_t)(\text{REV}_t - \text{TC}_t) & t = 1, 2, \ldots, N \\
\text{NIAT}_t &= \text{REV}_t - \text{TC}_t - \text{TAX}_t & t = 1, 2, \ldots, N \\
\text{NCI}_t &= \text{NIAT}_t + \text{DEP}_t - \text{WC}_t & t = 1, 2, \ldots, N \\
\text{SV}_n &= (\text{SV}_{n-1} - \text{DEP}_n)(1 + \text{IR}_n)
\end{array}
$$

If expropriation (EX_n) occurs in year n, determine loss suffered (LEX_n), then

$$
\text{TINF}_n = (1 - \text{LEX}_n)(\text{SV}_n + \text{NCI}_n)
$$

If war (WAR_n) occurs in year n, determine loss suffered (LWAR_n), then

$$
\text{TINF}_n = (1 - \text{LWAR}_n)(\text{SV}_n + \text{NCI}_n)
$$

PAYB_m = period i such that

$$
\text{INV} - \sum_{i=1}^{i} (\text{NCI}_t + \text{IC}_t) = 0
$$

NPV_m is determined in the usual way:

$$
\text{NPV}_m = \sum_{i=1}^{n} \frac{\dot{\text{NCI}}_t}{(1 + \text{KS})^t} - \text{INV}
$$

IRR_m = discount rate r such that

$$
\sum_{i=1}^{N} \frac{\text{NCI}_t}{(1 + r)^t} - \text{INV} = 0
$$

Empirical distributions are derived for each of these three methods based on all simulation runs. Of course, other criteria (e.g., discounted payback, equivalent annual savings, or growth in earnings per share) could be easily built into the model, depending on the needs of the individual firm.

Based on the empirical distributions described above, summary statistics (the expected value, standard deviation, measures of skewness, and so on) are computed and probability statements can be made about the likelihood that various ranges are achieved by each measure. The subsidiary will then have the necessary data to rank the proposal relative to all others under consideration (which have been run through the simulation) on the basis of its risk preferences and its evaluation of the risk-return trade-offs of the various proposals. Given this ranking of proposals, a recommendation will be made to the parent company concerning the set of proposals that the subsidiary feels should be adopted, depending on availability of capital.

Two details should be mentioned about the subsidiary simulation. First, the international variables dealing with inflation risks, expropriation risks, risk of war, and taxation have been built into the subsidiary simulation. The mechanics of handling inflation are discussed shortly and the treatment of host country taxation is straightforward. The occurrence of expropriation or war was obtained through a Monte Carlo determination in each year of the proposal's useful life. When it is established that either of these two events has taken place, the associated percentage loss is generated from the appropriate input distribution. This result is used to derive the terminal cash inflow of the project as a proportion of current salvage value, the yearly cash inflow, and working capital accumulated to date because of the project.

Second, the risk-free rate relevant to the subsidiary company (which will usually be different from the risk-free rate for the parent) is used in the computation of the

NPV and as the relevant hurdle rate for the final comparison in the IRR method. More will be said later about the risk-free rate.

Parent Company Simulation

The parent company takes a more global view in its evaluation of potential projects. It utilizes the empirical data relative to the project per se (i.e., project net income after taxes and net cash inflows) developed by the subsidiary simulation but also incorporates the critical international variables associated with the transfer of funds. These additional risks and uncertainties are built into the framework so that the parent can adequately assess the situation before it commits funds to a given project in a specific country. Table 26A–3 shows the cash flows from the parent's point of view.

Because the parent company simulation model closely parallels that of the subsidiary company shown in Table 26A–2 and Figure 26A–1, they are not repeated. It should be mentioned that the identities and operating equations for the parent show that all cash flows which cross international boundaries are subject to foreign exchange adjustment, international taxation, and quantitative controls. In addition, the benefits to the parent company are dependent upon the direct savings in the operations, which are a result of the project as well as the dividends, profits repatriated, royalties, and interest received from the subsidiary tied to the project. Both international and home country tax effects are taken into account in computing the net returns to the parent.

The same measures as before (i.e., internal rate of return, net present value, and payback) provide the criteria in the parent's evaluation of the worth of the project. Like each subsidiary, the parent can now rank all proposals on a worldwide basis using these empirical distributions and their associated statistics. The parent company's risk preferences and its evaluation of risk-return trade-offs of various proposals come into the analysis here. The parent company uses the relevant risk-free rate in the evaluation criteria.

Mechanics of the Simulation

As noted, the simulation is designed to be flexible and complete, yet not overly demanding on the user relative to data input requirements. However, it was also pointed out that the more precise the input specifications are, the more exact and helpful will be the results generated by the simulation. Thus, balancing these trade-offs, the decision maker is asked to specify the exogenous variables as accurately

Table 26A – 3   Parent Company Cash Flows

INFLOWS	OUTFLOWS
Direct savings generated by the project	Equity funds provided
Profit repatriated	Loans provided
Dividends	Labor, material, and other costs
Royalties and fees	Transportation costs
Interest and loan repayments	Taxes paid on dividends, royalties, and profit repatriated

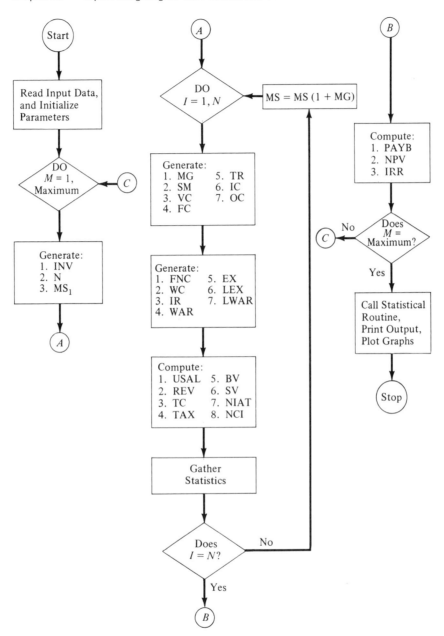

FIGURE 26A – 1   Flow Chart of Subsidiary Simulation

as he can for as many years into the future as possible. It is realized, of course, that the farther into the future a user must estimate distributions, the greater is the degree of uncertainty. Offsetting this shortcoming are two countermeasures:

1 The discounting process weighs more distant years less significantly.
2 Sensitivity analysis is used to determine the impact of changes in the input variables on the decision criteria.

To make the variable estimation process as painless as possible, the user is given many alternatives to the method of specifying inputs:

1 The user can provide the parameters of any well-known distribution (e.g., binomial, uniform, normal, beta, and so on).
2 The user can input any discrete distribution that he or she feels is appropriate.
3 The user can specify that the distribution is a composite of various distributions.

Inflation is dealt with in two ways. First, it can be taken into consideration in the estimation of the exogenous variables by the user specifying a different distribution for each year of the anticipated useful life of the project. Second, the distribution can be shifted to the right, every year, by the expected percent inflation. This operation can be done for selling price, variable cost, and so on. If a single distribution is specified for all periods, the inflation factor is built into the simulation and taken into consideration in the yearly revision of the distributions for the exogenous variables.

One of the important strengths of the model is the way in which it handles interdependencies among related variables. Some interrelationships can be reflected exclusively by means of an informed and careful specification of the input distribution's exogenous variables, whereas the simulation model has built in self-checks to handle other dependencies adequately. Examples of the former strategy would be where the user is reminded of the fact that expected high rates of inflation in any given year must be associated with larger expected changes in foreign exchange rates for that year; further, dividend rates and the percent of profits repatriated both should reflect those risks associated with a given host country—inflation risk, war and expropriation risks, taxation policies, and quantitative controls. The technique, using built-in checks, is necessitated by the fact that only after the value of an exogenous variable is generated by the simulation will the appropriate domain for a related variable be determined. For example, there is a trade-off between fixed and variable costs associated with producing a product—it is reasonable to assume that a high level of fixed costs is generally associated with a lower variable cost per unit; thus, the model restricts the feasible values of the variable-cost distribution to the lower tail whenever the value of total fixed cost generated comes from the upper tail, and vice versa. Similar relationships are built in to reflect the trade-offs between market size and market growth rate and among selling price, demand relationships, and market share.

One final important point should be mentioned. Because of the two-stage analysis of investment proposals—first by the subsidiary and then by the parent—two different risk-free rates are used. The subsidiary uses its own rate to determine the proposal's relative ranking, and whether the project should be recommended to the parent for acquisition. In a similar vein, the parent uses the risk-free rate of its home country to determine whether funds should be committed to the product. Such an approach gives a double, somewhat independent, more stringent screening of proposals. They must survive both cutoff points to be adopted by the multinational firm.

It must be strongly emphasized that both the parent and subsidiary simulations use the relevant risk-free rate (rather than the cost of capital or a risk-adjusted discount rate) in computing any project's net present value. Indeed, in both stages of the simulation, the discounting operation must reflect discounting only for futurity or the time value of money and not for the specific riskiness of the project under consideration. The risk element of each investment proposal is ascertained in the simulation runs themselves. As we have mentioned before in Chapter 21, and as Lewellen and Long point out, to discount cash flows on each simulation run "at a rate in excess of the default-free rate" (e.g., the risk-free rate) would impose improper double adjustment for uncertainty upon the project.[15] Thus, all that is required is to discount these empirical cash flows at the risk-free rate to arrive at an empirical NPV distribution which contains valuable information for both the expected return and the riskiness of the project under consideration.

Validation and Analysis of the Model's Output

The following discussion is aimed at providing insight to the users of the proposed simulation model in terms of interpreting the final results and utilizing them in the capital investment decision process. Several authors have pointed to a gap between theory and practice: Bower and Lessard[16] found in their empirical work that simulation models were not used because of "the inability to translate results into simple measures executives could reconcile with their intuition and experience and use, with other measures, to make a judgment"; Lewellen and Long[17] point to this problem by asking: "What do you do with that impressive distribution of possible outcomes once you have simulated? How should the information be digested?" Mao and Helliwell found that their three sample firms had difficulty in conceptualizing and quantifying risk-return trade-offs.[18]

The simulation methodology not only permits managers to evaluate and compare the expected performance of different potential investments, but also presents an analytical approach to determine relationships among project variables and international factors.

The main output consists of the two empirical profiles of net present value and internal rate of return for both the parent company and the subsidiary. Relevant statistical measures of central tendency variability and skewness are computed for each empirical distribution.

Figure 26A–2 gives an example of the main output. Curve I represents the IRR profile for the subsidiary, whereas curve II is for the parent. As can be quickly noted in this specific case, the IRR for the parent is everywhere lower than the subsidiary's

[15] W. G. Lewellen and M. S. Long, "Simulation vs. Single-Value Estimates in Capital Expenditure Analysis," *Decision Sciences*, 3, no. 4 (October 1972), 19–33.

[16] D. R. Lessard and R. S. Bower, "An Operational Approach to Risk Screening," *Journal of Finance* (May 1973), 245–247.

[17] W. G. Lewellen and M. S. Long, "Reply to Comments by Bower and Lessard and Gentry," *Decision Sciences*, 4, no. 4 (October 1973), 575–576.

[18] J. C. T. Mao and J. F. Helliwell, "Investment Decision Under Uncertainty: Theory and Practice," *Journal of Finance*, 24, no. 2 (May 1969), 323–338.

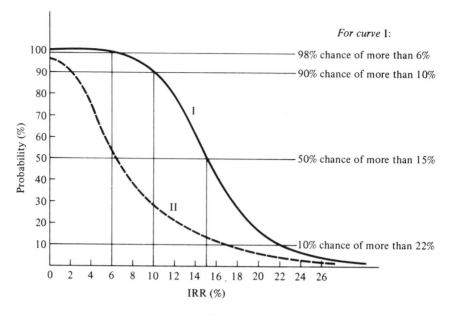

FIGURE 26A – 2

IRR. However, this need not always be the case (it would depend on the influence of such factors as foreign exchange rates, tax differentials, and the relevant risk-free rates). The purpose of these two profiles is to make sure that the worthiness of the investment can be evaluated by all groups (parent's managers and possible partners in the country of the investment) with their possibly different aspirations. Therefore, an investment is considered attractive by a particular group only if the proposal meets the acceptability criteria of that group.

How are these profiles used? As demonstrated by curve I of Figure 26A–2, there is a 98% probability that an IRR greater than or equal to 6% can be obtained, a 90% probability of the IRR exceeding 10%, a 50% probability of the IRR exceeding 15%, and a 10% probability of the IRR exceeding 22%. We know that the investment will be worthwhile (from the point of view of the subsidiary) if the IRR is at least equal to its risk-free rate. If we assume a subsidiary's risk-free rate of 10%, the chance of having an IRR $\geq$ 10% is 90 out of 100. The decision makers will have to decide whether they are ready to take the risk implied: 90 chances out of 100 of having a "profitable" investment, but 10 out of 100 of "losing money." The same analysis needs to be done with curve II from the point of view of the parent.

The statistics computed from the empirical distributions enable the subsidiary and the parent to evaluate risk-return trade-offs among various alternatives available. Furthermore, the analysis of the output data is rendered more sophisticated by the following elaborations. A statistical analysis subroutine using the multiple ranking criteria discussed by Kleijnen, Naylor, and Seaks analyzes and determines the order of the project desirability and whether statistically significant differences exist among the ranked projects.[19] The analysis is performed by each subsidiary and by the parent for

[19]J. P. C. Kleijnen, T. H. Naylor and T. G. Seaks, "The Use of Multiple Ranking Procedures to Analyze Simulations of Management Systems," *Management Sciences* (February 1972), 245–257.

all projects considered by the multinational firm. Such results are invaluable when the firms are faced with capital rationing and multiple, competing investment opportunities and risks.

Another significant benefit from the simulation approach is that sensitivity analysis can be performed. Decision makers can change the distribution of each exogenous variable one at a time or several at a time and have a good understanding of the importance each variable has on the attractiveness of the investment. It allows an increased comprehension of the relationships among variables and their impact on the decision process. This information is extremely valuable, especially for the evaluation of the international variables, in particular for foreign exchange rates, which are difficult enough to forecast. If, for example, the final results are found to be affected very little by changes in currency values, it is clear that the uncertainty of the investment is greatly reduced. On the contrary, high sensitivity to foreign exchange rates would warn the decision maker to give special forecasting attention to this variable and to consider the addition of an annual cost for hedging against this risk (i.e., a cost for "uncertainty absorption" discussed earlier).

Lease Analysis:
Lease/Buy and Lease/Sell

$$27$$

Leasing is a process whereby the owner of a particular asset (lessor) enters into an agreement (lease) with the user (lessee) so that the latter can use the asset for a specified period of time. The lessee pays a certain amount (lease payment) to the lessor for the use of the asset.

Real estate still constitutes the largest single category of leased items, but numerous types of equipment, such as airplanes, railroad cars, ships, specialized equipment for farming and the textile and oil industries, and computers, are being leased. Almost without exception, any type of equipment that a business can purchase, it can also lease. Within the consumer sector, leasing of durable goods, such as automobiles, washers, dryers, refrigerators, televisions, furniture, and the like, has also been increasing rapidly. The leasing industry has experienced a dynamic growth period and is becoming increasingly important as a means of financing for business, consumers, and to some extent, government operations.

ADVANTAGES OF LEASING

From the viewpoint of the lessee, there may be many advantages to leasing versus purchasing. Naturally, a primary consideration is cost. The cost of a lease may be more or less than the cost to purchase and may differ among lessees. For example, if a firm has been running at a very low profit, it might not be able to enjoy the tax benefits of accelerated cost recovery which are associated with the purchase of assets. A lessor could, however, take full advantage of the tax benefits and pass them along to the lessee by means of reduced lease payments. Also, the lessor may enjoy economies of scale which could make leasing a preferred alternative to purchasing.

Aside from the financial question, many other considerations become important in deciding whether to lease or to purchase. The general advantages, inherent to all leases, are described in the paragraphs that follow.

560

1   Leases provide an alternative source of obtaining facilities and equipment for firms that have limited capital budgets. In fact, capital projects can be analyzed on the basis of ownership or leasing and the respective NPV or IRR calculated for each alternative. Such a listing would provide wide visibility with respect to alternative capital acquisition plans. Some assets may be purchased and others leased, with the goal of selecting the most profitable combination.

2   Frequently, equipment may be leased over a longer period than would be available through conventional financing. Usually, equipment loans run for a period that is substantially shorter than the economic life of the asset, whereas leases can be obtained for nearly the total length of the asset's life. This spreads the cost over a longer time period.

3   Leases are normally quoted at fixed rates or may be tailored to meet the cash budgets of the lessee. This avoids the risks associated with short- or intermediate-term financing and refinancing. Recall that many intermediate-term loans have balloon repayment features, in which the bulk of the principal is due at the end of the loan and, if the firm maintains its credit rating, forms the basis for a new loan. Such refining exposes the firm to added risk, as interest rates may change.

4   Leasing may conserve existing sources of credit for other uses and usually does not restrict a firm's borrowing capacity. Many loan indentures do restrict additional borrowing. Further, some firms which cannot raise the needed capital to purchase assets due to marginal credit standings may be able to lease.

5   Leasing generally provides 100% financing, since a down payment is not required.

6   Leasing is quick and flexible as opposed to raising funds and making capital expenditures. The restrictive covenants usually found in loan indenture agreements are generally not included in lease agreements. Further, lease terms and options can be tailored to the specific need of the lessee. For example, lease payment schedules may be arranged to meet the seasonal cash flows of the lessee.

7   The total acquisition costs, including sales taxes, delivery and installation charges, and so on, may all be included in the lease payments. These front-end costs may be substantial and thereby result in heavy initial cash outflows if assets are purchased. This can be avoided through leasing.

8   Leasing can assist the process of cash budgeting by permitting accurate prediction of cash needs. This would be a desirable feature over short-term loans but less so over bond financing, which is long term.

9   The entire lease payment is tax deductible to the lessee. If land is involved in the lease, this is especially important, because land may not be depreciated.

10   Leasing avoids the costs of underwriting and floating new issues of stocks and bonds. Also, the public disclosure surrounding such offerings is avoided when a firm does not have to go to the capital markets to secure funds.

11   Leasing may avoid the risk of obsolescence. In fields that are changing rapidly, such as computer technology, ownership may be a distinct disadvantage when new products are introduced. But risk avoidance has a price, which will be factored into the cost of the lease by the lessor.

LEASE VERSUS PURCHASE: SOME KEY VARIABLES

1   *Depreciation.* The tax effects of depreciation represent an advantage of ownership that is lost under leasing. Since lease analysis is carried through on a cash flow basis, depreciation represents a tax savings, and accelerated depreciation, all things equal, tends to swing the decision in the direction of ownership by increasing cash flows in the early years. The terminology of accelerated depreciation has been changed by the Economic Recovery Act of 1981 to the accelerated cost recovery system (ACRS). The Tax Reform Act of 1986 further revised ACRS as described in Chapter 4.

2   *Obsolescence.* High rates of obsolescence (for instance, in computers and calculating equipment) increase the risks of ownership. This tends to make leasing a more attractive alternative.

3   *Operating and maintenance charges.* These represent an expense of ownership, although the gross charge is reduced by tax shields. If the lessor assumes these expenses as part of the lease agreement, the situation may make leasing a more attractive alternative and may reduce the overall cost of acquiring the use of the asset. This will occur if the lessor can more cheaply maintain and/or operate the asset by reason of the economies of scale.

4   *Salvage or residual values.* After allowance for tax effects, residual values are an advantage of ownership lost under leasing. But salvage value is a highly uncertain value. High salvage values lower the costs of ownership. The problem is to forecast salvage within a reasonable range 5 or 10 years in the future. This is not an easy assignment. On the side of the lessor, salvage value reduces the cost of leasing. Under the pressure of negotiation, the lessor may transfer some of his or her uncertainties to the future; that is, the lessor might anticipate a higher residual to keep the lease payments down and win the contract. In fact, many leases depend on a significantly higher actual residual asset value than the amount established for purposes of depreciation to make their profit.

5   *Discount rate.* This is perhaps one of the most controversial features in lease evaluation. It can swing the decision one way or the other. Leasing analysis uses cash flows, and these extend over several fiscal periods. The cash flows, therefore, have to be discounted for the time value of money and for risk. But the risk associated with each of the cash flows of ownership may differ significantly. There are differing degrees of risk associated with sales, operating expenses, interest charges, and residuals. By contrast, once agreed upon, lease payments are usually fixed and certain. We would, therefore, not use the same discount rate on each cash flow. How, for example, should we discount the after-tax operating costs or the tax savings of depreciation? We discuss this problem later in the chapter.

6   *Length of lease.* The length of time for which the lessee is committed to the lease payments and the extent of the penalties for premature cancellation greatly affect the flexibility of the firm and the risk associated with the acceptance of the lease.

7   *Timing of lease payments.* Since the analysis uses a discounted cash flow approach, the timing of the lease payments (payable annually, semiannually, quarterly, or monthly) may, in a close situation, affect the decision. Similarly, the timing of lease payments, whether they are payable in advance or at the end of a designated period, must be considered.

8   *Tax effects.* In Chapter 4 we discuss the implications of taxation on the cash flows derived from capital investments. With respect to leasing, it is important to note that lease payments are fully tax deductible by the lessee, while the lessor enjoys the advantages of depreciation. But another factor must be considered. Can the firm fully utilize the tax benefits associated with accelerated depreciation, and finance charges? That is, does the firm have sufficient levels of income to make the deductions worthwhile? For example, in recent years capital-intensive industries, such as railroads, airlines, maritime shipping, steel, aluminum, and public utilities, already deferred a large portion of their taxes and stood to lose permanently the tax benefits of accelerated depreciation on new projects. In like manner, oil and mining companies frequently resorted to leasing simply because depletion allowance held their effective tax rates below those of the lessor, the difference being used to reduce the lessee's net cost.

There are two caveats to the preceding enumeration of key variables in leasing. First, the variables express the dollar benefits and costs of leasing, while ignoring the convenience factor of the arrangement. Because lease analysis is frequently a "sharp-pencil" calculation, convenience could swing the decision in favor of leasing. Second, the key variables isolated above do not constitute a definitive list of the significant clauses typifying most leases. For example, the lease may require a pledge of collateral and contain express or implied warranties, restrictions on the use of the equipment, and/or provisions relating to such factors as redelivery, default, bankruptcy, damages, and insurance. These clauses, largely contingent, can have monetary implications as circumstances change. The lessee may find it advisable, therefore, to allow for other variables in his or her financial analysis as judgment dictates.

The question of leasing versus ownership represents a long-run financial planning decision and must be considered together with both capital budgeting and financial structure decisions. In some cases the asset to be leased or purchased will represent a mandatory investment; the project must be accepted, and the only decision is whether to acquire the asset by purchase or by lease. In such cases, lease analysis is essentially a financing decision, and we attempt to evaluate the lease against alternative ways of financing the asset. In other cases the lease arrangement itself is important in deciding whether to accept or reject a capital project. For example, some capital projects may only be available by lease; in other cases, it may not be sound financially to buy an asset, but leasing the same asset may be quite attractive. In this situation, lease proposals are incorporated in the capital budget as discrete projects, and the evaluation process should permit management to properly rank all proposed capital expenditures (including lease projects) in order of desirability.

LEASE VERSUS PURCHASE AS A FINANCING DECISION

The lessee desires to maximize present value. In our initial analysis, we make three assumptions relative to the lessee:

1 The project being considered is either mandatory, or the decision has been made to acquire the asset after an NPV analysis so all that remains is the question of how to finance the project. The lessee needs to know which method of financing (lease or purchase) is less costly.

2 Since leasing is a form of financing comparable to indebtedness, the asset, if purchased, will be financed by a bank loan. The underlying reasoning states that the borrowing capacity and cost of capital to a firm will be affected in about the same way by lease or debt financing.

3 The cash flows attributable to the project (except for residual value) will be discounted at the firm's after-tax cost of debt. This assumption will be discussed in greater detail later.

For the lessee, the financial analysis of lease versus purchase is quite simple: determine the yearly cost of each, discount to present value, and make the selection based on minimizing the present value of the cash outflows. But a word of caution is necessary. We have assumed that the project is mandatory or that the firm is committed to the project after an NPV analysis and must be included as an acquisition, whether it be purchased or leased. The decision we are presently examining is therefore one of financing rather than of capital expenditure. Thus, we ignore cash inflows from operations and rather seek to minimize the present value of the outflows over the project's life. The methodology for comparison is demonstrated in Example 1.

EXAMPLE 1

Lease Versus Purchase (Financing Decision)

Assume that a machine may be purchased by a lessee for $60,000, financed through a 12% bank loan, and depreciated using the cost recovery system of accelerated depreciation over its 3-year economic life. The loan would be paid back in *three* annual installments. The firm's cost of capital is 18%, a 20% rate is used to discount the residual value, and the marginal tax rate is 48% (federal and state). If leased, the rental would be $21,510 (if paid in advance) or $28,000 (if paid at the end of each period). There is a $1,000 yearly operating cost associated with ownership, but not with leasing. At the end of its economic life, the asset will have a residual value of $2,000, and the tax rate applied to the residual would also be 48%. Determine the NPVs of the three alternatives: lease with start-of-year payments, lease with end-of-year payments, and purchase, assuming that operating costs are the same whether the machine is leased or purchased.

SOLUTION: (a) Calculate the annual cost recovery. Based on a depreciable value of $60,000, the annual depreciation is

(1) PERIOD	(2) COST OF ASSET	(3) ACRS RATES*	(4) COST RECOVERY (2) × (3)
1	$60,000	0.33	$19,800
2	60,000	0.45	27,000
3	60,000	0.15	9,000
4	60,000	0.07	2,200
			$58,000

*Asset recovery under ACRS is limited to cost less residual value. The mandatory half-year convention under the Tax Reform Act of 1986 provides that only one-half the allowable cost of recovery be taken up in the first year and the remaining excess (less the residual value) recaptured in the period after the economic life of the asset. The rates shown in column (3) are taken from Table 4–5.

(b) Calculate the loan schedule needed to amortize the $60,000 over a 3-year period at 12% (Appendix B, column 6)

$$\text{loan repayment} = \$60,000(0.416348)$$

$$= \$24,981$$

The loan schedule appears in tabular form as follows:

PERIOD	REPAYMENT	INTEREST	PRINCIPAL	BALANCE
1	$24,981	$ 7,200	$17,781	$42,219
2	24,981	5,066	19,915	22,304
3	24,981	2,676	22,305	0
Total		$14,942	$60,000	

(c) Calculate the solutions required in the problem using the tabular format illustrated. Note that the figures used in column 10 for case 1 (after-tax lease cost) are found by multiplying the lease payment of $21,510 by 1 minus the marginal tax rate; similarly, the figures in column 8 for case 2 result when $28,000 is multiplied by 1 minus the tax rate. Note also that when lease payments are made in advance, the advantage to ownership is larger, whereas if the payments are made at the end of the year, the advantage to ownership is smaller. Finally, observe that the after-tax cash flows are discounted by the after-tax cost of debt capital (K_d).

Case 1: Lease Payment Made in Advance

PERIOD	(1) LOAN PAYMENT	(2) INTEREST	(3) PRINCIPAL	(4) BALANCE	(5) COST RECOVERY
0	—	—	—	—	$19,800
1	$24,981	$7,200	$17,781	$42,219	27,000
2	24,981	5,066	19,915	22,304	9,000
3	24,981	2,676	22,305	—	2,200
4					

(6) OPERATING COST	(7) TAX DEDUCTION (2) + (5) + (6)	(8) TAX SHIELD 48% of (7)	(9) NET OWNERSHIP COST (1) + (6) − (8)	(10) AFTER-TAX LEASE COST
—	—	—	—	$11,185
$1,000	$28,000	$13,440	$12,541	11,185
1,000	33,066	15,872	10,109	11,185
1,000	12,676	6,084	19,897	—
1,000	3,200	1,536	− 536	—

(11) ADVANTAGE TO OWNERSHIP (10) − (9)	(12) DISCOUNT FACTOR (K_d = 6.24%)	(13) PV TO OWN[†] (11) × (12)
+ $11,185	—	+ $11,185
− 1,356	0.941280	− 1,276
+ 1,076	0.886022	+ 953
− 19,897	0.833942	− 16,593
+ 536	0.785086	+ 421
+ 2,000 salvage	0.578704 (K_s = 20%)	+ 1,157
		− $ 4,153

[†]Note: If the solution is a *plus* value, ownership is preferred; if a negative value, leasing is the preferred option. In this illustration, since the PV to own is − $4,153, there is an advantage to leasing.

Case 2: Lease Payment Made at End of Period

PERIOD	(1) LOAN PAYMENT	(2) INTEREST	(3) PRINCIPAL	(4) BALANCE	(5) COST RECOVERY
0	—	—	—	—	—
1	$24,981	$7,200	$17,781	$42,219	$19,800
2	24,981	5,066	19,915	22,304	27,000
3	24,981	2,676	22,305	—	9,000
4	—	—	—		2,200

(6) OPERATING COSTS	(7) TAX DEDUCTION (2) + (5) + (6)	(8) TAX SHIELD 48% of (7)	(9) NET OWNERSHIP COST (1) + (6) − (8)
—			—
$1,000	$28,000	$13,440	$12,541
1,000	33,066	15,872	10,109
1,000	12,676	6,084	19,897
1,000	3,200	1,536	− 536

(10) AFTER-TAX LEASE COST	(11) ADVANTAGE TO OWNERSHIP (10) − (9)	(12) DISCOUNT FACTOR (K = 6.24%)
—	—	—
$14,560	+ $2,019	0.941280
14,560	+ 4,451	0.886022
14,560	− 5,337	0.833942
—	+ 536	0.785086
—	+ 2,000 salvage	0.578704 (K_s = 20%)

	(13) PV TO OWN (11) × (12)	
	—	
	+ $1,900	
	+ 3,944	
	− 4,451	
	+ 421	
	+ 1,157	
	+ $2,971	

The final value in column (13) shows that owning is preferred to leasing in the amount of $2,971 in present value terms.

The solution methodology demonstrated in Example 1 may be reduced to equation form by noting that the cost of the borrow-and-purchase alternative is the sum of the loan payments for each period plus operating expenses less interest, depreciation, and operating expense tax shields, less the after-tax salvage value discounted to present value at a discount rate appropriate to the cash flows.[1] The cost of borrowing and purchasing is expressed in Equation (1):

$$\text{cost to purchase} = \sum_{t=1}^{N} \frac{P + O_t - (I_t + D_t + O_t)t_c}{(1 + K_d)^t} - \frac{S_N - (S_N - B)t_g}{(1 + K_s)^N} \tag{1}$$

where P = loan payment (interest and amortization of principal)
  L_t = lease payment t
  I_t = interest payment in period t
  D_t = cost recovery in period t
  O_t = incremental operating costs of ownership in period t
  t_c = firm's marginal tax rate on ordinary income
  t_g = tax rate applicable to the disposal of assets (see Chapter 4)
  S_N = expected cash value of asset in period N
  B = book value of asset in period N
  K_d = explicit after-tax cost of new debt
  K_s = discount rate applied to residual value of the asset

[1] The next section, including Equations (1) through (3), is based upon the article by R. W. Johnson and W. G. Lewellen, "Analysis of the Lease or Buy Decision," *Journal of Finance*, 27 (September 1972), 815–823.

567 Chapter 27 Lease Analysis: Lease/Buy and Lease/Sell

Similarly, the cost to lease is the sum of the after-tax payments discounted by the after-tax cost of debt capital, as expressed in Equation (2):

$$\begin{matrix} \text{cost to lease} \\ \text{with end-of-} \\ \text{period payment} \end{matrix} = \sum_{t=1}^{N} \frac{L_t(1 - t_c)}{(1 + K_d)^t} \qquad (2)$$

If lease payments were made at the start of each period, we would sum from $t = 0$ to $t = N - 1$. This would have the effect of reducing the lease payment, as was demonstrated in case 1.

In many instances the question of lease versus purchase is not limited to a financial decision as was the case in this section. Rather, all alternatives must be examined to ascertain whether the project is acceptable based on its merits, and then the most advantageous method of securing it is determined.

The discount rate used in lease versus purchases analysis is a very controversial issue. How do we justify the use of the after-tax cost of debt capital as the appropriate discount rate? The choice depends upon the assessment of risk. The following considerations weigh heavily in our choice:

1   In this particular problem, the capital budgeting question has already been decided. The project is required. The expenditure is nondiscretionary. As such, the question is one of financing.

2   If the firm as a whole reasonably expects to generate sufficient taxable income from its overall operations to use all tax deductions, tax shields are to be discounted at a low rate, since they are virtually risk free.

3   The lease would enable management to avoid uncertain (risky) operating expenses; these amounts should also be discounted at a lower rate. In fact, the idea that a lease enables a firm to avoid risk leads some authorities to suggest a discount rate even lower than the risk-free rate, but, as a practical matter, debt cost is a reasonable approximation.

4   Some lease arrangements include lease payments that are contingent on future performance or other events; other leases are readily cancelable at the option of one of the parties involved. These types of situations also impact the choice of a discount rate. For example, a cancelable lease may actually be less burdensome than debt, since the face amount may be an upper limit with the lessee able, if necessary, to cancel and avoid losses. Here, the after-tax cost of debt might be too high a rate of discount.

5   The salvage value proceeds are generally a very uncertain amount, and if so, we logically discount them at a higher rate than the firm's average cost of capital. The rate reflects the firm's judgment about the estimate of the amount that can probably be recovered from the asset.

LEASE VERSUS PURCHASING AS A CAPITAL BUDGETING DECISION

In our discussion of lease versus purchase as a financing decision, we indicated that the capital budgeting decision had been made or the acquisition was mandatory and our concern lay in selecting the optimum mode for financing. Thus, we presumed conditions of certainty as to the financing and lease payment cash flows and discounted them at the after-tax cost of debt. By contrast, *if the firm were considering the lease proposal as a distinct capital project to be ranked against all other projects, the cash flows would not be considered certain. Sales and operating costs change, tax rates and the like change frequently with business conditions, and sometimes lease payments vary with business conditions. In this case, the financial manager would discount the separate cash flows of ownership or leasing at a rate appropriate to the level of risk.*

Moreover, it is axiomatic in capital budgeting that the return on investment be computed independently of the cost of financing. Yet in Example 1, interest charges were explicitly included in the ownership calculations. *The reason for including interest in the calculations was the need to find the difference in the after-tax cash flows between the leasing and borrowing alternatives. The project had already been accepted, and the decision was made independently of financing.* We had to look directly to those cash flows which would affect the financing decision. By contrast, in this section we view the question of purchase or lease as two distinct, independent, and mutually exclusive projects. Further, it is not necessary to make any assumption of borrowing to meet the purchase price of the asset. These modifications change the structure of the calculations in three ways:

1   It is necessary to calculate the difference between net present value of ownership and the net present value of leasing as a basis for the decision.
2   The approach follows the general rule in capital budgeting of separating the return on a project from the cost of financing: specifically, we delete the interest charges from the costs of ownership in determining net present value.
3   Allowance is made for the uncertainties of the operating cash flows, tax shields, and residuals by discounting the first two by the firm's cost of capital and the latter by a rate appropriate to the risk level.[2]

The net present value anticipated from purchase of the asset, then, is the sum of the present value of the net after-tax operating profits (revenues less operating costs) plus the discounted after-tax cash proceeds from salvage less the cost of the asset. Similarly, the net present value of the leasing project would be the present value of the revenues less the lease payments and other costs, if any, associated with leasing. In comparing the net present values of the two alternatives, the revenues are assumed to be the same in both cases, which allows their deletion from the analysis.

In practice, two steps are required. We first determine whether the project is acceptable if purchased. Then we compare the net present values of ownership versus leasing using Equation (3):

$$\Delta\text{NPV} = \text{NPV (purchase)} - \text{NPV (lease)}$$

$$= \sum_{t=1}^{N} \frac{t_c(D_t) - O_t(1 - t_c)}{(1 + K)^t} + \frac{S_N - (S_N - B)t_g}{(1 + K_S)^N} \tag{3}$$

$$- C + \sum_{t=1}^{N} \frac{L_t(1 - t_c)}{(1 + K_d)}$$

where ΔNPV = difference between NPV (purchase) and NPV (lease)
K = firm's marginal cost of capital

---

[2] The cost of capital would be applied for projects having the same degree of risk as the firm overall. For projects of differing risk, adjustment would be made as indicated in Part IV.

Excluding revenues from both NPV calculations, the net present value of ownership is the sum of the depreciation tax shield, $t_c(D_t)$, less the after-tax operating costs, $O_t(1 - t_c)$, for each period discounted at the firm's cost of capital (K) plus the after-tax salvage, $S_N - (S_N - B)t_g$, discounted at some higher rate (K_S) less the cost of the equipment (C). The present value of leasing in the comparison (again excluding revenues) is the sum of after-tax rental for each period, $L_t(1 - t_c)$, discounted at the cost of debt capital (K_d). This amount is added to the present value of ownership, since it represents a negative NPV because the lease involves exclusively cash outflows. If ΔNPV is positive, purchasing is preferred; if ΔNPV is negative, leasing is preferred.

The process of deciding between purchasing and leasing is demonstrated in Examples 2 and 3. In Example 2 we examine only the purchase, while in Example 3 we determine the difference in the purchase and lease costs using Equation (3) to determine which is preferable.

EXAMPLE 2
Purchase Decision

A corporation may purchase or lease equipment costing $60,000 and having a salvage value of $2,000. If purchased, the cost of the equipment would be recovered using ACRS rates over its 3-year life. If leased, the lease payment would be made at year's end, and the cost would be $28,000. In either case, operating revenues would be increased by $30,000 per year, and, if the equipment is purchased, operating costs would increase by $5,000 per year. The corporation's marginal tax rate is 48% (combined federal and state); its cost of capital, 20%; its after-tax cost of debt, 10%; and the risk-adjusted discount rate for salvage, 25%. The marginal tax rate also applies to the residual value. Determine the wisdom of purchase.

SOLUTION: The changes in the corporation's income statement and cash flows are tabulated as follows:

Changes in Corporation's Income Statement

	PERIOD 1	PERIOD 2	PERIOD 3	PERIOD 4
Revenues	$30,000	$30,000	$30,000	
Operating expenses	(5,000)	(5,000)	(5,000)	—
Cost recovery	(19,800)	(27,000)	(9,000)	(2,200)
Earnings before taxes	$ 5,200	$ (2,000)	$ 6,000	$(2,200)
Taxes at 48%	(2,496)	960	(7,680)	(1,056)
Earnings after taxes	$ 2,704	$ (1,040)	$ 8,320	$(1,144)

Change in Corporation's Cash Flows

	PERIOD 1	PERIOD 2	PERIOD 3	PERIOD 4
Cost recovery	$19,800	$27,000	$ 9,000	$2,200
Earnings after taxes	2,704	(1,040)	8,320	(1,144)
Cash flow	$22,504	$25,960	$17,320	$1,056

The cash flows are shown discounted to present value next. The 20% rate is applied to the operating cash flows, while 25% is applied to salvage value.

TIME	AMOUNT	DISCOUNT FACTOR	PRESENT VALUE
Present	− $60,000	1.000000	− $60,000
1	22,504	0.833333	18,753
2	25,960	0.694444	18,028
3	17,320	0.578704	10,023
3	2,000	0.512000 (at 25%)	1,024
4	1,056	0.482253	509
			NPV = − $11,663

Since the NPV of purchase is negative, the purchase is unacceptable. However, the lease may be acceptable. This determination is made using Equation (3).

EXAMPLE 3

Lease Versus Purchase Comparison

Using the information provided in Example 2, determine the ΔNPV of the lease and purchase employing Equation (3).

SOLUTION: Employing Equation (3) in a sequential manner, we have

$$\sum_{t=1}^{4} \frac{t_c(D_t) - O_t(1 - t_c)}{(1 + K)^t} = \{[\$19,800(0.48)] - [\$5,000(1 - 0.48)]\} \times 0.83333$$

$$= (\$9,504 - \$2,600) \times 0.83333 = \$5,753$$

$$\{[\$27,000(0.48)] - [\$5,000(1 - 0.48)]\} \times 0.694444$$

$$= (\$12,960 - \$2,600) \times 0.694444 = \$7,194$$

$$\{[\$9,000(0.48)] - [\$5,000(1 - 0.48)]\} \times 0.578704$$

$$= (\$4,320 - \$2,600) \times 0.578704 = \$995$$

$$\{[\$2,200(0.48)] - [0(1 - 0.48)]\} \times 0.482253$$

$$= (\$1,056 - 0) \times 0.482253 = \$509$$

$$= \$14,451$$

$$\sum_{t=1}^{3} \frac{L_t(1 - t_c)}{(1 + K_d)^t} = \$28,000(1 - 0.48)(0.909091) + \$28,000(1 - 0.48)(0.826446)$$

$$+ \$28,000(1 - 0.48)(0.751315)$$

$$= \$13,236 + \$12,033 + \$10,939$$

$$= \$36,208$$

$$\Delta\text{NPV} = \$14,451 + \$1,024 - \$60,000 + \$36,208$$

$$= - \$8,317$$

The negative ΔNPV means that leasing is preferable to purchase.

The analysis illustrates the impact of choosing discount rates unique to the cash flows of ownership and leasing. A higher degree of risk surrounds the cash flows associated with ownership; therefore, these are discounted at the firm's cost of capital with higher rates for salvage values. The lease cash flows, supported by contractual agreements, are discounted at the after-tax cost of debt capital.

In summary, if management has determined to acquire a project or if it is mandatory, the essential problem is to determine the lowest cost of financing. This problem was examined in the previous section. If, however, there is no presumption, the analysis looks at two mutually independent projects: one to purchase, the other to lease. Then, these projects are evaluated with all other projects being considered using the techniques detailed in Examples 2 and 3.

However, Equation (3) must be interpreted with care. It is possible that the asset acquisition may have a negative NPV whether purchased or leased. It may not be desirable to management on any grounds. Nonetheless, Equation (3) is valuable because it will always indicate the least undesirable alternative.

LEASE ANALYSIS: THE LESSOR'S PERSPECTIVE

Finance and accounting literature on leasing predominantly treats the position of the lessee. Professional journals mostly argue the merits of one particular financial model and the accounting presentation of leases in terms of the lessee's objectives. On the other hand, the lessor must address a more complicated set of issues under a greater variety of circumstances. From the perspective of the lessor, the lease may be offered by a lessor-dealer or lessor-manufacturer. The number of parties to the contract may range from two to seven. The methods of lease evaluation are similarly more diverse, although the same key variables form the substance of the analysis. Yet, whatever the nature of the lease transaction, the essential question for analysis remains constant: What lease payment should the lessor charge to accomplish the firm's objective of maximizing net present value?

Lessor-Dealer

The lessor-dealer acquires an asset with the intention of leasing it. Rent-a-car agencies come readily to mind. The lessor does not manufacture the asset, although the firm may maintain the asset in operating condition.

The lessor-dealer sets a minimum rental such that the present value of the after-tax rental cash inflows (R_t) equals or exceeds the cost of the asset (C) less the present value of the salvage (PV_S) and the present value of the depreciation tax shield (PV_{DT}) plus the present value of the after-tax operating expenses (PV_O) related to the lease. Consistent with capital budgeting conventions, cash flows are displayed on an after-tax basis.[3]

The expression becomes

$$C - PV_S - PV_{DT} + PV_O = \sum_{t=1}^{N} \frac{R_t}{(1 + K_{MC})^t} \tag{4}$$

[3] The Tax Reform Act of 1986 repealed the 10% investment tax credit (ITC) unless the company meets certain binding contract rules in effect on December 31, 1985, and the property is placed in service within a specified number of years.

EXAMPLE 4

Determining a Lease Payment — Lessor-Dealer

A lessor of construction equipment is writing a lease contract based upon the following data:

Lease term (N)	8 years
Asset life	10 years
Asset cost (C)	$2,000,000
Residual value (S)	$400,000 (at the end of the lease)
Lessor's marginal tax rate (t_c)	48% (combined federal and state)
Lessor's marginal cost of capital (K_{MC})	15% (after tax)
Discount rate on salvage (K_S)	20% (after tax)
Operating expense (O)	$2,000 (paid at end of each period)
Depreciation method	straight line

What should the lease charge be in each case?
(a) It is paid at end of each period.
(b) It is paid at beginning of each period.

SOLUTION: Based on Equation (4), we develop each of the necessary terms. The present value of salvage or residuals is[4]

$$PV_S = S \times \frac{1}{(1 + K_S)^N}$$

$$= \$400,000 \times \frac{1}{(1 + 0.20)^8}$$

$$= \$400,000 \times 0.23257$$

$$= \$93,028$$

The present value of operating expenses after taxes is

$$PV_O = O(1 - t_c) \times \sum_{t=1}^{N} \frac{1}{(1 + K_{MC})^t} \qquad (5)$$

$$= \$2,000(1 - 0.48) \times \sum_{t=1}^{8} \frac{1}{(1 + 0.15)^t}$$

$$= \$1,040 \times 4.487322$$

$$= \$4,667$$

The asset is depreciated on a straight-line basis over the 10-year life stipulated in the data. The problem assumes the book value of $400,000 is the same as the estimated market

---

[4]The economic life of the asset is 10 years. The term of the lease is 8 years. Depreciation is on a straight-line basis. Therefore, the residual value is $400,000 at the end of the eighth year, which represents the remaining depreciation of $200,000 per year over the 10-year life of the asset. At the end of the tenth year, there is no residual value.

value at the end of the 8-year lease. Therefore, at the end of the tenth year, the asset has no book value and no salvage.

$$\text{annual depreciation} = \frac{\$2,000,000}{10} = \$200,000 \tag{6}$$

$$PV_{DT} = (DT_t) \times \sum_{t=1}^{N} \frac{1}{(1 + K_{MC})^t}$$

$$= (\$200,000 \times 0.48) \times \sum_{t=1}^{8} \frac{1}{(1 + 0.15)^t}$$

$$= \$96,000 \times 4.487322$$

$$= \$430,783$$

For the lease payment, if paid at the end of each period refer to Equation (4):

$$C - PV_S - PV_{DT} + PV_O = \sum_{t=1}^{N} \frac{R_t}{(1 + K_{MC})^t}$$

$$\$2,000,000 - \$93,028 - \$430,783 + \$4,667 = R_t \times 4.487322$$

$$\$1,480,856 = 4.487322 R_t$$

$$\$330,009 = R_t$$

The \$330,099 is an after-tax lease payment. Thus must now be converted to the pretax lease payment, which will be paid by the lessee:

$$\text{pretax lease payment} = \frac{R_t(\text{after taxes})}{(1 - t_c)} \tag{7}$$

$$= \frac{\$330,009}{(1 - 0.48)}$$

$$= \$634,632$$

To compute rent if paid at the beginning of each period, we assume that all cash flows *except salvage and depreciation tax savings* are payable at the beginning of the period. Accordingly, Equation (4) is revised to allow for the new time sequence:

$$C - PV_S - PV_{DT} + PV_O = \left[1.0 + \sum_{t=1}^{N-1} \frac{1}{(1 + K_{MC})^t} \right] R_t \tag{8}$$

We revise the present value of operating expenses as follows:

$$PV_O = O(1 - t_c) \left[1.0 + \sum_{t=1}^{N-1} \frac{1}{(1 + K_{MC})^t} \right] \tag{9}$$

$$= \$2,000(1 - 0.48) \left[1.0 + \sum_{t=1}^{7} \frac{1}{(1 + 0.15)^t} \right]$$

$$= \$1,040(1.0 + 4.160420)$$

$$= \$1,040 \times 5.160420$$

$$= \$5,367$$

Then we complete Equation (8) to obtain the after-tax lease payment:

$$\$2,000,000 - \$93,028 - \$430,783 + \$5,367 = \left[1.0 + \sum_{t=1}^{7} \frac{1}{(1 + 0.15)^t} \right] R_t$$

$$\$1,481,556 = (1.0 + 4.160420) R_t$$

$$\$287,100 = R_t$$

Finally, we convert to obtain the pretax lease payment:

$$\frac{R_t(\text{after-tax})}{(1 - t_c)} = \frac{\$287,556}{(1 - 0.48)} = \$552,115$$

In summary, the lessor-dealer would post a rental of $634,632 if the cash flows were payable at the end of the period or $552,115 if the cash flows, except as noted, were payable at the beginning of the period.

Lessor-Manufacturer

As a manufacturer of the product, the lessor has the option of selling or leasing the equipment. Boeing may sell or lease aircraft. IBM and Xerox offer similar options. The lessor-manufacturer, furthermore, may decide to emphasize one or the other of the available options. He or she might, for example, stress the sell option by lowering the selling price, increasing trade allowances, or lowering the cost of full-service maintenance agreements. Alternately, the lessor-manufacturer might induce leasing by offering longer-term lease plans or lower lease payments. The decision to stress one or the other option depends upon the lessor-manufacturer's financial and tax position in relation to the state of the economy and the lessee trade. In any event, the lessor-manufacturer must determine the *minimum lease payment that would give him or her the same net present value as an outright sale*. Armed with this analysis, the company has the basis for a policy decision.

It is interesting to compare the lessor-manufacturer's posture with that of the lessor-dealer described earlier. The major differences emanate from the tax laws and include the following:

1 *Depreciation tax shield.* The lessor-manufacturer who elects to lease includes only the manufacturing cost in calculating the tax shield. The anticipated profit on sale of the asset does not form a part of his or her depreciable base. On the other hand, a dealer who purchases the equipment for subsequent lease capitalizes the manufacturer's profit included in the purchase price plus work-up costs. The same holds for a conventional lessee making a decision to lease or purchase.

2 *Gain or loss on sale of asset.* If the equipment is sold above its book value before its economic life is terminated, the IRS regards the excess as ordinary income for tax purposes. Since the depreciable tax base differs between the lessor-manufacturer and the purchaser, the tax obligations of the two parties also differ.

Financial analysis of the lessor-manufacturer's decision proceeds through three steps:

1   *Determine the net present value of outright sale.* This is the selling price less the cost of producing the asset multiplied by 1 minus the firm's marginal income tax rate.
2   *Determine the net present value of the cost of leasing.* The NPV of the leasing cost will equal the negative outflow of the asset cost to the manufacturer plus the present value of the investment tax credit inflow plus the present value of the depreciation tax savings plus the present value of the after-tax salvage value inflow.
3   *Determine the annual lease payment that will give the same net present value as selling the asset.* The NPV of outright sales will equal the net present value of the annual lease payments.

EXAMPLE 5
Determining a Lease Payment: Manufacturer-Lessor

Assume the following data for a manufacturer who has the option to sell or lease a product.

Selling price of asset (SP)	$500,000
Manufacturer's cost (C)	$200,000
Marginal tax rate (t_c)	48% 14% (combined federal and state)
Cost of capital (K_{MC}), after taxes	14%
Manufacturer's cost of new debt (K_d), after tax	6%
Selling price of asset at the end of the lease (S) (ignored in depreciation calculations)	$50,000
Depreciation	ACRS
Length of lease	8 years
Depreciation write-off period	10 years

Determine the net present value of pretax lease rental that will have the same net present value as outright sale.

SOLUTION: The net present value of an outright sale equals the net selling price (SP) less the cost of manufacturing the asset (C) times 1 minus the firm's marginal tax rate ($1 - t_c$) and then discounted back one period under the assumption that all cash flows take place at the end of year 1.

$$\text{NPV of outright sale} = \frac{(SP - C)(1 - t_c)}{(1 + K_{MC})^1}$$

$$= \frac{(\$500{,}000 - \$200{,}000)(1 - 0.48)}{(1 + 0.14)^1}$$

$$= \frac{\$156{,}000}{1.14}$$

$$= \$136{,}842$$

The NPV of the leasing cost equals the cash outflow of the asset to the manufacturer (C) plus the present value of the depreciation tax shield (PV_{DT}) plus the present value of the after-tax salvage value (PV_S).[5]

$$\text{NPV of lease cost} = -C + \sum_{t=1}^{N} \frac{D_t t_c}{(1 + K_d)^t} + \frac{(S - B)(1 - t_c)}{(1 + K_{MC})^N} \tag{10}$$

Calculating the components, we have the cost recovery tax shield:

$$PV_{DT} = \sum_{t=1}^{N} \frac{D_t t_c}{(1 + K_d)^t} \tag{11}$$

Then, we have the following depreciation schedule for the first 8 years of the asset's 10-year useful life

(1) PERIOD	(2) COST	(3) ACRS PERCENTAGE	(4) COST RECOVERY	(5) TAX DEDUCTION	(6) DISCOUNT ($K_d = 6\%$)	(7) PV OF TAX SAVINGS (5) × (6)
1	$200,000	0.10	$ 20,000	$ 9,600	0.943396	$ 9,057
2	200,000	0.18	36,000	17,280	0.889996	15,379
3	200,000	0.144	28,800	13,824	0.839619	11,667
4	200,000	0.115	23,000	11,040	0.792094	8,744
5	200,000	0.092	18,400	8,832	0.747258	6,600
6	200,000	0.074	14,800	7,104	0.704961	5,008
7	200,000	0.066	13,200	6,336	0.665057	4,213
8	200,000	0.066	13,200	6,336	0.627412	3,975
						$64,643

The last term of Equation (10) finds the present value of the after-tax proceeds of the sale of the asset at the end of the lease:

$$\frac{(S - B)(1 - t_c)}{(1 + K_{MC})^N} = \frac{(\$50,000 - \$32,600)(1 - 0.48)}{(1.14)^8}$$

$$= \$3,172$$

Finally, by Equation (10):

$$\text{NPV of lease cost} = -\$200,000 + \$64,643 + \$3,172$$

$$= -\$132,185$$

Minimum lease payment with the same net present value of outright sales is:

$$\text{NPV of outright sale} = \text{NPV of lease cost} + \text{NPV of annual lease payments}$$

---

[5]The after-tax cost of debt capital (K_d) is applied to the depreciation tax savings due to the higher level of certainty surrounding these cash flows.

If NPV of annual lease payments equals

$$R(1 - t_c) \sum_{t=1}^{N} \frac{1}{(1 + K_d)^t}$$

Then for the 8 year lease, we would find:

$$\$136{,}842 = - \$132{,}185 + R(1 - 0.48)(6.209794)$$
$$\$136{,}842 = - \$132{,}185 + R(0.52)(6.209794)$$
$$\$136{,}842 + \$132{,}185 = 3.2290928R$$
$$\$83{,}354 = R \quad (\text{pretax rental})$$

An annual lease payment of $83,354 on the proposed lease would yield the same NPV as would an outright sale of the asset to the lessor-manufacturer. The lease payment represents an indifference point between the policy of leasing or selling. Armed with this insight, the manufacturer can work toward an optimal mix of sales and leases to achieve particular financial objectives. If the firm wishes to encourage leasing and charge a lease payment of $83,354, the manufacturer might increase the sales price of the asset. Should the manufacturer take the opposite task, the firm might encourage sales by raising the rental above $83,354.

SUMMARY

The use of leasing has grown extensively in recent years, and for many firms it offers a viable alternative to purchasing. Thus it is necessary to examine leasing as an important part of the capital budgeting decision-making process.

Our discussion examined the various advantages of leasing, types of leases, and legal aspects of leasing. Then we analyzed the lessee's position, first as a financing decision when the assets involved represented mandatory expenditures, and later as a capital budgeting decision involving discretionary expenditures.

We then concentrated on the position of the lessor. Two kinds of lessors were recognized: the lessor-dealer and the lessor-manufacturer. The differences in position arise from the vagaries of the income tax law. In fact, it is probably fair to say that, except where the lessor has economies of scale, leasing would not survive but for tax legislation. That is, except where the lessor has economies of scale, ownership is preferred over leasing. The intervention of tax legislation upsets the natural economic equilibrium.

QUESTIONS*
——————
PROBLEMS

1. The investment tax credit (ITC) has been part of the federal tax law off-and-on over the last 25 years. This credit of 10% of the purchase cost of the asset was generally received in the first year after the purchase of the asset. The Tax Reform Act of 1986 repealed the ITC. Thus, none of the models in this chapter incorporated the ITC. If the ITC were reinstated, how should Equation (4) be modified?

*In carrying out the calculations for these problems, Table 4–5 should be used for ACRS rates and the half-year convention should be used for assets depreciated on a straight-line basis.

2. Discuss the rationale for using the firm's after-tax borrowing rate when making the lease versus purchase decision.

3. In many capital budgeting and leasing models, a relatively high discount rate is used to find the present value of anticipated salvage value. Given the fact that the recovery of salvage value is in the last period of the project's life (and very often out in the distant future), is using a high discount rate really necessary? Discuss.

4. Garrbadge Corporation is about to acquire a new piece of production equipment costing $100,000. The firm has the choice of borrowing the $100,000 at 10%, to be repaid in ten annual installments of $16,273 each, or of leasing the machine for $16,500 per year, with payments at year-end. The machine will be used for 10 years, at the end of which time its estimated salvage value will be $10,000. If the firm leases the equipment, maintenance cost is included in the lease payment; but if it purchases the machine, it must spend an estimated $2,000 a year on maintenance. (Note: The decision to acquire the production equipment was made previously as part of the capital budgeting process.) Determine whether the equipment should be leased or purchased if the effective income tax rate for the firm is 34%. The average after-tax cost of capital for Garrbadge Corporation is 10%, and the firm uses ACRS depreciation under the Tax Reform Act of 1986 and discounts salvage value at 12%.

5. U.S. Motors is considering the acquisition of retooling equipment to regain its share of the market. Before entering lease negotiations, the vice president and treasurer wish to know the maximum rental U.S. Motors can afford to pay. The facts of the case are: cost of the equipment, $200,000; salvage, $6,667; ACRS depreciation; operating cost of ownership, $10,000 per year; term of lease, 10 years; marginal cost of capital, 16%; discount factor applied to salvage, 20% after tax; cost of new debt, 12% before tax; marginal tax rate, 34%. What is the maximum lease payment U.S. Motors will pay if rents are payable at the end of the period?

6. The Mather Construction Company must either purchase or lease a new crane having a purchase price of $75,000. The lease would run 10 years, the estimated life of the crane. If the company purchases the crane, they have projected its salvage value to be $7,500. Because of the high risk of the assigned salvage value, a 20% discount will be applied. The company's cost of borrowing is 12% and it has a 34% tax rate bracket. The company uses ACRS rates.

   Whether the company leases or buys, operating costs will be the same. The lease agreement offers two plans of ten equal payments: (1) payment at the start of each year for $10,000 per year; (2) payment at the end of each year for $11,000 per year.

   Compare the lease with start of year payments, with the lease having end of year payments, and with the purchase option.

7. The Castaway Corporation makes disposable diapers in northeastern Pennsylvania and markets them locally. Recently, the market for Castaway Diapers has expanded so that they now need a fleet of 15 trucks for distribution purposes. The president is very traditional and believes in ownership of all equipment necessary to production and distribution; how-

ever, the finance department recommends an evaluation of leasing. Castaway will retain all drivers of the trucks regardless of the decision, and this will in no way affect the outsome of the decision.

Castaway knows that if they purchase the trucks at $36,000 each, they can finance them through the First National Bank of Smalltown at 9% interest paid in five equal annual installments. They can depreciate the trucks using ACRS rates. The firm's cost of capital is 12%. Salvage on the trucks is estimated to be $9,000 at the end of 5 years. As Castaway is uncertain as to what the mileage will actually be, they will assign the salvage a slightly higher discount rate at 15%. Maintenance on the trucks will be 5¢ per mile, with an additional $606 per year for licensing fees.

Pursky Leasing has offered Castaway an operating lease for the 15 trucks at $169,594.35 if paid in arrears for their 5-year life or $162,358.50 per year if paid in advance. The terms of the lease cover all services, including tires and towing charges and licensing.

All calculations are made on the basis of a 52-week year and 80,000 miles on all 15 trucks. Castaway is in the 34% tax bracket.

Determine which alternative would be the wiser choice. Show all work in tabular form. If leasing appears to be a viable alternative, explain why that is true.

8. The I-GOT-YA Company must acquire a computer costing $500,000. If they purchase the computer, a 14% loan must be taken out with the WE-GRAB-YOUR-MONEY Bank. Loan payments are required at the end of each year. I-GOT-YA Company uses ACRS rates. The computer is estimated to have a 5-year useful life with a salvage value of $20,000, so a 20% discount factor is applied to this period. Concurrently, the WE-LEASE-IT-ALL Company has offered to lease the same equipment to I-GOT-YA for 5 years, with the following terms and conditions:

(1) No maintenance expense required by I-GOT-YA.

(2) Annual rental of $117,523 if paid at the beginning of each year.

(3) Annual rental of $130,276 if paid at the end of each year.

If I-GOT-YA purchases the computer, they must incur an additional $1,000 of maintenance expense in addition to depreciation. The effective tax rate for I-GOT-YA is 34%.

Determine the advantage/disadvantage of lease versus purchase considering rental payments at both the end and the beginning of each year.

9. Assume a lease proposal with the following terms: lease term (N), 8 years; asset life, 10 years; asset cost, $1,000,000; salvage value (S), $200,000 at end of lease; lessor's combined federal and state marginal tax rate, 40%; lessor's marginal cost of capital (K_{mc}), 15% (after tax); discount on salvage (K_s), 20% (after-tax); operating expenses (O), $1,000 (paid at end of each period); cost recovery: ACRS. What rental should be charged in each case?

(a) Rents paid at end of period, after-tax and pretax.

(b) Rents paid at beginning of periods, after-tax and pretax.

10. NBM has the option of either selling or leasing its new computer. The company's financial officer presents the following data: selling price of asset, $300,000; manufacturer's cost, $250,000; marginal tax rate, 34%; marginal cost of capital, 10%; depreciation, straight-line, no salvage anticipated;

lessor's cost of new debt, 5% after-tax; length of lease and depreciable life of asset, 8 years. What is the pretax rental with the same NPV as outright sale?

REFERENCES

Allen, C. L., J. D. Martin, and P. F. Anderson. "Debt Capacity and the Lease-Purchase Problem: A Sensitivity Analysis." *Engineering Economist* (Winter 1978).

American Institute of Certified Public Accountants, Accounting Principles Board, *Opinion 5*, "Reporting of Leases in Financial Statements of Lessee" (September 1964); and *Opinion 31*, "Disclosure of Lease Commitments by Lessees" (June 1973).

Anderson, Paul E. *Financial Aspects of Industrial Leasing Decisions: Implications for Marketing.* East Lansing, Mich.: Division of Research, Graduate School of Business Administration, Michigan State University, 1977.

Ashton, D. J. "The Reasons for Leasing—A Mathematical Programming Framework." *Journal of Business Finance and Accounting* (Summer 1978).

Athanaspoulos, Peter J., and Peter W. Bacon. "The Evaluation of Leveraged Leases." *Financial Management*, 9 (Spring 1980), 76–80.

Axelson, Kenneth S. "Needed: A Generally Accepted Method for Measuring Lease Commitments." *Financial Executive*, 39 (July 1971), 40–52.

Benjamin, James J., and Robert H. Strawser. "Developments in Lease Accounting," *CPA Journal*, 46, 11 (November 1976), 33–36.

Bowman, R. G. "The Debt Equivalence of Leases: An Empirical Investigation." *Accounting Review* (April 1980).

Brealey, R. A., and C. M. Young. "Debt, Taxes and Leasing—A Note." *Journal of Finance* (December 1980).

Capettini, Robert, and Howard Toole. "Designing Leveraged Leases: A Mixed Integer Linear Programming Approach," *Financial Management*, 10 (Autumn 1981), 15–23.

Cason, Roger L. "Leasing, Asset Lives and Uncertainty: A Practitioner's Comments." *Financial Management* (Summer 1987).

Cooper, Kerry, and Robert H. Strawser. "Evaluation of Capital Investment Projects Involving Asset Leases." *Financial Management*, 4 (Spring 1975), 44–49.

Copeland, Thomas E., and J. Fred Weston. "A Note on the Evaluation of Cancellable Operating Leases." *Financial Management*, 11 (Summer 1982), 60–67.

Crawford, Peggy J., Charles P. Harper, and John J. McConnell. "Further Evidence on the Terms of Financial Leases," *Financial Management*, 10 (Autumn 1981), 7–14.

Davidson, Sidney, and Roman L. Weil. "Lease Capitalization and Inflation Accounting." *Financial Analysts Journal*, 34 (November–December 1975), 22–29.

Dyl, Edward A., and Stanley A. Martin, Jr. "Setting Terms for Leveraged Leases." *Financial Management*, 6 (Winter 1977), 20–27.

Fawthrop, R. A., and Brian Terry. "The Evaluation of an Integrated Investment in Lease-Financing." *Journal of Business Finance and Accounting*, 3 (Autumn 1976), 79–112.

Ferrara, William L. "The Case for Symmetry in Lease Reporting." *Management Accounting*, 59 (April 1978), 17–24.

Findlay, M. Chapman, III. "A Sensitivity Analysis of IRR Leasing Models." *Engineering Economics*, 20 (Summer 1975), 231–241.

Finnerty, Joseph E., Rick N. Fitzsimmons, and Thomas W. Oliver. "Lease Capitalization and Systematic Risk." *Accounting Review* (October 1980).

Franks, J. R., and S. D. Hodges. "Valuation of Financial Lease Contracts: A Note." *Journal of Finance*, 33 (May 1978), 617–639.

Gaumnitz, Jack E., and Allen Ford. "The Lease or Sell Decision." *Financial Management*, 7 (Winter 1978), 69–74.

Griesinger, F. K. "Pros and Cons of Leasing Equipment." *Harvard Business Review*, 33 (March–April 1955), 75–89.

Grimlund, Richard A., and Robert Capettini. "A Note on the Evaluation of Leveraged Leases and Other Investments." *Financial Management*, 11 (Summer 1982), 68–72.

Heaton, Hal. "Corporate Taxation and Leasing." *Journal of Financial and Quantitative Analysis* (September 1986).

Hindelang, Thomas J., and Robert E. Pritchard. *Making the Lease-Buy Decision*, 2nd ed. New York: AMACOM, 1984.

Hodges, Stewart D. "The Valuation of Variable Rate Leases." *Financial Management* (Spring 1985).

Honic, Lawrence E., and Stephen C. Colley. "An After-Tax Equivalent Payment Approach to Conventional Lease Analysis." *Financial Management*, 4 (Winter 1975), 28–35.

Idol, Charles R. "A Note on Specifying Debt Displacement and Tax Shield Borrowing Opportunities in Financial Lease Valuation Models." *Financial Management*, 9 (Summer 1980), 24–29.

Johnson, Keith B., and Thomas B. Hazuka. "The NPV-IRR Debate in Lease Analysis." *Mississippi Valley Journal*.

Keller, Thomas F., and Russell J. Peterson. "Optimal Financial Structure, Cost of Capital, and the Lease or Buy Decision." *Journal of Business Finance and Accounting*, 1 (Autumn 1974), 405–414.

Kim, E. Han, Wilbur G. Lewellen, and John J. McConnell. "Sale-and-Leaseback Agreements and Enterprise Valuation." *Journal of Financial and Quantitative Analysis*, 13 (December 1978), 871–883.

Knutson, P. H. "Leased Equipment and Divisional Return on Capital." *N.A.A. Bulletin* (November 1962), 15–20.

Levy, Haim, and Marshall Sarnat. "Leasing, Borrowing, and Financial Risk." *Financial Management*, 8 (Winter 1979), 47–54.

Levy, L. E. "Off Balance Sheet Financing." *Management Accounting*, 51 (May 1969), 12–14.

MacEachron, W. D. "Leasing: A Discounted Cash-Flow Approach." *Controller*, 29 (May 1961), 213–219.

Martin, John D., Paul E. Anderson, and Arthur J. Keown. "Lease Capitalization and Stock Price Stability: Implication for Accounting." *Journal of Accounting, Auditing and Finance*, 2 (Winter 1979), 151–164.

Middleton, K. A. "Lease Evaluation: Back to Square One." *Accounting and Business Research* (Spring 1977).

Miller, Merton H., and Charles W. Upton. "Leasing, Buying, and the Cost of Capital Services." *Journal of Finance*, 31 (June 1976), 787–798.

Peat, Marwick, Mitchell & Co. *1981 Economic Recovery Act Tax Act Leases*. New York: Peat, Marwick, Mitchell & Co., 1981.

Peller, Philip R., John E. Stewart, and Benjamin S. Neuhausen. "The 1981 Tax Act: Accounting for Leases." *Financial Executive* (January 1982), 16–26.

Sartoris, William L., and Ronda S. Paul. "Lease Evaluation—Another Capital Budgeting Decision." *Financial Management*, 2, 2 (Summer 1973), 46–52.

Sax, F. S. "Lease or Purchase Decision—Present Value Method." *Management Accounting*, 47 (October 1965), 55–61.

Schall, Lawrence D. "Analytic Issues in Lease vs. Purchase Decisions." *Financial Management* (Summer 1987).

Smith, Bruce D. "Accelerated Debt Repayment in Leveraged Leases." *Financial Management*, 11 (Summer 1982), 73–80.

Smith, Clifford W., Jr., and L. MacDonald Wakeman. "Determinants of Corporate Leasing Policy." *Journal of Finance* (July 1985).

Thulin, W. B. "Own or Lease: Underlying Financial Theory." *Financial Executive*, 32 (April 1964), 23–24, 28–31.

Vancil, Richard F. "Lease or Borrow: Steps in Negotiation." *Harvard Business Review*, 39 (November–December 1961), 238–259.

_____. "Lease or Borrow: New Method of Analysis." *Harvard Business Review*, 39 (September–October 1961), 122–136.

Weingartner, H. Martin. "Rejoinder." *Financial Management* (Summer 1987).

_____. "Leasing, Asset Lives and Uncertainty: Guides to Decision Making." *Financial Management* (Summer 1987).

Wiar, Robert C. "Economic Implications of Multiple Rates of Return in the Leverage Lease Context." *Journal of Finance*, 28 (December 1973), 1275–1286.

Wilson, C. J. "The Operating Lease and the Risk of Obsolescence." *Management Accounting*, 55 (December 1973), 41–44.

Table of the Normal Distribution

A

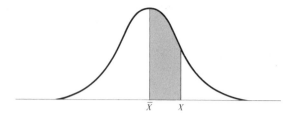

The table of areas of the normal curve between $\bar{X}$ and X for Z values is computed as follows:

$$Z = \frac{X - \bar{X}}{\sigma}$$

Z	.00	.01	.02	.03	.04	.05	.06	.07	.08	.09
0.0	.0000	.0041	.0080	.0120	.0160	.0199	.0239	.0279	.0319	.0359
0.1	.0398	.0438	.0478	.0517	.0557	.0596	.0636	.0675	.0714	.0753
0.2	.0793	.0832	.0871	.0910	.0948	.0987	.1026	.1064	.1103	.1141
0.3	.1179	.1217	.1255	.1293	.1331	.1368	.1406	.1443	.1480	.1517
0.4	.1554	.1591	.1628	.1664	.1700	.1736	.1772	.1808	.1844	.1879
0.5	.1915	.1950	.1985	.2019	.2054	.2088	.2123	.2157	.2190	.2224
0.6	.2257	.2291	.2324	.2357	.2389	.2422	.2454	.2486	.2517	.2549
0.7	.2580	.2611	.2642	.2673	.2704	.2734	.2764	.2794	.2823	.2852
0.8	.2881	.2910	.2939	.2967	.2995	.3023	.3051	.3078	.3106	.3133
0.9	.3159	.3186	.3212	.3238	.3264	.3289	.3315	.3340	.3365	.3389
1.0	.3413	.3438	.3461	.3485	.3508	.3531	.3554	.3577	.3599	.3621
1.1	.3643	.3665	.3686	.3708	.3729	.3749	.3770	.3790	.3810	.3830
1.2	.3849	.3869	.3888	.3907	.3925	.3944	.3962	.3980	.3997	.4015
1.3	.4032	.4049	.4066	.4082	.4099	.4115	.4131	.4147	.4162	.4177
1.4	.4192	.4207	.4222	.4236	.4251	.4265	.4279	.4292	.4306	.4319
1.5	.4332	.4345	.4357	.4370	.4382	.4394	.4406	.4418	.4429	.4441
1.6	.4452	.4463	.4474	.4484	.4495	.4505	.4515	.4525	.4535	.4545
1.7	.4554	.4564	.4573	.4582	.4591	.4599	.4608	.4616	.4625	.4633
1.8	.4641	.4649	.4656	.4664	.4671	.4678	.4686	.4693	.4699	.4706
1.9	.4713	.4719	.4726	.4732	.4738	.4744	.4750	.4756	.4761	.4767
2.0	.4772	.4778	.4783	.4788	.4793	.4798	.4803	.4808	.4812	.4817
2.1	.4821	.4826	.4830	.4834	.4838	.4842	.4846	.4850	.4854	.4857
2.2	.4861	.4864	.4868	.4871	.4875	.4878	.4881	.4884	.4887	.4890
2.3	.4893	.4896	.4898	.4901	.4904	.4906	.4909	.4911	.4913	.4916
2.4	.4918	.4920	.4922	.4925	.4927	.4929	.4931	.4932	.4934	.4936
2.5	.4938	.4940	.4941	.4943	.4945	.4946	.4948	.4949	.4951	.4952
2.6	.4953	.4955	.4956	.4957	.4959	.4960	.4961	.4962	.4963	.4964
2.7	.4965	.4966	.4967	.4968	.4969	.4970	.4971	.4972	.4973	.4974
2.8	.4974	.4975	.4976	.4977	.4977	.4978	.4979	.4979	.4980	.4981
2.9	.4981	.4982	.4982	.4983	.4984	.4984	.4985	.4985	.4986	.4986
3.0	.4987	.4987	.4987	.4988	.4988	.4989	.4989	.4989	.4990	.4990

Compound Interest and Annuity Tables*

B

*SOURCE: *Thorndike Encyclopedia of Banking and Financial Tables*, Warren, Gorham and Lamont, Inc., New York, pp. 6–352 through 6–373. Used with permission.

1.00 %
ANNUAL

		Amount Of 1	Amount Of 1 Per Period	Sinking Fund Payment	Present Worth Of 1	Present Worth Of 1 Per Period	Periodic Payment To Amortize 1	Constant Annual Percent	Total Interest	Annual Add-on Rate		
		What a single $1 deposit grows to in the future. The deposit is made at the beginning of the first period.	What a series of $1 deposits grow to in the future. A deposit is made at the end of each period.	The amount to be deposited at the end of each period that grows to $1 in the future.	What $1 to be paid in the future is worth today. Value today of a single payment tomorrow.	What $1 to be paid at the end of each period is a loan of $1. Value today of a series of payments tomorrow.	The mortgage payment to amortize a loan of $1. An annuity certain, payable at the end of each period, worth $1 today.	The annual payment, including interest and principal, to amortize completely a loan of $100.	The total interest paid over the term on a loan of $1. The loan is amortized by regular periodic payments.	The average annual interest rate on a loan that is completely amortized by regular periodic payments.		
		$S=(1+i)^n$	$S_{\overline{n}}=\dfrac{(1+i)^n-1}{i}$	$\dfrac{1}{S_{\overline{n}}}=\dfrac{i}{(1+i)^n-1}$	$V^n=\dfrac{1}{(1+i)^n}$	$A_{\overline{n}}=\dfrac{1-V^n}{i}$	$\dfrac{1}{A_{\overline{n}}}=\dfrac{i}{1-V^n}$					
YR												**YR**
1	1	1.010000	1.000000	1.00000000	0.990099	0.990099	1.01000000	101.00	0.010000	1.00	1
2	2	1.020100	2.010000	0.49751244	0.980296	1.970395	0.50751244	50.76	0.015025	0.75	2
3	3	1.030301	3.030100	0.33002211	0.970590	2.940985	0.34002211	34.01	0.020066	0.67	3
4	4	1.040604	4.060401	0.24628109	0.960980	3.901966	0.25628109	25.63	0.025124	0.63	4
5	5	1.051010	5.101005	0.19603980	0.951466	4.853431	0.20603980	20.61	0.030199	0.60	5
6	6	1.061520	6.152015	0.16254837	0.942045	5.795476	0.17254837	17.26	0.035290	0.59	6
7	7	1.072135	7.213535	0.13862828	0.932718	6.728195	0.14862828	14.87	0.040398	0.58	7
8	8	1.082857	8.285671	0.12069029	0.923483	7.651678	0.13069029	13.07	0.045522	0.57	8
9	9	1.093685	9.368527	0.10674036	0.914340	8.566018	0.11674036	11.68	0.050663	0.56	9
10	10	1.104622	10.462213	0.09558208	0.905287	9.471305	0.10558208	10.56	0.055821	0.56	10
11	11	1.115668	11.566835	0.08645408	0.896324	10.367628	0.09645408	9.65	0.060995	0.55	11
12	12	1.126825	12.682503	0.07884879	0.887449	11.255077	0.08884879	8.89	0.066185	0.55	12
13	13	1.138093	13.809328	0.07241482	0.878663	12.133740	0.08241482	8.25	0.071393	0.55	13
14	14	1.149474	14.947421	0.06690117	0.869963	13.003703	0.07690117	7.70	0.076616	0.55	14
15	15	1.160969	16.096896	0.06212378	0.861349	13.865053	0.07212378	7.22	0.081857	0.55	15
16	16	1.172579	17.257864	0.05794460	0.852821	14.717874	0.06794460	6.80	0.087114	0.54	16
17	17	1.184304	18.430443	0.05425806	0.844377	15.562251	0.06425806	6.43	0.092387	0.54	17
18	18	1.196147	19.614748	0.05098205	0.836017	16.398269	0.06098205	6.10	0.097677	0.54	18
19	19	1.208109	20.810895	0.04805175	0.827740	17.226008	0.05805175	5.81	0.102983	0.54	19
20	20	1.220190	22.019004	0.04541531	0.819544	18.045553	0.05541531	5.55	0.108306	0.54	20
21	21	1.232392	23.239194	0.04303075	0.811430	18.856983	0.05303075	5.31	0.113646	0.54	21
22	22	1.244716	24.471586	0.04086372	0.803396	19.660379	0.05086372	5.09	0.119002	0.54	22
23	23	1.257163	25.716302	0.03888584	0.795442	20.455821	0.04888584	4.89	0.124374	0.54	23
24	24	1.269735	26.973465	0.03707347	0.787566	21.243387	0.04707347	4.71	0.129763	0.54	24
25	25	1.282432	28.243200	0.03540675	0.779768	22.023156	0.04540675	4.55	0.135169	0.54	25
26	26	1.295256	29.525631	0.03386888	0.772048	22.795204	0.04386888	4.39	0.140591	0.54	26
27	27	1.308209	30.820888	0.03244553	0.764404	23.559608	0.04244553	4.25	0.146029	0.54	27
28	28	1.321291	32.129097	0.03112444	0.756836	24.316443	0.04112444	4.12	0.151484	0.54	28
29	29	1.334504	33.450388	0.02989502	0.749342	25.065785	0.03989502	3.99	0.156956	0.54	29
30	30	1.347849	34.784892	0.02874811	0.741923	25.807708	0.03874811	3.88	0.162443	0.54	30
31	31	1.361242	36.132740	0.02767573	0.734577	26.542285	0.03767573	3.77	0.167948	0.54	31
32	32	1.374941	37.494068	0.02667089	0.727304	27.269589	0.03667089	3.67	0.173468	0.54	32
33	33	1.388690	38.869009	0.02572744	0.720103	27.989693	0.03572744	3.58	0.179005	0.54	33
34	34	1.402577	40.257699	0.02483997	0.712973	28.702666	0.03483997	3.49	0.184559	0.54	34
35	35	1.416603	41.660276	0.02400368	0.705914	29.408580	0.03400368	3.41	0.190129	0.54	35
36	36	1.430678	43.076878	0.02321431	0.698925	30.107505	0.03321431	3.33	0.195715	0.54	36
37	37	1.445076	44.507647	0.02246805	0.692005	30.799510	0.03246805	3.25	0.201318	0.54	37
38	38	1.459527	45.952724	0.02176150	0.685153	31.484663	0.03176150	3.18	0.206937	0.54	38
39	39	1.474123	47.412251	0.02109160	0.678370	32.163033	0.03109160	3.11	0.212572	0.55	39
40	40	1.488864	48.886373	0.02045560	0.671653	32.834686	0.03045560	3.05	0.218224	0.55	40
41	41	1.503752	50.375237	0.01985102	0.665003	33.499689	0.02985102	2.99	0.223892	0.55	41
42	42	1.518790	51.878989	0.01927563	0.658419	34.158108	0.02927563	2.93	0.229576	0.55	42
43	43	1.533978	53.397779	0.01872737	0.651900	34.810008	0.02872737	2.88	0.235277	0.55	43
44	44	1.549318	54.931757	0.01820441	0.645445	35.455454	0.02820441	2.83	0.240994	0.55	44
45	45	1.564811	56.481075	0.01770505	0.639055	36.094508	0.02770505	2.78	0.246727	0.55	45
46	46	1.580459	58.045885	0.01722775	0.632728	36.727236	0.02722775	2.73	0.252476	0.55	46
47	47	1.596263	59.626344	0.01677111	0.626463	37.353699	0.02677111	2.68	0.258242	0.55	47
48	48	1.612226	61.222608	0.01633384	0.620260	37.973959	0.02633384	2.64	0.264024	0.55	48
49	49	1.628348	62.834834	0.01591474	0.614119	38.588079	0.02591474	2.60	0.269822	0.55	49
50	50	1.644632	64.463182	0.01551273	0.608039	39.196118	0.02551273	2.56	0.275637	0.55	50

COMPOUND INTEREST AND ANNUITY TABLE

2.00 %
ANNUAL

		Amount Of 1	Amount Of 1 Per Period	Sinking Fund Payment	Present Worth Of 1	Present Worth Of 1 Per Period	Periodic Payment To Amortize 1	Constant Annual Percent	Total Interest	Annual Add-on Rate	
		What a single $1 deposit grows to in the future. The deposit is made at the beginning of the first period.	What a series of $1 deposits grow to in the future. A deposit is made at the end of each period.	The amount to be deposited at the end of each period that grows to $1 in the future.	What $1 to be paid in the future is worth today. Value today of a single payment tomorrow.	What $1 to be paid at the end of each period is worth today. Value today of a series of payments tomorrow.	The mortgage payment to amortize a loan of $1. An annuity certain, payable at the end of each period, worth $1 today.	The annual payment, including interest and principal, to amortize completely a loan of $100.	The total interest paid over the term of $1. The loan is amortized by regular periodic payments.	The average annual interest rate on a loan that is completely amortized by regular periodic payments.	
		$S=(1+i)^n$	$S_{\overline{n}}=\dfrac{(1+i)^n-1}{i}$	$\dfrac{1}{S_{\overline{n}}}=\dfrac{i}{(1+i)^n-1}$	$V^n=\dfrac{1}{(1+i)^n}$	$A_{\overline{n}}=\dfrac{1-V^n}{i}$	$\dfrac{1}{A_{\overline{n}}}=\dfrac{i}{1-V^n}$				
YR											YR
1	1	1.020000	1.00000000	1.00000000	0.980392	0.980392	1.02000000	102.00	0.020000	2.00	1
2	2	1.040400	2.020000	0.49504950	0.961169	1.941561	0.51504950	51.51	0.030099	1.50	2
3	3	1.061208	3.060400	0.32675467	0.942322	2.883883	0.34675467	34.68	0.040264	1.34	3
4	4	1.082432	4.121608	0.24262375	0.923845	3.807729	0.26262375	26.27	0.050495	1.26	4
5	5	1.104081	5.204040	0.19215839	0.905731	4.713460	0.21215839	21.22	0.060792	1.22	5
6	6	1.126162	6.308121	0.15852581	0.887971	5.601431	0.17852581	17.86	0.071155	1.19	6
7	7	1.148686	7.434283	0.13451196	0.870560	6.471991	0.15451196	15.46	0.081584	1.17	7
8	8	1.171659	8.582969	0.11650980	0.853490	7.325481	0.13650980	13.66	0.092078	1.15	8
9	9	1.195093	9.754628	0.10251544	0.836755	8.162237	0.12251544	12.26	0.102639	1.14	9
10	10	1.218994	10.949721	0.09132653	0.820348	8.982585	0.11132653	11.14	0.113265	1.13	10
11	11	1.243374	12.168715	0.08217794	0.804263	9.786848	0.10217794	10.22	0.123957	1.13	11
12	12	1.268242	13.412090	0.07455960	0.788493	10.575341	0.09455960	9.46	0.134715	1.12	12
13	13	1.293607	14.680332	0.06811835	0.773033	11.348374	0.08811835	8.82	0.145539	1.12	13
14	14	1.319479	15.973938	0.06260197	0.757875	12.106249	0.08260197	8.27	0.156428	1.12	14
15	15	1.345868	17.293417	0.05782547	0.743015	12.849264	0.07782547	7.79	0.167382	1.12	15
16	16	1.372786	18.639285	0.05365013	0.728446	13.577709	0.07365013	7.37	0.178402	1.12	16
17	17	1.400241	20.012071	0.04996984	0.714163	14.291872	0.06996984	7.00	0.189487	1.11	17
18	18	1.428246	21.412312	0.04670210	0.700159	14.992031	0.06670210	6.68	0.200638	1.11	18
19	19	1.456811	22.840559	0.04378177	0.686431	15.678462	0.06378177	6.38	0.211854	1.12	19
20	20	1.485947	24.297370	0.04115672	0.672971	16.351433	0.06115672	6.12	0.223134	1.12	20
21	21	1.515666	25.783317	0.03878477	0.659776	17.011209	0.05878477	5.88	0.234480	1.12	21
22	22	1.545980	27.298984	0.03663140	0.646839	17.658048	0.05663140	5.67	0.245891	1.12	22
23	23	1.576899	28.844963	0.03466810	0.634156	18.292204	0.05466810	5.47	0.257366	1.12	23
24	24	1.608437	30.421862	0.03287110	0.621721	18.913926	0.05287110	5.29	0.268906	1.12	24
25	25	1.640606	32.030300	0.03122044	0.609531	19.523456	0.05122044	5.13	0.280511	1.12	25
26	26	1.673418	33.670906	0.02969923	0.597579	20.121036	0.04969923	4.97	0.292180	1.12	26
27	27	1.706886	35.344324	0.02829309	0.585862	20.706898	0.04829309	4.83	0.303913	1.13	27
28	28	1.741024	37.051210	0.02698967	0.574375	21.281272	0.04698967	4.70	0.315711	1.13	28
29	29	1.775845	38.792235	0.02577836	0.563112	21.844385	0.04577836	4.58	0.327572	1.13	29
30	30	1.811362	40.568079	0.02464992	0.552071	22.396456	0.04464992	4.47	0.339498	1.13	30
31	31	1.847589	42.379441	0.02359635	0.541246	22.937702	0.04359635	4.36	0.351487	1.13	31
32	32	1.884541	44.227030	0.02261061	0.530633	23.468335	0.04261061	4.27	0.363539	1.14	32
33	33	1.922231	46.111570	0.02168653	0.520229	23.988564	0.04168653	4.17	0.375656	1.14	33
34	34	1.960676	48.033802	0.02081867	0.510028	24.498592	0.04081867	4.09	0.387835	1.14	34
35	35	1.999890	49.994478	0.02000221	0.500028	24.998619	0.04000221	4.01	0.400077	1.14	35
36	36	2.039887	51.994367	0.01923285	0.490223	25.488842	0.03923285	3.93	0.412383	1.15	36
37	37	2.080685	54.034255	0.01850678	0.480611	25.969453	0.03850678	3.86	0.424751	1.15	37
38	38	2.122299	56.114940	0.01782057	0.471187	26.440641	0.03782057	3.79	0.437182	1.15	38
39	39	2.164745	58.237238	0.01717114	0.461948	26.902589	0.03717114	3.72	0.449675	1.15	39
40	40	2.208040	60.401983	0.01655575	0.452890	27.355479	0.03655575	3.66	0.462230	1.16	40
41	41	2.252200	62.610023	0.01597188	0.444010	27.799489	0.03597188	3.60	0.474847	1.16	41
42	42	2.297244	64.862223	0.01541729	0.435304	28.234794	0.03541729	3.55	0.487526	1.16	42
43	43	2.343189	67.159468	0.01488993	0.426769	28.661562	0.03488993	3.49	0.500267	1.16	43
44	44	2.390053	69.502657	0.01438794	0.418401	29.079963	0.03438794	3.44	0.513069	1.17	44
45	45	2.437854	71.892710	0.01390962	0.410197	29.490160	0.03390962	3.40	0.525933	1.17	45
46	46	2.486611	74.330564	0.01345342	0.402154	29.892314	0.03345342	3.35	0.538857	1.17	46
47	47	2.536344	76.817176	0.01301792	0.394268	30.286582	0.03301792	3.31	0.551842	1.17	47
48	48	2.587070	79.353519	0.01260184	0.386538	30.673120	0.03260184	3.27	0.564888	1.18	48
49	49	2.638812	81.940590	0.01220396	0.378958	31.052078	0.03220396	3.23	0.577994	1.18	49
50	50	2.691588	84.579401	0.01182321	0.371528	31.423606	0.03182321	3.19	0.591160	1.18	50

COMPOUND INTEREST AND ANNUITY TABLE

3.00 %
ANNUAL

		Amount Of 1	Amount Of 1 Per Period	Sinking Fund Payment	Present Worth Of 1	Present Worth Of 1 Per Period	Periodic Payment To Amortize 1	Constant Annual Percent	Total Interest	Annual Add-on Rate		
		What a single $1 deposit grows to in the future. The deposit is made at the beginning of the first period.	What a series of $1 deposits grow to in the future. A deposit is made at the end of each period.	The amount to be deposited at the end of each period that grows to $1 in the future.	What $1 to be paid in the future is worth today. Value today of a single payment tomorrow.	What $1 to be paid at the end of each period is worth today. Value today of a series of payments tomorrow.	The mortgage payment to amortize a loan of $1. An annuity certain, payable at the end of each period, worth $1 today.	The annual payment, including interest and principal, to amortize completely a loan of $100.	The total interest paid over the term on a loan of $1. The loan is amortized by regular periodic payments.	The average annual interest rate on a loan that is completely amortized by regular periodic payments.		
		$S=(1+i)^n$	$S_{\overline{n}}=\dfrac{(1+i)^n-1}{i}$	$\dfrac{1}{S_{\overline{n}}}=\dfrac{i}{(1+i)^n-1}$	$V^n=\dfrac{1}{(1+i)^n}$	$A_{\overline{n}}=\dfrac{1-V^n}{i}$	$\dfrac{1}{A_{\overline{n}}}=\dfrac{i}{1-V^n}$					
YR												**YR**
1	1	1.030000	1.000000	1.00000000	0.970874	0.970874	1.03000000	103.00	0.030000	3.00	1
2	2	1.060900	2.030000	0.49261084	0.942596	1.913470	0.52261084	52.27	0.045222	2.26	2
3	3	1.092727	3.090900	0.32353036	0.915142	2.828611	0.35353036	35.36	0.060591	2.02	3
4	4	1.125509	4.183627	0.23902705	0.888487	3.717098	0.26902705	26.91	0.076108	1.90	4
5	5	1.159274	5.309136	0.18835457	0.862609	4.579707	0.21835457	21.84	0.091773	1.84	5
6	6	1.194052	6.468410	0.15459750	0.837484	5.417191	0.18459750	18.46	0.107585	1.79	6
7	7	1.229874	7.662462	0.13050635	0.813092	6.230283	0.16050635	16.06	0.123544	1.76	7
8	8	1.266770	8.892336	0.11245639	0.789409	7.019692	0.14245639	14.25	0.139651	1.75	8
9	9	1.304773	10.159106	0.09843386	0.766417	7.786109	0.12843386	12.85	0.155905	1.73	9
10	10	1.343916	11.463879	0.08723051	0.744094	8.530203	0.11723051	11.73	0.172305	1.72	10
11	11	1.384234	12.807796	0.07807745	0.722421	9.252624	0.10807745	10.81	0.188852	1.72	11
12	12	1.425761	14.192030	0.07046209	0.701380	9.954004	0.10046209	10.05	0.205545	1.71	12
13	13	1.468534	15.617790	0.06402954	0.680951	10.634955	0.09402954	9.41	0.222384	1.71	13
14	14	1.512590	17.086324	0.05852634	0.661118	11.296073	0.08852634	8.86	0.239369	1.71	14
15	15	1.557967	18.598914	0.05376658	0.641862	11.937935	0.08376658	8.38	0.256499	1.71	15
16	16	1.604706	20.156881	0.04961085	0.623167	12.561102	0.07961085	7.97	0.273774	1.71	16
17	17	1.652848	21.761588	0.04595253	0.605016	13.166118	0.07595253	7.60	0.291193	1.71	17
18	18	1.702433	23.414435	0.04270870	0.587395	13.753513	0.07270870	7.28	0.308757	1.72	18
19	19	1.753506	25.116868	0.03981388	0.570286	14.323799	0.06981388	6.99	0.326464	1.72	19
20	20	1.806111	26.870374	0.03721571	0.553676	14.877475	0.06721571	6.73	0.344314	1.72	20
21	21	1.860295	28.676486	0.03487178	0.537549	15.415024	0.06487178	6.49	0.362307	1.73	21
22	22	1.916103	30.536780	0.03274739	0.521893	15.936917	0.06274739	6.28	0.380443	1.73	22
23	23	1.973587	32.452884	0.03081390	0.506692	16.443608	0.06081390	6.09	0.398720	1.73	23
24	24	2.032794	34.426470	0.02904742	0.491934	16.935542	0.05904742	5.91	0.417138	1.74	24
25	25	2.093778	36.459264	0.02742787	0.477606	17.413148	0.05742787	5.75	0.435697	1.74	25
26	26	2.156591	38.553042	0.02593829	0.463695	17.876842	0.05593829	5.60	0.454396	1.75	26
27	27	2.221289	40.709634	0.02456421	0.450189	18.327031	0.05456421	5.46	0.473234	1.75	27
28	28	2.287928	42.930923	0.02329323	0.437077	18.764108	0.05329323	5.33	0.492211	1.76	28
29	29	2.356566	45.218850	0.02211467	0.424346	19.188455	0.05211467	5.22	0.511325	1.76	29
30	30	2.427262	47.575416	0.02101926	0.411987	19.600441	0.05101926	5.11	0.530578	1.77	30
31	31	2.500080	50.002678	0.01999893	0.399987	20.000428	0.04999893	5.00	0.549967	1.77	31
32	32	2.575083	52.502759	0.01904662	0.388337	20.388766	0.04904662	4.91	0.569492	1.78	32
33	33	2.652335	55.077841	0.01815612	0.377026	20.765792	0.04815612	4.82	0.589152	1.79	33
34	34	2.731905	57.730177	0.01732196	0.366045	21.131837	0.04732196	4.74	0.608947	1.79	34
35	35	2.813862	60.462082	0.01653929	0.355383	21.487220	0.04653929	4.66	0.628875	1.80	35
36	36	2.898278	63.275944	0.01580379	0.345032	21.832252	0.04580379	4.59	0.648937	1.80	36
37	37	2.985227	66.174223	0.01511162	0.334983	22.167235	0.04511162	4.52	0.669130	1.81	37
38	38	3.074783	69.159449	0.01445934	0.325226	22.492462	0.04445934	4.45	0.689455	1.81	38
39	39	3.167027	72.234233	0.01384385	0.315754	22.808215	0.04384385	4.39	0.709910	1.82	39
40	40	3.262038	75.401260	0.01326238	0.306557	23.114772	0.04326238	4.33	0.730495	1.83	40
41	41	3.359899	78.663298	0.01271241	0.297628	23.412400	0.04271241	4.28	0.751209	1.83	41
42	42	3.460696	82.023196	0.01219167	0.288959	23.701359	0.04219167	4.22	0.772050	1.84	42
43	43	3.564517	85.483892	0.01169811	0.280543	23.981902	0.04169811	4.17	0.793019	1.84	43
44	44	3.671452	89.048409	0.01122985	0.272372	24.254274	0.04122985	4.13	0.814113	1.85	44
45	45	3.781596	92.719861	0.01078518	0.264439	24.518713	0.04078518	4.08	0.835333	1.86	45
46	46	3.895044	96.501457	0.01036254	0.256737	24.775449	0.04036254	4.04	0.856677	1.86	46
47	47	4.011895	100.396501	0.00996051	0.249259	25.024708	0.03996051	4.00	0.878144	1.87	47
48	48	4.132252	104.408396	0.00957777	0.241999	25.266707	0.03957777	3.96	0.899733	1.87	48
49	49	4.256219	108.540648	0.00921314	0.234950	25.501657	0.03921314	3.93	0.921444	1.88	49
50	50	4.383906	112.796867	0.00886549	0.228107	25.729764	0.03886549	3.89	0.943275	1.89	50

COMPOUND INTEREST AND ANNUITY TABLE   4.00 % ANNUAL

		Amount Of 1	Amount Of 1 Per Period	Sinking Fund Payment	Present Worth Of 1	Present Worth Of 1 Per Period	Periodic Payment To Amortize 1	Constant Annual Percent	Total Interest	Annual Add-on Rate	
		What a single $1 deposit grows to in the future. The deposit is made at the beginning of the first period.	What a series of $1 deposits grow to in the future. A deposit is made at the end of each period.	The amount to be deposited at the end of each period that grows to $1 in the future.	What $1 to be paid in the future is worth today. Value today of a single payment tomorrow.	What $1 to be paid at the end of each period is worth today. Value today of a series of payments tomorrow.	The mortgage payment to amortize a loan of $1. An annuity certain, payable at the end of each period, worth $1 today.	The annual payment, including interest and principal, to amortize completely a loan of $100.	The total interest paid over the term of $1. The loan is amortized by regular periodic payments.	The average annual interest rate on a loan that is completely amortized by regular periodic payments.	
		$S=(1+i)^n$	$S_{\overline{n}}=\dfrac{(1+i)^n-1}{i}$	$\dfrac{1}{S_{\overline{n}}}=\dfrac{i}{(1+i)^n-1}$	$V^n=\dfrac{1}{(1+i)^n}$	$A_{\overline{n}}=\dfrac{1-V^n}{i}$	$\dfrac{1}{A_{\overline{n}}}=\dfrac{i}{1-V^n}$				
YR											**YR**
1	1	1.040000	1.000000	1.00000000	0.961538	0.961538	1.04000000	104.00	0.040000	4.00	1
2	2	1.081600	2.040000	0.49019608	0.924556	1.886095	0.53019608	53.02	0.060392	3.02	2
3	3	1.124864	3.121600	0.32034854	0.888996	2.775091	0.36034854	36.04	0.081046	2.70	3
4	4	1.169859	4.246464	0.23549005	0.854804	3.629895	0.27549005	27.55	0.101960	2.55	4
5	5	1.216653	5.416323	0.18462711	0.821927	4.451822	0.22462711	22.47	0.123136	2.46	5
6	6	1.265319	6.632975	0.15076190	0.790315	5.242137	0.19076190	19.08	0.144571	2.41	6
7	7	1.315932	7.898294	0.12660961	0.759918	6.002055	0.16660961	16.67	0.166267	2.38	7
8	8	1.368569	9.214226	0.10852783	0.730690	6.732745	0.14852783	14.86	0.188223	2.35	8
9	9	1.423312	10.582795	0.09449299	0.702587	7.435332	0.13449299	13.45	0.210437	2.34	9
10	10	1.480244	12.006107	0.08329094	0.675564	8.110896	0.12329094	12.33	0.232909	2.33	10
11	11	1.539454	13.486351	0.07414904	0.649581	8.760477	0.11414904	11.42	0.255639	2.32	11
12	12	1.601032	15.025805	0.06655217	0.624597	9.385074	0.10655217	10.66	0.278626	2.32	12
13	13	1.665074	16.626838	0.06014373	0.600574	9.985648	0.10014373	10.02	0.301868	2.32	13
14	14	1.731676	18.291911	0.05466897	0.577475	10.563123	0.09466897	9.47	0.325366	2.32	14
15	15	1.800944	20.023588	0.04994110	0.555265	11.118387	0.08994110	9.00	0.349117	2.33	15
16	16	1.872981	21.824531	0.04582000	0.533908	11.652296	0.08582000	8.59	0.373120	2.33	16
17	17	1.947900	23.697512	0.04219852	0.513373	12.165669	0.08219852	8.22	0.397375	2.34	17
18	18	2.025817	25.645413	0.03899333	0.493628	12.659297	0.07899333	7.90	0.421880	2.34	18
19	19	2.106849	27.671229	0.03613862	0.474642	13.133939	0.07613862	7.62	0.446634	2.35	19
20	20	2.191123	29.778079	0.03358175	0.456387	13.590326	0.07358175	7.36	0.471635	2.36	20
21	21	2.278768	31.969202	0.03128011	0.438834	14.029160	0.07128011	7.13	0.496882	2.37	21
22	22	2.369919	34.247970	0.02919881	0.421955	14.451115	0.06919881	6.92	0.522374	2.37	22
23	23	2.464716	36.617889	0.02730906	0.405726	14.856842	0.06730906	6.74	0.548108	2.38	23
24	24	2.563304	39.082604	0.02558683	0.390121	15.246963	0.06558683	6.56	0.574084	2.39	24
25	25	2.665836	41.645908	0.02401196	0.375117	15.622080	0.06401196	6.41	0.600299	2.40	25
26	26	2.772470	44.311745	0.02256738	0.360689	15.982769	0.06256738	6.26	0.626752	2.41	26
27	27	2.883369	47.084214	0.02123854	0.346817	16.329586	0.06123854	6.13	0.653441	2.42	27
28	28	2.998703	49.967583	0.02001298	0.333477	16.663063	0.06001298	6.01	0.680363	2.43	28
29	29	3.118651	52.966286	0.01887993	0.320651	16.983715	0.05887993	5.89	0.707518	2.44	29
30	30	3.243398	56.084938	0.01783010	0.308319	17.292033	0.05783010	5.79	0.734903	2.45	30
31	31	3.373133	59.328335	0.01685535	0.296460	17.588494	0.05685535	5.69	0.762516	2.46	31
32	32	3.508059	62.701469	0.01594859	0.285058	17.873551	0.05594859	5.60	0.790355	2.47	32
33	33	3.648381	66.209527	0.01510357	0.274094	18.147646	0.05510357	5.52	0.818418	2.48	33
34	34	3.794316	69.857909	0.01431477	0.263552	18.411198	0.05431477	5.44	0.846702	2.49	34
35	35	3.946089	73.652225	0.01357732	0.253415	18.664613	0.05357732	5.36	0.875206	2.50	35
36	36	4.103933	77.598314	0.01288688	0.243669	18.908282	0.05288688	5.29	0.903928	2.51	36
37	37	4.268090	81.702246	0.01223957	0.234297	19.142579	0.05223957	5.23	0.932864	2.52	37
38	38	4.438813	85.970336	0.01163192	0.225285	19.367864	0.05163192	5.17	0.962013	2.53	38
39	39	4.616366	90.409150	0.01106083	0.216621	19.584485	0.05106083	5.11	0.991372	2.54	39
40	40	4.801021	95.025516	0.01052349	0.208289	19.792774	0.05052349	5.06	1.020940	2.55	40
41	41	4.993061	99.826536	0.01001738	0.200278	19.993052	0.05001738	5.01	1.050712	2.56	41
42	42	5.192784	104.819586	0.00954020	0.192575	20.185627	0.04954020	4.96	1.080688	2.57	42
43	43	5.400495	110.012382	0.00908989	0.185168	20.370795	0.04908989	4.91	1.110865	2.58	43
44	44	5.616515	115.412877	0.00866454	0.178046	20.548841	0.04866454	4.87	1.141240	2.59	44
45	45	5.841176	121.029392	0.00826246	0.171198	20.720040	0.04826246	4.83	1.171811	2.60	45
46	46	6.074823	126.870568	0.00788205	0.164614	20.884654	0.04788205	4.79	1.202574	2.61	46
47	47	6.317816	132.945390	0.00752189	0.158283	21.042936	0.04752189	4.76	1.233529	2.62	47
48	48	6.570528	139.263206	0.00718065	0.152195	21.195131	0.04718065	4.72	1.264671	2.63	48
49	49	6.833349	145.833734	0.00685712	0.146341	21.341472	0.04685712	4.69	1.295999	2.64	49
50	50	7.106683	152.667084	0.00655020	0.140713	21.482185	0.04655020	4.66	1.327510	2.66	50

COMPOUND INTEREST AND ANNUITY TABLE

**5.00 %
ANNUAL**

		Amount Of 1	Amount Of 1 Per Period	Sinking Fund Payment	Present Worth Of 1	Present Worth Of 1 Per Period	Periodic Payment To Amortize 1	Constant Annual Percent	Total Interest	Annual Add-on Rate		
		What a single $1 deposit grows to in the future. The deposit is made at the beginning of the first period.	What a series of $1 deposits grow to in the future. A deposit is made at the end of each period.	The amount to be deposited at the end of each period that grows to $1 in the future.	What $1 to be paid in the future is worth today. Value today of a single payment tomorrow.	What $1 to be paid at the end of each period is worth today. Value today of a series of payments tomorrow.	The mortgage payment to amortize a loan of $1. An annuity certain, payable at the end of each period, worth $1 today.	The annual payment, including interest and principal, to amortize completely a loan of $100.	The total interest paid over the term of $1. The loan is amortized by regular periodic payments.	The average annual interest rate on a loan that is completely amortized by regular periodic payments.		
		$S=(1+i)^n$	$S_{\overline{n}}=\dfrac{(1+i)^n-1}{i}$	$\dfrac{1}{S_{\overline{n}}}=\dfrac{i}{(1+i)^n-1}$	$V^n=\dfrac{1}{(1+i)^n}$	$A_{\overline{n}}=\dfrac{1-V^n}{i}$	$\dfrac{1}{A_{\overline{n}}}=\dfrac{i}{1-V^n}$					
YR												**YR**
1	1	1.050000	1.000000	1.00000000	0.952381	0.952381	1.05000000	105.00	0.050000	5.00	1
2	2	1.102500	2.050000	0.48780488	0.907029	1.859410	0.53780488	53.79	0.075610	3.78	2
3	3	1.157625	3.152500	0.31720856	0.863838	2.723248	0.36720856	36.73	0.101626	3.39	3
4	4	1.215506	4.310125	0.23201183	0.822702	3.545951	0.28201183	28.21	0.128047	3.20	4
5	5	1.276282	5.525631	0.18097480	0.783526	4.329477	0.23097480	23.10	0.154874	3.10	5
6	6	1.340096	6.801913	0.14701747	0.746215	5.075692	0.19701747	19.71	0.182105	3.04	6
7	7	1.407100	8.142008	0.12281982	0.710681	5.786373	0.17281982	17.29	0.209739	3.00	7
8	8	1.477455	9.549109	0.10472181	0.676839	6.463213	0.15472181	15.48	0.237775	2.97	8
9	9	1.551328	11.026564	0.09069008	0.644609	7.107822	0.14069008	14.07	0.266211	2.96	9
10	10	1.628895	12.577893	0.07950457	0.613913	7.721735	0.12950457	12.96	0.295046	2.95	10
11	11	1.710339	14.206787	0.07038889	0.584679	8.306414	0.12038889	12.04	0.324278	2.95	11
12	12	1.795856	15.917127	0.06282541	0.556837	8.863252	0.11282541	11.29	0.353905	2.95	12
13	13	1.885649	17.712983	0.05645577	0.530321	9.393573	0.10645577	10.65	0.383925	2.95	13
14	14	1.979932	19.598632	0.05102397	0.505068	9.898641	0.10102397	10.11	0.414336	2.96	14
15	15	2.078928	21.578564	0.04634229	0.481017	10.379658	0.09634229	9.64	0.445134	2.97	15
16	16	2.182875	23.657492	0.04226991	0.458112	10.837770	0.09226991	9.23	0.476319	2.98	16
17	17	2.292018	25.840366	0.03869914	0.436297	11.274066	0.08869914	8.87	0.507885	2.99	17
18	18	2.406619	28.132385	0.03554622	0.415521	11.689587	0.08554622	8.56	0.539832	3.00	18
19	19	2.526950	30.539004	0.03274501	0.395734	12.085321	0.08274501	8.28	0.572155	3.01	19
20	20	2.653298	33.065954	0.03024259	0.376889	12.462210	0.08024259	8.03	0.604852	3.02	20
21	21	2.785963	35.719252	0.02799611	0.358942	12.821153	0.07799611	7.80	0.637918	3.04	21
22	22	2.925261	38.505214	0.02597051	0.341850	13.163003	0.07597051	7.60	0.671351	3.05	22
23	23	3.071524	41.430475	0.02413682	0.325571	13.488574	0.07413682	7.42	0.705147	3.07	23
24	24	3.225100	44.501999	0.02247090	0.310068	13.798642	0.07247090	7.25	0.739302	3.08	24
25	25	3.386355	47.727099	0.02095246	0.295303	14.093945	0.07095246	7.10	0.773811	3.10	25
26	26	3.555673	51.113454	0.01956432	0.281241	14.375185	0.06956432	6.96	0.808672	3.11	26
27	27	3.733456	54.669126	0.01829186	0.267848	14.643034	0.06829186	6.83	0.843880	3.13	27
28	28	3.920129	58.402583	0.01712253	0.255094	14.898127	0.06712253	6.72	0.879431	3.14	28
29	29	4.116136	62.322712	0.01604551	0.242946	15.141074	0.06604551	6.61	0.915320	3.16	29
30	30	4.321942	66.438848	0.01505144	0.231377	15.372451	0.06505144	6.51	0.951543	3.17	30
31	31	4.538039	70.760790	0.01413212	0.220359	15.592811	0.06413212	6.42	0.988096	3.19	31
32	32	4.764941	75.298829	0.01328042	0.209866	15.802677	0.06328042	6.33	1.024973	3.20	32
33	33	5.003189	80.063771	0.01249004	0.199873	16.002549	0.06249004	6.25	1.062171	3.22	33
34	34	5.253348	85.066959	0.01175545	0.190355	16.192904	0.06175545	6.18	1.099685	3.23	34
35	35	5.516015	90.320307	0.01107171	0.181290	16.374194	0.06107171	6.11	1.137510	3.25	35
36	36	5.791816	95.836323	0.01043446	0.172657	16.546852	0.06043446	6.05	1.175640	3.27	36
37	37	6.081407	101.628139	0.00983979	0.164436	16.711287	0.05983979	5.99	1.214072	3.28	37
38	38	6.385477	107.709546	0.00928423	0.156605	16.867893	0.05928423	5.93	1.252801	3.30	38
39	39	6.704751	114.095023	0.00876462	0.149148	17.017041	0.05876462	5.88	1.291820	3.31	39
40	40	7.039989	120.799774	0.00827816	0.142046	17.159086	0.05827816	5.83	1.331126	3.33	40
41	41	7.391988	127.839763	0.00782229	0.135282	17.294368	0.05782229	5.79	1.370714	3.34	41
42	42	7.761588	135.231751	0.00739471	0.128840	17.423208	0.05739471	5.74	1.410578	3.36	42
43	43	8.149667	142.993339	0.00699333	0.122704	17.545912	0.05699333	5.70	1.450713	3.37	43
44	44	8.557150	151.143006	0.00661625	0.116861	17.662773	0.05661625	5.67	1.491115	3.39	44
45	45	8.985008	159.700156	0.00626173	0.111297	17.774070	0.05626173	5.63	1.531778	3.40	45
46	46	9.434258	168.685164	0.00592820	0.105997	17.880066	0.05592820	5.60	1.572697	3.42	46
47	47	9.905971	178.119422	0.00561421	0.100949	17.981016	0.05561421	5.57	1.613868	3.43	47
48	48	10.401270	188.025393	0.00531843	0.096142	18.077158	0.05531843	5.54	1.655285	3.45	48
49	49	10.921333	198.426663	0.00503965	0.091564	18.168722	0.05503965	5.51	1.696943	3.46	49
50	50	11.467400	209.347996	0.00477674	0.087204	18.255925	0.05477674	5.48	1.738837	3.48	50

COMPOUND INTEREST AND ANNUITY TABLE

6.00 %
ANNUAL

		Amount Of 1	Amount Of 1 Per Period	Sinking Fund Payment	Present Worth Of 1	Present Worth Of 1 Per Period	Periodic Payment To Amortize 1	Constant Annual Percent	Total Interest	Annual Add-on Rate	
		What a single $1 deposit grows to in the future. The deposit is made at the beginning of the first period.	What a series of $1 deposits grow to in the future. A deposit is made at the end of each period.	The amount to be deposited at the end of each period that grows to $1 in the future.	What $1 to be paid in the future is worth today. Value today of a single payment tomorrow.	What $1 to be paid at the end of each period is worth today. Value today of a series of payments tomorrow.	The mortgage payment to amortize a loan of $1. An annuity certain, payable at the end of each period, worth $1 today.	The annual payment, including interest and principal, to amortize completely a loan of $100.	The total interest paid over the term of $1. The loan is amortized by regular periodic payments.	The average annual interest rate on a loan that is completely amortized by regular periodic payments.	
		$S=(1+i)^n$	$S_{\overline{n}}=\dfrac{(1+i)^n-1}{i}$	$\dfrac{1}{S_{\overline{n}}}=\dfrac{i}{(1+i)^n-1}$	$V^n=\dfrac{1}{(1+i)^n}$	$A_{\overline{n}}=\dfrac{1-V^n}{i}$	$\dfrac{1}{A_{\overline{n}}}=\dfrac{i}{1-V^n}$				
YR											**YR**
1	1	1.060000	1.000000	1.00000000	0.943396	0.943396	1.06000000	106.00	0.060000	6.00	1
2	2	1.123600	2.060000	0.48543689	0.889996	1.833393	0.54543689	54.55	0.090874	4.54	2
3	3	1.191016	3.183600	0.31410981	0.839619	2.673012	0.37410981	37.42	0.122329	4.08	3
4	4	1.262477	4.374616	0.22859149	0.792094	3.465106	0.28859149	28.86	0.154366	3.86	4
5	5	1.338226	5.637093	0.17739640	0.747258	4.212364	0.23739640	23.74	0.186982	3.74	5
6	6	1.418519	6.975319	0.14336263	0.704961	4.917324	0.20336263	20.34	0.220176	3.67	6
7	7	1.503630	8.393838	0.11913502	0.665057	5.582381	0.17913502	17.92	0.253945	3.63	7
8	8	1.593848	9.897468	0.10103594	0.627412	6.209794	0.16103594	16.11	0.288288	3.60	8
9	9	1.689479	11.491316	0.08702224	0.591898	6.801692	0.14702224	14.71	0.323200	3.59	9
10	10	1.790848	13.180795	0.07586796	0.558395	7.360087	0.13586796	13.59	0.358680	3.59	10
11	11	1.898299	14.971643	0.06679294	0.526788	7.886875	0.12679294	12.68	0.394722	3.59	11
12	12	2.012196	16.869941	0.05927703	0.496969	8.383844	0.11927703	11.93	0.431324	3.59	12
13	13	2.132928	18.882138	0.05296011	0.468839	8.852683	0.11296011	11.30	0.468481	3.60	13
14	14	2.260904	21.015066	0.04758491	0.442301	9.294984	0.10758491	10.76	0.506189	3.62	14
15	15	2.396558	23.275970	0.04296276	0.417265	9.712249	0.10296276	10.30	0.544441	3.63	15
16	16	2.540352	25.672528	0.03895214	0.393646	10.105895	0.09895214	9.90	0.583234	3.65	16
17	17	2.692773	28.212880	0.03544480	0.371364	10.477260	0.09544480	9.55	0.622562	3.66	17
18	18	2.854339	30.905653	0.03235654	0.350344	10.827603	0.09235654	9.24	0.662418	3.68	18
19	19	3.025660	33.759992	0.02962086	0.330513	11.158116	0.08962086	8.97	0.702796	3.70	19
20	20	3.207135	36.785591	0.02718456	0.311805	11.469921	0.08718456	8.72	0.743691	3.72	20
21	21	3.399564	39.992727	0.02500455	0.294155	11.764077	0.08500455	8.51	0.785095	3.74	21
22	22	3.603537	43.392290	0.02304557	0.277505	12.041582	0.08304557	8.31	0.827003	3.76	22
23	23	3.819750	46.995828	0.02127848	0.261797	12.303379	0.08127848	8.13	0.869405	3.78	23
24	24	4.048935	50.815577	0.01967900	0.246979	12.550358	0.07967900	7.97	0.912296	3.80	24
25	25	4.291871	54.864512	0.01822672	0.232999	12.783356	0.07822672	7.83	0.955668	3.82	25
26	26	4.549383	59.156383	0.01690435	0.219810	13.003166	0.07690435	7.70	0.999513	3.84	26
27	27	4.822346	63.705766	0.01569717	0.207368	13.210534	0.07569717	7.57	1.043823	3.87	27
28	28	5.111687	68.528112	0.01459255	0.195630	13.406164	0.07459255	7.46	1.088591	3.89	28
29	29	5.418388	73.639798	0.01357961	0.184557	13.590721	0.07357961	7.36	1.133809	3.91	29
30	30	5.743491	79.058186	0.01264891	0.174110	13.764831	0.07264891	7.27	1.179467	3.93	30
31	31	6.088101	84.801677	0.01179222	0.164255	13.929086	0.07179222	7.18	1.225559	3.95	31
32	32	6.453387	90.889778	0.01100234	0.154957	14.084043	0.07100234	7.11	1.272075	3.98	32
33	33	6.840590	97.343165	0.01027293	0.146186	14.230230	0.07027293	7.03	1.319007	4.00	33
34	34	7.251025	104.183755	0.00959843	0.137912	14.368141	0.06959843	6.96	1.366346	4.02	34
35	35	7.686087	111.434780	0.00897386	0.130105	14.498246	0.06897386	6.90	1.414085	4.04	35
36	36	8.147252	119.120867	0.00839483	0.122741	14.620987	0.06839483	6.84	1.462214	4.06	36
37	37	8.636087	127.268119	0.00785743	0.115793	14.736780	0.06785743	6.79	1.510725	4.08	37
38	38	9.154252	135.904206	0.00735812	0.109239	14.846019	0.06735812	6.74	1.559609	4.10	38
39	39	9.703507	145.058458	0.00689377	0.103056	14.949075	0.06689377	6.69	1.608857	4.13	39
40	40	10.285718	154.761966	0.00646154	0.097222	15.046297	0.06646154	6.65	1.658461	4.15	40
41	41	10.902861	165.047684	0.00605886	0.091719	15.138016	0.06605886	6.61	1.708413	4.17	41
42	42	11.557033	175.950545	0.00568342	0.086527	15.224543	0.06568342	6.57	1.758703	4.19	42
43	43	12.250455	187.507577	0.00533312	0.081630	15.306173	0.06533312	6.54	1.809324	4.21	43
44	44	12.985482	199.758032	0.00500606	0.077009	15.383182	0.06500606	6.51	1.860266	4.23	44
45	45	13.764611	212.743514	0.00470050	0.072650	15.455832	0.06470050	6.48	1.911522	4.25	45
46	46	14.590487	226.508125	0.00441485	0.068538	15.524370	0.06441485	6.45	1.963083	4.27	46
47	47	15.465917	241.098612	0.00414768	0.064658	15.589028	0.06414768	6.42	2.014941	4.29	47
48	48	16.393872	256.564529	0.00389765	0.060998	15.650027	0.06389765	6.39	2.067087	4.31	48
49	49	17.377504	272.958401	0.00366356	0.057546	15.707572	0.06366356	6.37	2.119515	4.33	49
50	50	18.420154	290.335905	0.00344429	0.054288	15.761861	0.06344429	6.35	2.172214	4.34	50

COMPOUND INTEREST AND ANNUITY TABLE

7.00 %
ANNUAL

		Amount Of 1	Amount Of 1 Per Period	Sinking Fund Payment	Present Worth Of 1	Present Worth Of 1 Per Period	Periodic Payment To Amortize 1	Constant Annual Percent	Total Interest	Annual Add-on Rate
		What a single $1 deposit grows to in the future. The deposit is made at the beginning of the first period.	What a series of $1 deposits grow to in the future. A deposit is made at the end of each period.	The amount to be deposited at the end of each period that grows to $1 in the future.	What $1 to be paid in the future is worth today. Value today of a single payment tomorrow.	What $1 to be paid at the end of each period is worth today. Value today of a series of payments tomorrow.	The mortgage payment to amortize a loan of $1. An annuity certain, payable at the end of each period, worth $1 today.	The annual payment, including interest and principal, to amortize completely a loan of $100.	The total interest paid over the term of $1. The loan is amortized by regular periodic payments.	The average annual interest rate on a loan that is completely amortized by regular periodic payments.
		$S=(1+i)^n$	$S_{\overline{n}}=\dfrac{(1+i)^n-1}{i}$	$\dfrac{1}{S_{\overline{n}}}=\dfrac{i}{(1+i)^n-1}$	$V^n=\dfrac{1}{(1+i)^n}$	$A_{\overline{n}}=\dfrac{1-V^n}{i}$	$\dfrac{1}{A_{\overline{n}}}=\dfrac{i}{1-V^n}$			
YR											**YR**
1	1	1.070000	1.000000	1.00000000	0.934579	0.934579	1.07000000	107.00	0.070000	7.00	1
2	2	1.144900	2.070000	0.48309179	0.873439	1.808018	0.55309179	55.31	0.106184	5.31	2
3	3	1.225043	3.214900	0.31105167	0.816298	2.624316	0.38105167	38.11	0.143155	4.77	3
4	4	1.310796	4.439943	0.22522812	0.762895	3.387211	0.29522812	29.53	0.180912	4.52	4
5	5	1.402552	5.750739	0.17389069	0.712986	4.100197	0.24389069	24.39	0.219453	4.39	5
6	6	1.500730	7.153291	0.13979580	0.666342	4.766540	0.20979580	20.98	0.258775	4.31	6
7	7	1.605781	8.654021	0.11555322	0.622750	5.389289	0.18555322	18.56	0.298873	4.27	7
8	8	1.718186	10.259803	0.09746776	0.582009	5.971299	0.16746776	16.75	0.339742	4.25	8
9	9	1.838459	11.977989	0.08348647	0.543934	6.515232	0.15348647	15.35	0.381378	4.24	9
10	10	1.967151	13.816448	0.07237750	0.508349	7.023582	0.14237750	14.24	0.423775	4.24	10
11	11	2 104852	15.783599	0.06335690	0.475093	7.498674	0.13335690	13.34	0.466926	4.24	11
12	12	2.252192	17.888451	0.05590199	0.444012	7.942686	0.12590199	12.60	0.510824	4.26	12
13	13	2.409845	20.140643	0.04965085	0.414964	8.357651	0.11965085	11.97	0.555461	4.27	13
14	14	2.578534	22.550488	0.04434494	0.387817	8.745468	0.11434494	11.44	0.600829	4.29	14
15	15	2.759032	25.129022	0.03979462	0.362446	9.107914	0.10979462	10.98	0.646919	4.31	15
16	16	2.952164	27.888054	0.03585765	0.338735	9.446649	0.10585765	10.59	0.693722	4.34	16
17	17	3.158815	30.840217	0.03242519	0.316574	9.763223	0.10242519	10.25	0.741228	4.36	17
18	18	3.379932	33.999033	0.02941260	0.295864	10.059087	0.09941260	9.95	0.789427	4.39	18
19	19	3.616528	37.378965	0.02675301	0.276508	10.335595	0.09675301	9.68	0.838307	4.41	19
20	20	3.869684	40.995492	0.02439293	0.258419	10.594014	0.09439293	9.44	0.887859	4.44	20
21	21	4.140562	44.865177	0.02228900	0.241513	10.835527	0.09228900	9.23	0.938069	4.47	21
22	22	4.430402	49.005739	0.02040577	0.225713	11.061240	0.09040577	9.05	0.988927	4.50	22
23	23	4.740530	53.436141	0.01871393	0.210947	11.272187	0.08871393	8.88	1.040420	4.52	23
24	24	5.072367	58.176671	0.01718902	0.197147	11.469334	0.08718902	8.72	1.092536	4.55	24
25	25	5.427433	63.249038	0.01581052	0.184249	11.653583	0.08581052	8.59	1.145263	4.58	25
26	26	5.807353	68.676470	0.01456103	0.172195	11.825779	0.08456103	8.46	1.198587	4.61	26
27	27	6.213868	74.483823	0.01342573	0.160930	11.986709	0.08342573	8.35	1.252495	4.64	27
28	28	6.648838	80.697691	0.01239193	0.150402	12.137111	0.08239193	8.24	1.306974	4.67	28
29	29	7.114257	87.346529	0.01144865	0.140563	12.277674	0.08144865	8.15	1.362011	4.70	29
30	30	7.612255	94.460786	0.01058640	0.131367	12.409041	0.08058640	8.06	1.417592	4.73	30
31	31	8.145113	102.073041	0.00979691	0.122773	12.531814	0.07979691	7.98	1.473704	4.75	31
32	32	8.715271	110.218154	0.00907292	0.114741	12.646555	0.07907292	7.91	1.530333	4.78	32
33	33	9.325340	118.933425	0.00840807	0.107235	12.753790	0.07840807	7.85	1.587666	4.81	33
34	34	9.978114	128.258765	0.00779674	0.100219	12.854009	0.07779674	7.78	1.645089	4.84	34
35	35	10.676581	138.236878	0.00723396	0.093663	12.947672	0.07723396	7.73	1.703189	4.87	35
36	36	11.423942	148.913460	0.00671531	0.087535	13.035208	0.07671531	7.68	1.761751	4.89	36
37	37	12.223618	160.337402	0.00623685	0.081809	13.117017	0.07623685	7.63	1.820763	4.92	37
38	38	13.079271	172.561020	0.00579505	0.076457	13.193473	0.07579505	7.58	1.880212	4.95	38
39	39	13.994820	185.640292	0.00538676	0.071455	13.264928	0.07538676	7.54	1.940084	4.97	39
40	40	14.974458	199.635112	0.00500914	0.066780	13.331709	0.0750C914	7.51	2.000366	5.00	40
41	41	16.022670	214.609570	0.00465962	0.062412	13.394120	0.07465962	7.47	2.061045	5.03	41
42	42	17.144257	230.632240	0.00433591	0.058329	13.452449	0.07433591	7.44	2.122108	5.05	42
43	43	18.344355	247.776496	0.00403590	0.054513	13.506962	0.07403590	7.41	2.183543	5.08	43
44	44	19.628460	266.120851	0.00375769	0.050946	13.557908	0.07375769	7.38	2.245338	5.10	44
45	45	21.002452	285.749311	0.00349957	0.047613	13.605522	0.07349957	7.35	2.307481	5.13	45
46	46	22.472623	306.751762	0.00325996	0.044499	13.650020	0.07325996	7.33	2.369958	5.15	46
47	47	24.045707	329.224386	0.00303744	0.041587	13.691608	0.07303744	7.31	2.432760	5.18	47
48	48	25.728907	353.270093	0.00283070	0.038867	13.730474	0.07283070	7.29	2.495873	5.20	48
49	49	27.529930	378.999000	0.00263853	0.036324	13.766799	0.07263853	7.27	2.559288	5.22	49
50	50	29.457025	406.528929	0.00245985	0.033948	13.800746	0.07245985	7.25	2.622992	5.25	50

COMPOUND INTEREST AND ANNUITY TABLE   8.00 % ANNUAL

		Amount Of 1	Amount Of 1 Per Period	Sinking Fund Payment	Present Worth Of 1	Present Worth Of 1 Per Period	Periodic Payment To Amortize 1	Constant Annual Percent	Total Interest	Annual Add-on Rate		
		What a single $1 deposit grows to in the future. The deposit is made at the beginning of the first period.	What a series of $1 deposits grow to in the future. A deposit is made at the end of each period.	The amount to be deposited at the end of each period that grows to $1 in the future.	What $1 to be paid in the future is worth today. Value today of a single payment tomorrow.	What $1 to be paid at the end of each period is worth today. Value today of a series of payments tomorrow.	The mortgage payment to amortize a loan of $1. An annuity certain, payable at the end of each period, worth $1 today.	The annual payment, including interest and principal, to amortize completely a loan of $100.	The total interest paid over the term on a loan of $1. The loan is amortized by regular periodic payments.	The average annual interest rate on a loan that is completely amortized by regular periodic payments.		
		$S=(1+i)^n$	$S_{\overline{n}}=\dfrac{(1+i)^n-1}{i}$	$\dfrac{1}{S_{\overline{n}}}=\dfrac{i}{(1+i)^n-1}$	$V^n=\dfrac{1}{(1+i)^n}$	$A_{\overline{n}}=\dfrac{1-V^n}{i}$	$\dfrac{1}{A_{\overline{n}}}=\dfrac{i}{1-V^n}$					
YR												**YR**
1	1	1.080000	1.000000	1.00000000	0.925926	0.925926	1.08000000	108.00	0.080000	8.00	1
2	2	1.166400	2.080000	0.48076923	0.857339	1.783265	0.56076923	56.08	0.121538	6.08	2
3	3	1.259712	3.246400	0.30803351	0.793832	2.577097	0.38803351	38.81	0.164101	5.47	3
4	4	1.360489	4.506112	0.22192080	0.735030	3.312127	0.30192080	30.20	0.207683	5.19	4
5	5	1.469328	5.866601	0.17045645	0.680583	3.992710	0.25045645	25.05	0.252282	5.05	5
6	6	1.586874	7.335929	0.13631539	0.630170	4.622880	0.21631539	21.64	0.297892	4.96	6
7	7	1.713824	8.922803	0.11207240	0.583490	5.206370	0.19207240	19.21	0.344507	4.92	7
8	8	1.850930	10.636628	0.09401476	0.540269	5.746639	0.17401476	17.41	0.392118	4.90	8
9	9	1.999005	12.487558	0.08007971	0.500249	6.246888	0.16007971	16.01	0.440717	4.90	9
10	10	2.158925	14.486562	0.06902949	0.463193	6.710081	0.14902949	14.91	0.490295	4.90	10
11	11	2.331639	16.645487	0.06007634	0.428883	7.138964	0.14007634	14.01	0.540840	4.92	11
12	12	2.518170	18.977126	0.05269502	0.397114	7.536078	0.13269502	13.27	0.592340	4.94	12
13	13	2.719624	21.495297	0.04652181	0.367698	7.903776	0.12652181	12.66	0.644783	4.96	13
14	14	2.937194	24.214920	0.04129685	0.340461	8.244237	0.12129685	12.13	0.698156	4.99	14
15	15	3.172169	27.152114	0.03682954	0.315242	8.559479	0.11682954	11.69	0.752443	5.02	15
16	16	3.425943	30.324283	0.03297687	0.291890	8.851369	0.11297687	11.30	0.807630	5.05	16
17	17	3.700018	33.750226	0.02962943	0.270269	9.121638	0.10962943	10.97	0.863700	5.08	17
18	18	3.996019	37.450244	0.02670210	0.250249	9.371887	0.10670210	10.68	0.920638	5.11	18
19	19	4.315701	41.446263	0.02412763	0.231712	9.603599	0.10412763	10.42	0.978425	5.15	19
20	20	4.660957	45.761964	0.02185221	0.214548	9.818147	0.10185221	10.19	1.037044	5.19	20
21	21	5.033834	50.422921	0.01983225	0.198656	10.016803	0.09983225	9.99	1.096477	5.22	21
22	22	5.436540	55.456755	0.01803207	0.183941	10.200744	0.09803207	9.81	1.156706	5.26	22
23	23	5.871464	60.893296	0.01642217	0.170315	10.371059	0.09642217	9.65	1.217710	5.29	23
24	24	6.341181	66.764759	0.01497796	0.157699	10.528758	0.09497796	9.50	1.279471	5.33	24
25	25	6.848475	73.105940	0.01367878	0.146018	10.674776	0.09367878	9.37	1.341969	5.37	25
26	26	7.396353	79.954415	0.01250713	0.135202	10.809978	0.09250713	9.26	1.405185	5.40	26
27	27	7.988061	87.350768	0.01144810	0.125187	10.935165	0.09144810	9.15	1.469099	5.44	27
28	28	8.627106	95.338830	0.01048891	0.115914	11.051078	0.09048891	9.05	1.533689	5.48	28
29	29	9.317275	103.965936	0.00961854	0.107328	11.158406	0.08961854	8.97	1.598938	5.51	29
30	30	10.062657	113.283211	0.00882743	0.099377	11.257783	0.08882743	8.89	1.664823	5.55	30
31	31	10.867669	123.345868	0.00810728	0.092016	11.349799	0.08810728	8.82	1.731326	5.58	31
32	32	11.737083	134.213537	0.00745081	0.085200	11.434999	0.08745081	8.75	1.798426	5.62	32
33	33	12.676050	145.950620	0.00685163	0.078889	11.513888	0.08685163	8.69	1.866104	5.65	33
34	34	13.690134	158.626670	0.00630411	0.073045	11.586934	0.08630411	8.64	1.934340	5.69	34
35	35	14.785344	172.316804	0.00580326	0.067635	11.654568	0.08580326	8.59	2.003114	5.72	35
36	36	15.968177	187.102148	0.00534467	0.062625	11.717193	0.08534467	8.54	2.072408	5.76	36
37	37	17.2456	203.070320	0.00492440	0.057986	11.775179	0.08492440	8.50	2.142203	5.79	37
38	38	18.625276	220.315945	0.00453894	0.053690	11.828869	0.08453894	8.46	2.212480	5.82	38
39	39	20.115298	238.941221	0.00418513	0.049713	11.878582	0.08418513	8.42	2.283220	5.85	39
40	40	21.724521	259.056519	0.00386016	0.046031	11.924613	0.08386016	8.39	2.354406	5.89	40
41	41	23.462483	280.781040	0.00356149	0.042621	11.967235	0.08356149	8.36	2.426021	5.92	41
42	42	25.339482	304.243523	0.00328684	0.039464	12.006699	0.08328684	8.33	2.498047	5.95	42
43	43	27.366640	329.583005	0.00303414	0.036541	12.043240	0.08303414	8.31	2.570468	5.98	43
44	44	29.555972	356.949646	0.00280152	0.033834	12.077074	0.08280152	8.29	2.643267	6.01	44
45	45	31.920449	386.505618	0.00258728	0.031328	12.108402	0.08258728	8.26	2.716428	6.04	45
46	46	34.474085	418.426067	0.00238991	0.029007	12.137409	0.08238991	8.24	2.789936	6.07	46
47	47	37.232012	452.900152	0.00220799	0.026859	12.164267	0.08220799	8.23	2.863776	6.09	47
48	48	40.210573	490.132164	0.00204027	0.024869	12.189136	0.08204027	8.21	2.937933	6.12	48
49	49	43.427419	530.342737	0.00188557	0.023027	12.212163	0.08188557	8.19	3.012393	6.15	49
50	50	46.901613	573.770156	0.00174286	0.021321	12.233485	0.08174286	8.18	3.087143	6.17	50

COMPOUND INTEREST AND ANNUITY TABLE

9.00 %
ANNUAL

		Amount Of 1	Amount Of 1 Per Period	Sinking Fund Payment	Present Worth Of 1	Present Worth Of 1 Per Period	Periodic Payment To Amortize 1	Constant Annual Percent	Total Interest	Annual Add-on Rate		
		What a single $1 deposit grows to in the future. The deposit is made at the beginning of the first period.	What a series of $1 deposits grow to in the future. A deposit is made at the end of each period.	The amount to be deposited at the end of each period that grows to $1 in the future.	What $1 to be paid in the future is worth today. Value today of a single payment tomorrow.	What $1 to be paid at the end of each period is worth today. Value today of a series of payments tomorrow.	The mortgage payment to amortize a loan of $1. An annuity certain, payable at the end of each period, worth $1 today.	The annual payment, including interest and principal, to amortize completely a loan of $100.	The total interest paid over the term on a loan of $1. The loan is amortized by regular periodic payments.	The average annual interest rate on a loan that is completely amortized by regular periodic payments.		
		$S=(1+i)^n$	$S_{\overline{n}}=\dfrac{(1+i)^n-1}{i}$	$\dfrac{1}{S_{\overline{n}}}=\dfrac{i}{(1+i)^n-1}$	$V^n=\dfrac{1}{(1+i)^n}$	$A_{\overline{n}}=\dfrac{1-V^n}{i}$	$\dfrac{1}{A_{\overline{n}}}=\dfrac{i}{1-V^n}$					
YR												**YR**
1	1	1.090000	1.000000	1.00000000	0.917431	0.917431	1.09000000	109.00	0.090000	9.00	1
2	2	1.188100	2.090000	0.47846890	0.841680	1.759111	0.56846890	56.85	0.136938	6.85	2
3	3	1.295029	3.278100	0.30505476	0.772183	2.531295	0.39505476	39.51	0.185164	6.17	3
4	4	1.411582	4.573129	0.21866866	0.708425	3.239720	0.30866866	30.87	0.234675	5.87	4
5	5	1.538624	5.984711	0.16709246	0.649931	3.889651	0.25709246	25.71	0.285462	5.71	5
6	6	1.677100	7.523335	0.13291978	0.596267	4.485919	0.22291978	22.30	0.337519	5.63	6
7	7	1.828039	9.200435	0.10869052	0.547034	5.032953	0.19869052	19.87	0.390834	5.58	7
8	8	1.992563	11.028474	0.09067438	0.501866	5.534819	0.18067438	18.07	0.445395	5.57	8
9	9	2.171893	13.021036	0.07679880	0.460428	5.995247	0.16679880	16.68	0.501189	5.57	9
10	10	2.367364	15.192930	0.06582009	0.422411	6.417658	0.15582009	15.59	0.558201	5.58	10
11	11	2.580426	17.560293	0.05694666	0.387533	6.805191	0.14694666	14.70	0.616413	5.60	11
12	12	2.812665	20.140720	0.04965066	0.355535	7.160725	0.13965066	13.97	0.675808	5.63	12
13	13	3.065805	22.953385	0.04356656	0.326179	7.486904	0.13356656	13.36	0.736365	5.66	13
14	14	3.341727	26.019189	0.03843317	0.299246	7.786150	0.12843317	12.85	0.798064	5.70	14
15	15	3.642482	29.360916	0.03405888	0.274538	8.060688	0.12405888	12.41	0.860883	5.74	15
16	16	3.970306	33.003399	0.03029991	0.251870	8.312558	0.12029991	12.03	0.924799	5.78	16
17	17	4.327633	36.973705	0.02704625	0.231073	8.543631	0.11704625	11.71	0.989786	5.82	17
18	18	4.717120	41.301338	0.02421229	0.211994	8.755625	0.11421229	11.43	1.055821	5.87	18
19	19	5.141661	46.018458	0.02173041	0.194490	8.950115	0.11173041	11.18	1.122878	5.91	19
20	20	5.604411	51.160120	0.01954648	0.178431	9.128546	0.10954648	10.96	1.190930	5.95	20
21	21	6.108808	56.764530	0.01761663	0.163698	9.292244	0.10761663	10.77	1.259949	6.00	21
22	22	6.658600	62.873338	0.01590499	0.150182	9.442425	0.10590499	10.60	1.329910	6.05	22
23	23	7.257874	69.531939	0.01438188	0.137781	9.580207	0.10438188	10.44	1.400783	6.09	23
24	24	7.911083	76.789813	0.01302256	0.126405	9.706612	0.10302256	10.31	1.472541	6.14	24
25	25	8.623081	84.700896	0.01180625	0.115968	9.822580	0.10180625	10.19	1.545156	6.18	25
26	26	9.399158	93.323977	0.01071536	0.106393	9.928972	0.10071536	10.08	1.618599	6.23	26
27	27	10.245082	102.723135	0.00973491	0.097608	10.026580	0.09973491	9.98	1.692842	6.27	27
28	28	11.167140	112.968217	0.00885205	0.089548	10.116128	0.09885205	9.89	1.767857	6.31	28
29	29	12.172182	124.135356	0.00805572	0.082155	10.198283	0.09805572	9.81	1.843616	6.36	29
30	30	13.267678	136.307539	0.00733635	0.075371	10.273654	0.09733635	9.74	1.920091	6.40	30
31	31	14.461770	149.575217	0.00668560	0.069148	10.342802	0.09668560	9.67	1.997254	6.44	31
32	32	15.763329	164.036987	0.00609619	0.063438	10.406240	0.09609619	9.61	2.075078	6.48	32
33	33	17.182028	179.800315	0.00556173	0.058200	10.464441	0.09556173	9.56	2.153537	6.53	33
34	34	18.728411	196.982344	0.00507660	0.053395	10.517835	0.09507660	9.51	2.232604	6.57	34
35	35	20.413968	215.710755	0.00463584	0.048986	10.566821	0.09463584	9.47	2.312254	6.61	35
36	36	22.251225	236.124723	0.00423505	0.044941	10.611763	0.09423505	9.43	2.392462	6.65	36
37	37	24.253835	258.375948	0.00387033	0.041231	10.652993	0.09387033	9.39	2.473202	6.68	37
38	38	26.436680	282.629783	0.00353820	0.037826	10.690820	0.09353820	9.36	2.554452	6.72	38
39	39	28.815982	309.066463	0.00323555	0.034703	10.725523	0.09323555	9.33	2.636186	6.76	39
40	40	31.409420	337.882445	0.00295961	0.031838	10.757360	0.09295961	9.30	2.718384	6.80	40
41	41	34.236268	369.291865	0.00270789	0.029209	10.786569	0.09270789	9.28	2.801023	6.83	41
42	42	37.317532	403.528133	0.00247814	0.026797	10.813366	0.09247814	9.25	2.884082	6.87	42
43	43	40.676110	440.845665	0.00226837	0.024584	10.837950	0.09226837	9.23	2.967540	6.90	43
44	44	44.336960	481.521775	0.00207675	0.022555	10.860505	0.09207675	9.21	3.051377	6.93	44
45	45	48.327286	525.858734	0.00190165	0.020692	10.881197	0.09190165	9.20	3.135574	6.97	45
46	46	52.676742	574.186021	0.00174160	0.018984	10.900181	0.09174160	9.18	3.220113	7.00	46
47	47	57.417649	626.862762	0.00159525	0.017416	10.917597	0.09159525	9.16	3.304977	7.03	47
48	48	62.585237	684.280411	0.00146139	0.015978	10.933575	0.09146139	9.15	3.390147	7.06	48
49	49	68.217908	746.865648	0.00133893	0.014659	10.948234	0.09133893	9.14	3.475608	7.09	49
50	50	74.357520	815.083556	0.00122687	0.013449	10.961683	0.09122687	9.13	3.561343	7.12	50

COMPOUND INTEREST AND ANNUITY TABLE

10.00 %
ANNUAL

		Amount Of 1	Amount Of 1 Per Period	Sinking Fund Payment	Present Worth Of 1	Present Worth Of 1 Per Period	Periodic Payment To Amortize 1	Constant Annual Percent	Total Interest	Annual Add-on Rate		
		What a single $1 deposit grows to in the future. The deposit is made at the beginning of the first period.	What a series of $1 deposits grow to in the future. A deposit is made at the end of each period.	The amount to be deposited at the end of each period that grows to $1 in the future.	What $1 to be paid in the future is worth today. Value today of a single payment tomorrow.	What $1 to be paid at the end of each period is worth today. Value today of a series of payments tomorrow.	The mortgage payment to amortize a loan of $1. An annuity certain, payable at the end of each period, worth $1 today.	The annual payment, including interest and principal, to amortize completely a loan of $100.	The total interest paid over the term on a loan of $1. The loan is amortized by regular periodic payments.	The average annual interest rate on a loan that is completely amortized by regular periodic payments.		
		$S=(1+i)^n$	$S_{\overline{n}}=\dfrac{(1+i)^n-1}{i}$	$\dfrac{1}{S_{\overline{n}}}=\dfrac{i}{(1+i)^n-1}$	$V^n=\dfrac{1}{(1+i)^n}$	$A_{\overline{n}}=\dfrac{1-V^n}{i}$	$\dfrac{1}{A_{\overline{n}}}=\dfrac{i}{1-V^n}$					
YR												**YR**
1	1	1.100000	1.000000	1.00000000	0.909091	0.909091	1.10000000	110.00	0.100000	10.00	1
2	2	1.210000	2.100000	0.47619048	0.826446	1.735537	0.57619048	57.62	0.152381	7.62	2
3	3	1.331000	3.310000	0.30211480	0.751315	2.486852	0.40211480	40.22	0.206344	6.88	3
4	4	1.464100	4.641000	0.21547080	0.683013	3.169865	0.31547080	31.55	0.261883	6.55	4
5	5	1.610510	6.105100	0.16379748	0.620921	3.790787	0.26379748	26.38	0.318987	6.38	5
6	6	1.771561	7.715610	0.12960738	0.564474	4.355261	0.22960738	22.97	0.377644	6.29	6
7	7	1.948717	9.487171	0.10540506	0.513158	4.868419	0.20540550	20.55	0.437838	6.25	7
8	8	2.143589	11.435888	0.08744402	0.466507	5.334926	0.18744402	18.75	0.499552	6.24	8
9	9	2.357948	13.579477	0.07364054	0.424098	5.759024	0.17364054	17.37	0.562765	6.25	9
10	10	2.593742	15.937425	0.06274539	0.385543	6.144567	0.16274539	16.28	0.627454	6.27	10
11	11	2.853117	18.531167	0.05396314	0.350494	6.495061	0.15396314	15.40	0.693595	6.31	11
12	12	3.138428	21.384284	0.04676332	0.318631	6.813692	0.14676332	14.68	0.761160	6.34	12
13	13	3.452271	24.522712	0.04077852	0.289664	7.103356	0.14077852	14.08	0.830121	6.39	13
14	14	3.797498	27.974983	0.03574622	0.263331	7.366687	0.13574622	13.58	0.900447	6.43	14
15	15	4.177248	31.772482	0.03147378	0.239392	7.606080	0.13147378	13.15	0.972107	6.48	15
16	16	4.594973	35.949730	0.02781662	0.217629	7.823709	0.12781662	12.79	1.045066	6.53	16
17	17	5.054470	40.544703	0.02466413	0.197845	8.021553	0.12466413	12.47	1.119290	6.58	17
18	18	5.559917	45.599173	0.02193022	0.179859	8.201412	0.12193022	12.20	1.194744	6.64	18
19	19	6.115909	51.159090	0.01954687	0.163508	8.364920	0.11954687	11.96	1.271390	6.69	19
20	20	6.727500	57.274999	0.01745962	0.148644	8.513564	0.11745962	11.75	1.349192	6.75	20
21	21	7.400250	64.002499	0.01562439	0.135131	8.648694	0.11562439	11.57	1.428112	6.80	21
22	22	8.140275	71.402749	0.01400506	0.122846	8.771540	0.11400506	11.41	1.508111	6.86	22
23	23	8.954302	79.543024	0.01257181	0.111678	8.883218	0.11257181	11.26	1.589152	6.91	23
24	24	9.849733	88.497327	0.01129978	0.101526	8.984744	0.11129978	11.13	1.671195	6.96	24
25	25	10.834706	98.347059	0.01016807	0.092296	9.077040	0.11016807	11.02	1.754202	7.02	25
26	26	11.918177	109.181765	0.00915904	0.083905	9.160945	0.10915904	10.92	1.838135	7.07	26
27	27	13.109994	121.099942	0.00825764	0.076278	9.237223	0.10825764	10.83	1.922956	7.12	27
28	28	14.420994	134.209936	0.00745101	0.069343	9.306567	0.10745101	10.75	2.008628	7.17	28
29	29	15.863093	148.630930	0.00672807	0.063039	9.369606	0.10672807	10.68	2.095114	7.22	29
30	30	17.449402	164.494023	0.00607925	0.057309	9.426914	0.10607925	10.61	2.182377	7.27	30
31	31	19.194342	181.943425	0.00549621	0.052099	9.479013	0.10549621	10.55	2.270383	7.32	31
32	32	21.113777	201.137767	0.00497172	0.047362	9.526376	0.10497172	10.50	2.359095	7.37	32
33	33	23.225154	222.251544	0.00449941	0.043057	9.569432	0.10449941	10.45	2.448480	7.42	33
34	34	25.547670	245.476699	0.00407371	0.039143	9.608575	0.10407371	10.41	2.538506	7.47	34
35	35	28.102437	271.024368	0.00368971	0.035584	9.644159	0.10368971	10.37	2.629140	7.51	35
36	36	30.912681	299.126805	0.00334306	0.032349	9.676508	0.10334306	10.34	2.720350	7.56	36
37	37	34.003949	330.039486	0.00302994	0.029408	9.705917	0.10302994	10.31	2.812108	7.60	37
38	38	37.404343	364.043434	0.00274692	0.026735	9.732651	0.10274692	10.28	2.904383	7.64	38
39	39	41.144778	401.447778	0.00249098	0.024304	9.756956	0.10249098	10.25	2.997148	7.68	39
40	40	45.259256	442.592556	0.00225941	0.022095	9.779051	0.10225941	10.23	3.090377	7.73	40
41	41	49.785181	487.851811	0.00204980	0.020086	9.799137	0.10204980	10.21	3.184042	7.77	41
42	42	54.763699	537.636992	0.00185999	0.018260	9.817397	0.10185999	10.19	3.278120	7.81	42
43	43	60.240069	592.400692	0.00168805	0.016600	9.833998	0.10168805	10.17	3.372586	7.84	43
44	44	66.264076	652.640761	0.00153224	0.015091	9.849089	0.10153224	10.16	3.467418	7.88	44
45	45	72.890484	718.904837	0.00139100	0.013719	9.862808	0.10139100	10.14	3.562595	7.92	45
46	46	80.179532	791.795321	0.00126295	0.012472	9.875280	0.10126295	10.13	3.658096	7.95	46
47	47	88.197485	871.974853	0.00114682	0.011338	9.886618	0.10114682	10.12	3.753901	7.99	47
48	48	97.017234	960.172338	0.00104148	0.010307	9.896926	0.10104148	10.11	3.849991	8.02	48
49	49	106.718957	1057.189572	0.00094590	0.009370	9.906296	0.10094590	10.10	3.946349	8.05	49
50	50	117.390853	1163.908529	0.00085917	0.008519	9.914814	0.10085917	10.09	4.042959	8.09	50

COMPOUND INTEREST AND ANNUITY TABLE

11.00 %
ANNUAL

		Amount Of 1	Amount Of 1 Per Period	Sinking Fund Payment	Present Worth Of 1	Present Worth Of 1 Per Period	Periodic Payment To Amortize 1	Constant Annual Percent	Total Interest	Annual Add-on Rate	
		What a single $1 deposit grows to in the future. The deposit is made at the beginning of the first period.	What a series of $1 deposits grow to in the future. A deposit is made at the end of each period.	The amount to be deposited at the end of each period that grows to $1 in the future.	What $1 to be paid in the future is worth today. Value today of a single payment tomorrow.	What $1 to be paid at the end of each period is worth today. Value today of a series of payments tomorrow.	The mortgage payment to amortize a loan of $1. An annuity, certain, payable at the end of each period, to amortize a loan worth $1 today.	The annual payment, including interest and principal, to amortize completely a loan of $100.	The total interest paid over the term of $1. The loan is amortized by regular periodic payments.	The average annual interest rate on a loan that is completely amortized by regular periodic payments.	
		$S=(1+i)^n$	$S_{\overline{n}}=\dfrac{(1+i)^n-1}{i}$	$\dfrac{1}{S_{\overline{n}}}=\dfrac{i}{(1+i)^n-1}$	$V^n=\dfrac{1}{(1+i)^n}$	$A_{\overline{n}}=\dfrac{1-V^n}{i}$	$\dfrac{1}{A_{\overline{n}}}=\dfrac{i}{1-V^n}$				
YR											YR
1	1	1.110000	1.000000	1.00000000	0.900901	0.900901	1.11000000	111.00	0.110000	11.00	1
2	2	1.232100	2.110000	0.47393365	0.811622	1.712523	0.58393365	58.40	0.167867	8.39	2
3	3	1.367631	3.342100	0.29921307	0.731191	2.443715	0.40921307	40.93	0.227639	7.59	3
4	4	1.518070	4.709731	0.21232635	0.658731	3.102446	0.32232635	32.24	0.289305	7.23	4
5	5	1.685058	6.227801	0.16057031	0.593451	3.695897	0.27057031	27.06	0.352852	7.06	5
6	6	1.870415	7.912860	0.12637656	0.534641	4.230538	0.23637656	23.64	0.418259	6.97	6
7	7	2.076160	9.783274	0.10221527	0.481658	4.712196	0.21221527	21.23	0.485507	6.94	7
8	8	2.304538	11.859434	0.08432105	0.433926	5.146123	0.19432105	19.44	0.554568	6.93	8
9	9	2.558037	14.163972	0.07060166	0.390925	5.537048	0.18060166	18.07	0.625445	6.95	9
10	10	2.839421	16.722009	0.05980143	0.352184	5.889232	0.16980143	16.99	0.698014	6.98	10
11	11	3.151757	19.561430	0.05112101	0.317283	6.206515	0.16112101	16.12	0.772331	7.02	11
12	12	3.498451	22.713187	0.04402729	0.285841	6.492356	0.15402729	15.41	0.848327	7.07	12
13	13	3.883280	26.211638	0.03815099	0.257514	6.749870	0.14815099	14.82	0.925963	7.12	13
14	14	4.310441	30.094918	0.03322820	0.231995	6.981865	0.14322820	14.33	1.005195	7.18	14
15	15	4.784589	34.405359	0.02906524	0.209004	7.190870	0.13906524	13.91	1.085979	7.24	15
16	16	5.310894	39.189948	0.02551675	0.188292	7.379162	0.13551675	13.56	1.168268	7.30	16
17	17	5.895093	44.500843	0.02247148	0.169633	7.548794	0.13247148	13.25	1.252015	7.36	17
18	18	6.543553	50.395936	0.01984287	0.152822	7.701617	0.12984287	12.99	1.337172	7.43	18
19	19	7.263344	56.939488	0.01756250	0.137678	7.839294	0.12756250	12.76	1.423688	7.49	19
20	20	8.062312	64.202832	0.01557564	0.124034	7.963328	0.12557564	12.56	1.511513	7.56	20
21	21	8.949166	72.265144	0.01383793	0.111742	8.075070	0.12383793	12.39	1.600597	7.62	21
22	22	9.933574	81.214309	0.01231310	0.100669	8.175739	0.12231310	12.24	1.690888	7.69	22
23	23	11.026267	91.147884	0.01097118	0.090693	8.266432	0.12097118	12.10	1.782337	7.75	23
24	24	12.239157	102.174151	0.00978721	0.081705	8.348137	0.11978721	11.98	1.874893	7.81	24
25	25	13.585464	114.413307	0.00874024	0.073608	8.421745	0.11874024	11.88	1.968506	7.87	25
26	26	15.079865	127.998771	0.00781258	0.066314	8.488058	0.11781258	11.79	2.063127	7.94	26
27	27	16.738650	143.078636	0.00698916	0.059742	8.547800	0.11698916	11.70	2.158707	8.00	27
28	28	18.579901	159.817286	0.00625715	0.053822	8.601622	0.11625715	11.63	2.255200	8.05	28
29	29	20.623691	178.397187	0.00560547	0.048488	8.650110	0.11560547	11.57	2.352559	8.11	29
30	30	22.892297	199.020878	0.00502460	0.043683	8.693793	0.11502460	11.51	2.450738	8.17	30
31	31	25.410449	221.913174	0.00450627	0.039354	8.733146	0.11450627	11.46	2.549694	8.22	31
32	32	28.205599	247.323624	0.00404329	0.035454	8.768600	0.11404329	11.41	2.649385	8.28	32
33	33	31.308214	275.529222	0.00362938	0.031940	8.800541	0.11362938	11.37	2.749770	8.33	33
34	34	34.752118	306.837437	0.00325905	0.028775	8.829316	0.11325905	11.33	2.850808	8.38	34
35	35	38.574851	341.589555	0.00292749	0.025924	8.855240	0.11292749	11.30	2.952462	8.44	35
36	36	42.818085	380.164406	0.00263044	0.023355	8.878594	0.11263044	11.27	3.054696	8.49	36
37	37	47.528074	422.982490	0.00236416	0.021040	8.899635	0.11236416	11.24	3.157474	8.53	37
38	38	52.756162	470.510564	0.00212535	0.018955	8.918590	0.11212535	11.22	3.260763	8.58	38
39	39	58.559340	523.266726	0.00191107	0.017077	8.935666	0.11191107	11.20	3.364532	8.63	39
40	40	65.000867	581.826066	0.00171873	0.015384	8.951051	0.11171873	11.18	3.468749	8.67	40
41	41	72.150963	646.826934	0.00154601	0.013860	8.964911	0.11154601	11.16	3.573386	8.72	41
42	42	80.087569	718.977896	0.00139086	0.012486	8.977397	0.11139086	11.14	3.678416	8.76	42
43	43	88.897201	799.065465	0.00125146	0.011249	8.988646	0.11125146	11.13	3.783813	8.80	43
44	44	98.675893	887.962666	0.00112617	0.010134	8.998780	0.11112617	11.12	3.889552	8.84	44
45	45	109.530242	986.638559	0.00101354	0.009130	9.007910	0.11101354	11.11	3.995609	8.88	45
46	46	121.578568	1096.168801	0.00091227	0.008225	9.016135	0.11091227	11.10	4.101964	8.92	46
47	47	134.952211	1217.747369	0.00082119	0.007410	9.023545	0.11082119	11.09	4.208596	8.95	47
48	48	149.796954	1352.699580	0.00073926	0.006676	9.030221	0.11073926	11.08	4.315485	8.99	48
49	49	166.274619	1502.496533	0.00066556	0.006014	9.036235	0.11066556	11.07	4.422612	9.03	49
50	50	184.564827	1668.771152	0.00059924	0.005418	9.041653	0.11059924	11.06	4.529962	9.06	50

COMPOUND INTEREST AND ANNUITY TABLE

12.00 %
ANNUAL

		Amount Of 1	Amount Of 1 Per Period	Sinking Fund Payment	Present Worth Of 1	Present Worth Of 1 Per Period	Periodic Payment To Amortize 1	Constant Annual Percent	Total Interest	Annual Add-on Rate		
		What a single $1 deposit grows to in the future. The deposit is made at the beginning of the first period.	What a series of $1 deposits grow to in the future. A deposit is made at the end of each period.	The amount to be deposited at the end of each period that grows to $1 in the future.	What $1 to be paid in the future is worth today. Value today of a single payment tomorrow.	What $1 to be paid at the end of each period is worth today. Value today of a series of payments tomorrow.	The mortgage payment to amortize a loan of $1. An annuity certain, payable at the end of each period, worth $1 today.	The annual payment, including interest and principal, to amortize completely a loan of $100.	The total interest paid over the term on a loan of $1. The loan is amortized by regular periodic payments.	The average annual interest rate on a loan that is completely amortized by regular periodic payments.		
		$S=(1+i)^n$	$S_{\overline{n}}=\dfrac{(1+i)^n-1}{i}$	$\dfrac{1}{S_{\overline{n}}}=\dfrac{i}{(1+i)^n-1}$	$V^n=\dfrac{1}{(1+i)^n}$	$A_{\overline{n}}=\dfrac{1-V^n}{i}$	$\dfrac{1}{A_{\overline{n}}}=\dfrac{i}{1-V^n}$					
YR												**YR**
1	1	1.120000	1.000000	1.00000000	0.892857	0.892857	1.12000000	112.00	0.120000	12.00		1
2	2	1.254400	2.120000	0.47169811	0.797194	1.690051	0.59169811	59.17	0.183396	9.17		2
3	3	1.404928	3.374400	0.29634898	0.711780	2.401831	0.41634898	41.64	0.249047	8.30		3
4	4	1.573519	4.779328	0.20923444	0.635518	3.037349	0.32923444	32.93	0.316938	7.92		4
5	5	1.762342	6.352847	0.15740973	0.567427	3.604776	0.27740973	27.75	0.387049	7.74		5
6	6	1.973823	8.115189	0.12322572	0.506631	4.111407	0.24322572	24.33	0.459354	7.66		6
7	7	2.210681	10.089012	0.09911774	0.452349	4.563757	0.21911774	21.92	0.533824	7.63		7
8	8	2.475963	12.299693	0.08130284	0.403883	4.967640	0.20130284	20.14	0.610423	7.63		8
9	9	2.773079	14.775656	0.06767889	0.360610	5.328250	0.18767889	18.77	0.689110	7.66		9
10	10	3.105848	17.548735	0.05698416	0.321973	5.650223	0.17698416	17.70	0.769842	7.70		10
11	11	3.478550	20.654583	0.04841540	0.287476	5.937699	0.16841540	16.85	0.852569	7.75		11
12	12	3.895976	24.133133	0.04143681	0.256675	6.194374	0.16143681	16.15	0.937242	7.81		12
13	13	4.363493	28.029109	0.03567720	0.229174	6.423548	0.15567720	15.57	1.023804	7.88		13
14	14	4.887112	32.392602	0.03087125	0.204620	6.628168	0.15087125	15.09	1.112197	7.94		14
15	15	5.473566	37.279715	0.02682424	0.182696	6.810864	0.14682424	14.69	1.202364	8.02		15
16	16	6.130394	42.753280	0.02339002	0.163122	6.973986	0.14339002	14.34	1.294240	8.09		16
17	17	6.866041	48.883674	0.02045049	0.145644	7.119630	0.14045673	14.05	1.387764	8.16		17
18	18	7.689966	55.749715	0.01793731	0.130040	7.249670	0.13793731	13.80	1.482872	8.24		18
19	19	8.612762	63.439681	0.01576300	0.116107	7.365777	0.13576300	13.58	1.579497	8.31		19
20	20	9.646293	72.052442	0.01387878	0.103667	7.469444	0.13387878	13.39	1.677576	8.39		20
21	21	10.803848	81.698736	0.01224009	0.092560	7.562003	0.13224009	13.23	1.777042	8.46		21
22	22	12.100310	92.502584	0.01081051	0.082643	7.644646	0.13081051	13.09	1.877831	8.54		22
23	23	13.552347	104.602894	0.00955996	0.073788	7.718434	0.12955996	12.96	1.979879	8.61		23
24	24	15.178629	118.155241	0.00846344	0.065882	7.784316	0.12846344	12.85	2.083123	8.68		24
25	25	17.000064	133.333870	0.00749997	0.058823	7.843139	0.12749997	12.75	2.187499	8.75		25
26	26	19.040072	150.333934	0.00665186	0.052521	7.895660	0.12665186	12.67	2.292948	8.82		26
27	27	21.324881	169.374007	0.00590409	0.046894	7.942554	0.12590409	12.60	2.399411	8.89		27
28	28	23.883866	190.698887	0.00524387	0.041869	7.984423	0.12524387	12.53	2.506828	8.95		28
29	29	26.749930	214.582754	0.00466021	0.037383	8.021806	0.12466021	12.47	2.615146	9.02		29
30	30	29.959922	241.332684	0.00414366	0.033378	8.055184	0.12414366	12.42	2.724310	9.08		30
31	31	33.555113	271.292606	0.00368606	0.029802	8.084986	0.12368606	12.37	2.834268	9.14		31
32	32	37.581726	304.847719	0.00328033	0.026609	8.111594	0.12328033	12.33	2.944970	9.20		32
33	33	42.091533	342.429446	0.00292031	0.023758	8.135352	0.12292031	12.30	3.056370	9.26		33
34	34	47.142517	384.520979	0.00260064	0.021212	8.156564	0.12260064	12.27	3.168422	9.32		34
35	35	52.799620	431.663496	0.00231662	0.018940	8.175504	0.12231662	12.24	3.281082	9.37		35
36	36	59.135574	484.463116	0.00206414	0.016910	8.192414	0.12206414	12.21	3.394309	9.43		36
37	37	66.231843	543.598690	0.00183959	0.015098	8.207513	0.12183959	12.19	3.508065	9.48		37
38	38	74.179664	609.830533	0.00163980	0.013481	8.220993	0.12163980	12.17	3.622312	9.53		38
39	39	83.081224	684.010197	0.00146197	0.012036	8.233030	0.12146197	12.15	3.737017	9.58		39
40	40	93.050970	767.091420	0.00130363	0.010747	8.243777	0.12130363	12.14	3.852145	9.63		40
41	41	104.217087	860.142391	0.00116260	0.009595	8.253372	0.12116260	12.12	3.967667	9.68		41
42	42	116.723137	964.359478	0.00103696	0.008567	8.261939	0.12103696	12.11	4.083552	9.72		42
43	43	130.729914	1081.082615	0.00092500	0.007649	8.269589	0.12092500	12.10	4.199775	9.77		43
44	44	146.417503	1211.812529	0.00082521	0.006830	8.276418	0.12082521	12.09	4.316309	9.81		44
45	45	163.987604	1358.230032	0.00073625	0.006098	8.282516	0.12073625	12.08	4.433131	9.85		45
46	46	183.666116	1522.217636	0.00065694	0.005445	8.287961	0.12065694	12.07	4.550219	9.89		46
47	47	205.706050	1705.883752	0.00058621	0.004861	8.292822	0.12058621	12.06	4.667552	9.93		47
48	48	230.390776	1911.589803	0.00052312	0.004340	8.297163	0.12052312	12.06	4.785110	9.98		48
49	49	258.037669	2141.980579	0.00046686	0.003875	8.301038	0.12046686	12.05	4.902876	10.01		49
50	50	289.002190	2400.018249	0.00041666	0.003460	8.304498	0.12041666	12.05	5.020833	10.04		50

COMPOUND INTEREST AND ANNUITY TABLE

13.00 %
ANNUAL

		Amount Of 1	Amount Of 1 Per Period	Sinking Fund Payment	Present Worth Of 1	Present Worth Of 1 Per Period	Periodic Payment To Amortize 1	Constant Annual Percent	Total Interest	Annual Add-on Rate		
		What a single $1 deposit grows to in the future. The deposit is made at the beginning of the first period.	What a series of $1 deposits grow to in the future. A deposit is made at the end of each period.	The amount to be deposited at the end of each period that grows to $1 in the future.	What $1 to be paid in the future is worth today. Value today of a single payment tomorrow.	What $1 to be paid at the end of each period is worth today. Value today of a series of payments tomorrow.	The mortgage payment including payment to amortize a loan of $1. An annuity certain, payable at the end of each period, worth $1 today.	The annual payment, including interest and principal, to amortize completely a loan of $100.	The total interest paid over the term of $1. The loan is amortized by regular periodic payments.	The average annual interest rate on a loan that is completely amortized by regular periodic payments.		
		$S=(1+i)^n$	$S_{\overline{n}}=\dfrac{(1+i)^n-1}{i}$	$\dfrac{1}{S_{\overline{n}}}=\dfrac{i}{(1+i)^n-1}$	$V^n=\dfrac{1}{(1+i)^n}$	$A_{\overline{n}}=\dfrac{1-V^n}{i}$	$\dfrac{1}{A_{\overline{n}}}=\dfrac{i}{1-V^n}$					
YR												**YR**
1	1	1.130000	1.000000	1.00000000	0.884956	0.884956	1.13000000	113.00	0.130000	13.00	1
2	2	1.276900	2.130000	0.46948357	0.783147	1.668102	0.59948357	59.95	0.198967	9.95	2
3	3	1.442897	3.406900	0.29352197	0.693050	2.361153	0.42352197	42.36	0.270566	9.02	3
4	4	1.630474	4.849797	0.20619420	0.613319	2.974471	0.33619420	33.62	0.344777	8.62	4
5	5	1.842435	6.480271	0.15431454	0.542760	3.517231	0.28431454	28.44	0.421573	8.43	5
6	6	2.081952	8.322706	0.12015323	0.480319	3.997550	0.25015323	25.02	0.500919	8.35	6
7	7	2.352605	10.404658	0.09611080	0.425061	4.422610	0.22611080	22.62	0.582776	8.33	7
8	8	2.658444	12.757263	0.07838672	0.376160	4.798770	0.20838672	20.84	0.667094	8.34	8
9	9	3.004042	15.415707	0.06486890	0.332885	5.131655	0.19486890	19.49	0.753820	8.38	9
10	10	3.394567	18.419749	0.05428956	0.294588	5.426243	0.18428956	18.43	0.842896	8.43	10
11	11	3.835861	21.814317	0.04584145	0.260698	5.686941	0.17584145	17.59	0.934256	8.49	11
12	12	4.334523	25.650178	0.03898608	0.230706	5.917647	0.16898608	16.90	1.027833	8.57	12
13	13	4.898011	29.984701	0.03335034	0.204165	6.121812	0.16335034	16.34	1.123554	8.64	13
14	14	5.534753	34.882712	0.02866750	0.180677	6.302488	0.15866750	15.87	1.221345	8.72	14
15	15	6.254270	40.417464	0.02474178	0.159891	6.462379	0.15474178	15.48	1.321127	8.81	15
16	16	7.067326	46.671735	0.02142624	0.141496	6.603875	0.15142624	15.15	1.422820	8.89	16
17	17	7.986078	53.739060	0.01860844	0.125218	6.729093	0.14860844	14.87	1.526343	8.98	17
18	18	9.024268	61.725138	0.01620085	0.110812	6.839905	0.14620085	14.63	1.631615	9.06	18
19	19	10.197423	70.749406	0.01413439	0.098064	6.937969	0.14413439	14.42	1.738553	9.15	19
20	20	11.523088	80.946829	0.01235379	0.086782	7.024752	0.14235379	14.24	1.847076	9.24	20
21	21	13.021089	92.469917	0.01081433	0.076798	7.101550	0.14081433	14.09	1.957101	9.32	21
22	22	14.713831	105.491006	0.00947948	0.067963	7.169513	0.13947948	13.95	2.068549	9.40	22
23	23	16.626629	120.204837	0.00831913	0.060144	7.229658	0.13831913	13.84	2.181340	9.48	23
24	24	18.788091	136.831465	0.00730826	0.053225	7.282883	0.13730826	13.74	2.295398	9.56	24
25	25	21.230542	155.619556	0.00642593	0.047102	7.329985	0.13642593	13.65	2.410648	9.64	25
26	26	23.990513	176.850098	0.00565451	0.041683	7.371668	0.13565451	13.57	2.527017	9.72	26
27	27	27.109279	200.840611	0.00497907	0.036888	7.408556	0.13497907	13.50	2.644435	9.79	27
28	28	30.633486	227.949890	0.00438693	0.032644	7.441200	0.13438693	13.44	2.762834	9.87	28
29	29	34.615839	258.583376	0.00386722	0.028889	7.470088	0.13386722	13.39	2.882150	9.94	29
30	30	39.115898	293.199215	0.00341065	0.025565	7.495653	0.13341065	13.35	3.002320	10.01	30
31	31	44.200965	332.315113	0.00300919	0.022624	7.518277	0.13300919	13.31	3.123285	10.08	31
32	32	49.947090	376.516078	0.00265593	0.020021	7.538299	0.13265593	13.27	3.244990	10.14	32
33	33	56.440212	426.463168	0.00234487	0.017718	7.556016	0.13234487	13.24	3.367381	10.20	33
34	34	63.777439	482.903380	0.00207081	0.015680	7.571696	0.13207081	13.21	3.490407	10.27	34
35	35	72.068506	546.680819	0.00182922	0.013876	7.585572	0.13182922	13.19	3.614023	10.33	35
36	36	81.437412	618.749325	0.00161616	0.012279	7.597851	0.13161616	13.17	3.738182	10.38	36
37	37	92.024276	700.186738	0.00142819	0.010867	7.608718	0.13142819	13.15	3.862843	10.44	37
38	38	103.987432	792.211014	0.00126229	0.009617	7.618334	0.13126229	13.13	3.987967	10.49	38
39	39	117.505798	896.198445	0.00111582	0.008510	7.626844	0.13111582	13.12	4.113517	10.55	39
40	40	132.781552	1013.704243	0.00098648	0.007531	7.634376	0.13098648	13.10	4.239459	10.60	40
41	41	150.043153	1146.485795	0.00087223	0.006665	7.641040	0.13087223	13.09	4.365761	10.65	41
42	42	169.548763	1296.528948	0.00077129	0.005898	7.646938	0.13077129	13.08	4.492394	10.70	42
43	43	191.590103	1466.077712	0.00068209	0.005219	7.652158	0.13068209	13.07	4.619330	10.74	43
44	44	216.496816	1657.667814	0.00060326	0.004619	7.656777	0.13060326	13.07	4.746543	10.79	44
45	45	244.641402	1874.164630	0.00053357	0.004088	7.660864	0.13053357	13.06	4.874011	10.83	45
46	46	276.444784	2118.806032	0.00047196	0.003617	7.664482	0.13047196	13.05	5.001710	10.87	46
47	47	312.382606	2395.250816	0.00041749	0.003201	7.667683	0.13041749	13.05	5.129622	10.91	47
48	48	352.992345	2707.633422	0.00036933	0.002833	7.670516	0.13036933	13.04	5.257728	10.95	48
49	49	398.881350	3060.625767	0.00032673	0.002507	7.673023	0.13032673	13.04	5.386010	10.99	49
50	50	450.735925	3459.507117	0.00028906	0.002219	7.675242	0.13028906	13.03	5.514453	11.03	50

COMPOUND INTEREST AND ANNUITY TABLE

**14.00 %
ANNUAL**

		Amount Of 1	Amount Of 1 Per Period	Sinking Fund Payment	Present Worth Of 1	Present Worth Of 1 Per Period	Periodic Payment To Amortize 1	Constant Annual Percent	Total Interest	Annual Add-on Rate	
		What a single $1 deposit grows to in the future. The deposit is made at the beginning of the first period.	What a series of $1 deposits grow to in the future. A deposit is made at the end of each period.	The amount to be deposited at the end of each period that grows to $1 in the future.	What $1 to be paid in the future is worth today. Value today of a single payment tomorrow.	What $1 to be paid at the end of each period is worth today. Value today of a series of payments tomorrow.	The mortgage payment to amortize a loan of $1. An annuity certain, payable at the end of each period, worth $1 today.	The annual payment, including interest and principal, to amortize completely a loan of $100.	The total interest paid over the term on a loan of $1. The loan is amortized by regular periodic payments.	The average annual interest rate on a loan that is completely amortized by regular periodic payments.	
		$S=(1+i)^n$	$S_{\overline{n}}=\dfrac{(1+i)^n-1}{i}$	$\dfrac{1}{S_{\overline{n}}}=\dfrac{i}{(1+i)^n-1}$	$V^n=\dfrac{1}{(1+i)^n}$	$A_{\overline{n}}=\dfrac{1-V^n}{i}$	$\dfrac{1}{A_{\overline{n}}}=\dfrac{i}{1-V^n}$				
YR											**YR**
1	1	1.140000	1.000000	1.00000000	0.877193	0.877193	1.14000000	114.00	0.140000	14.00	1
2	2	1.299600	2.140000	0.46728972	0.769468	1.646661	0.60728972	60.73	0.214579	10.73	2
3	3	1.481544	3.439600	0.29073148	0.674972	2.321632	0.43073148	43.08	0.292194	9.74	3
4	4	1.688960	4.921144	0.20320478	0.592080	2.913712	0.34320478	34.33	0.372819	9.32	4
5	5	1.925415	6.610104	0.15128355	0.519369	3.433081	0.29128355	29.13	0.456418	9.13	5
6	6	2.194973	8.535519	0.11715750	0.455587	3.888668	0.25715750	25.72	0.542945	9.05	6
7	7	2.502269	10.730491	0.09319238	0.399637	4.288305	0.23319238	23.32	0.632347	9.03	7
8	8	2.852586	13.232760	0.07557002	0.350559	4.638864	0.21557002	21.56	0.724560	9.06	8
9	9	3.251949	16.085347	0.06216838	0.307508	4.946372	0.20216838	20.22	0.819515	9.11	9
10	10	3.707221	19.337295	0.05171354	0.269744	5.216116	0.19171354	19.18	0.917135	9.17	10
11	11	4.226232	23.044516	0.04339427	0.236617	5.452733	0.18339427	18.34	1.017337	9.25	11
12	12	4.817905	27.270749	0.03666933	0.207559	5.660292	0.17666933	17.67	1.120032	9.33	12
13	13	5.492411	32.088654	0.03116366	0.182069	5.842362	0.17116366	17.12	1.225128	9.42	13
14	14	6.261349	37.581065	0.02660914	0.159710	6.002072	0.16660914	16.67	1.332528	9.52	14
15	15	7.137938	43.842414	0.02280896	0.140096	6.142168	0.16280896	16.29	1.442134	9.61	15
16	16	8.137249	50.980352	0.01961540	0.122892	6.265060	0.15961540	15.97	1.553846	9.71	16
17	17	9.276464	59.117601	0.01691544	0.107800	6.372859	0.15691544	15.70	1.667562	9.81	17
18	18	10.575169	68.394066	0.01462115	0.094561	6.467420	0.15462115	15.47	1.783181	9.91	18
19	19	12.055692	78.969235	0.01266316	0.082948	6.550369	0.15266316	15.27	1.900600	10.00	19
20	20	13.743490	91.024928	0.01098600	0.072762	6.623131	0.15098600	15.10	2.019720	10.10	20
21	21	15.667578	104.768418	0.00954486	0.063826	6.686957	0.14954486	14.96	2.140442	10.19	21
22	22	17.861039	120.435996	0.00830317	0.055988	6.742944	0.14830317	14.84	2.262670	10.28	22
23	23	20.361585	138.297035	0.00723081	0.049112	6.792056	0.14723081	14.73	2.386309	10.38	23
24	24	23.212207	158.658620	0.00630284	0.043081	6.835137	0.14630284	14.64	2.511268	10.46	24
25	25	26.461916	181.870827	0.00549841	0.037790	6.872927	0.14549841	14.55	2.637460	10.55	25
26	26	30.166584	208.332743	0.00480001	0.033149	6.906077	0.14480001	14.49	2.764800	10.63	26
27	27	34.389906	238.499327	0.00419288	0.029078	6.935155	0.14419288	14.42	2.893208	10.72	27
28	28	39.204493	272.889233	0.00366449	0.025507	6.960662	0.14366449	14.37	3.022606	10.80	28
29	29	44.693122	312.093725	0.00320417	0.022375	6.983037	0.14320417	14.33	3.152921	10.87	29
30	30	50.950159	356.786847	0.00280279	0.019627	7.002664	0.14280279	14.29	3.284084	10.95	30
31	31	58.083181	407.737006	0.00245256	0.017217	7.019881	0.14245256	14.25	3.416029	11.02	31
32	32	66.214826	465.820186	0.00214675	0.015102	7.034983	0.14214675	14.22	3.548696	11.09	32
33	33	75.484902	532.035012	0.00187958	0.013248	7.048231	0.14187958	14.19	3.682026	11.16	33
34	34	86.052788	607.519914	0.00164604	0.011621	7.059852	0.14164604	14.17	3.815965	11.22	34
35	35	98.100178	693.572702	0.00144181	0.010194	7.070045	0.14144181	14.15	3.950463	11.29	35
36	36	111.834203	791.672881	0.00126315	0.008942	7.078987	0.14126315	14.13	4.085473	11.35	36
37	37	127.490992	903.507084	0.00110680	0.007844	7.086831	0.14110680	14.12	4.220952	11.41	37
38	38	145.339731	1030.998076	0.00096993	0.006880	7.093711	0.14096993	14.10	4.356857	11.47	38
39	39	165.687293	1176.337806	0.00085010	0.006035	7.099747	0.14085010	14.09	4.493154	11.52	39
40	40	188.883514	1342.025099	0.00074514	0.005294	7.105041	0.14074514	14.08	4.629806	11.57	40
41	41	215.327206	1530.908613	0.00065321	0.004644	7.109685	0.14065321	14.07	4.766781	11.63	41
42	42	245.473015	1746.235819	0.00057266	0.004074	7.113759	0.14057266	14.06	4.904052	11.68	42
43	43	279.839237	1991.708833	0.00050208	0.003573	7.117332	0.14050208	14.06	5.041590	11.72	43
44	44	319.016730	2271.548070	0.00044023	0.003135	7.120467	0.14044023	14.05	5.179370	11.77	44
45	45	363.679072	2590.564800	0.00038602	0.002750	7.123217	0.14038602	14.04	5.317371	11.82	45
46	46	414.594142	2954.243872	0.00033860	0.002412	7.125629	0.14033860	14.04	5.455571	11.86	46
47	47	472.637322	3368.838014	0.00029684	0.002116	7.127744	0.14029684	14.03	5.593951	11.90	47
48	48	538.806547	3841.475336	0.00026032	0.001856	7.129600	0.14026032	14.03	5.732495	11.94	48
49	49	614.239464	4380.281883	0.00022830	0.001628	7.131228	0.14022830	14.03	5.871186	11.98	49
50	50	700.232988	4994.521346	0.00020022	0.001428	7.132656	0.14020022	14.03	6.010011	12.02	50

COMPOUND INTEREST AND ANNUITY TABLE

**15.00 %
ANNUAL**

		Amount Of 1	Amount Of 1 Per Period	Sinking Fund Payment	Present Worth Of 1	Present Worth Of 1 Per Period	Periodic Payment To Amortize 1	Constant Annual Percent	Total Interest	Annual Add-on Rate
		What a single $1 deposit grows to in the future. The deposit is made at the beginning of the first period.	What a series of $1 deposits grow to in the future. A deposit is made at the end of each period.	The amount to be deposited at the end of each period that grows to $1 in the future.	What $1 to be paid in the future is worth today. Value today of a single payment tomorrow.	What $1 to be paid at the end of each period is worth today. Value today of a series of payments tomorrow.	The mortgage payment to amortize a loan of $1. An annuity certain, payable at the end of each period, worth $1 today.	The annual payment, including interest and principal, to amortize completely a loan of $100.	The total interest paid over the term on a loan of $1. The loan is amortized by regular periodic payments.	The average annual interest rate on a loan that is completely amortized by regular periodic payments.
		$S=(1+i)^n$	$S_{\overline{n}}=\dfrac{(1+i)^n-1}{i}$	$\dfrac{1}{S_{\overline{n}}}=\dfrac{i}{(1+i)^n-1}$	$V^n=\dfrac{1}{(1+i)^n}$	$A_{\overline{n}}=\dfrac{1-V^n}{i}$	$\dfrac{1}{A_{\overline{n}}}=\dfrac{i}{1-V^n}$			
YR										**YR**
1	1	1.150000	1.000000	1.00000000	0.869565	0.869565	1.15000000	115.00	0.150000	15.00	1
2	2	1.322500	2.150000	0.46511628	0.756144	1.625709	0.61511628	61.52	0.230233	11.51	2
3	3	1.520875	3.472500	0.28797696	0.657516	2.283225	0.43797696	43.80	0.313931	10.46	3
4	4	1.749006	4.993375	0.20026535	0.571753	2.854978	0.35026535	35.03	0.401061	10.03	4
5	5	2.011357	6.742381	0.14831555	0.497177	3.352155	0.29831555	29.84	0.491578	9.83	5
6	6	2.313061	8.753738	0.11423691	0.432328	3.784483	0.26423691	26.43	0.585421	9.76	6
7	7	2.660020	11.066799	0.09036036	0.375937	4.160420	0.24036036	24.04	0.682523	9.75	7
8	8	3.059023	13.726819	0.07285009	0.326902	4.487322	0.22285009	22.29	0.782801	9.79	8
9	9	3.517876	16.785842	0.05957402	0.284262	4.771584	0.20957402	20.96	0.886166	9.85	9
10	10	4.045558	20.303718	0.04925206	0.247185	5.018769	0.19925206	19.93	0.992521	9.93	10
11	11	4.652391	24.349276	0.04106898	0.214943	5.233712	0.19106898	19.11	1.101759	10.02	11
12	12	5.350250	29.001667	0.03448078	0.186907	5.420619	0.18448078	18.45	1.213769	10.11	12
13	13	6.152788	34.351917	0.02911046	0.162528	5.583147	0.17911046	17.92	1.328436	10.22	13
14	14	7.075706	40.504705	0.02468849	0.141329	5.724476	0.17468849	17.47	1.445639	10.33	14
15	15	8.137062	47.580411	0.02101705	0.122894	5.847370	0.17101705	17.11	1.565256	10.44	15
16	16	9.357621	55.717472	0.01794769	0.106865	5.954235	0.16794769	16.80	1.687163	10.54	16
17	17	10.761264	65.075093	0.01536686	0.092926	6.047161	0.16536686	16.54	1.811237	10.65	17
18	18	12.375454	75.836357	0.01318629	0.080805	6.127966	0.16318629	16.32	1.937353	10.76	18
19	19	14.231772	88.211811	0.01133635	0.070265	6.198231	0.16133635	16.14	2.065391	10.87	19
20	20	16.366537	102.443583	0.00976147	0.061100	6.259331	0.15976147	15.98	2.195229	10.98	20
21	21	18.821518	118.810120	0.00841679	0.053131	6.312462	0.15841679	15.85	2.326753	11.08	21
22	22	21.644746	137.631638	0.00726577	0.046201	6.358663	0.15726577	15.73	2.459847	11.18	22
23	23	24.891458	159.276384	0.00627839	0.040174	6.398837	0.15627839	15.63	2.594403	11.28	23
24	24	28.625176	184.167841	0.00542983	0.034934	6.433771	0.15542983	15.55	2.730316	11.38	24
25	25	32.918953	212.793017	0.00469940	0.030378	6.464149	0.15469940	15.47	2.867485	11.47	25
26	26	37.856796	245.711970	0.00406981	0.026415	6.490564	0.15406981	15.41	3.005815	11.56	26
27	27	43.535315	283.568766	0.00352648	0.022970	6.513534	0.15352648	15.36	3.145215	11.65	27
28	28	50.065612	327.104080	0.00305713	0.019974	6.533508	0.15305713	15.31	3.285600	11.73	28
29	29	57.575454	377.169693	0.00265133	0.017369	6.550877	0.15265133	15.27	3.426888	11.82	29
30	30	66.211772	434.745146	0.00230020	0.015103	6.565980	0.15230020	15.24	3.569006	11.90	30
31	31	76.143538	500.956918	0.00199618	0.013133	6.579113	0.15199618	15.20	3.711882	11.97	31
32	32	87.565068	577.100456	0.00173280	0.011420	6.590533	0.15173280	15.18	3.855450	12.05	32
33	33	100.699829	664.665524	0.00150452	0.009931	6.600463	0.15150452	15.16	3.999649	12.12	33
34	34	115.804803	765.365353	0.00130657	0.008635	6.609099	0.15130657	15.14	4.144423	12.19	34
35	35	133.175523	881.170156	0.00113485	0.007509	6.616607	0.15113485	15.12	4.289720	12.26	35
36	36	153.151852	1014.345680	0.00098586	0.006529	6.623137	0.15098586	15.10	4.435491	12.32	36
37	37	176.124630	1167.497532	0.00085653	0.005678	6.628815	0.15085653	15.09	4.581692	12.38	37
38	38	202.543324	1343.622161	0.00074426	0.004937	6.633752	0.15074426	15.08	4.728282	12.44	38
39	39	232.924823	1546.165485	0.00064676	0.004293	6.638045	0.15064676	15.07	4.875224	12.50	39
40	40	267.863546	1779.090308	0.00056209	0.003733	6.641778	0.15056209	15.06	5.022483	12.56	40
41	41	308.043078	2046.953856	0.00048853	0.003246	6.645025	0.15048853	15.05	5.170030	12.61	41
42	42	354.249540	2354.996933	0.00042463	0.002823	6.647848	0.15042463	15.05	5.317834	12.66	42
43	43	407.386971	2709.246473	0.00036911	0.002455	6.650302	0.15036911	15.04	5.465872	12.71	43
44	44	468.495017	3116.633443	0.00032086	0.002134	6.652437	0.15032086	15.04	5.614118	12.76	44
45	45	538.769269	3585.128460	0.00027893	0.001856	6.654293	0.15027893	15.03	5.762552	12.81	45
46	46	619.584659	4123.897729	0.00024249	0.001614	6.655907	0.15024249	15.03	5.911154	12.85	46
47	47	712.522358	4743.482388	0.00021082	0.001403	6.657310	0.15021082	15.03	6.059908	12.89	47
48	48	819.400712	5456.004746	0.00018328	0.001220	6.658531	0.15018328	15.02	6.208798	12.93	48
49	49	942.310819	6275.405458	0.00015935	0.001061	6.659592	0.15015935	15.02	6.357808	12.98	49
50	50	1083.657442	7217.716277	0.00013855	0.000923	6.660515	0.15013855	15.02	6.506927	13.01	50

COMPOUND INTEREST AND ANNUITY TABLE

16.00 %
ANNUAL

		Amount Of 1	Amount Of 1 Per Period	Sinking Fund Payment	Present Worth Of 1	Present Worth Of 1 Per Period	Periodic Payment To Amortize 1	Constant Annual Percent	Total Interest	Annual Add-on Rate
		What a single $1 deposit grows to in the future. The deposit is made at the beginning of the first period.	What a series of $1 deposits grow to in the future. A deposit is made at the end of each period.	The amount to be deposited at the end of each period that grows to $1 in the future.	What $1 to be paid in the future is worth today. Value today of a single payment tomorrow.	What $1 to be paid at the end of each period is worth today. Value today of a series of payments tomorrow.	The mortgage payment to amortize a loan of $1. An annuity certain, payable at the end of each period, worth $1 today.	The annual payment, including interest and principal, to amortize completely a loan of $100.	The total interest paid over the term on a loan of $1. The loan is amortized by regular periodic payments.	The average annual interest rate on a loan that is completely amortized by regular periodic payments.
		$S=(1+i)^n$	$S_{\overline{n}}=\frac{(1+i)^n-1}{i}$	$\frac{1}{S_{\overline{n}}}=\frac{i}{(1+i)^n-1}$	$V^n=\frac{1}{(1+i)^n}$	$\frac{1}{A_{\overline{n}}}=\frac{i}{1-V^n}$	$\frac{1}{A_{\overline{n}}}=\frac{i}{1-V^n}$			

YR											YR
1	1	1.160000	1.000000	1.00000000	0.862069	0.862069	1.16000000	116.00	0.160000	16.00	1
2	2	1.345600	2.160000	0.46296296	0.743163	1.605232	0.62296296	62.30	0.245926	12.30	2
3	3	1.560896	3.505600	0.28525787	0.640658	2.245890	0.44525787	44.53	0.335774	11.19	3
4	4	1.810639	5.066496	0.19737507	0.552291	2.798181	0.35737507	35.74	0.429500	10.74	4
5	5	2.100342	6.877135	0.14540938	0.476113	3.274294	0.30540938	30.55	0.527047	10.54	5
6	6	2.436396	8.977477	0.11138987	0.410442	3.684736	0.27138987	27.14	0.628339	10.47	6
7	7	2.826220	11.413873	0.08761268	0.353830	4.038565	0.24761268	24.77	0.733289	10.48	7
8	8	3.278415	14.240093	0.07022426	0.305025	4.343591	0.23022426	23.03	0.841794	10.52	8
9	9	3.802961	17.518508	0.05708249	0.262953	4.606544	0.21708249	21.71	0.953742	10.60	9
10	10	4.411435	21.321469	0.04690108	0.226684	4.833227	0.20690108	20.70	1.069011	10.69	10
11	11	5.117265	25.732904	0.03886075	0.195417	5.028644	0.19886075	19.89	1.187468	10.80	11
12	12	5.936027	30.850169	0.03241473	0.168463	5.197107	0.19241473	19.25	1.308977	10.91	12
13	13	6.885791	36.786196	0.02718411	0.145227	5.342334	0.18718411	18.72	1.433393	11.03	13
14	14	7.987518	43.671987	0.02289797	0.125195	5.467529	0.18289797	18.29	1.560572	11.15	14
15	15	9.265521	51.659505	0.01935752	0.107927	5.575456	0.17935752	17.94	1.690363	11.27	15

17.00 %
ANNUAL

YR											YR
1	1	1.170000	1.000000	1.00000000	0.854701	0.854701	1.17000000	117.00	0.170000	17.00	1
2	2	1.368900	2.170000	0.46082949	0.730514	1.585214	0.63082949	63.09	0.261659	13.08	2
3	3	1.601613	3.538900	0.28257368	0.624371	2.209585	0.45257368	45.26	0.357721	11.92	3
4	4	1.873887	5.140513	0.19453311	0.533650	2.743235	0.36453311	36.46	0.458132	11.45	4
5	5	2.192448	7.014400	0.14256386	0.456111	3.199346	0.31256386	31.26	0.562819	11.26	5
6	6	2.565164	9.206848	0.10861480	0.389839	3.589185	0.27861480	27.87	0.671689	11.19	6
7	7	3.001242	11.772012	0.08494724	0.333195	3.922380	0.25494724	25.50	0.784631	11.21	7
8	8	3.511453	14.773255	0.06768989	0.284782	4.207163	0.23768989	23.77	0.901519	11.27	8
9	9	4.108400	18.284708	0.05469051	0.243404	4.450566	0.22469051	22.47	1.022215	11.36	9
10	10	4.806828	22.393108	0.04465660	0.208037	4.658604	0.21465660	21.47	1.146566	11.47	10
11	11	5.623989	27.199937	0.03676479	0.177810	4.836413	0.20676479	20.68	1.274413	11.59	11
12	12	6.580067	32.823926	0.03046558	0.151974	4.988387	0.20046558	20.05	1.405587	11.71	12
13	13	7.698679	39.403993	0.02537814	0.129902	5.118280	0.19537814	19.54	1.539916	11.85	13
14	14	9.007454	47.102672	0.02123022	0.111019	5.229299	0.19123022	19.13	1.677223	11.98	14
15	15	10.538721	56.110126	0.01782209	0.094888	5.324187	0.18782209	18.79	1.817331	12.12	15

COMPOUND INTEREST AND ANNUITY TABLE

18.00 % ANNUAL

		Amount Of 1	Amount Of 1 Per Period	Sinking Fund Payment	Present Worth Of 1	Present Worth Of 1 Per Period	Periodic Payment To Amortize 1	Constant Annual Percent	Total Interest	Annual Add-on Rate	
		What a single $1 deposit grows to in the future. The deposit is made at the beginning of the first period.	What a series of $1 deposits grow to in the future. A deposit is made at the end of each period.	The amount to be deposited at the end of each period that grows to $1 in the future.	What $1 to be paid in the future is worth today. Value today of a single payment tomorrow.	What $1 to be paid at the end of each period is worth today. Value today of a series of payments tomorrow.	The mortgage payment to amortize a loan of $1. An annuity certain, payable at the end of each period, worth $1 today.	The annual payment, including interest and principal, to amortize completely a loan of $100.	The total interest paid over the term on a loan of $1. The loan is amortized completely by regular periodic payments.	The average annual interest rate on a loan that is completely amortized by regular periodic payments.	
		$S=(1+i)^n$	$S_{\overline{n}}=\dfrac{(1+i)^n-1}{i}$	$\dfrac{1}{S_{\overline{n}}}=\dfrac{i}{(1+i)^n-1}$	$V^n=\dfrac{1}{(1+i)^n}$	$A_{\overline{n}}=\dfrac{1-V^n}{i}$	$\dfrac{1}{A_{\overline{n}}}=\dfrac{i}{1-V^n}$				
YR											YR
1	1	1.180000	1.000000	1.00000000	0.847458	0.847458	1.18000000	118.00	0.180000	18.00	1
2	2	1.392400	2.180000	0.45871560	0.718184	1.565642	0.63871560	63.88	0.277431	13.87	2
3	3	1.643032	3.572400	0.27992386	0.608631	2.174273	0.45992386	46.00	0.379772	12.66	3
4	4	1.938778	5.215432	0.19173867	0.515789	2.690062	0.37173867	37.18	0.486955	12.17	4
5	5	2.287758	7.154210	0.13977784	0.437109	3.127171	0.31977784	31.98	0.598889	11.98	5
6	6	2.699554	9.441968	0.10591013	0.370432	3.497603	0.28591013	28.60	0.715461	11.92	6
7	7	3.185474	12.141522	0.08236200	0.313925	3.811528	0.26236200	26.24	0.836534	11.95	7
8	8	3.758859	15.326996	0.06524436	0.266038	4.077566	0.24524436	24.53	0.961955	12.02	8
9	9	4.435454	19.085855	0.05239482	0.225456	4.303022	0.23239482	23.24	1.091553	12.13	9
10	10	5.233836	23.521309	0.04251464	0.191064	4.494086	0.22251464	22.26	1.225146	12.25	10
11	11	6.175926	28.755144	0.03477639	0.161919	4.656005	0.21477639	21.48	1.362540	12.39	11
12	12	7.287593	34.931070	0.02862781	0.137220	4.793225	0.20862781	20.87	1.503534	12.53	12
13	13	8.599359	42.218663	0.02368621	0.116288	4.909513	0.20368621	20.37	1.647921	12.68	13
14	14	10.147244	50.818022	0.01967806	0.098549	5.008062	0.19967806	19.97	1.795493	12.82	14
15	15	11.973748	60.965266	0.01640278	0.083516	5.091578	0.19640278	19.65	1.946042	12.97	15

19.00 % ANNUAL

YR											YR
1	1	1.190000	1.000000	1.00000000	0.840336	0.840336	1.19000000	119.00	0.190000	19.00	1
2	2	1.416100	2.190000	0.45662100	0.706165	1.546501	0.64662100	64.67	0.293242	14.66	2
3	3	1.685159	3.606100	0.27730789	0.593416	2.139917	0.46730789	46.74	0.401924	13.40	3
4	4	2.005339	5.291259	0.18899094	0.498669	2.638586	0.37899094	37.90	0.515964	12.90	4
5	5	2.386354	7.296598	0.13705017	0.419049	3.057635	0.32705017	32.71	0.635251	12.71	5
6	6	2.839761	9.682952	0.10327429	0.352142	3.409777	0.29327429	29.33	0.759646	12.66	6
7	7	3.379315	12.522713	0.07985490	0.295918	3.705695	0.26985490	26.99	0.888984	12.70	7
8	8	4.021385	15.902028	0.06288506	0.248671	3.954366	0.25288506	25.29	1.023080	12.79	8
9	9	4.785449	19.923413	0.05019220	0.208967	4.163332	0.24019220	24.02	1.161730	12.91	9
10	10	5.694684	24.708862	0.04047131	0.175602	4.338935	0.23047131	23.05	1.304713	13.05	10
11	11	6.776674	30.403546	0.03289090	0.147565	4.486500	0.22289090	22.29	1.451800	13.20	11
12	12	8.064242	37.180220	0.02689602	0.124004	4.610504	0.21689602	21.69	1.602752	13.36	12
13	13	9.596448	45.244461	0.02210215	0.104205	4.714709	0.21210215	21.22	1.757328	13.52	13
14	14	11.419773	54.840909	0.01823456	0.087567	4.802277	0.20823456	20.83	1.915284	13.68	14
15	15	13.589530	66.260682	0.01509191	0.073586	4.875863	0.20509191	20.51	2.076379	13.84	15

COMPOUND INTEREST AND ANNUITY TABLE

**20.00 %
ANNUAL**

		Amount Of 1	Amount Of 1 Per Period	Sinking Fund Payment	Present Worth Of 1	Present Worth Of 1 Per Period	Periodic Payment To Amortize 1	Constant Annual Percent	Total Interest	Annual Add-on Rate	
		What a single $1 deposit grows to in the future. The deposit is made at the beginning of the first period.	What a series of $1 deposits grow to in the future. A deposit is made at the end of each period.	The amount to be deposited at the end of each period that grows to $1 in the future.	What $1 to be paid in the future is worth today. Value today of a single payment tomorrow.	What $1 to be paid at the end of each period is worth today. Value today of a series of payments tomorrow.	The mortgage payment to amortize a loan of $1. An annuity certain, payable at the end of each period, worth $1 today.	The annual payment, including interest and principal, to amortize completely a loan of $100.	The total interest paid over the term on a loan of $1. The loan is amortized by regular periodic payments.	The average annual interest rate on a loan that is completely amortized by regular periodic payments.	
		$S=(1+i)^n$	$S_{\overline{n}}=\dfrac{(1+i)^n-1}{i}$	$\dfrac{1}{S_{\overline{n}}}=\dfrac{i}{(1+i)^n-1}$	$V^n=\dfrac{1}{(1+i)^n}$	$A_{\overline{n}}=\dfrac{1-V^n}{i}$	$\dfrac{1}{A_{\overline{n}}}=\dfrac{i}{1-V^n}$				
YR											**YR**
1	1	1.200000	1.000000	1.00000000	0.833333	0.833333	1.20000000	120.00	0.200000	20.00	1
2	2	1.440000	2.200000	0.45454545	0.694444	1.527778	0.65454545	65.46	0.309091	15.45	2
3	3	1.728000	3.640000	0.27472527	0.578704	2.106481	0.47472527	47.48	0.424176	14.14	3
4	4	2.073600	5.368000	0.18628912	0.482253	2.588735	0.38628912	38.63	0.545156	13.63	4
5	5	2.488320	7.441600	0.13437970	0.401878	2.990612	0.33437970	33.44	0.671899	13.44	5
6	6	2.985984	9.929920	0.10070575	0.334898	3.325510	0.30070575	30.08	0.804234	13.40	6
7	7	3.583181	12.915904	0.07742393	0.279082	3.604592	0.27742393	27.75	0.941967	13.46	7
8	8	4.299817	16.499085	0.06060942	0.232568	3.837160	0.26060942	26.07	1.084875	13.56	8
9	9	5.159780	20.798902	0.04807946	0.193807	4.030967	0.24807946	24.81	1.232715	13.70	9
10	10	6.191736	25.958682	0.03852276	0.161506	4.192472	0.23852276	23.86	1.385228	13.85	10
11	11	7.430084	32.150419	0.03110379	0.134588	4.327060	0.23110379	23.12	1.542142	14.02	11
12	12	8.916100	39.580502	0.02526496	0.112157	4.439217	0.22526496	22.53	1.703180	14.19	12
13	13	10.699321	48.496603	0.02062000	0.093464	4.532681	0.22062000	22.07	1.868060	14.37	13
14	14	12.839185	59.195923	0.01689306	0.077887	4.610567	0.21689306	21.69	2.036503	14.55	14
15	15	15.407022	72.035108	0.01388212	0.064905	4.675473	0.21388212	21.39	2.208232	14.72	15

**25.00 %
ANNUAL**

YR											**YR**
1	1	1.250000	1.000000	1.00000000	0.800000	0.800000	1.25000000	125.00	0.250000	25.00	1
2	2	1.562500	2.250000	0.44444444	0.640000	1.440000	0.69444444	69.45	0.388889	19.44	2
3	3	1.953125	3.812500	0.26229508	0.512000	1.952000	0.51229508	51.23	0.536885	17.90	3
4	4	2.441406	5.765625	0.17344173	0.409600	2.361600	0.42344173	42.35	0.693767	17.34	4
5	5	3.051758	8.207031	0.12184674	0.327680	2.689280	0.37184674	37.19	0.859234	17.18	5
6	6	3.814697	11.258789	0.08881950	0.262144	2.951424	0.33881950	33.89	1.032917	17.22	6
7	7	4.768372	15.073486	0.06634165	0.209715	3.161139	0.31634165	31.64	1.214392	17.35	7
8	8	5.960464	19.841858	0.05039851	0.167772	3.328911	0.30039851	30.04	1.403188	17.54	8
9	9	7.450581	25.802322	0.03875620	0.134218	3.463129	0.28875620	28.88	1.598806	17.76	9
10	10	9.313226	33.252903	0.03007256	0.107374	3.570503	0.28007256	28.01	1.800726	18.01	10
11	11	11.641532	42.566129	0.02349286	0.085899	3.656403	0.27349286	27.35	2.008421	18.26	11
12	12	14.551915	54.207661	0.01844758	0.068719	3.725122	0.26844758	26.85	2.221371	18.51	12
13	13	18.189894	68.759576	0.01454343	0.054976	3.780098	0.26454343	26.46	2.439065	18.76	13
14	14	22.737368	86.949470	0.01150093	0.043980	3.824078	0.26150093	26.16	2.661013	19.01	14
15	15	28.421709	109.686838	0.00911686	0.035184	3.859263	0.25911686	25.92	2.886753	19.25	15

**30.00 %
ANNUAL**

YR											**YR**
1	1	1.300000	1.000000	1.00000000	0.769231	0.769231	1.30000000	130.00	0.300000	30.00	1
2	2	1.690000	2.300000	0.43478261	0.591716	1.360947	0.73478261	73.48	0.469565	23.48	2
3	3	2.197000	3.990000	0.25062657	0.455166	1.816113	0.55062657	55.07	0.651880	21.73	3
4	4	2.856100	6.187000	0.16162922	0.350128	2.166241	0.46162922	46.17	0.846517	21.16	4
5	5	3.712930	9.043100	0.11058155	0.269329	2.435570	0.41058155	41.06	1.052908	21.06	5
6	6	4.826809	12.756030	0.07839430	0.207176	2.642746	0.37839430	37.84	1.270366	21.17	6
7	7	6.274852	17.582839	0.05687364	0.159366	2.802112	0.35687364	35.69	1.498115	21.40	7
8	8	8.157307	23.857691	0.04191521	0.122589	2.924702	0.34191521	34.20	1.735322	21.69	8
9	9	10.604499	32.014998	0.03123536	0.094300	3.019001	0.33123536	33.13	1.981118	22.01	9
10	10	13.785849	42.619497	0.02346344	0.072538	3.091539	0.32346344	32.35	2.234634	22.35	10
11	11	17.921604	56.405346	0.01772882	0.055799	3.147338	0.31772882	31.78	2.495017	22.68	11
12	12	23.298085	74.326950	0.01345407	0.042922	3.190260	0.31345407	31.35	2.761449	23.01	12
13	13	30.287511	97.625036	0.01024327	0.033017	3.223277	0.31024327	31.03	3.033163	23.33	13
14	14	39.373764	127.912546	0.00781784	0.025398	3.248675	0.30781784	30.79	3.309450	23.64	14
15	15	51.185893	167.286310	0.00597778	0.019537	3.268211	0.30597778	30.60	3.589667	23.93	15

COMPOUND INTEREST AND ANNUITY TABLE

		Amount Of 1	Amount Of 1 Per Period	Sinking Fund Payment	Present Worth Of 1	Present Worth Of 1 Per Period	Periodic Payment To Amortize 1	Constant Annual Percent	Total Interest	Annual Add-on Rate	
		What a single $1 deposit grows to in the future. The deposit is made at the beginning of the first period.	What a series of $1 deposits grow to in the future. A deposit is made at the end of each period.	The amount to be deposited at the end of each period that grows to $1 in the future.	What $1 to be paid in the future is worth today. Value today of a single payment tomorrow.	What $1 to be paid at the end of each period is worth today. Value today of a series of payments tomorrow.	The mortgage payment to amortize a loan of $1. An annuity certain, payable at the end of each period, worth $1 today.	The annual payment, including interest and principal, to amortize completely a loan of $100.	The total interest paid over the term on a loan of $1. The loan is amortized by regular periodic payments.	The average annual interest rate on a loan that is completely amortized by regular periodic payments.	
		$S=(1+i)^n$	$S_{\overline{n}}=\dfrac{(1+i)^n-1}{i}$	$\dfrac{1}{S_{\overline{n}}}=\dfrac{i}{(1+i)^n-1}$	$V^n=\dfrac{1}{(1+i)^n}$	$A_{\overline{n}}=\dfrac{1-V^n}{i}$	$\dfrac{1}{A_{\overline{n}}}=\dfrac{i}{1-V^n}$				
YR											YR
1	1	1.350000	1.000000	1.00000000	0.740741	0.740741	1.35000000	135.00	0.350000	35.00	1
2	2	1.822500	2.350000	0.42553191	0.548697	1.289438	0.77553191	77.56	0.551064	27.55	2
3	3	2.460375	4.172500	0.23966447	0.406442	1.695880	0.58966447	58.97	0.768993	25.63	3
4	4	3.321506	6.632875	0.15076419	0.301068	1.996948	0.50076419	50.08	1.003057	25.08	4
5	5	4.484033	9.954381	0.10045828	0.223014	2.219961	0.45045828	45.05	1.252291	25.05	5
6	6	6.053445	14.438415	0.06925968	0.165195	2.385157	0.41925968	41.93	1.515558	25.26	6
7	7	8.172151	20.491860	0.04879987	0.122367	2.507523	0.39879987	39.88	1.791599	25.59	7
8	8	11.032404	28.664011	0.03488695	0.090642	2.598165	0.38488695	38.49	2.079096	25.99	8
9	9	14.893745	39.696415	0.02519119	0.067142	2.665308	0.37519119	37.52	2.376721	26.41	9
10	10	20.106556	54.590160	0.01831832	0.049735	2.715043	0.36831832	36.84	2.683183	26.83	10
11	11	27.143850	74.696715	0.01338747	0.036841	2.751884	0.36338747	36.34	2.997262	27.25	11
12	12	36.644198	101.840566	0.00981927	0.027289	2.779173	0.35981927	35.99	3.317831	27.65	12
13	13	49.469667	138.484764	0.00722101	0.020214	2.799387	0.35722101	35.73	3.643873	28.03	13
14	14	66.784051	187.954431	0.00532044	0.014974	2.814361	0.35532044	35.54	3.974486	28.39	14
15	15	90.158469	254.738482	0.00392559	0.011092	2.825453	0.35392559	35.40	4.308884	28.73	15

YR											YR
1	1	1.400000	1.000000	1.00000000	0.714286	0.714286	1.40000000	140.00	0.400000	40.00	1
2	2	1.960000	2.400000	0.41666667	0.510204	1.224490	0.81666667	81.67	0.633333	31.67	2
3	3	2.744000	4.360000	0.22935780	0.364431	1.588921	0.62935780	62.94	0.888073	29.60	3
4	4	3.841600	7.104000	0.14076577	0.260308	1.849229	0.54076577	54.08	1.163063	29.08	4
5	5	5.378240	10.945600	0.09136091	0.185934	2.035164	0.49136091	49.14	1.456805	29.14	5
6	6	7.529536	16.323840	0.06126010	0.132810	2.167974	0.46126010	46.13	1.767561	29.46	6
7	7	10.541350	23.853376	0.04192279	0.094865	2.262839	0.44192279	44.20	2.093460	29.91	7
8	8	14.757891	34.394726	0.02907422	0.067760	2.330599	0.42907422	42.91	2.432594	30.41	8
9	9	20.661047	49.152617	0.02034480	0.048400	2.378999	0.42034480	42.04	2.783103	30.92	9
10	10	28.925465	69.813664	0.01432384	0.034572	2.413571	0.41432384	41.44	3.143238	31.43	10
11	11	40.495652	98.739129	0.01012770	0.024694	2.438265	0.41012770	41.02	3.511405	31.92	11
12	12	56.693912	139.234781	0.00718211	0.017639	2.455904	0.40718211	40.72	3.886185	32.38	12
13	13	79.371477	195.928693	0.00510390	0.012599	2.468503	0.40510390	40.52	4.266351	32.82	13
14	14	111.120068	275.300171	0.00363240	0.008999	2.477502	0.40363240	40.37	4.650854	33.22	14
15	15	155.568096	386.420239	0.00258786	0.006428	2.483930	0.40258786	40.26	5.038818	33.59	15

Answers to Selected Problems

C

CHAPTER 2

3. (a) $9,441.12; (b) $9,563.09; (c) $9,628.24 (d) $9,673.36.
4. $1,349.90
6. $6,863.93
9. $690.29
10. $4,953.03
11. $4,801.02
13. (a) $79,058.19; (b) $83,801.68
14. $41,583.80
16. (a) $193,332.44; (b) $182,389.08
17. $206,723.29
21. $1,183.52
23. $4,860.72 versus $3,607.59

CHAPTER 3

12. $20,456.03
14. $14,205.15
16. $42,818.29
18. $717.34
20. $400,000
21. $636,547.87, $74,367.57

22. $8,291.14
24. (a) $1,598.89
    (b) $190,330.15
    (c) $52,616.01
    (d) $1,937.82

CHAPTER 4

5. (a) Year 1: $11,000; Years 2–9: $13,000; Year 10: $11,000; Year 11: $2,000. (c) Year 1: $17,000; Year 2: $21,800; Year 3: $16,680; Years 4 and 5: $13,600; Year 6: $2,320.
7. Year 1: $55,160; Year 2: $1,406,400.
9. $2,955,000.

CHAPTER 5

1. 4.54 years
3. Project A: 3 years, B = 4 years, C = $3\frac{3}{4}$ years
5. Discounted payback period is 12 years.
7. Select Project B
8. $3,605

CHAPTER 6

2. $NPV_A = \$1,009.16$, $NPV_B = \$2,326.29$, $PI_A = 1.05$, $PI_B = 1.08$
4. IRR = 18.125%
6. $NPV = -\$5,055$, PI = .922
7. $EAC_{New} = \$4,703,487$, $EAC_{Rebuild} = \$5,447,401$
9. Project should be abandoned after 3 years where $NPV^m = \$695$

CHAPTER 7

12.

Year 1 Cash Flows

K	I	II
20%	$25,000	$20,000
30%	23,077	20,000
40%	21,429	20,000
45%	20,690	20,000
49%	20,134	20,000

15. Present value of $5860 = $5051.72; $NPV_I = \$19,726.52$; $NPV_{II} = \$14,673.01$; $NPV_I - NPV_{II} = \$5053.51$ (error due to rounding)
17. I and Loan combined becomes $8,000 in period 2 versus $10,000 for Project II.

CHAPTER 8

7. (a) $NPV_A = \$6,699$, $NPV_B = \$7,135$
   (b) $IRR_A \cong 21.86\%$, $IRR_B \cong 18.20\%$
   (e) $NPV_A^* > NPV_B^*$
9. $NPV_{GR}^* = \$1,810$, $NPV_{RZ}^* = \$1,265$.
11. $NPV_{HG}^* = \$13,428$, $NPV_S^* = \$7,197$.
13. $NPV_A^* = \$4,443$, $NPV_B^* = \$2,689$
15. $NPV_A^* = \$3,923$, $NPV_B^* = \$2,206$
17. $NPV_O^* = \$13,632$, $NPV_P^* = \$54,816$
19. $NPV_{Be}^* = \$4,505$, $NPV_{Bo}^* = \$10,679$

CHAPTER 10

7. $K_e = 9.4\%$, $_nK_e = 10.05\%$
9. $K_i = 5.94\%$
10. Marginal cost of capital is 8.28%

CHAPTER 11

5. (a) $\bar{R}_A = \$4,000$, $\bar{R}_B = \$4,000$; (b) $MAD_A = \$400$, $MAD_B = \$800$;
   (c) $\sigma_A^2 = \$300,000$, $\sigma_B^2 = \$1,200,000$; (d) $\sigma_A = \$548$, $\sigma_B = \$1,095$;
   (e) $SV_A = \$150,000$, $SV_B = \$600,000$; (f) $D_A = .137$, $D_B = .274$
7. (a) $\bar{A}_w = \$3,500$, $\bar{A}_x = \$4,390$, $\bar{A}_y = \$4,900$, $\bar{A}_z = \$4,750$;
   (b) Only a .03 increase in the probability of a "good" economy will shift the preferred alternative from Y to Z.
8. $\bar{A} = \$1,153.58$, $\sigma_A = \$264.69$

CHAPTER 12

1. $\overline{CE} = \$6,352$
3. $\overline{RAR}_A = \$9,549$; $\overline{RAR}_B = \$4,152$
5. $\overline{RAR} = -\$5,127$; $\overline{CE} = \$263$

CHAPTER 13

5. (b) $\sigma_1 = \$7.75$; $\sigma_2 = \$13.575$; $\sigma_3 = \$4.58$
   (c) $\sigma_{CE} = \$14.64$; (d) $\sigma_{CE} = \$23.24$
7. (b) Load Shedder $\sigma_{CE} = \$2,443$ (independent)
   $\sigma_{CE} = \$4,215$ (perfectly correlated)
   Air Conditioner $\sigma_{CE} = \$3,664$ (independent)
   $\sigma_{CE} = \$6,322$ (perfectly correlated)

CHAPTER 14

1. $\sigma_A = \$16,426$, $\sigma_B = \$66,394.65$, $\text{Cov}_{AB} = \$89,735,217.46$
2. $\sigma_{12}^2 = 0.19$, $\sigma_{13}^2 = 2.82$, $\sigma_{14}^2 = 0.94$, $\sigma_{23}^2 = 1.324$, $\sigma_{24}^2 = 3.4406$, $\sigma_{34}^2 = 0.94$
3. $\overline{R}_x = \$200$, $\overline{R}_y = \$175$, $\sigma_x^2 = 2,000$, $\sigma_y^2 = 6,875$, $\sigma_p^2 = 2,218.75$
10. Portfolio 2 is optimal: $L = 0.1413$

CHAPTER 15

1. $\alpha = 0.047$, $\beta = 0.5$
3. (a) 0.0001; (b) 0.00017; (c) 0.000025; (d) 0.0001933
5. $\pm 2.37\%$
6. (a) $E(R_p) = 0.10088$; (b) 0.884; (c) 0.0111
7. 2 and 3 are overpriced
9. (a) $\beta_1 = .24$, $\beta_2 = 1.62$, $\beta_3 = .56$; (b) 1 and 2 overpriced

CHAPTER 16

1. (a) $E(R_1) = 0.115$, $\beta_1 = 3.154$, $E(R_2) = 0.037$, $\beta_2 = 1,426$, $E(R_3) = 0.07$, $\beta_3 = 0.4776$;
   (b) $\text{Cov}(R_{P_1}, R_m) = .012745$, $\text{Cov}(R_{P_2}, R_m) = .005761$, $\text{Cov}(R_{P_3}, R_m) = .00193$
   (c) $\beta_1 = 3.154$, $\beta_2 = 1.426$, $\beta_3 = .4776$
   (d) $R_1^0 = .019$, $R_2^0 = .0415$, $R_3^0 = .054$

CHAPTER 17

5. (a) $E(\overline{R}_{1t}) = 1.2933$, $E(\overline{R}_{2t}) = .2595$, $E(\overline{R}_{3t}) = .2724$
   (b) $\beta_1 = 21.3101$, $\beta_2 = 6.1560$, $\beta_3 = 4.8429$
   (c) $E(R_1) = 2.5572$, $E(R_2) = .8587$, $E(R_3) = .70116$
   (d) Reject all three projects

CHAPTER 18

1. 133.3 units of product X; 500 units of product Y; \$3,649.99 profit
3.

Value	S_1	S_2	S_3	S_4	S_5
Δ^+	∞	25	∞	∞	100
Δ^-	116.667	200	650	16.667	50

5. $P_2 = \$2.00$, $P_5 = \$2.50$, $P_1 = P_3 = P_4 = 0$

7. (a) $X_1 = 250$ acres, $X_2 = 625$ acres, $X_3 = 0$
(b) Profit $= \$32,500$
(c) $S_3 = 125$
(d) \$.125 for each additional dollar of capital; \$2.50 for each additional man-day of labor; nothing for additional acreage
(f) This is the amount by which the objective function decreases if the farmer is forced to plant 1 acre of soybeans.
(g) $\$28.75 = (70)(1.25) + (8)(2.50) + (1)(0)$

9.

Value	S_1	S_2	S_3
Δ^+	\$3.33	\$2.86	\$8.75
Δ^-	\$2.00	\$4.00	∞

11. $X_1 = 500$; $X_2 = 450$; $S_3 = 50$; profit $= \$33,000$

CHAPTER 19

1. Completely accept projects 5, 6, 8, and 10; partially accept projects 4 and 9. NPV $= \$300.88$

5. (a) Completely accept projects 1, 2, 3, 4, 5, 6, 8, and 11; partially accept projects 9, 10, and 12; all budgeted funds are exhausted.

PROJECT	SHADOW PRICE
11	\$144.64
6	85.67
2	39.11
3	29.64
5	21.90
4	18.72
1	5.74
8	0.14

6. Completely accept projects 1, 2, 3, 4, 5, 6, 8, 11, and 12; partially accept projects 7 and 10; cash inflow $= \$2237.71$

CHAPTER 20

1. Constraints are: $X_1 + X_3 + X_5 \leq 1$
$$X_6 \leq X_3$$
$$X_2 + X_4 + X_7 + X_{10} \geq 2$$
$$2X_7 \leq X_8 + X_9$$
$$X_5 + X_9 + X_{59} \leq 1$$
$$X_1 + X_2 + X_3 + X_4 + X_5 + X_6 + X_7 + X_8 + X_9 + X_{10} \geq 5$$

2. The Integer LP formulation for the TUB Company is:

$$\text{Max NPV} = 60X_1 + 80X_2 + 55X_3 + 50X_4 + 25X_5 + 100X_6$$
$$+ 90X_7 + 40X_8 + 75X_9 + 75X_{10} + 156X_{11}$$

Subject to:

Budget Year 1: $250X_1 + 300X_2 + 275X_3 + 225X_4 + 150X_5$
$+ 400X_6 + 200X_7 + 350X_8 + 250X_9 + 175X_{10}$
$+ 446.25X_{11} \leq 2000$

Budget Year 2: $200\ X_1 + 250X_2 + 250X_3 + 225X_4 + 250X_5$
$+ 150X_6 + 150X_7 + 50X_8 + 100X_9 + 175X_{10}$
$+ 403.75X_{11} \leq 1500$

Budget Year 3: $100X_1 + 150X_2 + 175X_3 + 50X_4 + 150X_5$
$+ 0X_6 + 100X_7 + 25X_8 + 150X_9 + 175X_{10}$
$+ 170X_{11} \leq 1000$

Project Interrelationships:

(1) $X_6 + X_7 \leq 1$
(2) $X_2 + X_6 \leq 1$
(3) $X_7 \leq X_8$
(4) $X_9 + X_{10} = 1$
(5) $X_2 + X_4 + X_{11} \leq 1$

Project Acceptance:

$$X_j = \{0, 1\}\ j = 1, 2, \ldots, 10, 11$$

Note: Decision variable X_{11} is the acceptance of the complementary Project X_2 and X_4.

CHAPTER 21

4. (a) $\overline{\text{NPV}} = \$21,970$ and $\sigma_{\text{NPV}} = \$12,305$
   (b) $\text{Pr}\{\text{NPV} > 0\} = .9629;\ \text{Pr}\{\text{NPV} > \$10,000\} = .8340$

CHAPTER 23

4. (a) $W_A = \$43.05;\ W_{GA} = \$40.99$
   (b) $W_{A+GA} = \$40.95$
   (c) Maximum $= 1.07$ shares; Minimum $= .88$ shares

CHAPTER 24

1. (a) i. a. $g^* = .2615$; b. $g^* = .28052$
   (b) i. a. $g_R^* = .13878$; b. $g_R^* = .163$
   (c) i. a. $g^* = .45787$; b. $g^* = .46565$
4. $P = .4385;\ g^* = .50687$

CHAPTER 25

4. Hold project until the end of its useful life NPV^4 = $24,580

CHAPTER 27

4. Present value to own = ($2,927)
8. a) Beginning of year lease payments: present value to own = ($37,938)
    b) End of year lease payments: present value to own = ($33,106)
10. Pretax rental = $43,136.67

Index